RETAILING
Critical Concepts

RETAILING
Critical Concepts

**Edited and with a new introduction by
Anne M. Findlay and Leigh Sparks**

VOLUME I

The Evolution and Development of Retailing

London and New York

First published 2002
by Routledge
11 New Fetter Lane, London EC4P 4EE

Simultaneously published in the USA and Canada
by Routledge
29 West 35th Street, New York, NY 10001

Routledge is an imprint of the Taylor & Francis Group

Typeset in Times by Graphicraft Limited, Hong Kong
Printed and bound in Great Britain by TJ International Ltd, Padstow, Cornwall

British Library Cataloguing in Publication Data
A catalogue record for this book is available from the British Library

Library of Congress Cataloging in Publication Data
Retailing : critical concepts / edited by Anne M. Findlay and Leigh Sparks.
        p.   cm.
    Includes bibliographical references and index.
    1. Retail trade.   I. Findlay, A. M.   II. Sparks, Leigh.

    HF5429.R479   2001
    658.8′7 – dc21   2001019348

ISBN 0-415-08723-6 (Set)
ISBN 0-415-08719-8 (Volume I)

Disclaimers

Contents

Acknowledgements   xii
Chronological table of reprinted articles and chapters   xix

General introduction: the domain of retailing   1

Volume I   The evolution and development of retailing

   Introduction   23

PART I   The study of retailing: research agendas   27

  1 Retailing at century end: some challenges for management
    and research   *J. A. Dawson*   29
  2 Next revolution in retailing   *A. F. Doody and W. R. Davidson* 63
  3 A rearview mirror might help us drive forward: a call for
    more historical studies in retailing   *S. C. Hollander*   75
  4 The distributive trades in the Second World War and the
    post-war years, 1939–1950: and suggestions as to future trends
    J. Jeffreys   80
  5 1949–1989: retail reflections   *M. L. Mayer*   99
  6 Trends in large-scale retailing   *M. P. McNair*   105
  7 Looking back to see ahead: writing the history of American
    retailing   *R. Savitt*   118

PART II   Theories of retail change   145

II(a)   Paradigms and their influence on retailing

  8 Postmodernism, the wheel of retailing and will to power
    S. Brown   147

9 Gap on the map? Towards a geography of consumption and
   identity   *L. Crewe and M. Lowe*   174
10 Rethinking retail capital   *K. Ducatel and N. Blomley*   197

II(b)   Macro theories of retail development

11 Institutional change in retailing: a review and synthesis
   S. Brown   219
12 Concepts in comparative retailing   *E. W. Cundiff*   256
13 The retail life cycle   *W. R. Davidson, A. D. Bates
   and S. J. Bass*   264
14 Applying evolutionary models to the retail sector   *K. Davies* 278
15 The retailing ecology model: a comprehensive model of
   retail change   *M. Etgar*   294
16 The wheel of retailing   *S. C. Hollander*   314
17 Notes on the retail accordion   *S. C. Hollander*   322
18 The transformation of retailing institutions: beyond the wheel
   of retailing and life cycle theories   *R. J. Markin and
   C. P. Duncan*   334

II(c)   Location modelling

19 Reilly's challenge: new laws of retail gravitation which define
   systems of central places   *M. Batty*   349
20 Retail location theory – the legacy of Harold Hotelling
   S. Brown   395
21 Retail location at the micro-scale: inventory and prospect
   S. Brown   414
22 New laws of retail gravitation   *P. D. Converse*   447
23 A retail market potential model   *T. R. Lakshmanan and
   W. G. Hansen*   456
24 A stated choice model of sequential mode and destination
   choice behaviour for shopping trips   *H. J. P. Timmermans*   471

Volume II   The environments for retailing   1

Introduction   3

PART I   Consumer environment   7

25 The impact of a market spoiler on consumer preference
   structures (or, what happens when Wal-Mart comes to town)
   S. J. Arnold, J. Handelman and D. J. Tigert   9
26 Situational variables and consumer behavior   *R. W. Belk*   34
27 Life-style retailing: competitive strategies for the 1980s
   R. D. Blackwell and W. W. Talarzyk   47

28 Shopping motives, emotional states and retail outcomes
 S. J. Dawson, P. H. Bloch and N. M. Ridgway 65
29 A motivation-based shopper typology *R. A. Westbrook
 and W. C. Black* 82

PART II Public policy 105

30 Planning for women to shop in postwar Britain *S. R. Bowlby* 107
31 The retail revolution, the carless shopper and disadvantage
 R. D. F. Bromley and C. J. Thomas 135
32 Trade barriers in East and South East Asia: the implications
 for retailers *K. Davies* 160
33 Controls over the development of large stores in Japan
 J. A. Dawson and T. Sato 180
34 Controlling new retail spaces: the impress of planning policies
 in western Europe *C. M. Guy* 192
35 Regulation, retailing, and consumption *T. Marsden and
 N. Wrigley* 225

PART III Financial and property environment 247

36 The evolution of shopping center research: a review and
 analysis *M. J. Eppli and J. D. Benjamin* 249
37 Numbers of shops and productivity in retail distribution
 in Great Britain, the United States and Canada
 M. Hall and J. Knapp 279
38 Learning to multiply: the property market and the growth
 of multiple retailing in Britain 1919–39 *P. Scott* 303
39 Sunk capital, the property crisis and the restructuring of
 British food retailing *N. Wrigley* 328
40 Is the 'golden age' of British grocery retailing at a watershed?
 N. Wrigley 337

PART IV Built environment 349

41 Major shopping centres in England and Wales, 1961
 W. I. Carruthers 351
42 The changing High Street *J. A. Dawson* 375
43 The 'magic of the mall': an analysis of form, function, and
 meaning in the contemporary retail built environment *J. Goss* 392
44 The invention of the mall: Eureka in Edina, Minnesota
 W. Kowinski 434
45 Comparative retail structure of British and American cities:
 Cardiff (UK) and Charlotte (USA) *J. D. Lord and C. M. Guy* 442

Volume III(i)   Retail practices and operations   1

   Introduction   3

PART I   Relationships between retail businesses – strategy   7

I(a)   Competition and strategy

46 Concentration in retail distribution: measurement and
    significance   *G. Akehurst*   9
47 The emergence of cost-based strategies in retailing
    R. Dickinson and B. Cooper   30
48 A taxonomy of competitive retailing strategies   *J. M. Hawes
    and W. F. Crittenden*   43

I(b)   Case studies

49 Marks and Spencer: the geography of an image   *J. H. Bird and
    M. E. Witherwick*   59
50 The Carrefour Group – the first 25 years   *S. Burt*   78
51 The locations of Wal-Mart and Kmart supercenters:
    contrasting corporate strategies   *T. O. Graff*   101
52 Reciprocal retail internationalisation: the Southland
    corporation, Ito-Yokado and 7–Eleven convenience stores
    L. Sparks   117

PART II   Relationships between retailers and other businesses   155

53 Changing consumption patterns: impacts on retailers and
    their suppliers   *S. Bowlby, J. Foord and C. Tillsley*   157
54 A theory of channel control   *L. P. Bucklin*   175
55 The puppet show: changing buyer–supplier relationships within
    clothing retailing   *L. Crewe and E. Davenport*   191
56 The move to administered vertical marketing systems by
    British retailers   *J. A. Dawson and S. A. Shaw*   216
57 Power measurement in the distribution channel
    A. I. El-Ansary and L. W. Stern   229
58 Retail restructuring and the strategic significance of food
    retailers' own-labels: a UK–USA comparison   *A. Hughes*   240
59 Organisation and control in retail buying groups
    S. A. Shaw and J. A. Dawson   271
60 Economies of scale in UK supermarkets: some preliminary
    finds   *S. A. Shaw, D. J. Nisbet and J. A. Dawson*   284
61 The transformation of physical distribution in retailing:
    the example of Tesco plc   *D. L. G. Smith and L. Sparks*   301

Volume III(ii)   Retail practices and operations

PART III   Within business operations   1

III(a)   Formats

62 Warehouse retailing: a revolutionary force in distribution?
   A. D. Bates   3
63 Structural-spatial relationships in the spread of hypermarket
   retailing   *J. A. Dawson*   14
64 Innovation adoption in food retailing: the example of
   self-service methods   *J. A. Dawson*   39
65 Diffusion of large-scale food retailing in France: supermarché
   et hypermarché   *E. Langeard and R. A. Peterson*   48
66 The outlet/off-price shopping centre as a retailing innovation
   J. D. Lord   67

III(b)   Management and customer service

67 Store atmosphere: an environmental psychology approach
   R. J. Donovan and J. R. Rossiter   77
68 The personality of the retail store   *P. Martineau*   98
69 Refinement and reassessment of the SERVQUAL scale
   A. Parasuraman, L. L. Berry and V. A. Zeithaml   114
70 SERVQUAL: a multiple-item scale for measuring consumer
   perceptions of service quality   *A. Parasuraman, V. A. Zeithaml
   and L. L. Berry*   140

III(c)   Products and prices

71 'Checkout'; the analysis of oligopolistic behaviour in the UK
   grocery retail market   *G. Akehurst*   162
72 Clarifying the difference between manufacturers' brands and
   distributors' brands   *L. de Chernatony and G. McWilliam*   216
73 Own brands in food retailing across Europe   *H. Laaksonen
   and J. Reynolds*   225
74 The role of brands in European marketing   *R. Mårtenson*   236
75 A multi-dimensional framework for retail pricing
   P. J. McGoldrick   247
76 Brands versus private labels: fighting to win   *J. A. Quelch
   and D. Harding*   270
77 Are store brands perceived to be just another brand?
   P. S. Richardson   286
78 Resale price maintenance: the main economic issues
   B. S. Yamey   303

Volume IV   Comparative and international retailing   1

Introduction   3

PART I   Internationalisation and globalisation   7

79 Trends in the internationalization of grocery retailing:
   the European experience   *S. Burt*   9
80 Internationalization of retailing operations   *J. A. Dawson*   38
81 Alternatives for growth and internationalization in retailing
   L. Pellegrini   56
82 The internationalisation of retailing   *W. J. Salmon and
   A. Tordjman*   84
83 International opportunities for American retailers
   M. Y. Yoshino   100

PART II   Leading markets   111

84 European retailing: dynamics, restructuring and development
   issues   *J. Dawson and S. Burt*   113
85 Japan's distribution system: institutional structure, internal
   political economy, and modernization   *A. Goldman*   140
86 Exploring corporate culture and strategy: Sainsbury at
   home and abroad during the early to mid 1990s   *R. Shackleton*   167
87 Foreign retail capital on the battlefields of Connecticut:
   competition regulation at the local scale and its implications
   N. Wrigley   193

PART III   Emerging markets   209

88 Temporal lags in comparative retailing   *J. Arndt*   211
89 The new retail trade and services and their emerging location
   patterns in St. Petersburg   *K. E. Axenov, E. Bondarchuk
   and I. Brade*   222
90 Market-place trading and the transformation of retail
   space in the expanding Latin American city
   R. D. F. Bromley   246
91 Trading places: the evolution of the retail sector in the new
   German *Länder* since unification   *T. Coles*   274
92 Adoption of supermarket shopping in a developing country:
   the selective adoption phenomenon   *A. Goldman*   298
93 Supermarkets in China: the case of Shanghai   *A. Goldman*   310
94 Retail development in East Germany: the example of
   the city of Jena   *G. Meyer*   333
95 From suq to supermarket in Tunis   *J.-M. Miossec*   350

PART IV   New retail forms: e-commerce   365

96 Interactive home shopping: consumer, retailer, and
   manufacturer incentives to participate in electronic
   marketplaces   *J. Alba, J. Lynch, B. Weitz, C. Janiszewski,*
   R. Lutz, A. Sawyer and S. Wood   367
97 Exploring the implications of the Internet for consumer
   marketing   *R. A. Peterson, S. Balasubramanian and*
   B. J. Bronnenberg   400
98 The revolution in distribution: challenges and opportunities
   L. W. Stern and B. A. Weitz   430

Index   441

Acknowledgements

The publishers would like to thank the following for permission to reprint their material:

American Marketing Association for permission to reprint Cundiff, E. W., 'Concepts in comparative retailing', *Journal of Marketing* 29, 1965: 59–63; Hollander, S. C., 'The wheel of retailing', *Journal of Marketing* 24, 1960: 37–42; Converse, P. D., 'New laws of retail gravitation', *Journal of Marketing* 14, 1949: 379–384; Bucklin, L. P., 'A theory of channel control', *Journal of Marketing* 37, 1973: 39–47; Arndt, J., 'Temporal lags in comparative retailing', *Journal of Marketing* 36, 1972: 40–45; Alba, J., Lynch, J., Weitz, B., Janiszewski, C., Lutz, R., Sawyer, A. and Wood, S., 'Interactive home shopping: consumer, retailer and manufacturer incentives to participate in electronic marketplace', *Journal of Marketing* 61(3), 1997: 38–53 and El-Ansary, A. I. and Stern, L. W., 'Power measurement in the distribution channel', *Journal of Marketing Research* 9, 1972: 47–52.

The American Real Estate Society for permission to reprint Eppli. M. and Benjamin, J., 'The evolution of shopping center research: a review and analysis', *Journal of Real Estate Research* 9(1), 1994: 5–32.

Blackwell Publishers for permission to reprint Ducatel, K. and Blomley, N., 'Rethinking retail capital', *International Journal of Urban and Regional Research* 14, 1990: 207–227; Hall, M. and Knapp, J., 'Numbers of shops and productivity in retailing distribution in Great Britain, the United States and Canada', *Economic Journal* 65, 1955: 72–88; Goss, J., 'The "magic of the mall": an analysis of form, function, and meaning in the contemporary retail built environment', *Annals of the Association of American Geographers* 83(1), 1993: 18–47; Graff, T., 'The locations of Wal-Mart and Kmart supercenters: contrasting corporate strategies', *Professional Geographer* 50(1), 1998: 46–57.

California Management Review for permission to reprint Bates, A. D., 'Warehouse retailing: a revolutionary force in distribution?', *California Management Review* 20(2), 1977: 74–80. © 1977 by The Regents of the University of California. Reprinted by the permission of The Regents.

Cambridge University Press for permission to reprint Jefferys, J., 1954 'The distributive trades in the Second World War and the post-war years, 1939–1950: and suggestions as to future trends', in J. Jeffreys, *Retail Trading in Britain*, pp. 101–120.

Elsevier Science for permission to reprint Coles, T., 'Trading places: the evolution of the retail sector in the new German *Länder* since unification, *Applied Geography* 17(4), 1997: 315–333; Etgar, W., 'The retailing ecology model: a comprehensive model of retail change', *Research in Marketing* 7, 1984: 41–62; Arnold, S., Handelman, J. and Tigert, D., 'The impact of a market spoiler on consumer preference structures (or, what happens when Wal-Mart comes to town)', *Journal of Retailing and Consumer Services* 5(1), 1998: 1–13; Stern, L. W. and Weitz, B. A., 'The revolution in distribution: challenges and opportunities', *Long Range Planning* 30(6), 1997: 823–829.

Frank Cass for permission to reprint Brown, S., 'Retail location at the micro-scale: inventory and prospect', *Service Industries Journal* 14(4), 1994: 542–576; Dawson, J. A. and Sato, T., 'Controls over the development of large stores in Japan', *Service Industries Journal* 3(2), 1983: 136–145; Scott, P., 'Learning to multiply: the property market and the growth of multiple retailing in Britain, 1919–39', *Business History* 36(3), 1994: 1–28; Akehurst, G. P., Concentration in retail distribution: measurement and significance, *Service Industries Journal* 3(2), 1983: 161–179; Sparks, L., 'Reciprocal retail internationalisation: the Southland corporation, Ito-Yokado and 7–Eleven convenience stores', *Service Industries Journal* 15(4), 1995: 57–96; Dawson, J. A., 'Innovation adoption in food retailing: the example of self-service methods', *Service Industries Journal* 1(2), 1981: 22–35; Lord, J. D., 'The outlet/off-price shopping centre as a retailing innovation', *Service Industries Journal* 4(1), 1984: 9–18; Akehurst, G., ' "Checkout"; the analysis of oligopolistic behaviour in the UK grocery retail market', *Service Industries Journal* 4(2), 1984: 189–242.

The Geographical Association for permission to reprint Bird, J. and Witherwick, M., 'Marks and Spencer: the geography of an image', *Geography* 70(4), 1986: 305–319.

Greenwood Publishing Group Inc. for permission to reprint Dawson, J. A., 'Structural-spatial relationships in the spread of hypermarket retailing', in E. Kaynak, and R. Savitt (eds), *Comparative Marketing Systems*, New York: Praeger, 1984, pp. 156–182. © 1984 by Greenwood Publishing Group Inc., Westport, CT.

Harvard Business Review for permission to reprint McNair, M. P., 'Trends in large-scale retailing', *Harvard Business Review* 10, 1931: 30–39. © Copyright 1931 by the President and Fellows of Harvard College: all rights reserved. Doody, A. F. and Davidson, W. R., 'Next revolution in retailing', *Harvard Business Review* 45, 1967: 4–20. © Copyright 1967 by the President and Fellows of Harvard College: all rights reserved. Davidson, W., Bates, A. and Bass, S., 'The retail life cycle', *Harvard Business Review* 55(6), 1976: 89–96. Copyright 1976 by the President and Fellows of Harvard College: all rights reserved. Martineau, P., 'The personality of the retail store', *Harvard Business Review* 36, 1958: 47–55. Copyright 1958 by the President and Fellows of Harvard College: all rights reserved. Quelch, J. and Harding, D., 'Brands versus private labels: fighting to win', *Harvard Business Review*, January–February 1996: 99–109. Copyright 1996 by the President and Fellows of Harvard College: all rights reserved.

Haworth Press Inc. for permission to reprint Dickinson, R. and Cooper, B., 'The emergence of cost-based strategies in retailing', *Journal of Marketing Channels* 2(1), 1992: 29–45. © 1992 The Haworth Press, Inc.; Shaw, S. and Dawson, J., 'Organisation and control in retail buying groups', *Journal of Marketing Channels* 4(4), 1995: 89–103. © 1995 The Haworth Press, Inc.

Henry Stuart Publications for permission to reprint Laaksonen, H. and Reynolds, J., 'Own brands in food retailing across Europe', *Journal of Brand Management* 2(1), 1994: 37–46; Mårtenson, R., 'The role of brands in European marketing', *Journal of Brand Management* 2(4), 1995: 243–251.

John Wiley & Sons Ltd. For permission to reprint Dawson, J. A. and Burt, S. L., 'European retailing: dynamics, restructuring and development issues', in D. Pinder, *The New Europe: Economy, Society and the Environment*, 1998, pp. 157–176. © 1998, John Wiley & Sons, Ltd.; Hawes, J. M. and Crittenden, W. F., 'A taxonomy of competitive retailing strategies', *Strategic Management Journal* 5(3), 1984: 275–287. © 1984, John Wiley & Sons, Ltd.

The Journal of the American Planning Association for permission to reprint Lakshmanan, T. R. and Hansen, W. G., 'A retail market potential model', *Journal American Institute of Planners* 31, 1965: 134–143.

Kluwer Academic Publishers for permission to reprint Axenov, K. E., Bondarchuk, E. and Brade, I., 'The new retail trade and services and their emerging location patterns in St Petersburg', *GeoJournal* 42(4), 1997: 403–417.

Leonard N. Stern School of Business for permission to reprint Hollander, S., 'A rearview mirror might help us drive forward – a call for more historical studies in retailing', *Journal of Retailing* 62(1), 1986: 7–10; Mayer, M., '1949–1989: retail reflections', *Journal of Retailing* 65(3), 1989: 396–401; Savitt, R.,

'Looking back to see ahead: writing the history of American retailing', *Journal of Retailing* 65(3), 1989: 326–355; Hollander, S. C., 'Notes on the retail accordion', *Journal of Retailing* 42, 1966: 29–40, 54; Brown, S., 'Retail location theory – the legacy of Harold Hotelling', *Journal of Retailing* 65(4), 1989: 450–470; Blackwell, R. D. and Talarzyk, W. W., 'Life-style retailing: competitive strategies for the 1980s', *Journal of Retailing* 59(4), 1983: 7–27; Dawson, S. J., Bloch, P. H. and Ridgway, N. M., 'Shopping motives, emotional states and retail outcomes', *Journal of Retailing* 66(4), 1990: 408–427; Westbrook, R. A. and Black, W. C., 'A motivation-based typology', *Journal of Retailing* 61(1), 1985: 78–103; Langeard, E. and Peterson, R., 'Diffusion of large-scale food retailing in France: supermarché et hypermarché', *Journal of Retailing* 51(3), 1975: 43–63, 80; Donovan, R. J. and Rossiter, J. R., 'Store atmosphere: an environmental psychology approach', *Journal of Retailing* 58(1), 1982: 34–57; Parasuraman, A., Zeithaml, V. A. and Berry, L. L., 'SERVQUAL: a multiple-item scale for measuring consumer perceptions of service quality', *Journal of Retailing* 64(1), 1988: 12–37; Yoshino, M.Y., 'International opportunities for American retailers', *Journal of Retailing* 42, 1966: 1–10, 76; Goldman, A., 'Japan's distribution system – institutional structure, internal political economy and modernization', *Journal of Retailing* 67(2), 1991: 154–183. Parasuraman, A., Berry, L. L. and Zeithaml, V. A., 'Refinement and reassessment of the SERVQUAL scale', *Journal of Retailing* 67(4), 1991: 420–450.

Leslie de Chernatony for permission to reprint de Chernatony, L. and McWilliam, G., 'Clarifying the difference between manufacturers' brands and distributors' brands', *Quarterly Review of Marketing*, Summer 1988: 1–5.

MCB University Press for permission to reprint Brown, S., 'Institutional change in retailing: a review and synthesis', *European Journal of Marketing* 21(6), 1987: 5–36; Dawson, J. and Shaw, S., 'The move to administered vertical marketing systems by British retailers', *European Journal of Marketing* 23(7), 1989: 42–52; McGoldrick, P. J., 'A multi-dimensional framework for retail pricing', *International Journal of Retailing* 2(2), 1987: 3–26; Salmon, W. J. and Tordjman, A., 'The internationalisation of retailing', *International Journal of Retailing* 4(2), 1989: 3–16; Richardson, P., 'Are store brands perceived to be just another brand?', *Journal of Product and Brand Management* 6(6), 1997: 388–404; Goldman, A., 'Adoption of supermarket shopping in a developing country: the selective adoption phenomenon', *European Journal of Marketing* 16(1), 1982: 17–26; Burt, S., 'The Carrefour Group – the first 25 years', *International Journal of Retailing* 1(3), 1986: 54–78 and Shaw, S. A., Nisbet, D. J. and Dawson, J. A., 'Economics of scale in UK supermarkets: some preliminary finds', *International Journal of Retailing* 4(5), 1989: 12–26.

Orion Books for permission to reprint Yamey, B., 'The main economic issues', in B. Yamey, *Resale Price Maintenance*, 1966, pp. 1–22.

Pion Limited for permission to reprint Crewe, L. and Lowe, M., 'Gap on the map? Towards a geography of consumption and identity', *Environment and Planning A* 27, 1995: 1877–1898; Batty, M., 'Reilly's challenge: new laws of retail gravitation which define systems of central places', *Environment and Planning A* 10(2), 1978: 185–219; Timmermans, H., 'A stated choice model of sequential mode and destination choice behaviour for shopping trips', *Environment and Planning A* 28(1), 1996: 173–184; Bowlby, S., 'Planning for women to shop in postwar Britain', *Environment and Planning D: Society and Space* 2, 1984: 179–199; Wrigley, N., 'Is the "golden age" of British grocery retailing at a watershed?', *Environment and Planning A* 23, 1991: 1537–1544; Hughes, A., 'Retail restructuring and the strategic significance of food retailers' own-labels: a UK–USA comparison', *Environment and Planning A* 28, 1996: 2201–2226; Shackleton, R., 'Exploring corporate culture and strategy: Sainsbury at home and abroad during the early to mid 1990s', *Environment and Planning A* 30, 1998: 921–940; Marsden, T. and Wrigley, N., 'Regulation, retailing and consumption', *Environment and Planning A* 27, 1995: 1899–1912; Wrigley, N., 'Sunk capital, the property crisis and the restructuring of British food retailing', *Environment and Planning A* 24, 1992: 1521–1530 and Wrigley, N., 'Foreign retail capital on the battlefields of Connecticut: competition regulation at the local scale and its implications', *Environment and Planning A* 29, 1997: 1141–1152.

Royal Geographical Society for permission to reprint Dawson, J. A., 'The changing High Street', *Geographical Journal* 154(1), 1988: 1–22.

Sage Publications for permission to reprint Markin, R. and Duncan, C., 'The transformation of retail institutions: beyond the wheel of retailing and life cycle theories', *Journal of Macromarketing* 1(1), 1981: 58–66. © 1981 Sage Publications. Reprinted by permission of the publisher. Peterson, R., Balasubramanian, S. and Bronnenberg, B., 'Exploring the implications of the Internet for consumer marketing', *Journal of the Academy of Marketing Science* 25(4), 1997: 329–346. Reprinted by permission of the publisher.

Taylor and Francis Limited for permission to reprint Dawson, J. A., 'Retailing at century end: some challenges for management and research', *International Review of Retail, Distribution and Consumer Research* 10(2), 2000: 119–148. http://www.tandf.co.uk/journals/; Brown, S., 'Postmodernism, the wheel of retailing and will to power', *International Review of Retail, Distribution and Consumer Research* 5(3), 1995: 387–414. http://www.tandf.co.uk/journals/; Davies, K., 'Applying evolutionary models to the retail sector', *International Review of Retail, Distribution and Consumer Research* 8(2), 1998: 165–181. http://www.tandf.co.uk/journals/; Davies, K., 'Trade barriers in East and South East Asia: the implications for retailers', *International*

Review of Retail, Distribution and Consumer Research 3(4), 1993: 345–365. http://www.tandf.co.uk/journals/; Lord, J. D. and Guy, C. M., 'Comparative retail structure of British and American cities: Cardiff (UK) and Charlotte (USA)', *International Review of Retail, Distribution and Consumer Research* 1, 1991: 391–436. http://www.tandf.co.uk/journals/; Bowlby, S., Foord, J. and Tillsley, C., 'Changing consumption patterns: impacts on retailers and their suppliers', *International Review of Retail, Distribution and Consumer Research* 2, 1992: 133–150. http://www.tandf.co.uk/journals/; Smith, D. and Sparks, L., 'The transformation of physical distribution in retailing: the example of Tesco plc', *International Review of Retail, Distribution and Consumer Research* 3(1), 1993: 35–64. http://www.tandf.co.uk/journals/; Burt, S. L., 'Trends in the internationalization of grocery retailing: the European experience', *International Review of Retail, Distribution and Consumer Research* 1, 1991: 487–515. http://www.tandf.co.uk/journals/; Pellegrini, L., 'Alternatives for growth and internationalization in retailing', *International Review of Retail, Distribution and Consumer Research* 4, 1994: 121–148. http://www.tandf.co.uk/journals/; Goldman, A., 'Supermarkets in China: the case of Shanghai', *International Review of Retail, Distribution and Consumer Research* 10(1), 2000: 1–21. http://www.tandf.co.uk/journals/; Meyer, G., 'Retail development in East Germany: the example of the city of Jena', *International Review of Retail, Distribution and Consumer Research* 2(3), 1992: 245–261; Findlay, A., Paddison, R., and Dawson, J. A. 'From suq to supermarket in Tunis', in J.-M. Miossec, *Retailing Environments in Developing Countries*, 1990, pp. 227–242. http://www.tandf.co.uk/journals/; Guy, C., 'Controlling new retail spaces: the impress of planning policies in Western Europe', *Urban Studies* 35(5–6), 1998: 953–979; Carruthers, W. I., 'The major shopping centres in England and Wales 1961', *Regional Studies* 1, 1967: 65–81; Bromley, R., 'Market-place trading and the transformation of retail space in the expanding Latin American city', *Urban Studies* 35(8), 1998: 1311–1333.

Transactions of the Institute of British Geographers for permission to reprint Bromley, R. D. F. and Thomas, C. J., 'The retail revolution, the carless shopper and disadvantage', *Transactions of the Institute of British Geographers* 18(2), 1993: 222–236 and Crewe, L. and Davenport, E., 'The puppet show: changing buyer–supplier relationships within clothing retailing', *Transactions of the Institute of British Geographers* 17, 1992: 183–197.

The University of Chicago Press for permission to reprint Belk, R. W., 'Situational variables and consumer behaviour', *Journal of Consumer Research* 2, 1975: 157–164.

Westburn Publishers Ltd for permission to reprint Dawson, J. A., 'Internationalization of retailing operations', *Journal of Marketing Management* 10, 1994: 267–282. © Westburn Publishers Ltd. 1995. www.westburn.co.uk.

William Severini Kowinski for permission to reprint Kowinski, W. S., 'The invention of the mall: Eureka in Edina, Minnesota', in W. Kowinski, *The Malling of America*, 1985, pp. 115–124. © 1985 by William Severini Kowinski. By permission of the author.

The publishers have made every effort to contact authors/copyright holders of works reprinted in *Retailing: Critical Concepts*. This has not been possible in every case, however, and we would welcome correspondence from those individuals/companies we have been unable to trace.

Chronological Table of Reprinted Articles
and Chapters

Date	Author	Article/Chapter	Source	Vol.	Chap.
1931	Malcolm P. McNair	Trends in large-scale retailing	*Harvard Business Review* 10: 30–39.	I	6
1949	P. D. Converse	New laws of retail gravitation	*Journal of Marketing* 14: 379–384.	I	22
1954	J. Jeffreys	The distributive trades in the Second World War and the post-war years, 1939–1950: and suggestions as to future trends	J. Jeffreys, *Retail Trading in Britain*, Cambridge: Cambridge University Press, pp. 101–120.	I	4
1955	M. Hall and J. Knapp	Numbers of shops and productivity in retail distribution in Great Britain, the United States and Canada	*Economic Journal* 65: 72–88.	II	37
1958	Pierre Martineau	The personality of the retail store	*Harvard Business Review* 36: 47–55.	III	68
1960	Stanley C. Hollander	The wheel of retailing	*Journal of Marketing* 24: 37–42.	I	16
1965	Edward W. Cundiff	Concepts in comparative retailing	*Journal of Marketing* 29: 59–63.	I	12
1965	T. R. Lakshmanan and Walter G. Hansen	A retail market potential model	*Journal American Institute of Planners* 31: 134–143.	I	23
1966	Stanley C. Hollander	Notes on the retail accordion	*Journal of Retailing* 42: 29–40, 54.	I	17
1966	B. S. Yamey	Resale price maintenance: the main economic issues	B. Yamey, *Resale Price Maintenance*, London: Weidenfeld & Nicolson, pp. 1–22.	III	78
1966	M. Y. Yoshino	International opportunities for American retailers	*Journal of Retailing* 42: 1–10, 76.	IV	83
1967	W. I. Carruthers	Major shopping centres in England and Wales, 1961	*Regional Studies* 1: 65–81.	II	41
1967	Alton F. Doody and William R. Davidson	Next revolution in retailing	*Harvard Business Review* 45: 4–20.	I	2
1972	Johan Arndt	Temporal lags in comparative retailing	*Journal of Marketing* 36: 40–45.	IV	88
1972	Adel I. El-Ansary and Louis W. Stern	Power measurement in the distribution channel	*Journal of Marketing Research* 9: 47–52.	III	57
1973	Louis P. Bucklin	A theory of channel control	*Journal of Marketing* 37: 39–47.	III	54

Year	Author	Title	Source	Vol.	Ch.
1975	Russell W. Belk	Situational variables and consumer behavior	*Journal of Consumer Research* 2: 157–164.	II	26
1975	Eric Langeard and Robert A. Peterson	Diffusion of large-scale food retailing in France: supermarché et hypermarché	*Journal of Retailing* 51(3): 43–63, 80.	III	65
1976	William R. Davidson, Albert D. Bates and Stephen J. Bass	The retail life cycle	*Harvard Business Review* 55(6): 89–96.	I	13
1977	Albert D. Bates	Warehouse retailing: a revolutionary force in distribution?	*California Management Review* 20(2): 74–80.	III	62
1978	M. Batty	Reilly's challenge: new laws of retail gravitation which define systems of central places	*Environment and Planning A* 10(2): 185–219.	I	19
1981	John A. Dawson	Innovation adoption in food retailing: the example of self-service methods	*Service Industries Journal* 1(2): 22–35.	III	64
1981	Rom J. Markin and Calvin P. Duncan	The transformation of retailing institutions: beyond the wheel of retailing and life cycle theories	*Journal of Macromarketing* 1(1): 58–66.	I	18
1982	Robert J. Donovan and John R. Rossiter	Store atmosphere: an environmental psychology approach	*Journal of Retailing* 58(1): 34–57.	III	67
1982	Arieh Goldman	Adoption of supermarket shopping in a developing country: the selective adoption phenomenon	*European Journal of Marketing* 16(1): 17–26.	IV	92
1983	Gary Akehurst	Concentration in retail distribution: measurement and significance	*Service Industries Journal* 3(2): 161–179.	III	46
1983	Roger D. Blackwell and W. Wayne Talarzyk	Life-style retailing: competitive strategies for the 1980s	*Journal of Retailing* 59(4): 7–27.	II	27
1983	John A. Dawson and Toshio Sato	Controls over the development of large stores in Japan	*Services Industries Journal* 3(2): 136–145.	II	33
1984	Gary Akehurst	'Checkout': the analysis of oligopolistic behaviour in the UK grocery retail market	*Service Industries Journal* 4(2): 189–242.	III	71
1984	S. R. Bowlby	Planning for women to shop in postwar Britain	*Environment and Planning D. Society and Space* 2: 179–199.	II	30

Date	Author	Article/Chapter	Source	Vol.	Chap.
1984	John A. Dawson	Structural-spatial relationships in the spread of hypermarket retailing	E. Kaynak and R. Savitt (eds), *Comparative Marketing Systems*, New York: Praeger, pp. 156–182.	III	63
1984	Michael Etgar	The retailing ecology model: a comprehensive model of retail change	*Research in Marketing* 7: 41–62.	I	15
1984	Jon M. Hawes and William F. Crittenden	A taxonomy of competitive retailing strategies	*Strategic Management Journal* 5(3): 275–287.	III	48
1984	J. Dennis Lord	The outlet/off-price shopping centre as a retailing innovation	*Service Industries Journal* 4(1): 9–18.	III	66
1985	W. Kowinski	The invention of the mall: Eureka in Edina, Minnesota	W. Kowinski, *The Malling of America*, New York: Harper Collins, pp. 115–124.	II	44
1985	Robert A. Westbrook and William C. Black	A motivation-based shopper typology	*Journal of Retailing* 61(1): 78–103.	II	29
1986	J. H. Bird and M. E. Witherwick	Marks and Spencer: the geography of an image	*Geography* 70(4): 305–319.	III	49
1986	Steve Burt	The Carrefour Group – the first 25 years	*International Journal of Retailing* 1(3): 54–78.	III	50
1986	Stanley C. Hollander	A rearview mirror might help us drive forward: a call for more historical studies in retailing	*Journal of Retailing* 62(1): 7–10.	I	3
1987	Stephen Brown	Institutional change in retailing: a review and synthesis	*European Journal of Marketing* 21(6): 5–36.	I	11
1987	Peter J. McGoldrick	A multi-dimensional framework for retail pricing	*International Journal of Retailing* 2(2): 3–26.	III	75
1988	Leslie de Chernatony and Gil McWilliam	Clarifying the difference between manufacturers' brands and distributors' brands	*Quarterly Review of Marketing*: 1–5.	III	72
1988	John A. Dawson	The changing High Street	*Geographical Journal* 154(1): 1–22.	II	42

Year	Author(s)	Title	Source	Part	No.
1988	A. Parasuraman, Valarie A. Zeithaml and Leonard L. Berry	SERVQUAL: a multiple-item scale for measuring consumer perceptions of service quality	*Journal of Retailing* 64(1): 12–37.	III	70
1989	Stephen Brown	Retail location theory – the legacy of Harold Hotelling	*Journal of Retailing* 65(4): 450–470.	I	20
1989	John A. Dawson and Susan A. Shaw	The move to administered vertical marketing systems by British retailers	*European Journal of Marketing* 23(7): 42–52.	III	56
1989	Morris L. Mayer	1949–1989: retail reflections	*Journal of Retailing* 65(3): 396–401.	I	5
1989	Walter J. Salmon and André Tordjman	The internationalisation of retailing	*International Journal of Retailing* 4(2): 3–16.	IV	82
1989	Ronald Savitt	Looking back to see ahead: writing the history of American retailing	*Journal of Retailing* 65(3): 326–355.	I	7
1989	Susan A. Shaw, Donald J. Nisbet and John A. Dawson	Economies of scale in UK supermarkets: some preliminary finds	*International Journal of Retailing* 4(5): 12–26.	III	60
1990	S. J. Dawson, P. H. Bloch and N. M. Ridgway	Shopping motives, emotional states and retail outcomes	*Journal of Retailing* 66(4): 408–427.	II	28
1990	Ken Ducatel and Nicholas Blomley	Rethinking retail capital	*International Journal of Urban and Regional Research* 14: 207–227.	I	10
1990	Jean-Marie Miossec	From suq to supermarket in Tunis	A. Findlay, R. Paddison and J. A. Danson (eds), *Retailing environments in developing countries*, London: Routledge, pp. 227–242.	IV	95
1991	Steve Burt	Trends in the internationalization of grocery retailing: the European experience	*International Review of Retail, Distribution and Consumer Research* 1: 487–515.	IV	79
1991	J. Dennis Lord and Clifford M. Guy	Comparative retail structure of British and American cities: Cardiff (UK) and Charlotte (USA)	*International Review of Retail, Distribution and Consumer Research* 1: 391–436.	II	45
1991	Arieh Goldman	Japan's distribution system: institutional structure, internal political economy, and modernization	*Journal of Retailing* 67(2): 154–183.	IV	85

Date	Author	Article/Chapter	Source	Vol.	Chap.
1991	A. Parasuraman, Leonard L. Berry and Valarie A. Zeithaml	Refinement and reassessment of the SERVQUAL scale	*Journal of Retailing* 67(4): 420–450.	III	69
1991	N. Wrigley	Is the 'golden age' of British grocery retailing at a watershed?	*Environment and Planning A* 23: 1537–1544.	II	40
1992	S. Bowlby, J. Foord and C. Tillsley	Changing consumption patterns: impacts on retailers and their suppliers	*International Review of Retail, Distribution and Consumer Research* 2: 133–150.	III	53
1992	Louise Crewe and Eileen Davenport	The puppet show: changing buyer–supplier relationships within clothing retailing	*Transactions of the Institute of British Geographers* 17: 183–197.	III	55
1992	Roger Dickinson and Bixby Cooper	The emergence of cost-based strategies in retailing	*Journal of Marketing Channels* 2(1): 29–45.	III	47
1992	Günter Meyer	Retail development in East Germany: the example of the city of Jena	*International Review of Retail, Distribution and Consumer Research* 2(3): 245–261.	IV	94
1992	N. Wrigley	Sunk capital, the property crisis and the restructuring of British food retailing	*Environment and Planning A* 24: 1521–1530.	II	39
1993	Rosemary D. F. Bromley and Colin J. Thomas	The retail revolution, the carless shopper and disadvantage	*Transactions of the Institute of British Geographers* 18(2): 222–236.	II	31
1993	Keri Davies	Trade barriers in East and South East Asia: the implications for retailers	*International Review of Retail, Distribution and Consumer Research* 3(4): 345–365.	II	32
1993	Jon Goss	The 'magic of the mall': an analysis of form, function, and meaning in the contemporary retail built environment	*Annals of the Association of American Geographers* 83(1): 18–47.	II	43
1993	David L. G. Smith and Leigh Sparks	The transformation of physical distribution in retailing: the example of Tesco plc	*International Review of Retail, Distribution and Consumer Research* 3(1): 35–64.	III	61

Year	Author	Title	Source	Vol.	No.
1994	Stephen Brown	Retail location at the micro-scale: inventory and prospect	*Services Industries Journal* 14(4): 542–576.	I	21
1994	John A. Dawson	Internationalization of retailing operations	*Journal of Marketing Management* 10: 267–282.	IV	80
1994	Mark J. Eppli and John D. Benjamin	The evolution of shopping center research: a review and analysis	*Journal of Real Estate Research* 9(1): 5–32.	II	36
1994	Harri Laaksonen and Jonathan Reynolds	Own brands in food retailing across Europe	*Journal of Brand Management* 2(1): 37–46.	III	73
1994	Luca Pellegrini	Alternatives for growth and internationalization in retailing	*International Review of Retail, Distribution and Consumer Research* 4: 121–148.	IV	81
1994	Peter Scott	Learning to multiply: the property market and the growth of multiple retailing in Britain 1919–39	*Business History* 36(3): 1–28.	II	38
1995	Stephen Brown	Postmodernism, the wheel of retailing and will to power	*International Review of Retail, Distribution and Consumer Research* 5(3): 387–414.	I	8
1995	L. Crewe and M. Lowe	Gap on the map? Towards a geography of consumption and identity	*Environment and Planning A* 27: 1877–1898.	I	9
1995	T. Marsden and N. Wrigley	Regulation, retailing, and consumption	*Environment and Planning A* 27: 1899–1912.	II	35
1995	Rita Mårtenson	The role of brands in European marketing	*Journal of Brand Management* 2(4): 243–251.	III	74
1995	Susan A. Shaw and John A. Dawson	Organisation and control in retail buying groups	*Journal of Marketing Channels* 4(4): 89–103	III	59
1995	Leigh Sparks	Reciprocal retail internationalisation: the Southland corporation, Ito-Yokado and 7-Eleven convenience stores	*Services Industries Journal* 15(4): 57–96.	III	52

Date	Author	Article/Chapter	Source	Vol.	Chap.
1996	A. Hughes	Retail restructuring and the strategic significance of food retailers' own-labels: a UK–USA comparison	*Environment and Planning A* 28: 2201–2226.	III	58
1996	John A. Quelch and David Harding	Brands versus private labels: fighting to win	*Harvard Business Review*: 99–109.	III	76
1996	H. J. P. Timmermans	A stated choice model of sequential mode and destination choice behaviour for shopping trips	*Environment and Planning A* 28: 173–184.	I	24
1997	Joseph Alba, John Lynch, Barton Weitz, Chris Janiszewski, Richard Lutz, Alan Sawyer and Stacy Wood	Interactive home shopping: consumer, retailer, and manufacturer incentives to participate in electronic marketplaces	*Journal of Marketing* 61(3): 38–53.	IV	96
1997	Konstantin E. Axenov, Evgeniy Bondarchuk and Isolde Brade	The new retail trade and services and their emerging location patterns in St Petersburg	*GeoJournal* 42(4): 403–417.	IV	89
1997	Tim Coles	Trading places: the evolution of the retail sector in the new German *Länder* since unification	*Applied Geography* 17(4): 315–333.	IV	91
1997	Robert A. Peterson, Sridhar Balasubramanian and Bart J. Bronnenberg	Exploring the implications of the Internet for consumer marketing	*Journal of the Academy of Marketing Science* 25(4): 329–346.	IV	97
1997	Paul S. Richardson	Are store brands perceived to be just another brand?	*Journal of Product and Brand Management* 6(6): 388–404.	III	77
1997	Louis W. Stern and Barton A. Weitz	The revolution in distribution: challenges and opportunities	*Long Range Planning* 30(6): 823–829.	IV	98
1997	N. Wrigley	Foreign retail capital on the battlefields of Connecticut: competition regulation at the local scale and its implications	*Environment and Planning A* 29: 1141–1152.	IV	87

Year	Author(s)	Title	Source	Vol.	Page
1998	Stephen J. Arnold, Jay Handelman and Douglas J. Tigert	The impact of a market spoiler on consumer preference structures (or, what happens when Wal-Mart comes to town)	*Journal of Retailing and Consumer Services* 5(1): 1–13.	II	25
1998	Rosemary D. F. Bromley	Market-place trading and the transformation of retail space in the expanding Latin American city	*Urban Studies* 35(8): 1311–1333.	IV	90
1998	Keri Davies	Applying evolutionary models to the retail sector	*International Review of Retail, Distribution and Consumer Research* 8(2): 165–181.	I	14
1998	John Dawson and Steve Burt	European retailing: dynamics, restructuring and development issues	D. Pinder, *The New Europe: Economy, Society and the Environment*, Chichester: Wiley, pp. 157–176.	IV	84
1998	Thomas O. Graff	The locations of Wal-Mart and Kmart supercenters: contrasting corporate strategies	*Professional Geographer* 50(1): 46–57.	III	51
1998	Clifford M. Guy	Controlling new retail spaces: the impress of planning policies in western Europe	*Urban Studies* 35(5–6): 953–979.	II	34
1998	R. Shackleton	Exploring corporate culture and strategy: Sainsbury at home and abroad during the early to mid 1990s	*Environment and Planning A* 30: 921–940.	IV	86
2000	John A. Dawson	Retailing at century end: some challenges for management and research	*The International Review of Retail, Distribution and Consumer Research* 10(2): 119–148.	I	1
2000	Arieh Goldman	Supermarkets in China: the case of Shanghai	*International Review of Retail, Distribution and Consumer Research* 10(1): 1–21.	IV	93

General introduction: the domain of retailing

Retailing is a distinct, diverse and dynamic sector of many economies. The ubiquitous presence and independent organisational structure of retail outlets – a multitude of small local shops – had, however, for a long time blinded many to the challenges that the practice of retailing has to meet. With the emergence of modern techniques of retailing and the rise of large retail companies and new retail forms and formats, retailing has become more visible. Reflecting as it does cultures and consumers, retailing is a primary conduit for production and consumption linkages in economies. The pace of change in the various environments with which retailing interacts, together with the complex and distinct features of modern retailing, make it an exciting and challenging topic for study. The diversity of retailing, both within and amongst countries, adds further to the richness of the subject.

This collection of articles on retailing is intended to serve a number of purposes. First, it offers a miniature library of retailing, as developed in English language academia over the past 50 years or so. As such it consolidates material which is representative of the development of the study of retailing. A context for otherwise disparate individual articles is therefore provided. Second, the collection provides insights into previous and current research agendas and situates the research effort. Third, the different traditions of development of the subject across the globe has meant an inevitable dispersal of the research literature. As a subject asserts its own domain and becomes increasingly synthetic, a concomitant consolidation of the literature base often occurs. The value of these volumes is in bringing together key elements of the literature from the period when the discipline was emerging, and thus providing a 'route-map' to the study of the subject. Finally, the collection illustrates the distinctiveness, dynamism and diversity of retailing, as seen through its academic study. The themes of change and difference are never far away and the key contributions in the theoretical and conceptual study of retailing (and more generally) are highlighted.

The aim of this set is to provide an informed guide to retailing rather than a miscellaneous collection of the 100 most cited articles. The volumes are intended to offer a presentation of the discipline of retailing comprising its development as a subject, its progress in research and the key interest areas of the subject. By introducing critical concepts for, and in, the study of retailing, it is hoped more people can be encouraged to greater research efforts.

These volumes thus represent the culmination of a considerable process of evaluation and assessment. Each of the individual volumes has a brief introduction (Volume III comprises two books – Volumes IIIi and IIIii – having been split into two parts, reflecting the breadth and interest in retail operations, with an Introduction appearing in Volume IIIi only). The individual introductions focus on the selected articles and their subject matter in that volume, whereas this general introduction takes the perspective of the discipline and subject as a whole. It seeks to identify the intrinsic interest of the subject, its distinctiveness, its diversity and its dynamism. Key themes of this introduction are the distinctive nature of retailing and its legitimacy as a discipline with a significant research portfolio and research agenda. To achieve this, a short first section introduces the domain and challenges of retailing, making the case for its study as a distinct and challenging subject.

This is followed by a brief introduction to the practice of retailing, focusing on its important components and differences. It is suggested that these elements inform both the overall study of retailing and thus the collection of articles (and indeed the structure of the collection) presented here. An introductory review of the development of the study of retailing as an academic discipline is then presented. This identifies different traditions and approaches, emphasising the emergence of the synthetic discipline and the development of the retail academy. It is concluded that the vitality and vibrancy we see in the practice of retailing is reflected in the best of the retail research output.

We then discuss the approach adopted in the development of this collection, i.e. how the articles were selected for inclusion. There are many ways to approach such a task, but it is believed that the combination of methods utilised here has produced a collection that whilst reflecting the best in retail research and the work of the leading scholars, also stresses the breadth of the subject material.

Finally, a brief section presents a shorthand guide to the broad subject matter of the four volumes. The details of the individual papers in the collection are not presented here, being reserved for the individual volume introductions, but instead the overall structure of the collection is outlined, volume by volume.

The domain of retailing: distinctiveness, diversity and dynamism

Retailing is an ancient business. Retailing as an academic area of study has a less extensive history. Viewed by many in a lesser light than productive industries, retailing has had to struggle, both to assert its centrality in contemporary society and to be a respectable focus for study. The legacy of this struggle is demonstrated in the academic development of the discipline. The academic work presented here demonstrates categorically that retailing is significantly different from other sectors of the economy. These differences and the economic and cultural importance of retailing make it both a legitimate field of academic study, but also a fascinating and ever-changing one.

Both at the level of its operating units and at the level of a whole business, retailing is distinctively different. For example, the issues in managing an electronics factory, a quarry or a petrochemical plant are vastly different to those in managing a hypermarket or a major department store. Equally, the development and control of a supermarket business or multiple outlet clothes retailing business are very different from those in the petrochemicals industry. The tasks involved, resources required, strategies to be developed, profit structures, range of products involved, service requirements, consumer relationships and the network of operational units are incomparably different. At another scale of operation, multinational retail operations are different from multinational production businesses.

By its nature, retailing is a distinct management activity linking production and consumption. Retailing can be seen as a reflection of culture. As such, retailing acts as a critical reflector of a country's culture and consumers, transmitting these influences into productive and other sectors of the economy. Some would argue further that retailing is active in changing societal views and the very cultural environment it inhabits. Our understanding of the world can no longer be taken solely from an industrial perspective, but has to encompass this 'retail' view. This collection on critical concepts in retailing emphasises this point above all others.

The dynamism and diversity of retailing are also key aspects of the intrinsic interest of the subject, and help mark out retailing as distinctive from other industry sectors. They are key challenges to retailers and to retail researchers. The economic significance of the retail sector has become manifest as the size of the businesses involved, and their roles within domestic economies and internationally, have become more obvious to governments, the financial world and consumers. As a whole, the sector has undergone considerable change over the past century as new types of business (franchises), new scales of business (Wal-Mart), new formats and locations for trading (hypermarkets, mega-malls), new markets (electronics, lifestyle, emerging) and new methods of operation (e-retailing, outsourced logistics) have been introduced or developed. These changes have brought new demands in understanding the sector better, particularly with the greater financial risks associated with the increased scale and scope of businesses.

This very dynamism is a distinctive dimension of the sector. Whilst many traditional industries have come and gone and many contemporary industries have only a short history, retailing remains a dynamic and evolving industry. It also remains an entrepreneurial sector. Consequently, different challenges and research questions confront the researcher from those in other industry sectors. The increased size of the sector and the many businesses within it have drawn the subject into the business school arena, but the diversity and different challenges of the industry have also stimulated other lines of essential research, more commonly found outside the business or management schools.

The distributed nature of the industry and the critical role of matching consumer, product and selling environments make retailing distinctive. It is also a sector characterised by immense diversity, probably not matched in other sectors. Within the practice of retailing, there is an immense diversity of types of business, scale and methods of operation, business goals, built environments, consumer bases and cultural environments. As globalisation continues and as new markets emerge, this retail diversity takes on new dimensions challenging both retailers and researchers. There is also therefore diversity in the breadth of topics with which the academic study of the subject must engage. Academics have to range from the environments in which retailing operates, to the detailed operations of retail businesses themselves. The academic discipline has to engage with this diversity in different ways. These volumes, implicitly in most cases, but explicitly in others, demonstrate this through the vitality, richness and excitement of its academic study.

The practice of retailing

Retailing is traditionally defined as the sale of articles, either individually or in small numbers, directly to the consumer. Whilst this might sound straightforward, it is but a simplistic statement about a complex set of processes and relationships. This section of the introduction takes the key components of the practice of retailing and demonstrates the distinctive nature of the retail sector. This section moves from consideration of aspects of the retail environment, to the places and locations where retailing takes place. It then examines the inter-relationships involving retail businesses with other organisations and finally the businesses themselves, through considering the people who take on the running of retail businesses and individual shops, and the nature of the selling and retailing processes, the supply and sale of goods. It is recognised that other elements might be introduced, but it is believed that this construction is both explanatory and pedagogically useful.

Retailing begins with the environments within which it takes place. In terms of the distinctiveness of the sector the very specific relationships retailing has with *culture and consumers* are crucial. Retailing must be responsive to the culture within which it operates. This creates a great diversity in terms of regulatory environments, shopping environments, service standards and store format and layout. Japanese culture and societal behaviours are fundamentally different to the cultural norms and values of, say, Saudi Arabia or the southern United States. Whilst we might believe that a global culture is emerging, and certainly we have to agree that cultures evolve, in reality, retailing adapts to the local situation and norms in most instances.

These cultural norms are derived from societal and economic situations. Retailing is both an economic transaction but also, in many cases, a fundamental social interaction. The norms of economic and social behaviour permeate, inform and on occasion constrain, the retail operations. The opening hours allowed (or agreed to) in much of Germany are a legal recognition of cultural dimensions to the running of society, and have long-standing roots. The advertising of retail wares through weekly newspaper 'fliers' in Denmark or the United States have different origins and obligations, but nonetheless inform and constrain the retailer and retail practice. Limits on what can be advertised or sold in Islamic countries reflect cultural and religious norms.

This emphasis on culture demands that retailers are embedded in the culture of the economy and society. This may be best achieved by being part of that economy and society, or at least understanding it, and is mainly accomplished through an understanding of the local consumers. Knowledge of what drives local consumers and what they need and want (in product and service terms) is fundamental to the operation of retailing. This embeddedness may be derived from the local operations, companies or managers or may be achieved by a thoroughly researched knowledge of the local consumer base. There is a radical difference for retailing here, when compared to most other management activities, where the problems of consumers do not intrude in the same way.

Consumers are a dynamic grouping. In whatever way we consider consumers, we have to allow for their propensity to change and for alterations in their behaviours over time. Norms of consumer behaviour that were once thought to be inviolate or immutable have altered considerably. As economies and societies have developed, so the consumer desires have changed. What is important to the society or to groups of consumers has evolved. The way in which time and money are inter-related is one illustration of the process. Consumers in many economies use time very differently to previous generations. Equally they have different potential for travel for shopping. The implications of this for retailing are fundamental. Changing attitudes towards vegetarianism or meat consumption may be another example. Consumers' needs, and their ability to satisfy these needs, have altered dramatically, giving rise to retailing concepts such as organic superstores, lifestyle shopping, outlet malls, convenience stores and fast food.

This emphasis on culture and consumers is reflected in the criticality that is afforded by retailers to the places where retailing takes place – the *location* of retailing. This is in itself a distinctive dimension of the retail industry as few industries involve such a diverse and dispersed type of outlet network. Whilst the old adage 'location, location, location' has probably been overplayed, it has some truth, and above all it is an identifying characteristic of the retail trade. Retailers must understand the spaces within which consumers operate and try to match these in terms of their locational and operational decisions.

Retailing not only has a distinctive locational dimension, but is further distinguished by the diversity of retail location. Furthermore, locations have a dynamic dimension. Some are fixed in the most visible of ways as with Harrods in London or Bloomingdales in New York. Others are more transient, such as wet or night markets, car-boot sales and other similar activities. Whilst some locations clearly have a premium for retail activity such as Ginza in Tokyo, others come and go from retail activity. Town centres and city centres are for many economies the main concentration of retailing and the centre of this economic and social interaction. Market spaces in historic cities illustrate this well. Corner shops have a similar function at a different scale. In other economies this central emphasis may often have been disturbed by the decentralisation of much retail activity.

The most developed car-borne and thus decentralised retail economy is the United States. In many town and city centres the central area (the downtown) is a desolate, retail-free zone. The retail activity mainly occurs in suburban malls and strip centres along important highways or at key road intersections. The location for retailing has thus been fundamentally altered over time. This locational shift has also had important implications for the form of much of the retail infrastructure. The internalisation and privatisation of retail space in a mall is one outcome of this process.

Whilst we can argue that much retailing must prioritise micro-locational factors in the location selection process, this is not always the case. Some retailers or locations have an international reputation and attract visitors in very different ways (e.g. Mall of America). Selected forms of retailing (e.g. mail-order) are to some extent location-free. It could be argued that virtual or Internet retailing has the potential to release retailing from its various locational strait-jackets. By contrast some retailers have become clear destinations in their own right and as a result transform the locational landscape wherever they appear. For example a Wal-Mart Supercenter is clearly a destination store. The large number of shuttered Wal-Marts in the United States as the company's locational demands evolve, bear silent witness to their extensive construction of retail landscapes. These closed stores illustrate the volatility of retail demand and supply, but also the way in which some retailers can manipulate demand and consumer decision-making. Different cultures and economies have different views on how space should be constructed and used, and how land should be utilised for retailing.

The nature of retail business is also distinctive and diverse in terms of those who take on the management and operation of retail businesses – *the shopkeepers and retail managers*. Retailing remains numerically dominated in almost every country by independent retailers, i.e. retailers who operate single stores with shopkeepers who are both owner and manager. This local form of retailing has been central to retail operations throughout history. However, the independent retailer is but one form of business organisation in retailing. Four other forms can be identified:

- In some countries, the government is a major retailer controlling and operating many stores (e.g. as in the past in communist Poland) or reserving control for particular product lines (e.g. government liquor stores in Alberta, Canada).
- More commonly, there are corporate retailers. These are businesses operating as a company entity and having more than one store. Typically, such companies dominate the trading component of retailing in many countries and can be enormous businesses (e.g. Wal-Mart), sometimes with operations in many countries across the globe (e.g. Carrefour or Ahold).
- Historically, consumer co-operatives have been strong in many countries and remain so in some (e.g. Finland and Denmark). These businesses are owned by members and typically are run for mutual benefit not shareholder profit.
- Finally, many previously independent retailers have given up some degree of independence by becoming part of a contractual chain or a franchise. The contractual forms vary from operation to operation (e.g. Spar, 7–Eleven Japan, Body Shop) but all attempt to maximise buying and other powers to improve overall performance, in the belief that working together enhances their competitive position.

The balance of power amongst these business organisational forms varies from country to country and has altered over time. As a general rule centrally controlled and large organisations (running chains of large and small stores) have gained power and market share from other forms. Corporate retailers are the dominant commercial forms in many countries. This illustrates the economies of scale and scope available to retailers, but also suggests more distancing of the business from the local situation if retailers are not careful. The role and function of store management in a chain organisation has consequently become more critical over time, though the boundaries of central versus local control remain flexible and variable amongst companies. Local retailers with local knowledge and an ability to satisfy local needs and wants can be successful over a long period.

The growth of large retail companies such as Wal-Mart, Ahold, Ito-Yokado or Carrefour also illustrates another fundamental difference between retailing and other forms of business. To a much greater extent, than for example manufacturing, retailers have to construct structures for managing multi-plant operations with much greater variety and variability in concept and transactions. Retail management at the highest level is very different to other production-based businesses and is at the local level much more open to local demand vicissitudes. The role of technology in data capture and transmission and in chain control has therefore increased substantially. The business of retailing involves the selection and assembly of goods for sale, i.e. the process of *product sourcing*. This process is also one dominated by variety – of types of good, sourcing strategy and product mix. Retailers sell a wide variety of items. Some are concentrated in a narrow line of business (specialist stores, e.g. Bath and Body Works) whereas others are much wider in their scope (general stores, e.g. K Mart). The balance amongst items may change for some retailers over time. In any event, retailers have to obtain a source for their product range. This involves the retailers themselves dealing with particular suppliers (perhaps local suppliers), with a wholesaler or some other form of intermediary.

The products that are sourced have changed over time. Whilst there always has been a market for exotic and non-local products, the expectations of many consumers and the abilities of many retailers have transformed the supply position. A reliance on local (i.e. immediate area) sourcing is now not the normal relationship. For many retailers, products from around the world can be standard elements to be included in the product mix, although some would question the economic and environmental benefits of this.

In obtaining products, retailers have a choice to make over what products to sell, but also under what name to sell them. This might be simply the choice of the name of the store, but retailers themselves have also become names or brands of note. The approach to retailer branding varies across the globe, but large retailers are becoming much more concerned in managing their own retail names or brand. In the United Kingdom, retailers such as Tesco have developed a very sophisticated branding strategy, which has allowed them to leverage their name and reputation into sectors other than their core business.

The process of retailing involves *relationships with other businesses* and these too have their own distinctive characteristics. The requirement to source products, combined in some instances by concerns over branding, inevitably means that retailers are concerned with relationships with business partners, as well as relationships with staff and consumers. These business relationships can take many forms and many variants, but essentially retailers can choose to have either collaborative or transactional (sometimes conflictual) relationships.

Product sourcing involves a number of elements, but retailers are attempting to purchase and obtain products at a given price and quality position. For some retailers price is the over-riding concern and retailers will always seek the lowest price for products they know their customers will purchase. This inevitably means that the relationships they have with individual suppliers are transient and focus on transactional price components alone. The relationship in that sense is straightforward, but often comes down to a conflict about price.

More complex, but of importance to many retailers, is the notion of a collaborative relationship with suppliers which involves all parties in something rather more than simply a transaction based on price. The relationship might be to secure a source of supply or to obtain a given quality and quantity of a product. It might be to develop a product line or to ensure product consistency and quality. If a retailer is branding the product then the collaborative arrangement may be about ensuring certain standards. For many retailers therefore, whilst price may well be very important, there could well be other aspects of the business relationship that need to be in place.

Retailers of course have business relationships beyond product sourcing. Relationships exist with an array of service providers depending on the operation. Finance is a good example of such relationships, with independent retailers seeking bank finance and multiple or corporate retailers searching for institutional finance to enable them to develop their store portfolios. One of the most important relationships occurs in the physical supply of products to the retailer. Product sourcing in a transactional sense has been identified above, but products have to be delivered to the retail store to be available for merchandising and for sale. Logistics systems and logistics providers, therefore, may be key components of another set of business relationships.

As might be imagined, with product sourcing complexities, expansion in the number of stores and their spatial breadth in many companies and the increased expectations of consumers with respect to product quality and availability, logistics supply systems have become more and more important. For many retailers, being in retailing is sufficient and logistics systems are often out-sourced to logistics services providers. This requires another set of relationships to be managed. Further relationships (e.g. store-fitting, legal, property) could also be considered.

A final and fundamental component of retailing is the *merchandising and selling* of the products either in the stores or through other means. The issues are rather different from those involved in marketing products in other industries. Theories and practices developed elsewhere do not necessarily find an application in the processes of selling and merchandising. Indeed retailing, although often subsumed within marketing, has agendas that are distinct from those in marketing.

For many outside retailing, selling is often viewed as the same as retailing but selling is only one component of the retail operation. Selling itself varies, of course, with the move to self-service in many product categories and retailers reducing the sales role in the store. In other retailers, the skills of the sales staff are critical in the delivery of customer service and the repeat patronage of the consumers. The art and science of selling and the quality of the sales staff are of fundamental importance for much business success. In other situations, the lack of quality or knowledge of the staff acts as a negative influence on consumers.

Store and selling design varies enormously by situation. The emphasis on design, staff knowledge and staff competency may be vital in some situations, but of no consequence in others. The retail offer has become more disparate overall as retailers have attempted to match their offer to the demands of the customer. Some stores are dramatic (e.g. Sephora), some are functional (e.g. Aldi), others playful (e.g. REI). Some have many staff selling, others simply have takers of money. All, however, are based on retailers' understanding of what works with their customers.

Store based selling has its own distinctive characteristics. How the product is merchandised and the ways in which design and display interact are important to attracting consumers and obtaining their custom. As a result much effort is expended in laying out the store and in ensuring that products are presented appropriately. This presentation includes aspects of visual display, as well as essential product information. Depending on the product lines involved and the approach of the retailer, such merchandising may be of lesser or greater importance. Even in supposedly simple retailers, such as markets, product display can be sophisticated. Mail order retailers may have similar objectives, but a different set of tasks and expectations to manage.

The practice of retailing can not be adequately described or analysed in a few thousand words. It is believed that the above quick review of the major activities of retail operations has shown that it is a distinctive sector, which demands its own study and research. Retailing's dynamism and diversity, both of the sector and the environments within which it operates, mean that it is difficult to achieve useful generalisations, providing ready-made solutions to retail problems, which are then immediately transferable across cultures and societies. Looking towards an analysis of the retail research agenda, we conclude this section with some broad thoughts about retail practice:

1) Retail forms of all types can be found across the globe, i.e. there is no one 'better' application that fits all situations, and many types co-exist (and compete) in many markets;
2) There is an emerging set of retailers that have global pretensions. They are not there yet, but internationalisation of all aspects of retailing is a key business issue for the future;
3) This internationalisation requires management and organisational skills to avoid the problems of mis-managing local cultures and a mal-adaptation to local needs and wants. Understanding consumers is vital;
4) Retailing is about relationships. These relationships, whether they are consumer or supplier focused, are more and more important to the successful practice of retailing. The pace of consumer change, leading to inherent dynamism and change in retailing, implies that relationships need constant re-evaluation;
5) It needs to be emphasised again that retailing is distinctive and does require different skills to pursue its practice. Many have an idealistic view of the simplicity of retailing – open a shop and they will come. Retailing, however, is no field of dreams but instead is at the cutting edge of much

business and management practice, because of its extraordinarily demanding nature. This has found a parallel in the study of retailing.

The study of retailing

As retailing has changed and become more central to contemporary society and certainly to economies, so too the academic study of the subject has developed and expanded. There is a need to write a history of the academic study of retailing but this is not the place for that. Rather, this section highlights two themes – the differences in traditions of academic study of retailing between the US and UK and the different impact of these traditions on the synthetic nature of the subject.

The development of the discipline reflects different academic contexts. These traditions have been influenced by the demands of the market, as well as by the structure of academia and the prevalent research ethos. The direction of research agendas is also influenced by the changes in the paradigms being explored in academic thought at a broader level. In particular, we might distinguish between research where retailing is the focus of that research and researcher, and research where retailing is but an example or illustration of the broader subject pursued by the researcher. In recognising the now synthetic nature of the subject, this distinction has become more important. Research should also remain accessible to the industry and the research agenda should engage with issues of concern to the industry and to policy-makers. Equally, as a discipline, retail study must be able to engage with the broader debates in business and social sciences, hopefully influencing as well as being influenced by them. It is debatable to what extent this has been achieved thus far.

In the same way that the American market is large and is thus a magnet for large indigenous and overseas retailers, so too the American academic study of retailing has a longer history and can not, nor should it, be ignored. The study of retailing in American universities is long-standing and indeed many of the gurus of retail study are found in the early pioneers of American retail research. It is noteworthy of course that the longest (70+ years) established journal in the field – *The Journal of Retailing* – is American in origin, base and approach.

A number of the pioneers of retail research are represented in this collection (see below). Their fields of study are spread throughout the volumes. It is interesting to consider the work of Stan Hollander and to counterpoint it to the current concerns and approaches to the subject, as exemplified in the *Journal of Retailing* over the last decade or two. Gone are the broad concerns and exciting theorising and conceptualisations. Gone are the concerns in many cases with real retailers and a direct link to practice. In its place, in much American work, is a highly standardised, rigorous and mathematical approach, a trend reflecting a narrow interpretation of the subject domain by many retail academics. This 'scientific' slant is often orientated to micro-problems, using sophisticated mathematical tools. There is undoubtedly a place for mathematical solutions to certain retail problems, but one might question whether the balance is appropriate currently, and it is certainly in stark contrast to the agendas of the early retail researchers.

There remains much to interest and excite about American retail research. The historical papers presented in the collection and the historical approach is generally popular and involving. Some of the leading retail research universities (Florida, Texas A&M, California) are producing cutting-edge work on new retail situations and operational projects. Interestingly, much of this work is not finding a home in the *Journal of Retailing*, but is being published elsewhere, including some targeted at practitioners. There are many good universities involved in retail research or with centres of retail study. The involvement of retail companies in funding such work, either directly or in kind with data and other resources, is notable, as evidenced in the widespread sponsorship of academic posts, student internships and a number of executive/retail academic conferences. These linkages between academic and retailer agendas are important in maintaining a continuing dialogue, though it would be hard to identify these in much of the core retail published work.

Against the American approach, should be placed the approach that has emerged in Europe and particularly in the United Kingdom. Whilst Europe had significant retail scholars in earlier decades, the real flowering of retail research in the United Kingdom and Europe came in the 1970s onwards when, after initial failings, retailing became a subject of study in a number of key institutions (e.g. Stirling, Manchester, Bocconi). This has been followed by further development of centres and foci across Europe as the subject gathered interest. Retail companies, however, do not appear to be involved to the same extent as in the US, in such institutions, and there is a paucity of meeting points between academia and industry.

In Europe, the publication in English of retail research has been more problematic than in the United States, because of the lack of a core retail journal. In academic terms, the real beginnings are at the end of the 1980s when *The International Review of Retail, Distribution and Consumer Research* came into being and *The International Journal of Retail and Distribution Management* attempted to cast-off its trade origins and mainly practitioner and news orientation. Subsequently, these have been joined by the *Journal of Retailing and Consumer Services*, edited in The Netherlands. As a result there is now a range of core English-language retail publishing options in Europe. In addition to these English language publications, specialist outlets in Spanish, Italian and other languages have also become important.

In the United Kingdom, the academic approach that has emerged towards the subject is very different to that in the United States. Many of those engaged in retail research in the 1970s and 1980s were geographers by original training. As they developed their interest in retailing they moved increasingly towards the business academy. The American interest in micro-scale topics and their fascination with mathematical solutions was not replicated in the UK, although it does have adherents in parts of Europe. Rather, UK researchers took a much broader perspective, showing much more interest in the live retail operations, retail companies and the environments in which retailing operates. Retail research in the UK has probably had to work much harder to assert its distinctiveness. Awareness and advocation of the nature of that distinctiveness, as outlined in the earlier section on the practice of retailing, has been formative in shaping the subject and has contributed to the impetus and initiative present in contemporary research.

Whilst many retail researchers have some geography in their past, it is also the case that other disciplines have also helped develop the research approach. An emerging interest in all aspects of services research and a strong growth in marketing as a subject have spread the forms of academic approach and the outlets for publication. Established disciplines such as economics, sociology and psychology have on occasions also shown some interest in retailing.

There is perhaps one other difference between the European and the American approach. In the past twenty years there seems to have been a much stronger interest in Europe on the issue of retail internationalisation. Given the lead of Hollander, amongst others, in the late 1960s, it is ironic that until very recently there was limited work on the subject in the United States. This is probably a reflection of the business situation in each region, as Europe has lived with internationalisation for much longer and in a more extensive way than have the Americans.

Inevitably in a collection with a focus on English as the language of publication, this collection reflects the biases above. Retailing, of course, occurs across the globe and a conscious effort has been made to incorporate retail practices in 'other' markets into these volumes. As retailer practice has become international, so too the study of retailing has spread its geography, and work on retailing in virtually any country could be found if one tried hard enough. Some of that work is included here.

The disparate disciplinary origins of research, particularly in the UK, have resulted in two approaches by academics to the study of retailing. First, there are those who clearly see retailing and the retail firm as but one object of their study. They would approach retailing as an example for their work, but would classify themselves as, for example, human resource specialists, marketing scholars, psychologists, economists and geographers. Second, by contrast there are those who see retailing as their subject of study and would describe themselves as retailing scholars. Their interest lies in the 'retailing difference' and they would perceive retailing as a whole as their subject of study.

This dichotomy is not necessarily bound by disciplinary categorisation, with some well informed retail work undertaken by other disciplinary specialists (and some of that work is included here). Neither is the distinction necessarily as sharp in reality as portrayed here, but increasingly the difference between the two groups in their approach will reflect their own disciplinary agendas and research portfolios. Indeed the legacy of the lack of recognition of the distinctiveness of the retail sector lives on in the approaches taken to retail research by some non-retail specialists. With the establishment of a synthetic subject of retailing, has come its own agendas and body of substantive research. On a more positive note the legacy has helped the subject to establish its legitimacy, through its appreciation of the diversity of the subject of retailing. Equally, it brings to the subject a wider awareness of contemporary discourses and paradigms, as well as affording greater opportunity for collaboration.

The recency of much of the retail research and to some extent the retail researchers, as well as the sense of a subject area, is reflected by the lack of really credible professional bodies in the subject. It is possible to identify the activities of two such bodies, the American Collegiate Retailing Association established in 1949 and the European Association of Education and Research in Commercial Distribution founded in 1990. Whilst both are worthy and important bodies, it is questionable whether they have the same standing as say the equivalent economics, geography and/or psychology associations. Indeed, the special interest groups of each country's Marketing Association might argue for primacy and 'ownership' of retailing.

The study of retailing is not of course confined solely to research issues. Education of students about retailing remains a key component of academic life. These students sometimes go on to major careers in retailing, can become academics or may simply be more informed about a major sector of the economy and its interactions. The length of time retailing has been studied in the United States means that there is a much longer established pedagogical tradition in the subject. More universities are involved and their linkages with practice are perhaps more profound, informed and probably better funded. This recognises the more long-standing position of retailing as a subject. In the United Kingdom and Europe, teaching about retailing is more recent, but has expanded considerably in the last decade.

The description of the academic study of retailing presented here, is a somewhat divided one therefore. There are fault-lines in the approach to the study of the subject and these will be evident to the reader of the collection. A further fault-line not yet mentioned involves the linkage between the practice and study of the subject. To what extent does either inform the other in the published work? Should retail research be understandable and readable by informed practitioners? Or should academia somehow maintain a 'purity' despite its interest in 'grubby' commercial activities? Our answer to this is unambiguous; retail research has to address both academic and practitioner/policy maker audiences. Failure to do so will leave it ever more marginalised on the big economic and operational issues of the day.

These fault-lines are possibly better seen as symptomatic of a dynamic and emerging subject. The emergence of retailing as a subject worthy of study has attracted scholars from across many disciplines. Those of us fascinated by retailing and convinced of its difference from other subject areas should welcome this interest. The emergence of a number of journals in this and related fields is further evidence of the dynamism and interest in the subject, as well as an affirmation of its distinctiveness. The more involving European approach to retail research seems to continue to flourish and inform, setting challenging and relevant research agendas.

The selection of the articles for this set (see below) was not an easy task. Whilst we might criticise aspects of the retail literature canon, we must at the same time be impressed by the amount of work, the variety of approaches and the quality of the work. Hopefully our wrestling with the literature has produced a collection that adequately reflects the development of the subject, as it in turn has reflected the ever-changing practice of retailing and consumption.

The approach adopted

Given the practice of retailing and the history of its academic study, the selection of the articles to be included in this collection could have been approached in any number of ways.

A very tight definitional approach to the categories or structure of the volumes could have been adopted. This would have identified sections of volumes and then set about a search for the appropriate articles within these pre-defined headings.

Alternatively, an open approach to the subject matter could have been adopted. By utilising the knowledge of the literature, the 'best' articles could have been identified and then a structure overlain on this at the end of the selection process.

Equally, we could have taken an approach based on key personnel in influential research and teaching institutions. However, the previous section on the different ways the discipline has developed has shown that this alone would have missed much that has come to be distinctive about the subject that is retailing today.

All these approaches have some merit. They also raise important questions about the selection of the material. It might be possible to identify the 'best' articles on some measure or other. For example, an attempt could be made to identify the most influential pieces either by citation analysis or through a survey of experts. But the inclusion of others in the selection process also complicates the approach itself – are they being asked for the 'best' or a rounded view of retailing through a slate of papers? Are they defining the 'best' in the same way? Moreover, these volumes have our two names on the covers. We probably have to bear some responsibility for the contents, rather than passing it over to a 'panel of others'.

So, what was the approach adopted? Retailing as a new subject area with only recent journal expansion (outside the long-established *Journal of Retailing*) could be considered through its own subject base. The problem with this is that excellent retail papers have often been presented in a variety of different journals, from a variety of disciplinary backgrounds. It has to be recognised that in addition to retailing being a distinct subject in its own right, others have viewed retailing as a destination or object for their study, from their disciplinary base, or have moved into retailing study via a journey from another subject. The core retail literature therefore is not enough alone. Our approach relied consequently on three elements in producing these volumes.

First, we undertook a citation analysis using the Social Science Citation Index (SSCI). This has many problems in its treatment of retailing, chiefly deriving from its inadequate coverage of the core subject over time (both 'historical' and recent) and the time taken to include new journals and to obtain a full citation history after the publication of any article. Its strength is that it does have an established name and approach to citation analysis and it is successful in this case in identifying retail work in major non-retail publications. Whilst citation analysis has flaws and should not be relied on exclusively, it was felt to be valuable in this case.

Second, we took the most recent journals in the core subject area (*International Review of Retail Distribution and Consumer Research, Journal of Retailing and Consumer Services, International Journal of Retail and Distribution Management*) and developed our own analysis of their citation rates and citing journals. This provided us with some understanding of the way in which this material was being received and utilised. It illustrated how the body of research was interacting and developing in an increasingly synthetic way. In addition, to some extent this provided a European balance to the more American content of SSCI. On completion of this we also looked closely in the same way at the *Journal of Retailing*, which is included in the SSCI.

Third, we utilised a variety of bibliographic sources, including an SSRC sponsored database from the 1970s and 1980s (developed by John Dawson), research monographs and textbooks as well as other resources available through the Internet. Recent enhancements in technology have vastly improved the availability of bibliographic material, though in many cases much effort has to be expended in discerning quality from the considerable quantity. We attempted in this to search for 'key' articles in the minds of bibliographic producers and researchers. To these we then added our own personal lists of key articles in retailing, drawn from our own experiences and research.

The outcome of this was a long list of potential articles! Clearly there was some overlap amongst the various sources. Nonetheless, the long list of articles was substantially more than could be incorporated in the volumes, the total extent of the volumes having been set by the publishers. The intent was to try to get each volume approximately similar in length (though in the event we failed on this and have had to split the texts into separate parts). At that stage, the professional librarian expertise of one of the editors came to the fore, as we began to organise the material to match our developed understanding of the subject of retailing. As might be imagined, once we had a structure that seemed to make some sense (see below) we were able to examine the proposed entries section by section, on the assumption of approximate broad equity of treatment under each heading.

The discussion phase lasted a considerable time. Some decisions on what to include or exclude were easy, others were very hard. What is left is our view of the most critical ways of looking at retailing. Some may cavil at the inclusion or exclusion of favourites (or their own published material). Some may say we have missed the contribution of one key person or another. What we present, however, is our view of the subject matter of retailing, supported by a range of articles drawn from those heavily cited and those we believe illustrate the themes of vitality, critical enquiry and knowledge accumulation in a subject which is different, dynamic and diverse. As with any list of 'best' (or 'worst') there will be disagreements over the merits of the selection. We welcome that. That debate and discussion is also a key aim of the editors in preparing this collection. If you want to tell us your views, and suggest pieces we should have included or excluded, then please contact us. Please do remember this is not a 'top 100' citation collection (which could have been done mechanically), but rather is a guide to the subject area as a whole.

Once the selection was finalised, a mechanistic process of identifying and contacting the copyright owners took over. We had only one refusal to allow reprinting of an article (on the reasonable grounds that it was only just published) and one refusal on a copyright issue. Other than those, the selection is as originally conceived. All publishers, authors and other copyright holders are thanked for their assistance in this process: see the full list of Acknowledgements in this volume.

The outcome of this process, discussed in detail below and in the individual introductions to each volume, is a collection of 98 papers, primarily articles, though with some selections from books to capture a particular position or topic. These 98 articles are divided into five volumes (Volume III – on practice and operations – having been split into two volumes, reflecting the breadth and interest in retail operations).

The articles are drawn from two main journals, supported by a large number of other publication outlets. The American literature is dominated by the *Journal of Retailing* although vital contributions from *Harvard Business Review* and the *Journal of Marketing* are also included on many occasions. We feel this reflects the history and approach in American research in the subject. On the European side, the dominant journal is the *International Review of Retail, Distribution and Consumer Research*. Significant numbers of other papers are included from *Service Industries Journal*, reflecting the wider services concern in the UK, and from *Environment and Planning A*, reflecting the strong geographical tradition of retail research.

The scholars included in this collection are some of the most famous and influential in the study of retailing. Some would describe themselves as retail scholars and have been instrumental in the furthering of the discipline as an independent subject. Others are from related disciplines, where they are clearly influential in their own right, but where they have produced work that has enhanced considerably our knowledge of retailing. We did not set out to ensure we included so-called retail gurus, but the process we have undertaken in assembling this collection has resulted in the inclusion of many of the leading lights. Some authors might not regard the article selected as their best article but the selection is intended to exemplify particular advances in the subject.

Thus from the American side, major academics such as McNair, Hollander, Mayer and Davidson represent the origins of the study of the subject. Belk, Blackwell and Stern are illustrative of senior academics from associated subjects. Berry and Weitz are among more recent scholars and are both located at key retail research universities. The contribution of these scholars not only to the body of published research, but also in terms of the establishment of educational and academic centres and in positions of influence in learned societies and editorial boards, has been fundamental to the development of the subject.

A similar situation exists among academics from outside the United States. Outwith the UK scholars such as Timmermans, Martenson, Pellegrini and Goldman have been fundamental to our understanding of the subject. Within the UK, Akehurst and Wrigley are examples of academics influential in their own subject or area of research. Early leaders of the subject include Jefferys, Hall and Yamey. Dawson is the pre-eminent retail academic in Europe. Others come from leading retail research centres in the UK, e.g. McGoldrick (Manchester), Reynolds (Oxford) and Burt and Sparks (Stirling). Burt is the first president of the European Association for Education Research and Commercial Distribution. Editors of a number of leading retail journals are also represented. The standing of those included is undeniable, given their publication record both in journals (the UK tradition) and textbooks (the US tradition).

Retailing – Critical Concepts : the volumes

Each of the individual volumes has an introduction to the articles included. It is not the intention to summarise those details here, nor to duplicate that material. Rather, this final section of the overall introduction paints in broad terms the outline of the volumes and the topics covered. As mentioned previously, the final selection of articles is divided into five volumes, with in most cases some subdivision into sections.

Volume I is entitled The Evolution and Development of Retailing: background, development and theory. Retailing has been described above and the study of retailing has been shown to have had a particular geographical (or locational) bias in some countries. This volume presents material from academics that both describes where academics think they are in their understanding of retailing and also in terms of their theorising about retail change. The latter section includes elements of locational modelling, emphasising the centrality of location to much of the understanding and practice of retailing. In covering theoretical issues about retailing change we include the Wheel of Retailing, which remains one of the few conceptual contributions that might yet be recognised as distinctly retailing in origin, though it remains a controversial conceptualisation.

Volume II examines The Environments for Retailing. Following our examination of the practice of retailing above, this volume covers four of the most critical environments in which retailing has to operate. Beginning with the consumer environment, the volume examines the changing consumer patterns, motives and benefits. Public policy constraints on retailing are then considered, with academic analysis from various parts of the world. The financial and property environments are combined for these purposes, illustrating the way in which land and property have become such a major financial component. Finally, the built environment and the changes in the built retail and urban forms are reviewed. A theme of this volume is the dynamics of change in retail environments.

Volume III focuses on Retail Practices and Operations, and in particular on management, strategy and operations. This is, as noted earlier, the largest of the volumes and is in two parts. This is a reflection of both the distinctiveness and breadth required by retail management and the many tasks involved, and also the interest that academics have developed in retail practice. Of all the volumes, it is probably the one that most directly utilises details of retail companies, thereby meeting the aim of illustrating the excitement and diversity of companies in the business.

The volume is divided into three main sections, with additional subsections. First, relationships amongst retail businesses are considered, i.e. horizontal relationships, and examples of retail strategies are presented. Second, relationships between retailers and other businesses are presented, i.e. vertical relationships. Finally, the operations within companies are examined, focusing on formats, management and customer service and products and prices.

Volume IV takes a different tack by presenting material on Comparative and International Retailing. Academic work on retail internationalisation has picked up strongly in recent years and this is reflected in the section on internationalisation and globalisation. It can be argued that retail research here is ahead of similar business research generally. However retailers and academics operate in individual markets and so sections examine such markets and their retailing under the headings of leading and emerging markets. Finally, and looking towards changes in future retailing practice, developments in e-commerce are presented. The academic papers in this section probably lag behind the business practice, but hopefully they ask more fundamental questions about the economic and/or social nature of what we know as retailing, and where this might be going.

Conclusions

Retailing varies in quality, approach and success. Its management and operations are distinctive and different to other sectors. It is inherently vibrant and dynamic, due to its relationships with consumers and other environments. Such is the pace of change in some locations that capturing the essence of the moment is hard. Retailing's diversity adds another layer of complexity and interest. The papers here try to give a broad picture and flavour of retail research. We hope you find the collection interesting, useful, but above all stimulating. We understand some things as retail academics, but there is much more to research and learn.

Anne M. Findlay
Leigh Sparks
Institute for Retail Studies,
University of Stirling

The evolution and development of retailing

Introduction

Retailing is ever-changing. Academics have examined its changing nature and attempted to understand it and to theorise about the development of retailing and retail institutions. This first volume of the collection contains papers which provide an introduction to what might be described as the 'making of retailing' as a subject of study in its own right, but which also outlines the development of the practice of retailing.

This volume has been subdivided into two major sections, with the latter section further divided into three components. The initial section presents papers on the study of retailing and the identification of research agendas by academics. The second section presents the theoretical background to retail change. This second section is divided into articles on paradigm shifts and their influence on retail study, the macro-theories of retail change and, reflecting the importance of location to retailing, a final grouping on location modelling.

The study of retailing: research agendas

The seven papers in this section have been selected so as to provide a research review of the subject and to allow some tracing of the development of the subject. The contributors also include some of the most influential and important figures in retailing research.

Large-scale businesses in retailing are not a new phenomenon, despite some claims today. McNair's (1931) paper provides one of the earliest attempts to theorise retail change and to envisage future retail change. The paper was published in the *Harvard Business Review* and is one of a number in this collection from that journal. It illustrates the important theoretical contributions that have come from the USA, including others by McNair himself, and also the significance of the *Harvard Business Review* as an outlet for leading-edge research. The paper by Doody and Davidson, very forward looking for 1967, is another example.

The papers by Hollander, Mayer and Savitt are review papers that all appeared in the *Journal of Retailing*. This journal has been influential in the development of retail study and as Mayer notes 'it serves and has served as a barometer and conscience of the discipline of retailing'. The three selected papers represent an age when the *Journal of Retailing* was a stronger and broader journal than presently. All the papers share the breadth of thought and the willingness to learn from other disciplines that is perhaps lacking today, as represented by the *Journal of Retailing*. Hollander and Mayer are giants of retail study, both ACRA Hall of Fame members amongst many other honours.

The final two inclusions in this section are European in origin, though in this section there is little of a European–American divide in approach. Jefferys' book *Retail Trading in Britain* is a classic, landmark study of the state of retailing in Britain and this work, and his other work from his base in Paris, mark out Jefferys as a pioneer of British and European retail research. This selected chapter is an illustration of his scope and vision. The final piece is a contemporary one by the leading European authority on retailing, John Dawson. Its inclusion here reviews the research of the last hundred years and looks to future challenges. As Dawson points out, so much remains to be done and an extensive agenda of interesting questions exists.

Theories of retail change

Paradigms and their influence on retailing

Retail research, as noted in the introduction to this collection, has been linked to practice and to understanding the retail world. Some of the papers in the first section call for the inclusion of other subject specialisms in the study of retailing. This section focuses on the way in which recent academic developments have found a voice in retailing. It is of interest that these papers are in European journals, reflecting the broader disciplinary origins of the subject.

The papers show how wider academic influences can be brought into retail study and can inform the discipline. Brown's move into postmodernism is emblematic of a postmodern turn generally. The geographers Crewe and Lowe exemplify the cultural turn in the subject in their studies of geographies of consumption. Ducatel and Blomley, again geographers, point out some academic criticisms of being 'close to practice' and call for a more developed and arms-length understanding of how economies operate.

Macro theories of retail development

There are eight papers in this section spread across both Europe and America. The paper by Brown provides an overview of theory development for retail change. This is a valuable introductory piece, although it is written in stark counterpoint to his later work, also included here. His categorisation of retail theories is important and the other contributions in this section are, in many cases, the originators or the best examples of theory development for that particular category of theory.

Perhaps the most famous, or infamous, theoretical development in retailing is the Wheel of Retailing. The 1960 paper by Stan Hollander is a good exposition of the original idea. Its links to the retail life cycle concept are clear as the Davidson, Bates and Bass paper and the Markin and Duncan paper show. Hollander, of course, has been significant in theory development in retailing and a second paper by him, on the retail accordion, is also included here. The Etgar paper on retail ecology is one of the clearest statements of early thinking on this subject. The ecological and environmental approaches have received considerable enhancement in recent years, through developments in other fields, as illustrated in the paper by Davies. An outlier in one sense in this section, the paper by Cundiff, is an interesting precursor to much of the work on internationalisation (covered in Volume IV), and is included here to show how our theoretical developments have moved across spatial scales.

In addition to the papers, which show clearly how much solid theoretical work has been achieved in retailing, it is of interest that they have been published in a broad variety of outlets. The link to marketing, present in much retail study, is shown by the various marketing publications, including the influential *Journal of Marketing*, though as with the *Journal of Retailing* it is notable that the *Journal of Marketing* has changed direction and approach radically in recent decades.

Location modelling

Retailers never stray far from the importance of location to the business. It is no surprise therefore that academics have considered location in great depth and detail. Early considerations of aspects of locational decisions and their impact are represented by the papers by Converse, Lakshmanan and Hansen and *inter alia* by Batty's consideration of Reilly's 'law'. The papers by Brown again provide a good overview of the area of study. The final paper by Timmermans is representative of a large body of advanced quantitative literature on trip selection and store choice modelling. This modern work has moved a long way from the origins of considerations of retail location and shows how modern mathematical techniques may be of help in making locational choices.

Two of the papers in this section are taken from *Environment and Planning A*, one of the leading UK journals, and one which has had a long-standing and strong interest in retailing.

The 24 papers in this volume hopefully provide a broad introduction to the subject of retailing. They focus on the theoretical developments in the subject, in a variety of ways, and also examine the research agendas at various points in time. Whilst covering a broad range, it is believed there is enough cohesion to excite the reader to tackle the challenges ahead in understanding retailing and retail change.

Anne M. Findlay
Leigh Sparks
Institute for Retail Studies,
University of Stirling

PART I: The study of retailing: research agendas

1

Retailing at century end: some challenges for management and research

John A. Dawson

Source: *The International Review of Retail, Distribution and Consumer Research* 10(2) (April 2000): 119–148.

Abstract

The aim of this paper is to take stock of key issues facing retail executives and researchers. The synthesis presented is the result of an extended series of interviews and discussions with retailers, their advisors and academics across Europe. The aim is to generate discussion of the issues rather than consider any one issue in depth. The in-depth analysis of specific issues is the subject of further work. Six challenges have been identified for managers as: i) the need to grow continually and the consequent pressures associated with 'bigness', ii) the changing nature of brands in retailing, iii) impending over-capacity of retail space, iv) the turbulent nature of environmental, including consumer, change, v) the balance between externalization and internalization of functions and vi) the unknown impact of e-retail. For the researchers it is suggested that research should move from current descriptive paradigms to more explanatory ones with a stronger theoretical base. The six areas of retail research suggested as important for the next five years are, i) considerations of the nature of the retail firm, ii) risk assessment and evaluation, iii) modelling the organization, establishment and channel relationships, iv) the role of corporate culture and organizational learning, v) understanding the economics of competition and vi) the role of retailing as a catalyst for economic growth in transitional economies. The challenges identified may help to frame strategic thought in the sector and the creation of an agenda for academic research.

Keywords

European retailing, trends, forecasts, managerial issues, research agenda.

Introduction

Retailing continues to be in rapid structural transformation. At the end of the twentieth century, e-commerce appeared to be taking off at last. New ways are being found to manage retailing as an international business. The fragmentation of consumer demand is serviced through the application of expanded information on consumers. Demand chains are becoming more efficient as new ways are implemented to add value within the chain. Retailers are exploring ways to diversify their businesses. These changes in present-day retailing in Europe have been reviewed elsewhere (Costa *et al.* 1997; Dawson 1999). The aim of this paper is to consider the issues that will shape retailing in the early years of this century. Retailing in Europe remains, however, as it has all last century, a response to local European culture. European consumer society is evolving rapidly. As the European political ideal progresses to encompass Central Europe so the pressures for divergence in consumer values and cultures increase, with a plurality of consumer cultures from Poland to Portugal. Many aspects of retailing show features of divergence rather than convergence.

The aim of this paper is to review and take stock of the challenges resulting from these changes and which, in consequence, senior managers and researchers of retailing face as the new century begins. One aim is to provoke discussion of a research agenda. The start of the century generates an opportunity, albeit rather artificial and self-indulgent, to pause and reflect on past research before moving on for the next hundred years.

The paper is divided into three parts. First, there is a brief excursion into history to emphasize the importance of seeing retailing, whether from a managerial or academic perspective, as an evolving process. Retailing this century will contain many of the attributes it presently exhibits but these will have evolved into new forms. Second, the current managerial challenges facing retailers are explored. Bartlett and Peterson (1992) drew up, from a North American perspective, a long agenda to launch retail management into the twenty-first century. This paper limits itself to six major challenges which management face at the start of this century. Some broad themes are common to Bartlett and Peterson and this paper. The third part of this paper consists of a consideration of research challenges that face academics. This list also is arbitrarily limited to six. The paper draws on managerial and academic publications and on an extensive ongoing programme of interviews and discussions, over several hundred hours, with European retail executives and their advisors. The perspective is dominantly European and at times essentially British.

A brief look backwards

A hundred years ago, at least in Europe, retailing was very different from today. Nonetheless, many of the big changes of the twentieth century were already present in incipient form. Winston Churchill claimed that 'The further backward you look, the further forward you can see'. At the start of the twentieth century we can see precursors of the present:

- while most products were named, but not 'branded', by retailers there was the emergence of manufacturer branding. Customers knew retailers by their company name and their products were named by association but this was not always a conscious use of a brand name. The retailer was the brand. This was most pronounced with inns and taverns but by 1900 there were notable brands of product retailer (Mathias 1967). Lipton's 250 or so stores in the UK accounted for 10 per cent of the retail market for tea (Davis 1966). Manufacturers of consumer goods, however, were starting to realize the importance of brand names in enhancing consumer recognition of their products and so communicating brand values;
- while the independent family-owned retailer dominated the market there were already, by 1900, larger organizations appearing both in the consumer co-operative sector and in the capitalist sector. Jefferys (1954) estimates that by 1900 there were ninety-four firms with twenty-five or more branches in the UK. Notable were the footwear trades, newspaper retailers and grocers. By 1914 there were seven firms each with over 500 branches;
- conflicts were arising between small retailers and the emergent large retail firms, notably in Belgium, Germany and France (Boddewyn 1971; Gellately 1974);
- direct relationships between retailers and manufacturers were already present. Jefferys points out that 'the significant developments were the beginnings of national marketing direct to retailers by large-scale producers, and of bulk purchasing by large-scale retailing organizations direct from the manufacturers' (1954: 11);
- new technologies, particularly in construction and transport, were making an impact on retail operations, plate glass, steel-framed building construction, elevators, mass passenger transportation by rail were influencing the design, operation and location of stores;
- international sourcing was already being practised, albeit in a limited way and mainly by department stores (Pasdermadjian 1954; Ferry 1961; Lancaster 1995);
- city centres were becoming major foci of comparison retailing as middle-income consumers grew in number and mass transport focused on city centres;
- shopping centres planned as central city arcades and as railway company shopping parades at suburban railway stations had been built in many large European cities (Geist 1983; MacKeith 1986)

Faure writes in the conclusion of his analysis of retailing in late nineteenth-century Paris:

> To ignore the competition from the large scale store is to misunderstand the general evolution of trade . . . in grocery the large store and small ones gradually effected a sharing out both of geographical space and of clientèles. The losers in this process were the traditional grocers of the city centre. This state of non-competition was reached because of the total contrast between the different clientèles' purchasing powers, between their purchasing habits and between their attitudes towards the grocer and his merchandise.
>
> (Faure 1984: 172)

This could easily have been written about late twentieth century Paris or much of Europe.

Many of these developments were not limited to Europe. Monod (1996) relates the complexity of retailer–supplier relationships in Canada in the late nineteenth century when retailers began to buy directly from producers. Friedman's (1998) account of the information technology company's efforts to sell hardware to retailers in America at the turn of the nineteenth century has many echoes of the same activity today. Then it was selling NCR equipment; now it is different IT solutions. Lebhar (1959) showed the emerging strength of the chain store by the end of the nineteenth century in USA. Perkins and Meredith (1996) indicate the evolutionary nature of managerial ideas during this period.

While it is interesting to see precursors of the present in the retailing of 100 years ago, it is, however, more instructive to examine the last fifty years if we seek to understand the substantive antecedents of the challenges facing present-day retailing. Davies (1998) argues coherently for an evolutionary view of retailing development. Retailing is not a new industry, unlike the electronics or the aerospace industries. The retail sector of today results from a continuous process of structural change and adjustment within a very varied base of resources across the constituent firms. Some retail networks, buildings, management practices and many companies of today were in operation in mid-century. European retailing in 1950 was emerging from wartime product and labour shortages and the destruction of the fabric of retailing. Many of the seeds of current retailing were sown in the post-war reconstruction undertaken at this time.

The privations of post-war Germany generated in West Germany the opportunity for investment in networks of discount stores for everyday goods, typified by Aldi. There was also the reconstruction of the city centre department stores (Gerlach 1988), for example in Cologne. In East Germany the political belief that retailing did not add value to products resulted in virtually no investment in retail networks and their management. This legacy has led to a dichotomy of provision in post-unification Germany and presents particular challenges for retailers in the Eastern Länder.

In the UK by 1950, self-service was already in place in the more innovative grocery retailers, particularly the consumer co-operatives (Stacey and Wilson

1958). Attempts to manage the supply chain were under way by Sainsbury, W.H. Smith and Marks and Spencer. Retailers were also pursuing the benefits of larger-scale shops and of larger organizations (Westwood and Westwood 1955). The Town and Country Planning Act of 1947 had begun to limit the unrestricted expansion of retail floor-space and to focus investment on city centres (Ford and Thomas 1953; Burns 1959). Ideas of the urban hierarchy were applied to shopping and the different grades of centre were being determined (Smailes 1955; Carol 1960). New Towns were pioneering the ideas of planned and managed shopping centres with pedestrian-only areas – ideas stimulated by contemporary developments in Sweden (Jones 1969). Although many of today's issues were present there were two major differences which made retailing in the 1950s radically different, namely a legacy of recent product rationing and resale price maintenance. Not only was there not a surfeit of product but also there was little price competition possible for retailers. Manufacturers controlled the channel.

Elsewhere in Europe there were elements familiar today and which have helped shape the current challenges for retailers. Jefferys and Knee (1962), in their classic account, describe the state of retailing at this time and there are many aspects of the processes they describe which are familiar today. Store size was being steadily increased with the advent of self-service (Bauman 1956; Henksmeier 1960; Thygesen 1951). The Chambers of Commerce in France and Italy were already exhibiting a powerful role and ideas of growth poles as ways to stimulate economic development were emerging. Dickinson's (1951) study of the history of the West European city pointed to the importance of retailing in sustaining city centres. Relationships between retailers and suppliers were hotly debated within a public policy framework as the consensus grew for the abolition of RPM (Boggis 1966).

The region of radical change, of both structure and resource base, has been Central Europe. Change after 1989 has fundamentally altered the retail landscape. Not only have form and function changed (Riley 1997; Pütz 1998) but the processes of retailing have changed substantially through internal transformation and with the influx of West European capital into retailing (Michalak 1999a; Plichta and Swiatowiec 1998).

In order to understand many of the challenges facing retailers today we need to be aware of the origins of the present patterns of retailing. In order to explore solutions to these challenges we need to be aware of the processes which created them. Understanding the historical development of retailing is important to solving some of the problems and dilemmas present in retailing at century end. The economic, political and social change have revolutionized structure while internal entrapreneurialism and foreign investment have created great variety in the resource base of retail firms. These processes continue to be powerful factors generating change in retailing.

Challenges facing retail management

The legacy of the past fifty years has created some major managerial challenges for the retail sector at the start of the new century.

Bigness

First and foremost, and perhaps the most difficult, is the challenge of 'bigness'; 'how big should I grow?' Wal-Mart, with sales in 1998–9 of £138 billion and 830,000 employees, suggests that most retailers have some way to go before they can contemplate not growing. In comparisons with other economic sectors, retailing on a global scale is not a concentrated industry. In several other sectors, for example automobile manufacture, computer hardware, aerospace/defence, oil, airlines, etc., the largest five companies account for over 50 per cent of global sales. By this measure Wal-Mart and others have considerable growth potential. Nonetheless, 'bigness', even by retail standards, raises some substantial managerial challenges.

Retailers continue to pursue the benefits of large scale. While large stores have been evident for many decades, in the form of department stores, the search for scale-related benefits of operation has moved into other types of shop (Colla 1995). More importantly, the search for scale-related economies at the level of the organization rather than the shop has become almost mesmerizing. This, in itself, is not new. Levy pointed out that 'The large retail business . . . is imbued with a natural and almost unlimited ambition for expansion of the business' (1948: 201). What is new is the magnitude of the businesses that continue to grow.

Large retailers are growing, at least measured by sales, at a significantly faster rate than growth in the market. Table 1 shows the growth through the 1990s of the largest firms measured by sales volume. In general, their growth is outstripping the growth in the market but there are some notable exceptions of large firms which have stagnated over the decade. Metro, with sales of US$54.7 billion in 1998, is still some way smaller than Wal-Mart but is still big. In 1998 there were twelve European companies with sales of over US$25 billion compared with eight in 1997. Of the twenty-five companies with sales of over $20 billion, seventeen had increased their sales by more than 100 per cent during the 1990s. Extensive multinational operation is not necessarily a feature of these companies with six of the seventeen operating in three or fewer countries. The low growth companies, however, are characterized by operation in few countries. With some exceptions, large growth in sales is associated with a substantial increase in stock market value, which to some extent explains the managerial cynosure with sales growth.

Concentration ratios are increasing both across all retailing and also within the various sectors of retailing. M + M Eurodata (1999) calculate for Europe that the top ten retailers in 1997 accounted for 36.2 per cent of food and grocery sales. This had increased from 27.8 per cent in 1992 when the single

Table 1 Change in sales, market value and operations of large retail firms

	Sales – $US mill.			Market value[1] – $US mill.			Number of shops		Number of countries
	1990	*1998*	*% change*	*1991*	*1998*	*% change*	*1990*	*1998*	*1998*
Wal-Mart	32,602	137,594	322	43,875	181,116	313	1,721	3,599	9
Metro	18,810	54,700	191		26,633	N/A		2,085	20
Kroger	20,260	43,080	113		24,935		2,214	3,370	1
ITM Enterprises*	16,030	40,860	155	N/A	N/A	N/A	2,320	3,148	6
Ahold	9,305	38,930	318		21,153		789	3,927	17
Carrefour	13,675	37,797	171	4,074	29,150	616	369	1,661	20
Sears, Roebuck	32,690	36,808	13	11,988	16,300	36	1,765	5,132	2
Albertson's	8,220	35,870	383	6,285	26,188	317	531	2,563	1
Rewe*	16,810	33,823	101	N/A	N/A	N/A	7,800	11,509	9
Kmart	29,775	33,673	13	8,190	7,554	–8	4,082	2,161	1
Tengelmann*	18,600	32,090	73	N/A	N/A	N/A	5,022	7,853	11
Edeka	13,920	31,020	123	N/A	N/A	N/A	11,598	11,746	2
Dayton Hudson	14,739	30,950	110	4,961	23,970	383	708	1,182	1
J.C. Penney	16,735	30,455	82	6,308	11,720	86	2,577	4,578	4
Aldi*	14,750	30,440	106	N/A	N/A	N/A	2,600	4,020	9
Home Depot	3,815	30,220	692	6,263	90,280	1341	145	761	3
Ito-Yokado	17,910	28,700	60	12,188	28,845	137	4,684	18,494	19
Tesco	9,720	28,380	192	8,597	19,103	122	384	821	8
Safeway Inc	14,870	27,090	82		29,875		1,121	1,623	3
Sainsbury*	12,005	26,850	124	9,183	14,790	61	439	823	2
Auchan	11,925	26,325	121	N/A	N/A	N/A	269	1,527	11
Centres Leclerc	14,940	25,790	73	N/A	N/A	N/A	576	823	4
Costco	4,060	23,830	487		15,750		119	294	6
Promodès	10,560	22,890	117	1,105	13,770	1146	2,738	4,711	12
Daiei	21,450	22,065	3	3,988	1,620	–59	5,075	8,871	2
Jusco	14,524	21,660	49	3,618	6,745	86	1,804	2,355	9

Sources: annual reports of companies, specialist trade press, stockbrocker reports

Notes
1 Market value at year end
* tax included
N/A Not applicable

market became operative. The challenge of 'bigness' does not lie with managing large shops but with managing, in ever more concentrated markets, the large retail organization of perhaps 2,000 or more shops spread across several countries and operating in several sectors of retailing. Conglomerates in the manufacturing sector have fallen into disrepute just as conglomerates in the consumer service sector are in the ascendancy. This is one of several contrasts which exist between the retailing and manufacturing sectors.

What in reality are the challenges of bigness? While the benefits of large scale in organizations are conceded to be substantial and are listed in Table 2, these benefits bring certain challenges which are less frequently considered.

Retaining consumer responsiveness

A major challenge, as the organization gets more diffuse and store numbers increase, is to remain in touch with and responsive to customers. Large stores have been developed to respond to consumer needs more than to reap establishment-scale economies (Messinger and Narasimhan 1997), but the customer responsiveness also has to be at organizational level. Developments in late 1998 in Marks and Spencer, for example, show the problems when a large company loses touch with consumer needs. In the autumn of 1998 it is estimated that in about four months the company lost £300 million in profit through not having the right product at the right prices, and failing to push new product development in the right direction. P. Salsbury, Chief Executive, admitted, 'We lost touch with our customers and forgot about the competition' (*Economist* 1999). The challenge is to enable the store management to maintain links to the buyers and strategists in head office as well as to the customers but within the structure of a very large firm.

Keeping a focus on competition

With increasing size and diversification the number of potential competitors increases and there is a danger of losing sight of competition. Metro was facing this problem in the mid-1990s, prior to its recent moves to dispose of retailing activities which were peripheral to the core business, for example, Vobis computer stores and the food discount chains. In the UK the acquisition in 1989 of Ward White by Boots enlarged the company significantly in terms of sales volume but moved it into new markets in which the competition was not understood. There were, in consequence, difficulties in managing the newly acquired activities and the increased size did not bring financial benefits.

Entering new markets

As organizations become bigger it is necessary to enter new markets either geographical or sectoral in order to sustain the growth. While for European retailers the opening of Central Europe, particularly Poland, has offered a timely bonus of new and proximate geographical markets, these are not without challenges (Dawson and Henley 1999). Very different institutional

Table 2 Some sources of scale-related benefits in retail organizations

Functional area	Activity	Selected benefits related to larger organizations
Sourcing	Discounts from suppliers	Volume related
		Additional discounts negotiated
	Search costs	Spread over more products
	Buyer expertise	More buyers with specialist knowledge
	Transaction costs	Volume related
	Buying organization	Foreign buying offices become cost effective
	Logistics costs	Better terms – volume related
	Quality management	Reduced unit cost with larger volumes
Product development	Retail brand products	Lower unit development costs with more products
Procurement	IT equipment	Volume discounts
	Advertising rates	Volume discounts
	Professional services	Volume discounts
Marketing	Support from suppliers	Promotions with better terms
		New store opening
		Special packaging due to volume
	Advertising effectiveness	Wider exposure
	Corporate branding	More public relations
	Market research	Larger customer base
	Pricing	More flexibility over the range
R&D	NPD	More information on market response
	Site evaluation	More experience
	New format design	Economies of replication
Finance	Cash-flow	Capital projects from revenue
	Loan capital	Lower cost
Operations	IT	Hardware costs shared
		Bespoke software
		More responsive support
	Maintenance, security, etc.	Volume discounts
HRM	Training and development	Volume-related costs
	Labour scheduling	More flexibility
	Management development	More flexibility and internal transfers of know-how
Logistics	RDCs	Lower unit cost logistics
	Outsourcing	Open book accounting

frameworks, a new supply base, unknown consumer demands with little market research and an under-developed logistics system are typical problems being faced by Tesco, Carrefour, Ahold, Metro and others as they enter Central European markets. Even greater challenges are posed when retailers either enter already crowded markets, for example Wal-Mart's entry into

Germany and UK and Kingfisher's entry into France and Germany, or move into distant and emergent markets, for example Carrefour's and Tesco's entry into China, Thailand and Korea. The nature of retailing and its close connection to consumer culture, compared to manufacturing, means that this aspect of retail brand-name recognition can be a particular difficulty in becoming established in new markets.

Entering new diversifications

In pursuit of growth, a sectoral diversification strategy is sometimes pursued. Examples are into banking by Tesco, Sainsbury and Safeway in the UK, moves by El Cortes Ingles into travel services in Spain, moves in the 1980s into cleaning and entertainment services by Vendex in the Netherlands. All present new challenges in respect of becoming involved in sectors in which different managerial paradigms and constraints apply. Not all have been successful. Moves into banking, for example where some successes are evident, involve not only adherence to sector specific legal codes and requirements in terms of financial regulation and security but also developing customer relationships of a quite different form to those associated with the retailing of products. The organizational culture of some organizations may find these challenges of diversification difficult to accommodate. Again, organizational diversification presents distinctive challenges for retailers compared with manufacturers.

Relationships with suppliers and retail buying

Large size in retailing gives potential power over many aspects of buying relationships. Having this power also brings the responsibility to use or not use it. A challenge of size is to establish to what extent, for what purpose and how the channel power should be used in relationships with suppliers. Managing these power relationships requires a level of managerial sophistication which sometimes takes time to evolve. A second area of managerial challenge in respect of large retailers and their position in the channel is the extent to which channel integration policies, both formal and informal, should be pursued. The larger the retailer, the greater is the extent to which integration becomes feasible. For example, Kingfisher has a property development subsidiary, Marks and Spencer has substantial integration over product design and development, Promodès and Carrefour are involved in shopping-centre development and Tesco has joint ventures with firms in the consumer finance sector. While informally administered integration may be favoured in product channels, more formal ownership structures are apparent in service channels. This makes an interesting comparison with manufacturing.

Relationships with other retailers

With increasing size of company, so more opportunities arise to explore co-operative alliances with other retailers with whom, at another level, there is intense competition. An issue for management in the large retailers is the extent to which they become involved in this 'co-opetition' (Brandenburger and Nalebuff 1996). While 'co-operate to compete' might simply be the call of the embattled multinational, nonetheless, new strategic paradigms via alliances (Nooteboom 1999; Håkansson and Sharma 1996) and the idea of a networked company (Haugland and Lunman 1996) become available as retail companies expand beyond a critical size. These new strategic choices present a challenge consequent on 'bigness'. The evaluation of the benefits from such alliances requires some different considerations from those addressed by management operating exclusively under competitive conditions, for example the issues of external access to information, system design and supplier terms.

Management of mergers and acquisitions

With larger size the only realistic mode for substantial growth is through merger and acquisition. This presents some difficulties as the speed of such activity quickens. For example, Laurus, the new name for the combined Vendex-De Boer company made twelve acquisitions in barely a year in 1998/9 and Ahold has quickened its acquisition activity in the late 1990s in USA and in Spain. There are not only difficulties in integrating acquisitions which may combine firms with different cultures, for example Wal-Mart's purchase of Spar Germany and the cross-border merger of ICA and Hakon, in late 1998, but also it is increasingly difficult to make acquisitions at realistic prices. As the companies get larger so the cost of merging also becomes high. The merger of Promodès and Carrefour announced in August 1999 will cost 1,500 million FFr, as estimated by Herve Deffroy, the CFO. The cut in operating costs of the merger is estimated at 4,000 million FFr over the three years following merger (Woodruff and Carreyrou 1999). One of the important factors behind the success of Ahold as an international retailer is claimed to be its ability to integrate new acquisitions quickly. In respect of the acquisition by Ahold of Giant in May 1998 and Pathmark in March 1999:

> The economies of scale are yielding significant synergy effects in distribution and production, store operation, and information technology. A major factor is the savings coming from synergies in buying and merchandising ... We also see Giant–Landover giving Ahold a pool of talented retail professionals to populate other sister companies in the U.S. and abroad. That helps our globalization process.
>
> (Van der Hoven 1999: 78)

The Pathmark acquisition has raised other issues, notably the relationship with competition authorities.

Marketing execution

Large size of firm in retailing also generates particular marketing problems of consistency of execution. These may be compounded because the large firm often becomes multinational, with pricing, product and promotional policies having to be different in different countries. Exceptional managerial discipline is needed to execute, correctly in all the stores, the promotions, merchandising changes, category management layouts and even price changes. The larger the firm and chain of stores, the greater the likelihood that promotions and merchandising will be complex and difficulties will occur. The challenges for large firms are to keep systems simple, to motivate large numbers of store-level staff and really to know what is going on at store level. The problems are lessened if the firm, in effect, has a single store format and tightly defined systems, for example Aldi. With increasing size, however, it becomes difficult to operate only a single format. It also becomes more difficult to determine the extent to which a store's financial performance is due to the store format or to the performance of the store management. With large firms the difficulties and costs of making minor adjustments to marketing implementations increase with the size of the firm – one of the dis-benefits of scale.

Relationships with financial institutions

Large size brings with it changes in the nature of relationships with the institutional investors. The imperative to meet short-term tactical targets becomes stronger as institutional investor involvement increases and becomes more active. The financial analysts working in these institutions require ever more sophisticated and potentially commercially sensitive information. Retail tactics and strategies have to explained and specified with quantitative targets against which performance is assessed. Deviation from plans has to be communicated before any surprises happen. This openness on issues of strategy and performance can create difficulties in competitive terms, with the copying of tactics and strategies widespread in retailing.

Relationships with governments

The challenge here is to establish mutually beneficial relationships with public policy agencies, particularly those concerned with competition and the right of establishment. Competition policies and their control agencies view large firms as likely violators of policy (Pilat 1997; Rey and Caballero-Sanz 1996). Acquisition activity is scrutinized and interventions occur. The European Commission blocked the whole merger of Kesko-Tuko in Finland. In 1999 the European Commission ruled on the Rewe acquisition of Meinl in Austria. Rewe acquired Bila in Austria in 1996, giving Rewe substantial market share but with no major intervention from the competition agencies. In 1998 Rewe then acquired Julius Meinl in Austria, comprising Pam Pam hypermarkets, Julius Meinl supermarkets, Meinl Gourmet and Jééé discount. This would have increased the national market share from 30 to 37 per cent and to even higher levels in Vienna and East Austria. The competition authority of the European Commission ruled that only 162 of the original 300 stores could be acquired. The importance of the ruling is that the European Commission considered regional and local markets. In 1999, the referral to the UK Competition Commission of all the large and medium-sized firms in the grocery sector provides a further example of intervention by competition authorities. This referral followed extensive debate over the potential abuse of retailer power in respect of consumers and suppliers (Dobson and Waterson 1996, 1998; London Economics 1997). As firms become very large the roles of competition policy and the right of establishment policies become interconnected. Permissions to open new stores under land-use planning policies or licensing policies may become more difficult to obtain when the firm already has a substantial market share. The agreement of competition agencies to acquisitions may become more difficult if firms have strong local positions due to the operation of land-use or licensing policies.

There are other challenges for the large retailer inherent in the 'bigness' factor in respect of simply managing the large number of staff, handling the large number of products, accounting the large number of transactions, etc. These are challenges of big numbers, and can be handled by sophisticated management science. The challenges outlined above are the challenges to strategies and of processes. It is the issue of processes being different in large firms compared to medium-sized ones where the major challenges reside. In all this, it is unclear whether, if at all, there is a maximum effective size of retail firm. It is also not clear why retail firms continue to grow; this is an issue not limited to retailers (Geroski 1999). It is not clear how big a retailer has to become before these difficulties outweigh the benefits of 'bigness' outlined in Table 2.

Brands and brand extension

A second big challenge for management in retailing is in the area of brands and branding. Retailer branded product is well-established (Mills 1995; Raju *et al.* 1995; Dhar and Hoch 1997; Richardson 1997) and of increasing importance. Retailers are finding new ways to exploit brand concepts, to extend their brand and move product branding into new areas (Nijssen and van Trijp 1998). The issue for management is to implement profitably the several approaches to branding in a retail context.

Retail branding has moved through several stages of *product branding*. Laaksonen and Reynolds (1994) suggest that, in the mid-1990s grocery re-tailers were at a fourth stage, having moved through phases of generics, own label, un-supported retail brand and into the fourth phase where there is extensive innovative product development, sub-branding and support for the retail brand. The challenge in the grocery sector is to determine what is to be phase 5 in product branding. In non-foods, retailer branding of products has become very complex, with the extensive development of sub-brands.

Alongside the development in retail brand products are developments in *store branding*. Stores have become brands with brand images and values associated with their names, for example, Mamouth, IKEA, Dia, B&Q, Hennes and Mauritz, etc. Some companies have moved into brand extension with multiple format operation. Tesco, for example, in August 1998 had *Tesco Superstore* for their 470 large food stores, typically over 2,600 sq. m. and with 25–30,000 skus, *Tesco Compact* for their fifty-nine small-town supermarkets of less than 2,600 sq. m. and with around 13,000 skus, *Tesco Extra* for their two hypermarkets with over 45,000 skus, *Tesco Metro* for their forty town-centre stores typically between 400 and 1,000 sq. m. with 6–8,000 skus, *Tesco Express* for their fifteen convenience store and filling stations of 150–230 sq. m. with approximately 2,000 skus. Others are following this multi-format model of brand extension, for example GB, Casino and Ahold. This multi-format strategy is one way to use brand concepts to expand market share in strongly contested markets.

At a further level there is *retailer (corporate) branding*. Kingfisher has become a brand although no stores carry that name. The brand is used not to final consumers but for other stakeholders in the company, notably but not exclusively the financial institutions. This is one way of building relationships with financial institutions in response to the issues of large size discussed above.

How far can a retail brand be extended? In product terms several large retailers, for example Tesco and Wal-Mart, already export their retail brand products. Marks and Spencer has formalized the export activity into a form of franchising with branded products available in several European Countries, South Africa, Middle East, East Asia through export and franchise arrangements. Since 1998, Sainsbury has been making its retail brand products available to selected village shops in the UK. This distribution to others may be one direction for retail brand products. There may be further development of retail brands with them being the only brand in the store. This is already the case in some large stores. Marks and Spencer is an example, although it is interesting, and indicative of the challenge posed by retail brands, that the strategic review undertaken in 1999 by Marks and Spencer is considering introducing other brand names into the store. There are many other examples of single-brand stores: IKEA, Disney Store, Thorntons, Benetton, Gap, Laura Ashley, etc., in the medium-sized range of firms. In these cases the product, store and corporate brand work together. Therein lies a challenge of keeping the consistency of the brand across all activities.

There were three trends apparent in branding in the late 1990s:

- Brand extension to open new sectoral markets. Moves into banking, food service, travel services, para-medical services and internet–web services have been made by different European retailers attempting to use their brand in new areas. In these cases the wish is to create a single brand which has wide applicability.

- Sub-branding. This is being undertaken with different assortments in the store carrying different brand names, for example the George clothing range in ASDA, the several brands in C&A and Decathlon.
- Use of the brand to support international activity. This may take place despite the brand name having few customer values in the country of entry. Marks and Spencer's entry into, and subsequent withdrawal from, Germany is an example, with the Marks and Spencer brand having little meaning in a German context. Tesco, B&Q and Carrefour use their store brand prominently in their entries into countries in Central Europe and East Asia, but the names mean little to consumers in those countries. Nonetheless the names are used in preference to names of chains that they acquire or to names more easily acknowledged by the local consumers.

At the end of the twentieth century there was already great variety and confusion in the tactical and strategic use of brands by retailers. How to use these techniques of branding generates difficult questions for retailers in their various relationships with consumers (Auty and Elliott 1998), suppliers (Narasimhan and Wilcox 1998), and competitors (East and Hogg 1997). There are likely, in the twenty-first century, to be new uses of brands by retailers – and yet more questions over their exploitation. Sorting out the confusions represents a significant managerial challenge.

Over-supply of retail floor-space

A third challenge for retail managers is the impending over-capacity in retail floor-space. This is perhaps more of a challenge for the property sector to find alternative users for the excess space, but it is also of concern to retailers. Many stores are not trading at an optimum level partly because of over-supply of space. Store refurbishments seek to increase the productivity of the floor-space. This adds to the over-capacity. There are several reasons for the over-capacity:

- The potential for increased sales productivity from existing space. Higher levels of efficiency in retail operations and improved effectiveness of marketing, for example through ECR, mean that more sales can potentially be made from existing space. In addition, the higher levels of mobility of consumers result in more shops becoming potential shopping destinations. Thus, from a retailer perspective, the potential trade area of a store can increase.
- Non-store retailing gaining a larger share of retail sales. While there are many different estimates of the volume of sales through e-commerce, even the low estimates suggest there will be need for less retail floor-space in the future. It is noteworthy, however, that several firms in electronic retailing are linking with store-based companies to provide multi-channel distribution.

- Switch from goods to services in consumer spending. Spending on goods is increasing at a lower rate than consumer spending generally and spending on services in particular. This underpins some moves by product retailers into retailing services in attempts to use store-space more efficiently.
- A continuing development of new retail space. This is due to shopping-centre development in new types of location, for example, transport inter-changes, and with new marketing approaches, for example, factory-outlet centres.
- Expansion strategies of large firms. It is increasingly difficult for large firms to acquire smaller firms with appropriate store formats in order to gain market share in mature markets and in consequence the large firms expand, in these markets, through building new stores.
- A tendency for governments to de-regulate controls on store location. There have been moves in recent years, in several countries, to reduce restrictions on new store openings but at the same time to encourage new store development in town and city centres (Guy 1998a; Davies 1995).

The over-capacity will have an impact on company balance sheets as property values stabilize or fall over the next few years. It may also mean that inter-firm and inter-type competition increase in intensity through both price and non-price competition (Langston *et al.* 1998). This is one of the drivers towards lower costs. Large retailers will find it difficult, however, to reduce their floor-space in response to over-capacity as this will probably mean a reduction in sales volumes. Reductions in space may come from the exit from the market of small retailers, but their market share is already small in many sectors. Failure of some medium-sized firms, for example the bankruptcy of Eatons in Canada in mid-1999, also may take some space out of the retail sector.

Turbulence in the retail environment

The external environment in which retailers operate is changing in new ways. Globalization and a single currency in Europe create more unknowns in the market environment (Salto 1999). In globalization, for example, it is unclear what direction this trend will take over the next five to ten years (Lehmann 1999). Is globalization a long-term trend? Can retailers reap the benefits of globalization in the same way as manufacturing companies? Several very large retailers are committing their strategy very strongly to a belief in the continuance of globalization. There are, however, several realistic alternative scenarios about globalization to which probabilities can be applied. In each case the implications for retailers are different. Examples of these alternatives are:

- Crises in Asia. This draws a parallel between Asia at century end and Europe in the late nineteenth century and the West, more generally, in the 1930s. The Cold War is still present in Asia and might intensify. As of 1999, a banking and financial collapse in Japan was still possible, leading to worldwide depression. There could be, in this case, a collapse of 'globalization' as Asia stagnates.

- The West builds barriers to rest of world. As the US trade deficit increases so trade conflicts with the European Union increase and Europe becomes protectionist. The trade disagreement generates strong political and cultural animosity to the West. Again, there would be a collapse of 'globalization' as the West protects itself.

- Evolutionary survival. This is a no-change scenario. Globalization unleashes a strong search for competitiveness, with increased merger, acquisition and alliance activity. Only the strongest and best-managed firms survive as the ends justify the means in commercial behaviour, but corruption increases. The landscape comprises global winners and national losers with big gaps in corporate wealth.

- Post-modern global capitalism. Globalization continues but there is learning from previous mistakes. Pragmatism and transparency become important. Environmentalism, human rights and inter-government organizations all increase in power. IT results in increased commercial transparency. Monopoly power is controlled, taxed and reduced. Globalization of operations also brings global responsibility which is accepted, but with an increase in the cost base of firms.

- New world order. Russia transforms to be a successful liberal democracy and sustained economic growth occurs in former communist economies. Political and economic liberalization occurs in China. Japan revives economically. The Euro is a success in Europe and becomes a major currency. WTO grows in power and credibility. Emerging markets emerge rather than submerge and multinationals accept global responsibilities. Global statesmanship and responsibilities become recognized.

Each of these scenarios has very different implications for retailing. Each is possible. Some have higher probabilities that others. Lehmann (1999) suggests either evolutionary survival or post-modern global capitalism as the most likely. Given such possible scenarios, globalization is not a secure concept. While the global picture is important for retailing now and the large retailers do not operate only in local markets, nonetheless globalization as a basis for long-term strategy raises issues for debate.

The environmental turbulence is also seen in changes in consumers' demands and behaviours. The fragmentation of consumer demand, the need to personalize retail offers, the demands for more choice from consumers, and an increasingly critical consumer constituency have been present for some years and are generating retail responses (Leefland and Van Raaji 1995). More difficult to respond to are the concerns about product quality, the fall in confidence in the fairness of retailer activity and the ageing of the European population (Hall and White 1995).

The concerns about quality are seen particularly clearly in the food sector. The Eurobarometer survey in spring 1998 (European Commission 1998) asked about perceptions of food safety. The date is important as this is before the concern over dioxin contamination of food in Belgium. In the survey across fifteen European countries only 39 per cent of respondents thought pre-cooked meals were a safe food to buy. In Sweden the percentage was 71 per cent and in UK 61 per cent, but this falls to 7 per cent in Greece and 12 per cent in Italy. Even with frozen foods, only 20 per cent of respondents in Greece believed them safe and 78 per cent believed them to be actually unsafe. Confidence in these processed foods is low. With fresh foods, the picture is disquieting but not as bad. Only 34 per cent in Germany believe fresh meat is safe and 40 per cent in Belgium. Given Denmark's agricultural industry, it is surprising that 44 per cent believe fresh meat unsafe. Table 3 summarizes the results of this large European-wide survey. Many questions are raised by such data. How should European food retailers respond to such figures, which may well now show lower levels of confidence, given the dioxin scare in Belgium in 1999? Should retailer branding be pursued in pre-prepared meals in this environment?

Externalization or internalization of functions

Retailers continue to grapple, but with increased intensity from the late 1990s, with the issue of what functions to keep within the firm and what to externalize. The extent to which functions are carried out within the firm or the extent to which they are subcontracted has been of concern for a long time. The potential for externalization has increased. The decisions of retailers on this issue influence the structure of the sector and the ways that competitive processes operate. There are a number of areas, for example advertising, where externalization has been widespread for many years. Other functions, notably finance, remain internalized. There are, however, some functions where there are notable changes taking place in the responsibility and control of these functions in the distribution sector.

Externalization or subcontracting is of increasing importance in logistics, security and maintenance, software development, inventory ownership and staff recruitment. In each case, there are successful specialist companies serving the retail sector. Even in the area of store management there is an externalization of responsibility to be seen with the continuing growth of franchise-type arrangements in several sub-sectors of retailing.

There are many reasons for this externalization of activity. In some cases they are undertaken purely for accounting and financial reasons to change the financial structure of the firm – moving costs off the balance sheet and onto the profit and loss account. In other cases the externalization of activity enables retail management to focus more sharply on retail issues. The firm focuses on its core managerial competencies in order to seek competitive advantage in these areas. It is also possible in many cases for the retailer to

Table 3 Percentage[1] of respondents answering 'safe' and 'unsafe' to the question 'For each of the following food products, please tell me if you think it is safe or not safe'

	Pre-cooked meals		Frozen foods		Eggs		Fresh meat		Fresh fish	
	safe	*unsafe*	*safe*	*unsafe*	*safe*	*unsafe*	*safe*	*unsafe*	*safe*	*unsafe*
Belgium	36	55	57	36	78	18	40	55	65	31
Denmark	35	51	62	30	45	53	54	44	71	25
Germany	40	46	49	39	53	40	34	57	42	49
Greece	7	89	20	78	71	27	63	35	77	21
Spain	41	51	55	39	83	15	82	17	88	11
France	40	53	57	39	68	29	48	48	68	29
Ireland	36	49	67	24	83	12	63	27	77	16
Italy	12	69	41	44	89	7	85	10	77	15
Luxembourg	29	66	44	51	65	33	55	42	61	35
Netherlands	55	32	87	9	84	12	72	22	75	17
Austria	40	52	63	29	76	19	75	19	58	34
Portugal	19	71	41	52	68	20	47	50	71	28
Finland	56	32	78	17	93	5	81	15	86	10
Sweden	70	18	84	10	90	7	78	15	84	10
UK	61	27	86	9	78	16	67	23	84	11
EU 15	39	49	58	34	73	22	60	34	69	25

Source: European Commission 1998

Note

1 The difference between the 'safe' and 'unsafe' and 100% is the 'Don't Know' group

specify precisely the nature of the service although there is no need to be the actual supplier. In the case of logistics, for example, the retailer can specify quality and service levels and the specialist logistics company works to these levels, in some cases through physical facilities dedicated to a single retailer (Fernie 1990; IGD 1998). Such an approach has become widespread in food and non-food areas. Specialist firms, for example Tibbett and Britten, operate a number of distribution centres each dedicated to the needs of a particular retailer. They also operate shared specialist facilities but even in these centres it is the retailers who define the service levels and related performance measures. A question for retailers is: 'What other functional areas can benefit from the successful experience gained in outsourcing logistics?'

The extent and form of externalization may be related to size of firm. In small businesses we see the externalization of the buying function to central buying agencies being used as a means to gain organizational-scale economies for these firms (Lachner and Täger 1997). Euromadi in Spain has a network of over 2,000 stores linked in the single buying group; Intersport has created a European-wide buying network for member firms. Within large firms, buying is most certainly internalized as this is the way for these firms to achieve the scale economies in supply-chain management while externalizing the logistics function (GEA 1994; Lamey 1996). Nonetheless, some selective joint buying may be undertaken by large firms who have entered into international buying alliances, but the value of products purchased in this way is small compared with total sales volumes (Robinson and Clarke-Hill 1995). Such alliances of large firms can be fragile, as indicated more generally by Serapio and Cascio (1996), and questions can be raised over their long-term stability in retailing.

There are also areas of increased internalization by the retailer. Notable in this respect are product development, quality auditing and customer communications. In these cases, retailers are becoming more directly involved in functions which were previously undertaken by other firms. In the case of product development, for example, retailers have become heavily involved in the design, development, packaging and quality monitoring of retailer brand products. Given customer perceptions of safety, food retailers certainly wish to ensure that suppliers adhere to quality-control procedures. The retailers often do not own the production facility but have considerable effective control over the production process (Kaas 1993). The substantial expansion of retail brand products in the product ranges of retailers, of all types, increases the extent of this internalization of product development (A C Nielsen 1998). As retail-brand-product developments have become more sophisticated so internalization of processes has increased. The future optimal balance between internalization and externalization is far from clear.

e-retail

One of the great unknowns over the next five years is whether or not e-commerce will become a significant force in satisfying consumer markets and so make electronic retailing a serious competitor to fixed store retailing. Much is promised but little has been delivered (Stern and Weitz 1997; Jones and Biasiotto 1998). Michalak points out that academics have not provided much guidance to managers on this issue, arguing that, 'There is a paucity of research identifying and articulating issues that could guide business managers in the use of internet commerce' (1999b: 1). e-commerce has grown in the business-to-business market but remains small in final consumer markets. Some authors suggest major growth in this channel but with little hard evidence (de Kare-Silver 1998). Some of it is written by those groups who will benefit most from the growth of the channel and so must be viewed with caution. Nonetheless, if there is growth, the implications for existing retailers could be considerable. There are several key questions here for senior retail executives.

- What are the product and service areas in which e-commerce will grow first and in which will it take market share from fixed store retailers? We see development in books, toys and recorded entertainment, but will these be profitable areas?
- Which customer groups will use it?
- From where will customers access the shopping sites?
- Will either existing store-based firms or new firms or both supply e-retail services to consumers?
- Will the market become concentrated or very fragmented? Boston Consulting Group (1998) suggests that the ten largest companies involved in 1998 accounted for 50 per cent of sales volumes. How will this level of concentration change?
- What form will inter-firm competition take when it is on an electronic channel? Will price be all-important or will service, in terms of accuracy of order fulfilment, delivery, security, packaging, brand integrity, etc., have a role to play (Alba *et al.* 1997)?
- What logistics support systems will be needed for the new channel? Will these be externalized and/or shared?
- What will be the cost and value drivers in the total value chain?
- Will there be significant first mover advantages?
- How will the various national rules on consumer redress and data protection apply across Europe?

While it is possible to surmise answers to all these questions there is little certainty about any of the answers. The whole area is presently at a very early stage of development. Whether development will continue and, if it does, what direction it will take is a major forecasting challenge facing managers in retailing. Paradigm shifts in retailing which render existing core skills and assets obsolete happen very rarely; more commonly, firms improve by doing existing things better and doing new things within existing paradigms. Some retailers and commentators think that the Internet and electronic retailing represent the first paradigm shift in retailing for over fifty years. What strategy should be followed until the pattern becomes clearer?

Challenges for research in retailing

Some challenges to retail research reflect these managerial challenges. There are also research challenges, which relate to the theory of retailing.

Who does what and why?

Within retailing we are seeing great variation in the functions performed by the firms called retailers. How is this portfolio of functions changing? Why is this so? How is the value chain changing such that firms internalize and externalize functions? What is the structure of transaction costs? The nature of the retail firm is difficult to define when it is selling banking services, health services and travel services in addition to its established product ranges over which it is exerting controls over production, development and quality monitoring.

Before this type of question is answered we need to have a better way of measuring what is happening in retail firms. The difficulties in measuring performance in retailing are compounded by the dis-aggregated nature of retail operations and the volume of data which has to be aggregated. The value chain has a significant spatial component to it in retailing. This is often not the case to the same extent in manufacturing industry. In addition, the value chain is dis-aggregated through many products; this can be across 200,000 or more product items in a department store. Tracking and measuring added value in the service sector presents some conceptual issues which have not yet been solved. These compound the empirical problems resulting from the distinctive characteristics of retail activity.

A related area is in the measurement of productivity of the various assets in retailing. Productivity measurement in the service sector generally remains one of the big challenges for research in management. Measurement in retailing of the productivity of capital, floor-space, employees, marketing spend, etc., presents theoretical as well as empirical difficulties linked to the determination of the functions being performed by the retailer (Anderson *et al.* 1997; Ratchford and Brown 1985). Work by Oi (1992) waits to be developed further. This area of performance measurement presents a noteworthy theoretical and empirical research challenge.

When we have better ways of measuring performance, particularly productivity, then it will be easier to theorize and analyse the way the portfolio of functions is changing and why it is changing.

Risk assessment

Risk evaluation is of increasing importance in retailing. The change in retailing from being supply driven to being demand driven, the changes in the structure of the retail sector and changing dynamics of retail operations all make risk evaluation of increasing importance in retailing. Very little research has been carried out on risk in retailing either generally or in component sub-systems. The only substantial exception is the work on consumers (Mitchell and McGoldrick 1996). Recent concerns about food safety, for example, suggest that the consumers' and retailers' ways of evaluating risk are different. The consequences of food retailers moving into banking suggest that the risks of these moves were inadequately analysed in some cases.

Within the retail context it is unclear whether the levels of different types of risk are increasing or decreasing from the viewpoint of the various participants. There is an extensive literature on risk within a general business context (Ansell and Wharton 1992) and also considerable research on the different, but related, concepts of financial risk. How applicable the existing theoretical and conceptual studies are to retailing has not been established. Do the dis-aggregated nature of activity in retailing and the large number of retailers potentially at risk, for example, affect the applicability of this existing research?

It may be possible, for example, to consider some of the recent internationalization of retailing within a framework of risk analysis. Risk levels at the various points in the value chain are different in different spatial contexts. By taking the spatial dimension, to the value chain in addition to its quantitative and qualitative dimensions, so we might be able to explore modes of entry and adaptation to local markets within a risk analytical framework. The apparent pattern of standardization for back-store systems with adaptation at the front-store to accommodate new markets may become explicable within a risk-based theory of market entry which considers risk throughout the retail demand chain.

Given the levels of investment and the dynamism of processes within retailing it is surprising that risk has featured so slightly in research on retailing.

Modelling the sector

Many of the models of activity in the sector have got stuck in analogues of wheels and cycles. A considerable amount of research and publication on retailing has become mesmerized by these ideas. Perhaps with the new century we can relegate these models to useful historical ideas and explore some new models of the industry, the organization and the establishment (Ratchford and Stoops 1992). In developing explanatory, rather than descriptive, models we need to consider the processes through which decisions are made and the range of choices considered by managers, customers and public policy agents. Research on how decisions are made is not easy because we often do not know what the decisions are that are being taken. In many cases we do not have a clear understanding of how the retail organization functions or indeed what the information flows are in a highly dis-aggregated organization of the type present in retailing.

In considering models of the organization we should consider, perhaps, whether all the organizations in retailing are of the same type and should fit into a common model. Can a model be generic for Ahold, Leclerc, Migros, Benetton and Harrods? If so, is it of any value? If not, then on what dimensions should we discriminate different types of retail organization, which would have coherence for modelling? Only then can we begin to think about the structure of the models, which might be used to consider the internal workings of retailers and their intra-type and inter-type relationships. From these models we might then gain some insights into, among many things, why some retail organizations have to grow and develop to survive and others do not.

Our modelling of the retail establishment is little better than our modelling of the organization. We do not have a good classification system for establishments, although it is perhaps better than our non-attempts to classify organizations. Casual terms have been incorporated into use such that we use the terms discount store, department store, convenience store with no consistency in our interpretation. Guy (1998b) suggests the problem extends to the classification of locations. Helffrich *et al.* (1997) suggest a similar lack of definitions is to be seen in concepts of international retailing. How can we model the performance of a department store when we do not have agreement on what it is? Perhaps we need to look afresh at the retail establishment and decide what dimensions we should use to differentiate different types, if indeed there are different types. Research on this aspect of retailing which applies the established taxonomic techniques could be a way forward. We can then begin to establish how to measure and model the performance of different formats and the aspects of format which make a difference in performance, for example building on the work of Magi and Julander (1996).

In addition to the models of organizations and establishments, a third group of models which still need development is of those which explain relationships between retailers and other organizations in the demand chain, including suppliers. There has been considerably more work undertaken on these relationships when they involve manufacturer relationships with their suppliers than when retailers are involved. Nonetheless, the possibilities of applying some of the conceptual work into the retail area are present if it is feasible to obtain reliable empirical information from retailers and other sources (Messinger and Narsimhan 1995). Recent work by Artz (1999) and Heide and Stump (1995) which explores issues of asset specificity and the performance of channel relationships might form the basis for work involving retailer relationships with suppliers. A second direction this type of work might take is extending current work (Parkhe 1998; Das and Teng 1998; Inkpen and Beamish 1997; Smeltzer 1997; Kramer and Tyler 1996) on trust and knowledge into the context of retailer relationships. This general topic, however, remains a difficult one given the very confidential nature of many of the relationships between retailers and their suppliers. Some conceptual work may even be possible with current levels of knowledge and judicious use of in-depth qualitative case studies.

Organizational learning

Retail organizations have variable levels of ability to change in response to relationships with external agents, notably consumers, suppliers and public policy agencies. The speed of response, even of some large organizations, is often rapid. In other organizations, response has been too slow and commercial failure has occurred. There are interesting research questions about how this rapid change takes place and the role of innovation and organizational learning in these response patterns (Pontiggia and Sinatra 1997).

The nature and origins of innovation in retailing have not been a focus for research. It is accepted that investment in R&D by retailers is relatively low in comparison with other sectors so the question arises: 'From where does innovation come?' Retailer responsiveness to the changes in the environment suggests that considerable innovation is present. Is it only present in short-term marketing initiatives or is there more fundamental innovation within the retail organization?

Being a consumer-orientated industry, which depends on consumer access to its operations, retailing is a very open industry in that retailers can see easily what other retailers are doing. Retailers can therefore learn not only from within their organization but also from what other organizations are doing (Dierkes and Berthoin-Antal 1985). As such, retailing could be a suitable industry in which to test and extend some of the theories of organizational learning (Hatch 1993). While there has been some work on the international transfer of managerial expertise in retailing (Kacker 1985) this is an area where there are many unanswered questions. Some of the large retailers are now widespread in their international operations, both sourcing and shop operation. To what extent has this enabled the transfer of expertise back into the retail firm? Has the increase in the use of alliances for international expansion increased the intensity of organizational learning? What is the role of external agents, for example suppliers, trade associations and consultants, in the transfer and diffusion of practices, for example ECR? To what extent can retailers retain competitive advantage in areas that are open to competitor inspection? How influential is the CEO in the transfer of ideas? Answers to these and other related questions would give us a much better understanding of innovation in retailing.

Economics of competition

The models of competition traditionally developed by economists often do not fit comfortably with retailing. Over thirty years ago McClelland (1967) was uncomfortable about the seeming mismatch between competition as viewed by an economist and the reality in retailing. Even earlier Weld (1923) was doubtful about the translation into distribution of some economic concepts developed in manufacturing. More recently Oi (1992) has raised a similar concern. Economic theory has moved forward dramatically in many ways but seldom making the application into retailing with much confidence. It is interesting, for example, to see central place theory, abandoned as a retailing concept, being born again by quantitative economists (Fujita *et al.* 1999). Notable exceptions to the lack of economic theory in retailing are the works of Bliss (1988) and Ratchford and Stoops (1992). Several causes can be hypothesized for the lack of applicability to retailing of some recent advances in economics:

- the spatial element of horizontal competition, the complexity of the vertical dis-intermediation of functions and the co-operation of retailers under some circumstances cause complications for the analysis of competitive processes;
- it has already been suggested we are not sure of what we mean by 'type' in inter- and intra-type competition;
- the use of power relationships by retailers to compete and co-operate vertically in order to improve horizontal competitiveness makes models of competition difficult to formalize;
- the large number of products and services across which competition can be undertaken within a single firm also causes problems as not all the products are of the same competitive importance, and so substitution is complex in both time and space;
- the use of a variety of promotional tools, both in price and in non-price sales promotion, makes empirical work complex because of the difficulty in getting a sound basis for inter-firm and inter-type comparisons;
- increasingly the competition is between total supply/demand chains not between organizations at one stage of the chain;
- the difficulty of establishing a sound base for empirical comparisons of performance (Burt and Sparks 1997);
- a general unwillingness for economics and strategic management to converge (Knudsen 1995).

A major challenge facing retail research is to get better models of retail competition and co-operation and to find ways of testing them. The need is to integrate the models developed from the managerial perspective, for example those of Corstjens and Corstjens (1995), with new perspectives from economies. We see some developments in the work of Smith (1999) and Wrigley (1992, 1995) but much more is needed.

A related area for research is into the exact nature of scale and scope economies in the retail sector as it is now structured. Scale economies operate in different ways at establishment and organization level in that they affect different aspects of cost structure but the inter-relationships are not clear. The same situation holds for economies of scope but these have been explored even less in retailing despite their being at the heart of assortment planning in the firm and at the store. A potentially complicating issue here is associated with branding and the way this might influence economies of scope and possibly even scale.

Retailing as an economic stimulus

A somewhat different research challenge is to get a better understanding of the nature of the economic and social stimulus provided by retail activity. Retailing is an activity that is commonplace around the world in societies with vastly different levels of income and expenditure. In all these societies it adds value in the economy. Can retailing be better used as a vehicle to generate social and economic advancement? If so, then how can this be done? The historic evidence in the richer countries is that retailing has provided a mechanism for improvement in social conditions and capital accumulation. In the immediate aftermath of World War II the number of retailers in France increased by 116,000 between 1946 and 1952 (Stacey and Wilson 1958). More recently, shopping-centre development has been used as a vehicle for wider economic regeneration. Are these experiences transferable to countries where there is a pressing need to close the huge gap between the few rich and the many poor?

In the economic transformation in Central Europe after 1989 an explosion took place in the number of small retail operations. Retailing provided a mechanism for many people to gain a basic understanding of pricing and profit-driven business. It remains unclear whether many of these new informal organizations will grow into fully fledged formal retailers. At the same time, the entry into these countries by well-established and often large retailers from Western Europe generated growth in suppliers and the transfer of managerial expertise into the larger firms already present. How might it be possible to get a trickle-down effect of this expertise to the smaller firms? The role of IKEA, for example, in generating new investment in the furniture manufacturing sector in Poland and in the development of shopping centres is one example of major transfers of expertise and generation of added value in the economy. What has been the effect on the smaller furniture retailer and manufacturer? We can hypothesize positive and negative effects but there is no confirmatory evidence either way. There are gaps both in the theoretical and empirical work.

Retailing plays a significant role in meeting popular aspirations as consumers gradually increase their purchasing power. It also may play a much more direct role in generating increases of purchasing power through the jobs generated directly and in suppliers. Research on this aspect of retailing, not only in Central Europe but also across many countries, would help in understanding the nature of retailing as a creator of economic growth and so perhaps influence public policy in this area.

In many Third World countries there is an extensive informal sector of retailing which has received some notable research in recent years (Lubell 1991; Ranis and Stewart 1999) What remains unclear is the extent of interaction between formal and informal sectors. Are the supply chains quite distinct even when the informal sector is selling branded items? While the retail sector cannot solve the gap between the haves and have-nots in these societies there is certainly scope for more research, both theoretical and empirical, to try to understand better the role retailing has as a stimulant to social and economic transformation.

Conclusion

Retailing is an evolving industry. While much is talked about a 'retail revolution', there is in reality little evidence of either major paradigm shifts or of change of a revolutionary nature. Many of the features of European retailing at the century's end reflect the evolution of the sector over fifty years or more. Given this evolutionary nature it should be possible to hypothesize with some accuracy the evolution of present trends over the next ten years, although perhaps not the timing of change. The likely changes bring particular challenges for managers and academic researchers. These challenges are dissimilar to those in manufacturing.

This paper considers six topics that are suggested as major challenges for management in the next decade. These changes illustrate the ways that retailing, and its management, is somewhat different from the manufacturing sector and that there is limited crossover of relevant managerial knowledge. Retailing is distinctive in many ways, for example in its responsiveness to local culture, the spatially dis-aggregated and dispersed nature of operations, the large number of items which constitute the product and service range, the low profit per employee per item, the large extent of the network of operational units, etc. These differences have been explored elsewhere (Dawson 1994). In considering the next ten years these particular features of the industry are important determinants of change.

The increase in scale of retail firms, as they seek both greater market penetration and new markets, provides some difficult issues which retailers will have to resolve. While there are benefits to large scale there are also problems associated with 'bigness'. These problems and benefits associated with large and increasing scale of operation also present theoretical and empirical challenges for academic researchers.

The nature of competition in retailing is changing as a greater understanding of the value chain is gained. Again there are challenges for academics and managers in better understanding the processes of competition. Branding issues have become more important in managerial considerations of competition but they have not yet been introduced successfully into the academic models of retail competition.

Impending excess provision of retail floorspace, and the associated aspects of format development and productivity evaluation, provide new problem areas for managers and researchers. The extent to which consumers will accept an e-commerce retail format is one of the big questions hanging over retailing. This reinforces the need for addressing the potential over-supply of space and its potential absorption by the diversification activity of retailers. Electronic retailing is an area where retailers have to take a view and to evaluate the strategic and operations risks of that view. Risk assessment in retailing is little understood and a notably under-researched topic. Retail managers making decisions about involvement in e-commerce will not get much help, unfortunately, from the academic literature.

Research on retailing has some way to go before it can provide rigorous realistic models of structure and behaviour at establishment, organizational and sectoral levels. In some aspects the foundations of research, namely accepted definitions of terms, are absent. In other aspects there are significant studies on which advances of knowledge can be built. The academic study of retailing has advanced considerably in recent years but there is still some way to go before we have an understanding of many of the processes and relationships in the sector. To address the research gaps and to provide support to management there is need for a major investment in the new century in developing expertise to understand the processes and their management in retailing and its associated demand chain.

Acknowledgements

Work on this paper developed during a period as Visiting Professor at the University of South Africa, Pretoria. Thanks are due to Professors Cronje, Cant and Strydom who made the visit possible and stimulating. Thanks are also due to Professor Donald Harris and several referees for insightful comments during the development of the paper.

References

A.C. Nielsen (1998) *International Private Label Retailing*, Henley-on-Thames: NTC.
Alba, J. *et al.* (1997) 'Interactive home shopping: consumer, retailer and manufacturer incentives to participate in electronic marketplaces', *Journal of Marketing*, 61(3): 38–53.
Anderson, E.W., Fornell, C. and **Rust, R.T.** (1997) 'Customer satisfaction, productivity and profitability: differences between goods and services', *Marketing Science*, 16(2): 129–45.
Ansell, J. and **Wharton, F.** (1992) *Risk: Analysis, Assessment and Management*, Chichester: Wiley.
Artz, K.A. (1999) 'Buyer-seller performance: the role of asset specificity, reciprocal investments and relational exchange', *British Journal of Management*, 10: 113–26.
Auty, S. and **Elliott, R.** (1998) 'Fashion involvement, self-monitoring and the meaning of brands', *Journal of Product and Brand Management*, 7(2): 109–23.
Bartlett, D.C. and **Peterson, R.A.** (1992) 'A retailing agenda for the year 2000', in Peterson, R.A. (ed.) *The Future of US Retailing*, Westport, CT: Quorum.

Bauman, W. (1956) *Das Selbstbedienungssystem in den Migros-Genossenschaften*, Zürich: Migros.

Bliss, C. (1988) 'A theory of retail pricing', *Journal of Industrial Economics*, 36: 375–92.

Boddewyn, J.J. (1971) *Belgian Public Policy towards Retailing*, East Lansing: Michigan State University.

Boggis, F.D. (1966) 'The European Economic Community', in Yamey, B. (ed.) *Resale Price Maintenance*, London: Weidenfeld & Nicolson.

Boston Consulting Group (1998) *The State of On-line Retailing*, Boston, MA: B.C.G.

Brandenburger, A.M. and **Nalebuff, B.J.** (1996) *Co-opetition*, New York: Doubleday.

Burns, W. (1959) *British Shopping Centres*, London: Leonard Hill.

Burt, S. and **Sparks, L.** (1997) 'Performance in food retailing: a cross-national consideration and comparison of retail margins', *British Journal of Management*, 8: 133–50.

Carol, H. (1960) 'The hierarchy of central functions in the city', *Annals of the Association* of *American Geographers*, 50: 419–38.

Colla, E. (1995) *La Grande Distribuzione in Europa*, Milan: Etas.

Corstjens, J. and **Corstjens, M.** (1995) '*Store Wars: The Battle for Mindspace and Shelfspace*', Chichester: Wiley.

Costa, C. *et al.* (1997) '*Structures and Trends in the Distributive Trades in the European Union*', Munich: Ifo Institut.

Das, T.K. and **Teng, B-S.** (1998) 'Between trust and control: developing confidence in partner cooperation alliance', *Academy of Management Review*, 23(3): 491–512.

Davies, B.K. (1998) 'Applying evolutionary models to the retail sector', *International Review of Retail, Distribution and Consumer Research*, 8(2): 165–81.

Davies, R.L. (ed.) (1995) *Retail Planning Policies in Western Europe*, London: Routledge.

Davis, D. (1966) *A History of Shopping*, London: Routledge & Kegan Paul.

Dawson, J.A. (1994) 'Internationalization of retailing operations', *Journal of Marketing Management*, 10: 267–82.

Dawson, J.A. (1999) 'The evolution and future structure of retailing in Europe', in Jones, K. (ed.) *The Internationalisation of Retailing in Europe*, Toronto: Centre for the Study of Commercial Activity.

Dawson, J.A. and **Henley, J.S.** (1999) 'Recent developments and opportunities in retailing in Poland', *Distribucion y Consumo*, in press.

de Kare-Silver, M. (1998) *e-shock: The Electronic Shopping Revolution*, London: Macmillan.

Dhar, S.K. and **Hoch, S.J.** (1997) 'Why store brand penetration varies by retailer', *Marketing Science*, 16(3): 208–27.

Dickinson, R.E. (1951) *The Western European City*, London: Routledge & Kegan Paul.

Dierkes, M. and **Berthoin-Antal, A.** (1985). 'Umweltmanagement Konkret: Erfahrungen aus acht jahen entwicklung beim Migros-Gennossenschaftsbund', *VDI Impuls*, 1: 25–35.

Dobson, P.W. and **Waterson, M.** (1996) 'Vertical restraints and competition policy', *Office of Fair Trading, Research Paper*, 12.

Dobson, P.W. and **Waterson, M.** (1998) 'The welfare consequences of the exercise of buyer power', *Office of Fair Trading, Research Paper*, 16.

East, R. and **Hogg, A.** (1997) 'The anatomy of conquest: Tesco versus Sainsbury', *Journal of Brand Management*, 5(l): 53–60.

Economist (1999) 'Marks and Spencer: food for thought', *The Economist*, 10 July: 76.

European Commission (1998) *Standard Eurobarometer: Public Opinion in the European Union Report 49*, Brussels: Directorate-General X.

Faure, A. (1984) 'The grocery trade in nineteenth century Paris', in Crossick, G. and Haupt, H-G. (eds) *Shopkeeping and Master Artisans in Nineteenth Century Europe*, London: Methuen.

Fernie, J. (1990) 'Third party or own account: trends in retail distribution', in Fernie, J. (ed.) *Retail Distribution Management*, London: Kogan Page.

Ferry, J.W. (1961) *A History of the Department Store*, New York: Macmillan.

Ford, P. and **Thomas, C.J.** (1953) *Shops and Planning*, Oxford: Blackwell.

Friedman, W.A. (1998) 'John H. Paterson and the sales strategy of National Cash Register Company, 1884–1922', *Business History Review*, 72: 552–84.

Fujita, M., Krugman, P. and **Mori, P.** (1999) 'On the evolution of hierarchical urban systems', *European Economic Review*, 43(2): 209–51.

GEA (1994) *Supplier–Retailer Collaboration in Supply Chain Management*, London: Coca-Cola Retailing Research Group – Europe.

Geist, J.F. (1983) *Arcades: The History of a Building Type*, trans. Newman, J.O. and Smith, J.H., Boston, MA: MIT Press.

Gellately, R. (1974) *The Politics of Economic Despair: Shopkeepers and German Politics, 1890–1914*, London: Sage.

Gerlach, S. (1988) *Das Warenhaus in Deutschland*, Stuttgart: F. Steiner.

Geroski, P. (1999) 'The growth of firms in theory and practice', *London Business School, CEPR Discussion Paper*, 2092.

Guy, C. (1998a) 'Controlling new retail spaces: the impress of planning policies in Western Europe', *Urban Studies*, 35(5–6): 953–79.

Guy, C. (1998b) 'Classification of retail stores and shopping centres: some methodological issues', *GeoJournal*, 45: 255–64.

Håkansson, H. and **Sharma, D.D.** (1996) 'Strategic alliances in perspective', in Iacobucci, D. (ed.) *Networks in Marketing*, London: Sage.

Hall, R. and **White, P.** (eds) (1995) *Europe's Population: Towards the Next Century*, London: UCL Press.

Hatch, M.J. (1993) 'The dynamics of organizational culture', *Academy of Management Review*, 18(4): 657–93.

Haugland, S.A. and **Lunman, R.** (1996) 'Core competencies in a network organization', in Falkenberg, J. and Haugland, S.A. (eds) *Rethinking the Boundaries of Strategy*, Copenhagen: Handelshöjskolens Forlag.

Heide, J.B. and **Stump, R.L.** (1995) 'Performance implications of buyer–seller relationships in industrial markets: a transaction cost explanation', *Journal of Business Research*, 37: 57–66.

Helfferich, E., Hinefelaar, M. and **Kasper, H.** (1997) 'Towards a clear terminology on international retailing', *International Review of Retail, Distribution and Consumer Research*, 7(3): 287–307.

Henksmeier, K.H. (1960) *The Economic Performance of Self Service in Europe*, Paris: OEEC.

IGD (1998) *Retail Distribution*, Watford: Institute of Grocery Distribution.

Inkpen, A.C. and **Beamish, P.W.** (1997) 'Knowledge, bargaining power and the instability of international joint-ventures', *Academy of Management Review*, 22: 177–202.

Jefferys, J.B. (1954) *Retail Trading in Britain 1850–1950*, Cambridge: Cambridge University Press.

Jefferys, J.B. and **Knee, D.** (1962) *Retailing in Europe*, London: Macmillan.

Jones, C.S. (1969) *Regional Shopping Centres*, London: Business Books.

Jones, K. and **Biasiotto, M.** (1998) 'Internet retailing: current hype or future reality?', *International Review of Retail, Distribution and Consumer Research*, 9(1): 69–79.

Kaas, K.P. (1993) 'Symbiotic relationships between producers and retailers in the German food market?', *Journal of Institutional and Theoretical Economics*, 149(4): 741–7.

Kacker, M.P. (1985) *Transatlantic Trends in Retailing*, Westport, CT: Greenwood.

Knudsen, C. (1995) 'Theories of the firm, strategic management, and leadership', in Montgomery, C.A. (ed.) *Resource Based and Evolutionary Theories of the Firm*, Boston, MA: Kluwer.

Kramer, R.M. and **Tyler, T.R.** (1996) (eds) *Trust in Organizations: Frontiers of Theory and Research*, Thousand Oaks, CA: Sage.

Laaksonen, H. and **Reynolds, J.** (1994) 'Own branding in food retailing across Europe', *Journal of Brand Management*, 2(l): 37–46.

Lachner, J. and **Täger, U. Chr.** (1997) *Entwicklungen in den Handelskooperationen unter Handels und Wettbewerbspolitischen Aspekten*, Munich: Ifo Institut.

Lamey, J. (1996) *Supply Chain Management*, London: Pearson.

Lancaster, B. (1995) *The Department Store*, London: Leicester University Press.

Langston, P., Clarke, G.P. and **Clarke, D.B.** (1998) 'Retail saturation: the debate in the mid 1990s', *Environment and Planning*, A30: 49–66.

Lebhar, G.M. (1959) *Chain Stores in America, 1859–1959*, New York: Chain Store Publishing.

Leefland, P. and **Van Raaji, W.** (1995) 'The changing consumer in the European Union', *International Journal of Research in Marketing*, 12: 373–87.

Lehmann, J-P. (1999) 'Scenarios for the coming decade', *EFMD Forum*, 99(1): 9–12.

Levy, H. (1948) *The Shops of Britain*, London: Kegan Paul, Trench Trubner.

London Economics (1997) 'Competition in retailing', *Office of Fair Trading, Research Paper*, 13.

Lubell, H. (1991) *The Informal Sector in the 1980s and 1990s*, Paris: OECD.

M+M Eurodata (1999) *Top-Firmem*, Frankfurt am Main: M+M.

McClelland, W.G. (1967) *Costs and Competition in Retailing*, London: Macmillan.

MacKeith, M. (1986) *The History and Conservation of Shopping Arcades*, London: Mansell.

Magi, A. and **Julander, C-R.** (1996) 'Perceived service quality and customer satisfaction in a store performance framework', *Journal of Retailing and Consumer Services*, 3(l): 33–41.

Mathias, P. (1967) *Retail Revolution*, London: Longman.

Messinger, P.R. and **Narasimhan, C.** (1995) 'Has power shifted in the grocery channel?', *Marketing Science*, 14(2): 189–223.

Messinger, P.R. and **Narasimhan, C.** (1997) 'A model of retail formats based on consumers' economizing on shopping time', *Marketing Science*, 16(l): 1–22.

Michalak, W.Z. (1999a) 'Foreign direct investment and Polish retail', in Jones, K. (ed) *The Internationalisation of Retailing in Europe*, Toronto: Centre for the Study of Commercial Activity.

Michalak, W.Z. (1999b) 'Internet commerce', *Ryerson Polytechnic University, Centre for the Study of Commercial Activity, Research Report*, 6.

Mills, D.E. (1995) 'Why do retailers sell private label', *Journal of Economics and Management Strategy*, 4(3): 509–28.

Mitchell, V-W. and **McGoldrick, P.** (1996) 'Consumers' risk-reduction strategies: a review and synthesis', *International Review of Retail, Distribution and Consumer Research*, 6(1): 1–33.

Monod, D. (1996) *Store Wars: Shopkeepers and the Culture of Mass Marketing*, Toronto: University of Toronto Press.

Narasimhan, C. and **Wicox, R.T.** (1998) 'Private labels and the channel relationship: a cross category analysis', *Journal of Business*, 71(4): 573–600.

Nijssen, E.J. and **van Trijp, H.C.M.** (1998) 'Branding fresh products: exploratory empirical evidence from the Netherlands', *European Review of Agricultural Economics*, 25: 228–42.

Nooteboom, B. (1999) *Inter-firm Alliances*, London: Routledge.

Oi, W.Y. (1992) 'Productivity in the distributive trades: the shopper and the economics of massed reserves', in Griliches, Z. (ed.) *Output Measures in Service Sectors*, Chicago: University of Chicago Press.

Parkhe, A. (1998) 'Understanding trust in international alliances', *Journal of World Business*, 33(3): 219–40.

Pasdermadjian, H. (1954) *The Department Store: Its Origins, Evolution and Economics*, London: Newman.

Perkins, J. and **Meredith D.** (1996) 'Managerial developments in retailing: the department and the chain store, 1890–1940', *University of New South Wales, School of Economics, Discussion Paper*, 96/8.

Pilat, D. (1997) 'Regulation and performance in the distribution sector', *OECD, Economics Department Working Papers*, 180.

Plichta, J. and **Swiatowiec, J.** (1998) 'Inwestycje Zagraniczne w Polskim Handlu: Stan faktyczny I opinie konsumentow (Foreign Investment in Retailing and Wholesaling: Current position and consumer views)', in Szrommik, A. (ed.) *Warunki funkcjonowania I rozwoju handlu w Polsce*, Cracow: Cracow University of Economics.

Pontiggia, A. and **Sinatra, A.** (1997) 'Learning for growth: the United Colors of Benetton', in Sinatra, A. (ed.) *Corporate Transformation*, Dordrecht: Kluwer.

Pütz, R. (1998) *Einkelhandel im Transformatioonsprozess*, Passau: L.I.S.

Raju, J.S., Raj, K.S. and **Dhar, S.L.** (1995) 'The introduction and performance of store brands', *Management Science*, 41: 957–78.

Ranis, G. and **Stewart, F.** (1999) 'V-goods and the role of the urban informal sector in development', *Economic Development and Cultural Change*, 47(2): 259–88.

Ratchford, B. and **Brown, J.R.** (1985) 'A study of productivity changes in food retailing', *Marketing Science*, 4(4): 292–311.

Ratchford, B. and **Stoops, G.** (1992) 'An econometric model of a retail firm', *Managerial and Decision Economics*, 13: 223–31.

Rey, P. and **Caballero-Sanz, F.** (1996) 'The policy implications of the economic analysis of vertical restraint', *European Commission, Directorate General for Economic and Financial Affairs, Economic Papers*, 119.

Richardson, P.S. (1997) 'Are store brands perceived to be just another brand?', *Journal of Product and Brand Management*, 6(6): 388–404.

Riley, R. (1997) 'Retail change in post communist Poland: with special reference to ulica Piotrkowska, Lodz', *Geography*, 82(l): 27–37.

Robinson, T. and **Clarke-Hill, C.M.** (1995) 'International alliances in European retailing', *International Review of Retail, Distribution, and Consumer Research*, 5(2): 167–84.

Salto, L. (1999) 'Towards global retailing: the Promodès case', in Dupuis, M. and Dawson, J. (eds) *Cases in European Retailing*, Oxford: Blackwell.

Serapio, M.G. and **Cascio, W.F.** (1996) 'End games in international alliances', *Academy of Management Executive* 10(l): 62–73.

Smailes, A.E. (1955) *The Geography of Towns*, London: Hutchinson.

Smeltzer, L.R. (1997) 'The meaning and origin of trust in buyer–seller relationship', *International Journal of Purchasing and Materials Management*, 33(Winter): 40–8.

Smith, H. (1999) 'Supermarket choice and supermarket competition market equilibrium', *Oxford University Applied Economics Discussion Paper*, 207.

Stacey, N.A.H. and **Wilson, A.** (1958) *The Changing Pattern of Distribution*, Oxford: Pergamon.

Stern, L.W. and **Weitz, B.A.** (1997) 'The revolution in distribution: challenges and opportunities', *Long Range Planning*, 30(6): 823–9.

Thygesen, J. (1951) *Om Selvebetjening*, Köbenhavn: FDB.

Van der Hoven, C. (1999) 'Royal Ahold: a global strategy based on local independence', *International Trends in Retailing*, 16(l): 73–80.

Weld, L.D.H. (1923) 'Do principles of large scale production apply to merchandising?', *American Economic Review Supplement*, 13: 185–97.

Westwood, B. and **Westwood, B.** (1955) *The Modern Shop*, London: Architectural Press.

Woodruff, D. and **Carreyrou, J.** (1999) 'French retailers create new Wal-Mart rival', *Wall Street Journal*, 31 August: A14, A19.

Wrigley, N. (1992) 'Sunk capital, the property crisis and the restructuring of British food retailing', *Environment and Planning*, A24: 1521–27.

Wrigley, N. (1995) 'Sunk costs and corporate restucturing: British food retailing and the property crisis', in Wrigley, N. and Lowe, M.S. (eds) *Retailing, Consumption and Capital: Towards a New Economic Geography*, London: Longman.

2

Next revolution in retailing

Alton F. Doody and William R. Davidson

Source: *Harvard Business Review* 45 (1967): 4–20.

SCENE: *The large and comfortably furnished family room of the two-story, four-bedroom suburban home of Jim and Susan Brown. The sturdy, rustic furniture gives evidence of casual family living. A modern kitchen can be seen through a large entrance upstage. A door to the right opens into the master bedroom. The time is 11:15 p.m. on a Thursday night in the 1970s. Jim is sprawled on the sofa, thumbing through a magazine; Susan is sitting in an easy chair, knitting. Jim drops the magazine on the floor and stretches.*

JIM: I think I'll hit the hay. Are you coming?

SUSAN: In a few minutes. Just as soon as I do the shopping.

JIM: Order me another 25-foot length of that flexible plastic garden hose we got last week, will you?

As Jim retires to the bedroom, Susan goes into the kitchen and sits at her planning desk. A tiny color television screen is mounted on the wall at eye level from where she is sitting. Settling comfortably into her chair, Susan lifts the protective cover from the Direct-Shop console on the desk and presses a set of buttons that connects her directly with the Customer Communications Department of City-Wide Distribution Center, Incorporated.

For several minutes Susan is busy at her desk, placing her order by punching various keys. Images of many kinds of merchandise appear on the screen, some fleetingly and some held several seconds for her examination. As she continues to push buttons Susan seems to get impatient, and finally she pushes a tally button on the console. In a second a recap of her order appears on the screen. It itemizes her purchases and shows a total. She examines the recap and with a nod of approval pushes another button to confirm and clear the order, authorizing City-Wide to begin processing the order and clearing payment from her checkless bank account.

Susan smiles with the satisfaction of someone who has just completed an irksome task. She yawns as she walks back from the kitchen and into the bedroom. From the bedroom we hear:

JIM: How was the shopping expedition?

SUSAN (*jokingly*): Oh! It was absolutely exhausting. It took ten whole minutes. I'm going to get it down to five or six some night!

*   *   *

This little glimpse into the future is not meant simply to portray the dream castle of our fictional couple, the Browns. It is intended, rather, to illustrate a mode of consumer buying that will become commonplace sometime in the 1970s. The technology necessary for it is already here, and the market conditions that will help create the demand for it are fast materializing.

In fact, a paradox is developing in the traditional concept of mass merchandising. Historically, "convenience" goods — staple groceries, toiletries, drug sundries, standard household supplies, and other frequently purchased items of standard quality and low unit price — have been sold, as the name implies, at the *convenience* of the consumer. Convenience in this sense has always meant geographic convenience. (This is opposed to another current use of the term to describe so-called ready-mixed or "convenience" food products.) Since the consumer has always visited the store to do his buying, the merchandise has had to be placed as close as possible to his doorstep or along the routes that he travels to and from work and other activities. In other words, the distribution of such goods has spawned great numbers of retail outlets in separate locations.

The emerging paradox is that convenience and staple items are adaptable more readily than most other types of goods to highly centralized, mechanized, and computerized distribution techniques.

In the not too distant future a substantial share of these items may be marketed through a relatively few large central distribution facilities in each major market area. Consumers will never set foot inside these centers, except possibly for guest tours. Instead, retail transactions will be made by electronic telecommunications and push-button devices installed in private homes and hooked on-line to date processing networks.

Such a radical change in retail merchandising is bound to reach wide and deep. Virtually no segment of marketing will go untouched. Just as the development of supermarkets revolutionized the food industry in the 1930s, and the appearance of discount houses shook the traditional concepts of retailing in the 1950s, so too will the central distribution facility bring a major upheaval in mass merchandising in the 1970s.

To understand how such an upheaval may come about and how it will affect other marketing institutions and other industries, let us look further at the hypothetical experience of Susan Brown. Through her we can visualize how millions of American housewives may be doing their shopping a few years from now.

Success of City-Wide

City-Wide is the retail center where Susan Brown buys most of her groceries, many basic household goods, and some personal care items. It is obviously not a "store" in the old sense of the word; except for the products displayed on her Tele-Shopper screen, Susan never sees the merchandise that she buys until it is delivered to her home.

City-Wide was the first of several competing merchandising centers to be opened in Susan's community and one of the earliest to appear anywhere in the country. It was founded by two men who had been systems analysts for a large food chain. They had tried to interest their former employers in the idea of central distribution, and they had shown top management a plan for a high-volume and low-cost warehouse-to-consumer system for staples and convenience goods. But the president had turned them down.

He told them their ideas looked good on paper but would never work in practice because consumers weren't ready to accept such a drastic change in their buying habits. "People have to be physically exposed to merchandise," he argued. "They've got to have the chance to see the goods and handle them. That's how you get impulse buying."

The two would-be innovators knew, of course, that a highly automated warehouse-to-consumer system would not be appropriate for all the goods typically handled by modern supermarkets, drugstores, hardware and variety stores, and other mass merchandise-oriented retail outlets. But they were convinced that there were plenty of high-volume items whose demand patterns were stable enough to make the idea workable. For example, once a person has established a preference for a certain brand of toothpaste, he does not need to examine the item when he wants to buy it again. Furthermore, they believed that brand preference for certain items, especially some of the nationally distributed labels of foods, was not so strong that consumers would not accept substitutes. For instance, to many people one well-known brand of canned pineapple, paper napkins, or aspirin tablets is almost equally substitutable for another.

So the two men struck out on their own, starting a business unique not only in physical make-up, but also in terms of conglomerate merchandise assortments not offered by existing retail stores. Judging from City-Wide's healthy growth in its first four years, their ideas were well founded. From a modest start they have built the original operation into an $11 million annual sales volume. And a new distribution center that they opened only last year in another city is already doing $7 million.

Competition develops

Where they initially had the field to themselves, however, they are now facing growing competition. So far, one other locally owned company and several national chains, including their old employers, have set up operations similar to City-Wide; and many others are believed to have plans on their drawing boards. Before they began construction, the major chains waited to assure themselves that the new merchandising approach was not a fad.

Susan Brown, of course, still shops at supermarkets, neighborhood drug-stores, and other conventional stores. For one reason, City-Wide does not stock "big ticket" or low-volume merchandise or items that require a fit or personal inspection to determine quality or identify special features. Susan visits stores, too, when she is not sure what she wants or when she needs the product information supplied by a sales clerk. When she started with City-Wide, she continued to rely on conventional stores for information on new or unfamiliar products.

Now, however, she finds that City-Wide's advertising is supplying more of this information, and the company has recently improved its system so as to provide more detailed product data on the Tele-Shopper screen. (According to a recent company announcement, City-Wide plans to add a printer to home consoles, permitting the housewife to keep a copy of information such as recipes if she so desires.)

Susan also takes a shopping trip when she must be extra particular in her buying. She may be planning a dinner party, and so she wants to tell the butcher precisely how to cut and prepare the roast.

City-Wide, however, is her chief source for most standard foods, household supplies, and convenience goods that she needs repeatedly. She patronizes City-Wide because it is quick and convenient. The demands on Susan's time and energy of raising children, working part-time as a secretary, an active social life, and membership in several organizations are heavy; and the ease of buying from City-Wide is invaluable to her.

Susan at the console

To see more clearly how central distribution will function on the consumer's level, let us look at Susan's typical buying routine.

Once she is connected with City-Wide's ordering system, Susan can order at random anything from the inventory by simply punching on her home console (rental: $3 a month) a five-digit product code and indicating on a sixth key the quantity she needs. Before doing this, however, she usually orders her staple requirements by punching a single six-digit code which is programmed especially for her. This code tells City-Wide's computer to process the regular weekly Brown family order for predetermined quantities of products such as butter, milk, eggs, bread, cigarettes, and other basic goods that the family uses regularly.

This procedure is sufficiently flexible to allow Susan to make changes at any time she wishes. If she wants to increase the quantity of any item, she makes a separate unprogrammed item request. If, on the other hand, she wants to buy less of anything that appears on her regular program, she first punches the product code, then a "subtract" key, and finally the quantity key to indicate the amount she wants subtracted. To make substantial or perhaps permanent changes in her regular program, Susan of course does not want to go through so many keyboard manipulations. In this case she merely phones City-Wide's programming department and tells it what to do. She may make such basic changes by telephone up to four hours before placing an order through her home console.

To select items that are not on her regular program, Susan shops the "weekly specials" shown on her color Tele-Shopper screen. By pressing a "weekly display" button, she can view the currently featured items individually, with their prices and order codes.

When she wishes, Susan can also request a screening of any portion of City-Wide's entire 6,000-item assortment of foods, drugs, and sundries. To do this she presses a "total stock" key and then a two-digit code representing the classification code of the merchandise in which she is interested. The Tele-Shopper screen then shows individually, and with prices and code numbers, all of the items in whatever classification she has selected, such as "dairy products," "laundry supplies," or "men's toiletries."

Normally such extensive screening is unnecessary. To begin with, since most of the goods Susan buys from City-Wide are repeat purchases, they are included in her regular program and no further screening is needed except when she becomes dissatisfied with a product and wishes to replace it with a new or different brand. Secondly, most new products, as well as seasonal items and specialties, are introduced through the weekly specials. And finally, every month City-Wide sends her a product code book containing descriptions, codes, and prices for all the items in stock. The book is kept up to date with all additions and deletions of merchandise and with changes in prices, sizes, quantities, or other assortment factors.

Fast shopping 'trips'

When she is in no great hurry and is carefully shopping the weekly specials, it takes Susan about 15 minutes a week to do her City-Wide buying. But if she is rushed, she can fill nearly all the family's needs in 10 minutes. Actually, she prefers to take the time to shop carefully about every second week, and for the week between she merely reorders from her regular program while giving a quick glance at the specials.

Susan's weekly order averages about $35, which is safely above City-Wide's minimum single-order requirement of $25. A few weeks ago she received in the mail a brochure from a competitor, the Consumer Central Shopping Company (CCS), promoting its minimum of $15 per order. To Susan this lower requirement represented no particular advantage, although a couple of her friends considered it enough of an inducement to cancel their City-Wide service and switch to CCS.

The order that Susan placed at 11:15 this evening will be delivered by midmorning tomorrow. She could, in fact, wait till as late as 2 a.m. and still get delivery before noon. Orders placed between 2 a.m. and noon, however, are delivered in the afternoon of the same day, while orders placed in the afternoon until 6 p.m. are scheduled for early morning delivery the following day.

All in all, Susan is quite happy with City-Wide service, and she sometimes wonders how she got along without it before.

"Oh sure," she said to a friend, "I was skeptical when they first opened up. They were advertising how fast and easy it would be. And I just thought there was too much machinery in it. Computers and all that, you know. I told Jim it would either cost too much or they'd be getting everybody's packages mixed up and charging us for somebody else's orders. But we've just had wonderful service. And when I think how much time we used to spend running back and forth to the shopping center!"

How City-Wide functions

Keeping Susan happy by providing her and thousands of other housewives with that "wonderful service" she spoke of poses a tremendous challenge for the new central distribution organizations.

Companies like City-Wide must develop an integrated, total systems approach to merchandising in order to mesh the many separate steps in the shopping and buying process into a smoothly functioning operation. From the time Susan presses the first button on her console to the time the merchandise is delivered to her door, a series of interlocking and inter-dependent activities must be coordinated. And even before Susan pushes a button, of course, the system has to be ready to receive her input and respond to it. It must be ready to record, interpret, and process her order; it has to have a means of scheduling delivery, of separating perishable goods for special packaging protection while in transit, and of posting the transaction to her checkless account.

The first step in processing her order after she has confirmed and cleared it on the console is separation of the order into two categories — one part to be filled from the "automatic" warehouse and the other from the "conventional" warehouse.

Items in the first category are sufficiently standardized in size and shape to be handled by automatic equipment. Engineers expect more and more items to fall into this category as manufacturers awake to the potential of centralized distribution and begin to standardize their products and redesign their packages. City-Wide's engineering consultant feels that this trend will permit almost all centrally distributed goods eventually to be handled automatically. As he told City-Wide's owners:

"I really can't think of any item that won't someday be packaged for this kind of handling. And I'm even including meats and produce. After all, just because an item is an odd size or shape doesn't mean it has to be put in an odd-sized or -shaped package.

"You can see it coming. The technology of packaging is already pretty advanced. And so is the design of materials handling equipment. They're both very sophisticated industries, and there's no question but that they'll come up with what we need once it's proven to everybody concerned that central distribution is here to stay."

But now, in the early stages of development, City-Wide's automatic warehouse is able to handle only 40% of the company's total item assortments. The remaining 60% is processed through the conventional warehouse, an operation built on the latest design principles and employing the best available manual equipment. Through this facility the average customer order of 30 items can be filled in about 7 minutes. By comparison, a housewife shopping in a supermarket takes 30 minutes or more to assemble the same amount of merchandise.

After an order is combined from both warehouses, it is spot-checked for accuracy against the preprinted invoice. Next it is sent to the packing room, where all frozen foods are separated from the other goods and placed in a special container that keeps them at zero temperature for 24 hours. Other perishables are placed in another container that maintains a 35- to 40-degree temperature for the same period. The two refrigerated packs are then placed with the nonperishable goods in box-like containers two feet square. These "boxes," made of inexpensive, lightweight, weatherproof materials, are machine-sealed, and then they are stamped with the customer's name and address.

Computer sorting

Before the orders reach the loading and delivery area, they are sorted by computer for geographic delivery. The computer programs for these territory assignments are so complete that they even tell the truck drivers what freeway entrance and exit ramps to use in reaching their destinations.

The trucks are special-purpose vans, each built to hold 208 of City-Wide's standardized delivery packs. The trucks are loaded according to the sequence in which deliveries will be made; and to prevent confusion, each order is numbered to show its place in the sequence.

A typical order fills three to four containers, which means that each van, making morning and afternoon runs, can make about 100 deliveries a day.

The drivers are instructed to deposit the containers at the place designated by the customer, ring the doorbell, and leave. They are discouraged from entering the customer's house, since this slows the delivery schedule. Besides, there is really no need for the driver ever to see the customer.

With the customer's bank account number programmed into its computer, City-Wide uses a "telephone-cash" system for collection. When the total value of an order is calculated on the computer and flashed on the customer's Tele-Shopper screen at home, it is also transmitted via a switching computer to the customer's bank. The bank automatically debits her account and credits City-Wide by the same amount. In this way City-Wide is able, in effect, to receive payment even before the order is filled; and as a result, the company has no expense for collection efforts, no bad debt losses, and no capital tied up in accounts receivable.

These savings, as well as other economies of central distribution, have enabled City-Wide and its competitors to maintain low prices. Susan, who had expected City-Wide to be too expensive, learned that she can buy there at *lower* prices than those offered by conventional supermarkets. Like most American housewives, she is not sure how much she is saving, but she estimates 10%.

She remembers something the guide told her during a tour for prospective customers of City-Wide's facilities. He said that the cost of operating a conventional retail store in the 1970s takes anywhere from one fourth to more than a third of every sales dollar. In a food store, he said, operating costs account for 27 cents of each sales dollar, and in a drugstore they amount to 37 cents, based on latest figures. (This is considerably higher than in the 1960s.)

"It just isn't necessary," he said, "for some consumer products to be handled and rehandled, when it costs so much."

Winning Susan's neighbors

To assume that all consumers, during the period of initial rapid growth in the 1970s, would adopt this innovation as readily as did Susan Brown would be to defy the lessons of marketing history. Look at some of the reactions of Susan's neighbors.

As an early convert, Susan became a rather important word-of-mouth promoter of the new service.[1] She persuaded her nextdoor neighbor, Jane Brooks, to try it. Another neighbor, Lorna Sullivan, was skeptical of the handling of meats and fresh produce. Susan made a point to ask about this when she took Lorna to visit City-Wide, and the answer they got was convincing enough to break down Lorna's resistance:

> "Look at it this way. Why should we have any more trouble with meat and produce than a supermarket? After all, just about any farm product

you get these days is so much improved over what it used to be that there's not even a good comparison. You know, what we used to classify as prize-winning meats or vegetables are just the standard quality nowadays. Of course, this means, for one thing, that produce stays fresh longer; a seller like City-Wide, who's planning his inventory sensibly, can have a constant flow of fresh food and not get stuck with anything over age. I think you'll find it'll work out very well. With the consistently highgrade foods we have today and fast shipping from the farm to City-Wide, it isn't necessary for the lady of the house to personally inspect every tomato or head of cabbage before she buys it."

Susan, Jane, and Lorna have since found very little to complain about where meats and produce are concerned, and in fact Lorna is the only one of the three who has ever sent anything back. She was unhappy once with a bunch of bananas.

Of the 16 families on Susan's block, all but 3 are now buying from either City-Wide or CCS. One of the holdouts is Mrs. O'Malley, who feels her buying volume is not big enough to justify central distribution service. Her children have married and moved away, so she buys only for herself and her husband. Another nonsubscriber is Mrs. Endicott, a widow; the third is Miss Little, a teacher who does little of her own cooking. Mrs. Endicott and Miss Little, moreover, have a lot of free time on their hands, and both of them enjoy shopping and browsing in conventional stores.

Far-reaching implications

Services like those offered by City-Wide Distribution Center in our fictional account will have an important influence on the housewife of the 1970s. If she were weekend shopping for groceries and other convenience goods in the traditional manner at the supermarket, it would take her at least 10 minutes to drive there and a half hour or so in the store. The aggravation of waiting in the check-out lines, fighting traffic, and competing for parking space is something to consider, too. The benefits of speed and ease, regardless of any price savings, will represent a strong advantage for an operation like City-Wide. In short, the customer service aspects of central distribution are undeniably attractive, and they will become even more attractive as our lives get busier and more complex.

Many housewives of the 1970's will have grown up with color television, push-button telephones, and computerized banking services. Indeed, these and other products of a highly sophisticated technology are already commonplace. The young matron of the 1970s probably will have a college education and have a greater variety of interests and activities than her mother did. And she will enjoy greater economic security and comfort than did the women of her mother's generation.

All these things add up to the certainty that she will demand more and different services, and new marketing institutions will have to be developed to meet these demands.

Central distribution, of course, may not come about precisely the same way or with exactly the same features as we have portrayed it. But technological, social, and competitive changes will make it inevitable that something very similar to the City-Wide illustration will be a reality in the 1970s and will have far-reaching effects on business — not just on retailing, but also on many other industries.

The whole institutional structure of marketing in foods, drugs, and convenience goods will be drastically affected. A successful central distribution company like City-Wide will offer powerful competition not only to conventional supermarkets and drug stores in its trading area but to other mass merchandisers as well. At the same time it will pose an important challenge to established wholesale organizations, since its new methods of merchandising will make it possible for the first time to circumvent the established pattern of wholesale–retail relationships.

The upheaval in retailing and wholesaling, like the supermarket challenge in the 1930s, will probably begin not so much by taking business away from established outlets, but rather by exploiting most of the growth that they would otherwise have achieved. Then, once established as a major merchandising institution, central retail distribution will rapidly begin to cut into the volume of conventional stores. To survive, many conventional stores will have to either adopt some of the methods of central distribution or find strong competitive alternatives.

Some stores and chain organizations will convert to the new methods on a large scale and will become leaders in central distribution themselves. Few conventional operators, however, will be able to stand still and survive unchanged.

Will history repeat?

Upstarts, rather than well-established companies, historically have initiated most retailing innovations. If history repeats itself, this would mean that City-Wide's owners — and their counterparts throughout the country — would do what companies like King Kullen, Big Bear, and Albers did to the existing food industry in the 1930s when they began the supermarket revolution. It is well known that by the time the established chains finally reacted to the new competition, the successful supermarket innovators were well entrenched. To this day, of course, they account for a substantial share of the total market.

Will things be different this time? Recognizing the nature and the magnitude of the challenge, perhaps progressive managements will learn from history and begin now to plan for the types of radical organizations appropriate for the future. There is no reason why the great companies in the industry today cannot turn this challenge into opportunity. Although the central distribution concept requires some "far out" planning, it can be done — even in a systematic way.

In addition, today's established companies have one tremendous advantage over the upstarts. Unlike many past retailing innovations, the central distribution system will require a sophistication and a magnitude of investment totally different from, for example, the early supermarkets. This means that those who enter the battle of the future will have to be armed with new weapons.

It is interesting to speculate that these will be largely in the realm of human resources. Effective implementation of this innovation will require bright people with a high level of education in systems theory, quantitative analysis, communications, information technology, and electronic data processing. They will need to work under conditions where organizational rigidities do not thwart creative effort. Perhaps they will not function well within an established division of a corporation long committed to a traditional form of distribution. Instead it may be advisable to spin off their operation into a separate unit, giving them the freedom to operate like entrepreneurs.

Impact on others

The influence of central distribution will also be felt acutely in such areas as advertising, sales promotion, and national brand programs.

Mass media advertising will become even more important than it is today, and sales promotion in foods and convenience goods will be focused on nonstore activities because, in effect, there will be much less in-store selling and fewer opportunities for point-of-sale promotions. Producers of convenience goods will be obliged to pre-sell their products harder, and brand image will become immensely more important.

These shifts in advertising and sales promotion will, of course, affect such industries as television and radio, newspaper and national magazine publishing, direct mail promotion, and advertising.

The packaging industry, too, will be seriously affected. Packaging will become less important as a sales promotion tool because the consumer will not be selecting merchandise from display shelves. Package design will have to be standardized to suit the handling procedures of central distribution, so that less individuality will be possible in the size and shape of packaged products.

Among others who will feel a significant impact from central distribution are the manufacturers and distributors of store fixtures, warehousing equipment, cash registers, and all the other tools of conventional retailing. The progressive companies in these industries will recognize and exploit the plentiful opportunities for new equipment tailored to the needs of central distribution. For example, new materials handling devices and better means of refrigeration and storage of perishables will be needed. Business machine manufacturers will have the chance to develop the customer ordering systems needed in central distribution. And the alert cabinet manufacturer will design a planning desk for Susan Brown's kitchen.

A list of the possible implications and effects of this coming upheaval in mass merchandising could run on and on, touching many additional industries and activities. But perhaps most dramatic and intriguing of all is the influence it will have on communications and data processing, bringing long-recognized technical capabilities into households as everyday shopping tools. The success of central distribution will depend on reliable record keeping and high-speed, accurate communications. When Susan Brown pushes a button, she will expect results; and when she checks her bank balance, she will not tolerate any errors in her direct payment account with City-Wide. What is more, she cannot shop with City-Wide without closed-circuit television and heavy reliance on product information from advertising in regular media.

A vast and very complex network of communications and information handling will be needed to keep Susan happy and City-Wide profitable. Someone will have to synthesize and coordinate the variety of separate components and operations that go into this network. The span of control will be tremendous — reaching from City-Wide's computers to Susan's kitchen to the bank, and covering many points between. An existing resource in the communications and data processing industries may rise to this challenge, or an entirely new institution may merge to provide the total system. In any event, solving this synthesis and control problem, along with manufacturing physical components and software and developing systems designs for the network, will be among the most promising business opportunities of the next decade.

These opportunities, however, as well as the opportunities in the other areas that will be affected by central distribution, belong only to those who have the vision to begin planning for them ahead of the field. Central distribution, today, is a vision — an expectation. The conditions that will demand its creation and the tools needed to accomplish it are fast becoming realities. Now it is time to plan, and in not too many tomorrows it will be time to act.

Note

1. See Ernest Dichter, "How Word-of-Mouth Advertising Works," HBR November–December 1966, p. 147.

3

A rearview mirror might help us drive forward: a call for more historical studies in retailing

Stanley C. Hollander

Source: *Journal of Retailing* 62(1) (1986): 7–10.

Merchants' historical interests are often limited to anniversary sales with dates determined more by promotional calendars than by commemorative precision. Retail scholarship is usually ahistorical or, at best, highly anecdotal. Certainly, historical studies that go beyond comparison of last year's and this year's sales will never constitute the main thrust of retail research, but longer-range, deeper, and more macroscopic analysis can illuminate many important retailing issues. The past is prologue, not prototype, so while history may not repeat itself, it will suggest useful questions and useful answers. Let us note just a few of these questions.

Aggressive versus traditional retailers

American (and foreign) retail history records numerous aggressive, volume-oriented/low-price retailers—such as the early department store, mail-order, chain store, supermarket, and discount store merchants—who gained market share from more traditional contemporaries. Various "patterns" or models, such as The Wheel of Retailing, The Retail Life Cycle, and the Hegelian Dialectic (the eventual synthesis of institutions and their opposition [see Gist 1971] have been advanced to describe and possiby explain the rise and sometimes decline of these types. Much conceptual and empirical historical research, however, is needed to verify, modify, or replace those models. To be most meaningful, this research should embrace both the highly successful retail types and the more transitory or limited ones. The latter include the bazaar stores of the 1920s or 1930s, the post-World War II closed-door hard goods discounters, and the 1970s furniture warehouses.

Intertype competition usually evokes calls for government intervention which sometimes ensues, occasionally with surprising results. The anti-chain store movement of the 1920s and 1930s produced discriminatory state licensing taxes, and minimum markup, resale price maintenance, and Robinson-Patman laws (Palamountain 1955). The current national mood is for deregulation; anti-chain fervor is dormant here, although still active in Europe (Migros Federation of Swiss Cooperatives 1983), and the controversy may now seem purely antiquarian. But sentiments can change, particularly if old economic pressures reemerge. Here we should note that the "liberal" economists, who once influenced so much political thinking, no longer exhibit their enthusiasm for big retailing as a counterweight to big manufacturing (Galbraith 1956). The currently dominant Chicagoans, for example, find resale price maintenance quite compatible with a laissez-faire economy. In fact, resale price maintenance recently enjoyed a very modest renaissance under the toleration of sympathetic FTC chairmen. We need to remain aware of the socioeconomic forces that have induced, and could induce, regulation of existing or future retail institutions.

Consumerism

Government has intervened in retailing in many inhibiting and supporting ways. Consumeristic groups have also exercised fluctuating influence throughout this century. Although certainly not ignored by historians, more scholars like Friedman (1985) should ask who worked for what changes in what ways for what reasons and with what results.

Personnel

After about 1920, department store trainers tried to impose a middle-class, customer-advisor role on their salespeople. Benson (1981) notes rather disastrous tensions between this decision-making, professional role and the perhaps necessary, but demeaning, security regulations (restricted employee entrances, package inspection) and service rules (dress codes, "customer is always right" policy, etc.). We should study whether and how role conflict has been reduced in some or most establishments.

One historically observable trend definitely indicates a need to refocus retail education. While pioneer institutions such as New York University and the Prince School may have started by training salesmanship trainers, collegiate work in retailing has for several decades appealed primarily to those who want to be department store buyers. A new breakdown in the 1982 Census of Retail Trade, however, shows that the conventional department stores have slipped from about eight percent of total retail trade to just about three percent. The replacement of single unit department stores by flagship and branch systems has also reduced the number of buyers needed. Now some major ownership groups (Federated, Macy, Dayton-Hudson,

Batus) are beginning to consolidate divisions. Increased centralization along with declining market share means that many who want to enter retailing will have to look for careers outside buying for conventional department stores.

Recurrent patterns and pertinent experience have occurred in other aspects of retail education and personnel management. What has been the importance of substantive content in retail education in comparison to the socialization or adjustment of students to retail careers? Varying results of graduate student recruitment; rapid versus more gradual training programs; installation, abandonment, and reappearance of internship and other experiential retailing educational methods; different compensation and reward systems; and centralized versus decentralized training are a few other such topics.

Organization

The constant tension between centralization and decentralization, and the numerous steps towards increasing the functional specialization of buyers and other executives, should provide some background for current attempts at organizational restructuring. The central question probably is: What organizational techniques have reduced communication difficulties and suboptimization and how have they done it?

Fashion

Since fashion change is a chronological process, fashion is especially susceptible to historical thinking and testing. Actually, we are well supplied with fashion theories (Bell 1979; Solomon 1985) that attribute style change to consumer, designer, and other commercial elites and influentials, external events, immutable cycles, social striving, conspicuous consumption, and consumer boredom. Much current, readily available literature, however, simply extolls selected designers. Increased testing, selection, modification, synthesis, and communication are needed. Historical fashion theory benchmarks could also help answer Bell's query as to whether fashion is becoming less important today.

Merchandising

History should tell us something about the merchandising issues that arise over and over again. Do retailers gain or lose in the long run when they emphasize supplier identities, as in the case of designer boutiques? What are the long-run impacts of high initial markup, high markdown policies? What

are the gains and losses when vendors and retailers regard purchase orders
not as firm commitments but as bargaining platforms susceptible to partial
and late delivery, cancellation, and negotiation of additional allowances?
In all such instances, can individual firms profitably deviate from prevailing
modes of behavior? The history of retail accounting experiments, particularly merchandise management accounting, may point up some guidelines
for current attempts to improve merchandising profitability measures.

Consumption

Social historians (Barth 1980; Fraser 1981; McKendrick, Brewer, and Plumb
1982, and many others) are beginning to study the interrelationships between
retailing practices and changes in consumption patterns. Further studies
that would add retailing-marketing perspectives to the historian's careful
examination of the environments in which change occurred could help us
understand what retailers have and could mean to consumers and society.
The sociological implications concern the way retailers have and do act as
gatekeepers and consumption modifiers. The economic development question
is how (if at all) can retailing stimulate consumption and production.

Macroretailing

Much interesting work (e.g., Bucklin 1972) has been done on another interesting macroretailing question: What are the forces that have shaped the
existing population (number and mix) of retail stores? This work should
continue, but attention should also be given to the changing role of retailing
in society. Retailers have lost much of their former, apparently important,
functions of providing recreational facilities, social leadership, and personal
advice. Although an increasingly specialized society is likely to continue to
force retail concentration on a service of supply, retrospection might indicate
some opportunities for restoring some of retailing's social influence.

A concluding caveat

This brief summary by no means exhausts the opportunities for historical
analysis. But no one should expect history to recur automatically. Each
historical event has occurred in its particular environment as a result of its
particular causes. What the historical overview can do is to give us another perspective, indicate many of the alternative solutions, and suggest many of the
relationships and interrelationships in the complex, evolving, and exciting
world of retailing.

References

Barth, Gunther P. (1980), *City People*, New York: Oxford.

Bell, Quentin (1979), *On Human Finery*, New York: Schocken.

Benson, Susan P. (1981), "The Cinderella Occupation: Managing the Work of Department Store Saleswomen 1900–1940," *Business History Review* **55** (Spring), 1–25.

Bucklin, Louis P. (1972), *Competition and Evolution in the Distributive Trades*, Englewood Cliffs, N.J.: Prentice-Hall.

Fraser, W. Hamish (1981), *The Coming of the Mass Market*, Hamden, Conn.: Archon.

Friedman, Monroe (1985), "Consumer Boycotts in the United States 1970–1980: Contemporary Events in Historical Perspective," *The Journal of Consumer Affairs* **19** (no.1), 96–117.

Galbraith, John K. (1956), *American Capitalism*, Boston: Houghton Mifflin.

Gist, Ronald (1971), *Basic Retailing*, New York: Wiley.

McKendrick, Neil, John Brewer, and J. H. Plumb (1982), *The Birth of a Consumer Society*, Bloomington: Indiana University Press.

Migros Federation of Swiss Cooperatives (1983), *Third Social Report of the Migros Community*, Zurich: The Federation.

Palamountain, Joseph C. (1995), *The Politics of Distribution*, Cambridge, Mass.: Harvard.

Solomon, Michael R., ed. (1985), *The Psychology of Fashion*. Lexington, Mass.: Lexington Books.

U.S. Bureau of the Census (1984), *Census of Retail Trade 1982*, vol. 1, U.S. Summary, Washington, D.C.: U.S. Government Printing Office.

4

The distributive trades in the Second World War and the post-war years, 1939–1950: and suggestions as to future trends

J. Jeffreys

Source: J. Jeffreys, *Retail Trading in Britain*, Cambridge: Cambridge University Press, 1954, pp. 101–120.

1. The war and post-war years

The distributive trades in the Second World War and post-war years were characterized by stability in methods and structure; by the maintenance of the *status quo* rather than by the emergence of new forces and new methods. This is not to say that no changes took place. The shortages of supplies, the controls direct and indirect over manpower, materials and capital, which existed in one degree or another throughout these years, affected the distributive trades in some respects more than any other sector of the economy. But the operation of these controls and the effects of the shortages resulted not in widespread reorganization or in the use of novel techniques but in the maintenance, practically intact, of the existing distributive framework, with fewer goods being distributed by fewer people.

The maintenance of the *status quo* was no accident, but the outcome of a deliberate and planned policy. The details of the various methods of control applied to the different trades at different times, ranging from the use of pre-war datum lines for allocations through distributive margin control to the insistence on licences to open and operate new shops, do not call for elaboration here. The principles upon which the policy of controls was based may, however, be stated briefly.

Government intervention in the working of the distributive trades was seen as a necessity and not a virtue. No attempt was made to reform, remodel or improve the main features of the system that had existed before the war. The overriding considerations of government policy were the maintenance of supplies to the consumers, the allocation of these supplies fairly, and, so far as was compatible with these aims, the reduction of the manpower employed in the distributive trades. These doctrines meant that the existing machinery was to be disturbed as little as possible for fear of inducing a breakdown in the flow of supplies, that new entrants to the trades were to be limited, and that changes and shifts in the methods and structure were to be discouraged. They also implied, as competitive bidding for scarce goods could not be allowed, that supplies to distributors should be determined on the basis of the number of customers and that margins should be fixed so that no exploitation of the public could take place and so that at the end of the emergency when controls could be lifted no sector or group would be either better off or worse off in relation to others than at the beginning. If necessity forced the curtailment of the activities of some distributive units or the merging of the activities of others, adequate safeguards were provided to ensure that when a return to free trading was possible such units should be the first to re-start operations. Even where direct government control did not operate or where the controls had been lifted, the shortage of supplies tended in the same way to maintain the existing relationships and the relative status of units and organizations. The fairest method and the method leading to least dispute was for producers to allocate scarce supplies evenly to their existing customers, and distributors had little hope of opening up new sources of supply of scarce goods.

Naturally no system of controls could succeed in eliminating all tendency towards change. Shifts in consumer habits, such as purchasing at shops close to hand during the years of heavy bombing rather than visiting shops further afield, and the destruction of shops by enemy action, for example, inevitably led to some changes from the pre-war pattern. But the pressure of government controls, the active part played by Trade Associations in fashioning these controls and sometimes in assisting in their enforcement, and the existence of a sellers' market in the post-war years which provided little inducement to develop or evolve new selling practices, combined to limit and contain the changes in the methods and structure of the distributive trades in these years.

The absence of change in distributive structure

Statistical data to illustrate this relative absence of significant change in the structure and organization of the distributive trades are not available for all aspects. Some examples can, however, be given of the absence of change in retail structure. There is no firm information about the change, if any, in the total number of retail shops between 1939 and 1950. While there is little doubt that the number declined in the war years as a result of rationing, shortages of goods and enemy action, it is not known whether the decrease had been made good by 1950.[1] Table 13 above, however, shows that the number of multiple shop branches increased only slightly. Between 1939 and 1950 there was an estimated increase of only 845, from 39,013 to 39,858, in the total number of branches of firms with 25 or more branches each. This compares with an increase of 8,439 in the years 1930 to 1939. The number of branches of Co-operative Societies increased by 1,140 between 1937–38 and 1946—from 23,954 to 25,094.[2] The increase in the number of department stores between 1939 and 1950 is thought to be less than 10.

The rationing statistics also show an absence of significant change between the early years of the war and 1950, though there were fluctuations in
the war and immediate post-war years. The total number of shops holding
registrations for meat, for example, was practically the same between 1942
and 1950. There were 45,489 retailers with meat registrations in 1942 and
45,022 in 1950. The decline in the number of grocery and provision dealers
holding registrations was rather greater, from 157,800 in 1940 to 145,100 in
1951. The share of the total number of sugar registrations held by independent or small-scale retailers was however practically unchanged between the
two dates—51.5% in 1940 and 50.6% in 1951. Finally, as shown in Table 19
above, the share of the large-scale retailers in the total retail trade of the
country is estimated to have increased by only 1.5% between 1939 and 1950,
from about 34.5% in 1939 to 36.0% in 1950. This compares with an increase
of 8.2% between 1930 and 1939.[3]

The virtual disappearance of bankruptcy among firms engaged in wholesale and retail trading in these years was another reflection of the stability
of the structure as a whole.[4] Price and margin control was in fact designed
to avoid bankruptcies as far as possible in order to prevent a breakdown in
supplies to the consumers. Further, the existence of price control combined
with resale price maintenance meant that over large sections of consumer
goods trades in these years there was no price competition between retailers.
The price controls, it is true, fixed maximum prices only, but few retailers
with limited supplies saw any advantages to be gained by selling below this
maximum. Similarly controls over new building and investment curtailed the
physical changes that could be made, though the shortage of supplies and
manpower may have led to some reduction in the actual number of shops in
existence.

The reduction in manpower

There were two developments however which, while they were the outcome
of the policy described above, may have long-term effects on the distributive
trades. The first of these developments was the decrease in the manpower
employed in the distributive trades which led to the disappearance of a
number of the pre-1938 practices. The second was the emphasis placed by
the government on reducing distribution costs and the practice of relying on
costings to determine margins. This led to the abandonment in many trades
of traditional mark-ups and margins.

There was a rapid decline in the numbers employed in the distributive
trades from 1939 onwards, until in 1944, the lowest point reached, the numbers were some one-third fewer than in 1938. From 1945 onwards the trend
was reversed and the numbers employed increased rapidly up to 1949, after
which the rate of increase slowed down. Changes in classification prevent a
direct comparison of the numbers employed in the pre- and post-war years,
but there is little doubt that the employment in these trades in 1950 was

below that of 1938, and certainly the distributive trades represented a smaller proportion of the total working population than in 1938.[5] At the same time there had been an increase in the proportion of women employed and a decrease in the proportion of juveniles.

This reduction in the manpower employed led to fewer services being provided for the consumer. Obvious examples are the curtailment of delivery of some goods, the reduction in the number of deliveries made, the employment of fewer assistants per customer and the development of self-service retailing units. The important consideration in relation to long-term trends was the indication that both the distributive trades and the consumers had begun to accept a situation in which less manpower was to be employed. The discussions and plans as to future developments were framed not in terms of a return to a period when manpower would be plentiful but in terms of methods and techniques of providing additional service to consumers without using additional manpower. The outlook differed markedly from that widely adopted in the inter-war years when the provision of extra services involving additional employment was considered as an answer to most problems of marketing. This change in outlook was in part a reflection of the difficulty of obtaining manpower. The raising of the school leaving age to 15 years, which reduced the supply of juvenile labour, was also of importance, as was the rise in wages cost relative to occupancy cost owing to the existence of many pre-1938 rent and lease agreements.

The shift from traditional mark-ups and margins to margins fixed by government control and based on costings encouraged the trend towards economy in the use of manpower. Price control, notably in the post-war years, led to a reduction in gross margins in many trades and made impossible a reversion to pre-1939 practices. Further, the reduction in gross margins in individual trades or in groups of commodities began to change many of the traditional relationships between trades. In some instances the reductions in margins meant that retailers who had sold the commodities as a side line no longer found it worth their while to stock the goods. In other instances the margins on the main groups of commodities had been so narrowed that specialist retailers felt compelled to add to the lines of goods sold to maintain their overall rate of profit. Trades such as confectionery, tobacco, bread and sections of the grocery and provisions trade were those most affected. Many of these forced shifts in the relative gross margins between different commodities will probably have permanent effects in that, even if price and margin controls are discontinued, it is most unlikely that any return to the earlier relationships will take place.

The effects of controls on the distributive trades

Apart from these two developments, however, and some others of a relatively minor character, the structure and organization of the distributive trades can best be described as 'frozen' during the war and immediate post-war years. Even in the early nineteen-fifties, when some of the controls had been lifted and some of the shortages ended, few new developments were to be observed. There can be no doubt that the controls, direct and indirect, over the distributive trades in these years achieved their main purpose. Goods in short supply were distributed consistently and equitably. Manpower and materials which might have been used in the distributive trades were otherwise employed, to the greater advantage of the nation as a whole. But the effects of these controls on the working and efficiency of the distributive trades were rarely the major consideration in determining policy, and some analysis of these effects is of value as an indication of the cost of securing these larger aims.

A distinction should perhaps be made between those controls that were the direct outcome of war conditions and shortages of supplies and those which were the outcome of attempts to plan the evolution of the economy as a whole. In the first category fall the *ad hoc* expedients such as rationing, limitation of entry to certain trades, and price and margin control. In the second category fall policies such as purchase tax, building licences and town planning schemes. A complete distinction between the two types of control is difficult to make in practice as the one clearly merges into the other, but in the following discussion the different origins or purposes of the controls will be kept in mind.

The main results of the controls, direct and indirect, over the distributive trades since 1940 may be suggested as the decline in competition in these trades, the relative absence of new entrants, and the strengthening of the position of existing or established firms. In those trades where shortages of goods and controls have persisted, the firms that were in the trades before the war were in a virtually monopolistic position. In the tobacco, confectionery, meat and milk trades and to a slightly smaller degree in the bread and grocery trades, the established wholesalers and retailers could hardly put a foot wrong and only the completely incompetent firms, once evacuation and bombing had been weathered, were likely to fail. Consumers it is true could change their retailer and to some extent the retailer could change his wholesaler, but shortages and price and margin control limited the advantage of such changes. In any event the entry of new firms, otherwise than by buying up existing firms at inflated prices, was practically out of the question. The magnitude of this problem may be seen from the fact that the trades listed above represented over one-half of total consumers' retail expenditure in 1950.

In other trades, when direct controls ended and supplies increased in the post-war years, competition played a slightly more important role in influencing developments. Here again however new entrants to the trades were limited in numbers owing partly to the difficulty of obtaining supplies of certain goods and partly to the difficulty of obtaining premises. Except in new housing areas and bombed areas, the building of new shops and warehouses was restricted. Only two new department stores, for example, were built in the whole of the United Kingdom between 1939 and 1951. New entrants could only come into a trade by taking over from existing and, for the most part, very prosperous retailers. The prices asked for the premises and the business were often completely uneconomic for a newcomer who had to build up his custom.

Similarly, existing retailers who wished to expand faced problems of high rentals and inflated property prices. Many firms preferred to postpone expansion rather than to pay a rent for a shop that was three or four times the pre-1938 rent already being paid for a similar-sized shop in the same town. Re-equipment and modernization of the wholesale and retail premises presented the same type of difficulty in that the cost of modernization was many times that of the pre-war cost. The newly-equipped shop would however have to compete with one that had been modernized in, say, 1938. If the differential in efficiency and operating costs between the recently modernized shop and the older shops was clear and attractive to the consumer, the higher costs of installation or re-building would have been met by higher turnover. The existence of price controls and of resale price maintenance however limited the possibility of such an appeal, and the attraction to the consumer of existing retailing units that were close at hand out-weighed in many trades the attractions of shops further afield that were using the new techniques. Only in one or two trades, such as footwear, women's clothing and to a minor extent grocery and provisions, were a few firms showing that capital outlay and new methods could bring an increased volume of turnover.

The high initial cost of entry, expansion and innovation relative to existing costs is a well-known problem in productive industry. The risks associated with extending plant or introducing a new product can to some extent be calculated and measured, and the capital organization of industry is geared to take such risks. The distributive trades on the other hand were facing this problem for practically the first time in the years after 1945, and in these trades far less had been done to measure and calculate the risks of innovation. A feature of the distributive trades hitherto had been the ease of entry to the trade and the relatively small amounts of capital required to do business. To the general rigidity in the distributive trades introduced by controls there was added therefore rigidity due to lack of knowledge and under-capitalization.

Some of the existing firms had resources as a result of re-investment of profits, or were able to raise funds on the market, and for these firms the problem of expansion was not insurmountable. In the post-war years many mergers took place between companies, particularly multiple shop firms. These firms found it easier to acquire a number of long-term leaseholds by taking over an existing multiple shop organization than by attempting to buy particular shops one by one. The growth in size of these larger firms did not however necessarily mean that re-equipment, experiment and innovation would follow. The majority of firms, both large and small, secure on their flanks by the obstacles to new entrants and able to maintain their turnover in a full employment economy, preferred, after making some adjustments for shortage of manpower, to follow existing practices and principles rather than to lead, and were content to delay reorganization as long as possible.

In the case of those commodities coming under direct governmental price control, an attempt was made to prevent this trend towards what may be called the ossification of the distributive trades from resulting in higher costs of distribution. The fixing of maximum margins based on examination of the costs of existing retailers and wholesalers is not however a policy aimed at improving efficiency in the distributive trades or at encouraging new methods and techniques. And viewing the economy as a whole there is some danger that the continuous improvements in production methods and techniques leading to lower real costs of production may in fact be more than offset by the use of the out-of-date methods, practices, equipment and buildings of the distributive trades.

The ending of shortages, of rationing and of price and margin control will undoubtedly lead to some return to competition in these trades. The exact moment in different trades to lift such controls is of course determined by the wider consideration of the advantages to the economy as a whole. In making such a decision however it is important that the effects of existing methods of control over the distributive trades and the possibility of using alternative systems of control that may not be subject to the same drawbacks should be taken fully into account. Moreover any easy assumption that the mere existence of a free market in the distributive trades would automatically lead to improvements in methods, techniques and organization and to an end of ossification is hardly justified on the basis of past experience. In the first place existing firms will have a cost advantage over newcomers for a very long time to come, apart from their dominant position in the trade resulting from over a decade of near-monopoly. In the second place the distributive trades, particularly retail trading, are a classic example of imperfect rather than of perfect competition. Competition in an imperfect market does not necessarily lead to the elimination of the economically inefficient firm, as such firms are protected from direct competition by many factors such as distance, the lack of special knowledge on the part of the consumer, and the minimum size of operating units. The twelve years of stability in the distributive trades have almost certainly increased the imperfections of the market rather than reduced them.

A policy of *laissez-faire* in the distributive trades, of freeing all goods from controls, may therefore be only slightly more effective in encouraging new developments than the system of controls in the past decade. There would however be a direct saving in the manpower employed to direct the controls. In regard to longer-term policies, and the problems of planning the uses of the national resources as a whole, attention has already been drawn to the danger of treating the distributive trades as a residual element, a sector of the economy for which a policy can be devised once the allocation of resources to the other sectors has been settled. Efficiency in the distributive trades is as essential as efficiency in productive industry. Of equal importance is the need to develop and devise yardsticks and standards which will enable differentiation to be made between sections and individual units in the distributive trades. Allocation of supplies, sites or capital on the basis of fair shares to all may be the simplest method. In certain fields this policy has much to commend it. But such a policy in the sectors of the economy where some firms and some methods are known to be superior to others tends to hold back and limit rather than to encourage efficiency.

2.   Future trends in the distributive trades

The scope for developments in the distributive trades in the future and the general direction of such developments will clearly be dependent upon the character of the economic framework within which these trades will operate in the future. This framework will be influenced by a number of factors. The size of the national income, the rate of increase of this income, the division of the income between different purposes, for example final consumption and investment, and the distribution of the income between classes is one factor. The rate of increase in the population, the age composition of the population and the total man and woman power available is another factor. Technical developments such as improvements in transport, an increase in the number of private motor cars and progress in preserving perishable goods will also directly influence the distributive trades, as will changes in social habits, for example in the size of families, in the size and frequency of purchase of certain goods and in the importance and incidence of fashion. Finally central and local government policies in relation to the use of resources, town planning, opening hours of shops, standards of hygiene and so on will in part determine the nature of such changes in the distributive trades as take place.

Speculation as to the possible character of economic setting in which the distributive trades will operate in the future would be a lengthy process and need not be undertaken here. There is, however, a case for glancing briefly at what would appear to be the most likely organizational and technical developments in the distributive trades in the future and relating these possible developments to the present problems facing large- and small-scale distributors.

As far as it is possible to distinguish future trends, there would appear to be little doubt that the use of large-scale methods of production of consumer goods will continue and be extended, and that manufacturers and producers will play an increasingly active part in the marketing of their products. Further, the flow of goods will almost certainly become more even, with gluts and fluctuations in supplies being avoided by the use of improved methods of storage such as freezing and of fuller data on consumer demand. The practice of manufacturers or producers taking over more and more tasks from retailers will be continued and may extend to tasks at present undertaken by consumers. For example, grading, identification, specification and information for the consumer will probably become the producer's function in practically all trades, and even such processes as cleaning, peeling, preparing or cooking at present undertaken by the consumer will in many instances be transferred to the producer. An important feature of this development will be greater progress in the direction of standardization and simplification of the design of goods and of their shapes and sizes, based on extensive knowledge of the needs and requirements of the great majority of the consumers. Such a trend will reduce considerably the costly and time-consuming tasks at present performed by the retail trades of measuring, fitting, adjusting and special ordering for each individual consumer.

The general effect of these developments will be to make the distributive process as such for a wide range of goods one of organization only, or, to use an American term, an engineering operation. The major problem will be that of devising ways and means of matching the demands and needs of millions of consumers with the controlled flow of commodities, without limiting in any serious way the personal choice of each consumer. In relation to standardized, staple goods that are needed at regular and frequent intervals by practically every household, the solution will probably lie in the direction of planned and intensive services to the home. The actual form taken by these services will, of course, depend at any given time on the relative cost of different factors such as manpower, vehicles, petrol and so on, but there can be little doubt that the mechanization and organization of these services will eventually lead to the supply of these basic commodities as smoothly, regularly and economically as the supply of other necessities such as water, gas or electricity. In relation to the less standardized goods, the goods purchased individually by consumers, the solution is likely to lie in the direction of very much larger shops in shopping centres, many of the shops selling goods of more than one trade. In these shops the retailing techniques will be those of open display of the different types of goods available and of self-selection, self-service or semi-self-service by the consumer. Given considerable improvements in standardization and simplification in size and quality the consumer need consult only himself as to style and taste.

These developments, it will be appreciated, would mean that the role of the retailer—if the term is still used—in guiding and advising the consumer will become less and less important. The need for technical skill and knowledge on the part of the retailer in relation to particular products will decline, and the boundaries between trades will be determined by considerations of the character of consumer demand and of consumer convenience rather than by traditional divisions. The functions of the retailer will become essentially those of providing an opportunity for consumers to make their selection and choice, and of engineering the flow of goods from the producer to the consumer. These developments suggest further that the consumer, without the guidance of the retailer, will not only have personal preferences but should also possess the knowledge and ability to make a correct choice and should be protected against fraud. At present information enabling the consumer to make a choice is provided by the manufacturers in many instances by way of branding and advertising. With the growth of large-scale production methods and the increasing concern of manufacturers with the marketing of their products this type of informational service will no doubt increase in importance. It may well be, however, that in the future the consumer will demand fuller and more impartial information than that provided by competitive branding and advertising. This may be secured through the development of systems such as national standards of performance and quality, consumers' advice bureaux, and the publication of results of tests made by independent bodies.

Given larger shops, shops selling a wider range of goods, open display to enable selection to be made, and adequate consumer knowledge, two types of organizational problems remain. First there are the problems of merchandising so that the goods stocked and displayed keep abreast of changes in consumer taste, of matching the consumer's selection of style and shade with his or her requirements in size, and of planning delivery to the consumer of the selection of goods made. These are straightforward problems of organization, though their solution will demand a large measure of expert specialization. Secondly there are the problems of maintaining the demand of consumers over time so that full use is made of the capacity of retail establishments. As consumers are human this problem will never be solved as completely as is possible in, say, a factory where the maintenance of a flow of raw materials presents few problems. But the use of open display and of one form or another of self-service will make possible greater utilization of the manpower employed in distribution in that the tasks can be planned without direct reference to the shopping whims of consumers. In addition, however, it is probable that other efforts will be made to solve the problem of the flow of customers by such devices as greater flexibility in the opening and closing hours of shops, increased use of automatic machinery and direct encouragement of off-peak shopping.

These suggestions as to possible trends in the organization of the distributive trades relate to developments in urban densely populated districts and, further, are hardly practicable in all sections of the consumer goods trades. Only when consumer demand is relatively concentrated both geographically and within certain ranges of goods can an engineering approach to distribution be adopted. In the small towns and rural areas, for example, the changes in methods are likely to be relatively small but, as in the past, developments in distributive methods in urban areas will probably spread in a modified form to the rural areas. The attraction of the larger shops in the towns for purchases of goods such as clothing and household goods will no doubt be maintained even though the spread of advertising and branding of such goods may assist the local shops. The supply of essential goods in rural areas is likely to become more organized through the use of travelling self-service shops and regular home deliveries. In respect of the range and type of goods demanded the specialist retailer providing skilled counter service will continue, both in the town and in the country, to play an important role. While the assumption is made that in the future the consumer will be more knowledgeable and better informed as to the exact type and quality of goods he or she requires, these conditions will apply only to the medium- and lower-priced goods purchased fairly regularly. For purchases made occasionally, for the purchase of goods requiring after-sales service, and for the purchase of high-priced articles, for example special types of tools, motor-cars, and certain types of electrical equipment, furniture and expensive clothing, the range of goods stocked and the knowledge and service of the specialist retailer will be essential.

If the above suggestions are accepted as indicating the probable lines of evolution in the distributive trades in the future, questions may be asked as to whether such evolution will be rapid or slow, whether it will be straightforward or involve painful adjustments. More specifically, questions may be asked as to whether the present short-term trends in the distributive trades point in this direction, and if not, what will be the main problems of adjustment.

In relation to the short-term trends mention was made above of the element of rigidity that was appearing in the structure, organization and techniques of the distributive trades in the years immediately preceding the Second World War. The circumstances of the war and post-war years strengthened this tendency. The exception in the pre-war years was the development of the new form of trading, the variety chain store, and in the war and post-war years the economies secured in the use of man-power, the move away from traditional margins, and the few experiments with self-service units. Certainly the express limitations on the development of new methods, techniques and policies brought about by controls and shortages tend to make very difficult any clear assessment of the type of changes that might result if these limitations disappeared. Some doubts may, however, be expressed as to whether widespread experimentation and new thinking in the distributive trades would necessarily follow the relaxation of controls.

There would appear to be two main problems arising from the present trends in the distributive trades which will need to be resolved if the evolution towards the kind of system outlined above is to be fairly rapid and relatively smooth. The first of these relates to the policies of manufacturers: the second to the present methods and structure of large-scale retailing.

Producers and the future trends in distribution

Reference has been made to the growing concern of manufacturers with the marketing of their products in the past fifty years or so. The continued growth of large-scale production methods will tend to increase this interest. In the past, however, the practices arising out of this concern, such as sales by manufacturers direct to retailers, advertising and branding, and resale price maintenance, have not in most cases encouraged the development of new forms and techniques distribution but rather the reverse. In the inter-war years, in those trades where the manufacturers' concern with marketing was greatest there was a tendency towards the maintenance of the existing framework of distribution, towards marketing through the small-scale re-tailer and towards increasing the number of outlets for the products. This is not to say that many advantages were not obtained as a result of these methods. As suggested above, there were considerable improvements in stan-dards and qualities of goods, the exact character of consumer demand was estimated more scientifically, and the concentration of demand on certain lines increased wholesale and retail stock turn and reduced holding costs. Manufacturers were not, however, alone in their introduction of these im-provements. The advantages and the rapid rise in importance of variety chain stores was directly related to the use of these methods of determination of demand, standardization and simplification. But whereas the variety chain stores were concerned with the reduction of the cost both of manufacture and of distribution and with the low price of their goods, the producers of branded advertised goods were concerned mainly with differentiating their product from similar products and with sales promotion. These efforts at sales promotion, including a very large number of outlets, extensive advertis-ing and free gifts and coupons, and even door-to-door salesmen, increased rather than decreased the complexity and cost of distribution and often off-set the advantages gained by way of more standardized production methods.

Shortages of goods, price controls, shifts in traditional mark-ups and margins and the existence of a sellers' market in many commodities have brought about some changes in policy, but if the future sees an increase in the control exerted by manufacturers over the marketing of their goods and the spread of this policy to new trades such as furniture and textiles will not the results be somewhat similar to those of the inter-war years? There would appear to be a need for manufacturers to examine closely their selling policies; and, while continuing to be concerned with the marketing of their products, to give encouragement in every way possible to the distribution of the goods through the most efficient and inexpensive channels and forms of retailing. Preoccupation with the total volume of sales must not be allowed to over-shadow the problem of the cost of sales, including the wholesalers' and retailers' margins. Such an approach would almost certainly mean some modification of resale price maintenance policies and of the relationship between the large-scale producers and the large-scale retailers. Examples of possible changes in selling policies are an adjustment of selling terms and the granting of permission for variations in the resale prices to those firms and organizations that can handle larger quantities at lower costs. Too often with present selling schedules and volume rebates the large buyer helps to subsidize the very small buyer either as a matter of manufacturers' sales policy or as a result of insufficiently detailed costings of individual accounts. But the producers aiming at the national market are often reluctant to make changes in their selling methods which would lead them to become dependent on a few large contracts. The danger of this is real, as is also the difficulty of one producer on his own making changes in his selling policies which might lead to his exclusion from the national market through the activities of competitors following traditional practices. The solution to neither problem is simple.

Retail organizations and the future trends in distribution

While it is possible, therefore, that manufacturers' marketing policies will undergo some change, the shifts in policy will be significant only if developments in the retailing structure make them essential. Further, the suggested developments in the distributive methods mentioned above all involve an increase in the scale and size of retailing operations. Questions may be asked therefore as to whether the present forms of large-scale retailing will continue to increase in importance, whether new forms of large-scale retailing will emerge, and whether the large-scale retailers will take the lead in introducing and developing new techniques of distribution and new relationships with manufacturers. The answers to all these questions would appear to be 'yes', but the 'yes' is conditional upon many adjustments being made in existing policies and practices. The problems of the chief types of large-scale retailers may be considered in turn.

In the case of department store trading, present trends suggest a slowing down in the rate of progress. The central stores are fighting a difficult battle against the geographical dispersion of their customers and against rising overhead costs. The suburban and smaller provincial stores are threatened with severe competition from specialist multiple shop retailers and have not yet achieved an accepted and distinctive position in the distributive framework such as that occupied in the first twenty-five years of the century by the older types of store. The department store method of trading is, however, well suited to mass distribution techniques combined with a fair measure of self-service. While there may always be a place for the individual, central store with a particular tradition of service and amenities, the future of the suburban and provincial department stores would appear to lie in a different direction. What would appear to be needed are specially built stores based on the principle of maximum display coupled, as far as practicable, with self-selection and perhaps semi-self-service. The type of goods stocked and the price ranges would differ from those of the variety chain stores, but many of the merchandising techniques of the latter would need to be adopted. And the development of small chains of provincial and suburban stores that cater for similar types of markets in different areas would enable the stores to compete on more equal terms with the specialist multiple shop firms.

The Co-operative Societies face different problems of expansion and adjustment. With no geographical 'Co-operative deserts' into which they can expand, the Societies will have to turn to intensifying their sales in the areas already covered and to branching out towards new sections of the market. In the mass distribution of essential goods such as foodstuffs the Societies are in a good position to lead the way with new forms and techniques. Already many Societies are prominent in opening self-service units in the grocery and provisions trade, and the Co-operative organization of the distribution of bread and milk is ahead of most. Again, as the trend is likely to be towards larger shops selling a wide range of foodstuffs the Co-operative Societies are well placed. The maintenance of this lead and the development of new techniques may, however, force the Societies to reconsider their traditional dividend policy and their buying preference for products of the Wholesale Societies. If a wider market is to be gained the appeal will have to stress efficiency and up-to-date methods of selling the goods the consumer demands, and not only the payment of dividends which in any event may be so small as to offer little attraction.

In relation to the trades other than food the central premises of many Co-operative Societies offer scope for large, attractive, well laid out semi-self-service stores. There are few signs, however, that this side of Co-operative trading will develop. The problems are clear enough. Specialization, employment of experts, prior claim to main-street sites, sales appeal directed to the public in general and not merely to members, and retail control over the wholesale production programmes are a few of the essential prerequisites, but the chances of these policies being adopted seem remote. Continued growth of the very large Societies which can afford to develop a measure of specialization will help to some extent, but what is needed is an entirely new approach by the Co-operative movement to the trades other than food.

Multiple shop retailing

The multiple shop form of retailing, because it comprises many different competing firms, would appear to be the most enterprising and the most likely to take the lead in developing the new methods and techniques mentioned above. Some difficulties will, however, have to be overcome. One of the most important of these is the problem of securing larger premises and selling a wider range of goods. In the foodstuffs trades, for example, any trend towards combination self-service stores, that is stores selling meat and vegetables and perhaps fish and poultry, as well as groceries and provisions, involves the abandonment of traditional frontage widths and the combination of many separate trades. Similar problems arise in the trades other than food. While some moves in these directions have been made by individual firms in the past, progress in the future is likely to be slow. A multiple shop firm in the butchery trade, for example, is unlikely to amalgamate with a multiple shop firm in the grocery and provisions trade, and even if this did happen the butchery and grocery premises would rarely be located next door to each other to enable a new combination store to be built. Again, two footwear firms which had branches in the same towns might amalgamate, but this would not lead necessarily to one larger shop in place of two separate branches. As pointed out above, the properties on either side of existing multiple shop branches are in most areas owned by other large-scale retailing organizations who are most unlikely to sell or move out. The bias in the past of multiple shop organizations towards specialization in trade, the tradition of 18 ft. and 24 ft. frontages in the main streets of most towns, and the occupation of practically all these sites by large-scale retailers, will tend to slow down the development of larger selling units handling a wider range of goods. In new housing estates, provided the local authorities do not insist on allocating shops according to traditional patterns, some development may take place, but with a slowly rising or stable population new building is not likely to be extensive. In older areas, while individual firms may succeed in increasing the size of their unit and the range of trade undertaken, it is difficult to envisage a general movement in this direction unless some arrangements for the exchange of shop properties are possible.

A second problem of the future development of multiple shop retailing and of other forms of large-scale trading is that of the relationship with the large-scale producers. A policy adopted by some multiple shop firms has been towards the integration of production and distribution units. In the past, however, this was rarely a complete solution. In order to give variety to the retail stock, firms found that some purchases had to be made from outside sources. In the future, with a trend towards shops selling a wider range of goods, the significance of integration is likely to be less. The solution to the problem will lie perhaps, as emphasis on display for selection and self-service develops, in the acceptance of a new division of functions between the large-scale producer and the large-scale distributor; the producer will take the responsibility of designing, planning, ascertaining demand and promoting the sale of the product, while the retailer takes the responsibility of displaying and pricing the product for the consumer to purchase if he wishes. The aim is a partnership of equals each respecting the other's function, rather than the domination of one by the other.

A final problem facing all types of large-scale retailers is that of raising the large amounts of capital required to finance such developments. There is a double problem here. First, the existing large-scale retailers already have extensive investments in property, equipment and good will. Secondly, practically all the developments envisaged involve additions to property or the erection of new buildings, and require increased amounts of fixed capital and the acquisition of property in shopping areas where the values are already inflated. Many of the existing assets are not easily realizable or adaptable to the newer methods of organization, and it is most unlikely that the additional outlay required can be met out of profits, at any rate in the initial stages. What will be needed if the new methods are to be developed fairly rapidly is much greater investment in the distributive trades than has been the case in the past. The practice in the United States of real estate companies, insurance companies and financial trusts building large shops and leasing them to retailers may be worth exploring in Britain.[6] But whether any particular priority can be given to investment in the distributive trades as against other forms of investment will depend on the economic position of the country as a whole and on the assessment of the relative importance of improvements in distributive techniques.

3.   Conclusion: the distributive trades, 1850–1950, and the future

The war and the immediate post-war years have been described as a period in which the developments in the structure and techniques of the distributive trades were few. In the future, however, these years may also be seen as marking the end of one phase of the history of the distributive trades and the beginning of another.

The distinctive feature of the past hundred years in the distributive trades has been the consistent growth in the significance of large-scale distribution. This growth has accompanied and has influenced the development of scale in production and importing. Large-scale retailing has led to some measure of integration between factory production and distribution, to the placing of large orders for specific types of standardized goods with manufacturers and producers, and to direct purchases in bulk from overseas producers. These practices have had the effect of reducing the number of separate links in the distributive chain, of enabling economies in production to be secured by the concentration of demand on a limited number of lines of goods and, in so far as large-scale retailers must place forward orders, of helping to stabilize manufacturing and production conditions and prices.

The growth of scale in distribution and the effects of this growth on productive organization and conditions varied between trades and between commodities. Distribution and production developments in the footwear trade for example in these years were in marked contrast to those in the fruit and vegetables trade. Further, in some instances, for example in the chocolate and sugar confectionery and tobacco goods trades, the growth of scale in production was not accompanied by any significant growth of scale in retailing organization. Contrariwise, the growth of scale in retailing in other instances, as for example in the women's wear trade and in the case of the department store form of large-scale retailing, was not accompanied by any significant changes in the size of productive units or in their methods of organization.

After allowances have been made for these exceptions, however, and the existence of unevenness and of differing rates of development between different trades has been accepted, the pattern of development appears to have been that of a parallel extension of the use of large-scale methods of organization in both production and distribution in the past hundred years. In most instances the new methods and techniques of producers and the rise of a mass demand for the goods made possible the development of scale in distribution. In a few instances the growth of scale in retailing and the consequent consolidation and concentration of demand, as in the case of variety chain stores and the wholesale bespoke tailors, made possible the introduction of large-scale methods and economies of scale on the manufacturing side.

There are no signs, whatever may be the specific problems in particular trades or the problems facing particular types of producers and distributors, that this trend towards large-scale production and distribution of consumer goods has reached a limit. In fact, given full employment, a continued rise in the standard of living, and a policy of redistribution of incomes by fiscal or other measures, there will probably be an increase in the volume of demand for many types of goods that are now semi-luxuries. Such an increase in demand will make possible the standardization and large-scale production and distribution of such goods. The existence of conditions favourable to the further development of scale can, however, only indicate the main direction of the probable trend. The detail of the pattern and the rate of progress in the future, as in the past, will be influenced by a host of other factors.

Taking as given the consistent growth in the importance of large-scale retailing, two main phases in the evolution of the distributive trades since the middle of the nineteenth century have been discussed in the foregoing chapters. The first was characterized by the wealth of new ideas and new methods that emerged in the last quarter of the nineteenth century and opening decade of the twentieth. The growth of large-scale production methods in many consumer goods trades, the large-scale imports of cheap foodstuffs, and the growing consistency of consumer demand combined to make possible and to make necessary division of labour and specialization on an important scale in the distributive process. There appeared alongside the small-scale, costly, leisurely and skilled methods of the one-shop retailer the impersonal, speedy and cheaper methods of the large-scale retailer. There followed radical changes in trading techniques and policies, and in the conception of the role of the retailer in the distributive process.

The second phase, the inter-war years, was characterized not so much by the development of new methods and forms of organization, with the exception of the variety chain store, as by the extended development of the trends of the pre-1914 era. Many of these trends were, however, modified. The slowing down in the rate of expansion of the economy and the unevenness of what expansion did take place were factors modifying the trends. The considerable improvements in the range, scale and techniques of the manufacture of consumer goods and the increasing concern, evidenced in the growth of sales promotion, branding, advertising and resale price maintenance, of the larger manufacturers with the marketing of their products were other factors. There followed a tendency to shift the emphasis in distributive method away from stress on price, on inexpensiveness and on crude mass distribution techniques towards stress on quality and standards, on display and siting, on choice and variety and on service to the consumer. Further, the trends in the distributive structure as a whole began to be influenced as much by the marketing policies of the large-scale producers as by the initiative of the units engaged in distribution alone.

It remains to be seen whether a third phase in the evolution of the distributive trades is about to begin. In such a phase large-scale retailing will continue to expand, not merely because of the inability of newcomers to enter the field or of existing small-scale retailers to compete in buying sites or in advertising, but as a result of the speeding-up and simplification of the distributive process through the further combination of the experience and advantages of large-scale methods of distribution with the knowledge and techniques of large-scale production. In such a phase the problems of consumer taste, preference, whims and habits will no longer be seen as intractable, and emphasis will not be placed on the need for elaboration of distributive organizations to cater for diversity. But instead it will be a phase in which, in respect of a wide sector of demand, the problem of matching in time and place the flow of goods with the needs of the consumer and his right to select individually will be seen as reducible to a number of relatively simple principles that call for close co-ordination and co-operation between producer and distributor.

Notes

1. See Appendix E for a summary of the Census of Distribution figures of the number of shops in existence in 1950.

2. J. A. Hough, *Co-operative Retailing*, p. 169.

3. The monthly figures of sales by different economic types of retailer published in the *Board of Trade Journal* since 1947 point to a rise in the sales of multiple shop retailers at a much faster rate than the increase in total retail sales between 1947 and 1950. This rapid increase, however, would appear in part to be a reflection of the efforts of multiple shop retailers to regain ground lost during the war owing to rationing, enemy action and the unwillingness of consumers to shop centrally.

4. Bankruptcies of retail businesses in the trades other than food were 1,280 in 1938 and 161 in 1941. (*House of Commons Debates*, vol. 382, col. 220.)

5. The Ministry of Labour 'old' series and 'new' series of employment cannot be compared directly, but the trend can be seen by placing the series side by side:

Year	Total working population	Total engaged in distribution	Proportion of total working population engaged in distribution %
1938 (*a*)	19,473,000	2,882,000	14.7
1948 (*a*)	20,274,000	2,354,000	11.5
1948 (*b*)	22,904,000	2,523,000	11.0
1950 (*b*)	23,327,000	2,643,000	11.3

(*a*) Old series.   (*b*) New series.

6 *Retailing*, Productivity Team Report, Anglo-American Council on Productivity, London and New York, 1952, p. 4. This report gives an admirable summary of the main features of retailing in the United States.

5

1949–1989: retail reflections

Morris L. Mayer

Source: *Journal of Retailing* 65(3) (1989): 396–401.

The Journal of Retailing *serves and has served as a barometer of the spirit and conscience of the discipline of retailing. An analysis of* JR *over a forty-year time span, including my entire retail business and academic career, has revealed the following four decades of retailing development: 1950s—The Era of "How to Do It"; 1960s—The Era of Transition and Conceptual Questions; 1970s—The Era of Upgraded Tools and Philosophy Development; 1980s—The Era of Strategic Marketing.*

In each era the paper addresses the following issues: (1) the status of retailing course(s) within business schools' curricula; (2) career focus and expectations; (3) academicians' interactions with and expectations of retail management; (4) the discipline's major emphasis and/or perspective; (5) issues or topics of major interest; and (6) major academic contributors.

When Avijit Ghosh, Editor of the *Journal of Retailing*, invited me to contribute to the 65th year commemorative issue of the journal, I was flattered and accepted immediately. That invitation has been responsible for a sentimental excursion into my past. Noted in the invitation was the basic idea that this anniversary issue could best be expressed by the old Iowa saying, "Look backwards to the future," or as quoted from my dear friend, Stan Hollander, "Drive with an eye on the rearview mirror"; thus my commitment to the project was established. And my framework seemed to be determined by the nature of the issue (and my own background).

Suddenly I was thrust back forty years to my matriculation, in 1949, at the New York University School of Retailing in the "Day Program" for full-time students working on Master of Science Degrees in Retailing. Some sixty students from almost as many institutions of higher education were to come together for a year in an intensive internship/classroom setting. During that year I experienced for the first time seeing my name (together with seven other committee members) in print in the Fall 1950 issue of the *Journal of Retailing*. Since at that time my interest in an academic career was nonexistent, I had no idea that the first article would become, almost four decades later, the inspiration for this invited article.

I left NYU and enjoyed a short career in retailing in New York City and Chicago. I have always thought that my experience in merchandising and management, though short, has provided a valuable dimension for my teaching. It also offers a significant perspective for this paper.

Framework for analysis and methodology

As noted, the inspiration for this piece derives from my association over the years with the *Journal of Retailing*. I can say with confidence that the *JR* serves and has served as a barometer of the spirit and conscience of the academic discipline of retailing. Academically, I have always been interested in investigating the evolution of ideas, concepts, and philosophies. Robert Bartels's writings on the history of marketing thought and classes under H. H. Maynard at The Ohio State University also influenced me to look at the times and conditions under which certain ideas have flourished.

Most of my real-world and academic time has been spent concentrating on retail marketing, and I have always believed that over the years retailing has changed dramatically. What were the changes? Could the periods of change be categorized into eras for analytical purposes? What would be a proper vehicle for this retrospective analysis? Obviously the *Journal of Retailing* is the appropriate source of academic development over time; also through careful analysis of the articles over the forty-year time span, if a clustering of trends or ideas becomes apparent, these eras can be identified. The *JR* analysis coupled with personal experiences from both practitioner and academic perspectives should provide a creditable base for the proposed analysis.

Analysis

The review of the volumes of the *Journal of Retailing* from 1950 to 1988 revealed that the four decades could be categorized as follows:

1950s—The Era of "How to Do It"
1960s—The Era of Transition and Conceptual Questions
1970s—The Era of Upgraded Tools and Philosophy Development
1980s—The Era of Strategic Marketing

In each era this paper addresses the following issues:

1. The status of retailing course(s) within business schools' curricula
2. Career focus and expectations

3. Academicians' interactions with and expectations of retail management
4. The discipline's major emphasis and/or perspective
5. Issues or topics of major interest
6. Major academic contributors

The 1950s—The Era of "How to Do It"

Following World War II, principles of retailing was taught as one of a number of marketing courses which might include, in addition to principles of marketing, wholesaling, credits and collections, salesmanship, sales management, purchasing, advertising principles (perhaps even copy and layout), and marketing research. It was not unusual for colleges and universities, especially those in which a faculty member or two had a particular interest in retailing, to offer several retailing courses such as retail merchandising and small store retailing. The retailing courses, as well as the other marketing courses, were descriptive, institutional, and "how to" in approach.

The structure of retailing/marketing courses in the 1950s was responding to the strong career focus of the era immediately following the war. Veterans were ready to learn how to enter the market and make it. The retailing courses stressed the role of the buyer in a single, downtown department store; branching was yet to occur, and realistically, career aspirations were middle management at best; courses addressed this reality. Retail management, in describing their junior executive trainee needs, talked in terms of intuitive, creative, fashion-oriented individuals. The food chains were not recruiting; the discounter was not on the horizon until late in the decade; marketing had not been "discovered" by retailers, and the department store or small entrepreneurial opportunity was virtually the only retail game in town.

It is not surprising that the retailing discipline, reading the environmental realities of the time, adopted the department store (or small entrepreneurial) perspective and that academicians provided pragmatic product information, merchandising tips, and training techniques, presenting the information in a descriptive, "how to" format. Items in the *Journal of Retailing* during that period addressed such topics as store policies (parking, evening openings, and services); branch storing potential and problems; personnel issues (selection, training, job evaluation, and unionization); automation; the impact of suburban shopping centers on downtowns; trading stamps; self selection; competition from the emerging discount house; government regulation impacts; and television as an advertising medium for retailers.

The academic contributors to the *Journal of Retailing* during that period were heavily New York University faculty, including T. Dart Elsworth, Karen Gillespie, Elmer O. Schaler, and Charles M. Edwards, Jr. Other names soon appeared and the discipline was enhanced by the contributions of Stanley Hollander, Lawrence Loxley, and Reavis Cox. The works of the 1950s need to be revisited; I encourage it. It was a rich era in many ways, and the seeds of future harvests were sowed.

The 1960s—The Era of Transition and Conceptual Questions

As was true for society in general, the 1960s were years of transition and questioning. The decade was not an easy one to live through; it is equally difficult to capture. The status of retailing as a subject area in business schools in this decade was predestined by the reports released by the Ford and Carnegie Foundations in the late 1950s which caused dramatic upheavals in business curricula. When the dust settled, some extremely descriptive, applied marketing courses disappeared from the course listings in many institutions. Retailing was a common victim. Business schools were charged to upgrade curricula and more quantitative, analytical tools evolved in response to the challenge.

In the trade, the growing mass merchandisers and food chains were perfectly content to hire high school graduates. Department and specialty stores, the traditional employers of retail-oriented students, were facing severe competition from other industries for the most promising graduates. Thus, the supply side (academe) was going through trauma while the demand side (business) was in some conflict. Facing such facts, it is not difficult to understand why communication between the academic community and the retail sector of business suffered. Neither side really understood the position of the other. The retailer felt somewhat betrayed as the pool of students was not being trained in the subject matter of interest to the executives, and the students were being hired by industries that out-bid the salaries offered by retail training programs. Add to this the 1960s anti-business attitude toward the end of the decade and into the next, and we see fertile ground for misunderstanding.

In academe, we found a critical, evaluative, and conceptual tone evolving from the very pragmatic focus of the past. Retailing courses that survived were broadening beyond the boundaries of the department store to other types of retail operations; students were being educated more broadly as marketing courses included such new titles as consumer behavior and more sophisticated marketing research courses were taking shape.

In the 1960s, contributors from the marketing mainstream were in evidence addressing retailing issues. Such names as William Lazer, Eugene Kelley, David Rachman, Louis Stern, Rom Markin, and Leonard Berry can be found among the authors of the period. The conceptual topics addressed included store image, conceptual modeling, shopping attitudes and behavior, channel control, diffusion theory, and segmentation. Continuing interest was displayed in issues such as sales evaluation, self-selection, electronic data processing, government regulation, trading stamps, the retailing mix, sales productivity, controls, and the shopping center's impact on the central business district.

As the decade of transition and conceptualization, the 1960s set the stage for the next decades.

The 1970s—The Era of Upgraded Tools and Philosophy Development

After the volatility within the marketing (and all business) curricula during the prior decade, the 1970s found marketing scholars no longer defensive about their discipline. They became more accepting of the sub-area of retailing, which once more became a popular offering at both the undergraduate and graduate levels. Career orientation was again accepted within the functional marketing courses, now offered on a more sophisticated level.

Direct and sound retail management/academic interaction was evidenced particularly through the newly conceived academic retail centers. The retailing discipline was moving toward a more scientific perspective with a focus on measurement, analyses, behavioral content, empiricism, and theory development. A marketing philosophy was being accepted in progressive firms in addition to merchandising as a guiding management statement.

The literature as observed, providing evidence of the upgraded tools and philosophy development, addressed such topics as follows: segmentation analysis, simulation, image measurement, role conflict and ambiguity, conceptual modeling, computerization, channel relationships, out-shopping behavior, strategy formulation, consumerism, social responsibility, atmospherics, generics, services retailing, and management by objectives. New marketing names such as Philip Kotler, Barry Mason, Ben Enis, and William Darden appeared as major contributors to the retailing literature.

The 1980s—The Era of Strategic Retailing

It is difficult to distinguish a difference between the 1970s and 1980s perception of the discipline vis-a-vis the business school versus the career orientation. From my vantage point, I conclude that the eras overlap on those two dimensions. I see even more evidence at the end of the 1980s of an expanded interaction between the worlds of academe and retailing practice. This interaction includes experiential learning, cooperative efforts to bring the real world to students by bringing executives to campus, seminars, speaker programs, and the like. Retailing centers continue to expand their programs and to proliferate throughout the nation.

During the 1980s, retailing as an academic discipline came of age. The emphasis was on strategic management and marketing rather than merchandise management. This new perspective is within a channel context with more predictive modeling in evidence. Supporting this conjecture as prominent issues of concern are: strategic planning, consumer complaint behavior, consumer dissatisfaction research, consumer alienation, image/positioning, merchandise information systems, lifestyle retailing, ethics, store choice models, channel conflict, structural equations approach, and forecasting. Names appearing in the 1980s addressing such topics were such established contributors as Elizabeth Hirschman, William Bearden, and Robert Lusch.

The 1990s

The objective of this essay was not to predict, but rather to reflect. It is diffi-cult not to look toward a new century and ask, "What's next?" If we learn anything from history, I believe we can expect a continuation of the strengths we have developed during the recent past. I urge colleagues to cherish and build on the received discipline structure. Improve our ability to predict and communicate with colleagues and practitioners, of course. But just as important, build strong relationships with retail organizations willing to be a part of our world. Be proud of our developing sub-marketing discipline, and never be defensive or apologetic. Those attitudes are relegated to the past.

6

Trends in large-scale retailing

Malcolm P. McNair

Source: *Harvard Business Review* 10 (1931): 30–39.

We usually speak of the industrial revolution in the past tense as if it were something that had happened a long time ago and were now a matter of interest only to the economic historians. Of course this is not true. The industrial revolution is still going on, as witness the Russian Five-year Plan, for instance. In the United States, however, the major scene of the industrial revolution for the present has definitely shifted from production to distribution. The economic historian of the future is likely to put his finger on the first three or four decades of the 20th century as the time when the marketing of commodities to consumers definitely developed away from the small-scale shopkeeping basis, parallel to the home industry or handicraft phase of manufacturing, towards a large-scale, fully capitalistic basis. The economic historian of the future, however, will have an advantage over us in being able to see this phase of the industrial revolution in something like a true perspective, whereas we are too close to it and almost too intimately concerned with its problems to be able to see clearly just what is going on. We can, however, name a few of the current trends which seem to give some clue to the general character of the change that is taking place.

(1) The trend from small-scale to large-scale operation of retail distributive enterprises has been sharply accelerated during the last ten years. Large-scale retail enterprises of the department store type are, of course, not new; nor are mail-order houses. In fact, following the initial period of development, when department stores and mail-order houses were subject to attacks less severe but of the same general character as those now being leveled at the chain store movement, these two types of retail enterprise apparently fitted into our marketing machinery without any very far-reaching effects. But since 1920 the growth of chain stores has been remarkable. Sales of the Great Atlantic & Pacific Tea Company, for instance, have increased from about $200,000,000 in 1922 to over $1,000,000,000 in 1929. According to the indices of the Federal Reserve

Board, the increase in chain store sales on the basis of the monthly average 1923–25 as 100 was, during the period from 1920 to 1929, from 66 to 234 in grocery chains, 64 to 164 in 5- and 10-cent chains, 78 to 204 in drug chains, and so on. At the same time, department store sales over the period from 1919 to 1925 showed a fairly strong rate of increase, although not so rapid as that of the chain stores. Finally, in the latter part of the decade just closed, the chain store movement definitely appeared in the department store field. During this period from about 1920 to about 1930, therefore, the development of large-scale distribution became unmistakably a major trend. For better or worse this distributive revolution is carrying us away from shopkeeping to mass distribution; and the really surprising thing is that the forces of mass production did not cause this development sooner.

(2) There has taken place during the last ten years a remarkable growth of what might be crudely termed scientific methods in distributive business. One cannot examine the voluminous literature of retail associations, controllers' congresses, merchandise managers' groups, and what not, without encountering repeatedly such terms as "merchandise budget," "unit control," "open-to-buy," "retail inventory method," "quota-bonus plan," "expense classification," "expense budget," and so on. All these are evidence of the general effort to get away from rule-of-thumb, expediency, hunch, guess work, and to develop some sounder methods of approach to the solution of business problems. It is quite proper to point out that more often than not the result of these efforts has been pseudo-science of the worst kind; but from the standpoint of long-time trends the important thing about these developments is the recognition that the old-time rule-of-thumb methods no longer are adequate to meet the problems of an increasingly complex distributive system.

(3) We have witnessed during recent years the increasingly rapid obliteration of recognized channels of distribution. Formerly there were fairly well-defined lines marking the boundaries between the respective functions of the manufacturer, the wholesaler, and the retailer. Furthermore, particular types of commodities had their own recognized channels of distribution and did not to any great extent flow over into other channels. Now we find that this picture is becoming more and more confused. It is an era of scrambled merchandising. Grocery stores sell cigarettes; drug stores sell grocery products; and tobacco stores sell razor blades. Grocery stores are on the way to becoming food department stores; department stores and variety chains operate luncheonettes and soda fountains. Functionally also the lines are breaking down. Manufacturers undertake to do their own retailing; retail chains undertake to do their own manufacturing; wholesalers seek to protect their increasingly precarious position sometimes by entering into manufacturing, sometimes by going into retailing through the formation of voluntary chains.

These three developments of the last ten years—the accelerated growth of large-scale retail enterprises, particularly of the chain store type, the marked interest in methods of management that promise to be more effective than guess and hunch, and the breakdown of recognized channels of distribution and spheres of activity—are among the significant symptoms of the distributive revolution which is taking place. We do not know whether this distributive revolution will continue for the next ten years at the same pace as during the last ten. If we are right, however, in the guess that we have hazarded in regard to the general direction of this movement, then we may expect the large-scale, fully organized type of retail distributive enterprise to increase in relative importance. At the present time the two major types of such institutions are department stores and chain stores. Developments of recent years suggest that we can disregard mail-order houses as an important separate type.

The preliminary figures for the Census of Distribution indicate a total volume of retail store sales in the United States of about $53,000,000,000. Figures are not yet available to indicate the precise breakdown of this total, but partial information so far released, together with estimates previously made by Dr. Nystrom[1] and others, seems to indicate that department store sales amount to 14% or 15% of the total and that chain store sales are perhaps 18% or possibly 20%. It was probably not until 1928 that chain store sales passed department store sales in total volume.

The outlook for department stores

What is the present outlook for department stores as compared with chains? Taking the department stores first, it is clear that they are being more seriously affected by the current business depression than are the chains. In fact, the department stores are suffering much more severely than they did in the last great business depression, in 1921. At that time the success of the department stores in weathering the storm was one of the factors which helped to develop the interest of the public in department stores as an investment possibility. In 1930, however, the average department store with sales over $2,000,000, according to the Harvard Bureau of Business Research, make a net gain, or net business profit, of only 2.7% of sales, or 4.9% of invested capital. The reason for this relatively poor showing of department stores in 1930 lies in unfavorable trends which began developing as far back as 1926. Over that period sales volume remained substantially unchanged until the decline in 1930, the gross margin percentage also remained stationary, and total expense increased sharply. Earnings in ratio to capital invested declined in 1927, 1928, and 1929, in sharp contrast to the earnings of manufacturing companies during this same period. For smaller department stores, those with sales under $500,000, there has been a steadily unfavorable trend since 1923. Over that period gross margin increased only from 27.6% to 29.0% of sales, while total expense increased from 25.9% to 32.2%. Stores in this classification apparently have felt the competition both of the large department stores and of chain store organizations. The principal point to be emphasized from these comparisons, however, is that the poor showing which department stores made in 1930 and which they are likely to make in 1931 is not to be attributed wholly to the business depression, but rather reflects in considerable part a culmination of unfavorable trends that began developing as far back as 1926. Department stores were headed for difficulties even if there had not been a business depression. In fact, it is not too much to say that many department stores were better off in 1921, a year of business depression, than they were in 1929, a year of supposedly great prosperity.

These trends suggest that there are certain elements of weakness in the situation of the average department store. Some of these are as follows:

(1) Management effort is dispersed over too many departments handling too wide a range of merchandise. Although the buying power of the organization as a whole is large, when it is divided into a hundred or more departments it does not compare favorably with the buying power of specialty chain organizations. Even more important, in the individual department of a department store there frequently is insufficient sales volume to justify hiring a really competent executive. The remarkable growth of leased departments during recent years is a tacit acknowledgment by department stores of this weakness.

(2) The cost of doing business in department stores has increased steadily for ten years. During that time the typical amount taken out of the consumer's sales dollar to meet costs of operation has increased from about 26 cents to about 34 cents. Measured by this standard the department store is not an efficient agency for the distribution of merchandise at retail. The relatively high cost of doing business in department stores is in the first instance attributable to their relatively low productivity. For department stores with sales over $10,000,000, average sales per square foot of total space are only about $29 or $30, and below that sales volume the output per square foot is lower. Chain stores, getting greater productivity from the space which they use, can and do pay higher rentals in percentages of net sales than can department stores. The productivity per capita of persons employed in the department store business is also low. For stores with sales of $10,000,000 or over, average annual sales per employee are $8,500. This low output per capita reflects in part the high proportion of nonselling employees in department stores. Usually from 50% to 60% of the total employees in a department store are in the nonselling classification. Both the low productivity per square foot and the low output per capita reflect in part the rather complicated physical and human mechanism apparently necessary to handle the wide variety of merchandise sold in these institutions.

(3) Competition in services among department stores has reached a point where it not only contributes considerably to the high cost of doing business but actually interferes with the effectiveness of selling. Returns of merchandise by customers in large department stores, for instance, amount to over 14% of net sales. Competition in credit terms is steadily lowering the turnover of accounts receivable. In at least one large city, one or two stores have taken the initiative in discontinuing the charge for alterations on women's garments.

(4) Certain changes not wholly favorable to department stores appear to be taking place in consumers' buying habits. Shopping in the old sense of the word not only has become less necessary with increasing standardization of merchandise and wider spread of style knowledge, but actually, because of traffic conditions, has become more difficult. At the same time, the growth of suburban shopping centers makes it easy for customers to buy many articles of merchandise at nearby points.

(5) Department stores still are organized predominantly as buying institutions rather than as selling institutions. It is too hard work to buy merchandise in the average department store. There is too much red tape, lost motion, annoyance, and so on. In spite of the lip service they render to the idea of acting as purchasing agents for their communities, department stores do not make it easy enough for consumers to buy merchandise.

Looking at the other side of the picture, we can see that there remain several important elements of strength in the department store situation:

(1) The convenience of filling a variety of needs under one roof is still a factor of strength, although perhaps less important now than in the past.

(2) Department stores occupy established locations in definitely recognized retail trading areas, in many cases owning their own physical properties. The volume of retail trade in such areas, even though it may eventually decline with the growth of suburban shopping centers, will remain large for many years to come. Conceivably, however, it will tend to change in character.

(3) Department stores render many services to which the consumer has become accustomed and which many other types of retail organizations do not offer.

(4) A substantial number of department stores have developed institutional prestige with consumers.

(5) The notion that department stores in general handle high-quality merchandise, and the corollary notion that chain stores do not handle high-quality merchandise, still operates in favor of the department store.

It must be admitted, however, that the points of strength in the department store situation are not so impressive as the elements of weakness. Furthermore, some of the points of strength are of such a character that they are likely to become gradually less important with the lapse of time. Consequently it appears that the average department store, if one may hazard a forecast, must shortly make a choice between a decline, even though gradual, in its relative importance as a type of retail distribution and such a vigorous reorientation of policies, methods, and organization as will give it a new lease of life, perhaps in considerably changed form.

Chain stores

To turn from the department store to the other important type of large-scale retail distribution, namely, chain stores, it must be at once observed that there are chains *and* chains. In fact, it is a misapprehension to speak of "the chain store" as if there were any such homogeneous entity. The grocery chain and drug chain, performing a combination of retail and wholesale functions and displacing both the independent unit retailer and the wholesaler, present management problems quite different from those which characterize chain variety stores, for instance, where actually little or no warehousing is done but rather this function is shifted back to sources of supply. Speaking of chains, furthermore, we must remember that while the term chain store immediately conjures up a picture of such great organizations as A & P, Liggett, Woolworth, and so on, actually the small chains, those with less than ten or even less than five stores each, greatly outnumber the large chains and in the aggregate handle a substantial volume of business. In the city of Chicago, for instance, according to the recent census report, 2,000 stores are operated by national chains, 1,400 belong to sectional chains, 2,311 are in local chains of four stores or more, 744 are three-store multiples, and 2,018 are two-store multiples.[2]

A few years ago it was a favorite sport of marketing experts to delimit the boundaries of the chain store movement and lay down the law as to the sorts of things which chains could not do. For instance, it was said confidently that grocery chains could not handle meats or perishable fruits and vegetables, that they were limited to packaged groceries. A little later it was stated with equal confidence that chains were limited to staple merchandise, that they could not handle style and fashion goods. In all these cases events proved these conclusions wrong. Students of marketing, therefore, have become a little chary of predicting what chains cannot do. When some of the bolder prophets say that of course chains are confined to the cash-and-carry type of business, that the great stronghold of the independent merchant lies in the services which he renders, one remembers past attempts to predict.

Until recently there has been little authentic information on the operating expenses of chain stores. A little over a year ago, however, the Harvard Bureau of Business Research, operating on a grant from The Two Hundred Fifty Associates of the Harvard Business School, undertook a study of the

margins, expenses, and profits of chain grocery stores in the year 1929, the
same year which is covered by the Census of Distribution. The first bulletin
of the Bureau on the chain store business, Bulletin No. 84, *Expenses and
Profits in the Chain Grocery Business in 1929*, was published in June, 1931.

In its study of the chain grocery business the Harvard Bureau of Business
Research received reports representing substantially half the chain grocery
business in the United States. In 33,171 chain grocery stores operated by
82 companies which reported their figures to the Bureau, consumers spent
slightly under $2,000,000,000 in 1929. Out of each of these consumers' dollars,
the grocery chains typically took an average of 19.4 cents as a gross margin,
from which to pay expenses and earn a profit. This figure means that the
typical net cost of this dollar's worth of merchandise to the chains was 80.6
cents, including freight and after deducting all discounts and merchandise
allowances.

Of this 19.4 cents, 18.2 cents was required to cover the cost of doing
business, including such items as pay roll, rent, advertising, and supplies,
and also including the interest on invested capital, leaving 1.2 cents out of
each dollar spent by consumers as the pure net profit, in the sense of a
reward for undertaking the risks of business enterprise. With the addition
to this figure of the interest on owned capital and other net revenue, the total
net gain, or, in everyday business language, the "net business profit," of
these companies amounted as a common figure to 1.9 cents of the consumer's
dollar, that is to say, 1.9% of net sales. Another way to look at this figure for
net gain is to measure it, not in relation to the dollar of sales, but in relation
to the dollar of invested capital. Looked at in this way the 1.9 cents of net
gain taken by the chain grocery concerns from the consumer's dollar amounted
to 19.5 cents for each dollar of invested capital, as represented by the net
worth of the companies.

It is natural that on the basis of these figures attention should be directed
toward comparison of marketing costs for the chain store channel of distribution with those for the wholesaler–retailer channel. Since the chain grocery company typically is both wholesaler and retailer, practically the only
type of comparison that is feasible is to balance the expenses and profits of
the chain grocery store, figured as percentages of the consumer's dollar,
against the combined expenses and profits of the independent grocery store
and the grocery wholesaler, also figured as percentages of the consumer's
dollar. There are many respects, of course, in which such a comparison is not
wholly satisfactory, since independent retailers do not buy entirely from
wholesalers, nor do all chains buy entirely from manufacturers and producers. Furthermore, there are no fully satisfactory recent figures available
for expenses and profits of wholesale and retail grocers. Waiving these difficulties, however, and taking as a basis of comparison sectional studies for
1929 in the wholesale grocery business made by the Ohio State University
and of the retail grocery business made by the University of Nebraska,

checked by studies of the Harvard Bureau of Business Research for earlier years, it appears that chain grocery companies in 1929, to cover their costs of doing business and profits, took out of the consumer's dollar approximately 8.8 cents less than did wholesale and retail grocers together. If the assumption is made that chain stores buy on the same terms as wholesalers, this difference in margins means that a chain grocery company buying merchandise at the same net cost as the wholesale grocer typically could have sold for approximately 90 cents merchandise which the retail grocer buying from the wholesaler normally would have had to sell for one dollar. It is probably a fair statement that a little less than half this difference represents the costs of credit and delivery service.

Viewing the chain store situation generally, with due recognition of the widely different problems faced by different types of chains, there are apparent certain fundamental elements of strength:

(1) Chain stores by and large are still in the expansion phase of their development. At present, for instance, with retail price levels substantially lower than a year ago, numerous chain store organizations are reporting dollar sales very nearly equal to their 1930 performance. Department stores, on the other hand, are falling about 9% behind the 1930 figures.

(2) Many types of chains have the advantage of a somewhat lower cost of doing business, not all of which is to be accounted for by differences in services rendered. That is to say, there is evidence that certain types of chains, particularly those which combine wholesale and retail functions under one overhead, are inherently more economical channels for the distribution of merchandise than are many of the institutions which they are displacing. The greater efficiency of grocery chains, for instance, may be measured by the time required to move merchandise from the manufacturer or producer to the consumer by this channel as contrasted with the wholesaler–retailer channel. According to the Harvard Bureau's study previously referred to, it normally requires $36\frac{1}{2}$ days to move goods from manufacturer or producer to consumer *via* chain grocery stores as contrasted with a total of $99\frac{1}{4}$ days required to move the same merchandise through the wholesaler–retailer channel.

(3) Chain stores have made it easier for customers to buy. The sales end of the chain store mechanism is not only more conveniently located but more simple and less time-consuming in its operation.

Turning to the unfavorable factors, we can discern certain distinct elements of weakness in the present situation of the chains:

(1) The chains have failed to develop goodwill sufficiently and consequently have left the door open for the present widespread anti-chain propaganda, most of which is not based on facts. It is true that some independent retailers and wholesalers have been put out of business, but trade

mortality studies indicate that plain inefficiency has been putting these people out of business for a good many years past, and that the rate of mortality in these trades is little if any higher than it was before the advent of the chains. It must be frankly admitted, however, that such far-reaching changes in the distributive system as are being caused by the chains cannot take place without injury to those who are unable or possibly unwilling to adapt themselves to new conditions. The present outcry against the chains is fundamentally parallel to the periodic outcries of hand laborers against machines which have characterized various phases of the industrial revolution. Because there has been and promises to be a certain amount of real injury to some independent retailers and wholesalers, because the chains have been slow in recognizing the importance of cultivating goodwill, because they have frequently been shortsighted in their dealings with manufacturers, and because the arts of propaganda and manufacturing public sentiment are well understood in our time, the anti-chain store agitation has developed unexpected proportions.

The recent decision of the United States Supreme Court in the Indiana tax case has given added impetus to the already widespread movement to curb chain store activities by means of special taxation. Apparently this decision opens the door for all kinds of discriminatory legislation. In the Commonwealth of Massachusetts, for instance, a bill was introduced last year proposing to license each individual store beyond one at the rate of $750 per year in towns under 5,000, with a sliding scale from there up to $2,750 a year in cities with population over 500,000. The purposes of this bill were frankly punitive and confiscatory. Following the decision of the Supreme Court in upholding the Indiana tax on chain stores we may expect to see this and similar measures reintroduced in nearly all the state legislatures. It is unfortunate also that this decision comes at a time when state legislatures are eagerly looking around for new sources of revenue. Clearly this decision definitely forces the chains to take their case to the bar of public opinion. They must now do what they previously should have done in the way of developing a favorable and articulate public opinion to the point where state legislators will realize that consumers are friendly to chain stores and that consumers have more votes than storekeepers.

(2) Another element of weakness is to be attributed in some instances to the rapidity of growth of chain store organizations. In the scramble for desired locations numerous leases have been made at rental figures which cannot be justified within any reasonable period. Many chains, therefore, do *not* have low operating costs. In other instances effective merchandise control has not kept pace with the rate of expansion. Furthermore, there are undoubtedly a few instances of chain store promotions in which the predominant motive was the cupidity of shortsighted

investment bankers. A particular type of chain expansion that has not always turned out to be sound is the development of chains by manufacturers primarily as outlets for their plants. This type of chain, especially in the shoe business, has been far from uniformly successful.

(3) Chain store organizations have been slow to recognize the existence of personnel problems. Comparatively few chains have systematically gone about recruiting the type of personnel needed to build favor with the public. In many instances too much reliance has been placed on the efficacy of system plus relatively low-grade personnel.

(4) Chains have needlessly antagonized many manufacturers.

In summarizing their relative position it is perhaps fair to say that both the factors of strength and the factors of weakness of the chain stores are characteristically those which accompany any new economic development. Chain store methods and policies frequently are crude, and chain stores encounter the opposition of those business interests which have the most to gain from the preservation of the *status quo*. Yet a majority of chain store managements are young, vigorous, resourceful, imaginative. In the same way, department stores have both the strengths and the weaknesses of the mature type of enterprise. They are well-intrenched in an established position; habit and custom operate in their favor. But their managements are a little too conservative, a little too complacent, a little too lacking in vigor and initiative.

Chain department stores

Of course any consideration of the pros and cons of department stores and chain stores must necessarily take into account that peculiar hybrid, the so-called "chain" department store. When this particular hybrid was hatched, there was a good deal of cackling, particularly in Wall Street. But with the drastic decline in the market valuation of many chain department store stocks not a few of the experts on the side lines are ready to proclaim the offspring an ugly duckling and decry the possibility of any good results issuing from such a union.

In the first place, it must be stated definitely that so far there is no such thing as a real chain department store. The A stores of Sears, Roebuck perhaps represent the closest approach, and next in order the J. C. Penney Company. Such organizations as the Associated Dry Goods Corporation, Gimbel's, and the May Company are, properly speaking, department store ownership groups rather than full-fledged chains. One of the most essential features of a chain store organization is the centralization of management; and this feature is not as yet present in such department store ownership groups.

At the outset promoters and investors expected too much of department store "chains" formed by the merger process. They were misled to some extent, presumably, by the mistaken idea that chains in the department store field could readily duplicate the success of chains in other fields. The analogy, however, does not bear close examination. Chains in other fields have for the most part displaced stores of the comparatively small one-man management type. Department stores are large compared with unit retail stores, and even small–medium department stores have a fairly well-defined internal organization that is almost entirely lacking in unit stores. Furthermore, the unit stores which chains are tending to replace are in general very poorly managed. This is not true of department stores. Again, in the fields where it has been most successful the chain typically has performed a combination of wholesale and retail functions. The opportunity to carry on such a combination of functions does not exist in the department store field, since department stores already buy largely from manufacturers. These are only a few of the differences, but they are sufficient to indicate that the supposed analogy of department store "chains" to other types of chain store organizations is of the most superficial character.

Great obstacles existed, furthermore, to the realization of any immediate economies in the operation of department store "chains." In the first instance it was necessary to develop some central organization, and such a central organization had to be superimposed on the existing organization of the stores. The immediate result of this situation was an increase rather than a decrease in expense. For the last three years the Harvard Bureau of Business Research has compared operating results for independently owned and for centrally owned department stores, and in each year the centrally owned stores have exhibited a higher ratio of operating expense than the independent stores. It is important to note, however, that the centrally owned stores frequently have achieved somewhat higher gross margins than the independent stores, the difference presumably reflecting savings from the pooling of purchasing power. It is particularly significant to note, however, that the expense of buying, as distinct from the cost of purchases, has usually run higher for centrally owned stores. These figures reflect the inevitable difficulties encountered at the outset in merging a group of large stores, each with a fairly complex organization. In the case of department stores, any transformation along chain lines is furthermore greatly handicapped by the fact that department stores, handling such a great variety of types of merchandise, have developed their buying on a decentralized basis, where it has been more or less inextricably interwoven with selling. Chains, on the other hand, specializing more narrowly in types of merchandise, have developed their buying on a centralized basis, where it has been sharply separated from the selling function. Hence the differences in practice, tradition, and point of view of the personnel concerned manifestly are too great to be overcome within any short period of time. Buyers in individual departments, for instance, are jealous of their prerogatives; they look with little favor on any steps which appear to diminish the importance of their positions.

It was foolishly optimistic, therefore, to expect that any immediate results of an outstandingly favorable character could be achieved by "chain" department stores. At the same time it is foolishly pessimistic to condemn these institutions out of hand and to see in them no possibilities for favorable development in the future. On the contrary, there are at least two considerations which should give pause to the managements of those independent department stores which have not yet seen their way clear to align themselves either formally or informally with groups of similar stores. These are as follows:

(1) Given the rate at which chain stores have expanded within the last ten years, and given the fact that as yet there seem to be no definite limitations as to the kinds of merchandise which chains can successfully handle, one cannot contemplate with equanimity the probable position of an independent department store, say 25 years hence, confronted with specialized chain competition in perhaps half its departments.

(2) The marked rise in the cost of doing business in department stores during the last ten years and the corollary failure of independent department stores to make any headway in their handling of this problem point strongly to the conclusion that economies in department store distribution can be obtained only through such a radical and far-reaching reorganization as can be brought about only through the application of chain methods to a group of stores under central ownership.

The immediate problems faced by "chain" department stores are particularly difficult. Time is an essential factor in their solution, but in the opinion of this writer the experiment is amply justified.

Conclusion

Finally, it is well to be reminded that in the course of this distributive revolution we may confidently expect the development of new forms of large-scale distribution. To judge from what has happened in the department store field and what is happening in the chain store field, it is a fair generalization that types of distributive enterprise tend to develop through three stages. They start off very largely on a price basis—as chain stores did, for instance—they catch the attention of the consumer by distributing merchandise at low prices because of a low overhead. That is the first stage. The next stage is the "trading up" of the quality of the merchandise handled. We can see chain stores going through that stage today. After they have traded up the quality of the merchandise handled, and some of the price advantage has been lost in the process, distributive enterprises develop into a third stage, characterized by competition in services of all kinds, for instance, in allowing customers to return merchandise; by high costs of doing business; by largely competitive advertising; and by an increase in the ratio of the fixed investment to the total investment. Department stores today are in that stage. More and more money is put into plant and a smaller proportion carried in liquid form, and with this solidifying of investment and the higher costs of doing business, a lower return is secured on the capital invested.

Along with that, in this third stage there also takes place more or less hardening of the arteries of management. Merchandising becomes imitative rather than creative. The forces of inertia become very strong. Managers are afraid to step out and do new and radical things. That is the situation in which many department stores find themselves today; and when a large number of distributive enterprises reach this third stage someone else starts all over again on the low overhead, low price basis. Only recently the executives of a chain drug company in California were complaining bitterly because a group of "illegitimate stores," as they termed them, occupying limited space and handling only fast-moving lines of toilet goods, had had the effrontery to cut the chain store prices.

As the rate of return on capital declines in older types of distributive enterprises, ingenuity will be directed to the discovery of new methods of distribution. This is even more likely to be the case in the near future because, for the time being at least, our current condition of overproduction may tend somewhat to discourage the invention of new processes for cheapening production, with a resultant diversion of some inventive genius toward the field of distribution. In the days to come, there will be Strauses and Woolworths, but they will not be in department stores or in the present types of chain stores.

Notes

1. See Nystrom, Paul H., "An Estimate of the Volume of Retail Business in the United States," HARVARD BUSINESS REVIEW, January, 1925, p. 158.

2. U. S. Department of Commerce, *Retail Trade in the City of Chicago, Ill.* (Preliminary Report of the Census of Distribution), Washington, Government Printing Office, 1930, p. 12.

7

Looking back to see ahead: writing the history of American retailing

Ronald Savitt

Source: *Journal of Retailing* 65(3) (1989): 326–355.

Looking at our own past is the best way to predict what the retail scholar of 100 years from now can learn about contemporary retailing. This article presents the challenges and the excitement of unravelling events of American retailing over the past three hundred years. Though not a history of American retailing, the discussion does look for the themes and writings that explore our own heritage.

Introduction

In our search for better ways of understanding contemporary retail institutions there has been a clear and growing interest in retail history. This article develops an understanding of what we should know about the past if it is to help us in looking at the present and the future. In great measure, the article is a response to Hollander's recent challenge to develop a framework for a synthetic history of retailing in the United States (Hollander 1986).

One way of viewing this issue is to think about what the retail historian and retail manager in 2089 would want to know about retailing and the events that affected it in our times. Contemporary scholarly pursuits, with their emphasis on improving the practice of retail management, have left little room for the contemplation of retail history. While academics have speculated about retail change, we have not fully explored the history of American retailing over the past centuries or fully laid the basis for understanding the events of our own period.

In the same way that the historian of the future will have difficulty in sorting out what we are about, we have difficulty in understanding what retailing was like 100, 200, or 300 years ago. To be certain there are important exceptions in our understanding of American retailing, but many of these are scattered threads, not woven into what we teach or what is understood by retail managers. All too often the textual literature focuses on selected firms, specific individuals, or obvious trends such as Macy's, John A. Wanamaker, and the movement to the suburbs.

There is little to be gained from arguing the importance of knowing history to prevent the mistakes of the past; that perspective is patently circular, for the future is unknowable. But a history of retailing can provide a broader understanding of how environmental factors have been accommodated in the decisions of retailers. It also provides an understanding about the process involved in these decisions. Because of the focus on analytical tools, we often forget the many important decisions that have been made under conditions that can never be factored into a decision model. In our treatment of individual firms we focus on what today is and what tomorrow might be, forgetting to acknowledge the nature of the firm and how it has evolved. What a retail firm is and "what it can do depend on what has been established through time" (Minkes 1987). Professor D. C. Coleman of the London School of Economics has suggested a more constructive way of looking at the past, focusing on "real people taking real decisions—primarily managers of business enterprises"; by doing so, "we may be able to learn how to make better decisions in the future" (Owen 1986). It is not for lack of methods but more for lack of commitment to process that we have ignored this perspective.

Hollander's challenge for a synthetic history of retailing calls for more than a narrative of people, places, dates, and events. A synthetic history would weave together the various individuals, institutions, events, trends, and themes (Hollander 1983). It would look at patterns: those that have come and gone, those that have dominated, and those that have remained in retailing and transcended into marketing history. Such a study requires agreement as to what should be included and what methods should be used to direct the work. There is no one best approach; as Hollander suggests, "Different goals will require different questions and different sets of data" (Hollander 1983).

I have attempted to raise some important issues about the history of American retailing in the following pages. The discussion focuses on patterns we should be aware of and ways we might tie them together. There is no attempt to be comprehensive; but there is a clear desire to point to that possibility. The ideas here should be viewed as examples of what a synthetic approach might look like, so that we can see what we can gain from it. Within this approach, I propose some ways that we might put historical data together, giving evidence of patterns. These should be considered as representing one way of looking at the subject matter, not as the sole or final approach. The article points to what we must look at in writing a history of American retailing by giving a brief glimpse of one part of that history.

Where do we stand in the history of American retailing?

Introduction

A journal article cannot cover all the issues that should be included in a history of American retailing. Some important issues of methodology and data, for example, are beyond the scope of the present discussion. Although historical methods for retailing have been discussed elsewhere (Savitt 1980, 1988a), access to relevant data is difficult. Oddly, the availability of primary data for American retailing in the recent past is less than it was 100 years ago. This is a result of the shift toward corporate structure and managerial capitalism and away from an entrepreneurial orientation. Hower's observation about the difficulty in obtaining "factual data regarding the major historical developments in the field" remains as true today as it was a half century ago (Hower 1935).

In terms of "where we stand" it is easy to oversimplify; however, my reading of the American literature is consistent with the observations of others. Conzen and Conzen, for example, two geographers who have studied American retailing, suggest that "American retailing history lacks scholarly synthesis on the order of the British treatments by David Alexander, *Retailing in England during the Industrial Revolution* (London 1970); Dorothy David, *A History of Shopping* (London 1966); or J. B. Jeffreys, *Retailing Trading in Britain, 1859–1950* (Cambridge 1954)" (Conzen and Conzen 1979). And an American business historian noted: "In this country the academic study of retailing history has so far been confined to the area most accessible to research—large individual firms" (Samson 1981).

Synthesis to date

Two of the most comprehensive, synthetic histories of American retailing were written by Paul Nystrom (1930) and Ralph Hower (1946). Each work, within its own framework and perspective, can be considered an important statement for its time. Although Nystrom was basically an economist, he employed a traditional historical approach in his examination of the progression of retailing. He identified five distinct periods: prehistoric Indian trade, the trading post period, the era of the general merchant, the rise and development of the independent single-line specialty store, and the "modern period" of the large-scale retailer including department stores, mail-order houses, and chain stores. As he noted, "These five stages have characterized the history of retail trade in practically all sections of the country" (Nystrom 1930).

Nystrom's study threaded a needle through retailing's various institutions and trends. He also provided brief but important sketches of many of the key retailers and their firms. As with much retail history, the central focus is on the events of the late nineteenth and early twentieth century. Nystrom's contribution not only provides us with a better sense of his times than we probably have of our own; it also establishes an approach for the writing of retail history.

Hower, on the other hand, provides us with an understanding of retail history by examining a single firm within the context of larger economic and historical forces; he says that [because] "most historians have written as if retailing had no place in daily life or even in commerce, we have little precise knowledge about the changes which have occurred in the history of retail trade; we also lack a careful analysis of the forces at work" (Hower 1946). (Hower turns our attention to the workings of R. H. Macy and his followers and their decisions in the context of the events that shaped them. Hower follows the thesis of N. S. B. Gras, his mentor at Harvard, who viewed economic and commercial development as a series of alternating movements between dominant forms of business practice.

> For a generation or more the prevailing movement is toward special-ization, with one firm after another splitting off an activity or commodity upon which to concentrate efforts. Then the tide reverses, and swing toward integration and diversification takes place. Neither tendency is so overwhelming at any time that instances in movements in the opposite direction do not occur. Nor, as these alternating currents bring forth new forms of retail organization, do they wipe out entirely the old forms (Hower 1946).

This movement between the two ends of the spectrum is in part affected by the environmental conditions of the American experience, which saw re-tailers performing many functions and providing a wide assortment of goods and services. There has been a tendency in the American character to avoid specialization. This is because specialists have always been viewed as elite, while the generalist has had more of the common person orientation. There is nevertheless a continual flux toward specialization that can be traced over the past 300 years. This continues to be a part of the general structure of retailing that we have been unable to fully understand. Hower remarked: "The forces behind this broad movement from nonspecialized to specialized business in America have never been carefully investigated" (Hower 1946). What we need is to understand the unique factors that have affected this flux in the American experience, factors which did not mirror the process in Europe. If it was the environment, what specific influences can be isolated? Were they part of the internal developments or part of the greater external forces? In regard to the latter, we must open our eyes to the fact that there has always been a world economy which affects all participants—more slowly than today's, but still present.

As with all patterns, there are exceptions to be considered. While non-specialization of retail trade can be linked in part to expansion of the economy (especially in the pre-Civil War period), there are examples of markets and retailers who did not move toward specialization from a base of general operations. Conzen and Conzen in a comprehensive study of urban retailing in Milwaukee suggested that "Milwaukee never really passed through the 'general store' phase often attributed to cities in the pedestrian era" (Conzen and Conzen 1979). They noted further that:

> The general trend, even allowing for imprecise data, was clearly toward increasing specialization of shop type between 1850 and 1870, followed by some signs of consolidation. Food stores retained the lowest customer threshold throughout, but the usually smaller customer bases of the earlier period imply low initial overheads and scales of operation in retailing more generally. By the 1870s, the entry of many new shops drove down thresholds for some specialized shops dealing in essential goods like fabrics, shoes and furniture (Conzen and Conzen 1979).

The retail institution and retail structure

Little is known about the structure of retailing in the United States before the twentieth century. Long-run structural studies on retailing have been limited by the scarcity of data. Systematic surveys of retail trade were only begun in this century as part of the Census of Business and even those suffer from an ever-changing set of definitions, arbitrary classification systems and irregularity of undertaking systems, as well as purposes beyond historical understanding. Yet, in spite of such limitations there have been important studies based on these surveys. The work of Cox, Goodman and Fischandler (1965), Bucklin (1972), as well as the extensive study of Hall, Knapp, and Winsten (1961) and the scholarly work of Barger (1955) have made significant contributions to our understanding of retailing in America.

Each of these pieces focuses on the importance of and the effects on the marketing system in the United States. Although each study provides insights about retailers, the primary concern is with the relationship between distribution activities and the economy. Barger's study is the most macro in orientation, and it was based on the widest variety of firm and industry data. (His Appendix C provides one of the most complete lists of data sources for retail statistics available.) The analytic framework in these studies stems from industrial organization theory, in which strong emphasis is given to measures of retail firms by size, by product and merchandise lines, by location, and in some cases by the degree of horizontal and vertical integration.

The operational categories employed by census agencies tend to impose homogeneity when we would like to see the heterogeneity that pervades markets. In order to discuss the changes in operations in a retail institution, one must concentrate on other structural elements than those for which data are traditionally collected; also, to the extent that these structural elements are required to make sense, they are probably best viewed and collected at the level of the individual firm. In this way comparisons among firms can reveal the similarities and differences of their structural elements rather than force the findings into fixed patterns. This approach is not only essential to the historian but also to the manager or entrepreneur who wants to use empirically based insights for making decisions.

Besides Bucklin's and Cox's studies, there have been other examinations of structural change. Entenberg (1961) studied changes in the competitive positions of department stores with regard to merchandise lines; Lebhar (1959), with a different agenda and methodology, looked at the development of the chain store from the mid-nineteenth to mid-twentieth century; and Mueller and Garoian (1961) looked at changes in the market structure of grocery retailing. More recent examples of structural studies are the works of Hirschman (1975) and Novakhtar and Widdows (1987). The former provides a nontraditional approach to defining retail markets based on merchandise functions while the latter examines changes in the structural conditions of general merchandise operations during 1953–1983. Although both provide additional dimensions to our understanding of retail change, the studies are locked into methods and data that do not fully meet our needs.

Only in Bucklin's (1972) chapter on "Structural Change in Retailing Since 1929" can we find a complete discussion of change in retailing. Not only does Bucklin present basic census data; he also subjects them to critical evaluation. Based on the 1929, 1939, 1948, 1958, and 1967 *Census of Business/Retail Trade*, Bucklin points to several major changes. He begins with the significant change in the scale of retail operations. He notes that the number of retail establishments increased only slightly in contrast to the significant increases in population. Using the "Ford Effect," which hypothesized that the decline in staple-goods was due to the economies of scale inherent in mass retailing, Bucklin examined the changes in retail store populations by changes in product lines (Bucklin 1972). His results supported the Ford hypothesis and linked changes in the number (downward) and size of establishment (upward) to competition reacting to differences in income levels. He notes:

> . . . the answer must lie in the mechanics of the adoption cycle for retail institutions. More specifically, it appears likely that the greater aggregate expenditures for staples in wealthier communities results in a demand for relatively more stores. The location of a number of such establishments close together does, in effect, stimulate greater competitive stress. In conjunction with the greater mobility of wealthier patrons (due to a higher incidence of car ownership), a low tolerance for obsolete store equipment, and little need for credit reliance other than as a service, shopkeepers in such communities are forced to remodel their facilities more frequently to retain patronage. The result is that the rich benefit first from the introduction of newer, and coincidentally, more efficient retail outlets (Bucklin 1972).

Let it be said that the richness of Bucklin's (1972) analysis deserves more attention than this paper can provide. To summarize, his analysis points to the increase in retail labor productivity that results from economies of scale, the increase in the size of retail transactions, and the introduction of automation in retailing. Interestingly, Bucklin defines automation in terms of self-selection and self-service. He gives important examples of developments in retailing including the supermarket, the discount house, and the automated store (which he does not see as a particularly beneficial operation because of increases in costs of capital and promotion). The analysis goes on to examine the role of the chain store, including the adjustment and reaction of the traditional department store to changes in the location of consumers, changes in population characteristics and demands, and the emergence of more competitive retailers such as discount houses.

Retailers and their stores

Historical work in retailing is most abundant in studies about department store founders. Among these works are important works in American retail history such as Hower's (1946) comprehensive study of Macy's and Emmet and Jeuck's (1950) masterful history of Sears. There are also a number of scholarly papers that focus on the individuals and their accomplishments and on the larger issues of retail history as well (Nystrom 1930, Ressequie 1962, 1964, 1965). Other books consist of self-serving, self-congratulatory writing, or are journalistic treatments with an eye for exposé rather than historical understanding (Marcus 1975, Harris 1980, Katz 1987). Retailers and their institutions have been chronicled in a number of places. Tom Mahoney's *The Great Merchants* provides snapshots of most of the major American institutions from The Hudson's Bay Company to Korvettes (Mahoney and Sloane 1966). A sample of nineteenth century retailers can be found in Table 1.

In spite of its weaknesses this vast and often controversial literature can be the source of a great number of artifacts that can be woven together to provide a comprehensive picture of this era. Such a picture would provide insights about the degree to which retailers influenced each other and the ways in which they were influenced by other events. An important line of research could be fashioned along the following:

> Thus it has happened in America that the retail of merchandise has engaged the talents of highly intelligent men, many of whom have studied the ways to make its operations more efficient. The same willingness to adopt innovations that caused an early desertion of periodic markets and fairs and the establishment of country general stores, appeared again and again in the creation of new channels of trade, and the adopting of old ones to fit changed conditions (Hotchkiss 1938).

There is simply no better study of retailers than Emmet and Jeuck's history of Sears, Roebuck and Company (Emmet and Jeuck 1950). It provides a comprehensive understanding of the company's development and the ways

Table 1 A Sampling of Major Nineteenth Century Retailers

Individual	Firm	Established
Morris Rich	Riches	1807
Henry S. Brooks	Brooks Brothers	1817
Roland H. Macy	Macy's	1837
Simon Lazarus	F & R Lazarus	1851
George H. Hartlow	A & P Tea Company	1859
August Brentano	Brentano's	1860
John Wanamaker	John Wanamaker	1861
Benjamin Altman	B. Altman & Co.	1865
Marshall Field	Marshall Fields	1865
Frank W. Woolworth	Woolworth	1879
William Filene	Filenes	1881
Joseph L. Hudson	J. L. Hudson	1881
Bernard H. Kroger	Kroger Company	1882
George Whelan	United Cigar	1892
George Romanta Kinney	G. R. Kinney	1894

Source: Selected materials in References.

its management learned to adapt to the world in which it existed; the volume also provides clear insights into the historian's craft. The work also reflects the cooperative effort required by scholar and manager in presenting the reader with an understanding of what took place within a holistic context. The authors were skillful not only in providing narration and analysis about "the marketing aspects" of Sears, but also in delving into all aspects of the firm, including accounting and personnel management.

The volume must be read and reread; its essence cannot be captured in a few paragraphs. (However, Chapter XXXIII "In Retrospect" might be considered a snapshot of the total work.) One point worthy of mention which might be helpful in understanding other firms, is the historic imprint that shaped Sears. Each of the company's early leaders—Richard Warren Sears, Julius Rosenwald, and Robert E. Wood—were well fitted to meet the conditions of their times. They all understood that Sears had to remain rooted in its earliest history: "the company has never been an innovator, on a scale large enough to merit serious note, in its merchandise items, although it has at every critical stage been something of an innovator in its techniques of buying and selling and related operating aspects . . ." (Emmet and Jeuck, 1950).

Some special cases: chain stores and supermarkets

Chain stores and supermarkets have received considerable attention because of their impact on American society. The major study of chain stores is Godfrey M. Lebhar's *Chain Stores in America, 1859–1959* (1959). Within this volume—whose purpose is more to defend the chain store against criticism than to present a history of the institution—the interested reader can find an excellent description of the individuals and the firms they founded. Little is said about the development of these firms or about the managerial systems that emerged in the context of a changing economic environment and in juxtaposition to other events in retailing. Much attention is given over to those forces that have brought the chain into existence. In spite of Lebhar's almost religious support of this concept, one cannot help but agree that chain stores are here to stay.

Although food retailing has always been important to American society, little attention has been paid to the area prior to the development of the supermarket in the first third of this century. While we recognize that the "supermarket did not suddenly appear one day in its present form," we have few insights about previous institutions (Appel 1972). The food industry before the development of the supermarket is lumped into such categories as "the pre-1930 industry," with only vague references to the patterns of food distribution in earlier eras and without any references to patterns in retailing in its larger context. A reading of this literature gives the impression that Americans were basically self-sufficient in the production of food and depended on highly specialized retailers for items not produced at home. As many scholars including Goldman point out, there were important predecessors to the supermarket (Goldman 1976). The "market store" embodied many of the characteristics of the department store and forecast many of the elements of the modern supermarket. "There is no question, however, that these stores contributed the two ideas of hugeness and the strategy of mass appeal to food retailing" (Goldman 1976). Where these stores fit in the progression of food retailing from earlier times and how they relate to other types of retailers operating at the same time are important areas of investigation.

The history of the supermarket has been fairly well documented through a classic series of studies including Zimmerman (1955), Charvat (1961), Mueller and Garoian (1961), Markim (1963), Appel (1972), and Goldman (1976). All document the development of the supermarket from the self-service innovation of the Piggly Wiggly through the development of Kroger and on to Safeway. Adelman documents the behavior of A&P and offers insights that might be applicable across the industry (Adelman 1959). The various studies provide an understanding of the basic reasons for the supermarket's development in the context of the changing economic and geographic structure of the American population.

In retrospect

As we have seen there are many important works of American retailing history. Most studies focus on firms, individuals, or merchandise and operating types rather than stretch across the variety of retail activities. As noted, these "are splendid studies that draw from a wide range of sources, and by referring to trends and events outside the immediate scope of their subjects, present a well-rounded view of large scale retailing" during the nineteenth and early twentieth century (Samson 1981). But what about the other types, other sizes, and other periods? And what about the linkage among all of these? What about their conflicts? These are questions to be investigated.

Developing a history of retailing

The major themes

If what we know and what we can discover through more research in the area of retailing are to come together into a synthetic history, we must organize our efforts around the discernable themes in retailing's development. All these themes would have as a central concern the issue of change. As we shall see, some themes have already been established as means for investigating retail history, although little work has been undertaken to develop them (Savitt 1988a). The purpose of this section is to review some of the possible themes and ideas around which a history could be developed. It should be said that there is no correct approach; each offers some direction, though some are more potent than others. The following sections will briefly examine three major themes that together might serve as the basis for retailing history. These are: (1) theories of retail change, (2) retailing and economic development, and (3) the progress of commerce.

Theories of retail change

Much has been written about theories of retail change; this probably stands as the most popular topic area in the entire marketing literature, receiving more credibility than it probably deserves. No attempt will be made here to review this literature since that has recently been done elsewhere (Brown 1988). What needs to be said first and foremost is that theories of retail change, regardless of how well they appear to explain retail events, should not be confused with a history of American retailing. Most of the various theories have not been subjected to historical data in any systematic fashion; while important to the understanding of specific events, they lack the intensity of effort that can be considered as historical. Secondly, their use in textual descriptions often fulfills the warning made by Karl Popper that the "divination of hidden purposes is far removed from the scientific way of thinking, it has left unmistakable traces upon the most modern historicism theories. Every version of historicism expresses the feeling of being swept into the future by irresistible forces" (Popper 1957).

These theories purport to be part of our understanding of the mosaic of American retailing; however they are really no more than artifacts of history rather than its substance. They represent what scholars have been interested in thinking about, namely a process, but not the essence of the discipline. While the studies may focus on one type of retail institution—the department store—textbook writers have been cavalier enough to use the findings as immutable laws of retailing. Major writers in marketing and retailing such as Kotler (1986) and Mason and Mayer (1984), for example, engage in extensive generalization about the validity of the basic theories of retail change, primarily the "wheel of retailing." The discussions do not represent the grand sweep of retail history, nor do they imply that there are alternative approaches; the writing is almost non-falsifiable. They are not links to a larger pattern of change and because of their limitation to primarily a single line of trade and to a short period, they may not even be correct when compared against the larger tapestry of retailing.

It is unfortunate that retailing scholarship has missed the important step between the development of hypothesis testing and historical testing; we have been unable to offer our students an understanding of retail change in the long run. The emphasis has been on short bites from a longer perspective and as a result we have neglected to see retailing in its larger, more complex context (Fullerton 1986).

Among the work in this area, perhaps only Alton Doody's development of the idea of incrementalism—based on the ideas of Ralph Hower (1946) and his mentor N. S. B. Gras (1939)—approaches a valid theory of change (Doody 1963). Doody's work is based on historical evidence and as such contains explanations that remain valid over relatively long periods of time. Unlike the more narrowly focused theories of retail change, Doody examines the basic social and economic underpinnings of retailing in the United States; by doing so, he establishes the perspective that change takes place slowly, that there are a number of exceptions to any visible change, that not all institutions change (and that those that do not are often as successful as those that do), and perhaps most importantly that there are precursors to change—it does not happen all at once and out-of-the-blue. Theories of retail change add to our understanding of American retailing by explaining variations from major themes and by providing alternatives to these themes that are supported by historical evidence. As they stand now, the theories provide challenges that can only be met by systematic evaluation.

Retailing and economic development

One of the most important historical issues is the relationship between retailing and economic development. Bucklin (1972) argues that there is a strong causal relationship between the development of an economy and the development of retail institutions. He has offered evidence to suggest such a relationship, though he has by his own admission not surveyed the full history of retailing in the United States. Relationships between retailing and economic development have been questioned and evaluated in a number of contexts and there has been a significant outpouring of research and publication in the larger area of "marketing and economic development." This research suggests, on one hand, that marketing and retailing are a driving force in economic development, and on the other, that marketing is determined by the progress of economic development (Savitt 1988b).

Without getting bound up in all of the subtle nuances involved in the relationships between institutions and economic development, it is fair to say that we basically know little about the relationships between retailing activities and economic development. What evidence we have generally comes from studies with small time horizons primarily on developing countries. Many of these studies rest their cases on beliefs about conditions in the United States, although there is very little data to substantiate the beliefs. We do have important historical studies that discuss the role of mass distribution as part of the evolution of the economy, such as *The Visible Hand: The Managerial Revolution in American Business* (Chandler 1977), but there are few studies with enough historical data to convincingly make the broader argument. Wood and Keyser's comprehensive case study of Sears Roebuck de Mexico S. A. provides important short-term evidence about the effects of modern retailing in a developing country (Wood and Keyser 1953). However we do not have such evidence in the domestic context.

To understand more complex issues, we need insights about the development of retail institutions and the impact they have had on economic development. The folklore of the Yankee Trader suggests that such retailers had an important effect on regional economic development and indeed they did to the extent that they brought goods into the hinterland and took surpluses back to market centers (Atherton 1939). On the other hand, they often engaged in barter, which did not provide the monetary surplus that allowed for investment and hence, in many ways, restricted local development.

Bucklin argues eloquently in this area. While he gives us reason to focus on retailing in terms of the basic demands emanating from total income and population, he also shows us that retailing structure is shaped by the level of economic development of the society and the distribution of social and cultural attributes in that society. "Economic development provides the necessary impetus to the growth of large-scale retail organizations" (Bucklin 1972). Such a hypothesis can be useful when, churning among the artifacts of the past, we work toward an understanding of American retailing.

The progress of commerce

In contrast to the narrower views of previous approaches to the organization of retail history, the progress of commerce idea entertains a more comprehensive approach to the development of history. Fernand Braudel's three-volume study of the development of civilization and capitalism provides the finest example of such an approach to history, although such a perspective has its own weaknesses (Braudel 1979). It so comprehensive in its breadth of coverage, for instance, that any specific institution may be lost to sight. In examining retail history, we want to back away from a scope as large as Braudel's without abandoning his holistic concerns.

Hower's (1946) work on Macy's is constructed along the same lines as N. S. B. Gras's 1939 treatise on *Business and Capitalism*, which provides great insights into the processes of historical writing and establishes a theme for understanding the development of American retailing (Gras 1939). Gras makes two significant points. First, analysis of any aspect of an institution— from production, to marketing, to transportation, to financing—must be done in the context of the larger economic system to which it belongs. Second, the progression of an institution is linked to the progression of the economic and social system; hence specific events from advances in technology, to depression, to "acts of nature" must be accounted for in the development of any specific institution.

For Gras, much like Braudel, the major force to be understood is the development of industrial capitalism. As it grew and spread there appear "wave-like alternating swings towards and away from specialization" (Hower 1946). Hower uses Gras's framework to discuss the "alternating movement in the dominant manner of operations. One swing is toward the specialization of functions performed or of the merchandise handled by the individual firms. The other is away from such specialization toward the integration of related activities under one management or the diversification of products handled by a single firm" (Hower 1946).

For retailing, Gras suggests that there have been three stages. The first stage focused on the development of production, and as a result there was little attention paid to any part of the marketing system. "Only a little real pioneering was done on the purely marketing side" (Gras 1939). The second stage exhibited a very different situation: "the problem was not to produce enough goods and services at a remunerative price in which it was not production that mattered but to sell them at any satisfactory price. In other words, the difficulty was over-supply at profitable prices." The third period in the history of retailing under the system of industrial capitalism sees "the partial elimination or absorption of either wholesaler or retailer or both" (Gras 1939).

Within Gras's system it is easy to link the activities of specific institutions both to the movement of the industrial capitalism and to individual events such as depression or social upheaval. Gras provides the analytic framework on which Hower's study is based, offering a discussion of changes in the department store as related to both the progress of industrial capitalism and the movement of the economy:

> First, there was the diversification of products and the departmentalization of store management. Second, there was the growth of multiple functions and their integration into an effective operating unit. Third, there was the formation of chains of department stores in the nineteenth century but chiefly in the 1920's (Gras 1939).

Built upon Gras (through Hower) is Doody's theory of incrementalism. Doody added the missing link, showing that changes—in spite of significant changes in the larger forces—came in small incremental steps. He argued that changes in retail operations have a tendency to be incremental over time because "there is a smaller amount of risk inherent in this type of change due to the greater predictability of its effects" and because the "pattern or history of competitive actions utilized by a firm conditions the character of its new moves" (Shapiro and Doody 1968). In spite of the rich potential of such a theme, it has not been extended beyond department stores. Researchers need to go back to the earlier mercantilistic stages to examine retail development in the United States in light of the shifts from industrial capitalism of the nineteenth century to managerial capitalism of the twentieth century.

This approach will take us beyond the boundaries of retailing and into social history. The two are inextricably intertwined—as noted by Daniel Boorstin, who views the growth and development of chain stores and department stores as central to the substance of the present world (Boorstin 1973). This is a point well understood by those writers who have taken a more critical view of retailing in American society (Benson 1979).

Some ideas about writing history

One major problem in writing history is that we are often attached to a format or approach that reflects the organization of the discipline itself. Such is the challenge of writing a history of American retailing. Since much historical writing begins with description before moving on to narration and analysis, there is a danger of absorbing the perspectives of economic structure. In marketing in general, and specifically in retailing, there is a great reliance upon structural perspectives. The heritage is obvious; we have borrowed both format and content from economics, making the task of understanding the events of the past even more difficult. Much of the important analysis of marketing institutions has been crafted within the context of industrial organization studies. Although this is a meaningful approach, it is only one way of viewing historical progression.

In using the notion of structure to understand change from period to period we often fail to recognize that not only does the structure of the institutions described change over time but also the definition of the structure itself changes. We often talk about the importance of the shift or change in number of department stores from one period to another as a measure of a change in structure, and then go on from that point to develop hypotheses about why such changes take place. While such events are important, we run the risk of confusing cause and effect. These are two very diverse pictures of different events.

Structure in the realm of the social sciences has less regularity than in the biological and physical sciences. What this indicates is that more attention must be paid to the variations. Forcing elements to comply with the standards of categories means that we lose some of the opportunity to understand why elements are different. While patterns of similarity may provide insights about the structure that define it, patterns of difference provide understanding about the forces of change. Looking at all the retailers that fit a particular structure will tell us something about the fact that they arrived at this point because something changed. Effects are interesting (even in the cases when their definitional characteristics may be artificial), but it is in the search for causes or origins that more can be learned. We must go beyond the structural classifications of the numbers and types of retailers to gain an appreciation of the functions underlying the structural patterns. What did the formative retailers do and how did they perform are more to the point. And these issues must be examined against some larger events. The next section provides a glimpse of this task for the colonial period.

Retailing in Colonial America
"But times do change and move continually" Edmond Spenser (1596)

In order to understand the progression of retailing it is necessary to know something about previous periods. The era of the American colonies is an obvious beginning point in establishing the recognized traditions that shaped further development in the progression of retailing. In this case, there are two sources: the Native Americans and the Europeans. Within the current discussion the former is recognized, but not included (see for example Nash 1982).

Although we know that the colonists came from countries in which there were well developed retail institutions, these institutions were not transferred to North America as directly or as quickly as one might suspect. This phenomenon is important in understanding how American retailing eventually developed in its own fashion rather than as a literal transplant of retailers from other countries. There were two major influences affecting this development: one was the mercantilist system which dominated the early colonial development; the other was the backgrounds of the settlers themselves.

Overview

The early trade of the American Colonies was part of a triangular pattern that included Great Britain, North America, and the Caribbean. Since production and supply of consumer goods was directed from London, specialization in retailing developed in Great Britain and was a result of her mercantilistic policies. By the same token, retail development was thwarted or at least hindered in North America because activity centered on the export, not the import of goods. This pattern is not very different from what we see in the developing countries of the world today, where production and marketing systems are organized toward the movement of goods from the hinterland, to the ports, to foreign markets.

While the circumstances surrounding the mercantilists' pursuits in North America are certainly different from colonial exploitation in other settings and other times (between Europeans and Africans, Asians, and South

American Indians, for example), the effects on retailing were some what similar—a slowing of the development of retailing, except for that required to sustain local demands. The slowing was only temporary, however; events changed in North America as the immigrants found themselves being treated differently in the new setting than they had been abroad. This was not true in the Caribbean however, and hence the ties and the control of commercial life were stronger and lasted longer.

Little is known about the extent and development of retail trade in North America in the early colonial period, 1620 to 1750. Economic historians have focused primarily on three groups engaged in retail trade: farmers, artisans and crafts people, and merchants. All to some degree were highly integrated units involved in production, wholesale, and retail trade. As part of everyday life, retailing was not viewed as a specialized economic activity. Farmers, artisans, merchants, and a host of others all participated in retail transactions; it was simply the means by which people bartered, purchased, or traded for the necessities of life they did not produce. Even those individuals who specialized in retailing were not divorced from wholesaling and production activities. The products they offered were often paid for in kind by surplus production from the consumers, and the merchants or traders then leveraged these items with other merchants and wholesalers to stock their inventories for retail customers. The generally held notion that marketing activities were simple and transactions easily accomplished has little validity.

To the extent that we can identify the people who were substantially involved in retailing, we learn that their operations were complex, especially in the financing of their inventories. There are many explanations of the origin of specialization by economic function: retailing related to environmental factors, for example, or internal economies of scale. Nevertheless, a major driving force may have been the desire for simplification of operations that was at foot. There are strong examples of highly complex, integrated farms in New England "spinning-off" various parts of their operations first into vertically integrated units such as in the production of shoes and leather goods, and finally into the retailing of shoes made and supplied by a number of other local firms. In this regard Mallen's hypotheses, tested with appropriate historical data, might go a long way in helping understand the diversification of retailing in this period (Mallen 1973).

Some of the literature focuses on the impact of European retailing on the development of American retailing. There is much to discover about the forms and the practice of retailing in the new world. Transfer of retail and marketing institutions from the European nations to the American continent was very limited during the colonial period. Although European and primarily British merchants had an important role to play in the New England colonies, neither the first individuals or their latter replacements possessed a retail orientation. Bailyn's exciting research about the peopling of the new world (Bailyn 1986a, 1986b) documents migration patterns to North America and offers information about the individuals who came. Many did not have a commercial background and were neither craftsmen or artisans. Their proximity to the world of commerce was minimal; they were the strong backs of agriculture and industry in pre-industrial revolution Europe. They were different from the merchants who were part of the original settlements—these individuals didn't come from a traditional retail-commercial class but they were still a part of the larger mercantilist society.

The original merchants, as the word itself connotes, were closely related to the mercantile objectives of the British government. The individuals and firms who comprised the merchants were selected to fulfill the larger political goals involving the development of colonies and government wealth, with only a limited regard to commercial orientation. Although goods and services had to be made available to the colonists, these activities were undertaken on a production-supply basis (Bailyn 1955). Even in the later colonial period, just before the American Revolution, the immigrants did not bring to the New World the current practices of European retailing. [See, for example, Harrison's discussion of shopping in sixteenth and seventeenth century Europe (Harrison 1975).]

What we can make of this period is that the institutional heritage of retail firms from Europe was not fully carried over to the colonies. The development of retail firms had its own American characteristics. Some grew out of the practices of traditional merchants who were unable to compete in the highly competitive export/import trade, and who exploited opportunities as the West opened up (Doerflinger 1983). Others grew out of the difficulties of making a living in the urban areas—hence trading activities in the hinterlands were developed, not by the romantic characters of traditional lore, but by a variety of itinerant artisans and an American version of the gypsy.

Retailing in New England to 1796

To understand New England retailing in the early colonial period to 1796 requires the development of a framework that identifies commercial and mercantile institutions and focuses on the retailing function of each area. In the earliest period, there were no retailers in the sense that we can identify them either in contemporary activities in Europe or in later years of this period. This is not to say that retailing was nonexistent; merely that the grounds for specialization of retail activities in contrast to the conditions in Europe were not sufficient to observe clearly defined establishments. Basic commercial enterprise was carried out by the merchants of the mercantile associations; they supplied goods and services for individuals as well as for the productive activities of the colony. For example, "The Massachusetts Bay Company seems to have maintained a 'company store,' in the modern phrase, at which the colonists might obtain clothing, fabrics, foodstuffs and supplies of all sorts" (Dow 1988). These early merchants were totally dependent on European sources for the supply of most goods, though as triangular trade between England, New England, and the Caribbean developed other sources also became available. There was also retail trade among the colonists in items that were not part of the larger trading networks.

Only with the development of specialized artisans and craftsmen do we begin to see more clearly the demarcation of enterprise activities that have the traditional characteristics we associate with retailing. These activities were primarily in leather goods and pottery, where specialization was easier to develop and surpluses were available. In the case of everyday items the opportunity to replace European supplies led to retail institutions. Within these groups there are distinct points at which the artisan moves from the producer to the retailer and even the wholesaler of such items. Important to the development of such opportunities were the increases in the size of both local and regional markets, as well as the inequalities in the distribution of basic resources.

Retail specialists of the early part of the eighteenth century dealt primarily in items that were not produced locally; among the most important were booksellers. Although often classified as specialists in the book trade, they should be more appropriately thought of as specialists in paper products, including publishing. One early bookseller as a result of seeing common ground among paper products became the first retail bookshop to offer wallpaper. "Michael Perry, a Boston Bookseller, who died in 1700, had in his stock '7 quires of painted paper (wall paper) and three reams of painted paper.'" His successor, Daniel Henchman, dealt in painted papers as appears from his account books commencing in 1712 (Dow 1988, "wall paper" added). Such retailers were in great part importers of the items they sold and also acted as suppliers for retailers in the ever developing hinterlands. And not all were men; the role of women in commerce of Colonial America, especially in retailing, was also imporant, although it is not well documented (Norton and Berkin 1979).

An important retailer of sorts in Colonial America was the probate court. For research purposes they provide important insights about the practices of merchants and retailers, the goods they stocked, and about what colonists purchased. However, they were also important sources of retail goods. At death estates had to be settled, and in a setting in which cash was short and taxes paid immediately, the courts often sold the inventory of the deceased to pay estate duties (Deetz 1977). Unlike the contemporary court sale and public auction, such sales were an important part of the retail supply system, although somewhat macabre in the cases in which heirs had to pay to receive items left to them.

The best known of the colonial retailers is the "Yankee Trader," better named "tin traders" as a result of the basic product lines they offered. Although some traders were involved in wholesale activities, primarily in the context of purchasing the goods of rural residents, their main activities were in the area of retailing. They were a significant form of retailer; they were mobile and made rounds in the countryside in ways not that different from the traders of medieval fairs (Moore 1985). Yankee traders provided a wide assortment of merchandise for people living in rural communities and as such were important sources for merchandise such as clothing and household equipment. Their contributions were not as great as we have been led to believe however. To portray them as noble instruments of trade is erroneous. Because of their reputations:

> All colonies regulated the peddling traffic, and in January 1767 New York forbade it entirely under a penalty of five pounds. Later, however, recognizing that it served a real need, not only to the countryfolk but to the merchants, New York reversed its position and permitted the chapmen to operate under a very strict licensing system, which imposed a fee of eight pounds for a horse and five pounds for wagons and sledges (Bridenbaugh 1955).

Along with the peddlers were general stores, serving the same markets though with different goods. Such retailers took advantage of the production of farm surplus, which also attracted numbers of craftspeople such as shoemakers, potters, and food products including butter and meat products (Hathaway 1832).[1] Unlike the peddler whose trade was often based on barter and hence was not instrumental in capital formation, the country store fulfilled other major economic functions as well.

As the hinterland populations increased, many traders settled into local communities and reverted back to the more classical merchant type with both wholesale and retail functions. Their operations differed from the general store in towns and cities or the country stores which were extensions of their city cousins. These stores were frequently the parlor or livingroom of the former itinerant trader's house. They were basically stocked with a very small inventory assortment, in many cases smaller than that carried by the trader.

The general store is a part of history that often remains hidden, though this is a retailer whose importance can still be measured in New England and elsewhere today (Wooster 1926). The general store has been often regarded as the first rung of the merchandise ladder because of their important influence on the development of the modern retail store as we know it today. The general store represented part of the shift from specialization to nonspecialized operations. "Country storekeepers provided critical services in the local economy. They were often the only convenient source of goods from the outside world whether 50 or 3,000 miles away . . ." (Perkins 1988). And their role had broader dimensions in the welfare of the community because they purchased, "collected and distributed the agricultural produce which supplied the cities and factories with foodstuffs and raw materials. Exchanging goods more often than money, local merchants played a dual role as the primary conduit between customers and markets" (Sloat 1968) and all of this took place in a manner not dissimilar to "collecting, sorting, and dispersing" (Vaile, Grether, and Cox 1953).

The frontier store, which was part of the western expansion of the population across the continent, was the direct descendant of the general store. They began their development at a level less sophisticated than the general store in the colonies, primarily as a result of frontier conditions and the more elongated transportation systems, but they soon caught up with their predecessors and by the mid-nineteenth century passed them by in complexity of operation and product assortment. As Atherton has noted, these had become some of the most important retail institutions (Atherton 1939). They were the harbingers of the department store.

Stepping back and moving forward

We can best think about this period as a movement from general, non-specialized merchants to general stores—with intervening types developing within the period as related to economic growth and geographic expansion. There is considerable overlap among the various types and there are periods and places in which one or more of the types became dominant. By 1796 the traditional merchants had spun-off in general retailing activities and indeed in many cases had become more specialized within their own product lines as a result of the growing internal markets (Doerflinger 1983). Some highly specialized retailers such as the tin traders moved to a more generalized operation such as the general store, while others moved from retailers of books (basically imported) to printers and publishers.

Retailing in this period can be characterized by a back-step progression in which each of the new types of retailers in New England took a step backward in terms of specialization. As each of the new types came into existence they engaged in practices often more "primitive" than that of their predecessor; but as they operated, they moved ahead. One can think of this as a series of progressions in which the various types had much more overlap in functions and structure than their names might imply. The company store of the original mercantile firms was less developed than what existed in England at the time as were each of the other types. The specialists were often organized around commonality in sources of supply and were often engaged in manufacturing, unlike their counterparts in England and Europe. Once developed they significantly advanced, becoming more complex and sophisticated than the types that had proceeded them. In turn they were confronted with simpler types.

In Table 2, I have tried to make some sense of the various types of retail establishments in order to give a structural description of the period. The classification or better, identification scheme, attempts to isolate establishments by merchandise types, sources of goods and customers, type of location, and functional activities of specialization.

Underlying changes in the structure of colonial retailing were numerous foreign and domestic factors which also deserve some attention. In the early

Table 2 Structural Development of New England Retailers: Early Colonial to 1796

Establishment Type	Source of Products	Location of Customers	Locational Characteristics	Primary Functional Orientation*
Merchants	Import	Local/ Regional	Fixed	W/R
Artisans (leather, pottery etc.)	Local	Local	Fixed	P/R
Retail specialists (books and paper)	Import	Local/ Regional	Fixed	R/P
"Tin Traders"	Import/ Domestic	Regional	Mobile	R/W/F
General Stores	Import/ Domestic	Regional	Fixed	R/W/F

* Primary functions include: P = production, R = retailing, W = wholesaling, and F = financing.

colonial period only Great Britain and its North American colonies—in contrast to France and Spain—found themselves in a period of strong economic development and growth. Significant changes within British society, primarily political and social, favored individual initiative and the accumulation of property and wealth. These forces, coupled with the bounties of nature that were found in North America, fostered opportunity for the development of a strong commercial system. Specifically, ". . . the real strength of the colonial economy was its prodigious agricultural production for local consumption and urban centers" (Perkins 1988). As a result of these forces and because of an increasing population there was an increase in the participation of the distributive trades in the colonies. One historian notes for Connecticut that between 1700 and 1770 the number of men engaged in trade: i.e., shopkeepers and merchants, increased "from four to five percent of the workforce at the beginning of the century up to seven percent by the 1770's" (Main 1985).

The eighteenth century merchants can best be described in terms of their roles as importers and exporters, primarily of raw agricultural and natural resource products along with some semi-finished and finished goods. Merchants then began to change their breadth of operations, though not in terms of the degree of specialization. The focus turned toward internal production and trade rather than foreign trade, though they did not begin to fully specialize in specific product areas. For example, smaller merchants who basically had interests related to leather and pottery, still offered a wide variety of very diverse products for sale.

What was common among these merchants was their concentration in the larger cities and towns and the high incidence of credit financing provided by them for wholesale and retail transactions. The career of a merchant was a choice made at least partly because of the lack of other employment opportunities, opportunities which would have been the primary source of jobs for many such individuals in Europe. These opportunities would emerge when the industrial revolution reached the American continent. It is worth noting again that many of these individuals did not stem from merchant classes in England, Scotland, Germany, and Switzerland (Bailyn 1986b). They had to develop their own patterns of operations, without a long-standing tradition behind them. Their creativity may well have affected the development of some of the unique practices and institutions in American retailing.

The view from 2089

What will the view be from 2089? Certainly what we choose to study about retailing and how we study it will be important artifacts for the future. However, the most important part of the view will be how we in 1989 and beyond have looked back to evaluate the events of our own recent and distant past. To continue work that never stretches beyond the totally normative or short-run study means that there will be little say about retail history (except in those terms).

The challenge we face is to put the themes of the past into a synthetic pattern that will allow the future scholar an opportunity to confirm or deny their existence and their validity. Such work demands more than linking all the possible short runs; it establishes a need to stand back and to look at the entire process. The future historian will see what we have done that goes past our theories of change, for example, and will see how well we have stretched our work to look for the patterns of behavior. It may well be that many short-run elements will fit these patterns, but the critical issue is establishing the pattern framework itself. How the future historian eventually interprets what we see as our present will be greatly influenced by the ways in which we handle both our past and our future.

Research methods for retail history

As stated earlier, the goal of historical research in American retailing should be the development of synthetic patterns rather than the accumulation of artifacts and records. The latter represent only one part of the whole. It is not necessary to believe that one type of history, such as the documentation of an individual's efforts or the history of a single store, is more or less valuable than the synthesis of detail into a larger pattern. Both must exist; one feeds on the other. The detailed data about specific retailers and their efforts is the grist for a synthesis and the synthesis provides the basis for understanding what must be sought in the field.

Unfortunately, much of what we know about the history of American retailing comes from secondary sources, all too often accepted as part of the discipline without adequate confirmation. Many pieces of retail history are assembled from journalistic sources and are often viewed as primary sources, which they are not. A history of retail prices cannot be built from newspapers and trade journals of the day, even though they are an important source of information. The journalistic sources are biased in favor of what is most interesting at a particular time and may not include other events that are important in shaping the behavior to come. In any case, these are not scholarly efforts; there is a filtering of ideas and concepts through the eyes of people who may distort events simply because of the need to look at the world in a positivistic, ahistorical way.

Other parts of our knowledge come from secondary sources in sister disciplines such as economics, geography, history, and sociology; these sources provide insights into events but should not be the sole basis for synthesis. Information and ideas stemming from such sources are important only in comparison to what is seen by the retail scholar who understands the issues of the retailing context. An economist's interpretation of the growth of retailing, as in the case of Bucklin (1972) and Cox et al. (1965) will reflect certain constructs; these can be a testing ground for other data and can be used as springboards for further research. Historians often have their own agendas and unique perspectives and these can be helpful in understanding the conditions of change, even if they are not focused on specific institutions. However the most astute historian may overlook particularly important subtleties. Doerflinger, a scholar of significant note, has studied issues of commercial specialization in the Philadelphia merchant community and shown that: "The central contention . . . that the paradigm of the all-purpose merchant does not accurately describe the trading community of America's largest port in the four decades after 1750" (Doerflinger 1983). Within this perceptive study he does not however fully develop the specialization of retailers into specific lines of trade, a movement which was to have substantial impact on the ways retail trade was to develop in the hinterlands of the mid-Atlantic region in future decades.

To be truly synthetic a history of retailing has to be cast in terms of supply, production, and wholesaling on one hand and consumption on the other. Also the material must be placed within the context of an analytical framework. Several frameworks have been proposed in this article but there are still others to develop. Vance, the geographer, has created a model for American wholesaling which has much to offer the retailing historian. Vance examines the economic landscape in terms of various institutions and the functions they perform as well as the organizational forms and behaviors that are pursued (Vance 1970). He begins with basic propositions that others have established and hones them with evidence from individual tests of hypotheses. This results in a framework that clarifies both the past and present and also offers direction for speculation about the future. His work could be an excellent model for retailing.

Note

1. Development in New England was not uniform. Retailing in the first third of the nineteenth century differed little from practices of 50 years before elsewhere. There are interesting aspects of diffusion of innovation to be examined.

References

Adelman, M. A. (1959), *A & P: A Study in Price-Cost Behavior*, Cambridge, MA: Harvard University Press.
Alexander, D. (1970), *Retailing in England during Industrial Revolution*, London: Athlone Press.
Appel, D. (1972), "The Supermarket: Early Development of an Institutional Innovation," *Journal of Retailing*, **48** (Spring), pp. 39–53.
Atherton, L. E. (1939), "The Pioneer Merchant in Mid-America," *The University of Missouri Studies* **XIV** (April), 5–135.
Bailyn, B. (1955), *The New England Merchants in the Seventeenth Century*, Cambridge, MA: Harvard University Press.
—— (1986a), *The Peopling of British North America: An Introduction*, New York, NY: Vintage.
—— (1986b), *Voyagers to the West: A Passage in the Peopling of America on the Eve of the Revolution*, New York, NY: Vintage.
Barger, H. (1955), *Distribution's Place in the American Economy since 1869*, National Bureau of Economic Research, Princeton, NJ: Princeton University Press.
Bensen, S. P. (1979), "Palace of Consumption and Machine for Selling: The American Department Store, 1880–1940," *Radical History Review*, **21** (Fall), 199–211.
Boorstin, D. (1973), *The Americans, The Democratic Experience*, New York, NY: Random House.
Braudel, F. (1979), *Civilization and Capitalism, 15th–18th Century*, Volume 1, *The Structures of Everyday Life*; Volume 2, *The Wheels of Commerce*; and, Volume 3, *The Perspective of the World*, New York, NY: Harper & Row.
Bridenbaugh, C. (1955), *Cities in Revolt: Urban Life in America, 1743–1776*, New York, NY: Oxford University Press.
Brown, S. (1988), "The Wheel of the Wheel of Retailing," *International Journal of Retailing*, **3** (1), 16–37.
Bucklin, P. L. (1972), *Competition and Evolution in the Distributive Trades*, Englewood Cliffs, NJ: Prentice Hall.
Chandler, A. D., Jr. (1977), *The Visible Hand: The Managerial Revolution in American Business*, Cambridge, MA: Belknap Press of Harvard University Press.
Charvat, F. J. (1961), *Supermarketing*, New York, NY: Macmillan.
Conzen, M. P., and K. N. Conzen (1979), "Geographical Structure in Nineteenth Century Urban Retailing: Milwaukee, 1836–90," *Journal of Historical Geography*, **5** (1), 45–66,
Cox, R., C. S. Goodman, and T. C. Fischandler (1965), *Distribution in a High Level Economy*, Englewood Cliffs, NJ: Prentice-Hall.
Davis, D. (1966), *A History of Shopping*, Boston, MA: Routledge & Kegan.
Deetz, J. (1977), *On Small Things Forgotten: The Archeology of Early American Life*, Garden City, NY: Doubleday Anchor.
Doerflinger, T. M. (1983), "Commercial Specialization in Philadelphia's Merchant Community, 1750–1791," *Business History Review*, **LVII** (Spring), 20–49.

Doody, A. F. (1963), "Historical Patterns in Marketing Innovation," in W. S. Decker, ed., *Emerging Concepts in Marketing*. Chicago, IL: American Marketing Association, 245–253

Dow, G. F. (1988), *Every Day Life in the Massachusetts Bay Colony*, Mineola, NY: Dover. Reprint of 1935 edition published by The Society for the Preservation of New England Antiquities, Boston, MA.

Drew-Baer, R. (1970), *Mass Merchandising: Revolution and Evolution*, New York, NY: Fairchild.

Emmet, B., and J. E. Jeuck (1950), *Catalogues and Counters: A History of Sears, Roebuck and Company*, Chicago, IL: University of Chicago Press.

Entenberg, R. D. (1961), *The Changing Competitive Position of Department Stores in the United States by Merchandise Lines*, rev. ed., Pittsburgh, PA: The University of Pittsburgh Press.

Fullerton, R. A. (1986), "Understanding Institutional Innovation and System Evolution in Distribution: The Contribution of Robert Nuschlag," *International Journal of Research in Marketing*, (3), 273–382.

Goldman, A. (1976), "Stages in the Development of the Supermarket," *Journal of Retailing*, **51** (Winter), 49–64.

Gras, N. S. B. (1939), *Business and Capitalism: An Introduction to Business History*, New York, NY: F. S. Crofts & Co.

Hall, M., J. Knapp, and C. Winsten (1961), *Distribution in Great Britain and North America*, London: Oxford University Press.

Harris, L. (1980), *Merchant Princes*, New York, NY: Berkeley Books.

Harrison, M. (1975), *People and Shopping: A Social Background*, London: Earnest Benn Ltd.

Hathaway, W. (1832), *Accounts and Journals*, Personal materials in Kent Museum Archives, Calais, Vermont.

Hirschman, E. C. (1975), "A Descriptive Theory of Retail Market Structure," *Journal of Retailing*, **54** (Winter), 29–48.

Hollander, S. C. (1983), "Who and What is Important in Retailing and Marketing History," in S. C. Hollander and R. Savitt, eds., *Proceedings of the First North American Workshop on Historical Research in Marketing*, East Lansing, MI: Department of Marketing and Transportation Administration, Michigan State University, 35–40.

—— (1986), "A Rearview Mirror Might Help Us Drive Forward—A Call for More Historical Studies in Retailing," *Journal of Retailing*, **62** (Spring), 7–10.

Hotchkiss, G. B. (1938), *Milestones of Marketing*, New York, NY: Macmillan.

Hower, R. M. (1935), "Wanted: Material on the History of Marketing," *Bulletin of the Business Historical Society*, **IX** (October), 79–81.

—— (1936), *History of Macy's of New York, 1858–1919*, Cambridge, MA: Harvard University Press.

Jefferys, J. B. (1954), *Retail Trading in Britain, 1859–1950*, Cambridge, MA: Cambridge University Press.

Katz, D. R. (1987), *The Big Store: Inside the Crisis and Revolution at Sears*, New York, NY: Viking.

Kotler, P. (1986), *Principles of Marketing*, 3rd ed., Englewood Cliffs, NJ: Prentice-Hall.

Lebhar, G. M. (1959), *Chain Stores in America: 1859–1959*, New York, NY: Chain Store Publishing Corporation.

Mahoney, T., and L. Sloane (1966), *The Great Merchants: America's Foremost Retail Institutions and the People Who Made Them Great*, New York, NY: Harper & Row.

Main, J. T. (1985), *Society and Economy in Colonial Connecticut*, Princeton, NJ: Princeton University Press.

Mallen, B. (1973), "Functional Spin-Off: A Key to Anticipating Change in Distribution Structure," *Journal of Marketing*, 37 (July), 18–25.

Mann, L. (1923), "The Importance of Retail Trade in the United States," *American Economic Review*, XIII (December), 609–617.

Marcus, S. (1975), *Minding the Store*, New York, NY: New American Library.

Markim, R. J. (1963), *The Supermarket: An Analysis of Growth, Development, and Change*, Pullman, WA: Washington State University Press.

Mason, B. J., and M. L. Mayer (1984), *Modern Retailing: Theory and Practice*, Plano, TX: Business Publications.

Minkes, A. L. (1987), *The Entrepreneurial Manager: Decisions, Goals and Business Ideas*, New York, NY: Viking Penguin.

Moore, E. W. (1985), *The Fairs of Medieval England: An Introductory Analysis*, Toronto, Ontario: Pontifical Institute of Medieval Studies.

Mueller, W. F., and L. Garoian (1961), *Changes in the Market Structure of Grocery Retailing*, Madison, WI: University of Wisconsin.

Nash, G. (1982), *Red, White and Black: The Peoples of Early North America*, Englewood Cliffs, NJ: Prentice-Hall.

Norton, M. B., and C. R. Berkin (1979), "A Cherished Spirit of Independence: the Life of an Eighteenth-Century Boston Business Woman," in C. R. Berkin, M. B. Norton, eds., *Women of America: A History*, Boston: Houghton Mifflin Co., 48–67.

Novakhtar, S., and R. Widdows (1987), "Research Note: The Structure of the General Merchandise Retailing Industry 1959–1983: An Empirical Analysis," *Journal of Retailing*, 63 (Winter), 426–435.

Nystrom, P. H. (1930), *Economics of Retailing*, 3rd ed. Vols. I and II. New York, NY: Ronald Press.

Owen, G. (1986), "What History Can Teach Managers," *The Financial Times* (November 14), p. 23.

Perkins, E. J. (1988), *The Economy of Colonial America*, 2nd ed., New York, NY: Columbia University Press.

Popper, K. (1957), *The Poverty of Historicism*, New York, NY: Harper & Row.

Ressequie, H. E. (1962), "Decline and Fall of the Commercial Empire of A. T. Stewart," *Business History Review*, 36 (Spring), 255–286.

—— (1964), "A. T. Stewart's Marble Palace: The Cradle of the Department Store," *New York Historical Society Quarterly*, XLVIII (April), 131–167.

—— (1965), "Alexander Turney Stewart and the Development of the Department Store, 1823–1876," *Business History Review*, 39 (Autumn), 301–322.

Samson, P. (1981), "The Department Store, Its Past and Its Future: A Review Article," *Business History Review*, LV (Spring), 28–34.

Savitt, R. (1980), "Historical Research in Marketing," *Journal of Marketing*, 44 (Fall), 52–58.

—— (1988a), "A Personal View of Historical Explanation in Marketing and Economic Development," in T. Nevett and R. A. Fullerton, eds., *Historical Perspectives in Marketing Essays in Honor of Stanley C. Hollander*, Lexington, MA: Lexington Books, 113–132.

—— (1988b), "State-of-the-Art of Marketing and Economic Development," in E. Kumcu and F. Firat, eds., *Marketing and Development Toward Broader Domains. Research in Marketing*, edited by J. Sheth. Greenwich, CN: JAI Press (in press).

Shapiro, S. J., and A. F. Doody, eds. (1968), *Readings in the History of American Marketing: Settlement to Civil War*, Homewood, IL: Irwin.

Sloat, C. F. (1985), "The Center of Local Commerce: the ABA Knight Store of Dummerston, Vermont," *Proceedings of the Vermont Historical Society*, **53** (4), 205–220.

Smalley, O. A. (1961), "Market Entry and Economic Adaptations: Spiegel's First Decade in Mail Order," *Business History Review*, **XXXV** (Autumn), 372–401.

Tonning, W. A. (1955), "Department Stores in Down State Illinois, 1887–1943," *Business History Review*, **XXIX** (December), 335–349.

Vaile, R. S., E. T. Grether, and R. Cox (1953), *Marketing in the American Economy*, New York, NY: The Ronald Press.

Vance, J. E., Jr. (1970), *The Merchant's World: The Geography of Wholesaling*, Englewood Cliffs, NJ: Prentice Hall.

Wood, R., and V. Keyser (1953), *United States Business Performance Abroad: The Case of Sears, Roebuck de Mexico, S. A.*, Washington, DC: National Planning Association.

Wooster, H. (1926), "A Forgotten Factor in American Industrial History," *American Economic Review*, **XVI** (March), 14–27.

Zimmerman, M. M. (1955), *The Supermarket: A Revolution in Distribution*, New York, NY: McGraw-Hill.

PART II: Theories of retail change

Section II(a): Paradigms and their influence on retailing
Section II(b): Macro theories of retail development
Section II(c): Location modelling

Postmodernism, the wheel of retailing and will to power

Stephen Brown

Source: *International Review of Retail, Distribution and Consumer Research* 5(3) (July 1995): 387–414.

Abstract

Postmodernism has been described as something everyone has heard of, but no-one can quite explain what it is. This paper explores the nature of the postmodern condition and examines its epistemological implications for one of retailing's longest established, most cited and vigorously debated concepts, Malcolm P. McNair's wheel of retailing theory. The analysis reveals that, although the concept is premised on assumptions that are anathema to many postmodern thinkers, the wheel is not entirely out of place in a postmodern world of fragmentation, difference and plurality. Indeed, like postmodernism itself, the wheel of retailing theory owes an enormous debt to the philosophical principles of Friedrich Nietzsche. McNair's original exposition, in particular, represents a paradigmatic example of Nietzsche's principal constructs: *Übermensch*, eternal recurrence and will to power

Keywords

Postmodernism, wheel of retailing theory, Friedrich Nietzsche.

It is certainly not the least charm of a theory that it is refutable: it is precisely with this charm that it entices subtler minds.

(Nietzsche 1990: 18)

Introduction

According to the celebrated German philosopher Friedrich Nietzsche (1986: 33), a word is like 'a pocket into which now this, now that, now several things at once have been put'. Although this pocket metaphor is true of innumerable words – just think of the diverse and ever-changing interpretations of retail marketing terms such as 'convenience', 'involvement', 'internationalization', 'superstore' or indeed 'retailing' itself – there is perhaps no word to which this analogy is more applicable than 'postmodernism'. Not only has a whole host of different phenomena been placed in the terminological pocket called postmodernism, but, if the sheer volume of contemporary academic discourse is any indication, the pocket is virtually bursting at the seams. As a glance at any of the copious postmodern 'readers' or introductory texts bears witness, the postmodern 'condition' has affected the A to Z of academic disciplines, albeit with varying degrees of success (e.g. Jencks 1992; Waugh 1992; Doherty 1993; Hollinger 1994; Dickens and Fontana 1994).

Although the recent rise of postmodernism has been dismissed as an artefact of the *fin de siècle*, the latest pseudo-intellectual fashion, a soon to be forgotten scholarly fad or a cultural bandwagon that is already on the point of departure (O'Neill 1995; Simons and Billig 1994), an ever-increasing number of marketing academics begs to differ (e.g. Ogilvy 1990; Rothman 1992; Elliott 1993; van Raaij 1993). Firat and Venkatesh (1993: 227), for instance, celebrate postmodernism as 'the new perspective on life and the human condition that is sweeping across the globe'. Foxall (1992: 403) describes it as 'the most intellectually demanding challenge facing consumer researchers'. And Brown (1995a: 234) maintains that 'Postmodernism provides a perspective on, and means of conceptualising, the dramatic changes that are taking place in the marketing arena, whether it be the fragmentation and turbulence of markets and competition, the emergence of strategic alliances and boundary-less corporations, the rise of the retro product and . . . the latter-day preoccupation with authenticity, reality and the nature of time'.

Postmodernism, however, is not just a fashionable position from which to view the ambiguous, paradoxical and disorientating marketing environment of the late twentieth century. It also has important theoretical and epistemological implications (Firat, Dholakia and Venkatesh 1995). Postmodernism, in other words, is pertinent to the nature of our knowledge – our very understanding – of retail marketing phenomena. In an attempt, therefore, to illustrate some of these epistemological issues, this paper will endeavour to examine the ramifications of postmodernism for one of retail marketing's most celebrated, frequently cited and vigorously debated concepts, the 'wheel of retailing' theory. It commences with an overview of the postmodern condition; continues with a summary of the extensive wheel of retailing literature; culminates with an assessment of the wheel theory's place in today's postmodern world; and concludes with a consideration of the parallels between the wheel of retailing theory and the work of a philosophical progenitor of postmodernism, Friedrich Nietzsche.

The postmodern condition

Postmodernism has been aptly described as 'one of those irritating things that everyone has encountered or heard of, but no-one can quite explain

precisely what it is' (Fielding 1992: 21). The irritation, not to say bewilder-
ment, that accompanies most people's introduction to the postmodern phenomenon is attributable to several interrelated factors (see Brown 1993,
1994). These include the notorious lack of a clear-cut definition, the widely
divergent and by no means immutable opinions of the movement's prime
movers, the sheer impenetrability of the source material, the oppositional
tenor of the accompanying debate, its proponents' propensity to indulge in
pretentious flights of pseudo-intellectual fancy and, not least, the counter-
intuitive – some would say absurd – nature of certain postmodern precepts.
As Adair (1992: 12) adroitly points out, 'few "isms" have provoked as much
perplexity and suspicion as postmodernism, no doubt because of the way in
which that already contentious word "modern" is sandwiched between a
prefix and suffix, each as dubious as the other'.

Modernism

In endeavouring to comprehend the fascinating yet frustrating phenomenon
that is postmodernism, perhaps the most obvious point of departure is from
that which it claims to be 'post'. Indeed, virtually every commentator on the
postmodern condition emphasizes that it represents some kind of reaction
to, extension of or break with, the 'modern'. Although the nature and characteristics of modernism have been subject to almost as much discussion as
postmodernism, there is a degree of agreement that the modern world emerged
from a series of profound political, economic, social and cultural transformations which began with the Age of Discovery in the fifteenth century; saw the
creation of the modern nation state in the sixteenth; witnessed the gradual
secularization-cum-democratization of Western society in the seventeenth;
experienced an efflorescence of scientific and intellectual endeavour in the
Enlightenment of the eighteenth; and which climaxed in the Agricultural and
Industrial Revolutions of the nineteenth century (Johnson 1991; Toulmin
1990; Wagner 1994).

As the copious volumes on the movement amply demonstrate (see Hall,
Held and McGrew 1992), modernity is a complex process involving a variety
of tightly interwoven, often contradictory, developments operating over an
extended time-scale. But, if it had to be summarized in a single word, that
word would probably be *progress*. The modern condition is characterized,
above all, by a belief that humanity 'has advanced in the past . . . is now
advancing, and will continue to advance through the foreseeable future'
(Nisbet 1980: 4–5). Although the idea of inexorable human progress is a
relatively recent development – prior to the Enlightenment the prevailing
assumption was that the past was superior to the present and that life was
lived against a backdrop of irredeemable decline (Bowler 1989; Gordon
1991) – there is no question that substantial 'progress' has been made in the
past four hundred years. Compared to the bestiality, squalor and degradation
of earlier times, it is our good fortune to be born into the modern world. We

are better fed and educated, more affluent and live longer than our ancestors, we are free to think and say what we like, and live in the reasonable expectation that things will continue to improve, diseases will be conquered, technological breakthroughs achieved and, periodic economic crises notwithstanding, our material well-being maintained (Kumar 1986; Toulmin 1990).

Postmodernism

Just as the project of modernity was distinguished by the complex interpenetration of several contrasting components, so too the postmodern moment is made up of a multiplicity of highly diverse, often antithetical, elements. Indeed, perhaps the single most important point to note about 'postmodernism' is that it is a portmanteau or umbrella term comprising a number of interdependent strands, three of which are particularly important.[1]

The first, and for most people, probably the most clearly identifiable aspect of postmodern condition is a very distinctive post-war artistic and cultural movement known as 'postmodernism' (some authorities restrict use of the term 'postmodernism' – and its predecessor 'modernism' – to this particular arena, hence the terminological confusion that often arises). In essence, postmodernism in the arts comprises a latter-day reaction against the, once radical and challenging but subsequently tamed and canonized, 'modern' movement of the first half of the present century, and a tongue-in-cheek return to pre-modern precepts of representation. Whether it be fine art, architecture, literature, music, dance, design, drama or whatever, the postmodern movement is characterized by the belief that there is no artistic orthodoxy or single overarching style. All traditions have some merit; there is a smorgasbord of choice; the challenge is to combine elements of existing traditions in an eclectic, hybrid, ironic style; and the traditional boundary between élite and popular cultural pursuits no longer exists. Just as popular preoccupations have been appropriated by 'high' culture (vernacular architecture, pop-art, science fiction, etc.), so too serious treatment is now accorded to what were once dismissed as 'low' or degraded cultural forms – film, television, popular music, fashion, football, comic books, hairstyles and, indeed, marketing, retailing and advertising (Burgin 1986; Boyne and Rattansi 1990; Denzin 1991; Hughes 1991; Beadle 1993).

The second element of the postmodern project, which is often accorded the epithet 'postmodernity', pertains to a series of significant post-war social and economic developments (Turner 1990; Bocock and Thompson 1992; Smart 1993; Lyon 1994). Socially, these include the decline of organized religion; the fragmentation of nation states and political blocs; the collapse of traditional party politics; the demise of the nuclear family; and the proliferation of media and communications technologies, which, according to the high priest of postmodernism, Jean Baudrillard (1983, 1988), has created a depthless world of simulation where images bear no discernible relationship to external 'reality' and where artifice is even better than the real thing. In

economic terms, moreover, recent years have witnessed a post-Fordist revolution in the workplace, where the computer-aided, flexible production of
specialized or semi-bespoke products for niche markets has superseded the
traditional Fordist regime of the mass production of standardized products
for mass-markets (Murray 1989; Cooke 1990; Kenny and Florida 1993). This
has been accompanied by the emergence of an increasingly information-
and services-driven post-industrial order. In effect, Silicon Glen rather than
Clyde shipbuilding, science parks rather than steel plants, building societies
rather than bricks and mortar, and mining museums rather than working
pits (Rose 1991; Walsh 1992; Lash and Urry 1994).

The third and much the most convoluted and impenetrable aspect of
the postmodern moment derives from the work of several prominent 'post-
structuralist' thinkers, principally Jacques Derrida, Roland Barthes, Michel
Foucault, Jacques Lacan and Jean-François Lyotard (see Boyne 1990; Young
1990; Best and Kellner 1991; Shumway 1992; Rylance 1994). Although the
contributions of these post-structuralists are many and varied, ranging across
fields as diverse as linguistics, literary theory, philosophy, history and psycho-
analysis, they all exhibit a concern with textuality, narrative, discourse and
language. Language, according to this perspective, does not *reflect* reality
but actively *constitutes* it. The world, in other words, is not composed of
meaningful entities to which language attaches names in a neutral and mi-
metic fashion. Language, rather, is involved in the construction of reality,
the understandings that are derived from it, the sense that is made of it (for
example, when an English speaker looks at an Arctic landscape, he or she
sees 'snow', whereas an Eskimo, with over fifty words for snow, sees something quite different when looking at the exact same landscape). Language
precedes and exceeds us; it is something we are initiated into; our every
utterance is governed and shaped by language; and we are not free to deploy
it whenever we write or speak. Human subjects are not so much the *producers* of language as the *products* of it. Language, moreover, is by no means
translucent, its meanings are not unequivocal and, indeed, there may be no
discernible relationship to any extra-linguistic or textual referents at all
(Sturrock 1979, 1993).

Retroactive retrospection

Although, as is often pointed out, postmodernism is characterized by idiosyncrasy, heterogeneity, eclecticism and its espousal of difference – the
so-called four Ps of paradox, plurivalence, polysemy and proliferation –
perhaps its single most distinctive feature is an all-pervasive air of finality
and failure. If, as noted earlier, modernism was characterized by the notion
of inexorable human progress, postmodernism is distinguished by the complete opposite. While it is undeniable that the project of modernity has
provided unimaginable material well-being, incalculable knowledge accumulation, astonishing aesthetic accomplishment and incredible technological

innovation, postmodernists argue that the material benefits of modernity and its promise of perpetual plenitude have been achieved at a very heavy social, environmental and political price. They recognize that, although 'progress' may have been made by certain groups of people (white, male, heterosexual, university professors in the Western world, for instance), the same is not necessarily true for others – coloured, female, homosexual, unemployed, non-Westerners, the marginal, the underprivileged, the different, the 'deviant'. For many postmodernists, Foucault (1990) and Lyotard (1984) in particular, it is time to abandon the Western 'metanarrative' of progress, to acknowledge instead the voices of the hitherto excluded, the silenced, the 'other' and to admit that the aspirations of the Enlightenment project are utopian and unattainable.

Whereas, in other words, modernism was predicated on advance, achievement, amelioration, betterment, breakthrough, exuberance, innovation and inexorable forward movement, postmodernism is suffused with stasis, debilitation, dissipation, disillusion, despair, enfeeblement, entropy, stagnation, cessation and termination (Brown 1995a). In point of fact, almost all of the movement's leading lights stress this particular symptom of the postmodern condition. Barthes (1977), for example, describes 'the death of the author', Derrida (1991) foresees the 'end of man', Lacan (1977) kills off Freud's mechanistic model of the unconscious, Foucault (1972) announces the 'death of the subject' and Vattimo (1991) predicts the demise of Western philosophy. Jameson (1985, 1991), moreover, maintains that artistic innovation is no longer possible, Lyotard (1984) argues that the same is true of science (and predicts the end of metanarratives, for good measure), and Gilbert Adair (1992: 15) considers postmodernism to be nothing less than 'the last gasp of the past'.

For Jean Baudrillard (1988, 1989), furthermore, every possibility in art, life, theory, politics and society has already been tried. Originality is impossible, history has ended, the future has already happened and all that remains is to play with the pieces among the anorexic ruins. In other words, the only available option is to re-work, re-arrange, re-organize, re-discover, re-combine and re-use the forms, styles, genres, approaches, techniques and methods that already exist, usually in an ironic, irreverent, iconoclastic manner. Indeed, in his most recent book, *The Illusion of the End*, Baudrillard (1994: 26–7) goes even further, arguing that 'History . . . that living lump of waste, that dying monster which, like the corpse in Ionesco, continues to swell after it has died . . . will not come to an end, since the leftovers, all the leftovers – the Church, communism, ethnic groups, conflicts, ideologies – are infinitely recyclable. What is stupendous is that nothing one thought superseded by history has really disappeared. All the archaic, anachronistic forms are there ready to emerge, intact and timeless, like the viruses deep in the body. History has only wrenched itself from cyclical time to fall into the order of the recyclable'.

The wheel of retailing

Just as discussions of postmodernism are all-pervasive in academic and intellectual life generally, so too analyses of retail change are dominated by the wheel of retailing. Along with location theory, it occupies pride of place in retail marketing's – admittedly limited – conceptual repertoire. The wheel theory and its manifold variants feature in almost every introductory marketing and retailing textbook. It surfaces periodically in the primary retailing journals and hardly a conference season goes by without some scholarly cogitation on the evolution of retailing institutions. Indeed, the wheel has variously been described as 'one of the five most influential concepts in marketing thought' (Robinson and Smith 1980: 249) and 'the most popular topic area in the entire marketing literature' (Savitt 1989: 336). It is appropriate, therefore, that any consideration of retail marketing epistemology in a postmodern era should commence with the wheel of retailing theory.

As originally conceived by McNair (1958), the wheel theory states that new forms of retailing (department stores, supermarkets, discount houses, etc.) commence as cut-price, low-cost, narrow-margin operations which subsequently trade up. Improvements in display, more prestigious premises, increased advertising and the provision of credit, delivery and many other customer services all serve to drive up expenses, margins and prices. Eventually, they mature as high-cost, conservative and moribund retail institutions with a sales policy based on quality goods and services rather than price appeal. This, in turn, opens the way for a next low-cost, cut-price retailing format; and so the wheel revolves.

Since McNair's pioneering contribution, the wheel of retailing theory has given rise to prolonged, occasionally acrimonious and ultimately inconclusive academic debate. At one extreme, it has been described as 'powerful and fascinating' (Stern and El-Ansary 1977: 243), 'the dominant concept in retailing' (Greyser 1976: iii) and 'a great achievement in the study of marketing' (Brown 1990: 143). At the other extreme, it has been castigated for having 'limited clarity' (Savitt 1988: 38), being 'vaguely conceived' (Gripsud 1986: 252) and for failing to 'meet the criteria for formal theory' (Hirschman and Stampfl 1980: 72). More to the point perhaps, the wheel theory has generated literally hundreds of associated publications. Broadly speaking, these commentaries and extensions can be divided into four major categories: applications of the concept to various US retailing institutions; examinations of its utility within different (non-US) cultural contexts; considerations of the causes of the trading-up process; and attempts to modify the wheel model or develop alternative analogies of retailing change.

Applications of the wheel

Although some academic authorities on the wheel of retailing literature would disagree, the manifold empirical studies of American retailing institutions reveal that there is considerable, albeit largely anecdotal, evidence in support of the wheel theory. It would appear that many innovative retailing forms – such as department stores, mail-order houses, variety stores, supermarkets, discount stores, catalogue showrooms, warehouse clubs, box stores, off-price outlets and shopping centres, home shopping networks and a host of retail services including hotels, gas stations and fast food outlets – began, as the wheel suggests, by selling a limited range of merchandise at below-average prices in a low-rent, restricted services environment and progressively evolved into higher-cost, quality-orientated, service-rich modes of distribution (Allvine 1968; Brand 1963; Bush and Hair 1976; Hollander 1960; Kaikati 1985; Lord 1984; May and Greyser 1989; Oxenfeldt 1960; Teeple 1979).

These studies have also shown, however, that a substantial number of American retailing innovations did not evolve as the wheel theory predicts. Boutiques, convenience stores, auto dealers, super-specialists, certain chain stores and, as noted in a celebrated early critique by Hollander (1960), planned shopping centres, automatic vending machines and branch department stores all entered the market on a high-cost basis (see Hollander 1962, 1980; May 1989; Moyer and Whitmore 1976; Thomas, Anderson and Jolson 1986). Goldman (1975), moreover, has also made the point that not every department store, supermarket or discounter in the United States began life as a cut-price, no frills operation; there were significant variations on each theme.

Utility outside America

Even though the wheel theory was formulated with respect to the evolution of retailing institutions in the United States, it has since been applied in several other national settings. In the main, these studies reveal that the characteristic cut-price/trading-up pattern is supported, at least for certain retailing institutions, by the experiences of developed nations like Australia (Blizzard 1976), Great Britain (Scott 1989), Belgium (Knee and Walters 1985), Germany (Nieschlag and Kuhn 1980), Norway (Arndt 1972), Denmark (Agergaard, Olsen and Allpass 1970), Italy (Lugli 1987) and, to a lesser extent, France (Filser 1984) and Finland (Makinen 1986).

If, however, the wheel has some relevance to the evolution of retailing institutions in high-level economies, the same cannot be said of the developing world (Bucklin 1976). Studies in Turkey (Kaynak 1979), Israel (Goldman 1974), China (Mun 1988), Guatemala (Ortiz-Buonofina 1987), Saudi Arabia (Alawi 1986), Malaysia (Zain and Rejab 1989) and Hong Kong (Ho and Lau 1988), among others, have demonstrated that retailing innovations tend to enter at the high end of the cost spectrum, appeal to high-income groups in the host country and only gradually trade down. This has been described as a 'reversed' wheel of retailing (Mun 1988), though Hollander (1970), borrowing from fashion theory, prefers to term it the 'trickle down' hypothesis.

The trading-up debate

While many academic commentators concur that the wheel theory is mean-ingful, if by no means universally applicable, there is less consensus on the causes of trading up. The process has been variously attributed to a progress-ive deterioration in managerial competence (Dreesmann 1968), an unholy alliance of equipment manufacturers and the trade press (Regan 1961), a statistical quirk caused by changes in the merchandise mix (Bucklin 1972), an unavoidable reduction in the initial, inordinately high levels of productiv-ity and capacity utilization (Hollander 1980), the increasing costs of labour (Bucklin 1983), a vicarious fulfilment of the originator's unattainable retailing vision (Berens 1980), the ossifying effects of scientific management systems (Dickinson 1983) and what can only be described as an immutable natural law (Berman and Evans 1979).

The two most frequently espoused explanations of trading up, however, consider secular trends in the retailing environment and inter-outlet competi-tion to be the principal driving forces of the upgrading process. The secular hypothesis treats trading up as a natural and enlightened retailing response to growing consumer affluence and the associated demand for a wider range of quality goods and services (Markin and Duncan 1981). The competition-based explanation, on the other hand, regards the process as an inevitable outcome of retailers' unending search for differentiation and competitive advantage; in other words, an irreversible ratchet-like progression of cost and margin increases stemming from inter- and intra-type competition (Dreesmann 1968).

Re-inventing the wheel

A milestone in retailing thought though it undoubtedly is, even the staunch-est supporters of the wheel theory would acknowledge that it is not a comprehensive conceptualization of institutional evolution. Accordingly, the associated literature abounds with attempts to formulate alternative theor-ies of retailing change. For the purposes of discussion, these can be divided into two basic types: those that are related to the wheel, in that they employ a similar cyclical analogy; and those that do not rely upon the recurrence of past patterns of development. The best-known examples of the former are the retail accordion, which hypothesizes perpetual alternation between generalist and specialist outlets (Hollander 1966), and the retail life cycle, which like the PLC upon which it is based, predicts an institution's inexor-able progression through the stages of birth, growth, maturity and decline (Davidson, Bates and Bass 1976).

The non-cyclical frameworks, by contrast, see the evolution of retailing institutions either in terms of the influence of the external environment or as a consequence of the inter-type conflict that occurs when innovative retailing formats appear (in this respect, they represent elaborations of the secular trends and competition-based explanations of trading up). According to the environmental approach, new forms of retailing are a manifestation of changes in underlying economic, social, demographic, legal and technological conditions (Meloche, di Benedetto and Yudelson 1988). Indeed, some proponents of this perspective have gone so far as to suggest that a form of economic ecology or 'natural selection' prevails, whereby only the fittest retailing species are likely to survive and prosper in the long run (Etgar 1984). Set against this, conflict-based standpoints attempt to explain retailing change in terms of the rivalry between new and established retailing institutions. Once again, a number of models of competitive interaction exist, most notably Gist's (1968) dialectical theory, which emphasizes the mutual adaptation between old and new institutions, and the crisis-response model, which predicts four distinct stages from the emergence of a novel retailing format to the resolution of the inter-institutional strife (Dawson 1979).

Postmodern epistemology and the wheel theory

In light of the voluminous literature that surrounds the wheel theory and given the manifold diagnoses of the postmodern condition, it almost goes without saying that a postmodern interpretation of the wheel is far from straightforward. Apart from the fact that in a postmodern world there is no basis for evaluating and comparing rival interpretations of the facts (or 'readings' of the 'texts'), any attempt to apply postmodern principles to the wheel theory faces a number of serious obstacles. The first of these pertains to the domain of the wheel; the second concerns the characteristics of postmodernism; and the third and most important revolves around the ambiguous outcome of any such endeavour.

The wheel's domain

As summarized in the previous section, the wheel theory has been subject to innumerable empirical analyses and spawned all manner of alternative models of change. Besides the above noted analyses of retailing 'institutions', the concept has been applied to individual retail organizations (Teeple 1979), at various geographical scales (Jeffreys 1985; Martenson 1981), to elements of the retailing mix, such as location (Holmes and Hoskins 1977), product policy (Hawes and Crittenden 1979) and promotional activities (Fox 1968), and, indeed, to a host of non-retailing phenomena. Wheels of marketing (Peckham 1981), wholesaling (Bucklin 1972), segmentation (Stone 1989) and consumer behaviour (Peter and Olson 1993) have all been identified, a wheel of marketing theory exists (Brown 1995a) and, to cite another instance of its pervasiveness, Michael Porter's (1990) book, *The Competitive Advantage of Nations*, bears the unmistakable stamp of the wheel theory. Likewise, there have been many attempts to develop a comprehensive model of retailing change. As exemplified by the formulations of McNair and May (1976), Diederick and Dodge (1983), Agergaard, Olsen and Allpass (1970) and Sampson and Tigert (1993), these typically comprise amalgamations of the wheel theory and one or more of the alternative conceptualizations that now exist. The inevitable upshot of these elaborations, adaptations and extrapolations is the obfuscation of the original model. What began as a succinct, coherent and clear-cut concept has become decidedly bloated, diffuse and amorphous. So much so that some latter-day explications of the wheel appear to describe a pattern of development that bears little or no resemblance to McNair's original exposition (e.g. May 1989).

The characteristics of postmodernism

Just as the domain of the wheel theory is by no means clearly defined, so too postmodernism has come to mean different things in different fields (Connor 1989; Featherstone 1991). Depending on which authority one consults, the exact same phenomena, ranging from systems analysis and the Pompideau Centre to the novels of Saul Bellow and James Joyce, have been cited as exemplars of modern and postmodern conditions (Hassard 1993; Jencks 1989; Rosenau 1992). For the cynical, indeed, the only discernible point of consensus among postmodernists is their lack of consensus on postmodernism. Some regard it as a continuation of modernism (Berman 1983), others consider it to be a complete break with the past (Bell 1976). Some deem postmodernism to be degenerative and destructive (Habermas 1987), others revel in its irreverence and cynicism (Kroker, Kroker and Cook 1989). Some date its commencement to the 1960s–1970s cusp (Harvey 1989), others to the avant-garde artistic movements of mid-nineteenth-century Paris (Lash 1990) and yet others to the Augustinian subversion of disembodied power in the fourth century AD (Kroker and Cook 1986). In these circumstances, therefore, it comes as little surprise to discover that the scholars most closely associated with the movement have, almost without exception, distanced themselves from and publicly repudiated postmodernism!

Anyone for ambiguity?

The dilemmas posed by a postmodern reading of the wheel of retailing theory are not confined to the sheer vagueness of postmodernism, which enables it to be cited as evidence for or against almost every conceivable position. Nor, for that matter, is it simply a question of the increasing uncertainty over the wheel's domain. Even if discussion is limited to McNair's original exposition and the analysis relies largely on the insights of postmodernism's principal thinkers, the implications are still less than unequivocal. This uncertainty, it must be emphasized, is *not* primarily due to the ambiguities inherent in postmodernism (though these do not make the investigation any easier). After all, the implications of postmodernism for other prominent marketing principles, such as the stages of internationalization theory and the hierarchy of advertising effects, are comparatively straightforward (Brown 1995a). The difficulties rather derive from the nature of the wheel theory itself.

On the surface, the wheel of retailing contravenes several key precepts of postmodernism and, accordingly, ought to be condemned to conceptual perdition. First, the theory is universalist. In other words, it assumes the same low-cost/trading-up pattern applies to every retailing institution, in every socio-economic setting. Admittedly, McNair had no such imperialistic aspirations, confining his discussion to the United States and to a limited number of retailing innovations (the department store, supermarket and discount house). The manifold empirical exercises, what is more, indicate that the concept is not universally applicable, though these studies are by no means above criticism. Nevertheless, it is generally accepted – thanks largely to Hollander's early intervention – that the wheel theory represents, or aspires to be, a universal retailing truth. Postmodernism, by contrast, is opposed to any overarching principle or totalizing concept. It emphasizes difference, uniqueness, idiosyncrasy, heterogeneity, local narratives and, indeed, would appear to lend more weight to the empirical refutations of the wheel than to the examples of conformity.

Second, the wheel of retailing is subject centred. It is premised on the actions of conscious, free-thinking, self-determining, individual human beings, the so-called 'subjects' of Cartesian discourse. McNair's original exposition, in particular, stressed the all-important part played by creative, risk-taking entrepreneurs – outsiders with a 'bright new idea' – in the emergence of retailing innovations. Indeed, in an otherwise highly circumscribed account he specifically mentioned John Wanamaker, Frank Woolworth, General Wood, Michael Cullen and Eugene Ferkauf. Similarly, several of the hypothesized causes of trading up, most notably the 'fat cats', managerial deterioration syndrome, rely on the decision-taking behaviours of individual human subjects. Once again, however, this perspective is incompatible with postmodernism. Despite the apparent lack of consensus on the distinguishing characteristics of the postmodern condition, it is widely accepted that the 'death of the subject' is a central conceit (Sarup 1993). Individual human beings, their utterances and behaviours are held to be governed by and artifacts of the pre-existing, albeit unstable, structures of language. In postmodernism, the human subject is effectively demoted from a constitutive to a constituted status.

From a postmodern perspective, the third and ostensibly most damning shortcoming of the wheel is its assumption that history has a pattern or shape. True, the cyclical, rise and decline trajectory is common to several other prominent marketing principles (the product life cycle, the fashion cycle, innovation diffusion theory, etc.), a mainstay of thinking in many other academic disciplines including economics, literary theory, sociology and regional science, and one of the most venerable evolutionary analogies

(Brown 1991). However, postmodernists tend to subscribe to the view, most forcibly propounded by Michel Foucault, that history is discontinuous, fragmented, contingent, context and locality dependent, uncertain, unpredictable and, above all, shapeless. Indeed, the very act of imposing a shape on history is implicated in the pursuit of power and the will to knowledge (Poster 1984).

Although the case against the wheel of retailing would appear to be compelling, a close reading to the 'text' of postmodernism suggests – somewhat typically – that things are not quite so clear-cut. There is, of course, the obvious point that postmodernists place great store by epistemological plurality, multiple interpretations and individual 'readings'. Hence, they have no grounds for passing judgement on a wheel-based interpretation of retailing change. More importantly perhaps, many postmodern authorities, drawing largely upon Lyotard, contend that, as ultimate truth is unattainable, the critical criterion for evaluating any scientific endeavour is 'performativity', its success or otherwise in the marketplace of ideas. In this respect, even the sternest critics of the wheel theory would be prepared to conceded that the concept has performed well in the agora of academic life. With the obvious exceptions of central place theory and the gravity model, very few retailing concepts come close to the wheel in terms of the sheer volume of citations, published papers and associated commentary.

Another significant consideration is the simple fact that the wheel of retailing is a prime example of the metaphorical reasoning that postmodernists enthusiastically endorse. Whereas positivist epistemology regards figurative language in general and metaphor in particular to be 'deviant and parasitic' (Ortony 1979: 2), postmodern philosophers and post-structuralist literary theorists maintain that knowledge claims are inherently metaphorical. Tropes, they argue, lie at the very heart of our understanding of the world and figurative thinking is central to the process of theory articulation (Norris 1991). The wheel, in addition, is more than a mere common-or-garden trope, it is an ancient and compelling metaphor. Not only does it contain overtones of the Greco-Roman 'wheel of fortune', particularly in the implication that the managerial sloth of the maturity stage is a harbinger of decline, but the cyclical conceptualization of time ('time's cycle') occupies a distinguished position in both Western and non-Western traditions of thought (Newton-Smith 1980; Whitrow 1988; Adam 1995). Granted, the linear metaphor ('time's arrow') dominates Judeo-Christian philosophy and the mindset of the modern, Western world – with, in the case of the latter, the idea of progress substituting for the eschaton – but the cyclical view of change retains a powerful almost primordial appeal, not least for the retailing community (see for example IGD 1994).

Interestingly, the debate over time's arrow/time's cycle is one of the issues that lies at the heart of the postmodern condition. Although postmodernism is premised on the notion that history is shapeless, it is also true to say that the shape postmodernists particularly revile is time's arrow. The idea of progress, the ascent of man, the triumphal, ever-upward trajectory of human achievement, which underpins Marxian and liberal democratic consciousness alike, is anathema to the majority of postmodern thinkers. There is considerably less hostility to time's cycle, however (e.g. Giddens 1984; Jencks 1989; Burrell 1994; Debord 1994). As noted earlier, whether it be art, architecture, literature, music, science, linguistics, philosophy, the rebarbative ruminations of Jean Baudrillard or, indeed, the rise of the retro product in contemporary marketing practice, postmodernists are characterized by their preparedness to plunder the past, to recycle history and ideology and to replace 'new and improved' with 'as good as always' (Brown 1995a).

Even Michel Foucault, widely regarded as *the* historian of discontinuity, does not dismiss the notion of cyclical time completely. On the contrary, in *The Order of Things* he emphasizes that the radical breaks discernible in the history of thought (*epistemes* in his terminology) actually exhibit elements of recurrence. Foucault (1972) argues, in short, that when one *episteme* replaces another, certain patterns repeat themselves – changing only in the arrangement of the elements – and do so again during succeeding epistemological transformations. The parallels with the wheel of retailing theory are clear: albeit premised on a cyclical analogy, the wheel does not contend that (say) department stores and supermarkets are locked in a continual low-cost/high-cost/low-cost cycle. It stresses radical discontinuity, the emergence of new, dynamic retail formats that challenge moribund incumbent institutions, but which go through a similar pattern of development and decline.

The wheel of retailing and will to power

The ambivalence that postmodernism's leading thinkers exhibit towards cyclical models of historical development is almost certainly attributable to the influence of the infamous German philosopher Friedrich Nietzsche. Although the postmodern movement is often portrayed as the latest intellectual fashion from Paris, many of its premises were anticipated by Nietzsche in the late nineteenth century. These include anti-foundationalism, an eschewal of progress, a belief in the end of history, the espousal of relativism ('perspectivism', in Nietzsche's phrase), a rejection of grand, systematic, overarching systems of thought, the assumption that art and aesthetics represent 'authentic' forms of knowledge and, not least, a bleak, cynical, nihilistic yet paradoxically exuberant view of the human condition. Even the unconventional style of writing, which, like Baudrillard's, is often dazzling in its brilliance, and the blurring of the distinction between philosophy and literature, which is common to many postmodern thinkers, formed an integral part of the Nietzschean project. Along with Heidegger, indeed, Nietzsche is often considered to be a postmodernist *avant la lettre* (Koelb 1990; Lampert 1993).

Although Nietzsche's thought has had an enormous (and widely acknowledged) impact on continental philosophy, and although it influenced
the work of such literary giants as Yeats, Shaw, Lawrence, Mann, Malraux
and Pirandello, it is still regarded with a degree of suspicion in the Anglo-
American world. Many primers on Western thought omit all discussion of
Nietzsche (Kuper 1987; Scruton 1984), as do overviews of the philosophy
of science for mainstream, academic marketing audiences (Hunt 1991;
O'Shaughnessy 1992) and the social sciences generally (e.g. Boyd, Gasper
and Trout 1991; Gordon 1991). The popular belief that Nietzsche is 'unsound'
is largely attributable to the appropriation of his work by the Nazi party
– 'mad genius', 'evil Teuton' and 'satanic mind' characterizations remain
all-too prevalent (Stern 1978; Sautet 1990) – though his aphoristic style and
unwillingness to systematize his thought have led some philosophers to down-
grade his 'contribution' (Solomon and Higgins 1988). Nevertheless, the three
interrelated conceits at the centre of Nietzsche's non-systematic philosophical system – *Übermensch*, eternal recurrence and will to power – are highly
pertinent to cyclical models of marketing evolution generally and the wheel
of retailing in particular (Brown 1995b). As the name implies, the *Übermensch*
or Superman is a 'great' man, a giant among pygmies, who is true to his own
beliefs and lives life to the full in an uninhibited, untrammelled, free-spirited
manner, irrespective of convention, constraint or criticism. The eternal return
of the same represented a rejection of the then (late nineteenth century)
fashionable idea of inexorable human progress, and its replacement with the
contention that the whole of history moves in cycles, vast cycles, so that
events occur again and again in perpetuity. The will to power, what is more,
is the driving force within the world, the source of man's strength, the
motivation or mechanism that sweeps aside and destroys all that is comfort-
able, complacent and mediocre.

As described above, the wheel of retailing theory has become encrusted
with academic barnacles and all manner of modifications, alternatives and
explanations have been propounded in its brief forty-year history. It is
undeniable, however, that McNair's original exposition exhibited strong
Nietzschean overtones. He stressed the importance of the 'great man', the
dynamic innovator of vision and self-belief, who is deprecated by his rivals,
but who succeeds against the odds in establishing a novel retailing format. He
contended that a recurrent, cyclical pattern of low-cost/high-cost/low-cost
development is evident in the case of every successful retailing innovation.
And he highlighted the process of creative destruction, the condition of com-
placency, stasis and ossification that the retailing visionary rips asunder,
only to fall eventual victim to its attractions. Thus, in Nietzschean terms, the
Dionysian spirit of chaos and abandon is superseded by the Apollonian
qualities of order and restraint. McNair, of course, may never have read
Nietzsche, though he grew up, and studied literature, at a time when the
philosopher's thought was influencing avant-garde artistic endeavour and

intellectual life generally (Lawrence, Yeats, Picasso, Spengler, Le Corbusier and so on). What is more, he once considered writing a doctoral dissertation on 'utopianism', which is informed by, if not infused with, Nietzschean perspectives (Manuel and Manuel 1979). Yet, it is difficult not to read the famous concluding section of *The Will to Power* without reflecting on its remarkable similarity to the wheel of retailing theory,

> This world: a monster of energy, without beginning, without end . . . a sea of forces flowing and rushing together, eternally changing, eternally flooding back, with tremendous years of recurrence, with an ebb and flood of its forms; out of the simplest forms striving toward the most complex, out of the stillest, most rigid, coldest forms toward the hottest, most turbulent, most self-contradictory, and then again returning home to the simple out of this abundance, out of the play of contradictions back to the joy of concord. . . . Do you want a name for this world? A solution for all its riddles? . . . This world is the will to power – and nothing besides. And you yourselves are also this will to power – and nothing besides!
>
> (Nietzsche 1967: 1067)

Irrespective of the philosopher's direct influence, or otherwise, on Malcolm P. McNair, recent postmodern Nietzschean scholarship raises a number of important issues for the wheel of retailing theory. Drawing upon Derrida's technique of deconstruction, Magnus, Stewart and Mileur (1993) maintain that *Übermensch*, will to power and, especially, eternal recurrence are examples of 'self-consuming concepts'. By this they mean that any given concept requires, as a condition of its intelligibility, the very contrast it attempts to set aside. The theory of eternal recurrence, therefore, depends upon the notion of linear time to distinguish a specific occurrence from recurrence. In other words, if the state of the world *at this instant* were to recur, it would have to occur at a future point in (linear) time. More importantly perhaps, Magnus, Stewart and Mileur (1993: 23) emphasize that self-consuming concepts are so vivid and arresting that they remain perennially fresh and insightful even after it is recognized that their force is achieved at the cost of incorporating the premises they oppose. Despite the concepts' internal contradictions, 'their appeal is not diminished by exposure . . . they seem plausible somehow, they continue to recommend themselves to us'.

When transposed to the wheel of retailing theory, this perspective provides a means of comprehending both the undeniable inadequacy of the wheel concept and its continuing academic appeal (as, indeed, it does for many other frequently 'refuted' marketing constructs like the product life cycle, the 4 Ps and the marketing concept itself). Thus, the wheel's cyclical view of retail institutional change presupposes a linear underpinning, the ordered and predictable pattern it portrays necessitates the notion of disorder and unpredictability, and McNair's 'great man' assumption, the will to power of driven retailing innovators, implies the existence of conducive environmental conditions. The wheel, in effect, is self-refuting because the concept incorporates its own negation. Conversely, of course, it follows that the copious attempts to formulate alternative theories of retail institutional change, or develop comprehensive models which seek to integrate the wheel theory with one or more of its numerous substitutes, are all-but doomed to failure. The latter merely end up as mixed metaphors and, hence, lose any impact they might otherwise have had. (Consider, for example, attempts to combine the wheel, a mechanical trope, with the biological and warfare-based metaphors of the environmental and conflict perspectives respectively.) The latter not only face the all-but impossible task of competing with the wheel in the marketplace of retailing ideas, but, as they derive much of their resonance from the fact that they are *not* the wheel theory, their very existence serves only to enhance, albeit implicitly, the standing of the concept they are endeavouring to supersede. In effect, every critique of the wheel merely adds to its attraction. Every refutation of the wheel helps ensure its continuation. Every alternative to the wheel of retailing theory simply perpetuates the prototype. The wheel may be 'disconfirmed' but it can never be discounted nor, for that matter, destroyed.

Discussion

Postmodernism, according to Gellner (1992: 22–3), 'is a contemporary movement. It is strong and fashionable. Over and above this, it is not altogether clear what the devil it is'. In its attempt to outline what the devil it is, the present paper does not contend that postmodernism is the perfect solution to marketing's current malaise or the 'new paradigm' of retailing that some commentators are calling for (Lee and Vryza 1994). On the contrary, it acknowledges that the postmodern movement is subject to severe and mounting criticism. All three component parts of the alleged epochal shift – artistic postmodernism, postmodernity and post-structuralism – have been examined in detail and found wanting (Callinicos 1989; Best and Kellner 1991; Smart 1992). Postmodernists, moreover, stand accused of decadence, narcissism and impotence in so far as they subvert the old theoretical, epistemological and ontological certitudes of rationality, truth and progress, yet refuse to provide a replacement. Postmodernism does not attempt to offer any definitive answers, while its proponents denigrate the endeavours of those who do. 'The postmodern mind', as one critic points out, 'seems to condemn everything, propose nothing. Demolition is the only job the postmodern mind seems to be good at. Destruction is the only construction it recognises' (Bauman 1992: ix).

Postmodernism, like all philosophical and intellectual positions, undoubtedly suffers from significant shortcomings. Nevertheless, it poses some very interesting questions, provides all manner of arresting insights and raises several important issues which have never been addressed (in the wheel of retailing literature) hitherto. The first of these issues is the above-mentioned point that every attempt to replace, reject, extend or supersede the wheel, every word of criticism no matter how damning, merely promulgates the concept's position as the predominant model of retailing change. Indeed, the very act of engaging in the debate about the wheel (as with postmodernism itself) only serves to perpetuate the theory! In these circumstances, as Baudrillard (1990) emphasizes, the only effective forms of resistance are apathy and silence. It follows, therefore, that the wheel of retailing may eventually disappear, but not because it has been refuted 'once and for all'. The concept will fade from the intellectual agenda when – and only when – it is ignored, when retail marketing academics get bored with the wheel and decide to move on to other things.

A second pertinent point arising from the advent of postmodernism concerns the nature of history and time. The postmodern project reminds us that time and history are human constructs and that there is more than one way of interpreting these particular phenomena (Berger and Luckmann 1967; Hassard 1990; Adam 1995). The notion of linear time and a forward-looking, 'future' orientation may dominate the modern Western worldview, but the ancient Greeks (to cite a single example) not only subscribed to the idea of cyclical time but also held that humans faced towards the past, with the future, so to speak, appearing over our shoulders from behind (Pirsig 1974). Some postmodernists, as noted earlier, cleave to the postulates of cyclical time and others contend that history is shapeless (though to contend that history has no shape is to state, as Giddens (1990) demonstrates, that history has a shape but that the shape is shapeless). From the perspective of the wheel of retailing theory, however, these differences in temporal interpretation are immaterial compared to the key fact that, in an intellectual environment informed by postmodernism, concepts predicated on non-linear time are no longer routinely dismissed as fallacious, untenable or indeed outdated. Quite the reverse.

A third important aspect of postmodern implications for the wheel theory concerns the theory laden-ness of observation. It is conventionally assumed that the wheel captures, albeit imperfectly, some of the changes that are taking place in the real-world retailing environment. The world, however, is not composed of brute facts waiting to be captured or observed (Peter 1991). On the contrary, 'facts' and 'observations' only make sense within the context of existing theory. Theory determines what is seen and what counts as factual (Hughes 1990). Theory, according to Derrida, *creates* the truth it purports to portray; it affects, not simply reflects, how external 'reality' is interpreted; the wheel-like 'pattern' of retailing evolution was brought into being by the articulation of the theory, not the other way around. In other words, prior to the theory (and its prototypes), the wheel-like pattern of retailing evolution was not recognized as such – *it did not exist.*

Regardless of the acceptability of this admittedly counter-intuitive suggestion, it is arguable that the wheel of retailing theory can never be *definitively*
'proved' or 'disproved' by empirical analysis. No matter how carefully ex-
ecuted the study or impressive the hypotheses under examination, it is always
possible to challenge the execution or contest the underlying premises. As
Kuhn, Lakatos, Feyerabend and several other 'postmodern' philosophers of
science have shown, empirical evidence is never decisive when it comes to
theory testing or the retention/refutation of established principles (see Gordon
1991; O'Shaughnessy 1992). This state of affairs is very clearly illustrated in
the wheel of retailing literature, where almost every innovation in retailing
can be cited as evidence of both the concept's inadequacy and its continuing
utility. Consider, for example, two recent studies of US warehouse clubs, one
of which concluded that the wheel pattern pertained and the other deduced
that the theory was inappropriate (Dickinson 1991; Sampson and Tigert 1993).
A similar disagreement is also evident in contrasting analyses of latter-day
trends in British grocery retailing (Brown and Quinn 1993; Sparks 1993).

The wheel of retailing theory, therefore, appears to be in the paradoxical,
albeit characteristically postmodern, position of being both inadequate and
irreplaceable. It cannot be decisively confirmed or refuted by empirical analysis
alone and attempts to develop alternative theories of retail institutional change
are destined forever to remain in its shadow. In these circumstances, it would
seem that the most promising alternative is – in Derrida's term – to 'bore from
within'; in other words, to consider the linguistic structures, figurative premises
and rhetorical devices upon which the wheel of retailing and the associated
body of literature are predicated. Thus, the real question is no longer whether
the wheel theory can be proved or disproved, or indeed if it can be sup-
planted by a more comprehensive model of retail change, but why the concept continues to exert such a powerful hold on the imaginations of some
retailing academics and drives others to paroxysms of refutational rage.[2]

Conclusion

Although, for the cynical, the postmodern condition 'means never having to
say you're sorry for not having an original idea in your head' (Beaumont
1993: 43), it has much to contribute to our understanding of retail marketing. This paper has examined the enigma that is postmodernism and
explored its implications for the wheel of retailing, one of the oldest, most
celebrated and energetically debated concepts in retail marketing's theoretical canon. The outcome of the exercise was (characteristically) ambiguous,
in that the wheel was neither supported nor rejected. Although the concept is
premised on assumptions that are anathema to many postmodern thinkers,
the wheel is not entirely out of place in a postmodern world of fragmentation, difference, plurality and neo-Nietzschean recurrence.

The ambiguities that arise from a postmodern interpretation of the wheel theory may prompt many to conclude that postmodernism is complex, otiose, uninsightful and, hence, unworthy of serious attention and further exploration. After all, it is arguable that the wheel theory is sufficiently imprecise as it stands without endeavouring to add another unnecessary, and unnecessarily vague, epistemological layer. Although a disdainful or dismissive reaction to postmodernism is eminently understandable, it is equally arguable that postmodernism poses interesting problems and raises important issues which have never been explored in the wheel of retailing literature (or, indeed, in marketing thought generally) and therefore the epistemological implications of the postmodern condition warrant very careful consideration. If nothing else, postmodernism serves to highlight the limits of empirical analysis, the theory laden-ness of observation and, thanks to recent Nietzschean scholarship, the self-consuming nature of many retailing and marketing concepts.

Notes

1. A fourth strand, known as 'postmodern science', is also sometimes identified (see Brown 1995a). This is predicated on a repudiation of the mechanistic, deterministic and static worldview of 'modern' science in favour of a new paradigm based on the principles of uncertainty, indeterminacy and change (e.g. chaos theory, quantum mechanics, fuzzy logic and so on).

2. In our attempts to answer this question, it may be worthwhile examining the field of cultural studies, especially the 'uses and gratifications' literature. Instead of focusing on the content of the 'text' itself (which can be films, books, television programmes, etc.) or the intentions of the author, students of 'uses and gratifications' concentrate on the diverse needs, activities and interpretations of the audience. Ang's (1985) classic study of the television series *Dallas*, for example, distinguished between three (largely self-explanatory) types of viewer: Dallas-haters, Dallas-lovers and 'ironists', those who adopt an ironical viewing attitude. This audience-centred approach to textual phenomena has recently been introduced into the marketing arena, thanks to an innovative study of the uses and gratifications young people derive from advertising (O'Dohonoe 1994), and it may also be adaptable to academic 'users' of marketing concepts, such as the wheel of retailing theory. Thus, it is possible to distinguish between wheel-haters, scholars who dismiss the concept out of hand (e.g. Savitt, Wrigley); wheel-lovers, those who consider it an interesting and empirically testable hypothesis (recent examples include IGD 1994; Freathy 1994); and ironists, the sort of unsavoury individual who employs it for tongue-in-cheek case studies, book reviews and, not least, figurative pegs for academic papers on postmodernism!

References

Adair, G. (1992) *The Postmodernist Always Rings Twice*, London: Fourth Estate.
Adam, B. (1995) *Timewatch: The Social Analysis of Time*, Cambridge: Polity.

Agergaard, E., Olsen, A. and **Allpass, J.** (1970) 'The interaction between retailing and the urban centre structure: a theory of spiral movement', *Environment and Planning*, 2(1): 55–71.

Alawi, H.M.A. (1986) 'Saudi-Arabia: making sense of self-service', *International Marketing Review*, 3(1): 22–38.

Allvine, F.C. (1968) 'The supermarket challenged! New competitive strategies needed', *Business Horizons*, 11(October): 61–72.

Ang, I. (1985) *Watching Dallas: Soap Opera and the Melodramatic Imagination*, London: Methuen.

Arndt, J. (1972) *Norsk Detaljhandel Frem Til 1980*, Oslo: Johan Grundt Tanum Forlag.

Barthes, R. (1977) 'The death of the author', in *Image Music Text*, trans. S. Heath, London: Fontana, pp. 142–8.

Baudrillard, J. (1983) *Simulations*, trans. P. Foss, P. Patton and P. Beitchman, New York: Semiotext(e).

Baudrillard, J. (1988) 'The year 2000 has already happened', in A. Kroker and M. Kroker (eds) *Body Invaders: Panic Sex in America*, Montreal: The New World Perspectives, pp. 35–44.

Baudrillard, J. (1989) 'The anorexic ruins', in D. Kamper and C. Wulf (eds) *Looking Back on the End of the World*, New York: Semiotext(e), pp. 29–45.

Baudrillard, J. (1990) *Fatal Strategies*, trans. P. Beitchman and W.G.J. Niesluchowski, London: Pluto.

Baudrillard, J. (1994) *The Illusion of the End*, trans. C. Turner, Cambridge: Polity.

Bauman, Z. (1992) *Intimations of Postmodernity*, London: Routledge.

Beadle, J.J. (1993) *Will Pop Eat Itself?* London: Faber.

Beaumont, P. (1993) 'Postmodernism', *The Observer*, 9 May: 43.

Bell, D. (1976) *The Cultural Contradictions of Capitalism*, New York: Basic Books.

Berens, J.S. (1980) 'Capital requirements and retail institutional innovation – theoretical observations', in C.W. Lamb and P.M. Dunne (eds) *Theoretical Developments in Marketing*, Chicago: American Marketing Association, pp. 248–50.

Berger, P. and **Luckmann, T.** (1967) *The Social Construction of Reality: A Treatise in the Sociology of Knowledge*, Harmondsworth: Penguin.

Berman, B. and **Evans, J.R.** (1979) *Retail Management: A Strategic Approach*, New York: Macmillan.

Berman, M. (1983) *All That is Solid Melts Into Air*, London: Verso.

Bertens, H. (1995) *The Idea of the Postmodern: A History*, London: Routledge.

Best, S. and **Kellner, D.** (1991) *Postmodern Theory: Critical Interrogations*, Basingstoke: Macmillan.

Blizzard, R.T. (1976) 'The competitive evolution of selected retail institutions in the United States and Australia: a culture ecological analysis', unpublished PhD thesis, University of Colorado.

Bocock, R. and **Thompson, K.** (1992) *Social and Cultural Forms of Modernity*, Cambridge: Polity Press.

Bowler, P.J. (1989) *The Invention of Progress*, Oxford: Blackwell.

Boyd, R., Gasper, P. and **Trout, J.D.** (1991) *The Philosophy of Science*, Cambridge: MIT Press.

Boyne, R. (1990) *Foucault and Derrida: The Other Side of Reason*, London: Unwin Hyman.

Boyne, R. and **Rattansi, A.** (1990) 'The theory and politics of postmodernism: by way of introduction', in R. Boyne and A. Rattansi (eds) *Postmodernism and Society*, Basingstoke: Macmillan, pp. 1–45.

Brand, E.A. (1963) *Modern Supermarket Operation*, New York: Fairchild, reprinted in R.R. Gist (ed.) *Management Perspectives in Retailing*, New York: Wiley, pp. 19–21.

Brown, S. (1990) 'The wheel of retailing: past and future', *Journal of Retailing*, 66(2): 143–9.

Brown, S. (1991) 'Variations on a marketing enigma: the wheel of retailing theory', *Journal of Marketing Management*, 7(2): 131–55.

Brown, S. (1993) 'Postmodern marketing?', *European Journal of Marketing*, 27(4): 19–34.

Brown, S. (1994) 'Marketing as multiplex: screening postmodernism', *European Journal of Marketing*, 28(8/9): 27–51.

Brown, S. (1995a) *Postmodern Marketing*, London: Routledge.

Brown, S. (1995b) 'Nietzsche marketing', *Irish Marketing Review*, 8, in press.

Brown, S. and **Quinn, B.** (1993) 'Reinventing the retailing wheel: a postmodern morality tale', in P.J. McGoldrick (ed.) *Cases in Retail Management*, London: Pitman, pp. 26–39.

Bucklin, L.P. (1972) *Competition and Evolution in the Distributive Trades*, Englewood Cliffs, NJ: Prentice-Hall.

Bucklin, L.P. (1976) 'Channel change agents in developing countries', *International Journal of Physical Distribution and Materials Management*, 7(1): 59–68.

Bucklin, L.P. (1983) 'Patterns of change in retail institutions in the United States with special attention to the traditional department store', *International Journal of Physical Distribution and Materials Management*, 13(5/6): 153–68.

Burgin, V. (1986) *The End of Art Theory: Criticism and Postmodernity*, Basingstoke: Macmillan.

Burrell, G. (1994) 'Modernism, postmodernism and organisational analysis 4: the contribution of Jürgen Habermas', *Organisation Studies*, 15(1): 1–19.

Bush, R.F. and **Hair, J.F.** (1976) 'Consumer patronage determinants of discount versus conventional motels', *Journal of Retailing*, 52(2): 41–50, 91.

Callinicos, A. (1989) *Against Postmodernism: A Marxist Critique*, Cambridge: Polity Press.

Connor, S. (1989) *Postmodernist Culture: An Introduction to Theories of the Contemporary*, Oxford: Blackwell.

Cooke, P. (1990) *Back to the Future: Modernity, Postmodernity and Locality*, London: Unwin Hyman.

Davidson, W.R., Bates, A.D. and **Bass, S.J.** (1976) 'The retail life cycle', *Harvard Business Review*, 54(November–December): 89–96.

Dawson, J.A. (1979) *The Marketing Environment*, London: Croom Helm.

Debord, G. (1994) *The Society of the Spectacle*, trans. S.F. Rendall, Cambridge: MIT Press.

Deiderick, T.E. and **Dodge, H.R.** (1983) 'The wheel of retailing rotates and moves', in J. Summey *et al.* (eds) *Marketing: Theories and Concepts for an Era of Change*, Carbondale: Southern Marketing Association, pp. 149–52.

Denzin, N.K. (1991) *Images of Postmodern Society*, London: Sage.

Derrida, J. (1991) *A Derrida Reader: Between the Blinds*, P. Kamuf (ed.), Hemel Hempstead: Harvester Wheatsheaf.

Dickens, D.R. and **Fontana, A.** (1994) *Postmodernism and Social Inquiry*, London: UCL Press.

Dickinson, R.A. (1983) 'Innovations in retailing', *Retail Control*, 51(June–July): 30–54.

Dickinson, R.A. (1991) 'Cost driven (based) retailing in the United States' in R.A. Thurik, and H.J. Gianotten (eds) *Proceedings: Sixth World Conference on Research in the Distributive Trades*, Zoetermeer: EIM, pp. 10–16.

Doherty, T. (1993) *Postmodernism: A Reader*, London: Harvester Wheatsheaf.

Dreesmann, A.C.R. (1968) 'Patterns of evolution in retailing', *Journal of Retailing*, 44(Spring): 64–81.

Elliott, R. (1993) 'Marketing and the meaning of postmodern consumer culture', in D. Brownlie *et al.* (eds) *Rethinking Marketing*, Coventry: Warwick Business School Research Bureau, pp. 134–42.

Etgar, M. (1984) 'The retail ecology model: a comprehensive model of retail change', in J.N. Sheth (ed.) *Research in Marketing*, Vol. 7, Greenwich, Conn.: JAI Press, pp. 41–62.

Featherstone, M. (1991) *Consumer Culture and Postmodernism*, London: Sage.

Fielding, H. (1992) 'Teach yourself post-modernism', *The Independent on Sunday*, 15 November: 21.

Filser, M. (1984) 'Les analyses mechanistes des formules de distribution: etat de l'art, apports et voies de recherche', *Revue Francaise du Marketing*, 99(3): 3–18.

Firat, A.F. and **Venkatesh, A.** (1993) 'Postmodernity: the age of marketing', *International Journal of Research in Marketing*, 10(3): 227–49.

Firat, A.F., Dholakia, N. and **Venkatesh, A.** (1995) 'Marketing in a postmodern world', *European Journal of Marketing*, 29(l): 40–56.

Foucault, M. (1972) *The Order of Things: An Archaeology of the Human Sciences*, trans. A. Sheridan, London: Tavistock.

Foucault, M. (1990) *The Care of the Self: The History of Sexuality*, Vol. 3, trans. R. Hurley, Harmondsworth: Penguin.

Fox, H.W. (1968) *The Economics of Trading Stamps*, Washington, DC: Public Affairs Press.

Foxall, G.R. (1992) 'The consumer situation: an integrative model for research in marketing', *Journal of Marketing Management*, 8(4): 383–404.

Freathy, P. (1994) 'Employment theory and the wheel of retailing: segmenting the circle', paper presented at American Collegiate Retailing Association conference, Richmond, October.

Gellner, E. (1992) *Postmodernism, Reason and Religion*, London: Routledge.

Giddens, A. (1984) *The Constitution of Society*, Cambridge: Polity.

Giddens, A. (1990) *The Consequences of Modernity*, Cambridge: Polity.

Gist, R.R. (1968) *Retailing: Concepts and Decisions*, New York: Wiley.

Goldman, A. (1974) 'Growth of large food stores in developing countries', *Journal of Retailing*, 50(Summer): 50–60.

Goldman, A. (1975) 'The role of trading up in the development of the retailing system', *Journal of Marketing*, 39(January): 54–62.

Gordon, S. (1991) *The History and Philosophy of Social Science*, London: Routledge.

Greyser, S. (1976) 'Foreword', in M.P. McNair and E.G. May *The Evolution of Retail Institutions in the United States*, Cambridge: Marketing Science Institute, pp. iii–iv.

Gripsrud, G. (1986) 'Market structure, perceived competition and expected competitor reactions in retailing', in L.P. Bucklin and J.M. Carman (eds) *Research in Marketing*, Vol. 8, Greenwich, Conn.: JAI Press, pp. 251–71.

Habermas, J. (1987) *The Philosophical Discourse of Modernity*, Cambridge: Polity.

Hall, S., Held, D. and **McGrew, T.** (1992) *Modernity and its Futures*, London: Polity.

Harvey, D. (1989) *The Condition of Postmodernity*, Oxford: Blackwell.

Hassard, J. (1990) *The Sociology of Time*, Basingstoke: Macmillan.

Hassard, J. (1993) *Sociology and Organisation Theory*, London: Cambridge University Press.

Hawes, J.M. and **Crittenden, W.F.** (1979) 'Generic grocery products and the wheel of retailing', *Mid-south Quarterly Business Review*, 3(3): 8–10.

Hirschman, E.C. and **Stampfl, R.W.** (1980) 'Retail research: problems, potentials and priorities', in R.W. Stampfl and E.C. Hirschman (eds) *Competitive Structure in Retail Markets: The Department Store Perspective*, Chicago: American Marketing Association, pp. 68–77.

Ho, S-C. and **Lau, H-F.** (1988) 'Development of supermarket technology: the incomplete transfer phenomenon', *International Marketing Review*, 5(Spring): 20–30.

Hollander, S.C. (1960) 'The wheel of retailing', *Journal of Marketing*, 24(July): 37–42.

Hollander, S.C. (1962) 'Retailing: cause or effect?', in W.S. Decker (ed.) *Emerging Concepts in Marketing*, Chicago: American Marketing Association, pp. 220–30.

Hollander, S.C. (1966) 'Notes on the retail accordion', *Journal of Retailing*, 42(Summer): 29–40, 54.

Hollander, S.C. (1970) *Multi-national Retailing*, East Lansing: MSU International Business and Economic Studies.

Hollander, S.C. (1980) 'Oddities, nostalgia, wheels and other patterns in retail evolution', in R.W Stampfl and E.C. Hirschman (eds) *Competitive Structure in Retail Markets: The Department Store Perspective*, Chicago: American Marketing Association, pp. 78–87.

Hollinger, R. (1994) *Postmodernism and the Social Sciences: A Thematic Approach*, Thousand Oaks, Calif.: Sage.

Holmes, J.H. and **Hoskins, W.R.** (1977) 'Using the life cycle in store location decisions', *Pittsburg Business Review*, 46(June): 1–6.

Hughes, J. (1990) *The Philosophy of Social Research*, Harlow: Longman.

Hughes, R. (1991) *The Shock of the New*, London: Thames & Hudson.

Hunt, S.D. (1991) *Modern Marketing Theory: Critical Issues in the Philosophy of Marketing Science*, Cincinnati: South-Western Publishing.

IGD (1994) *The Long Term Viability of Discount Grocery Retailing in the UK*, Letchmore Heath: Institute of Grocery Distribution.

Jameson, F. (1985) 'Postmodernism and consumer society', in H. Foster (ed.) *Postmodern Culture*, London: Pluto Press, pp. 111–25.

Jameson, F. (1991) *Postmodernism, or, The Cultural Logic of Late Capitalism*, London: Verso.

Jeffreys, J.B. (1985) 'Multinational retailing: are the food chains different?', in M.P. Kacker (ed.) *Transatlantic Trends in Retailing: Takeovers and Flow of Know-how*, Westport, Conn.: Quorum, pp. 141–4.

Jencks, C. (1989) *What is Postmodernism?*, London: Academy Editions.

Jencks, C. (1992) *The Post-modern Reader*, London: Academy Editions.

Johnson, P. (1991) *The Birth of the Modern: World Society 1815–1830*, London: Weidenfeld & Nicolson.

Kaikati, J.G. (1985) 'Don't discount off-price retailers', *Harvard Business Review*, 63 (May–June): 85–92.

Kaynak, E. (1979) 'A refined approach to the wheel of retailing', *European Journal of Marketing*, 13(7): 237–45.

Kenny, M. and **Florida, R.** (1993) *Beyond Mass Production: The Japanese System and its Transfer to the U.S.*, Oxford: Oxford University Press.

Knee, D. and **Walters, D.** (1985) *Strategy in Retailing: Theory and Application*, Oxford: Philip Allan.

Koelb, C. (1990) *Nietzsche as Postmodernist*, Albany: State University of New York Press.

Kroker, A. and **Cook, D.** (1988) *The Postmodern Scene: Excremental Culture and Hyper-aesthetics*, London: Macmillan.

Kroker, A., Kroker, M. and **Cook, D.** (1989) *Panic Encyclopedia: The Definitive Guide to the Postmodern Scene*, Basingstoke: Macmillan.

Kumar, K. (1986) *Prophecy and Progress: The Sociology of Industrial and Post-industrial Society*, Harmondsworth: Penguin.

Kuper, J. (1987) *Key Thinkers, Past and Present*, London: Routledge.

Lacan, J. (1977) *Écrits: A Selection*, trans. A. Sheridan, London: Routledge.
Lampert, L. (1993) *Nietzsche and Modern Times*, New Haven: Yale University Press.
Lash, S. (1990) *Sociology of Postmodernism*, London: Routledge.
Lash, S. and **Urry, J.** (1994) *Economies of Signs and Space*, London: Sage.
Lee, J. and **Vryza, M.** (1994) 'The paradigm of retailing revisited: directions for theory and research development', *Journal of Retailing and Consumer Services*, 1(1): 53–5.
Lord, J.D. (1984) 'The outlet/off-price shopping centre as a retailing innovation', *The Service Industries Journal*, 4(March): 9–18.
Lugli, G. (1987) 'Per una revisione della teoria della "wheel of retailing"', *Commercio*, 25: 5–19.
Lyon, D. (1994) *Postmodernity*, Buckingham: Open University Press.
Lyotard, J-F. (1984) *The Postmodern Condition: A Report on Knowledge*, Manchester: Manchester University Press.
McNair, M.P. (1958) 'Significant trends and developments in the post-war period', in A.B. Smith (ed.) *Competitive Distribution in a Free, High-level Economy and its Implications for the University*, Pittsburg: University of Pittsburg Press, pp. 1–25.
McNair, M.P. and **May, E.G.** (1976) *The Evolution of Retailing Institutions in the United States*, Cambridge: Marketing Science Institute.
Magnus, B., Stewart, S. and **Mileur, J-P.** (1993) *Nietzsche's Case: Philosophy as/and Literature*, New York: Routledge.
Makinen, E.H. (1986) 'Predictions of changes in food wholesale trade in Finland', in E. Kaynak (ed.) *World Food Marketing Systems*, London: Butterworths, pp. 313–28.
Manuel, F.E. and **Manuel, F.P.** (1979) *Utopian Thought in the Western World*, Cambridge: The Belknap Press.
Markin, R.J. and **Duncan, C.P.** (1981) 'The transformation of retailing institutions: beyond the wheel of retailing and life cycle theories', *Journal of Macromarketing*, 1(spring): 58–66.
Martenson, R. (1981) *Innovations in Multi-national Retailing: Ikea on the Swedish, Swiss, German and Austrian Furniture Markets*, Gothenburg: Department of Business, University of Gothenburg.
May, E.G. (1989) 'A retail odyssey', *Journal of Retailing*, 65(3): 356–67.
May, E.G. and **Greyser, S.** (1989) 'From-home shopping: where is it leading?', in L. Pellegrini and S.K. Reddy (eds) *Retail and Marketing Channels*, London: Routledge, pp. 216–33.
Meloche, M.S., di Benedetto, C.A. and **Yudelson, J.E.** (1988) 'A framework for the analysis of the growth and development of retail institutions', in R.L. King (ed.) *Retailing: Its Present and Future*, Charleston: American Collegiate Retailing Association, pp. 6–11.
Moyer, M.S. and **Whitmore, N.M.** (1976) 'An appraisal of the marketing channels for automobiles', *Journal of Marketing*, 40(July): 35–40.
Mun, K-C. (1988) 'Chinese retailing in a changing environment', in E. Kaynak (ed.) *Transnational Retailing*, Berlin: de Gruyter, pp. 211–26.
Murray, R. (1989) 'Fordism and post-Fordism', in S. Hall and M. Jacques (eds) *New Times*, London: Lawrence & Wishart, pp. 38–53.
Newton-Smith, W.H. (1980) *The Structure of Time*, London: Routledge & Kegan Paul.
Nieschlag, R. and **Kuhn, G.** (1980) *Binnenhandel und Binnenhandelspolitik*, Berlin: Duncker & Humblot.
Nietzsche, F. (1967 [1901]) *The Will to Power*, trans. W. Kaufmann and R.J. Hollingdale, New York: Vintage.

Nietzsche, F. (1986 [1878]) *Human, All Too Human: A Book for Free Spirits*, trans. R.J. Hollingdale, Cambridge: Cambridge University Press.

Nietzsche, F. (1990 [1886]) *Beyond Good and Evil*, trans. R.J. Hollingdale, Harmondsworth: Penguin.

Nisbet, R. (1980) *A History of the Idea of Progress*, New York: Basic Books.

Norris, C. (1991) *Deconstruction: Theory and Practice*, London: Routledge.

O'Dohonoe, S. (1994) 'Advertising uses and gratifications', *European Journal of Marketing*, 28(8/9): 52–75.

Ogilvy, J. (1990) 'This postmodern business', *Marketing and Research Today*, 18(1): 4–21.

O'Neill, J. (1995) *The Poverty of Postmodernism*, London: Routledge.

Ortiz-Buonofina, M. (1987) 'The economic efficiency of channels of distribution in a developing society: the case of the Guatemalan retail sector', *Journal of Macromarketing*, 7(Fall): 17–25.

Ortony, A. (1979) 'Metaphor: a multidimensional problem', in A. Ortony (ed.) *Metaphor and Thought*, Cambridge: Cambridge University Press, pp. 1–16.

O'Shaughnessy, J. (1992) *Explaining Buyer Behaviour: Central Concepts and Philosophy of Science Issues*, Oxford: Oxford University Press.

Oxenfeldt, A.R. (1960) 'The retailing revolution: why and whither', *Journal of Retailing*, 36(Fall): 157–62.

Peckham, J.O. (1981) *The Wheel of Marketing*, Scarsdale: A.C. Nielsen.

Peter, J.P. (1991) 'Philosophical tensions in consumer inquiry', in T.S. Robertson and H.H. Kassarjian (eds) *Handbook of Consumer Behaviour*, Englewood Cliffs, NJ: Prentice Hall, pp. 533–47.

Peter, J.P. and **Olson, J.C.** (1993) *Consumer Behaviour and Marketing Strategy*, 3rd edition, Homewood, Ill.: Irwin.

Pirsig, R.M. (1974) *Zen and the Art of Motorcycle Maintenance*, London: Vintage.

Porter, M.E. (1990) *The Competitive Advantage of Nations*, New York: The Free Press.

Poster, M. (1984) *Foucault, Marxism and History*, Cambridge: Polity.

Regan, W.J. (1961) 'Full cycle for self-service', *Journal of Marketing*, 25(April): 15–21.

Robinson, L. and **Smith, R.B.** (1980) 'The continuing relevance of foundation literature in marketing: implications for marketing education in the 1980s', in J.H. Summey and R.D. Taylor (eds) *Evolving Marketing Thought for 1980*, Carbondale: Southern Marketing Association, pp. 168–79.

Rose, G. (1991) *The Post-modern and the Post-industrial: A Critical Analysis*, Cambridge, Cambridge University Press.

Rosenau, P.M. (1992) *Postmodernism and the Social Sciences*, Princeton, NJ: Princeton University Press.

Rothman, J. (1992) 'Postmodern research and the arts', *Journal of the Market Research Society*, 34(4): 419–35.

Rylance, R. (1994) *Roland Barthes*, Hemel Hempstead: Harvester Wheatsheaf.

Sampson, S.D. and **Tigert, D.J.** (1993) *The Impact of Warehouse Membership Clubs: The Wheel of Retailing Turns One More Time*, Babson Park: Babson College Working Paper, Babson College.

Sarup, M. (1993) *An Introductory Guide to Post-structuralism and Postmodernism*, Hemel Hempstead: Harvester Wheatsheaf.

Sautet, M. (1990) *Nietzsche for Beginners*, New York: Writers & Readers Publishing.

Savitt, R. (1988) 'Comment: the wheel of the wheel of retailing', *International Journal of Retailing*, 3(1): 38–40.

Savitt, R. (1989) 'Looking back to see ahead: writing the history of American retailing', *Journal of Retailing*, 65(3): 326–55.

Scott, I. (1989) *Retail Warehousing*, London: Fletcher King.

Scruton, R. (1984) *A Short History of Modern Philosophy: From Descartes to Wittgenstein*, London: Ark.

Shumway, D.R. (1992) *Michel Foucault*, Charlotte: University Press of Virginia.

Simons, H.W. and **Billig, M.** (1994) *After Postmodernism: Reconstructing Ideology Critique*, London: Sage.

Smart, B. (1992) *Modern Conditions, Postmodern Controversies*, London: Routledge.

Smart, B. (1993) *Postmodernity*, London: Routledge.

Solomon, R.C. and **Higgins, K.** (1988) *Reading Nietzsche*, Oxford: Oxford University Press.

Sparks, L. (1993) 'The rise and fall of mass marketing? Food retailing in Great Britain since 1960', in R.S. Tedlow and G. Jones (eds) *The Rise and Fall of Mass Marketing*, London: Routledge, pp. 58–92.

Stern, J.P. (1978) *Nietzsche*, London: Fontana.

Stern, L.W. and **El-Ansary, A.I.** (1977) *Marketing Channels*, Englewood Cliffs, NJ: Prentice-Hall.

Stone, M. (1989) 'Competing with Japan – the rules of the game', in B. Lloyd (ed.) *Entrepreneurship: Creating and Managing New Ventures*, Oxford: Pergamon, pp. 62–76.

Sturrock, J. (1979) *Structuralism and Since: From Lévi-Strauss to Derrida*, Oxford: Oxford University Press.

Sturrock, J. (1993) *Structuralism*, London: Fontana.

Teeple, E.C. (1979) 'Look out McDonald's: the "wheel" is rolling', in H.S. Gitlow and E.W. Wheatley (eds) *Developments in Marketing Science*, Vol. II, Miami: Academy of Marketing Science, p. 379.

Thomas, S.M., Anderson, R.E. and **Jolson, M.A.** (1986) 'The wheel of retailing and non-store evolution: an alternative hypothesis', *International Journal of Retailing*, 1(2): 18–29.

Toulmin, S. (1990) *Cosmopolis: The Hidden Agenda of Modernity*, Chicago: University of Chicago Press.

Turner, B.S. (1990) *Theories of Modernity and Postmodernity*, London: Sage.

van Raaij, W.F. (1993) 'Postmodern consumption', *Journal of Economic Psychology*, 14(3): 541–63.

Vattimo, G. (1991) *The End of Modernity: Nihilism and Hermeneutics in Postmodern Culture*, trans. J.R. Snyder, Baltimore: Johns Hopkins University Press.

Wagner, P. (1994) *A Sociology of Modernity: Liberty and Discipline*, London: Routledge.

Walsh, K. (1992) *The Representation of the Past: Museums and Heritage in the Postmodern World*, London: Routledge.

Waugh, P. (1992) *Postmodernism: A Reader*, London: Edward Arnold.

Whitrow, G.J. (1988) *Time in History: Views of Time from Prehistory to the Present Day*, Oxford: Oxford University Press.

Wilson, E. (1990) 'These new components of the spectacle: fashion and postmodernism', in R. Boyne and A. Rattansi (eds) *Postmodernism and Society*, Basingstoke: Macmillan, pp. 209–36.

Wyver, J. (1989) 'Television and postmodernism', in L. Appignanesi (ed.) *Postmodernism ICA Documents*, London: Free Association Books, pp. 155–63.

Young, R. (1990) *Untying the Text: A Post-structuralist Reader*, London: Routledge.

Zain, O.M. and **Rejab, I.** (1989) 'The choice of retail outlets among urban Malaysian shoppers', *International Journal of Retailing*, 4(2): 35–45.

9

Gap on the map? Towards a geography of consumption and identity

L. Crewe and M. Lowe

Source: *Environment and Planning A* 27 (1995): 1877–1898.

Abstract

The current blurring of the boundaries between economic, cultural, and social geography has placed issues of consumption and identity firmly on the research agenda. In this paper, we address the question of the spatiality of retailing and consumption and argue that emergent microgeographies of consumption are challenging the simplicity of the globalisation thesis. We argue that retailers are in the business of creating particular urban landscapes and that qualitative differences are emerging between areas as consumption centres. By focusing on the spatial outcomes of the complex mediation between retailers, advertisers, and consumers, we examine the complex *political-economic relations* which enable the production of consumption. The project is thus an attempt to mesh production-oriented and culturally derived understandings of consumption and identity.

1 Introduction

The current blurring of the boundaries between economic, social, and cultural geography has placed issues of consumption and identity firmly on the research agenda. To date, however, there has been relatively little attention paid to the geographies of consumption and identity 'on the ground'. On the basis of research in progress on pioneering clothing retailers in the United Kingdom, in this paper we move towards such a geography via a consideration of the creation of 'differentiated spaces of consumption'. We argue that through their organisation of consumption retailers are creating particular urban landscapes and that qualitative differences are emerging between areas as consumption centres. By focusing on the complex mediation between retailers, advertisers, and consumers we question how retail spaces become invested with particular identities.

In the following discussion we are attempting to plug three particular 'gaps on the map' of research into geographies of retailing, consumption, and identity. First, we are shifting the research focus away from dominant accounts of the malling of retail space and of global homogeneity, and are focusing instead on the complexity and differentiation of retail spaces. In so doing we aim to move away from 'the tyranny of the single site' (Jackson and Thrift, 1995), and towards a consideration of the heterogeneity of retailing and consumption spaces. To suggest that the globalisation of culture is destroying the essence of place, and creating the "ageographical city, a city without a place attached to it" (Sorkin, 1992, page xi) misses the point that places, like people, have multiple meanings and identities (Massey, 1991). Second, in order to explore such localised spaces we are considering the geographies of retailing and consumption 'on the ground' and at a variety of scales. Third, we are attempting to mesh production-oriented and culturally derived understandings of consumption and identity,[1] and suggest that the combined analysis of material processes and symbolic representations produces a rich understanding of the production and reproduction of place-based meanings (see McDowell, 1994; Zukin, 1988; 1991). To date, there has been a tendency to focus on economic readings of global spaces, most notably the processes of investment, speculation, and capital switching underpinning the rise of global cities (see Budd and Whimster, 1992; Corbridge et al, 1994; Fainstein, 1994; Fainstein et al, 1992; Sassen, 1991), and to neglect the cultural determinants of uneven development (although see here Anderson and Gale, 1992; Burgess and Wood, 1988; Kearns and Philo, 1993; Watson, 1991; Zukin, 1991). We argue against research which takes its cue only from political economy and treats consumption as only an aspect of the circulation of capital. Such analyses must move on from being one-sidedly productionist, and must grasp the extent to which culture, aesthetics, and symbolic processes have penetrated the economy (see also Lash and Urry, 1994; Lipietz, 1993). To formulate "consumption as an opposite and independent position from production—is to be tripped up" (Laurier, 1993, page 272), the two are intertwined, and it may be argued that consumption is *the* social activity which unites above all others economy and culture (Lee, 1993). In this sense we are advocating an approach which simultaneously considers the cultural *and* the economic strands of retailing and consumption, recognising the need to understand how sociocultural processes intersect with material-economic processes in shaping consumption. Our focus on retailing is a useful starting point here because, we argue, retailers occupy a pivotal role within society, working at the critical intersection between production and consumption (Sayer and Walker, 1992). If, as Crawford suggests, "the ethos of consumption has penetrated every sphere of our lives ... [and] increasingly constructs the way we see the world" (1992, page 11), then retailers must be seen as central institutions in this process. It has further been suggested that "retailing is in many ways redefining the economic and cultural horizons of contemporary Britain" (and, we would argue, much of the developed market economies) (Mort, 1989, page 168).

Our approach is thus one which attempts to capture the ways in which retailing and consumption create and recreate place-specific identities, and how cultural attributes and capital gain are intrinsically bound together. Consumption spaces are fascinating precisely because they reflect cultural as well as economic processes, and the constant shifts in the meanings and practices of particular places remind us that "the building and revolutionising of an urban landscape is never just physical and economic; it is also social, cultural and political . . . urban change then is never pregiven or guaranteed . . . it is in this competition that the intersection of cultural and economic speculation plays such a crucial role" (Goodwin, 1993, page 149).

2   Globalising tendencies

Our starting point is the recognition by, amongst others, Jackson and Thrift (1995) and Amin and Thrift (1992), that "geographical perspectives on consumption—and on the dialectics of globalisation and localisation . . . — have begun to command attention across the social sciences as part of a growing interdisciplinary concern with 'mapping the futures'" (Jackson and Thrift, 1995, page 3). Although it is clear that we are seeing "a new 'globalised' localism" emerging (Thrift, 1994), it is also both conceptually and methodologically complex to hold together simultaneously the "most local of local detail and the most global of global structure in such a way as to bring them simultaneously into view" (Geertz, 1983, page 69; see also Cox, 1995; Crewe and Lowe, 1996a; McDowell, 1994; Thrift, 1994). As a result, debate has tended to be polarised between the globalising and the localising, creating a seemingly impassable conceptual dialectic of the global and the local.

Yet one of the most significant world changes that has taken place in recent years has been the emergence of "new configurations in which both the local/regional *and* the transnational/global scale have risen to prominence" (Swyngedouw, 1992, page 40). On the one hand the globalisation of retailing continues to weave complex interdependencies between geographically distant locations and tends towards global interconnection and dedifferentiation. On the other hand new patterns of regional specialisation are emphasising the importance of place and reinforcing local uniqueness. As a consequence, "one of the most fascinating aspects of place in recent years is that it has become more homogenous in some ways and more heterogenous in others" (Zukin, 1991, page 12). This interplay of the local and the global is particularly interesting in the case of fashion which is at once a symbol of personal identity and a global industry which has united (and differentiated) consumers the world over (Crewe and Lowe, 1996a). Fashion is also an interesting example because, it has been argued, its volatility and its power as a cultural signifier allow the fashion system to offer some important clues into the links between economic and cultural change which lie at the heart of 'new times' (Craik, 1994; Crewe and Forster, 1993a; Hall and Jacques, 1989; McRobbie, 1994).

The tendency for the spread of global culture to weaken local distinctiveness is now well documented (King, 1990; Sack, 1988; Shields, 1992; Zukin, 1991), and the idea that globalising forces are resulting in the emergence of an international culture is now a common one. Thus the global transmission of fashion trends and retail concepts, and the serial reproduction of a mall culture under 'shopping centre capitalism' is a recurrent theme (Jameson, 1984, page 33). This homogenisation of consumption practices and spaces is particularly apparent through the 'mailing' of retail space (Crawford, 1992; Jacobs, 1984; Kowinski, 1985; Shields, 1992; Sorkin, 1992). The resulting landscapes "appear to be pastiches, disorienting, unauthentic and juxtaposed" (Sack, 1988, page 642). Certainly, much previous work on the geography of consumption and identity has, as Jackson and Thrift have recently suggested, tended to focus on the shopping mall and those detailed studies of such consumption sites that have been carried out tend to emphasise a homogenous set of processes producing only homogeneity.[2]

Although we would not wish to deny that such globalisation processes are resulting in increased homogeneity at a global scale, we would like to argue that a finer grained approach is needed to the study of retailing and consumption. It is not possible to simply read off the local effects of global processes. Rather, we would argue that there are distinct regional and local landscapes of consumption quite apart from the dominant accounts of megamalls, and that these microgeographies are much less well understood and documented. We are aiming to redress this research imbalance and are focusing instead on the localisation tendencies of fashion. By considering the localisation end of the global–local complex and taking a much more fine-grained approach we hope to expose the complexity of consumption spaces. We take as our starting point the suggestion by Sack that consumption is one of the most pervasive place-building processes in the world (Sack, 1988, page 643). The way in which particular localities are being reconstructed and sold not as centres of production but of consumption is important here, as are new patterns of regional specialisation reflecting the selective location of highly valued economic activities (Zukin, 1991). Increasingly, what distinguishes one place from another is the strength of their 'consumptional identities' (Corner, 1994), the complexes of services which are available. As places compete for limited investment funds, their vitality and viability increasingly depend upon sustaining and nurturing an image, and central to such place-selling strategies is "a conscious and deliberate manipulation of culture in an effort to enhance the appeal and interest of places" (Kearns and Philo, 1993, page 3). So "of course, by place we mean in part image [and] . . . what is distinct about the contemporary remaking of place [is] the importance of image" (Lash and Urry, 1994, page 326). Places are thus being promoted and sold not simply as centres of economic growth, but also as culturally rich places in which to live and work (see Ashworth and Voogd, 1990; Boyle and Hughes, 1991; Burgess, 1982; Deakin and Edwards, 1993; Harvey, 1989; Judd and Parkinson, 1990; Lim, 1993; Lowe, 1993; Roger Tym and Partners, 1987; Sadler, 1993; Zukin, 1991), and the quality and quantity of consumption opportunities are critical elements in generating such place myths. What is critical here, then, is how contemporary consumption is intrinsically linked to quality of life, the key being the symbolic content of such services (Lash and Urry, 1994). Clearly, we need to explore the ways in which these economic and culturally rooted imaging strategies connect in particular places. And thus, although it was originally suggested that the internationalisation of retail services would eliminate differences between places, we would argue that retail location decisions often entail increased sensitivity to local features—a process which Massey terms "a global sense of place" (1991, page 29).

3   Pioneering retailers and their creation of differentiated spaces of consumption

In many localities, then, there has been a remaking of the character of the place, in which services and consumption differences have become primary. In view of this, there is a strong case for exploring the links between retailing, consumption, and urban image, as they work out in particular places. In moving away from the simplicity of the globalising tendencies highlighted above, we intend to begin to address the question of the spatiality of retailing and the consumer society, viewing this through the lens of what we have termed 'pioneering clothing retailers'. We define pioneers here as retailers who are innovative in terms of their product image, who are successfully expanding in an otherwise depressed marketplace, and whose locational choices reflect a certain awareness of both the economic *and* the cultural attributes of particular places. In this examination of pioneering retailers we focus on their strategies of growth, their locational preferences, and their creation of an exclusive image, and then move on to suggest that the activities of such retailers are creating particular urban landscapes and that it is as a result of such strategies that qualitative differences are emerging between areas as consumption centres. We will then use the example of Nottingham to demonstrate how there are distinctive *micro-geographies* of consumption and identity emerging, in addition to the regional geographies displayed by the pioneering retailers studied. The choice of our two case studies enables us to take a first cut into the complex geographies of consumption and identity as they are currently emerging in particular places.

   The retailers we have selected for this section of our empirical work are a group of design-oriented, quality women's fashion retailers who have all successfully positioned themselves between designer stores and the middle market, who retail through a limited number of outlets in a personalised way, and who are independent in the sense that they do not form part of a multiple chain (Hobbs Ltd, Monsoon Ltd, Oasis Stores Ltd, Jigsaw, Whistles, and Boules Ltd). Moreover, the assets of the companies remain very tightly controlled by the original founders. These pioneers have, in addition, been extremely successful in bucking current retail trends and have experienced phenomenal growth at a time when the UK high street has been in crisis (for example, see *The Times* 1990; *The Independent* 1991; *The Sunday Telegraph* 1993a), and when the middle-market chain stores in particular have faced falling rates of profitability (see Crewe and Forster, 1993a). In moving towards an understanding of how such retailers have successfully expanded during the 1990s, it becomes clear that we must look towards both economic and culturally rooted factors.

3.1   Market position

All of the above shops have been extremely successful in positioning themselves—and hence filling the gap—between mass-market and designer fashion. Hobbs, for example, markets clothes that are "exclusive but not expensive and fill the gap between mass market and designer fashion" (*Drapers Record* 1987), and claim to offer "high design at above average but affordable prices" (Green, 1994). Similarly, Jigsaw intends also to "fill the fashion gap between . . . 'the rather naff image' of much mass market high street clothing and the faddish dictates of the designer labels" (*Daily Telegraph* 1989). Indeed Whistles even suggest that in recession people are encouraged to spend "20% more on our product than on something from Next because it seems less ephemeral" (*Independent on Sunday* 1990).

3.2   Unique identity

In addition to filling a particular 'gap' in the market, but as part and parcel of the same strategy, the above companies are all keen to discourage a corporate identity, preferring instead to emphasise their exclusivity and identity. In the case of Jigsaw, for example, " 'Chain' is a word Jigsaw shies away from, although the shops may have the same generic make up and at least 90% of the same stock, they are quite individual in character (cool and woody in Richmond, streetwise and zappy in Kensington)" (*The Times* 1990).

Similarly, this notion of individual identity is sharply apparent in the case of Hobbs, who have succeeded in fostering an image of understated style and class with associations of traditional English quality such that "every branch of Hobbs is a little oasis of Englishness. The fruitwood interior, the dark green logo—even the shop name sounds like Dickens" (Green, 1994). Hobbs maintains a personalised management style which again enables the strong element of individuality to persist. It remains a family-run business with director Marilyn Anselm adhering to a classic English outlook: the clothes are manufactured in the United Kingdom and the emphasis is on attention to detail and classical longevity which can be individually interpreted. According to Hobbs's managing director, the concept is "all about Marilyn's sense of style. The rest of us just package and sell it" (Anselm, 1994). Certainly it would appear that consumption changes and continued recession, particularly in terms of property will make way for more independents to open once again, increasing choice for consumers. The retail analyst group Mintel, for example, predict that small chains will emerge from 1993 onwards, many from a regional base, offering something different from the multiples in fashion terms. Mintel (1993) suggest that "shoppers generally find department stores too 'anonymous' and are once again demanding old-fashioned, more intimate surroundings and a greater degree of personal attention" (see Lowe and Crewe, 1991; 1996). Clearly, this offers some pointers to the recent success of the small pioneers discussed here.

3.3   Site selection

Figure 1 shows maps of the geography of these retail pioneers in 1993. As is evident all are overwhelmingly concentrated in the south and east of the United Kingdom with centres such as Guildford and Bath figuring prominently. Large provincial cities such as Nottingham—arguably with strong fashion identities—are also popular locations. It is also interesting to note that none of the six design-based retailers studied report the use of geodemographic or other packages in their site-location strategies. Rather, the decisionmakers rely closely on 'hearsay', 'intuition', 'instinct', or 'reputation'. Hobbs, for example, report that "A branch in Croydon's Drummond Centre was forced to close and the company now says it will not open in a shopping centre again as the environment is wrong. Ideal sites are situated in affluent centres which are pleasant and house other more exclusive shops" (*Drapers Record* 1987).

   In addition *within* these centres many of these design-based small independents adopt rather unusual sites for their outlets, often outside of the main high street or megamall locations. In this sense the evidence for 'identity-based' rather than economically determined location preferences is significant. Indeed, it is extremely tempting to search for an explanation of the geography of these small independent design-based retailers in terms of notions of *city identity*, and to question what it is about centres such as Guildford, Nottingham, Cheltenham, and Glasgow which make them key-site location choices for these relatively upmarket retailers—and hence important centres of consumption tailored to specific niches. And similarly what is peculiar about the identity or image of Little Clarendon Street in Oxford or the Hockley area of Nottingham's Lace Market, and how might this account for the concentration of upmarket, design-based, and individual fashion retailers? Yet although we have no desire to dismiss these kinds of questions—indeed we argue that there is a need for much more work on this—we would also emphasise that it is important to go beyond notions of image and to

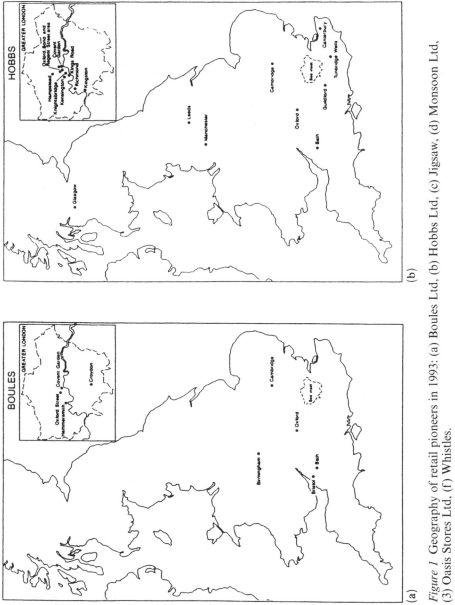

Figure 1 Geography of retail pioneers in 1993: (a) Boules Ltd, (b) Hobbs Ltd, (c) Jigsaw, (d) Monsoon Ltd, (3) Oasis Stores Ltd, (f) Whistles.

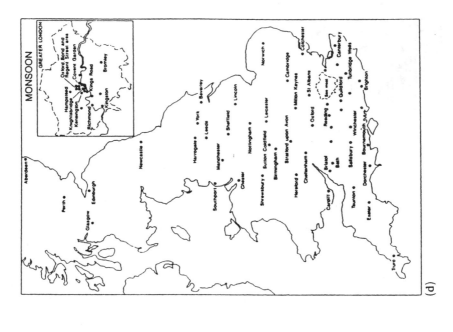

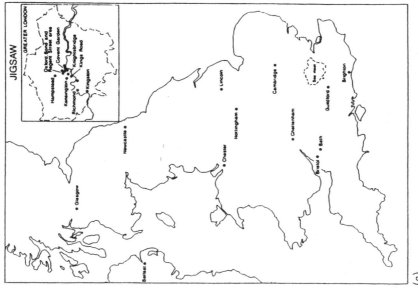

Figure 1 (continued)

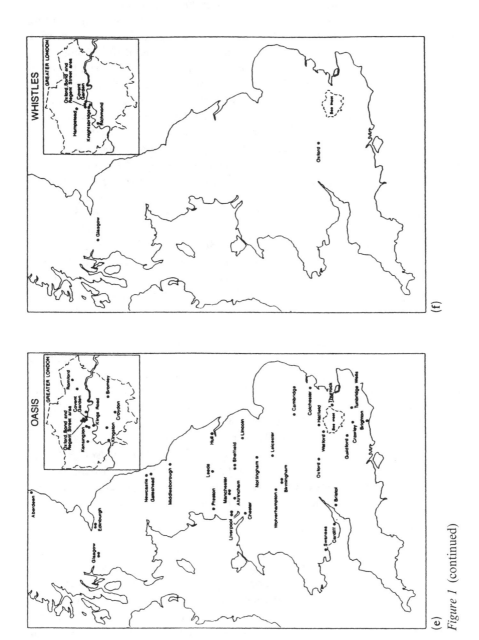

(f)

(e)

Figure 1 (continued)

suggest that on closer examination it is the complex interaction between *sociocultural* issues and their mediation by *political-economic* relations that is central to the site locations identified above. When we look again more closely at the particular locational strategies adopted by our pioneering retailers, we begin to see the interconnections between 'identity', 'image', and economics with some clarity. In the case of Whistles, for example, the company avoids the prime site locations and opts for sites which are 'off the beaten track' within each city.[3] Of course, this also means cheaper rents and rates, and such stores are thus also pioneering in the sense that they are prepared to take risks in their site-selection process and to inhabit formerly undesirable locations which then undergo a process of gentrification. Moreover, where high-street locations have been chosen by such retailers it has been at the right time, that is, when the recession has lowered rental levels. In the case of Monsoon, for example, Managing Director John Spooner comments: "We were not prepared to pay the dizzy rents and premiums of the late 1980s and saw the recession as an opportunity to get the right slots in the high street" (*The Sunday Telegraph* 1993b). There is here, then, clear evidence of an interaction between economics and identity. These connections between retailer image, place image, and economics can be further exemplified through studying the operating strategies of the retailers identified above.

3.4   Restriction of growth

We would argue that the restriction of growth is a key element underlying the contemporary success of our pioneers. Certainly, many of the retailers pointed to above highlight the significance of restricted growth to their commercial success. To expand, Marilyn Anselin at Hobbs does not want Hobbs to turn into a giant clothing chain: "People come from Leeds and Harrogate to our shop in Manchester which proves we are doing it right. You have got to keep it special. Other retailers have reached the saturation point where people no longer find them exciting" (*The Independent* 1990). "If you have a shop in Bath, there is no point opening another in Bristol. Buying your clothes from Hobbs should be a special enough experience to make it worth your while travelling to Bath" (*Fashion Weekly* 1988).

3.5   Rapid response

The companies are also all extremely quick to respond to changing market demands. Whistles, for example, state that they have "A three weeks turnaround in the looks they sell. This does not mean stock is changed every three weeks but that the approach to the stock is. New things are added to keep it looking up to the minute" (*Country Life* 1987). Similarly at Oasis, the Chairman, Michael Bennett, comments "High street fashion is a bit like sailing a boat—to get from A to B you have to keep making slight adjustments according to the wind or tide. We just make these adjustments quickly" (*The Sunday Telegraph* 1993a). Clearly, then, we can only begin to understand the recent successes of such retail specialists by unravelling the complex interactions between store image and location, product design and quality, production flexibility and rapid response, and consumption preferences.

4   Microgeographies of retailing and consumption: the case of Nottingham's Lace Market

In this section we would like to shift the level of analysis to a yet finer scale and to consider microgeographies of consumption, with particular reference to part of one provincial British city, Nottingham, which has been identified above as a city with a distinctive fashion identity, and one in which many of our retail pioneers are located. Here we see how complex geographies of retailing and consumption are apparent, and how one formerly redundant city space has been reimaged and revamped in the last decade, to become an alternative retail arena characterised by an agglomeration of small, predominantly independent, design-oriented fashion outlets whose product offerings and store, product, and staff images appeal to a broad range of consumers who are seeking an alternative to the highly controlled chain-store culture of the conventional retail centre in Nottingham. In this sense, then, the Lace Market area of Nottingham has been both physically restored, organisationally restructured, and culturally redefined. It is to an exploration of both the cultural and the economic processes underpinning such a transformation that we now turn. In so doing we can begin to read landscapes of consumption and identity in different ways and to challenge the dominant ideas regarding class, spatial specificities of retailing, and consumption spaces. As this case study reveals, "there is no imminent danger of a homogenous geography of advanced capitalism despite the efforts of fast-food outlets and developers" (Walker, 1978, footnote 20), and thus the bold generalisations identifying postmodernity with dedifferentiation are too simplistic to apply geographically to the processes defining the landscapes and spaces of consumer society (Clarke, 1991), as this local case study reveals.

For the purposes of this discussion we restrict our analysis of retailing, consumption, and identity to the specialist retail area of Hockley in the Lace Market (for a fuller discussion, see Crewe and Forster, 1993a; Crewe, 1996). The Lace Market is an industrial quarter of Nottingham lying to the east of the city centre and immediately adjacent to the retail core. It has a long history dominated by lace and latterly by garment production. The fashion sector in the Lace Market comprises just over 100 firms involved in fashion, including designers, retailers, and manufacturers, and employs approximately 1300 people. The following discussion is based around a series of in-depth, semistructured interviews with a sample of 78 of these firms. These were then supplemented by discussions with Nottingham City and County Councils, The Fashion Centre, and trade and industry associations. Customised interview schedules were compiled for each group of 'players' within the Lace Market fashion system, and the sampling frame covers the full spectrum of organisations in terms of age, size, product category, and market orientation, ranging from export-oriented international designer–retailers such as Paul Smith Ltd, through to small boutiques which source garments exclusively from local suppliers, to individual designers operating from workshops in the Fashion Centre. As with the examples above, we can look to both the cultural and the economic determinants of the retail space under consideration.

4.1   Design-based production and consumption

Retail provision in the Lace Market comprises a quirky mixture of small student-oriented 'ethnic', 'retrostyle', or rave outlets, including several secondhand boutiques. Alongside are more expensive higher quality designer showroom come stores. The key features of their product ranges are individuality and exclusivity, with ranges being variously described as "design-based", "exclusive and up-market" and even "deadly"! (retailer interviews[4]). All are operating on the basis of design, and are competing on factors other than price. Almost all offer very small batches or even one-offs, and see this exclusivity as one of the major reasons for their success. It is design and difference which characterise such outlets, as one retailer acknowledged, "Our competitive success relies on individuality and design". Certainly, recent consumer surveys in Nottingham (Crewe and Forster, 1993a) revealed that the major complaints about British fashion were first the lack of variety, with consumers consistently suggesting that clothes were too "mass market" with chainstores lacking in flair and adventure. Second, and linked to this, was a common concern that there was insufficient 'affordable' quality. In many cases it was argued that the price for variety was too high and there was a feeling that there was a lack of "middle priced quality": garments were either "exclusive designer wear" or "tacky and cheap". Third, there was a sense in which British fashion did not carry well from the designer to the retail outlet. If designer garments did reach the intended outlets, consumers felt that they were often prohibitively expensive. Clearly, the pioneering retailers above and the agglomeration of designer stores in the Lace Market would both appear to be responding perfectly to current consumption signals.

4.2   Exclusivity and restricted supply

Again, it is the recognition of the importance of exclusivity which accounts in part for the success of the retailers in the Lace Market. To quote Paul Smith, an international designer–retailer of Nottingham origin (see Crewe and Lowe, 1996a for a fuller discussion), "The problem in the UK is that there is just too much of everything. Everything just needs slimming down. The nice, individual, interesting shops have all gone" (Paul Smith, authors' interview, December 1991). This problem of lack of variety in retail provision is particularly apparent in the British case, where almost half of all retail sales go through just five stores (Marks & Spencer, Burtons, Sears, Storehouse, Next). Certainly, there is a sense in which consumers are tiring of their force-fed diet of middle-market chains and are searching for exclusivity. As one consumer told us, "If you do not want to dress like a New York street rapper, casual to the point of sloppiness, or decked out in a tailored 'Next style uniform' you will find it hard to get stylish, unusual, well-made clothes to suit your individuality". Similarly, a recent survey revealed that 68% of customers felt that high street stores were not satisfying their needs (*The Clothes Show Magazine* 1991).

We would argue that the success of retail provision in the Lace Market is in part related to the ability to satisfy this desire for exclusivity and difference. Certainly, the typical consumer profiles identified by retailers in Hockley, which range from "discerning" to "stylish", "people who like something different and do not mind paying. Not fashion victims", would appear to support this argument.

Although five of the retailers interviewed revealed that their customer base is exclusively 'wealthy' people by virtue of the price tags, the remaining outlets offer more affordable ranges and have a broader customer profile including students and design-conscious customers. This latter group of retailers frequently mention the 'exclusivity' element of shopping in Hockley, "People who shop here have a real snobbery. It's just not cool to shop on the high street" (authors' interviews).

4.3 Branding and local labels

Linked to this, a strong sense of identity through branding emerged from survey work with local designers, retailers, and consumers. The majority of small independent retailers in the Lace Market use a mix of own-brand and designer labels. Aside from the big designer labels such as Nicole Farhi, Betty Jackson, and Bruce Oldfield, then, are a variety of more affordable, often locally derived labels such as Pax, Wild, G Force, and Paul Smith. There is a clear recognition of the value consumers place upon identifiable brands. As one retailer quoted, "We carry four big designer street labels. They are as important as the international designer names. Street labels are the designer labels of today" (authors' interview). By sourcing from local designers and suppliers, retailers in the Lace Market may thus be able to retain their reputation for exclusivity through offering rare or unique brands and labels. Also important is the peer and media pressure to 'sport the right label', particularly for the young. As Haug recognises, "branding represents the concentration into one named character of all the aesthetic, visual and verbal communications contained in the styling of the commodity" (1986, page 25). Such stylistic self-consciousness is well served by smaller design-based stores where "articles are on exhibit as much as on sale—these consumption places restore an older ... experience of shopping as looking, strolling seeking new sensory delights" (Zukin, 1991, page 41). Linked to quality and design-based competition is the importance of staging and presentation, both of goods for sale and of salespeople themselves. Customer service is another element in the competitive environment of the 1990s, where discerning consumers are attracted by image and presentation. The small retailers interviewed in the Lace Market are fully aware of the importance of customer care and of the image and style of their employees: "customer care is all-important . . . I try to make the shopping experience as pleasant as possible for the consumer", and "Shop staff training is critical: we turn the tables and make the staff customers for a while" (authors' interviews). Certainly the shopping experience in a store such as Alicia Kite where staff are trained to help customers and where individual attention is offered, including refreshments and style magazines in elegant surroundings, is far removed from the frenzied 'snatch and grab' of the chain stores. In one sense, then, the success of retailing in the Lace Market relies in part on 'indirect commodification' where atmospheres and images (of stores and personnel) are juxtaposed with the commodities for sale in order to enhance the consumptive experience. Certainly, in such an overcrowded marketplace, "imagery has become increasingly critical as a way of attracting particular shops and facilitating acts of consumption" (Crawford, 1992, page 26).

4.4 A space with a unique identity

Hockley is thus very much a space with a unique local identity. The distinguishing feature of the area is the sense of individuality and uniqueness which is far removed from the glitzy, highly controlled, placeless tone of the indoor malls which form the conventional retail core. It is dominated by small independent largely locally based designer stores with, on its fringes, exclusive international boutiques including Paul Smith, Limeys, and Valentina. When asked "why Nottingham?" retailers were quick to point out that Nottingham has a "reputation for fashion". It also has a special and unique identity: "Because there is no Nottingham 'look', unlike, for example, Manchester, it gives designers greater freedom. The Manchester scene may serve to increase the number of designers but it may also act as a straitjacket". In part this is connected to the long historical tradition of clothing in Nottingham, "I feel the Lace Market history and fame gives me a competitive edge". Also important is the international reputation of the fashion design course at Trent University and latterly the support of the Nottingham Fashion Centre, the City and County Council, and a generally supportive local policy environment, keen to preserve and enhance the reputation as 'Nottingham, City of Fashion' (Crewe and Totterdill, 1994a; 1994b). "Nottingham is a brilliant place to work. It's known at all the trade fairs." "Hockley is vital and it's going to become better." "I use the Lace Market logo for PR—it is a prestigious location."

The important point is that the development of the Lace Market as a retail quarter has developed incrementally, and its particular role as an individual retail and cultural space has rather more to do with consumption preferences and property shifts than with some grand vision on the part of urban planners and civic salespeople. Indeed, many retailers and designers felt that they had been rather neglected by local planning agencies: "we chose this area because there were available shops at the time. This is a trendy area now but Hockley was a little bit disowned by the City Council. In nine years they haven't done anything to help Hockley. It's still very distinct and separate." "We came here nine years ago. The Lace Market was an up-and-coming area because of the rents and rates. It's an exciting little area but it was derelict three years before that." In this sense early neglect of this former industrial space may ironically have been one of the mainstays in preserving the individuality and identity of the area. Similarly, "we located here [nine years ago] because the premises were cheap and the workroom was close. When we came to the Lace Market it didn't have an image". In this sense it is a grass-roots reaction by small designers and retailers against both the extortion associated with prime sites and as a backlash against the purpose-built retail monoculture of the malls, capitalising both on lower rental structures and on certain historic and cultural associations.

4.5 Integrated supply chain

Yet the importance of the Lace Market as a new and differentiated retail space relates not only to market orientation and identity through branding but, as with the case of the retail pioneers discussed in section 3, is also bound up with the particular production chain which underpins such retail provision. Again, then, we must look towards the ways in which political-economic relations intertwine with cultural attributes of particular retail spaces if we are to understand the creation of differentiated landscapes of consumption. In this sense we echo Thrift's suggestion that we must understand more clearly "how the process by which context has been commodified can be connected back into economic relations" (1994, page 226). Such aesthetic attributes as store and product image and exclusivity are firmly underpinned in the Lace Market by a system of economic organisation which is rarely found outside certain continental European, and particularly Italian, centres of fashion. What we find here is a production chain (Jackson and Thrift, 1995) where 68% of firms employ fewer than 10 people, where 80% of firms have no minimum order size, and where 75% of firms have a lead time of less than 4 weeks. The advantages in terms of small batch availability, rapid style change, and exclusivity of design are obvious.

Most significantly, production and consumption are spatially and organisationally coincident in the Lace Market with dense local sourcing and supply chains being an important feature. Of all firms in the Lace Market 85% have local sourcing and supply chains, with local networks being important to the functioning of the complex. Similarly 70% of small designer studios also serve a retail function, thereby linking local designers to the marketplace in a very direct way. The result is an intricate web of subcontractual and sourcing arrangements with all elements of the fashion chain being linked through formal and informal alliances. Thus more than half of the local retail outlets source from local designers and producers, who in turn source fabrics, trims, etc from local manufacturers. Many local firms in turn use local designers, many of whom are located in the designer workshops in the Fashion Centre. Local intelligence is a key resource. All designer firms obtain intelligence about suppliers, customers, and sub-contractors "through the local grapevine" by "reputation" and "word of mouth". "It's easy here. Most firms know each other. We only have to go 50 yards for threads, trims, fashion forecasting information!" Issues such as product marketing, design, and distribution become comparatively easy under such circumstances. The value of local networks in streamlining the production–consumption pipeline cannot be underestimated, "our relationship with suppliers is good and involves the personal touch". "Proximity to suppliers is important. Our location in the Lace Market is important to customers, suppliers, and sub-contractors" (authors' interviews). Such linkages reinforce the importance of the local. In this sense, then, we can see clear economic dimensions to the creation of such a retail space. Most importantly, it shows the value of understanding the entire production of the fashion pipeline, from sourcing through design, production, retailing, advertising, marketing, and consumption (for a fuller discussion, see Crewe and Davenport, 1992; Crewe and Forster, 1993a; 1993b; Phizaklea, 1992). Clearly we need to understand the material processes which link together the production of consumption, that is, we need to focus attention on the 'production' dimension of the circuit of culture.

4.6 Mediation of conventional class distinctions

It has been suggested that certain spaces of consumption are associated with certain classes, and the evidence we have produced today would at first sight appear to support this (although see section 5). As Jackson and Thrift (1995, page 207) have argued "There is a symbiotic relationship between this new stage of commodification and particular social groups. Specifically, members of the new middle classes are usually revealed in the narrative as the cheerleaders for new forms of consumerism". We would, however, argue that such correspondence between social group and emergent landscapes of consumption is overstated. Such explanations disregard the importance of the multiplicity of meanings embedded in the consumption practices associated with the Lace Market. Although we would not dispute that certain places are associated with certain social groups or classes, we also think it is important to challenge the simplicity of such polarities, and to interrogate the issue of class cleavages in consumption practices with more rigour. Certainly, what is interesting about the Lace Market is its inability to fit into conventional class-based analyses. Rather than reading the landscape of the Lace Market (and indeed other consumption spaces) as ones identifiable with fairly rigid and class-specific meanings, we prefer to see them as places characterised by a multiplicity of meanings which cross class divisions and coexist at the level of the individual (for a fuller discussion, see Gregson and Crewe, 1994). For some, principally those on limited incomes such as students, there is little doubt that the Lace Market, and particularly secondhand stores such as Wild, provide a chance to buy stylish clothes cheaply. Yet for others the area may be much more of a landscape of curiosity and discovery, a place to search out a 'real find'. The urban cheerleaders described by Jackson and Thrift are thus a diverse group and in this sense we are responding to the criticism which Jackson and Thrift among others level at the broad brush approach to consumption change whereby "it can seem as though what is being constructed is a packaged landscape devoid of any local detail" (1995, page 206).

5 Research agendas: the geographies of consumption

In this paper we have made a preliminary attempt to balance production-centred consensual accounts of consumption change with more critical accounts which recognise that the strategies which shape consumption and identity are multiple and are dependent on political, economic, and cultural processes. In so doing we have tried to demonstrate the various ways in which consumption, identity, place, and accumulation are all inextricably linked, and how the uncovering of these various processes is an essential element in an understanding of contemporary geographical change. As Sack (1988) has argued, it is important to trace the processes of consumption back into the social relations of production. In that sense we are calling for approaches which reintegrate the production element in the circuit of culture (Jackson and Thrift, 1995).

Second, we have begun to address the issue of differentiated landscapes of consumption 'on the ground'. This we feel is an important area of enquiry, yet one which has hitherto largely been ignored. Certainly, the retailers we have studied here are clearly in the business of constructing identities not only in terms of their products but also in terms of the spaces in which they display their goods (where? alongside whom? etc). This relationship between place identities, product identities, and personal identities and the ways in which retailers are appropriating certain spaces and the interrelationship between familiar products and unfamiliar settings is clearly important here and is identified by Knox and others as reinvigorating the shopping experience (Knox, 1991; Crawford, 1992).

Third, and following on from this focus on landscapes of consumption 'on the ground', we acknowledge that the specialised pioneer retailers discussed above are but one 'segment' of a highly fragmented and differentiated retail system. Clearly, other forms of retailing and consumption are equally important in the creation of particular identities of place. Here we would signal the importance of informal spaces of consumption such as the car boot fair (see Gregson and Crewe, 1994), which suggest that "despite the growing homogeneity of international cultural production . . . there are spaces of resistance" (McDowell, 1994, page 166). Also important is the role of discount retailing which is currently the most rapidly growing segment of retailing in the United Kingdom and retail predictions are suggesting that the UK system will follow the North American route where more than 50% of clothing sales are made through discounters and budget chains such as K-Mart and Wal-Mart. Clearly, like our pioneering retailers above, discounters are bucking the recessionary trend. And, like the design-based retailers, the discounters also shy away from prime retail spaces and prefer secondary sites. Clearly, the geographies of consumption and identity which emerge from this apparent polarisation of retailing deserve further research attention.

In conclusion, then, we have here presented the beginnings of an attempt to interrogate the creation of differentiated spaces of consumption and identity with a more critical eye. The project clearly entails both an empirical and a theoretical reworking. The key elements we would identify in terms of shaping future research are as follows. First, there is a need to consider 'the production of consumption' as an integrated circuit which embraces production, retailing, and consumption. The interconnections between these processes are, we argue, difficult to disentangle but of course fascinating to trace. As Lee argues, "What appeared initially as a rather common sense and trivial observation—that commodities are produced by people under particular industrial circumstances—slowly began to assume quite profound dimensions. Why, for example when the commodity arrives in our shops should it show no manifest trace of all the labour that was invested in it during its production?" (1993, page xii). The tracking of such social relations of production has begun to be addressed through, for example, studies into buyer–supplier links in clothing retailing (Crewe and Davenport, 1992), into the 'unpacking' of the global fashion sector (Phizaklea, 1992), and more recently through consideration of labour processes and the employment experience of retailing (see Lowe, 1991; Lowe and Crewe, 1991; 1996). This tracking both backwards into production and forwards into cycles of consumption, use, and reuse is an area which, we suggest, requires further scrutiny.

Second, we have asserted that the confluence of recent economic and sociocultural changes is resulting in the emergence of distinctive new urban spaces. And, like Knox, we suggest that geographers have been slow to come to terms with the emergence and significance of new urban landscapes. As Knox argues, 'We have to contend with new economic and socio-cultural trends . . . changing patterns of economic and cultural differentiation. Most of this has to be mapped out and set within appropriate theoretical frameworks" (1991, page 204). It is to this project that we intend to contribute further.

Third and by way of conclusion, we have emphasised the need to recognise the importance of scales of analysis: global, local, and regional approaches reveal very different landscapes of consumption. And we would argue that, although the global scale is now more accurately understood, the regional and local dimensions of change have been neglected. In particular, it is impossible to 'read off' local impacts from global processes. In this sense we are arguing for a much finer grained approach to the study of consumption and identity. The suggestion, for example, that North America represents a model of consumption centring around malling, theming, merging of retail and leisure and so on, to which others will gravitate, is overstated (see Featherstone, 1993). There is, we would argue, limited evidence to suggest that the internationalisation of retailing and consumption will eliminate differences between places. In this sense we would follow Clarke's argument that there are "important differences between the European and North American consumer societies that require further geographical investigation" (1991, page 25). And this is where we return to our opening argument, that it is vitally important to consider the *specific* interactions between globalising and localising tendencies as they meet and are played out 'on the ground' (see Crewe and Lowe, 1996a; 1996b). This, we argue, would begin to fill some of the currently underinvestigated 'gaps on the map of consumer society'.

Acknowledgements

Versions of this paper were presented at the AAG annual conference in San Francisco and at the History of Design course held by the Victoria and Albert Museum and the Royal College of Art in London. We are grateful to all those who offered comments as well as two anonymous referees and also to the Economic and Social Research Council who in part funded the Lace Market study under award number R000233588, and to the research grants awarded by the University of Nottingham and the University of Southampton Research Fund (award number B200608).

Notes

1. Here we follow Jackson and Thrift (1995) who suggest that "there is a tendency for studies of consumption to be exclusively 'cultural', paying insufficient attention to other parts of the 'circuit of culture' such as the social relations of production".

2. To be fair there have been some recent attempts to move away from this emphasis, particularly by Jackson and Holbrook in their study of Brent Cross and Wood Green shopping centres in north London. See also Crewe (1996) on localisation.

3. London Fashion Library records.

4. All retailer, designer, manufacturer, and consumer interviews in the Lace Market were undertaken during 1992–94.

References

Amin A, Thrift N, 1992, "Neo-Marshallian nodes in global networks" *International Journal of Urban and Regional Research* **16** 571–587

Anderson K, Gale F, 1992 *Cultural Geography: Ways of Seeing* (Longman, Melbourne)

Anselm Y, 1994, "Relative strength" *Drapers Record* **14** May, pp 18–19

Ashworth G, Voogd H, 1990 *Selling the City: Marketing Approaches in Public Sector Urban Planning* (Belhaven, London)

Boyle M, Hughes G, 1991, "The politics of the representation of the 'real' discourses from the Left on Glasgow's rule as European city of culture, 1990" *Area* **23** 217–228

Budd L, Whimster S (Eds), 1992 *Global Finance and Urban Living* (Routledge, London)

Burgess J, 1982, "Selling places: environmental images for the executive" *Regional Studies* **16** 1–17

Burgess J, Wood P, 1988, "Decoding Docklands: place advertising and decision-making strategies of the small firm", in *Qualitative Methods in Human Geography* Eds J Eyles, D Smith (Polity Press, Oxford) pp 1–17

Clarke D, 1991, "Towards a geography of the consumer society", WP-91/3, School of Geography, University of Leeds, Leeds

Corbridge S, Martin R, Thrift N, 1994 *Money, Power and Space* (Basil Blackwell, Oxford)

Corner J, 1994, "Consumption editorial" *Media, Culture and Society* **16** 371–374

Country Life 1987, "Whistling", 5 February

Cox K, 1995 *The Global and the Local: Making the Connections* (Guilford, New York)

Craik J, 1994 *Cultural Studies in Fashion* (Routledge, London)

Crawford M, 1992, "The world in a shopping mall", in *Variations on a Theme Park* Ed. M Zorkin (Hill and Wang, New York) pp 3–30

Crewe L, 1996, "Material culture: embedded firms, organisational networks and the local economic development of a fashion quarter" *Regional Studies* **30**(3) forthcoming

Crewe L, Davenport E, 1992, "The puppet show: buyer supplier relations in clothing retailing" *Transactions of the Institute of British Geographers* **17** 183–197

Crewe L, Forster Z, 1993a, "The role of the small independent retailer in the workings of the fashion system" *Environment and Planning D: Society and Space* **11** 213–229

Crewe L, Forster Z, 1993b, "A Canute policy fighting economics: local economic policy in an industrial district: the case of Nottingham's Lace Market" *Policy and Politics* **21** 275–287

Crewe L, Lowe M, 1996a, "Global products, local processes", in T*he Global and the Local: Making the Connections* Ed. K Cox (Guilford, New York) forthcoming

Crewe L, Lowe M, 1996b, "United colors? Globalisation and localisation tendencies in fashion retailing", in *Retailing, Consumption and Capital* Eds N Wrigley, M Lowe (Longman, Harlow, Essex) forthcoming

Crewe L, Totterdill P, 1994a, "The institutional environment for clothing", final report to Economic and Social Research Council; copy available from the authors

Crewe L, Totterdill, 1994b, "Nottinghamshire fashion", final report to the Economic and Social Research Council; copy available from the authors

Daily Telegraph 1989, "Jigsaw: right pieces, right prices", 27 April

Deakin N, Edwards J, 1993 *The Enterprise Culture and the Inner City* (Routledge, London)

Drapers Record 1987, "Merchandise for all ages", 10 October

Fainstein S, 1994 *The City Builders* (Basil Blackwell, Oxford)
Fainstein S, Gordon I, Harloe M, 1992 *Divided Cities: New York and London in the Contemporary World* (Basil Blackwell, Oxford)
Fashion Weekly 1988, "Hobbs choice", 25 February
Featherstone M, 1993, "Global and local cultures", in *Mapping the Futures: Local Cultures, Global Change* Eds J Bird, B Curtis, T Putnam, G Robertson, L Tickner (Routledge, London) pp 169–187
Geertz C, 1983 *Local Knowledge: Further Essays in Interpretive Anthropology* (Basic Books, New York)
Goodwin M, 1993, "The city as commodity: the contested spaces of urban development", in *Selling Places: The City as Cultural Capital, Past and Present* Eds G Kearns, C Philo (Pergamon, Oxford) pp 145–162
Green T, 1994, "Relative strength" *Drapers Record* **4** May, pp 18–19
Gregson N, Crewe L, 1994, "Beyond the high street and the mall: car boot fairs and the new geographies of consumption in the 1990s" *Area* **26** 261–267
Hall S, Jacques M (Eds), 1989 *New Times: The Changing Face of Politics in the 1980s* (Lawrence and Wishart, London)
Harvey D, 1989, "From managerialism to entrepreneurialism: the transformation of urban governance in late capitalism" *Geografiska Annaler* **71B** 3–17
Haug W, 1986 *Critique of Commodity Aesthetics* (Polity Press, Cambridge)
Independent on Sunday 1990, "Lucille has a ball" 16 December
Jackson P, Holbrook B, 1995, "Multiple meanings: shopping and the cultural politics of identity" *Environment and Planning A* **27** 1913–1930
Jackson P, Thrift N, 1995, "Geographies of consumption", in *Acknowledging Consumption* Ed. D Miller (Routledge, London) forthcoming
Jacobs J, 1984 *The Mall: An Attempted Escape from Everyday Life* (Waveland Press, Prospect Heights, IL)
Jameson F, 1984, "Postmodernism, or the culture logic of late capitalism" *New Left Review* number 146, 53–92
Judd D, Parkinson M (Eds), 1990 *Leadership and Urban Regeneration* (Sage, Beverly Hills, CA)
Kearns G, Philo C, 1993 *Selling Places: The City as Cultural Capital, Past and Present* (Pergamon, Oxford)
King R, 1990, "Architecture, capital and the globalisation of culture" *Theory, Culture and Society* **7** 397–411
Knox P, 1991, "The restless urban landscape: economic and socio-cultural change and the transformation of metropolitan Washington DC" *Annals of the Association of American Geographers* **81** 181–209
Kowinski W, 1985 *The Mailing of America: An Inside Look at the Consumer Paradise* (William Morrow, New York)
Lash S, Urry J, 1994 *Economies of Signs and Spaces* (Sage, Beverly Hills, CA)
Laurier E, 1993, "Tackintosh: Glasgow's supplementary gloss", in *Selling Places: The City as Cultural Capital, Past and Present* Eds G Kearns, C Philo (Pergamon, Oxford) pp 267–290
Lee M, 1993 *Consumer Culture Re-born: The Cultural Politics of Consumption* (Routledge, London)
Lim H, 1993, "Cultural strategies for revitalising the city: a review and evaluation" *Regional Studies* **27**(6) 589–595
Lipietz A, 1993, "The local and the global: regional individuality or interregionalism?" *Transactions of the Institute of British Geographers* **18** 8–18
Lowe M, 1991, "Trading places: retailing and local economic development at Merry Hill, West Midlands" *East Midland Geographer* **14** 31–48

Lowe M, 1993, "Local hero! An examination of the role of the regional entrepreneur in the regeneration of Britain's regions", in *Selling Places: The City as Cultural Capital, Past and Present* Eds G Kearns, C Philo (Pergamon, Oxford) pp 211–230
Lowe M, Crewe L J, 1991, "Lollipop jobs for pin-money" *Area* **23** 344–347
Lowe M, Crewe L J, 1996, "Shop work: image, customer care and the restructuring of retail employment", in *Retailing, Consumption and Capital* Eds N Wrigley, M Lowe (Longman, Harlow, Essex) forthcoming
McDowell L, 1994, "The transformation of cultural geography", in *Human Geography: Society, Space and Social Science* Eds D Gregory, R Martin, G Smith (Macmillan, London) pp 146–173
McRobbie A, 1994 *Postmodernism and Popular Culture* (Routledge, London)
Massey D, 1991, "A global sense of place" *Marxism Today* June, pp 24–29
Mintel, 1993 *Market Intelligence* December, Mintel International Group, 18 Long Lane, London EC1A 9HE
Mort F, 1989, "The politics of consumption", in *New Times: The Changing Face of Politics in the 1980s* Eds S Hall, M Jacques (Lawrence and Wishart, London) pp 160–172
Phizaklea A, 1992 *Unpacking the Fashion Industry* (Routledge, London)
Roger Tym and Partners, 1987, "Greater Manchester Retail Enquiry: proof of evidence", Roger Tym and Partners, 9 Sheffield Street, London WC2A 2EZ
Sack R, 1988, "The consumers world as context" *Annals of the Association of American Geographers* **78** 642–664
Sadler D, 1993, "Place marketing, competitive places and the construction of hegemony in the 1980s", in *Selling Places: The City as Cultural Capital, Past and Present* Eds G Kearns, C Philo (Pergamon, Oxford) pp 175–192
Sassen S, 1991 *The Global City* (Princeton University Press, Princeton, NJ)
Sayer A, Walker R, 1992 *The New Social Economy* (Blackwell, Oxford)
Shields R, 1992 *Lifestyle Shopping: The Subject of Consumption* (Routledge, London)
Sorkin M (Ed.), 1992 *Variations on a Theme Park* (Hill and Wang, New York)
Swyngedouw E, 1992, "The Mammon quest. Globalisation, interspatial competition and the monetary order: the construction of new scales", in *Cities and Regions in the New Europe* Eds M Dunford, G Kafkalas (Belhaven, London) pp 39–67
The Clothes Show Magazine 1991, "The British high street and you", August, pp 40–41 (BBC Publications, London)
The Independent 1990, "From power dressing to ladies frocks", 24 March
The Independent 1991, "Today we are full of the joys of Jigsaw" 3 October
The Sunday Telegraph 1993a, "Monsoon's head storms to £3.6m pay", 30 May
The Sunday Telegraph 1993b, "Oasis in a cold climate", 14 November
The Times 1990, "Making the pieces fit for the high street", 8 May
Thrift N, 1994, "Taking aim at the heart of the region", in *Human Geography: Society, Space and Social Science* Eds D Gregory, R Martin, G Smith (Macmillan, London) pp 200–231
Walker R, 1978, "Two sources of un-even development under capitalism: spatial differentiation and capital mobility" *Review of Radical Political Economics* **10** 28–37
Watson S, 1991, "Gilding the smokestacks: the new symbolic representations of deindustrialised regions" *Environment and Planning D: Society and Space* **9** 59–71
Zukin S, 1988 *Loft Living: Culture and Capital in Urban Change* (Radius, London)
Zukin S, 1991 *Landscapes of Power: From Detroit to Disneyworld* (University of California Press, Berkeley, CA)

10

Rethinking retail capital

Ken Ducatel and Nicholas Blomley

Source: *International Journal of Urban and Regional Research* 14 (1990): 207–227.

I Introduction

This paper derives from a dissatisfaction with the wholly inadequate analysis of retailing and retail change that has characterized the literature. Traditional accounts of retailing and retail change appear to lack a systematic theoretical account of retail capital (Brown, 1987). Similarly, within the 'new' economic geography, it appears that retailing has not received the attention it deserves (Scott and Storper, 1986). This neglect both underplays the substantive importance of retail capital (given, for example, the size of its labour force, and its contribution to GNP in late capitalist economies) and undervalues the importance of retail capital in the valorization process, of vital importance to enlarged capital reproduction. To understand capitalism, we maintain, we need to theorize retailing.

Some theoretically informed considerations of the broader service sector are, however, at last being attempted (Daniels, 1985; Urry, 1987). These have been allied with some work on the retail sector itself (Noyelle, 1987; Bluestone *et al.*, 1981; Benson, 1978; 1979; Agnew, 1979; Wrigley, 1988). Many useful insights have been gained in this research, but these studies seem to illustrate the need for a rigorous theorization both of the service sector (although see Walker, 1985) and retail capital in order to place them in their position as components of contemporary capitalism.

This paper is a first attempt at filling this theoretical gap from a marxist perspective. In so doing we are trying to bring the study of retail capital onto the research agenda. We will argue that retail capital can only be conceived of as a moment of a larger circuit of total capital. Also, it is evident that retail capital has a specific function in this wider circuit. This specificity needs to be highlighted, as does the unique logic and institutional expression of retail capital. The concept of the 'separation in unity' of retail capital is essential to our argument and structures our analysis of both the accumulation of retail capital, and the manner in which retailing restructures in time and space.

This paper is thus the first attempt at what we see as a sustained and unfolding project which seeks to incorporate a recognition of the specificity of retail capital into theoretical accounts of overall capital accumulation. Our energies, in this paper, are focused on unravelling the specificity of retail capital and its often problematic location within a larger productive ensemble. Given space constraints, we are therefore obliged to leave to one side, for the most part, many of the undoubtedly important geographic aspects of retail capitalism and retail restructuring. Similarly, we have not attempted to explore the integration of the spheres of exchange and consumption in any depth. These are areas that we see as part of a continuing research agenda that we hope to address at a later date.

In the following sections, we introduce the marxist concept of the 'circuit of capital' in order to isolate one specific moment of capital, that of commercial capital. Leading on from this, we move towards an examination of the specific form, function and logic of retail capital. By *form*, we mean the specific expression which capital adopts as it moves from one phase of its circuit to another. By *function*, we mean the specific role which each form effects in the overall movement of capital. Each form of capital has its own *logic*, which is not reducible to its function. This logic is the internal rationale for the chronic application of investment capital in a specific form of capital.

In moving from form through function to logic, we proceed from the abstract towards the specific. We maintain that we can only approach the concrete via a procedure of derivation. To focus exclusively on the concrete is to fetishize and to make ideological distinctions (for example, the separability of 'consumption' as a discrete sphere, logically prior to production). Thus:

> When the dialectical method is applied to the study of economic problems, economic phenomena are not viewed separately from each other, as bits and pieces, but in their inner connection as an integrated totality, structured around, and by, a basic predominant mode of production. This totality is analyzed in all its apsects and manifestations, as determined by certain given laws of motion, which relate also to its origins and its inevitable disappearance. These laws of motion . . . are discovered to be nothing but the unfolding of the inner contradictions of that structure, which define its very nature (Mandel, 1977: 18).

II   Circuits of capital

Following Marx, we root our analysis in a consideration of the nature of commodities. Commodities are imbued with value through inputs of productive human labour. This labour value is realized by the owners of the means of production in the act of sale. At this moment, the value form of capital changes from commodity capital into money capital. The transformation of this sum of money into the means of production and labour power (occurring in the sphere of circulation) is necessary for the next phase of commodity production. This phase is complete as soon as the means of production have been converted into commodities whose value exceeds that of their component parts. These commodities must then be thrown back into the sphere of circulation, their value must be realized, this money must be transformed into capital, and so on. Each cycle of capital can be seen of as one circuit of productive capital. Simply put, the process can be defined as below:

$$M - C \quad \overset{L}{\underset{mp}{....P....C' - M' - C}} \quad \overset{L}{\underset{mp}{....P....C' - M' etc...}}$$

```
------------------------------     ------------------------------
        circuit 1                          circuit 2
```

where, M = money capital
C = commodity capital
P = productive capital
L = labour power
mp = means of production

This cycle is dependent on the dual nature of a commodity as having both use value and exchange value. Clearly, at different stages in the circulation of capital, different commodities have either use value or exchange value. In the process of purchase ($M - C$), commodities have use value for the industrial capitalist. Conversely, in the act of realization ($C' - M'$), the reverse applies. The industrial capitalist exchanges a use value for an exchange value.

This larger circuit of capital can be broken down into three distinct forms: money capital, productive capital and commodity capital. In other words, capital changes form as it passes through various phases in its overall circuit. First, we can identify a stage of money capital where a sum of money is converted into a sum of commodities ($M - C$). Secondly, there is a circuit of productive capital at which stage the circulation of capital is interrupted. In other words, capital moves from a sphere of circulation into one of production. Commodities are productively consumed and value created. This is represented by $C ... P ... C'$ (the dots representing the interruption of circulation). Next, we can consider the third stage, commodity capital, wherein commodities valorized in the production process are exchanged for money capital.

It is the basic curse of capitalism that commodities must go through the phase in which they contain – in as yet unrealized form – the surplus-value produced by the working class. In other words, before money capital can return to its original form, swollen by surplus-value, it has to go through the intermediate stage of commodity-value – of value embodied in commodities which still has to pass the acid test by being sold (Mandel, 1981: 18).

This circuit can be considered schematically as $C' - M'$. In this way capital moves from the sphere of circulation into the sphere of production and thence back into circulation again.

Extra value is created in production which will be redeployed within the following circuit of capital. The redeployment of this extra value is vital not only for the continuation of social relations (simple reproduction, characteristic of precapitalism), but for its enlarged reproduction, characteristic of capitalism. If all surplus value were to be consumed in the form of luxury goods, no capitalist accumulation would take place at all. Enlarged reproduction presupposes that part of the surplus value expropriated by the capitalist class is transformed into additional capital and is used to engender new increments of surplus value, leading to a growth of capital. Under capitalism, economic growth is expressed as the accumulation of total capital.

Marx comments that 'it is only in the unity of the three circuits that the continuity of the overall process is realized' (1981: 184). He recognizes, however, that the process of accumulation is not an automatic process. The unity of the circuit of capital can only be a unity 'in so far as each different part of the capital runs in succession through the successive phases of the circuit, can pass over from one phase and one functional form into the other' (1981: 183). Volume II of *Capital* addresses this issue, notably the disjunctures that can occur in the process of the circulation of capital. For example, he notes that

'If $C' - M'$ comes to a halt in the case of one portion [of circulation], for example, if the commodity is unsaleable, then the circuit of this part is interrupted and its replacement by its means of production is not accomplished; the successive parts that emerge from the production process as C' find their change of function barred by their predecessors. If this continues for some time, production is restricted and the whole process is brought to a standstill. Every delay in the succession brings the coexistence into disarray, every delay in one stage causes a greater or lesser delay in the whole circuit (1981: 183).

The circulation of capital, and thus the reproduction of the relations of production is, therefore, not an unproblematic procedure, but one potentially riven with contradictions and tensions.

III   Commercial capital

So far we have identified a series of phases of capital which together make up the totality of capital, as well as the changes of form which take place in the overall production process. From this level of the overall circuit of capital we now move down a level of abstraction to consider the nature of capital which is specific to the sphere of circulation.

An analytically identifiable portion of total capital exists which is specific to the sphere of circulation. Part of total capital always exists as commodities on the market, about to be converted into money. Another portion exists as money, about to be converted into commodities. This, Marx refers to as commercial capital.

What function does commercial capital serve? Marx argues that:

> This money-capital serves its purpose as capital only by attending exclusively to the conversion of commodity capital into money-capital, and it accomplishes this by the continual purchase and sale of commodities. This is its exclusive work (1981: 322).

We can thus conceptualize the internal logic of commercial capital with the circuit $M - C - M'$.

Marx points to the distinctiveness of commercial capital, arguing that it is, of itself, not productive of value. Value can only be created in the act of production. The circulation of commodities thus represents one of the *faux frais* of production, or essentially, an overhead cost. The capital engaged in the transportation of commodities from the place of production to the place of consumption, however, is productive of value. Although the transportation of commodities appears at first sight to be a *faux frais*, Marx held that, in so far as commodities have to be transported before they can be consumed, the value of the commodity is increased. Thus, within merchant capital, the simple trading of commodities represent *faux frais*, but the necessary movement of commodities is productive of value. Commercial capital 'creates neither value nor surplus-value, but promotes only their realization and thereby the actual exchange of commodities' (1909: 331). Thus, if surplus value is realized by the sale of commodities, it is only because that surplus value already existed in them' (1909: 329). This would indicate something of a contradiction. For the continuance of enlarged social reproduction, the realization of the surplus value contained within a produced commodity is a necessary act. However, this is offset by the fact that a proportion of social capital is consequently held continually in the sphere of circulation and cannot, therefore, re-enter as productive capital.

The constant drain on profit rates, represented by as yet unrealized commodities, gives rise to the logical and institutional separation of productive and commercial capital. We expect, in other words, the formation of a functionally separable body of commercial capital engaged in $M - C - M'$ transactions, as opposed merely to $C - M$ conversions. Marx argues that the concentration of exchange within a specific commercial sector generates a number of economies. He argues, first, that as a result of this division of labour the capital devoted to buying and selling (and thus not engaged in directly productive activities) is smaller than it would be if the industrial capitalist were obliged to finance this part of business. Secondly, he argues that the:

> . . . exclusive occupation of the merchant with this business [of buying and selling] enables the producer to convert his commodities more rapidly into money, and permits the commodity-capital itself to pass more quickly through its metamorphosis; than it would in the hands of the producer (1909, 324).

This may be due to the manner in which commercial capital is able to effectively soak up commodities prior to their realization via the development of inventories. Thirdly, one turnover of the merchant's capital may represent not only one turnover of many capitals in one sphere of production, but the turnovers of a number of capitals in different spheres of production. The intensity with which the circulation of capital occurs is a function only of the velocity of production and the rate of consumption. A fourth, less intuitive, manner in which commercial capital contributes to the generation of surplus value, arises from Marx's theory of the equalization of the rate of profit. The effect of this is that the faster the commercial capitalist can sell goods, the smaller the amount of money capital extended in order to move a given value of commodities in a given amount of time. Thus the size of commercial capital declines relative to the of the goods it is servicing, and therefore, relative to total capital. As turnover increases, the general rate of profitability is caused to rise.

For the industrial capitalist, the prolongation of the moment of circulation implies a concentration of capital in a moment at which value is not being realized or produced. However, if the burden can be passed onto a second party:

> . . . instead of the industrial capitalist, the merchant now spends this prolonged time in the process of circulation; instead of the industrial capitalist, the merchant now advances additional capital for the circulation; or what amounts to the same, instead of a large portion of the industrial capital straying off continually into the process of circulation, the capital of the merchant is wholly tied up in it; and instead of the industrial capitalist making a smaller profit, he must yield a portion of his profit wholly to the merchant (Marx, 1909: 343).

The producer gives up some of the responsibility for the realization of commodities to an external agent, and in so doing, relinquishes ownership of a portion of surplus value.

> Thus the capitalist who produces surplus-value, i.e. who extracts unpaid labour directly from the workers and fixes it in commodities, is admittedly the first appropriator of this surplus-value, but he is by no means the

ultimate proprietor. He has to share it afterwards with capitalists who fulfil other functions in social production taken as a whole ... surplus-value is therefore split up into various forms. Its fragments fall to various categories of person, and take on various mutually independent forms (Marx, 1977: 709).

Effectively, if the industrial capitalist acted alone, capital would have to be advanced for the realization of the value of commodity capital which would reduce the rate of profit for industrial capital. If these additional circulation costs are transferred to the shoulders of commercial capital, Marx argues, a reduction in the rate of profit occurs, but not to the same degree.

Marx then goes on to consider the question of the circulation costs that commercial capital has to bear. For example, he deals with the issue of the commercial wage worker, arguing that although in some regards similar to the wage worker employed in production (for example, wages being determined by the costs of the production and reproduction of labour, not by the product of labour) it cannot be the case that the commercial labourer is directly productive of surplus value (Walker, 1985). The commercial labourer 'adds to the income of the capitalist not by creating any direct surplus-value, but by helping him to reduce the costs of the realization of surplus-value' (Marx, 1909: 354). Expenditure on commercial labour thus seems another necessary evil. This expenditure serves to reduce the rate of profit given an increase in advanced capital with no commensurate increase in surplus value.

Thus, to summarize, Marx argues that commercial capital must be seen as both part of capital in general, seeking enlarged accumulation, and as an analytically separate moment of that larger unity. In the first regard, we can see commercial capital as serving a necessary function in the realization of the surplus value created in the act of production, an act which, were it not to occur, would disallow enlarged reproduction. Secondly, Marx argues that we need to see commercial capital as distinct in form and function given its expression first, as concerned solely with the exchange values of commodities, not their use values, secondly, as nonproductive of value, and thirdly, as completing the process of the conversion of commodities into money capital in the hands of an agent other than the industrial capitalist. In other words, a division of labour develops.

IV Retail capital

Our task now is to understand retailing in marxist terms, recognizing the 'indissoluble unity between the production of value and surplus-value on the one hand, and the circulation of commodities, the realization of value, on the other' (Mandel, 1981: 15–16). Unfortunately, Marx barely comments upon retailing in itself. However, his conception of circuits of capital indicates the path analysis must follow.

So far, we have moved from the identification of a circuit of total capital, which has its own form and function, to isolate one specific form of capital, which has the function of exchange within the wider circuit. From this we are now able, at a lower level of abstraction, to define the form, function and logic of a specific subform of commercial capital – retail capital. By way of definition, the form of retail capital is that part of total social capital which is located between productive capital and the final consumer. From this statement of form, it follows that the distinctive function of retail capital, within the wider circuit of capital, is the final exchange of commodities. The implication of this is that there are at least two quite different types of consumption. One of these is undertaken solely to further the accumulation of capital. In such transactions the purpose of the exchange is not to consume the commodity in itself but as part of the process of production. Retail capital, however, relates to the other type of consumption, that being consumption necessary to the maintenance of the private sphere of reproduction. For the purposes of this introductory paper, we assume that the logic of retail capital is the same as that of commercial capital. In other words, 'the purpose of commerce is not consumption, directly, but the gaining of money, of exchange value . . . In his exchange, the merchant is guided merely by the difference between the purchase and sale of commodities' (Marx 1973: 149). Clearly, some actions of retail capital may create value (for example, the transportation of goods). However, we would argue that the dominant logic of retail capital is that of exchange.

We will now consider the form of retail capital in more detail by considering, first, its interface with both production and consumption, and secondly, the way in which structural contradictions in capitalism are expressed through and mediated by retail capital.

First, we shall consider the relation between productive capital and commercial capital, of which retailing is one expression. The process is one whereby commodities imbued with surplus value are purchased by commercial capital and then reconverted into money capital on resale. Both commercial and productive capital are concerned not with the final consumption of these products (with the use value) but with their value in so far as they embody and preserve the exchange value. The profit for the commercial capital is expressed in the difference between M and M'. For the industrial capitalist, the profit is expressed as the difference between C and C'. However, each form of capital seeks, as part of its internal logic, to retain the largest share possible of the surplus value created in production. The anarchy of capitalist economic relations raises the contradiction that although each form of capital is functionally related, it must at the same time compete for its own share of the total social capital. Thus, as we shall argue below, the historical structures of the industries producing finished goods for consumer markets will be reflected in and upon the development of retail capital and its structure. Individual capitals on both side of the productive commercial divide will be locked into a system of contracts and negotiations. Hence, whilst retail capital and productive capital are dependent upon each other for their existence, the point of contact between these forms will be a potentially abrasive one in which retail capital will be inevitably implicated.

Secondly, we should consider the relation between commercial capital and the sphere of consumption. As noted above, when consumer and retailer meet, they do so for profoundly different reasons. The former seeks use value, the latter seeks to maximize exchange value. This indicates the potential for conflict and the negotiation of that conflict between retail capital and consumers in general. Clearly, such conflict can not be reduced to questions of price (and 'fair price') although that is clearly of relevance. It would imply that we need to consider the broader question of the social meaning of consumption for the consumer, and mediation by the retailer. Is demand being met, or created by retail capital in so far as it can be expressed as a commodity with exchange value? Is the arena as the disputation of relations of final exchange defined in terms of the priorities of retail capital, or by consumption needs? The savage irony of overstocked shelves in a city where the poor go hungry, or the congregation of the unemployed in those temples of consumption, the shopping mall, are cases in point.

Thus, retail capital is part of a larger circuit of capital, relating both to production and consumption. However, a marxist analysis also alerts us to other issues. The great power of Marx's analysis lies in its dynamism. Hence, we may consider the manner in which the capitalist mode of production and retail changes over time. Change, qualitative and quantitative, is inherently related to the inner contradictions of capitalism. If retail capital is, as we have argued, part of a larger entity, we should expect that broader systemic contradictions are being expressed within it, and that these contradictions are themselves functionally reshaping its specific historic expression.

Thus, the contradictions that Marx isolates within the process of production are clearly of importance in understanding restructuring given the relation between commercial capital and the surplus value generated within the productive sphere. Thus, the continual pressure to depress real wages and to increase the exploitation of productive wage labour given competitive pressure is of potential importance. We might expect that as capitalism staggers from one crisis to another, the degree to which this occurs will be intensified. Clearly this suppression of wages is beneficial both for individual capitalists, and, at first sight, for productive capital in general. However, the essential unity of consumption and production indicates that this can clearly have profound consequences for the realization of this extra surplus value given that less money capital will be available to consumers to bring to the market. Thus, Mandel points to the fact that 'the laws of motion of capitalism have the inherent tendency to develop the capacity of production (including the production of consumer goods) beyond the limits within which the mode of production confines the purchasing power of those condemned to sell their labour power' (1981: 32). Thus, 'to the extent that the productive power develops, it finds itself at variance with the narrow basis on which this condition of consumption rests' (Marx, 1981: 287). For the retailer, a crisis of this order is of serious import in that, any decline in the stock of money capital in the hands of consumers will endanger the very basis of commercial profits, given the need for the conversion of commodity capital into money capital.

Marx also isolates contradictions that are rooted less in production and more in circulation and consumption, specifically the problem of the realization of the value bound up in commodities. The issue is not one of 'overproduction', or of 'underconsumption', but reflects the dialectical relation of the two spheres of consumption and production. As Marx comments, the tension lies in the 'inner necessity of moments which belong together, and their indifferent, independent existence towards one another' (1973: 415). If the circuit of capital is to proceed, and social reproduction to continue, it is imperative that the surplus value locked up within commodities is realized. This can only occur in the act of exchange, when money capital is exchanged for commodity capital. Any disjunctures in that process are clearly of fundamental importance not only for commercial (and retail) capital, and for industrial capital, but also for the entire process of enlarged social reproduction. The severity of the crisis will be in part a function of the extent to which commercial capital is able to accommodate the effective overproduction.

Realization crises can be rooted in a number of factors. One is the volatility and the unpredictability of the consumptive sector. Unless we accord retail capital unlimited power in the definition of the consumptive agenda, it has to be recognized that the consumptive process is far from predictable. The body of consumers is clearly a dynamic one, accepting certain commodities as having a use value, others as not. Shopping is a social act, having meaning within the realm of privatized reproduction in and of itself. Certainly, it is an act of exchange; that is, it is essential to the realization of value in commodity production. The ultimate quantitative limit to this exchange is determined by the level of wages. However, the qualitative characteristics of retail exchange, located as it is between the sphere of privatized reproduction and the economic realms of production and circulation, are specifically problematic. Although the body of 'consumer demand' is clearly not an autonomous one, effectively setting the productive agenda, it is clear that it may, at any given time, seek differing commodities for different reasons. Mandel comments that 'the one freedom which cannot normally be taken away is the freedom to spend their wages as they wish – and there is no way in which it can be forecast with complete accuracy how they will do this' (1981: 32). However, as we have noted, the retailer and the consumer come to the market with a different purpose in mind. The retailer is engaged in the accumulation of capital, through engaging in repeated acts of exchange. The consumer only takes part in exchange in order to realize use value. However, the definition of that use value is determined by the commodities (i.e., use values and exchange values bound up together) which the retailer is seeking to convert into money capital. The implication of this is that only those use values which can be given an exchange value will be satisfied through the market. The central problem of realization for retailers, therefore, is to at least commodify the use values of consumers, or to invoke or encourage use values which they can approximate through the commodities in which they trade. Bourdieu's (1984) comments on the complex dialectic of supply and demand are informative. He argues that the consumption-retail nexus

> . . . is neither the simple effect of production imposing itself on consumption nor the effect of a conscious endeavour to serve the consumers' needs, but the result of the objective orchestration of two independent logics, that of the fields of production and the field of consumption . . . the tastes actually realized depend on the state of the system of goods offered; every change in the system of goods induces a change in tastes. But conversely, every change in tastes . . . will tend to induce . . . a transformation of the field of production (230–31).

The second issue of importance is situated in the capitalistic drive to extend consumption. In this regard, Marx's citation of a governmental report of 1879 is of interest in that it addresses the necessity of the fostering of effective consumer demand, that is the creation of a consumptive (and thus, productive) society:

> The working people have not kept up in culture with the growth of invention, and they have had things showered on them which they do not know how to use, and thus make no market for. There is no reason why the working man should not desire as many comforts as the minister, lawyer and doctor who is earning as much as himself . . . The problem remains, how to raise him as a consumer by rational and healthful processes, not an easy one as his ambition does not go beyond a diminution of his hours of labour, the demagogues rather inciting him to this than raising his condition by the improvement of his moral and mental powers' (1981: 591).

The prescription seems to be one of self-improvement through consumption. Mass consumption cannot be guaranteed, but must be engendered as a beneficial and even necessary social activity. To the extent that consumption is engendered, retail capital will clearly benefit.

So far, we have considered the form that retail capital takes, and the consequences of its linkages with phases of capitalist reproduction. We now intend to move down a step, and consider the institutional appearance of retail firms, and the internal consequences of this specific manifestation. At this point, we can at last bring into focus individual retailers, and make some sense of their historically specific character and subsequent transformations. Retail capital manifests itself as a number of competing retail firms. This expression needs to be understood in the light of the historical development of the retail capitalist in response to a number of factors.

Competition between retailers can be understood, at one level, as a struggle for a share of consumer expenditure, which at any one time is fixed by the total money capital attributable to wage labour and the bourgeois's consumption (which is subtracted from surplus value). At this level, the retail capitalists best able to approximate to the consumers' use value with the commodities in which they trade will gain a competitive advantage. The manner in which this occurs is, of course, complex. We shall consider this in a little more detail in later sections. Of course, this competitive advantage will only suit the logic of retail capital in so far as it contributes to the accumulation process. Ultimately, retailers (as with all capitalistic institutions) are engaged in a struggle for a share of that proportion of realized surplus value which is available to capitalists as investment capital. The apportionment of this investment capital is the basis for Marx's concept of a general rate of profitability. As was noted above, a faster turnover of commercial capital leads to a higher general rate of profit. However, the profit on each item sold falls. Paradoxically, therefore, a retailer's efforts to acumulate more than a competitor by increasing turnover, will eventually lead to a decline in the amount of profit realized from a given volume of goods. Thus the reality for retailers is that 'the merchant's profit is determined not by the mass of commodity capital he turns over, but rather by the amount of money capital he advanced to mediate this turnover' (Marx, 1981: 426).

Both types of competition are part of a basic contradiction of capitalist production. There is insufficient money capital to realize the total social product. That is, the total exchange value of the commodities produced is greater than the money capital available to realize it. So, as there are many individual capitalists, the competition for a share of finite money capital becomes a necessary part of accumulation. Within the total body of capitalists, of course, retail capitalists not only vie with other types of capital, but also with each other.

This internecine struggle between retail capitalists is of relevance in understanding a number of questions. One important issue involves the costs of circulation; the expenditure of money capital on essentially nonproductive but necessary fixed and variable capital within the sphere of circulation. Marx draws the analogy between the capital invested in circulation and that invested in fixed machinery. Thus, 'it is the same as if a part of the product was transformed into a machine that bought and sold the remaining part of the product. This machine makes a deduction from the product' (1981: 211). To the extent that this investment is nonproductive for the larger sphere of capital, and to the extent that it is drawn from the profits of the commercial capitalist, we should expect that there will be a drive towards a reduction of both fixed and variable capital investment costs. This, we might expect, may be intensified as the contradictions apparent within production and consumption become acute.

To summarize the main points of the argument so far:

1) At the highest level of abstraction, we can conceive of a circuit of total capital, composed of three forms of capital (money, commodity and productive capital). As capital moves through the circuit, it flows in and out of the spheres of production and circulation.
2) Each of these three forms has a specific function in the overall circuit of capital. Commercial capital describes the circuit of the exchange of money capital and commodity capital in the sphere of circulation, and has as its function the realization of the surplus value created in production, rather than the creation of value.
3) However, the specific logic of commercial capital is 'exchange for exchange's sake', in the process of accumulation of capital.
4) We can identify retail capital as a subform of commercial capital located between production and final consumption. In the final act of exchange, it has as its function the realization of the surplus value locked up in consumer commodities. Its primary logic is that of the accumulation of capital through exchange.
5) We need to be aware of the dynamic manner in which retail capital relates to other sectors (production and consumption) and any tensions that may result need to be explored.
6) In that retail capital is part of a larger circuit, we need to be aware of the manner in which the imperatives and contradictions inherent in the larger economic formation are expressed in and mediated by retail capital.
7) We also need to be concerned with the manner in which retail capital is expressed institutionally, as a number of competing firms. This competition for investment capital has a number of implications, including the attempted suppression of circulation costs.

V Retail restructuring

We have thus tried to place retail capital within a larger circuit of total capital. By adopting this conception, we attain a heightened awareness of the manner in which, first, the retail function is of relevance to this larger circuit, and secondly, the specific expression and motion of the larger circuit can have consequences for retail capital. Having said that, we need to be aware of the specificity of form, function and logic of retail capital, and the implications that this has not only for retail capital of itself, but also for the transformation of the larger social formation.

In this concluding section, we intend to briefly indicate the insights which a marxist theorization of retail capital yields. We intend to use the theoretical insights developed above to begin to bridge the gap between the abstract and the concrete by commenting on a number of historically specific expressions of retail capital. The three areas that we wish to comment on are, in turn, the marked concentration of retail capital over the last 40 years; the associated shift in power at the productive-commercial interface to the advantage of retail capital; and the attempt by retail capital to reduce circulation costs, itself an act with implications beyond that of retail capital itself. Clearly, we cannot follow through the full ramifications of this approach in the space of this paper. However, it is our contention that the perspective offered in this paper offers a basis for exciting and valuable analysis of the form and restructuring of the retail industry.

1   *The concentration of retail capital*

A key feature of both US and UK retail capital change since the second world war has been its increasing concentration. The twin faces of this concentration are the growth in market share attributable to the largest retailers and the local market concentration of retail outlets which, hand in glove, has accompanied this market concentration. In the USA, the five largest grocery chains attained combined sales of US $66 million by 1985, representing 23.5% of total grocery expenditure. This represented an increase of 1.5% over 1983 sales. Spatially, this concentration seems even more remarkable, given the phenomenon of local market concentration (Marion *et al.*, 1979). For the UK, concentration has been even more marked. For example, the market share of grocery multiples has increased from 59.2% in 1978, to 66.8% by 1983 (EUI, 1984). In 1980, there were 116 large gorcery retailers with a total turnover of £13 206 million. By 1982, the number of such outlets had fallen to 113, but turnover had increased by 26.5% to £16 703 million (Norkett, 1985).

We can make sense of such market share growth in terms not only of the tendential logic of all forms of capital towards centralization and concentration, but with reference to the specificity of retail capital. For retail capitalists, accumulation is constrained on the one hand by the surplus value already within production, and on the other, by the spending power of the mass of wage labourers and their families, which at any one time is fixed by the production process.

Historically, the first path toward concentration of retail capital has been its dynamic insurgence into areas of retailing which were traditionally dominated by petit bourgeois exchange relations. Petit bourgeois exchange stands at some distance from capitalistic exchange in that exchange does not necessarily occur for exchange's sake. The process of capital concentration in this instance has been fortified by the ability of larger retail capitalists to appropriate, from industrial capital, more of the surplus value in commodities through an enlarged market share. This issue, that of the struggle between sectors of capital, is taken up below. As they grow, retail capitalists gain further competitive strength through economies of scale in their operations, which do not accrue to management-intensive petty bourgeois retailers. Thus, retail capital has penetrated and restructured this sphere, driving out independent retailers through strategies such as direct price and quality competition, and through the ability to develop large stores in prime sites which operate at a higher turnover and require a larger staff than small-scale, owner-operator retailers can support.

Capitalism's usurpation of petit bourgeois retailing has proceeded both by the transmogrification of petit bourgeois firms into capitalist firms, and by the establishment of wholly new firms. This process has gone through several stages, first by the creation of localized chains of small stores (perhaps spread across a metropolitan system) and then through the merger and acquisition of these groupings of independent retail multiples into the regional and, in the UK, national retail capital groupings. For example, in the UK there has been a 7% decline in the number of small retail multiples between 1980 and 1983 (Euromonitor, 1984/85). In the USA, there has been a decline in the number of single-unit retail firms (falling from 87.8% of total units in 1954 to 78.4% in 1982). More importantly, market share for this sector has fallen from 69% to 45% over the same period. For those firms with more than 101 establishments, however the market share has increased from 12% to 30% between 1948 and 1982 (*US Retail Census*, 1948–82).

The extent of concentration now achieved by major retailers implies that capital has extended into the final consumption exchange relation as far as is presently possible. Given retail capital's limited ability to create value, further accumulation strategies have included both an extension of operations into new spatial arenas, and diversification into the retail of relatively underdeveloped product fields, such as home improvements. Below we discuss two further accumulation strategies which retailers seem to have been pursuing over the longer term: pressuring productive capital for a larger share of surplus value, and seeking generalized reductions in the costs of circulation.

2 The productive-commercial capital interface

We have theorized retail capital as located within a larger unity of capital. The points of contact between retail capital and other linked spheres were seen as necessary, yet potentially contradictory. This contradiction results from the coming together of the different logics which predominate in each sphere. The way in which these contradictions are resolved, or displaced, helps explain the dynamic restructuring of retail institutional form and, to some extent, the wider transformation of production and consumption.

Thus, we can consider the dynamic manner in which retail capitalists relate to those who produce the commodities which are realized in the sphere of exchange. One important dimension to this has been the steady rationalization of the institutional organization of the physical distribution process. In the UK, commodity distribution has traditionally been transacted through brokers and warehousemen, who were located between producers and retailers. Since the second world war, retailers have taken over distribution, eliminating these intermediaries (Stacey and Wilson, 1965).

This process of backward integration is bound up with the increased concentration of retail capital. As large retail capitals have increased in size, they have become better able to control delivery schedules to their stores, and overall inventory levels by centralizing the distribution function. The centralization of distribution means that they then can deal with producers and importers of commodities directly, rather than through intermediaries.

Individual retail firms now account for large proportions of some producer's total output. This has restructured the power relations that exist between productive and retail capital to the latter's benefit. For example, in the 1950s and early 1960s producers were able to institute and maintain retail price maintenance in their favour. Since then, the rise of the large-scale retail company has shifted this balance, as shown by such institutions as discriminatory discounts. It has been noted, for example, that if neither the top two UK grocery retailers, Sainsbury and Tesco, take a new product, the manufacturer may as well not bother marketing it (Randall, 1985). The growth of 'own-label' retail products has strengthened the bargaining power of those retailers who have adopted it (53% of Sainsbury's packaged goods, for example, were own label in 1983: Euromonitor, 1984/85) by effectively erasing the identity of the producer from the market. Under these new power relations, the co-operation that the producer gives the retailer 'is the co-operation the rabbit gives the stoat' (Randall, 1985: 77; see also Fannin, 1987).

We need to think of this restructuring in terms of the specific logics of both retail and productive capital. Both institutional types of capital share total surplus value, and will thus be in constant conflict for the lion's share. The growth in concentration of retail capital was at first beneficial to productive capital in that it increased the turnover of capital, as outlined above. Ultimately, this very concentration within retail capital has proved problematic for productive capital given the shift in power relations. Simply put, monopsony has restricted the number of avenues available for the realization of many commodities. This has given retailers a better position in bargaining for a greater share of surplus value, and in the determination of the commodities that will be presented to the consumer.

The implications of this development are of profound but often undervalued importance to urban and regional research. Concentrated retail capital is increasingly playing a determinate role in setting the agenda for productive capital. In many cases, it supplies the technical criteria for the production of commodities, defining the production batch sized and the profit margins under which productive capital must operate. In some cases, it even interferes with the nature of the labour process within individual factories and plants, through the stick and carrot of, respectively, sanctions against non-compliant suppliers, and investment support of new technology and management training. FitzSimmons (1983), for example, illustates the impact of increased concentration within the US grocery retail industry upon fresh produce production, to the point where by the mid-1970s, two firms controlled the production and marketing of more than 60% of the head lettuce sold in the USA. This concentration in production resulted from the privileged position that these firms enjoyed *vis-à-vis* retail capital. This restructuring of the productive/retail interface has led some producers to attempt to side-step the larger retail firms, and engage in the final sale of their own products themselves. The case of the apparel producer and retailer Benneton, is a case in point (Pitman, 1987; see also Gibbs, 1988; Rainnie, 1984).

3   *The reduction of circulation costs*

A key feature of the transformation of the retail industry has been that of the attempted reduction in circulation costs, by which we mean all those overhead costs associated with the final exchange function. These economies of operation are an instrument by which retail capitals have sought to protect themselves from competition in a sector which continues to exhibit low barriers to entry.

The first example of the process by which circulation costs have been reduced is that of the steady dismantling of a relatively skilled, male-dominated labour force, and its subsequent replacement by a low-skilled, lowly paid, feminized work force, coupled with the increasing use of part-time and juvenile labour. In the USA, for example, the percentage of women employees in overall retail employment has risen from 43% in 1961 to 52% in 1987. Average weekly hours worked have dropped from 39 in 1948 to 29 in 1986. Real hourly earnings, whilst rising through the 1960s and 1970s, declined during the early 1980s (*Employment and Earnings*, 1948–1986).

Given that the circulation costs incurred in capital do not contribute to the production of value, we should expect retail capitalists to reduce them as far as is possible. They do this in order to retain as large a share of the surplus value (which would otherwise be lost to the retail labour force or tied up in fixed capital) as they can. As far as productive capitalists are concerned, commercial capital is merely a cost. Any reduction in circulation costs will increase the surplus value available for reinvestment in the production process. Because of the nonproductive nature of retail capital, retail labour does not create value. This means that there is no immanent limit to the reduction of labour costs within retailing, as there is in production.

A second strand in the strategic reduction of circulation costs is seen in the new geography of store locations, with an increased centralization of provision, thus obliging consumers to undertake more of the work of exchange and consumption (Preteceille and Terrail, 1985). The deskilling of the grocery trade's labour force was aided in the postwar period (prewar in the

USA) by the process by which new stores increasingly became self-service, subsequently supermarkets, and lately superstores and hypermarkets. Thus, in the postwar period, a major fixed capital investment strategy for the retail trade has been the development of larger stores. Although representing a considerable capital outlay, such units have allowed retailers to address larger geographic markets as well as directly reducing a number of circulation costs. Between 1973 and 1986, for example, Tesco, the UK grocery chain, reduced the number of its outlets from 772 to 395, whilst increasing average selling space from 5100 square feet to 19 000 square feet (*Tesco Company Reports*, 1973–86). Size garners a number of efficiencies. Stock turnover can be increased (in Tesco's case from 8.8 to 17.6 between 1980 and 1986). The adoption of more efficient distribution systems can be adopted, including the use of just-in-time deliveries and direct deliveries from company warehouses. For example, the US chain, Montgomery Ward, rationalized its distribution system by reducing 150 distribution centres to 43. This led to a 24% increase in handling efficiency (Chain Store Age, 1984). Closely allied to this has been the investment in a variety of technologies, such as the use of laser scanning, computer-assisted stock control and personnel deployment, EFTPOS and remote shopping. In the UK, the ratio of net book value of plant assets (£000s) to total number of employees has increased from 3.9 to 8.5 between 1980 and 1986 for the top 12 grocery retailers (Ducatel, 1987).

As we noted above, the centralization of retail facilities requires a renegotiation of the work of consumption between retailers and consumers. In the power relation between retailers and consumers, the consumer undertakes more of the work of exchange in return for the lower costs and wide range of goods which the costs structures and sheer size of larger stores can accommodate. It is not surprising to reflect, therefore, that a correlate in the success story of supermarkets was the diffusion of automobile ownership across the class structure.

However, there is a second dimension to the negotiation of the consumptive/retail nexus which is also explicitly geographic. One important (and again, historically specific) characteristic of this relation is that, overwhelmingly, it is worked out in the privatized space of the retail store. This point has already been implied in preceding sections. This gives retail capital considerable leverage when it comes to defining the consumption process. Thus, it seems clear that the manner in which store organization and layout is constructed is clearly of importance in shaping the extent and intensity of purchasing activity by the consumer. Indeed, there is considerable evidence that retail capital has simultaneously become increasingly concerned with, and sophisticated in, the premediatated configuration of retail space in an attempt to induce consumption (Blomley, 1988). The skilful use of lighting and directed flooring, for example, can be used to direct consumer traffic towards as large a number of items as possible (Novak, 1977). One example is that of the recent remodelling of the Massachussetts-based 'Big Y' chain during the period 1985–87 (Chain Store Age, 1987). Recognizing that, in the past, 'Big Y stores had been designed as an architectural showplace instead of a selling machine' (p. 76), the designer broke with conventional 'grid-iron' walkway designs, and instead attempted to lure the potential consumer through the entire complex by placing 'items of control' (e.g., bakery and meat counters) at strategic points in the store. 'The philosophy of placement is to keep presenting another exciting department wherever you can to keep the customer in the store a little longer' (p. 77). Confidence in these techniques is high. One design analyst comments that, through a variety of techniques, 'we can control the customer both emotionally and psychologically' (Chain Store Age, 1985).

The rationale behind these strategies seems to be that by exposing the consumer to as many commodities as possible, the chances are increased that consumers will spend more of the limited funds available to them in any given store at one time, as opposed to in a competitor's store or at a later date. This is another way in which retailers compete for the finite amount of money capital. Clearly, the example given above is part of this process. We should note, however, that these strategies (given the specificities of the retail-consumer relation) are not unproblematic. Thus, there seems an increasing recognition (at least within the USA) of the dangers of product exposure, especially that of stock pilferage, associated with such store configurations. Thus, although attempting to configure retail space so as to ensure maximal product exposure, US retailers are also keen to cut the estimated US $30 billion annual 'shrinkage' bill. Again, however, spatial configuration and store design can be used to extend the control of the retailer of the use of the space within the unit itself. To give one example, the high end US specialty store, Neiman-Marcus, uses a device called a Trojan Horse, an eight foot high tall pillar covered with smoke two-way mirror glass. From inside this portable device, security personnel can watch customers unobserved (Groves, 1988).

VI   Concluding comments

This paper has been a first attempt at what is undoubtedly a complex task. We have tried to lay the groundwork for a more detailed theoretically informed analysis of retail capital. Any such analysis, we contend, should have at its centre the concept of 'separation in unity'. That is, retail capital is part of a larger circuit of capital and value realization, yet also driven by a unique logic. Not only is this is a necessary first step in developing an understanding of the transformation of retail capital, but it is also instructive in making sense of the motion of other spheres of capital.

In this paper we have argued that retail capital is a subform of commercial capital which itself plays a crucial role in accumulation by facilitating the realization of the value locked up in commodities. A division of labour between commercial and productive capital aids accumulation by disarticulating the rate of reinvestment in production from the rate of consumption of finished commodities. In mass-consumer society, therefore, retail capital plays an important role in ensuring continuous enlarged reproduction.

The primary characteristic of commercial capital, according to Marx, is 'exchange for exchange's sake'. It adds nothing to the value of a commodity. Retail capital is also predominantly unproductive. Thus, in order to accumulate capital retail capital must partake of the surplus value already in the commodities which represent its stock in trade. Thus, the conflict between final producers and retailers is likely to be crosscut by conflict over the distribution of surplus value. We would argue, furthermore, that the concentration of retail capital in recent years, has swung the balance of power in favour of large retail capitals to such an extent that major retail firms are now strong arbiters of the terrains of production, work *and* consumption (Scott and Storper, 1986).

The unique location of retail capital, between production and consumption, at the very edge of the economic sphere's boundary with the private sphere, also means that its struggles with productive capital will be mirrored in its relations with consumers. Retailing, however, is an inherently geographical phenomenon. Its major institutional changes are related to the employment of technology in the resolution of the historical difficulty of addressing markets which are spatially dispersed in order to expand accumulation or to reduce the costs of circulation (Ducatel, 1987).

We have tried to demonstrate the utility of this perspective by exploring a number of examples from the USA and the UK. Clearly, there is a great potential for much exciting and insightful work. For example, the spatial expression and manifestation of retail restructuring (which we have only touched on) can usefully be investigated from a marxist perspective. The vital role of distance and transport costs in the development of specific institutional forms of retail capital, the manner in which retail capital actively explores and penetrates specific spaces at a number of scales, and the way in which retailers manipulate spatial layout and design are cases in point. Finally, the processes outlined above do not occur in some Olympian sphere, but are mediated by real people, rooted in time and space. A theoretically informed examination of the historical development of retail capital would be useful not only in understanding retailing in itself, but also as part of the unravelling of the complex relations between production, consumption and the spatiality of society.

Two points in conclusion. First, we feel that retail capital, and its transformation, is a vital and relevant topic for research and demands urgent attention. Secondly, however, we feel that this analysis must occur in a rigorous manner. The marxist perspective outlined in this paper, we contend, provides the only adequate framework.

Acknowledgements

The authors gratefully acknowledge the comments of Sophie Bowlby, Susan Christopherson, Peter Daniels, Margaret FitzSimmons, Peter Garside, Allen Scott, Michael Storer and Nigel Thrift. They should in no way be held responsible for the arguments made in this paper.

VII References

Agnew, J. 1979: The threshold of exchange: speculations on the market. *Radical History Review* 21, 99–118.

Benson, S.P. 1978: The clerking sisterhood: rationalization and the work culture of saleswomen in American department stores, 1890–1960. *Radical America* 12(2), 41–55.

  1979: Palace of consumption and machine for selling: the American department store, 1880–1940. *Radical History Review* 21, 199–221.

Blomley, N.K. 1988: *Consumption space; production space.* Unpublished paper, Department of Geography, Boston University.

Bluestone, B., Hanna, P., Kuhn, S. and Moore, L. 1981: *The retail revolution.* Boston MA, Auburn House

Bourdieu, P. 1984: *Distinctions: a social critique of the judgement of taste.* Cambridge, MA: Harvard University Press.

Brown, S. 1987: Institutional change in retailing: a geographical perspective. *Progress in Human Geography* 11, 181–206.

Chain Store Age, 1984 Supermarket design takes bold strides. *Chain Store Age Executive* May, 37–43.

  1985: Progressive change pays off at Montgomery Ward. *Chain Store Age Executive* February, 30–36.

  1987: Big Y redesigns its selling machine. *Chain Store Age Executive* October, 76–78.

Daniels, P.W. 1985: *Service industries.* London: Methuen.

Ducatel, K.J. 1987: *Teleshopping and retail change: a Marxist perspective.* Unpublished PhD thesis, Department of Geography, University of Bristol.

EUI 1984: Strategies in grocery rctailing. *Retail Business* 340, 21–24. London: Economist Publications.

Euromonitor, 1984/85: *The retail trade in the United Kingdom.* London: Euronomonitor Publications.

Fannin, R. 1987: Bring a bag of money. *Marketing and Media* June, 38–45.

FitzSimmons, M. 1983: *Environmental and social consequences of agricultural industrialization in the Salinas Valley 1947–1978.* Unpublished PhD dissertation, University of California, Los Angeles.

Gibbs, D.C. 1988: Restructuring in the Manchester clothing industry: technical change and interrelationships between manufacturers and retailers. *Environment and Planning A* 20, 1219–33.

Groves, M. 1988: To catch a thief. *Los Angeles Times*, 18 January Part IV, 5.

Mandel, E. 1977: Introduction to Marx, K. *Capital: a critique of political economy*, Volume I. New York: Vintage Books.

  1981: Introduction to Marx, K. *Capital: a critique of political economy*, Volume II. New York: Vintage Books.

Marion, B.W., Mueller, W.F., Cotterill, R.W., Geithman F.E. and Schmeizer, J.R. 1979: *The food retailng industry: market structure, profits and prices.* New York: Praeger Publishers.

218   *The evolution and development of retailing*

Marx, K. 1909: *Capital: a critique of political economy*, Volume III. Chicago: Charles Kerr and Co.
    1973: *Grundrisse.* Harmondsworth: Penguin Books.
    1977: *Capital: a critique of political economy*, Volume I. New York: Vintage Books.
    1981: *Capital: a critique of political economy*, Volume II. New York: Vintage Books.
Norkett, P. 1985: The key to supermarket success. *Accountancy* 96, 74–79.
Novak, A. 1977: *Store planning and design.* New York: Lebhar-Friedmann Books.
Noyelle, T. 1987: *Beyond industrial dualism: market and job segmentation in the new economy.* Boulder, Co: Westview Press.
Pitman, B. 1987: *Radical transformations of the market and the Benettonisation phenomenon: speculations on the spatial dimensions of retailing in late capitalism.* Unpublished paper, Graduate School of Architecture and Urban Planning, UCLA.
Preteceille, E. and **Terrail, J-P.** 1985: *Capitalism, consumption and needs.* Oxford: Basil Blackwell.
Rainnie, A.F. 1984: Combined and uneven development in the clothing industry: the effects of competition and accumulation. *Capital and class* 22, 141–56.
Randall, J. 1985: The battle for the brands. *Management Today* November, 74–79.
Scott, A.J. and **Storper, M.** 1986: *Production, work and territory: the geographical anatomy of industrial capitalism.* Winchester MA: Allen and Unwin.
Stacey, N.A.H. and **Wilson, A.** 1965: *The changing pattern of distribution.* London: Pergamon.
Urry, J. 1987: Some social and spatial aspects of services. *Environment and Planning D, Society and Space* 5, 5–26.
Walker, R.A. 1985 Is there a service economy? *Science and Society* XLIX, 42–83.
Wrigley, N. 1988: Retail restructuring and retail analysis. In Wrigley, N. *Store choice, store location and market analysis* London: Routledge, 3–34.

Institutional change in retailing: a review and synthesis

Stephen Brown

Source: *European Journal of Marketing* 21(6) (1987): 5–36.

It has often been said that the only constant in retailing is change[138, 194], and retail change, if never a burning issue, has been a constant feature of marketing thought. Analyses have ranged from quantitative insights into the evolution of national and intra-national retail systems[34, 41, 95], to case histories of individual retail firms or groups of firms[28, 96, 143, 221]. However, the bulk of academic endeavour has been devoted to the study of retail institutions, such as department stores, supermarkets and catalogue showrooms, and has sought to develop models or theories of institutional change. Although subject to innumerable overviews in the (invariably) opening chapters of "me-too" retail textbooks, this body of work has never, to the author's knowledge, been comprehensively reviewed. Such an examination is not only long overdue but, for several reasons, would appear to be particularly timely. The recent death, at 91, of Malcolm P. McNair, the founding father of this field of research, necessitates an evaluation of the work he set in train. Moreover, the thirtieth anniversary of his pioneering formulation, "the wheel of retailing"[152], is fast approaching. Finally, a number of recent contributions to this conceptual genre suggest that a new era in the study of institutional change has commenced. The time is ripe, therefore, for a state-of-the-art survey and this issue will explore, at some length, the various schools of institutional thought. After outlining the basic theories of retail change and considering some less familiar applications of the hypotheses, discussion will turn to the manifold attempts to combine the basic models into a more comprehensive explanation of institutional evolution. In addition, the issue will endeavour to highlight potentially fruitful areas for future investigation and it will conclude with a simple model of research activity hitherto.

Before commencing the review, however, it should be noted that, firstly, "theory" is a rather generous term for what have been described as little more than inductively derived generalisations[102]. Nevertheless, the descriptor shall be retained and used interchangeably with model, hypothesis, paradigm and conceptualisation throughout this issue. Similarly, the terms retail institution, technique, format and type will be considered synonymous. Secondly, the majority of these concepts were developed with reference to American retail experience, though similar patterns are apparent in most advanced nations. Thus, although the discussion to follow concentrates on the commercial context in which the theories originated, pertinent examples from Europe (and beyond) shall also be cited. Indeed, it is noteworthy that some of the most significant scholarly contributions of recent years have been European in origin.

Basic theories

The theories of retail institutional change have been classified in a variety of ways[65, 79, 85, 142], but, broadly speaking, three basic approaches can be discerned. The first, environmental theory, contends that changes in retailing are a function of developments in an institution's operational milieu. Cyclical theory, the second and by far the most common perspective, suggests that change takes place in a rhythmic fashion and is characterised by the recurrence of earlier patterns. The third school of thought, conflict theory, focuses attention on the inter-institutional strife that occurs when novel retail forms first appear.

Environmental theory

An environmental view of institutional evolution maintains that changes in the economic, demographic, social, cultural, legal and technological conditions of the marketplace are reflected in the structure of the retail system[12, 80, 193]. Institutional innovations will only occur, or rather prove successful, when operational conditions are favourable and only those techniques which possess the ability to adapt to alterations in their trading milieu are likely to survive and prosper in the longer term. Retail institutions, in short, emerge, develop, mature and decline in direct response to environmental circumstances[10, 95].

Certainly there is much to commend an environmental approach to institutional change. The department store, for example, could not have emerged in the mid-nineteenth century without the growth of middle-class demand, the appearance of efficient intra-urban transport systems, elevators and plate glass, and the willingness of customers to accept a fixed price policy[76, 145, 169]. Likewise, the American mail order trade owed its initial success to an extension of the railway network, improvements in the postal system, growing literacy and the pent-up demand among rural residents for a wider choice of goods than were locally available[28, 159, 163]. The supermarket, furthermore, was an outgrowth of the Great Depression, increased car and refrigerator ownership and technological breakthroughs in the packaging, processing and purveyance (self-service) of foodstuffs[9, 153]. Indeed, the economic recession of recent years, coupled with rampant inflation, periodic energy crises, the availability of both aging shopping centres and manufacturers with a backlog of unsold inventory, and, moreover, well-educated, price-sensitive consumers who were prepared to sacrifice selection but not quality, has also given rise to a new retail phenonemon — "off-price" shops and shopping centres[137, 178, 181].

Although the environmental factors underpinning the birth and development of all manner of retail techniques, ranging from variety stores[120, 169] and chain stores[15, 25] to discount houses[48, 159] and shopping centres[57, 150], have been extensively documented, the majority of these studies are anecdotal rather than analytical in nature. As noted at the start of this issue, however, several scholars have employed sophisticated statistical techniques in an attempt to quantify the relationship between the changing structure of retailing and an extensive range of socio-economic variables, including *per capita* income, employment, urban form and population size, density and rate of growth. Termed "macro-retailing" by Rosenbloom and Schiffman [185], these investigations have been undertaken at the international[95, 205], national[117], regional[116], urban[33], and intra-urban[6], levels of analysis, though the results of the latter two have tended to be somewhat less clear-cut than their larger scale counterparts.

Another less quantitative view of retail change, while recognising the variety of factors influencing institutional evolution, has focused attention upon specific elements of the environmental mix. Thomas[209] laid stress upon sociological forces, noting the role of middle-class self-esteem, or "status uncertainty", in the development of the department store. Beem[14], by contrast, considered legal constraints, such as antichain store legislation, to be very significant; though he, like Stevens[201], regarded technological development — mass transit, motor cars, telephones, computers and so forth — to be the single most important determinant of retail institutional evolution. Other commentators, however, consider economics to be the prime environmental mover. Besides the oft noted correlation between hard times and institutional innovation[67, 153], a number of models describing the relationship between economic development and the structure of retailing have been posited. Bucklin[34] identified five stages of institutional evolution from the periodic markets of pre-industrial societies to the conglomerate retailing of the developed world. A similar seven-stage formulation was put forward by Wadinambiaratchi[218], though others were less convinced of this relationship[68, 166, 190].

Nonetheless, at the start of the 1970s it was widely believed that models of this nature would enable marketers to predict retail trends in one nation from developments in other, more advanced, economies[44, 218]. Yet despite some initial successes, most notably Arndt's[10] prediction of the growth of self-service in Norway, the study of comparative retailing has not fulfilled early expectations[127]. It is now acknowledged that a universal model of retail development is unobtainable and although many retail innovations are transmitted from more to less economically advanced nations, the sheer variety of social, political, cultural, legal and historical forces at work within individual countries, indicates that institutional diversity rather than uniformity is the hallmark of retail evolution[56]. The environmental impediments which faced the transfer of the supermarket from developed to developing countries like Spain[59], Turkey[125, 126], Israel[81, 82, 86], Chile[17], and Saudi Arabia[2], have been described at length and, on a smaller scale, retailers' frequent inability to establish successful outlets in foreign lands bears witness to the diversity of national environmental conditions[108, 123, 219]. Examples include: Sears Roebuck's abortive adventures in Belgium and Spain, Marks and Spencers' lame duck operations in Canada and France and Matsuzukiya, Mikomoto and Takashimaya's unsuccessful attempts to crack the American market.

As noted earlier, environmental factors do not simply determine the introduction and acceptance of novel retail institutions, they also influence the maturation and survival of the techniques. Consequently, an ability to adapt to alterations in the operational milieu is widely regarded as a prerequisite for retail longevity[78, 138, 174]. To cite but three instances, Sears and Montgomery Ward, the pioneers of mail order trading, successfully adapted to changed environmental circumstances (rural-urban migration, growing car ownership and escalating costs) when they commenced their fixed store operations in the 1920s[70, 177, 210]. Many American department stores, on the other hand, were slow to recognise the market potential of the rapidly growing suburbs in the early post-war period and suffered as a result[74, 152]. Similarly, the Co-operative movement in the United Kingdom, once a pacesetter in retail innovation, has been heavily criticised for its inability to recognise and respond to the environmental opportunities of the 1970s and 1980s[37, 73].

According to Gist's[79] "adjustment theory", the retail institutions best adapted to prevailing environmental conditions are the ones most likely to avoid extinction. In other words, a form of economic "natural selection" prevails, whereby only the fittest retail species survive[51, 78]. This Darwinian view of institutional evolution has been reiterated and the ecological analogy further extended by Dreesman[69]. He contended that the emergence of a new retail species, such as a department or chain store, is sudden, violent and followed by a long period of incremental development (phenotypes around the genotype). What is more, economic parallels to ecological concepts like convergence, hypertrophy, regression and assimilation are also apparent. More recently Markin and Duncan[138] have considered retail phenomena in ecological terms (see Figure 1), highlighting parasitic relationships, where one institution depends on another for survival (supermarkets and trading

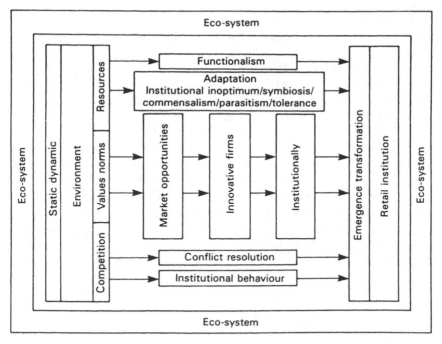

Figure 1 Ecological Model of Retail Institutional Change (Markin and Duncan)

stamp companies), commensalism, where different retail species share the same environment (tenants of shopping centres) and symbiosis, where institutions benefit from their mutual dependency (voluntary or buying groups).

Although the adoption of an ecological perspective has done much to release marketing from the tyranny of *homo economicus*[3, 4], the shortcomings of such a philosophy must also be acknowledged[180, 211]. Endowed as they are with a degree of foresight and an ability to initiate, choose and plan for change, human organisations cannot be treated in strict biotic terms. The environment does not *determine* what will occur; it creates *possibilities* which individuals or organisations are free to exploit or reject as they please. Thus, despite its intuitive appeal and widespread currency — *viz.*, Hirschman's [100, 101] concept of "natural dominance" — the ecological model of retailing remains unproven. Yet, there is no denying the almost universal adoption of an adaptive approach to doing business. Modern retail organisations devote considerable time and resources to environmental monitoring and the projection of operational scenarios. Indeed, the marketing literature is replete with prognostications upon short and long-term trends in the retail environment[66, 98, 136], the industry's likely response to these opportunities and threats[23, 144, 214], discussions of strategic planning[149, 183, 130] and visions of future retail formats[15, 27, 154].

Cyclical theory

The various cyclical theories of retail institutional evolution maintain that change occurs in an oscillatory manner, involving the repetition of earlier trends. Pattern analysis of this nature has taken pride of place in investigations of institutional change, the four most important conceptual contributions being the retail accordion, the wheel of retailing, the retail life cycle and, arguably, the polarisation principle.

The retail accordion

The retail accordion or general-specific-general cycle, describes the evolution of the modern commercial system in terms of the number of lines of merchandise handled by the preponderant institutional form[78, 107]. A rhythmic pattern of development, dominated in turn by establishments selling a wide variety of wares and shops specialising in a narrow range of goods is clearly apparent, if difficult to prove[79]. In the United States, for instance, the general store of the nineteenth-century gave way to the specialist, single-line businesses of the twentieth, which were themselves superseded by the mass merchandisers of the early post-war era[28]. Of late, however, highly specialised outlets selling ski equipment, computers, ties and socks, fine wines, gourmet foods and so on, have come once more to the fore[51, 149, 199]. Similar trends are evident in other advanced countries such as the United Kingdom, where, broadly speaking, the one-stop bandwagon of the 1970s has made way for the highly focused retail formats of today[59].

This cyclical pattern in merchandise assortments was first noted by Hower[114] and identified subsequently by Hall, Knapp and Winsten[95] and Brand[28], but it was Hollander[107] who extended the accordion principle to its fullest extent. He argued that in addition to the broad sweep of the general-specific-general cycle, individual institutions widen and narrow their inventories with the passage of time. Most American department stores began life as specialist establishments[75, 163, 169] but, as the nineteenth-century progressed, more and more lines of merchandise were added with the point of maximum diversification was attained at the start of the present century[103]. Since then a large number of departments have been discarded and many modern emporia are more akin to high fashion specialists than the "universal providers" of yore[171, 203].

By dint of its dynamic perspective, therefore, the retail accordion provides a salutary reminder that "merchandise, unlike eggs, can be unscrambled"[106]. In fact, at any one time some institutions may be in the throes of widespread inventory diversification while others are rationalising their range of goods and yet others are experiencing both. As Dawson[59] and Allvine[7] have demonstrated, the shopping centre and supermarket industries provide evidence of contemporaneous specialisation and diversification. The speciality shopping centre and limited line discount store are fine examples of the former, whereas megacentres and combination stores are typical of the latter trend.

The wheel of retailing

Variously described as a "useful Aunt Sally"[184] and the "dominant concept for those who practise and study (and teach) in the retailing field"[90], the wheel of retailing is undoubtedly the most famous and frequently cited theory of institutional change. It asserts that retail institutions commence as cut price, low cost, narrow margin operations which subsequently "trade up". Improvements in display, more prestigious premises, increased advertising and the provision of credit, delivery and many other customer services all serve to drive up expenses, margins and prices. Eventually the institutions mature as high cost, conservative and "top heavy" operations with a sales policy based upon quality goods and services rather than price appeal. This, in turn, opens the way for the next low cost innovator; and so the wheel revolves (see Figure 2).

The wheel theory is usually ascribed to Malcolm P. McNair's renowned 1957 paper, "Significant Trends and Developments in the Post-War Period"[152]. In actual fact, McNair had outlined the concept some 26 years earlier[151], though it was W.A. Lewis, a British economist, who first employed the cyclical metaphor[133]. Indeed, "Significant Trends" was also predated by a 1952 discussion in *Grey Matter*[184] and, a few years later, by Nieschlag's similar but independently derived formulation[161].

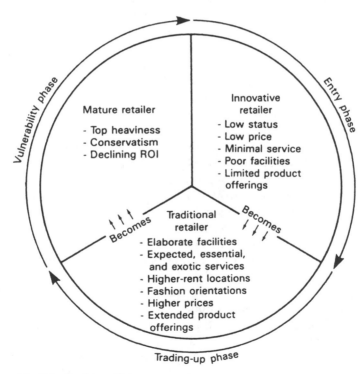

Figure 2 The Wheel of Retailing

Its antecedents notwithstanding, the wheel of retailing has inspired — and continues to generate — a great deal of scholarly debate. Discussions of the hypothesis centre upon two major areas; the universality of the concept and the causes of trading up. In support of the theory, there is considerable evidence that many institutional types, including department stores, mail order houses, discount stores, supermarkets and (evidently) off-price shops and shopping centres, began by selling merchandise at below average prices, evolved into high cost modes of distribution and thus created conditions conducive to new, low cost operations[28, 104, 124, 137, 164]. By the same token, however, a number of retail innovations did not commence at the low margin level. Boutiques, convenience stores, planned shopping centres, automatic vending machines and super-specialists all entered the market on a high cost basis[104, 105, 199]. Goldman[83] has also made the point that not every department store, supermarket or discount house began life as a cut-price, no-frills operation; there were significant variations on each theme[9, 48, 206]. What is more, although the wheel pattern is apparent in many economically advanced countries like the United Kingdom[170, 213], Belgium[155] and Germany[26, 223], retail innovations in developing nations tend to be introduced at the high end of the cost spectrum[44, 87, 108].

While most commentators agree that McNair's hypothesis is valid, if not universally applicable, there is less consensus on the causes of trading up; and several extensively discussed explanations of the process have been posited. It has been attributed to a deterioration in managerial ability[42, 69, 161]; an unscrupulous combination of trade magazines and equipment suppliers[134, 176]; a statistical quirk caused by changes in the merchandise mix[34, 35]; an unavoidable reduction in initial levels of plant utilisation[74, 109, 152]; the increasing cost of labour[35]; a vicarious fulfilment of the innovator's unattainable commercial vision[20]; and what can only be described as a law of nature[21]. Interestingly, however, the two most widely embraced explanations of trading up have their roots in the environmental and conflict-based traditions of institutional thought. The environmental view sees it as a natural and enlightened response to growing consumer affluence and the resultant increased demand for a wider range of customer services[34, 104, 138]. By contrast, the conflict-based perspective regards upgrading as a defensive search for differential advantage; in short, an irreversible progression of cost and margin increases stemming from intra-institutional non-price competition[12, 69]. In truth, neither hypothesis is entirely satisfactory as there is empirical evidence of both mature institutions abandoning customer services and indulging in price wars (contrary to the conflictual viewpoint)[8, 38, 135] and the emergence of no-frills institutions and severe price competition in eras of relative affluence (contrary to the environmental explanation)[67, 170].

Arguments over the causes of trading up, however, are becoming almost academic as it appears that the wheel of retailing is revolving much less rapidly than before[142, 216]. Recent years have witnessed the "rise of the conglomerchants", massive retail empires comprising numerous chain store groups each of which is orientated to a different segment of the market, or position on the wheel[215]. Examples include Dayton-Hudson in the United States, Migros in Switzerland, Ahold in the Netherlands, GB-Inno-BM in Belgium and Sears, Storehouse, Ward White and (increasingly) W.H. Smith in the United Kingdom. Whereas the wheel hypothesis contends that institutions trade up through time, conglomerchant-controlled chains of department stores, specialists, discount houses or whatever, are tailored to specific wheel positions and prevented from evolving into the niches already occupied by other arms of the empire. The wheel is effectively ossified and, as a result, new institutions are faced with an exceedingly difficult task of successful market entry against the firmly entrenched incumbents of each particular wheel position[142]. In addition, as retailing *per se* becomes more market segment orientated it is equally difficult for existing institutions to reposition themselves, as Montgomery Ward (USA), Hertie (West Germany) and Woolworths (UK) have discovered to their cost in the last few years.

The retail life cycle

Based upon marketing's hotly debated product life cycle conceptualisation (PLC)[18, 179], the retail life cycle maintains that institutions evolve through the anthropomorphic stages of birth, growth, maturity and decline[46, 148, 165]. When a retail institution endowed with significant competitive advantages over existing operators appears and achieves public acceptability, it enjoys a very rapid increase in sales[185]. Success, however, breeds imitation, the technique proliferates and enters the growth or accelerated development stage. Its volume of trade, profitability and market share all increase dramatically, but by the end of the period these are counterbalanced by escalating costs, a corollory of overzealous expansion. The maturity stage, therefore, is characterised by a dissipation of the institution's earlier vitality — a "shake out" often occurs — and the competitive assaults of new retail forms. Finally, the institution starts to decline. This is accompanied by a major loss of market share, reduced profitability and eventual withdrawal from the competitive arena[47] (see Figure 3).

Proponents of the life cycle contend that the process is inexorable and unavoidable; institutional decline cannot be prevented, only postponed[49]. Yet although there seems to be some evidence of the cycle in operation — variety stores and traditional counter service grocery stores are just two examples of institutions which evolved in the hypothesised manner[47, 142, 130] — the retail life cycle, as scion of the PLC, must be subject to the selfsame criticisms[138]. Many products are known to be immune from life cycle processes and others possess remarkable powers of recovery. Furthermore, a product's precise position on the cycle is often difficult to determine; nor is it possible to predict with any confidence how long the individual stages are likely to last[64, 62, 186]. Indeed, the use of both the model to predict future

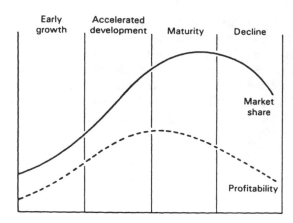

Figure 3 The Retail Life Cycle

sales and sales figures to determine the prevailing stage of the cycle has prompted Hunt[115] to dismiss the concept as "tautological . . . impotent and void of explanatory power". However, perhaps the major weakness of the PLC is its inherent determinism. A product's success, critics argue, depends upon managerial support and ability to cope with changing business conditions; not immutable evolutionary forces[62, 208]. Yet despite its manifold imperfections, the product life cycle is generally considered to be a useful conceptual device[157, 172, 212]. The retail life cycle is equally flawed but held in similar academic esteem[21, 65, 184].

As many scholars have noted[50, 51, 56, 153], there are clear parallels between the retail life cycle and the wheel of retailing. Both describe the introduction, development, maturation and demise of retail institutions. But, inasmuch as the wheel is slowing, there is evidence to suggest that the retail life cycle, like its PLC counterpart[175], is speeding up[13, 49, 56]. Although estimates of institutional maturation rates vary[47, 141, 148], it has been calculated that the department store took around 80 years to reach maturity, the supermarket approximately 35 and the hypermarket and home improvement centre 10 and 15 years respectively[47, 56] (see Table I). This apparent slowing wheel-speeding cycle contradiction, however, can be easily accounted for. Whereas the wheel of retailing argues that an institution evolves (from low to high cost) with the passage of time, the life cycle assumes that the technique remains unchanged. Alterations, admittedly, may occur in the maturity phase of the cycle, but these represent managerial attempts to postpone what would otherwise have transpired — the decline of the original institution. In fact, it is quite possible that the slowing of the wheel and the acceleration of the cycle are interrelated. If the wheel is unable to turn and an institution is incapable of evolving internally to meet changing market conditions, it follows that the institution will be more short-lived than might

Table I Life Cycle Characteristics of Five Retail Institutions

Institution	Approximate date of innovation	Approximate date of maximum market share	Approximate number of years required to reach maturity	Estimated maximum market share %	Estimated 1975 market share %
Department store	1860	1940	80	8.5[1]	1.1[1]
Variety store	1910	1955	45	16.5[2]	9.5[2]
Supermarket	1930	1965	35	70.0[3]	64.5[3]
Discount department store	1950	1970	20	6.5[1]	5.7[1]
Home improvement centre	1965	1980	15	35.0[4]	25.3[4]

1. Total retail sales.
2. General merchandise sales.
3. Grocery sales.
4. Hardware materials sales

Source: Davidson, Bates and Bass, 1976.

otherwise have been the case. Along with a general quickening of the pace of life, therefore,[66] the slowing of the wheel is one of the causes of accelerated institutional evolution.

The polarisation principle

First described by Dreesman[69] and Schary[190], though named and quantified by Kirby[129], the polarisation principle contends that the well documented trend towards fewer but larger retail institutions is counterbalanced by a renaissance of the small shop sector. The former is an outgrowth of the self-service technique of selling and a search for associated economies of scale, while the latter is a consequence of the tendency for large retail establishments, depending as they do upon extensive catchment areas, to be geographically dispersed[56, 59]. In America, Japan and Western Europe, recent years have witnessed the rapid development of hypermarket style operations and the modern convenience store[11, 60, 182]. Offering a wide range but limited assortment of fast moving merchandise and situated in easily accessible locations, convenience stores provide essential emergency and "topping up" facilities for onestop shoppers and cater for those unwilling or unable to patronise the larger, basically bulk order orientated, outlets. Small shops, according to the polarisation principle, complement rather than compete with their larger brethren.

Useful as it is, the polarisation principle describes but a single facet of the changing retail scene — the relationship between large and small institutions. In this respect, to be sure, it is not alone. The wheel of retailing is solely concerned with the interdependency of high and low cost techniques and the retail accordion with operations purveying wide and narrow ranges of goods (the retail life cycle does not take institutional interrelationships into account). It is apparent, however, that the dynamic processes described by the wheel, accordion and polarisation principles are themselves interconnected. The present retail landscapes of Great Britain and other advanced nations possess many examples of large outlets specialising in a relatively limited range of goods (discount electrical/carpet warehouses); small outlets handling a surprisingly wide variety of wares (modern convenience stores); price-cutting operations occupying sizeable premises (hypermarkets); and small stores with a service-orientated sales philosophy (boutiques, specialists). Indeed, it is arguable that retailing polarises simultaneously along each of the price, assortment and size dimensions and a model outlining this process has recently been presented[32]. The multi-polarisation model maintains that institutional developments along any of the aforementioned dimensions give rise to counter-balancing actions at one or more of the others (see Figure 4). Thus, the emergence of the superstore, selling a wide range of discounted goods from large premises, has paved the way for limited line discount stores, specialists in gourmet foods and modern convenience stores.

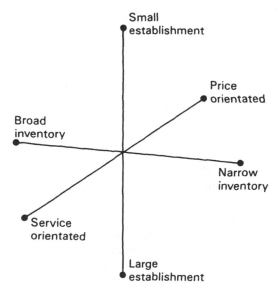

Figure 4 The Multi-Polarisation Model

The model, however, remains untested, though others have argued that the polarisation process may apply to the entire retail system, not just institutional evolution[54].

Conflict theory

Inter-institutional conflict is endemic to retailing and few significant innovations have failed to be greeted by a storm of protest from disaffected establishments. Department stores, mail order houses, co-operative societies, chain stores, supermarkets, discount houses and, more recently, hypermarkets and superstores were all maligned, boycotted, accused of unfair trading practices and subject to attempts to stifle their success[72, 94, 121, 146, 163, 164]. The term, "department store", for instance, was originally an epithet of opprobrium[103]; co-operative societies were initially portrayed as a "communistic and anti-Christian movement which seeks . . . the extinction of the private trade"[222]; and hypermarkets were once described as "neon lighted obscenities . . . which sprawl in the depths of the countryside like great leviathans stranded on a beach"[224]. Yet vituperation aside, many have argued that inter-institutional conflict is the propellant of retail change, the very essence of institutional evolution[56, 138, 147].

Although their philosophical perspectives differed, both Schumpeter[192] and Galbraith[77] concurred that the capitalist system is characterised by continual innovation. Indeed, according to the former, the intermittent internal upheaval brought about by innovation is the major way in which economic progress is attained under the capitalist mode of production. Vigorous competition between the old and the new — "the perennial gale of creative destruction"[192] — is capitalism's driving force. In terms of retail development, therefore, the competition that matters is not the "repetitive" day-to-day intra-institutional struggle but the "disruptive" competition — the "big disturbance" — brought about by the appearance of institutions like department stores, supermarkets, discount houses and shopping centres, those which command a decisive cost or quality advantage over the old[25, 192].

Invariably led by a dynamic individual from outside the retail establishment[93, 156, 162, 196], institutional innovations force conventional retailers to respond or adapt to the competitive challenge. Failure to do so invites disaster, though such is the imperfection of the marketplace that non-respondents are often able to survive, albeit with a reduced level of business[95]. Responses take a variety of forms — Martenson[140] identifies seven categories ranging from "rigid retailers" to "adoptive observers" — but these, broadly speaking, can be divided into two major types. As the methods of the innovator are rarely, if ever, patentable[5, 20], imitating some or all of its characteristics is one way of dealing with the threat[25, 72, 209]. The other is to attempt to sidestep direct competition by differentiating, where possible, the threatened institution from its challengers[25, 72, 125].

Thus, the emergence of the discount store in the United States prompted many traditional department stores to move further upmarket and abandon the lines handled by the no-frills institution. Imitative responses, on the other hand, included the wholesale cutting of prices and services, thereby matching those of the newcomer; establishing their own chains of discounters; and buying out the competition, which not only nullified a perceived threat but provided a useful insight into the operation of the innovator[20, 164]. Indeed, it is often the case that novel techniques of retailing are brought to fruition by the imitator of the idea, not the originator[20, 110]. The history of the supermarket in the United States[146] and the variety store in Belgium[39] represent classic examples of this commercial trait.

The nature of existing retail techniques may thus be altered as a result of interinstitutional strife; so much so in fact that completely new forms of retailing may emerge from the conflict. The voluntary group, for instance, was the independent retailers' response to the threat of the chainstore[200].

Appropriate responses to retail innovations, however, rarely appear overnight — indeed, a "wait and see" tendency is not unusual[5, 67] — and a range of responses may be considered, tested, and applied or rejected by the threatened institution. Attempts have been made to model this process. Swan[204] employed Parson and Smelser's[168] seven-stage model of social change to the chain store — voluntary group nexus, but on application the stages proved difficult to distinguish. Nevertheless, Swan felt that the theory's three basic elements, recognition of the problem, proposal and testing of possible solutions and adoption of the new trading format, were worthy of note.

Developed by Fink, Baek and Taddeo[76] for undifferentiated organisations and applied to marketing by Stern and El-Ansary[200] (though the process had been described some time earlier[91]), another model distinguishes four stages in the action — reaction sequence. These are: shock, defensive retreat, acknowledgement and adaptation. When an institutional innovation appears, the components of the retail system likely to suffer as a consequence enter the shock phase, but only when the crisis is perceived. This period is characterised by a refusal to recognise the extent of the threat and to try and explain it away[198]. The newcomer is regarded as either an ephemeral phenomenon or inferior to the existing system. Phase two, defensive retreat, sees the start of the reaction to the challenger. Pressure may be brought to bear on its suppliers[206] and attempts to discredit, control and generally impede the innovator are commonplace. McCammon[147] has studied this aspect in detail and argues that a range of factors including reseller solidarity, the size of the firm, organisational rigidity and channel politics underpin this hostility. Gradually, however, the group threatened by change realises that the assailant is likely to remain and becomes aware of the need for positive counter-measures; thus, phase three — acknowledgement — is entered. The final adaptive era represents the resolution of the conflict when a new power balance is created in the system. This, in turn, may initiate a crisis for another component of the system — often, but not necessarily, the original threat — and so conflict breaks out once more.

Dawson[56] has demonstrated the applicability of the Fink, Baek, Taddeo[76] model to changes in American and British grocery retailing. In America, the crisis was precipitated by the proliferation of chain stores, particularly after the First World War. The initial reaction of independents to this threat was to emphasise their own superiority but subsequently attempts were made to attract the attention of suppliers, the general public and the government to the "unfair" competitive practices of the chains. Anti-chain store legislation was called for and attained in many states, and campaigns to control price-cutting through the introduction of resale price maintenance were under-taken[167]. Eventually recognition of the need for positive counter-measures prevailed and voluntary groups, co-operative purchasing schemes, additional customer services and improved merchandise assortments were some of the competitive methods employed. The supermarket was yet another response by independents to the chain store threat. On this occasion, however, it was the chains who were forced to react and they did so in the same manner as the independents responded to them; ridicule and rejection, attempts to hamper the supermarkets' success, dabbling with the concept and, finally, widespread adoption of the new approach[146].

In many ways, the crisis-response model of retail institutional change is not dissimilar to Galbraith's[77] concept of countervailing power. In essence, his theory suggests that the emergence of a dominant group in any sector of the economy is counterbalanced by the appearance of another equally powerful opposing force. The market power of large-scale producers is held in check by large-scale purchasers which, in turn, may stimulate the creation of vociferous consumer groups. Likewise, large manufacturers beget large unions which necessitate large governments and so on. In a capitalist society, therefore, power tends to become organised in response to a given position of power. Although Galbraith is not acknowledged, Izraeli[118] has em-ployed his concept of countervailing power to describe changes in retail institutions. The growth of large-scale manufacturing, he argued, encouraged the development of multiple retail organisations, which exerted pressure on independent retailers and consumers, who responded with joint buying groups and the co-operative movement respectively[170]. In other words, whenever the relative economic positions of weaker members of marketing channels are threatened by a concentration of power elsewhere in the system, they will mobilise to counteract the competitive pressure and re-assert their pre-existing position. Any action thus instigates an equal and opposite reaction.

Perhaps the most important aspect of the crisis-response model, however, is its intimation that not only do threatened institutions evolve in response to a challenge, but *the attacker* is also altered by the hostilities. Termed challenge-evolution behaviour by Dickinson[65], the reaction of threatened institutions and the response of the attacker to the rejoinder of the retail establishment, combine to determine the post-conflict institutional structure. This often very rapid[215] action, reaction and resolution sequence has been formalised by Gist[78] in his dialectical theory of institutional change (see Figure 5). It regards retail evolution as a series of stages, each of which represents a rejection of the prior institutional orthodoxy. Derived from Marxist philosophy[24] and, incidentally, described as in Hollander (as retail Hegelianism) some years beforehand[105], Gist's dialectical model argues that the existing thesis is challenged by its antithesis and a synthesis eventually emerges from the melding of the two. The synthesis then becomes the thesis for a new round of negation and assimilation; and so the dialectical process continues. Thus, the trading philosophy espoused by the traditional counter-service grocery store may constitute a thesis, the supermarket its antithesis and the self-service grocery store the synthesis[52]. Similarly, the discount department store represents a synthesis of the department store and discount house[122]. The melding process, to be sure, is not inevitable and the dialectical model has been extended to include those establishments, noted earlier, that attempt to differentiate themselves from the initial attack and examples of both challenged and challenging institutions which remain unchanged throughout the hostilities[139]. According to the Hegelian theory, therefore, an increasingly diverse retail structure is the inevitable outcome of inter-institutional conflict.

Other applications

As the foregoing discussion, particularly the environmental section, indicates, analyses of retail institutional change are closely related to other areas of research interest including the economic development process, the product life cycle, the evolution of national and intra-national retail systems and even retail classification[21, 154]. However, just as institutional theory

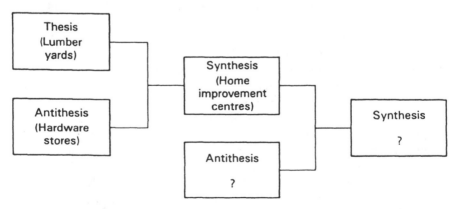

Figure 5 The Dialectical Process (Gist)

impinges upon and borrows from adjoining areas of academic concern, so too institutional conceptualisations have been employed in non-institutional settings. Besides the obvious utility of dialectics and the wheel of retailing to service industries like hotels[115], petrol stations[80, 139] and fast food restaurants[139, 207], Hollander[109] has noted accordion-like tendencies in store opening hours, advertising styles, vertical integration[see also 34, 114, 202], managerial systems and, in the grocery trade, the provision of credit, trading stamps and a delivery service[106]. The crisis-response model has been employed to describe the actions of combatants in a short but exceptionally vicious supermarket price war[16] and, as noted earlier, an attempt has also been made to extend the polarisation principle beyond the institutional arena[32]. Indeed, Hawes and Crittenden[97] contend that a "wheel of branding" is discernible in the American grocery business. When retailers' own brands were introduced in the 1950s they were low-quality products selling at prices well below equivalent manufacturers' brands. Through time, however, own brands were traded up, until by the late 1970s they were virtually indistinguishable in terms of quality, packaging and price from national brand competitors. This created an opportunity for the successful and widespread introduction of cut price ranges of generic goods which are likely, according to the authors, to go through the same upgrading process.

Interesting as these adaptations of institutional principles are, perhaps the most significant non-institutional applications involve, firstly, individual retail firms and, secondly, the location of retail activities. Although the validity of such an approach has been questioned[105, 111], Savitt[187, 188, 189] argued that the wheel of retailing, if set in a historical context[see also 67, 68], could provide a potentially useful insight into the evolution of specific retail firms. Regrettably, his analysis of Comet Radiovision, a British electrical discount chain, addressed few, if any, of the central issues of the wheel theory[188]. Nevertheless, this individualistic perspective has also been advocated by Davidson and Smallwood[50] with regard to the retail life cycle and employed in empirical studies of McDonalds, the fast-food operation[207] and IKEA, the Swedish flat-pack furniture retailer[140].

If firm-specific studies are still in their infancy, the application of institutional formulations to retail location is long established and all three schools of thought are evident. The environmental-cum-ecological view regards the development of retail establishments in certain areas as a response to favourable socio-economic circumstances (population growth, rising incomes, planning permission and so forth)[173, 191, 197, 217]. Hostile conditions, likewise, are the cause of deterioration and eventual demise of existing concentrations of commercial facilities[22]. Cyclically speaking, the decline and subsequent renaissance of the American city centre has been described as akin to a locational accordion[109] and it has been posited[55] — and empirically demonstrated[30] — that retail firms move from low rent to high rent locations in line with the wheel hypothesis. The parallel between geographical diffusion and the life cycle process has been pointed out on several occasions[55, 56, 147] and Holmes and Hoskins[112] even argue that individual locations go through an inexorable six-stage life cycle. Indeed, the very basis of the polarisation principle is the tendency for large retail establishments to be geographically dispersed, thereby creating suitable conditions in the interstices for small conveniently situated outlets. Conflict based conceptualisations have also been employed in a locational context. The reaction of city centres to the growth of out-of-town shopping centres provides a textbook illustration of the crisis-response process[24, 29, 66] and a similar action-reaction sequence is apparent in different locations as retail innovations spread out from their place of origin[56, 140].

Combined theories

For pedagogic purposes the present review has treated the environmental, cyclical and conflict-based approaches to retail institutional change as separate entities; yet, they are by no means unrelated. The retail life cycle, for example, possesses strong ecological overtones and, as described earlier, explanations of the wheel's trading up process have drawn upon both the environmental and conflictual schools of thought. In fact, Dreesman's biological analogy has been cited on several occasions as an example of a cyclical model[85, 187], as has Gist's retail Hegelianism[79, 85, 140], though the latter has also been deemed biological by one conceptual taxonomist[187]. Yet others have seen parallels between the wheel of retailing and the concept of countervailing power[118, 125]. The models, in short, are interdependent.

By the same token, however, none of the three basic perspectives provides an entirely satisfactory explanation of institutional evolution. The environmental view, by concentrating upon the conditions which beget retail innovations, suffers from its very environmental emphasis. The role of the innovator, while acknowledged, is considered to be of secondary importance. Although retail institutions are unlikely to survive in hostile trading milieux, it is equally true that favourable conditions will remain just that until recognised and exploited by perceptive businessmen. Retail institutions may act under environmental constraints, but they are certainly not passive. Cyclical models, admittedly, place greater stress upon the role of the innovator, yet suffer in turn from their determinism, preoccupation with pattern, lack of firm empirical support and the, possibly unsubstantiated[34], presupposition of a long term retail institutional equilibrium. Furthermore, they appear to revolve in a vacuum, with scant regard being paid to the reactions of conventional institutions when challenged by novel retail formats. Conflict theories, however, concentrate upon the interaction between the old and the new, but they too are incomplete explanations of institutional evolution. Very little attention is paid to the origins of institutions, the form they take and the reasons for their initial and continued success. What is more, most of the conflict theories fail to incorporate any external influences, all change is seen as a result of interinstitutional strife.

In these circumstances it is not surprising that a number of formal attempts to combine the three theoretical perspectives have been undertaken. In fact, every possible combination (environment-cycle, cycle-conflict, environment-conflict, environment-cycle-conflict) has been explored, some more extensively than others.

Environment-cycle

In the very first commentary on McNair's 1957 paper, Cox[43] contended that the wheel revolved within the context of a continually changing environment. Thus the cycle, by definition, moves on; it cannot return to its original starting point. A new retail institution may serve a similar function to one that has gone before, but as circumstances have changed in the interim it is not precisely the same as its predecessor. Since the late 1950s a number of environmental-cum-cylical conceptualisations have been published, with some tending towards the former and others the latter aspect of the combination. Broadly speaking, the environmental end of this theoretical continuum acknowledges the existence of cycle-like patterns of retail evolution but stresses that these are largely a reflection of environmental circumstances. Kaynak[125], in an analysis of supermarketing in Turkey, notes that the wheel of retailing can only revolve if cultural, socio-economic and legislative conditions permit. However, he went on to argue; as have others[88, 218], that these preconditions rarely pertain in the developing world. By contrast, Bucklin's[35] detailed analysis of the American department store between 1959 and 1980 demonstrated clear evidence of increasing margins and costs as the wheel theory intimates. Yet multivariate analysis revealed no indication of a moribund retail technique, as the wheel also hypothesises; rather, an institution able and willing to adapt to changes in its operational context was uncovered. Another study considered the utility of the wheel to non-store retailing and although evidence of trading up was discernible, this was regarded as an adaptive response to gradually increasing consumer affluence[210]. Consequently, an alternative "crescent theory", combining ecological and life-cycle elements, was presented for further consideration.

The cyclical end of the theoretical spectrum is exemplified by the work of Deiderick and Dodge[63]. In what is perhaps the single most elaborate extrapolation of the cyclical approach to institutional evolution, they argue that the original wheel theory is composed of three separate cycles pertaining to pricing, breadth of product line and geographical extent. This can be further combined with the organisational life cycle and the ever-changing environment, to produce a moving, rotating wheel which, the authors believe, provides the basis of a comprehensive model of retail change (see Figure 6).

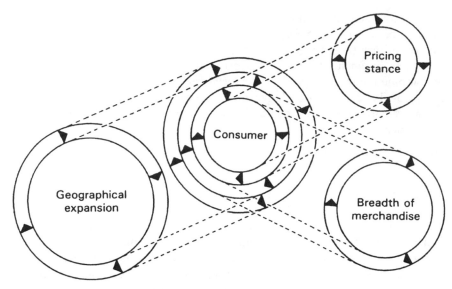

Figure 6 Revised Wheel of Retailing (Deiderick and Dodge)

Cycle-conflict

A long-standing criticism of cyclical theories of institutional development, particularly the wheel and life cycle, is their failure to accommodate conventional retailers' reactions to the threat of an innovative institution[119, 125, 160, 204]. In actuality, these accusations are somewhat unjustified as both conceptualisations consider, albeit briefly, possible responses to the newcomer. Nonetheless, their general preoccupation with pattern has given rise to a number of models seeking to combine the cyclical progress of retail institutions with the conflict they set in train. An early German study not only described what is now regarded as the "classic" wheel theory (low cost, high cost, low cost) but also an assimilation process whereby challenged institutions adopt elements of the innovation thus forcing it to trade up and become more akin to conventional retail forms[161]. A similar scenario was envisioned by Gist when he attempted to integrate the dialectical and wheel hypotheses[78]. The maturing institution, he maintained, represented the thesis, the innovation its antithesis and a synthesis resulted from the mutual modification or assimilation process. More recently, Martenson has brought together the life-cycle and crisis-response conceptualisations in her combined dynamic model[140]. In a detailed empirical study she demonstrated how the arrival and diffusion of a novel retail technique can instigate a wide range of responses among threatened institutions in a variety of economically advanced European countries.

Retail innovations, as noted above, can occur at both the cut price and prestige levels of the commercial hierarchy and several scholars share the view that just as a trading up process transpires at the low cost end so too a trading down process characterises top notch institutions[119, 160, 177]. However, empirical evidence of this procedure is rather thin on the ground and contradictory, moreover (some high end innovations, including shopping centres[89] and vending machines[210], have revealed a tendency to trade up). Be that as it may, an effort has been made to explain trading down in terms of Hotelling's[113] classic, if contentious[40, 71, 132], model of monopolistic competition[160]; though Izraeli[119], discussing the same phenomenon, preferred to emphasise the response of conventional retailers when exposed to top and bottom end competition. In his "three wheels of retailing" paradigm Izraeli contended that an ongoing assimilation process takes place at both extremes of the retail spectrum, thereby creating exploitable opportunities for nascent high and low cost institutions (see Figure 7).

Environment-conflict

If not specifically retail in orientation, Alderson's[4] theory of differential advantage encapsulates the environmental-conflict approach to institutional change. Taking an ecological or functionalist view of competition, Alderson demonstrated that organisations endeavour to differentiate themselves from

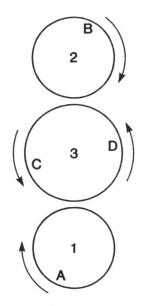

A - Low end innovation
B - High end innovation
C - Low end conventional retailer
D - High end conventional retailer

Figure 7 The Three Wheels of Retailing (Izraeli)

their rivals in the eyes of the consumer, thus carving out an unassailable niche in the marketplace. Opportunities for differential advantage, he argued, stemmed from technological, legal and economic developments in the business environment and when adopted force competitors to respond to the threat. Attempts to negate the advantages of the innovator and exploit potential differential advantages of their own subsequently ensue and this, in turn, forces the innovator to seek a further competitive edge — and so it goes on.

Advocates of an environment-conflict approach to retail institutional evolution comprise, firstly, those who have examined the cyclical modes of explanation and found them wanting and, secondly, independent observers of the changing retail scene. Indeed, one of the earliest contributions of the second of these categories predated McNair's pioneering paper of 1957. In 1954, Jeffreys explained the history of Britain's retail system in terms of a gradually increasing standard of living and intra-institutional strife[120]. These forces, furthermore, underpin both Regan's[177] multiplex model of institutional change and Guiltinan's[93] channel stage theory. Regan maintained that as a result of competitive dynamics and environmental circumstances, the product and service offerings of retail stores become increasingly complicated with the passage of time. Three initial levels of service and merchandise were identified and three ever more sophisticated combinations of goods and services — multiplex and omniplex — were predicted — (see Figure 8). Although devised with an individual outlet in mind, the subsequent "rise of the conglomerchant" and the history of certain retail institutions, such as the supermarket, have been cited as empirical proof of Regan's hypothesis[85, 148]. Guiltinan's observations on channel development are broadly similar, with a five-stage progression from rudimentary manufacturer-wholesaler-retailer relationships to the complexity of a vertically integrated channel of distribution[93].

While acknowledging the importance of underlying environmental change, Guiltinan considered the human decision maker to be the single most important factor influencing channel development. This view was shared by McNair and May in their comprehensive review of retail evolution in the United States[153]. Rejecting the wheel of retailing as "too narrow" an explanation of institutional change, they examined the economic, technological, marketing and, most importantly, managerial conditions surrounding the emergence of major retail techniques, including the department store, supermarket and discount house. The key role of the decision maker was also noted by Markin and Duncan[138], arch critics of the cyclical perspective, but their ecological model of institutional evolution emphasised broader environmental trends and the processes of conflict, co-operation and adaptation among institutional species. Davidson, Sweeny and Stampfl[51] went even further when they contended that all models of retail change were sub-sets of the environmental perspective, through another careful review of the literature concluded that institutional change was the combined result of environmental and situational influences and competition between retail forms[200].

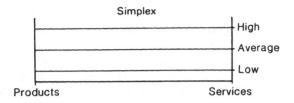

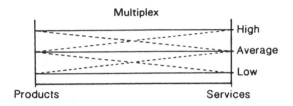

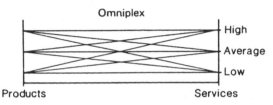

Figure 8 Simplex-Omniplex Theory of Retail Institutional Change (Regan)

Environment-cycle-conflict

Despite its obvious appeal, the all embracing approach to institutional evolution (environment-cycle-conflict) has attracted relatively few academic adherents. True, a number of scholars including Shaw[195], Kaynak[125], and Hall, Knapp and Winsten[95] have touched upon the relationship. Hunt[115] and Izraeli[118] also deserve mention for the former's integration of the wheel of retailing and the theory of differential advantage and the latter's cyclical-cum-environmental approach to the concept of countervailing power. McNair and May, moreover, predicted that the next turn of the wheel of retailing would be the result of environmental forces and give rise to inter-institutional conflict[154]. Yet only two, rarely cited, contributions have endeavoured to establish a formal link between the environmental, cyclical and conflictual schools of institutional thought.

In what is undoubtedly the most important conceptual advance since McNair's original hypothesis, Agergaard, Olsen and Allpass[1] argue that the pattern of retail evolution is more akin to a spiral than a cycle. Their theory of spiral movement maintains that institutions which trade up due to competitive pressure or place undue emphasis upon any aspect of the retail mix, such as a wide assortment, automatically create a vacuum at the opposite, low cost or specialist, ends of the trading spectrum. Novel retail techniques eventually emerge to capitalise upon these opportunities but because living standards have risen in the meantime, the original format is recreated on a slightly higher plane. According to the theory, therefore, the modern convenience store is simply a more sophisticated version of the former corner shop. Similarly, the discount food store harks back to the early days of the supermarket, though, once again, it is not quite so spartan. The evolution of the planned shopping centre can also be viewed from a spiral perspective[90]. In Britain, the early town centre shopping complexes were crude and fairly small scale but by the mid-1970s an era of major developments, epitomised by Newcastle's Eldon Square and Manchester Arndale, had dawned. Since then, the smaller centres have re-appeared, though they tend to be much more elaborate than their precursors of the 1960s[19, 99].

Central to the theory of spiral movement is a continued improvement in living standards with, presumably, higher or lower rates of economic growth being reflected in the slant of the spiral. The model, in addition, assumes unrestricted institutional development. As originally formulated, therefore, the hypothesis cannot accommodate constraints upon the evolutionary processes of retail techniques, such as anti-chain store legislation[131, 167] or restrictions on the construction of hypermarkets[36, 58]. In this respect, a slight modification of the spiral analogy to that of a coiled spring may be more appropriate. Thus, when the regulatory shackles on the institutional spiral are relaxed, a sudden surge of development can be expected. This observation would appear to be borne out by the spate of superstore construction which followed the British government's adoption of a less restrictive stance on such facilities in the late 1970s[53]. Indeed, a similar explosion of out-of-town regional shopping centres is being widely predicted at present, given the continuing relaxation of retail planning controls[59, 220].

The second comprehensive conceptualisation of institutional change, the diversity theory of market processes, holds that the history of retailing is composed of short and long cycles[15]. Long cycles begin in the classic Schumpeterian manner with the dramatic appearance of new forms of distribution, such as department stores, shopping centres and discount stores. A consequence of developments in the social and technological milieu, these institutions represent a distinct break from prior trading arrangements and possess considerable cost or quality advantages over the old. However, their advantageous attributes are quickly analysed, a process of imitation ensues and the gains accruing to the innovator are rapidly eroded. Short cycles, on the other hand, signify the subsequent replacement of inter-institutional by intra-institutional competition and are characterised by the unending search for differential advantage. As each competitor attempts to exploit its particular capabilities a number of variants of the original institution emerge, each emphasising different elements and combinations of the retail marketing mix. An increasingly diverse retail institutional structure thus transpires.

After outlining their basic diversity theory, Beem and Oxenfeldt combined it with the wheel of retailing to explain the evolution of the American food retailing system[see also 9, 84, 225]. Rapid urbanisation and customer price sensitivity in the early years of the present century, coupled with technological breakthroughs like the telephone, cash register and efficient accounting systems, gave rise to the economy chain store capable of selling at some 10 per cent below prevailing prices. Its initial success attracted numerous emulators and the gradual replacement of price by non-price competition. Gross margins were forced up and sellers became increasingly differentiated until the appearance of the supermarket — an outgrowth of economic depression and widespread car and refrigerator ownership — initiated the next long cycle and set the self-same wheel process in train. What is more, in a particularly perceptive passage, they predicted that by 1980 automated retail warehouses, accessed through interactive or teleshopping technology, would be operational.

Discussion

Although debating the pros and cons of institutional change has proved a perennial attraction to retail theorists, the utility and validity of this body of work has been questioned on a number of occasions[185, 187]. Hirschman and Stampfl, for instance, note that these "descriptive reasonings" fail to meet the criteria for formal theory, suffer from poorly defined concepts and causal linkages, lack validity, are tautological in their reasoning and, consequently, cannot hope to serve as the foundations for, sorely needed, retail theory[102]. Even renowned contributors to this field of study have stressed its manifold shortcomings. Hollander has argued that at best the models are descriptive rather than truly explanatory, lack predictive power, suffer from the subjectivity of the selected examples and are replete with ill-defined concepts like newness, merchandise mix, and vulnerability. The models, moreover, are extremely difficult to quantify and the patterns, like cloud formations, become "vaguer and vaguer as we approach them"[109].

Despite these harsh criticisms of the early 1980s, discussion of institutional change has continued unabated throughout the present decade. Interestingly, however, recent contributions appear to be moving away from the esoteric and self-indulgent analogies — geometrical forms, mechanical devices, household impedimenta and so on — that characterised earlier reflections on retail evolution. Today, the emphasis is firmly placed upon realism, quantification and, most importantly, managerial relevance. Examples include Bucklin's[35] detailed study of the US department store, Savitt's[188, 189] analysis of Comet Radiovision (UK), Martenson's[140] work on the geographical diffusion of IKEA and Deiderick and Dodge's[63] attempt to integrate institutional thought with Miller's[158] model of competitive strategy. Although this approach, particularly the application of institutional concepts to individual firms, is not without its critics[111] it is likely to continue to grow and develop.

Exciting as these new directions are, several significant problems with institutional theory as it stands needs must be addressed if the conceptual advances of recent years are to be maintained. The above mentioned institutional-individual controversy must be satisfactorily resolved with a clear definition of the scope of institutional thought. Prior contributions, remember, have ranged from specific products, through individual firms to the development of national retail systems; and while this adds to the eclecticism of the field of study it is also indicative of the lack of a clear research focus. It is equally important that the nature of retail institutions is unequivocally established and a comprehensive classification scheme devised[31, 109, 110]. Definitions of department stores, hypermarkets, discounters and so on vary from commentator to commentator, country to country, and time to time. Confusion, moreover, can result from the commonplace tendency to consider forms of organisation (chain stores, cooperative societies, etc) as institutional types. Chains of department stores and cooperative supermarkets are not unknown after all[61]. A closely related requirement concerns the internationalisation of institutional thought. Although the definitional problem is compounded when analysis is undertaken on an international scale[128], the bulk of studies hitherto have concentrated upon American retail experiences[187]. Granted, a number of important investigations have been conducted in Europe and various developing nations, but more — and more detailed — work remains to be done. As Savitt[187] and Hollander[109] point out, it is imperative that the validity of the models is carefully tested in a range of social and economic settings. A detailed comparison of the mix of institutions in contrasting countries and an examination of the same techniques in different environmental circumstances would prove particularly useful. With regard to the latter, Dawson's[58] recent work on the diffusion of the hypermarket represents an important step in the right direction, though much remains to be done.

Conclusion

Some 30 years ago in the course of an address on trends in retailing, McNair outlined what has become known as the wheel of retailing theory. Once described as "the most promising hypothesis yet advanced to explain retail development"[177] his concept has begat a prodigious body of scholarly research. Although a wide variety of approaches are evident, this work can be divided into three broad categories — environmental, cyclical and conflictual. The environmental approach to institutional evolution contends that change occurs as a consequence of developments in the socio-economic milieu; cyclical theories argue that it takes place in an oscillatory fashion;

and the conflictual perspective considers inter-institutional antagonism to be the mainspring of retail change.

It is generally recognised, however, that none of the three approaches provides a complete explanation of institutional evolution and a series of increasingly elaborate combination theories have been put forward. Although most model builders have been content to bring together a couple of conceptualisations, the most comprehensive picture is provided when all three are synthesised. The evolutionary process commences when changes in the business environment, be they technological (motor car and freezer ownership), economic (high inflation, increased consumer expenditure), legislative (planning regulations, shop hours), demographic (household size, age structure) or whatever, provide an opportunity for perceptive individuals. Those entrepreneurs who respond by developing new, or more usually, rearranging old[109, 162], methods of selling represent a threat to the remainder of the retail system. Inter-institutional strife then takes over until the new-found balance of power is once again upset by the next externally inspired parametric shock. Retail institutional change, in other words, is the outcome of external environmental influences and a cycle-like sequence of internal conflict.

In recent years, contributors to this area of academic endeavour have moved away from conceptual flights of fancy and adopted a more down-to-earth approach to institutional evolution. Quantification and managerial relevance, rather than aesthetically appealing but non-utilitarian formulations are the order of the present day. Despite D'Amico's[45] contention that it is "time for the wheel of retailing to roll off into the sunset", it seems that a whole new era of institutional thought has dawned. It remains to be seen whether a number of important definitional difficulties can be resolved, but the developments of the 1980s are encouraging in very many respects. Cross-national analyses, in particular, appear to offer many exciting possibilities for future research.

If, in conclusion, one were asked to encapsulate the 30 year history of retail institutional thought, it could perhaps be described as "the wheel of the wheel of retailing". From a bare-bones, 613 word hypothesis in 1957, a more and more elaborate conceptual edifice was constructed. By the early 1980s, however, disillusion with these vague "descriptive reasonings" had set in and since then a return to basic, factual analyses has taken place. (Proof positive of this sea change, if it be needed, is Hollander's[111] recent rejection of Savitt's historical endeavours[188]. An old line institutional theorist he reacted in the time-honoured manner to the threat posed by Savitt's factual, firm specific research. Still, given Hollander's massive contribution to the school of retail institutional thought, any published results of the — inevitable — assimilation process should prove very stimulating reading). Naturally, it is difficult, if not impossible, to determine whether the wheel of the wheel of retailing will continue to turn, but one can be fairly confident that for the foreseeable future retail institutional change will remain a major attraction for marketing theorists.

References

1. Agergaard, E., Olsen, P.A. and Allpass, J., "The Interaction between Retailing and the Urban Centre Structure: A Theory of Spiral Movement", *Environment and Planning*, Vol. 2, 1970, pp. 55–71.
2. Alawi, H.M.A., "Saudi-Arabia: Making Sense of Self-Service", *International Marketing Review*, Vol. 3, No. 1, 1986, pp. 21–38.
3. Alchain, A.A., "Uncertainty, Evolution and Economic Theory", *Journal of Political Economy*, Vol. 58, 1950, pp. 211–221.
4. Alderson, W., "*Marketing Behaviour and Executive Action*", Homewood, Illinois, Richard D. Irwin, 1957.
5. Alderson, W., "*Dynamic Marketing Behaviour: A Functionalist Theory of Marketing*", Homewood, Illinois, Richard D. Irwin, 1965.
6. Alderson, W. and Shapiro, S.J., "Towards a Theory of Retail Competition", in Cox, R., Alderson, W. and Shapiro, S.J. (Eds.), *Theory in Marketing*, Homewood, Illinois, Richard D. Irwin, Second Series, pp. 190–212.
7. Allvine, F.C., "The Supermarket Challenged! New Competitive Strategies Needed", *Business Horizons*, Vol. 11, October, 1968, pp. 61–72.
8. Allvine, F.C., "The Future for Trading Stamps and Games", *Journal of Marketing*, Vol. 33, January, 1969, pp. 45–52.
9. Appel, D., "The Supermarket, Early Development of an Institutional Innovation", *Journal of Retailing*, Vol. 48, Spring, 1972, pp. 39–53.
10. Arndt, J., "Temporal Lags in Comparative Retailing", *Journal of Marketing*, Vol. 36, October, pp. 40–45.
11. Aynsley, P., "Convenience Stores — USA", *Retail*, Vol. 2, No. 3, 1984, pp. 17–28.
12. Bartels, R., "Criteria for Theory in Retailing" in Stampfl, R.W. and Hirschman, E.C. (Eds.), *Theory in Retailing: Traditional and Non-traditional Sources*, Chicago, American Marketing Association, 1981, pp. 1–8.
13. Bates, A.D., "*Retailing and its Environment*", New York, Van Nostrand, 1979.
14. Beem, E.R., "Retailing in the 1980s" reprinted in Gist, R.R. (Ed.), "*Management Perspectives in Retailing*", second edition, New York, John Wiley, 1971, pp. 3–6.
15. Beem, E.R. and Oxenfeldt, A.R., "A Diversity Theory for Market Processes in Food Retailing", *Journal of Farm Economics*, Vol. 48, August, 1966, pp. 69–95.
16. Bell, J. and Brown, S., "Anatomy of a Supermarket Price War", *Irish Marketing Review*, Vol. 1, 1986, pp. 109–117.
17. Bennett, P.D., "Retailing Evolution or Revolution in Chile", *Journal of Marketing*, Vol. 30, July, 1966, pp. 38–41.
18. Bennett, R.C. and Cooper, R.G., "The Product Life Cycle Trap", *Business Horizons*, Vol. 27, No. 5, 1984, pp. 7–16.
19. Bennison, D.J. and Davies, R.L., "The Impact of Town Centre Shopping Schemes in Britain", *Progress in Planning*, Vol. 14, No. 1, Oxford, Pergamon, 1980.
20. Berens, J.S., "Capital Requirements and Retail Institutional Innovation — Theoretical Observations", in Lamb, C.W. and Dunne, P.M. (Eds.), *Theoretical Developments in Marketing*, Chicago, American Marketing Association, 1980, pp. 248–250.
21. Berman, B. and Evans, J.R., "*Retail Management: A Strategic Approach*", New York, Macmillan, 1979.
22. Berry, B.J.L., "Commercial Structure and Commercial Blight: Retail Patterns and Processes in the City of Chicago", Chicago, University of Chicago, Department of Geography, Research Paper No. 85, 1963.
23. Berry, L.L. and Wilson, I.H., "Retailing: The Next Ten Years", *Journal of Retailing*, Vol. 53, Fall, pp. 5–28.

24. Blake, W.J., *"Elements of Marxian Economic Theory and its Criticism"*, New York, Garden Company, 1939.
25. Bliss, P., "Schumpeter, the Big Disturbance and Retailing" reprinted in Gist, R.R. (Ed.), *Management Perspectives in Retailing*, New York, John Wiley, 1967, pp. 14–18.
26. Böcker, F. and Tries, B., "Distribution Systems and Distribution Research in the Federal Republic of Germany: A Synopsis" in Falk, T. and Julander, C.R. (Eds.), *Current Trends in Distribution Research*, Bradford, MCB University Press, 1984, pp. 53–67.
27. Bogart, L., "The Future of Retailing", *Harvard Business Review*, Vol. 51, November-December, 1973, pp. 16–32.
28. Brand, E.A., "Modern Supermarket Operation" reprinted in Gist, R.R. (Ed.) *Managerial Perspectives in Retailing*, New York, John Wiley, 1967, pp. 19–21.
29. Briggs, A., *Friends of the People: The Centenary History of Lewis's*, London, Batsford, 1956.
30. Brown, S., "Retail Location and Retail Change in Belfast City Centre", unpublished PhD thesis, Queen's University, Belfast, 1984.
31. Brown, S., "Retail Classification: A Theoretical Note", *Quarterly Review of Marketing*, Vol. 11, No. 2, 1986, pp. 12–16.
32. Brown, S., "An Integrated Approach to Retail Change: The Multi-Polarisation Model", *Service Industries Journal*, Vol. 6, No. 2, 1987, pp. 153–164.
33. Bruce, G.D., "The Ecological Structure of Retail Institutions", *Journal of Marketing Research*, Vol. 6, February, 1969, pp. 48–53.
34. Bucklin, L.P., *Competition and Evolution in the Distributive Trades*, Englewood Cliffs, Prentice Hall, 1972.
35. Bucklin, L.P., "Patterns of Change in Retail Institutions in the United States with Special Attention to the Traditional Department Store", *International Journal of Physical Distribution and Materials Management*, Vol. 13, Nos. 5/6, 1983, pp. 153–168.
36. Burt, S., "Hypermarkets in France: has the Loi Royer had any Effect?", *Retail and Distribution Management*, Vol. 12, No. 1, 1984, pp. 16–19.
37. Carson, D., Rushton, A. and Cameron, M., *Marketing*, Harmondsworth, Penguin, in press.
38. Cassady, R., "The New York Department Store Price War of 1951: A Micro-Economic Analysis", *Journal of Marketing*, Vol. 21, July, 1957, pp. 3–11.
39. Cauwe, M., "The Life Cycle of the Retail Business", *Retail and Distribution Management*, Vol. 7, No. 4, 1979, pp. 48–51.
40. Chamberlain, E.H., *The Theory of Monopolistic Competition*, Cambridge, Harvard University Press, 1933.
41. Collesei, U., Montovan, P. and Rispoli, M., "The Evolution of the Retail Structure in Italy: A Regional Analysis", in Angeli, F. (Ed.), *The Economics of Distribution*, Venice, Proceedings of the Second International Conference on the Economics of Distribution, 1983, pp. 13–78.
42. Converse, P.D., "Mediocrity in Retailing", *Journal of Marketing*, Vol. 23, 1959, pp. 419–420.
43. Cox, R., "Discussions" in Smith, A.B. (Ed.), *Competitive Distribution in a Free, High Level Economy and its Implications for the University*, Pittsburg, University of Pittsburg, 1958, pp. 48–60.
44. Cundiff, E.W., "Concepts in Comparative Retailing", *Journal of Marketing*, Vol. 29, 1965, pp. 143–162.
45. D'Amico, M., "Discussants Comments", in Summey, J.H. *et al.* (Eds.), *Marketing: Theories and Concepts for an Era of Change*, Carbondale, Proceedings Southern Marketing Association, 1983, p. 160.

46. Davidson, W.R., "Changes in Distributive Institutions", *Journal of Marketing*, Vol. 34, January, 1970, pp. 7–10.
47. Davidson, W.R., Bates, A. D. and Bass, S.J., "The Retail Life Cycle", *Harvard Business Review*, Vol. 54, November–December, 1976, pp. 89–96.
48. Davidson, W.R., Doody, A.F. and Lowry, J.R., "Leased Departments as a Major Force in the Growth of Discount Store Retailing", *Journal of Marketing*, Vol. 34, January, 1970, pp. 39–46.
49. Davidson, W.R. and Johnson, N.E., "Portfolio Theory and the Retailing Life Cycle" in Stampfl, R.W. and Hirschman, E.C. (Eds.), *Theory in Retailing: Traditional and Non-Traditional Sources*, Chicago, American Marketing Association, 1981, pp. 51–63.
50. Davidson, W.R. and Smallwood, J.E., "An Overview of Management of the Retail Life Cycle" in Stampfl, R.W. and Hirschman, E.C. (Eds.), *Competitive Structure in Retail Markets, the Department Store Perspective*, Chicago, American Marketing Association, 1980, pp. 53–62.
51. Davidson, W.R., Sweeny, P.J. and Stampfl, R.W., *Retailing Management*, fifth edition, New York, John Wiley, 1983.
52. Davies, R.L., *Marketing Geography; With Special Reference to Retailing*, Corbridge, Retail and Planning Associates, 1976.
53. Davies, R.L., *Retail and Commercial Planning*, London, Croom Helm, 1984.
54. Davies, R.L. and Kirby, D.A., "Current Trends in UK Distribution Research" in Falk, T. and Julander, C.R. (Eds.), *Current Trends in Distribution Research*, Bradford, MCB University Press, 1984, pp. 68–92.
55. Dawson, J.A., "Marketing" in Dawson, J.A. and Doornkamp, J.C. (Eds.), *Evaluating the Human Environment: "Essays in Applied Geography"*, London, Edward Arnold, 1973, pp. 134–158.
56. Dawson, J.A., *The Marketing Environment*, London, Croom Helm, 1979.
57. Dawson, J.A., *Shopping Centre Development*, London, Longman, 1983.
58. Dawson, J.A., "Structural-Spatial Relationships in the Spread of Hypermarket Retailing" in Kaynak, E. and Savitt, R. (Eds.), *Comparative Marketing Systems*, New York, Praeger, 1984, pp. 156–182.
59. Dawson, J.A., "Issues for Retail Planning", in Sparks, L. (Ed.), "Issues for Retail Planning in Scotland", University of Stirling, Department of Business Studies, Working Paper, 8503, 1985, pp. 5–18.
60. Dawson, J.A., "Change and Continuity in Japanese Retailing", *Retail and Distribution Management*, Vol. 13, No. 2, 1985, pp. 46–50.
61. Dawson, J.A. and Kirby, D.A., "Urban Retailing and Consumer Behaviour: Some Examples from Western Society" in Herbert, D.T. and Johnston, R.J. (Eds.), *Geography and the Urban Environment; Progress in Research and Applications: Volume Three*, London, John Wiley, 1980, pp. 87–132.
62. Day, G.S., "The Product Life Cycle: Analysis and Applications Issues", *Journal of Marketing*, Vol. 45, Fall, 1981, pp. 60–67.
63. Deiderick, T.E. and Dodge, H.R., "The Wheel of Retailing Rotates and Moves" in Summey, J. *et al.* (Eds.), *Marketing: Theories and Concepts for an Era of Change*, Carbondale, Proceedings Southern Marketing Association, 1983, pp. 149–152.
64. Dhalla, N.K. and Yuspeh, S., "Forget the Product Life Cycle Concept", *Harvard Business Review*, Vol. 54, January–February, 1976, pp. 102–112.
65. Dickinson, R.A., *Retail Management*, Texas, Austin Press, 1981.
66. Distributive Industry Training Board, *Political, Social, Economic and Technological Issues, Their Probable Effects on the UK Distributive Industry, 1980–1995*, Manchester DITB, 1980.

67. Doody, A.F., "Historical Patterns of Marketing Innovation", in Decker, W.S. (Ed.), *Emerging Concepts in Marketing*, Chicago, American Marketing Association, 1962, pp. 245–253.
68. Douglas, S.P., "Patterns and Parallels of Marketing Structures in Several Countries", *MSU Business Topics*, Vol. 19, Spring, 1971, pp. 38–48.
69. Dreesman, A.C.R., "Patterns of Evolution in Retailing", *Journal of Retailing*, Vol. 44, Spring, 1968, pp. 64–81.
70. Duncan, D.J., "Responses of Selected Retail Institutions to their Changing Environment", in Bennett, P.D. (Ed.), *Marketing and Economic Development*, Chicago, American Marketing Association, 1965, pp. 583–602.
71. Eaton, B.C. and Lipsey, R.G., "Comparison Shopping and the Clustering of Homogeneous Firms", *Journal of Regional Science*, Vol. 19, No. 4, 1979, pp. 421–435.
72. Edwards, C.M., "Discussions", in Smith, A.B. (Ed.), *Competitive Distribution in a Free, High Level Economy and its Implications for the University*, Pittsburg, University of Pittsburg, 1958, pp. 34–40.
73. Eliot, S., "The Crisis in the Co-operative Movement", *Retail and Distribution Management*, Vol. 11, No. 4, 1983, pp. 8–14.
74. Entenberg, R.D., "The Interaction of Consumer Behaviour and Market Competition on the Store of the Future", in Hindersman, C.H. (Ed.), *Marketing Precision and Executive Action*, Chicago, American Marketing Association, 1962, pp. 571–579.
75. Ferry, J.W., "*A History of the Department Store*", New York, Macmillan, 1960.
76. Fink, S.L., Baek, J. and Taddeo, K., "Organisational Crisis and Change", *Applied Behavioural Science*, Vol. 7, No. 1, 1971, pp. 15–37.
77. Galbraith, J.K., *American Capitalism: The Concept of Countervailing Power*, revised edition, Boston, Houghton Mifflin, 1956.
78. Gist, R.R., *Retailing: Concepts and Decisions*, New York, Wiley and Sons, 1968.
79. Gist, R.R., *Marketing and Society: A Conceptual Introduction*, New York, Holt, Rinehart and Winston, 1971.
80. Globerman, S., "Self-Service Gasoline Stations: A Case Study of Competitive Innovation", *Journal of Retailing*, Vol. 54, No. 1, 1978, pp, 75–86, 96.
81. Goldman, A., "Growth of Large Food Stores in Developing Countries", *Journal of Retailing*, Vol. 50, No. 2, 1974, pp. 50–60.
82. Goldman, A., "Outreach of Consumers and the Modernisation of Urban Food Retailing in Developing Countries", *Journal of Marketing*, Vol. 38, October, 1974, pp. 8–16.
83. Goldman, A., "The Role of Trading up in the Development of the Retailing System", *Journal of Marketing*, Vol. 39, January, 1975, pp. 54–62.
84. Goldman, A., "Stages in the Development of the Supermarket", *Journal of Retailing*, Vol. 51, No. 4, 1975–76, pp. 49–64.
85. Goldman, A., "Institutional Changes in Retailing: An Updated 'Wheel of Retailing' Theory" in Woodside, A.G. *et al.*, (Eds.), *Foundations of Marketing Channels*, Austin, Lone Star, 1978, pp. 189–211.
86. Goldman, A., "Transfer of a Retailing Technology into the Less Developed Countries: the Supermarket Case", *Journal of Retailing*, Vol. 57, Summer, 1981, pp. 5–29.
87. Goldman, A., "Adoption of Supermarket Shopping in a Developing Country: The Selective Adoption Phenomenon", *European Journal of Marketing*, Vol. 16, No. 1, 1982, pp. 17–26.
88. Goldman, A., "The Development and Implementation of a Marketing Based Economic Development Project in the Agricultural Sector — An Israeli Case"

in Kaynak, E. and Savitt, R. (Eds.), *Comparative Marketing Systems*, New York, Praeger, 1984, pp. 53–70.

89. Gosling, D. and Maitland, B., *Design and Planning of Retail Systems*, London, Architectural Press, 1976.
90. Greyser, S., "Foreword", in McNair, M.P. and May, E.G., *The Evolution of Retail Institutions in the United States*, Cambridge, Marketing Science Institute, 1976, pp. iii–iv.
91. Gross, W.L., "Strategies used by Major Department Stores to Compete with Low Margin Retailers", *Journal of Retailing*, Vol. 40, No. 2, 1964, pp. 11–28.
92. Guerin, J.R. "The Introduction of a New Food Marketing Institution in an Underdeveloped Economy: Supermarkets in Spain", *Food Research Institute Studies*, Vol. 3, 1965, pp. 217–227.
93. Guiltinan, P., "Planned and Evolutionary Changes in Distribution Channels", *Journal of Retailing*, Vol. 50, No. 2, 1974, pp. 79–91, 103.
94. Guy, C.M., "*Retail Location and Retail Planning in Britain*", Westmead, Gower, 1980.
95. Hall, M., Knapp, J. and Winsten, C., *Distribution in Great Britain and North America: A Study in Structure and Productivity*, London, Oxford University Press, 1961.
96. Harris, L., *Merchant Princes*, New York, Harper and Row, 1979.
97. Hawes, J.M. and Crittenden, W.F., "Generic Grocery Products and the Wheel of Retailing", *Mid-South Quarterly Business Review*, Vol. 3, No. 3, 1979, pp. 8–10.
98. Hensel, J.S., "Environmental Change and the Future Structure of Retailing", *Arizona Business*, Vol. 20, No. 2, 1973, pp. 14–20.
99. Hillier Parker Research, "*British Shopping Developments 1965–1982*", London, Hillier Parker May and Rowden, 1983.
100. Hirschman, E.C., "A Descriptive Theory of Retail Market Structure", *Journal of Retailing*, Vol. 54, No. 4, 1978, pp. 29–48.
101. Hirschman, E.C., "Retail Competitive Structure: Present and Potential" in Beckwith, N., *et al.* (Eds.), *1979 Educators Conference*, Chicago, American Marketing Association, 1979, pp. 401–405.
102. Hirschman, E.C. and Stampfl, R.W., "Retail Research: Problems, Potentials and Priorities", in Stampfl, R.W. and Hirschman, E.C. (Eds.), *Competitive Structure in Retail Markets: The Department Store Perspective*, Chicago, American Marketing Association, 1980, pp. 68–77.
103. Hollander, S.C., "Competition and Evolution in Retailing", *Stores*, Vol. 42, September, 1960, pp. 11–24.
104. Hollander, S.C., "The Wheel of Retailing", *Journal of Marketing*, Vol. 24, July, 1960, pp. 37–42.
105. Hollander, S.C., "Retailing: Cause or Effect", in Decker, W.S. (Ed.), *Emerging Concepts in Marketing*, Chicago, American Marketing Association, 1962, pp. 220–230.
106. Hollander, S.C., "Entrepreneurs Test the Environment: A Long Run View of Grocery Pricing" in Bennett, P.D. (Ed.), *Marketing and Economic Development*, Chicago, American Marketing Association, 1965, pp. 516–527.
107. Hollander, S.C., "Notes on the Retail Accordion", *Journal of Retailing*, Vol. 42, Summer, 1966, pp. 29–40, 54.
108. Hollander, S.C., *Multinational Retailing*, East Lansing, MSU International Business and Economic Studies, 1970.
109. Hollander, S.C., "Oddities, Nostalgia, Wheels and Other Patterns in Retail Evolution" in Stampfl, R.W. and Hirschman, E.C. (Eds.), *Competitive Structure in Retail Markets: "The Department Store Perspective"*, Chicago, American Marketing Association, 1980, pp. 78–87.

110. Hollander, S.C., "Retailing Theory: Some Criticism and Some Admiration", in Stampfl, R.W. and Hirschman, E.C. (Eds.), *Theory in Retailing: Traditional and Non-Traditional Sources*, Chicago, American Marketing Association, 1981, pp. 84–94.
111. Hollander, S.C., "If Small is Beautiful, Is a Very Small Sample even Prettier?", *European Journal of Marketing*, Vol. 20, No. 2, 1986, pp. 5–6.
112. Holmes, J.H. and Hoskins, W.R., "Using the Life Cycle in Store Location Decisions", *Pittsburg Business Review*, Vol. 46, No. 2, 1977, pp. 1–6.
113. Hotelling, H., "Stability in Competition", *Economic Journal*, Vol. 39, March, 1929, pp. 41–57.
114. Hower, R.M., *History of Macy's of New York, 1858–1919*, Cambridge, Harvard University Press, 1943.
115. Hunt, S.D., *Marketing Theory: Conceptual Foundations of Research in Marketing*, Colombus, Grid, 1976.
116. Ingene, C.A., "Intertype Competition: Restaurants versus Grocery Stores", *Journal of Retailing*, Vol. 59, No. 3, 1983, pp. 49–75.
117. Ingene, C.A. and Lusch, R., "A Model of Retail Structure" in Sheth, J. (Ed.), *Research in Marketing*, Vol. 5, 1981, pp. 101–164.
118. Izraeli, D., "The Cyclical Evolution of Marketing Channels", *British Journal of Marketing*, Vol. 5, No. 3, 1970, pp. 137–144.
119. Izraeli, D., "The Three Wheels of Retailing: A Theoretical Note", *European Journal of Marketing*, Vol. 7, No. 1, 1973, pp. 70–74.
120. Jeffreys, J.B., *Retail Trading in Britain 1850–1950*, Cambridge Cambridge University Press, 1954.
121. Jones, R., "Consumers' Co-operation in Victorian Edinburgh: The Evolution of a Location Pattern", *Transactions, Institute of British Geographers NS*, Vol. 4, 1979, pp. 292–305.
122. Jung, A.F., "Price Variations among Discount Houses and Other Retailers: A Re-appraisal", *Journal of Retailing*, Vol. 37, Spring, 1961, pp. 13–16, 51–52.
123. Kacker, M., "Coming to Terms with Global Retailing", *International Marketing Review*, Vol. 3, No. 1, 1986, pp. 7–20.
124. Kaikati, J.G., "Don't Discount Off-Price Retailers", *Harvard Business Review*, Vol. 63, No. 3, 1985, pp. 85–92.
125. Kaynak, E., "A Refined Approach to the Wheel of Retailing", *European Journal of Marketing*, Vol. 13, No. 7, 1979, pp. 237–245.
126. Kaynak, E. and Cavusgil, S.T., "The Evolution of Food Retailing Systems: Contrasting the Experience of Developed and Developing Countries", *Journal of the Academy of Marketing Science*, Vol. 10, No. 3, 1982, pp. 249–269.
127. Kaynak, E. and Savitt, R. (Eds.), *Comparative Marketing Systems*, New York, Praeger, 1984.
128. Kaynak, E. and Savitt, R., "Comparative Marketing: Integrative Statement", in Kaynak, E. and Savitt, R. (Eds.), *Comparative Marketing Systems*, New York, Praeger, 1984, pp. 3–13.
129. Kirby, D.A., "The North American Convenience Store: Implications for Britain", in Jones, P. and Oliphant, R. (Eds.), *Local Shops: Problems and Prospects*, Reading, Unit for Retail Planning Information, 1976, pp. 95–100.
130. Knee, D. and Walters, D., *Strategy in Retailing: Theory and Application*, Oxford, Philip Allan, 1985.
131. Lebhar, G.J., *Chain Stores in America: 1859–1962*, New York, Chain Store Publishing Co, 1963.
132. Lerner, A.P. and Singer, H.W., "Some Notes on Duopoly and Spatial Competition", *The Journal of Political Economy*, Vol. 45, No. 2, 1937, pp. 145–186.

133. Levy, H., *The Shops of Britain: A Study of Retail Distribution*, London, Kegan Paul, Trench, Trubner, 1948.
134. Lewis, W.A., "Competition in Retail Trade", *Economica*, Vol. 12, November, 1945, pp. 202–234.
135. Livesey, F., *The Distributive Trades*, London, Heinemann, 1979.
136. Livesey, F. and Hall, R.J., *Retailing: Developments and Prospects to 1985*, London, Staniland Hall, 1981.
137. Lord, J.D., "The Outlet/Off-price Shopping Centre as a Retailing Innovation", *Service Industries Journal*, Vol. 4, No. 1, 1984, pp. 9–18.
138. Markin, R.J. and Duncan, C.P., "The Transformation of Retailing Institutions: Beyond the Wheel of Retailing and Life Cycle Theories", *Journal of Macromarketing*, Vol. 1, No. 1, 1981, pp. 58–66.
139. Maronick, T.J. and Walker, B.J., "The Dialectic Evolution of Retailing", in Greenburg, B. (Ed.), *Proceedings, Southern Marketing Association*, Atlanta, Georgia State University, 1975, pp. 147–151.
140. Martenson, R., *Innovations in Multi-national Retailing: Ikea on the Swedish, Swiss, German and Austrian Furniture Markets*, Gothenburg, Department of Business Administration, University of Gothenburg, 1981.
141. Mason, J. B., "The Evolution of Retail Structure", *Survey of Business*, Vol. 16, No. 1, 1980, pp. 5–7.
142. Mason, J.B. and Mayer, M.L., *Modern Retailing: Theory and Practice*, third edition, Plano, Business Publications, 1984.
143. Mathias, P., *Retailing Revolution: A History of Multiple Retailing in the Food Trades Based upon the Allied Suppliers Group of Companies*, London, Longman, 1967.
144. May, E.G. and McNair, M.P., "Department Stores Face Stiff Challenge in Next Decade", *Journal of Retailing*, Vol. 53, Fall, 1977, pp. 47–58.
145. Mayfield, F.M., *The Department Store Story*, New York, Fairchild, 1949.
146. McAusland, R., "Supermarkets: 50 Years of Progress", *Progressive Grocer*, Vol. 59, No. 6, 1980, pp. 5–155.
147. McCammon, B.C., "Alternative Explanations of Institutional Change and Channel Evolution" in Greyser, S.A. (Ed.), *Toward Scientific Marketing*, Chicago, American Marketing Association, 1963, pp. 477–490.
148. McCammon, B.C., "Future Shock and the Practice of Management", in Levine, P. (Ed.), *Attitude Research Bridges the Atlantic*, Chicago, American Marketing Association, Marketing Research Techniques Series 16, 1975, pp. 71–89.
149. McCammon, B.C., Kasulis, J.J. and Lesser, J.A., "The New Parameters of Retail Competition: The Intensified Struggle for Market Share", in Stampfl, R.W. and Hirschman, E.C. (Eds.), *"Competitive Structure in Retail Markets: The Department Store Perspective"*, Chicago, American Marketing Association, 1980, pp. 108–118.
150. McKeever, J.R. and Griffin, N.M., *"The Community Builders Handbook"*, Washington DC, Urban Land Institute, 1977.
151. McNair, M.P., "Trends in Large Scale Retailing", *Harvard Business Review*, Vol. 10, October, 1931, pp. 30–39.
152. McNair, M.P., "Significant Trends and Developments in the Post War Period", in Smith, A.B. (Ed.), *Competitive Distribution in a Free High Level Economy and its Implications for the University*, Pittsburg, University of Pittsburg Press, 1958, pp. 1–25.
153. McNair, M.P. and May, E.C., *The Evolution of Retail Institutions in the United States*, Cambridge, Marketing Science Institute, 1976.
154. McNair, M.P. and May, E.G., "The Next Revolution of the Retailing Wheel", *Harvard Business Review*, Vol. 56, September–October, 1978, pp. 89–91.
155. Michel, M. and Vander Eycken, H., *"La distribution en Belgique"*, Gembloux, Ducalot, 1974.

156. Michman, R.D., "Channel Development and Innovation", *Marquette Business Review*, Vol. 15, Spring, 1971, pp. 45–49.
157. Midgley, D.F., "Toward a Theory of the Product Life Cycle: Explaining Diversity", *Journal of Marketing*, Vol. 45, Fall, 1981, pp. 109–115.
158. Miller, R., "Strategic Pathways to Growth in Retailing", *Journal of Business Strategy*, Vol. 1, Winter, 1981, pp. 16–29.
159. Moyer, M.S., "The Roots of Large Scale Retailing", *Journal of Marketing*, Vol. 26, October, 1962, pp. 55–59.
160. Nielsen, O., "Developments in Retailing" in Kjaer-Hansen, M. (Ed.), *Readings in Danish Theory of Marketing*, Amsterdam, North Holland Publishing Company, 1966, pp. 101–115.
161. Nieschlag, R., *Die Dynamik der Betriebsformen im Handel*, Essen, Rheinisch-Wertfalisches Institute Für Wirtschaftforschung, 1954.
162. Nieschlag, R., *Binnenhandel und Binnenhandelspolitik*, Berlin, Duncker and Humblot, 1959.
163. Nystrom, P., *The Economics of Retailing: Retail Institutions and Trends*, third edition, New York, Roland Press, 1930.
164. Oxenfeldt, A.R., "The Retailing Revolution: Why and Whither", *Journal of Retailing*, Vol. 36, Fall, 1960, pp. 157–162.
165. Oxenfeldt, A.R. and Kelly, A.O., "Will Successful Franchise Systems Ultimately Become Wholly-Owned Chains?", *Journal of Retailing*, Vol. 44, Winter, 1968, pp. 69–83.
166. Padburg, D.I. and Thorpe, D., "Channels of Grocery Distribution: Changing Stages in Evolution — A Comparison of USA and UK", *Journal of Agricultural Economics*, Vol. 25, 1974, pp. 1–19.
167. Palamountain, J.C., *The Politics of Distribution*, Cambridge, Harvard University Press, 1955.
168. Parsons, T. and Smelser, N.J., *Economy and Society*, New York, Free Press, 1956.
169. Pasdermadjian, H., "*The Department Store, Its Origins, Evolution and Economics*", London, Newman Books, 1954.
170. Pennance, F.G. and Yamey, B.S., "Competition in the Retail Grocery Trade, 1850–1939", *Economica*, Vol. 22, 1955, pp. 303–317.
171. Pennington, A.L., "The Department Store versus the Speciality Store", in Stampfl, R.W. and Hirschman, E.C. (Eds.), *Competitive Structure in Retail Markets: The Department Store Perspective*, Chicago, American Marketing Association, 1980, pp. 132–138.
172. Polli, R. and Cook, V., "Validity of the Product Life Cycle", *Journal of Business*, Vol. 42, 1969, pp. 385–400.
173. Potter, R.B., *The Urban Retailing System: Location, Cognition and Behaviour*, Aldershot, Gower, 1982.
174. Pumroy, J.T., "The Changing Structure of Retailing", in Greyser, S.A. (Ed.), *Toward Scientific Marketing*, Chicago, American Marketing Association, 1963, pp. 457–466.
175. Qualls, W., Olshavsky, R.W. and Michaels, R.E., "Shortening of the PLC — An Empirical Test", *Journal of Marketing*, Vol. 45, Fall, 1981, pp. 76–80.
176. Regan, W.J., "Full Cycle for Self-Service", *Journal of Marketing*, Vol. 25, April, 1961, pp. 15–21.
177. Regan, W.J., "The Stages of Retail Development", in Cox, R., Alderson, W. and Shapiro, S.J. (Eds.), *Theory in Marketing*, second series, Homewood, Illinois, Richard D. Irwin, 1964, pp. 139–153.
178. Richards, J., "Off-price", *Retail*, Vol. 1, Winter, 1983, pp. 21, 22, 31–35.
179. Rink, D.R. and Swan, J.E., "Product Life Cycle Research: A Literature Review", *Journal of Business Research*, Vol. 78, 1979, pp. 219–242.

180. Robson, B.T., "Human Ecology, Geography and Marketing", *British Journal of Marketing*, Vol. 3, 1969, pp. 164–169.
181. Rogers, D., "America's Maturing Institution: Off-price Apparel Stores", *Retail and Distribution Management*, Vol. 11, No. 5, 1983, pp. 29–31.
182. Rogers, D., "Changes in North American Supermarkets", *Retail and Distribution Management*, Vol. 12, No. 4, 1984, pp. 19–23.
183. Rosenbloom, B., "Strategic Planning in Retailing: Prospects and Problems", *Journal of Retailing*, Vol. 56, No. 1, 1980, pp. 107–120.
184. Rosenbloom, B., *Retail Marketing*, New York, Random House, 1981.
185. Rosenbloom, B. and Schiffman, L.G., "Retailing Theory: Perspectives and Approaches", in Stampfl, R.W. and Hirschman, E.C. (Eds.), *Theory in Retailing: Traditional and Non-Traditional Sources*, Chicago, American Marketing Association, 1981, pp. 168–179.
186. Rossum, R., "Is the Theory of Life Cycles Pure Humbug?", *Financial Times*, 23 August, Thursday, 1984, p. 14.
187. Savitt, R., "A Historical Approach to Comparative Retailing", *Management Decision*, Vol. 20, No. 4, 1982, pp. 16–23.
188. Savitt, R., "The 'Wheel of Retailing' and Retail Product Management", *European Journal of Marketing*, Vol. 18, No. 6/7, 1984, pp. 43–54.
189. Savitt, R., "Rejoinder to Stanley C. Hollander", *European Journal of Marketing*, Vol. 20, No. 2, 1986, pp. 6–7.
190. Schary, P.B., "Changing Aspects of Channel Structure in America", *British Journal of Marketing*, Vol. 5, Autumn, 1970, pp. 133–145.
191. Schell, E., *"Changes in Boston's Retail Landscape"*, New York, National Retail Merchants Association, 1964.
192. Schumpeter, J.A., *Capitalism, Socialism and Democracy*, second edition, London, George Allen and Unwin, 1947.
193. Shaffer, H., "How Retail Methods Reflect Social Change", *Canadian Business*, Vol. 46, No. 12, 1973, pp. 10–15.
194. Shaffer, H., "Will the Catalogue Supersede the Retailer?", *Canadian Business*, Vol. 48, No. 11, 1975, pp. 21–26.
195. Shaw, G., "Processes and Patterns in the Geography of Retail Change", University of Hull, Occasional Paper in Geography, No. 24, 1978.
196. Silk, A.J. and Stern, L.W., "The Changing Nature of Innovation in Marketing: A Study of Selected Business Leaders, 1852–1958", *Business History Review*, Vol. 37, 1963, pp. 182–199.
197. Simmons, J., *The Changing Pattern of Retail Locations*, University of Chicago, Department of Geography, Research Paper 92, 1964.
198. Slatter, S., "The Impact of Crisis on Managerial Behaviour", *Business Horizons*, Vol. 27, May–June, 1984, pp. 65–68.
199. Spalding, L.A., "The Superspecialists: A New Look at a Growing Challenge", *Stores*, Vol. 60, October, 1978, pp. 44–49.
200. Stern, L.W. and El-Ansary, A.I., *Marketing Channels*, Englewood Cliffs, Prentice Hall, 1977.
201. Stevens, R.E., "Retail Innovations: A Technological Model of Change in Retailing", *Marquette Business Review*, Vol. 19, No. 4, 1975, pp. 164–168.
202. Stigler, G.J., "The Division of Labour is Limited by the Extent of the Market", *Journal of Political Economy*, Vol. 59, No. 3, 1957, pp. 185–193.
203. Stone, E., "The Future of the Traditional Department Store", in Stampfl, R.W. and Hirschman, E.C. (Eds.), *"Competitive Structure in Retail Markets: The Department Store Perspective"*, Chicago, American Marketing Association, 1980, pp. 190–196.

204. Swan, J.E., "A Functional Analysis of Innovation in Distribution Channels", *Journal of Retailing*, Vol. 50, Spring, 1974, pp. 9–23, 90.
205. Takeuchi, H. and Bucklin, L., "Productivity in Retailing: Retail Structure and Public Policy", *Journal of Retailing*, Vol. 53, Spring, 1977, pp. 35–46.
206. Tallman, G.B. and Blomstrom, B., "Retail Innovations Challenge Manufacturers", *Harvard Business Review*, Vol. 40, No. 5, 1962, pp. 130–134.
207. Teeple, E.E., "Look out McDonalds; The 'Wheel' is Rolling", in Gitlow, H.S. and Wheatley, E.W. (Eds.), *Developments in Marketing Science, Vol. II*, Miami, Academy of Marketing Science, 1979, p. 379.
208. Tellis, G.J. and Crawford, C.M., "An Evolutionary Approach to Product Growth Theory", *Journal of Marketing*, Vol. 45, Fall, 1981, pp. 97–108.
209. Thomas, R.E., "Change in the Distribution Systems of Western Industrialised Economies", *British Journal of Marketing*, Vol. 4, Summer, 1970, pp. 62–69.
210. Thomas, S.M., Anderson, R.E. and Jolson, M.A., "The Wheel of Retailing and Non-Store Evolution: An Alternative Hypothesis", *International Journal of Retailing*, Vol. 1, No. 2, 1986, pp. 18–29.
211. Thorelli, H.B., "Ecology in Marketing", *Southern Journal of Business*, Vol. 11, 1967, pp. 19–25.
212. Thorelli, H.B. and Burnett, S.C., "The Nature of Product Life Cycles for Industrial Goods Businesses", *Journal of Marketing*, Vol. 45, Fall, 1981, pp. 97–108.
213. Thorpe, D., "Shopping Trip Patterns and the Spread of Superstores and Hypermarkets in Great Britain", Manchester Business School, Retail Outlets Research Unit, Research Paper No. 10, 1978.
214. Tietz, B., "The Future Development of Retail and Wholesale Distribution in Western Europe: An Analysis of Trends up to 1980", *British Journal of Marketing*, Vol. 5, No. 1, 1971, pp. 42–55.
215. Tillman, R., "Rise of the conglomerchant", *Harvard Business Review*, Vol. 49, November–December, 1971, pp. 44–51.
216. Tinsley, D.B., Brooks, J.R. and D'Amico, M., "Will the Wheel of Retailing Stop Turning?", *Akron Business and Economic Review*, Vol. 19, Summer, 1978, pp. 26–29.
217. Vance, J.E., "Emerging Patterns of Commercial Structure in American Cities", in Norborg, K. (Ed.), *The IGU Symposium on Urban Geography, Lund, 1960*, Lund, Gleerup, 1962, pp. 485–518.
218. Wadinambiaratchi, G.H., "Theories of Retail Development", *Social and Economic Studies*, Vol. 21, 1972, pp. 391–403.
219. White, R., "Multinational Retailing: A Slow Advance?", *Retail and Distribution Management*, Vol. 12, No. 2, 1984, pp. 8–13.
220. Whysall, P., "Changing Planning Policies for Large Stores", *Retail and Distribution Management*, Vol. 13, No. 1, 1985, pp. 8–12.
221. Winkler, J.K., *Nothing over Sixpence: The Fabulous Life of F.W. Woolworth*, London, Angus and Robertson, 1940.
222. Winstanley, M.J., *The Shopkeepers World: 1830–1914*, Manchester, Manchester University Press, 1983.
223. Woll, A., *Der Wettbewerb im Einzelhandel: Zur Dynamik der modernen Vertriebsformen*, Berlin, Duncker and Humblot, 1964.
224. Wrathall, J.E., "Out-of-Town Shopping Centres", Huddersfield Polytechnic, Department of Geography and Geology, Occasional Paper No. 1, 1974.
225. Zimmerman, M.M., *The Supermarket: A Revolution in Distribution*, New York, McGraw-Hill, 1955.

12

Concepts in comparative retailing

Edward W. Cundiff

Source: *Journal of Marketing* 29 (1965): 59–63.

The marketing systems that have evolved in different parts of the world clearly share certain common characteristics, but they also differ from each other in many important ways. Little is known about the degree and magnitude of these differences, and the degree, if any, to which they follow a logical, predictable pattern.

An understanding of such a pattern would be of great value to businessmen who wish to enter new markets or to predict developments in their own markets. At present, it is necessary to make a detailed study of each new market the businessman may propose to enter, because only rudimentary bases have been devised for comparing and generalizing about marketing systems.

These systems are at different stages of development throughout the world; and just as there are underdeveloped economies, there are underdeveloped marketing systems. By comparing economic systems at various stages, economists have attempted to devise ways of predicting future development in underdeveloped economies.[1] No equally comprehensive attempt has been made to explain the development of marketing systems.

Despite the lack of a theory of marketing development, marketing scholars have sometimes found to necessary to make predictions about foreign marketing systems by generalizing from their own systems.

An analysis of marketing in Finland indicated that, "Socio-economic conditions in Finland and the United States are sufficiently similar that our past is Finland's present and our present is seen evolving as Finland's future."[2] In their predictions for future retailing in Europe, Jefferys and Knee do little more than project existing American development.[3] To improve the value of such predictions, a better understanding of the evolution and development of marketing systems is needed.

Bartels has made an important preliminary contribution to this problem, by suggesting alternative methods of approaching the comparative study of marketing.[4] However, the preparation of a comprehensive explanation of the interrelationships among comparative marketing systems is a major job. One way of contributing to such an explanation is the development of hypotheses concerning specific aspects of marketing which may ultimately help to fill in the total picture. Since retailing is important in all systems, the hypotheses described herein were developed to help explain the comparative evolution and adaptation of retailing practices.

Evolution and adaptation in retailing

An orderly process of evaluation and adaptation of important retailing innovations in separate marketing systems seems to exist. An explanation of this process requires four postulates:

1. Innovation takes place only in the most highly developed systems. The retailers in other systems have more to gain from the adoption and adaptation of developments already tried and tested in the most highly developed systems.
2. The ability of a system to adapt innovations successfully of related directly to its level of economic development. Certain minimum levels of economic development are necessary to support anything beyond the most simple retailing methods.
3. When the economic environment is favorable to change, the process of adaptation may be either hindered or helped by local demographic-geographic factors, social mores, governmental action, and competitive pressures.
4. The process of adaptation can be greatly accelerated by the actions of aggressive individual firms.

The following discussion is a test of these hypotheses, by measuring the stages of adoption of some retailing innovations in a selected group of marketing systems.

Operating methods versus institutions

New retailing institutions would seem to be a logical kind of retailing innovation to study, since new institutions, such as supermarkets, are found in many nations. Yet such institutions are often too different from each other to justify comparison, having little in common beyond a name.

For example, there is little value in comparing American supermarkets with European supermarkets. Even a casual examination of the newly-developed "supermarkets" in Italy or England shows that the European institution is usually smaller, has a much more limited selection of merchandise, places far less emphasis on price appeals, makes less use of advertising, and makes no provision for parking.

American retailers themselves have used the term so loosely that it is necessary to define "real" supermarkets in terms of physical and operating criteria. Although *institutions* may evolve so differently and to preclude comparison, the basic retail *operating methods* are often the same in all marketing systems. The term "supermarket" may have different meaning in different markets; but a basic methods of retail operation, such as self-service, has the same meaning everywhere. For this reason, the four hypotheses will be tested against new methods of retail operations, not against new institutions.

Identification of new retail operating methods

For the purposes of this analysis, a new retailing development may be described as a new method of operating retail establishments, something that could be adopted by existing or newly-developed institutions, but that in no sense describes specific institutions. In this analysis it is necessary to confine attention only to *recent* innovations, because there is not enough historical information available about marketing methods in other notions to trace the pattern of adoption of earlier innovations.

At least four really new retail operating methods have evolved in the past half century. The best known and most widely adopted of these is self-service, which involves the displaying of merchandise in a manner so that the customer may if he wishes, examine it and make his purchase selection without the help and supervision of store employees. The aspect of self-service that is really new is not the open display of merchandise (which is as old as retailing itself), but the provision for customers to handle and select the merchandise themselves *without* supervision.

A second innovation is the use of unusually low markups made possible by strict limitation of inventories and strong emphasis on high stockturn. The new development here is the price-inventory stock-turn relationship, and should not be confused with price reductions resulting from other improvements in efficiency, such as increasing productivity of personnel.

A third development is the placement of large retail outlets or groups of retail outlets in suburban locations away from city congestion, as exemplified by planned shopping centers in the United States.

The fourth new development is automated retailing, providing the substitution of machines for people in the process of paying for and delivering possession of merchandise.

Selection of marketing systems of comparison

The paucity of information on marketing in other nations limits the comparisons that can be made. Census data are available for a large number of countries, but statistical information on retail operating practices is very limited. For this reason, it is necessary to rely to a large extent on descriptive material about foreign marketing institutions published by Americans who have visited and worked abroad.

Twenty nations were selected for comparison, including eleven European nations (Belgium, Denmark, Finland, France, Germany, Italy, the Netherlands, Spain, Switzerland, and the United Kingdom); four American nations (Canada, Mexico, the United States, and Venezuela); three Asian nations (India, Japan, and the Philippines); Australia; and the U.S.S.R. Unfortunately comparable economic information was not available for the U.S.S.R., and so it is not placed in rank order with the other nations.

Testing the hypotheses

Of the four new developments, self-service has been the most widely adopted in marketing systems around the world, so it provides the best information for comparison between systems. For this reason it will be considered first as a means of testing the four hypotheses. To the extent that information is available, the other three innovations will be used to check the experience with self-service.

Evolution and adaptation of self-service

Self-service, as an accepted method of retail operation, evolved in the United States primarily during or after the 1920s. Its development and dissemination in most of the highly-developed marketing systems throughout the world provides some support for the four hypotheses stated previously.

Hypothesis 1. The development of self-service supports the hypothesis that *retailing innovations evolve only in highly developed marketing systems.* On a purely *a priori* basis, the American marketing system is widely accepted as the most advanced in the world today, and was at least among the most advanced in the 1920s when self-service was first widely introduced.

Furthermore, there is no evidence of subsequent independent evolution of this method of operation in other marketing systems. The method appears to have spread primarily through adaptation of the original American idea.

Hypothesis 2. The spread of self-service into other marketing systems seems to support the hypothesis that *the ability to adapt innovations is related directly to the level of economic development of a system.* However, the identification and classification of stages of economic development is a problem challenging a number of economists today. A further complication is the wide variation in economic development that occurs within an economy. Just as the stage of economic development differs widely between New England and the Appalachian Mountain regions of the United States, so does it vary between the Amazon regions and the Rio de Janeiro–Sao Paulo areas in Brazil, and between the Piedmont and Sicilian areas of Italy. Thus, statistics on average economic development ignore the importance of highly developed subareas that may offer great potential for retail innovation.

Although it is beyond the scope of the present article to solve this problem of describing economic development, it is in order to have some basis for relating changes to economic differences, a number of factors for which comparable international data were sought. Only two factors were found— other data which showed promise of relating to economic development were not available on a current basis for all or most nations.

The first factor is an index of per-capita industrial productivity—percentage of value added in world industry divided by percentage of world population. The second is a measure of a nonessential semi-luxury good (telephones). These two economic factors, although offering promise as parts of a complex measure which may some day be devised to identify stages of economic development, are presented in this instance only as indicators of levels of economic development. Table 1 shows the measures of production and consumption, and the percentage estimates of self-service retail stores in all countries where information is available.

Table 1 A Comparative Ranking of Selected Nations with Respect to Economic Indices and Per Cent of Self-Service Stores[a]

Country	Index of production		Telephones in use		Self-service stores	
	Per capita	*Rank*	*Per capita*	*Rank*	*% of Total*	*Rank*
United States	7.7	1	.42	1	>10.0	1
United Kingdom	6.8	2	.16	7	1.3	8
Switzerland	6.7	3	.32	3	2.4	5
Canada	5.6	4	.315	4	>6.0	2
Germany	5.3	5	.12	11	3.6	4
Sweden	4.4	6	.36	2	5.35	3
Denmark	4.3	7	.245	5	1.4	6
Australia	4.1	8	.215	6	1.0	10
Belgium	3.7	9	.133	10	0.13	12
France	3.2	10	.101	12	0.24	11
Netherlands	3.0[b]	11	.1495	8	1.35	7
Venezuela	2.8[c]	12	.0285	16	0.005	16
Italy	1.9	13	.0805	13	0.02	13
Finland	1.6	14	.1464	9	1.1	9
Spain	1.05	15	.062	15	0.014	14
Japan	1.0	16	.065	14	(NA)	—
Mexico	0.7	17	.016	17	0.1	15
Philippines	0.05	18	.004	18	(NA)	—
India	0.03	19	.001	19	None	19
U.S.S.R.	—				<0.1	—

[a] *Sources*: Production and Telephone usage data were from *Statistical Yearbook, 1962*, Fourteenth Issue, Statistical Office of the United Nations, New York, 1963. Data on self-service penetration were collected from 16 sources.

[b] Production data understate level of economic development in this primarily trading nation.

[c] Production data overstate level of economic development because of the large production of oil for export.

When the nations are ranked with respect to industrial production and with respect to telephones per capita, the similarity in order is fairly close; in most instances where the change in rank order is more than two or three, the differences can be explained in terms of noneconomic factors. For example, the United Kingdom, which drops from second place on the production ranking to seventh place in telephones per capita, has a tradition of heavy reliance on mail and telegraph in situations where other nationals might more likely use the telephone. Also, the nationalized telephone system provides unusually extensive public telephone facilities.

A comparison of the data on production and consumption with self-service in the 20 countries shows a relationship between these factors. For example, 5 of the 6 leading nations in production are also leaders in penetration of self-service, or, to move further down the list, 11 of the top 12 are leaders in both. It would also be useful to know what level of productivity constitutes an absolute minimum below which there will be no self-service; but since this list comprises almost entirely highly developed or developing nations, there are insufficient data to locate a possible cutting point.

Hypothesis 3. The spread of self-service also provides some support for the hypothesis that *noneconomic factors may affect the level of marketing development that might otherwise have been predicted in terms of economic factors.* At least some of the variance between rank in production and consumption and rank in use of self-service can be explained by such factors. For example, the United Kingdom, second in value added in industry, is only eighth in penetration of self-service. The British government maintained rigorous restrictions on consumption long after the end of World War II, which served as a barrier to the introduction of new methods of retailing. Credit restrictions, for example, were not removed until 1958. The wide variance between production and consumption (as measured by installation of telephones) would appear to support this view.

As another example, Australia, which ranks sixth on the consumption index and eighth on the production index, is only tenth in adoption of self-service. This discrepancy can be explained at least partly by social pressures against strong business competition, and a history of cooperative action among retailers and manufacturers to oppose changes that might affect the status quo.

Hypothesis 4. As long as a marketing system has reached the minimum stage of development necessary to support retailing innovations, it seems likely that this process can be hastened by the actions of aggressive individuals or firms.*

For example, Sears Roebuck has dramatically influenced the retailing climate in Mexico since World War II, and may partially be responsible for the development of self-service in that nation at a more rapid rate than might be expected.

Also, in those instances where strong noneconomic forces may operate to prevent or delay the introduction of retailing innovations, an individual or firm may at least partially counteract these forces. Switzerland is a case in point where Gottlieb Duttweiler, through his Migros cooperative, worked almost single-handedly to overcome the organized opposition to change by entrenched retailers and wholesalers. Self-service has not developed as rapidly as might be expected in Switzerland, as indicated in Table 1; but might be nearly nonexistent without the Migros retail outlets and the examples set by Migros.

The price-inventory-stockturn relationship

The discount house provides the best example of an application of the price-inventory-stockturn relationship in most marketing systems, since it is by definition a price promoter. Other institutions, such as supermarkets, which emphasize price appeals in the United States, do not use this appeal consistently in different nations. Thus, the discount house provides a better basis for measuring the spread of the price-inventory-stockturn method of operation in *all* marketing systems.

Subjective descriptions of the development of retailing in other marketing systems provide evidence that discounting and the price-inventory-stockturn appeal has been adopted in the same manner as self-service—in a direct relation to the economic factors mentioned before. In those markets where it has met with almost no success thus far, there seem to be either legal, competitive, or social barriers to its adoption. In Melbourne, Australia, for example, new discount houses that were operating successfully were forced out of business by conventional retailers who were able to bring pressure on manufacturers and wholesalers to shut off their supplies of goods.

Decentralized locations

The decentralized location of retail stores also appears to be related to the stage of economic and marketing development. But it may be more strongly affected by noneconomic factors than the other retailing innovations.

For example, there seems to be a relationship between population concentrations, land costs, and the development of planned shopping centers. In Belgium, high population density and land cost have restricted the availability of parcels of land large enough for planned shopping centers. In addition, most decentralized retail locations are strongly dependent on the automobile as a means of transportation for the patrons. In those nations where excessive government taxes and restrictions have discouraged widespread ownership and use of automobiles (such as in Great Britain until recently) planned shopping centers have been slow to develop.

Automated retailing

Since an important end-result of automated retailing is the reduction of labor costs, it is potentially more valuable in those systems where labor is costly relative to capital. Also, it will flourish best in those systems where the level of consumption is high enough that there is a high priority on consumer convenience.

Australia provides an example of a situation where noneconomic factors can hasten the adoption of new developments. Union pressures for shorter working hours have resulted in legislation forbidding operation of retail stores on Saturday afternoons, Sundays, and evenings; and so retailers have turned to automatic vending of certain convenience goods (such as gasoline), to serve the needs of customers when stores must be closed.

Conclusions

Retailing institutions provide a part of the environment in which marketing decisions must be made. A better understanding of their evolution in different marketing systems helps to provide a framework for generalizing about comparative marketing systems. One factor, however, has been consciously ignored in this simplified explanation of retailing innovations. Retailing and the broader field of marketing are not only affected by the total economic environment, but, in turn, they may themselves affect this environment.

In societies with high discretionary income and abundant goods there are pressures for improvement in retailing efficiency. The degree to which these economic pressures result in the evolution and adoption of new methods of retailing operation depends on the total environment. Cultural acceptance of or resistance to change, demographic and geographic influences, the political and legal framework, the strength of pressure groups such as business competitors and unions—all of these may have an affect on retailing innovations. When these pressures are negative, the actions of aggressive individuals or firms may do much to achieve and hasten change.

Notes

1. W. W. Rostow, *The Stages of Economic Growth: A Non-Communist Manifesto* (Cambridge, England: The University Press, 1960), p. 4; Colin Clark, *The Conditions of Economic Progress*, 1st edition (London: Macmillan and Co., Ltd., 1940), pp. 337–338.

2. A. J. Alton, "Marketing in Finland," JOURNAL OF MARKETING, Vol. 27 (July, 1963), pp. 47–51.

3. James Jefferys and Derek Knee, *Retailing in Europe, Present Structure and Future Trends* (London: The Macmillan Company, 1963).

4. Robert Bartels, *Comparative Marketing: Wholesaling in Fifteen Countries*, sponsored by the American Marketing Association (Homewood, Illinois: Richard D. Irwin, Inc., 1963), pp. 1–6.

13

The retail life cycle

William R. Davidson, Albert D. Bates and Stephen J. Bass

Source: *Harvard Business Review* 55(6) (1976): 89–96.

Retail executives know about the "wheel of retailing" concept, the notion of the "marketing mix," the product life cycle, the so-called consumer revolution, and a number of other theories and philosophies, all of which have proved helpful in understanding business success in retailing. The following article introduces a concept that may be more significant still to retailers and suppliers. This is the concept of an *institutional* life cycle in retailing, a predictable series of stages that every major form of retailing is destined to go through. After describing the theory of this cycle, the authors look at some of its practical implications, including the kinds of strategies and policies needed to sustain profits at each of the four stages. For both retailers and their suppliers, turbulence and uncertainty are going to continue for some time to come, the authors believe, but the retail life cycle can be a helpful tool for adapting successfully to change.

For many years executives in manufacturing and retailing have sought to explain patterns of evolution among retail organizations and to forecast future retail innovations. Several meaningful efforts have been made to explain retail development, the most important being the "wheel of retailing" concept, originally advanced by Malcolm P. McNair.[1] In McNair's view new retailing concepts are oriented toward low costs and prices at first. Over time, the retail institution gradually trades up in terms of store decor, services offered, and merchandise stocked. Eventually the institution becomes vulnerable to a newer form of retailing operating with lower costs and prices.

Much of the progress in understanding institutional change can be attributed directly to the spark of controversy ignited by McNair's hypothesis. Efforts to expand, modify, or disprove the wheel of retailing concept have led to the development of numerous explanations of institutional development.[2] Some of the most widely discussed explanations are:

- *Demographic trends* – As the standard of living increases, retailers are naturally attracted by market segments with higher levels of income. This leads to increases in merchandise quality, prices, and the array of services.

- *Imperfect competition* – In efforts to avoid direct price competition, retailers place increasing emphasis on additional services, which can only be supported with higher margins.
- *Scrambled merchandising* – As retailers diversify their merchandise assortments, they tend to add higher-margin items that create the illusion of an evolutionary trading-up process.
- *Managerial evolution* – As company founders are replaced by second generation management, cost consciousness gives way to concerns over store appearance and image, thereby creating upward pressures on costs and prices.

Each of these approaches has merit as a basis for understanding the evolution of retail institutions. However, none of them seems entirely sufficient for explaining contemporary retail developments, which are of a decidedly different character from earlier retailing innovations. For instance, the wheel of retailing concept suffers from two important limitations:

1 It focuses almost exclusively on changing cost and gross margin relationships as the key to understanding evolutionary retail behavior. It assumes that breakthrough retailing institutions begin as low-cost concepts that gradually mature into higher-cost distribution mechanisms. This cost focus tends to make the concept somewhat limited in explaining the evolutionary behavior of newer, less price-oriented retail innovations, such as the convenience food store and the home improvement center.
2 It was never really intended to determine the pace with which retail innovations rise and fall. Given the somewhat frenetic rate at which new retailing concepts appear today, it is important to have a basis for appraising future developments.

The changing character of retail innovation and the apparent acceleration of innovative retail activity suggest that another expansion of the wheel of retailing concept is needed. We believe that the life cycle concept has considerable utility as a method for explaining and predicting institutional actions. In fact, detailed analyses using life cycle concepts can help management to project the direction and magnitude of future evolutionary processes.

Four stages of the life cycle

The product life cycle has a long and rich history in marketing and serves as a basis for many product line decisions, particularly in the consumer packaged goods field.[3] Much less well understood is the concept of the institutional life cycle. This theory argues that retailing institutions, like the products they distribute, pass through an identifiable life cycle.[4]

As *Exhibit I* shows, the retail life cycle, as we see it is divided into four distinct stages. While the stages are similar to those for the product life cycle, they have their own unique characteristics. We shall examine each stage in turn.

Exhibit I
The institutional life cycle in retailing

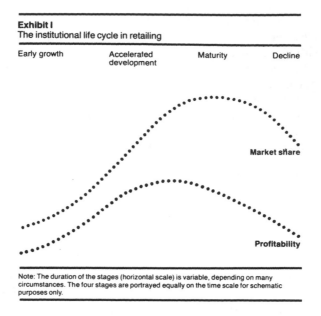

Note: The duration of the stages (horizontal scale) is variable, depending on many circumstances. The four stages are portrayed equally on the time scale for schematic purposes only.

1   Innovation

The first and most exciting stage of retail development is characterized by the emergence of a new, usually entrepreneurial, retail institution. The new concept typically represents a sharp departure from existing retailing approaches and as a result tends to enjoy a significant advantage. The advantage may arise from a tightly controlled cost structure that results in a favorable price position, but not always. The advantage may derive from a unique feature offered, such as a distinctive product assortment, ease of shopping, locational advantages, or even different advertising and promotional methods.

During the innovation period the new advantage produces a level of customer acceptance that causes sales to rise sharply. Profits, on the other hand, may lag as the new institution struggles with the operating problems associated with new ventures. Profits may also suffer because the company lacks the size to produce significant economies of scale, or because it incurs relatively large levels of start-up costs, many of which cannot be capitalized. Toward the end of the innovation period sales volume begins to increase even more rapidly, and profits also grow as the initial operating problems are overcome.

Let us look briefly at two examples with which many readers may be familiar:

- The supermarket of the 1930s is a classic example of a retail innovation based primarily on a cost and price advantage. By eliminating services such as credit, delivery, and telephone ordering, by utilizing self-service, and by achieving economies of scale, the supermarkets were able to operate on a gross margin of only 12% compared with 20% for more conventional food outlets. At the same time, the supermarkets produced a net profit margin fully 50% above conventional outlets, and some generated as much sales volume in two weeks as conventional food stores did in a year.

• In contrast to the supermarket, the home improvement center focused primarily on the "offer" of better combinations of related merchandise and services. Specializing in the sale of home repair and related do-it-yourself items, the home improvement center brings together at one place the tools, the application products, and the information necessary to do an entire home improvement job. The center's product variety and assortment cannot be matched by either hardware stores or building materials dealers. In addition, many home improvement centers provide extensive customer counseling, sponsor in-store seminars on home improvements, and often provide contractor assistance to do-it-yourselfers. Price in this total offer is a factor, but a relatively minor one.

As a result of its marketing efforts the home improvement center has been almost as spectacular a success as the supermarket. From a handful of outlets in the mid-1960s, such stores now account for more than 20% of total home improvement product sales, and they can be expected to increase that percentage steadily in future years.

2   Accelerated development

In the second stage of retail evolution, both sales volume and profits experience rapid rates of growth. During this period companies already established in the business are usually actively engaged in geographic expansion. Also, companies that were not innovators typically enter the new field. For example, once the discount department store was firmly established as a dynamic new form of retailing, mature corporations such as Kresge, Woolworth, Federated, and Dayton-Hudson made major comitments to their own discount operations.

As interest in the new concept surges, the market share of the innovating stores increases steadily and conventional outlets get hurt. As a result, companies that earlier had ignored the innovation begin to develop retaliatory programs. In most instances, though, the retaliatory programs are not completely thought through and are often ineffective. For example:

In the accelerated development phase of the discount department store, conventional department store outlets frequently attempted programs of retaliation on the theme of "we will not knowingly be undersold." This often proved ineffective because it focused on only one dimension of discount department store competition and did not give proper recognition to the discounter's nonprice advantages, including a suburban location, the convenience of night and Sunday operating hours, and the availability of open merchandising under a self-service formula.

During the early part of the accelerated development period there is normally a favorable impact on profits. Additional sales volume results in high levels of fixed expense leveraging, and substantial economies of scale are produced. However, toward the end of the period these favorable factors tend to be counterbalanced by cost pressures that arise from the need for a larger staff, more complex internal systems, increased management controls, and other requirements of operating large, multi-unit organizations. Consequently, near the end of the accelerated development period both market share and profitability tend to approach their maximum level.

3 Maturity

The third and most significant stage of development witnesses a dissipation of the earlier vitality of retailers. Market share levels off. As a result, a number of factors come together to create important operating problems.

First, entrepreneurial managers begin to face difficulties in controlling their large and complex organizations. Although they were excellent at maintaining the vitality and excitement of their organizations in the first two stages, they often lack the management skills necessary to direct large organizations in stable markets. Consequently, the quality of operations begins to slip.

Second, too much capacity becomes a problem. Retailers expand beyond the levels justified by the size of the total market, and in doing so they increase the level of total square footage to unprofitable levels. This situation persists until a major shakeout occurs, such as happened in the fast-food field in the late 1960s and among discount department stores in the early 1970s.

Finally, management finds itself facing direct frontal assaults from new forms of distribution. The upstart challengers run off with needed sales, creating profit problems which magnify other difficulties.

The result of such difficulties is a severe reduction in profitability. The discount department store industry offers a case in point.

This concept was pioneered by companies such as Masters, E. J. Korvette, and Two Guys from Harrison in the early 1950s. From this small base the industry grew quite rapidly, led for the most part by dynamic, highly creative, but not technically sophisticated managers. By 1960, the earliest year for which detailed trade data are available, the discount industry had more than 1,300 stores producing a total sales volume of approximately $2 billion. This volume put the industry well into the accelerated development stage of growth.

Sales and profits continued to advance during the early 1960s, spurred on by growth-oriented managements. Sales per store, sales per square foot, and market share rose continually, although not at the dramatic rates characteristic of previous years. At the same time, however, profitability started to fall as expenses outraced sales volume. In other words, the first signs of impending maturity were becoming apparent.

Despite this warning, entrepreneurs in the industry continued to open stores at an uninterrupted pace. "Overstoring" became an economic reality. Between 1965 and 1972, for example, the number of square feet of discount store space per household almost doubled, rising from 3.6 square feet to 6.5 square feet. As a result, sales per square foot fell precipitously throughout the 1960s and 1970s, as did profitability, despite the fact that market share continued to show increases through 1970.

Corporate executives did not start to correct these problems until about 1973, following a significant shakeout of weaker stores. As discount department stores continue to adapt to maturity as a way of life, profitability results can be expected to stabilize at economically sufficient levels. However, they are not likely ever to return to the exciting levels associated with the early stages of the life cycle.

4 Decline

The last era in the life cycle process is often avoided or greatly postponed by repositioning. By modifying its marketing concepts, management prolongs maturity and avoids decline. However, not all retail species are so lucky. Years ago, central city variety stores went into a downhill stage in most regions. In addition, some of the accustomed industry leaders may contract in size and importance. For example, the announcement in 1975 by A&P that it was closing approximately 1,250 stores was a concession that many of its units were economically obsolete in today's marketplace.

When decline occurs, the consequences are traumatic. Major losses of market share occur, profits are marginal at best, and a fatal inability to compete in the market becomes apparent to investors and competitors.

Is the life cycle growing shorter?

As the preceding discussion suggests, the institutional retail life cycle is a natural evolutionary process that is impossible to stop. Given the inevitability of the life cycle, management's responsibility in any one company is to anticipate changes in the stages and to adapt the organization to them as effectively as possible. *Exhibit II* highlights some of the activities that become important in different stages.

By utilizing different strategies at different stages of life cycle development, and by anticipating shifts from one stage to the next, both retailers and suppliers can maintain adequate profit levels. Difficulties arise in anticipating future developments, though, as the life cycle is far from being a stagnant concept.

Furthermore, innovative retail companies are typically small and relatively difficult to identify. Consequently, they are seldom given widespread notice until they reach the accelerated development stage. However, two

Exhibit II
Management activities in the life cycle

Area or subject of concern	Stage of life cycle development			
	1 Innovation	*2 Accelerated development*	*3 Maturity*	*4 Decline*
Market characteristics				
Number of competitors	Very few	Moderate	Many direct competitors Moderate indirect competition	Moderate direct competition Many indirect competitors
Rate of sales growth	Very rapid	Rapid	Moderate to slow	Slow or negative
Level of profitability	Low to moderate	High	Moderate	Very low
Duration of new innovations	3 to 5 years	5 to 6 years	Indefinite	Indefinite
Appropriate retailer actions				
Investment/growth/risk decisions	Investment minimization – high risks accepted	High levels of investment to sustain growth	Tightly controlled growth in untapped markets	Minimal capital expenditures and only when essential
Central management concerns	Concept refinement through adjustment and experimentation	Establishing a pre-emptive market position	• Excess capacity and "overstoring" • Prolonging maturity and revising the retail concept	Engaging in a "run-out" strategy

Use of management control techniques	Minimal	Moderate	Extensive	Moderate
Most successful management style	Entrepreneurial	Centralized	"Professional"	Caretaker
Appropriate supplier actions				
Channel strategy	Develop a pre-emptive market position	Hold market position	Maintain profitable sales	Avoid excessive costs
Channel problems	Possible antagonism of other accounts	Possible antagonism of other accounts	Dealing with more scientific retailers	Servicing accounts at a profit
Channel research	Identification of key innovations	Identification of other retailers adopting the innovation	Initial screening of new innovation opportunities	Active search for new innovation opportunities
Trade incentives	Direct financial support	Price concessions	New price incentives	None

widely discussed retail concepts are still at the innovation stage in the United States; both of them are in the food field. The first is the food warehouse, as exemplified by the Grocery Warehouse operation run by Allied Supermarkets in Detroit or the Magnamart division of Lucky Stores in San Antonio. The second is the hypermarket – very large-scale combination food and general merchandise stores – such as Jewel Grand Bazaar in Chicago or the newer units of Meijers Thrifty Acres in Michigan.

What is more, there is ample evidence to suggest that the length of the life cycle is contracting. The time between the introduction of a retail concept and the point at which it reaches maturity is growing progressively shorter.

At maturity, retailers tend to develop sophisticated inventory control procedures, develop five-year plans, and employ other modern management concepts. For suppliers, the main challenge is to hold on to the existing network while beginning to actively search for the next round of innovative companies that may eventually make existing relationships obsolete.

It is difficult to pinpoint the exact year in which a particular retail institution was established, since most innovations have important historical antecedents that can be traced back to the very beginnings of commerce. It is even more difficult to determine when a particular institution reached maturity. Market data are usually not sufficiently precise to indicate maturity, different geographic areas reach maturity at different points in time, and many individual firms run counter to prevailing trends.

Despite these limitations, it is possible to draw on trade data and historical studies to make realistic estimates of the approximate time of innovation and maturity for major retailing institutions.[5] *Exhibit III* documents the life cycle patterns for the downtown department store, the variety store, the supermarket, the discount department store, and the home improvement center.

As can be seen, the downtown department store enjoyed approximately 80 years of uninterrupted development from the time of its introduction to the time of achieving its maximum market share. But the pace of economic activity accelerated, the innovation and accelerated development stages contracted to 45 years for variety stores, 35 years for supermarkets, and 20 years for discount department stores.

Present patterns of change lead to the conclusion that the home improvement center probably will achieve its maximum market share by about 1980, only 15 or so years after the time of introduction. For future innovations, the period of market share growth could contract to as little as 10 years.

The institutional life cycle is not the only facet of economic activity that is accelerating. Futurists such as Alvin Toffler, Herman Kahn, and others have documented the accelerating pace of change in American society.[6] In addition, the product life cycle seems to be contracting. As an illustration consider the following observation made by the chief executive of General Electric Company:

Exhibit III
Life cycle characteristics of five retail institutions

Institution	Approximate date of innovation	Approximate date of maximum market share	Approximate number of years required to reach maturity	Estimated maximum market share	Estimated 1975 market share
Downtown department store	1860	1940	80	8.5% of total retail sales	1.1%
Variety store	1910	1955	45	16.5% of general merchandise sales	9.5%
Supermarket	1930	1965	35	70.0% of grocery store sales	64.5%
Discount department store	1950	1970	20	6.5% of total retail sales	5.7%
Home improvement center	1965	1980 (estimate)	15	35.0% of hardware and building material sales	25.3%

Sources: National Bureau of Economic Research, U.S. Department of Commerce, *Progressive Grocer, Discount Merchandiser,* National Retail Hardware Association, and Management Horizons, Inc.

"The honeymoon cycle of the new product is becoming shorter and shorter. We introduced the GE automatic toothbrush just two years ago. There are now 32 competitors. Our slicing knife, a product that we introduced approximately one year ago, now competes with 7 others, and at least that many more manufacturers are preparing to enter the marketplace."[7]

A sophisticated management group can slow the pace of its company's evolution, and it can hold profitability at adequate levels for an extended period of time. However, a return to exceptional levels of profitability can be achieved only by converting to new forms of distribution or by entering new lines of trade.

Implications and opportunities

The institutional life cycle represents more than just another way to conceptualize changes in retailer behavior and profitability patterns. It can be quite useful in projecting retail developments and planning marketing strategy. In particular, an analysis of current life cycle patterns suggests four important areas of management attention during the next decade.

Stay flexible

For retail executives, the shortening life cycle puts a premium on being able to adapt to changing trends and to work with new management ideas. To cope with continual change, retailers must consider the use of different management styles or even different management groups during succeeding stages of development. In large organizations with multiple types of outlets in various stages of development, this need could greatly increase the complexity of management. It also means, though, that a company can never afford to get "locked in" to some particular approach or philosophy.

An excellent example of a company that has employed different management styles in operations at different stages of development is Federated Department Stores. When setting up its Gold Circle discount division, the company established a management task force that was completely autonomous from the existing Federated management group. The task force was free to try new management concepts and operating procedures. With this approach, Federated had an innovative, free-wheeling management style for its discount division and a more conservative, controlled style for its conventional department store operation.

Merchandise suppliers are likely to have similar concerns about not being locked in to one type of retail outlet for a product. As a result of this concern suppliers probably will become more responsive to new retail ventures than they have been in the past. When, as in the past, manufacturers and wholesalers refrain from selling to new types of retailers for fear of disrupting existing channel relationships, they leave the door open for minor suppliers.

The latter can proceed to take market share away from the larger companies by selling to the innovative stores.

Analyze risks and profits

In order to lower the potential risks of failure in new ventures, retailers will become more analytical and innovative. To cut their risks, they are likely to utilize a variety of techniques for increasing sales and profits and decreasing investment requirements. For instance, they will:

- Look for second-use space – such as abandoned supermarkets – for new retail ventures.
- Place more emphasis on self-service in tasks where clerk service has been the mode.
- Emphasize more efficient merchandising techniques.
- Try to shift a greater portion of the investment burden back up the channel to merchandise suppliers. (This approach is especially important for financing inventory and fixture needs in the future.)

Suppliers face a dilemma in dealing with new retail concepts. While inclined to respond quickly to new forms of distribution which exhibit a strong customer appeal, they will need substantial financial support through the form of extended datings, floor planning of initial inventory, or even direct term loans. At present, few supply organizations have the ability to evaluate the prospects for innovations with any degree of precision. In order to do so, suppliers are going to be forced to become much more knowledgeable about retailing activities and possibly directly involved in the early operation of retail innovations.

Attempt to extend the maturity stage

As noted earlier, the duration of the four stages shown in *Exhibit I* on page 266 is variable. This fact is especially important for retailers in the third or maturity stage of the life cycle. As recognition of the life cycle grows, therefore, many retail executives can be expected to devote more attention to ways of attracting and appealing to new market segments; also, many managements will work on ways of renewing and recapturing the interest of their existing customers so as to keep their loyalty in the face of new forms of competition.

For an example of what can be done by alert maturity-stage retailers, consider the department store industry:

> Originally, the department store was a discount-oriented purveyor of a relatively wide range of basic merchandise. Over time the concept evolved into a mechanism for selling a broad variety of apparel, home furnishings, and general merchandise to a broadly defined middle-class customer base.
>
> But today, leading department stores are giving much more time, attention, inventory investment, and floor space to the sale of fashion merchandise – particularly apparel, fashion accessories, and fashion home

furnishings. Many of them see their main market as a more mobile, more affluent section of the middle class. While engaged in these changes and transitions, some conventional department stores have been able to maintain quite acceptable rates of profitability and interesting growth rates.

The marketing programs of key suppliers must evolve with the retail concepts they service. In the latter stages of the life cycle this means that suppliers must be able to cope with buying committees, vendor analysis programs, and similar efforts to assess the relative desirability of alternative supplier relationships. In addition, they must be able to function in programmed merchandising arrangements. Finally, they should be able to provide the product variations and other refinements that retailers will be looking for in order to shield conventional customers from innovative competitors. While doing all this, suppliers must also be able to service less mature retail outlets with less precise methods of operation.

In short, manufacturers will work up programs to satisfy multiple channel requirements. Like several of the other changes outlined, this development should result in a marked increase in the complexity of supplier operations.

Emphasize research

Given the risks in developing new retailing concepts, many retailers may prefer to leave the hard task of experimenting with new approaches to smaller, more entrepreneurial companies. The concepts that prove successful can then be copied – at least, if the large retailers discover the innovations soon enough.

Monitoring experimentation and innovation in the manner required calls for a more substantial and more sophisticated commitment to research than most retailers now employ. Such capabilities must be expanded in the future. Suppliers face an almost identical challenge in developing a monitoring system to identify potential new customers and anticipate their impact on the market.

In summary

The retail life cycle is a natural evolutionary process and executives can do very little to counteract it. What they can do is plan more effectively in order to sustain profitability in the different stages. Such planning implies continuous rethinking and revision of operations. This in turn means that retailing will continue to be an area of turbulence and uncertainty for some time to come.

Notes

1. Malcolm P. McNair, "Significant Trends and Developments in the Postwar Period," *Competitive Distribution in a Free High-Level Economy and its Implications for the University*, edited by Albert D. Smith (Pittsburgh: University of Pittsburgh Press, 1958).

2. For a more detailed discussion of these different hypotheses see Stanley C. Hollander, "The Wheel of Retailing," *Journal of Marketing*, July 1960, p. 37.

3. See, for example, Joel Dean, "Pricing Policies for New Products," HBR November–December 1950, p. 44 (repeated as HBR Classic in this issue, p. 141). Theodore Levitt, "Exploit the Product Life Cycle," HBR November–December 1965, p. 81; and Eberhard E. Schering, *New Product Management* (Hillside, Illinois: The Snyder Press, 1974). For a contrary view of the traditional approach, see Nariman K. Dhalla and Sonia Yuspeh, "Forget the product life cycle concept!" HBR January–February 1976, p. 102.

4. See William R. Davidson, Alton F. Doody, and Daniel J. Sweeney, *Retailing Management* (New York: The Ronald Press Co., 1975), p. 71; William R. Davidson, "Changes in Distributive Institutions," *Journal of Marketing*, January 1970, p. 9; and Bert C. McCammon, Jr. and Albert D. Bates, "Emerging Patterns of Distribution," *Strictly Wholesaling*, Spring 1971, p. 22.

5. For example, data on the sales and market share of retail institutions in the latter part of the nineteenth century and the first half of the twentieth century are found in Harold Barger, *Distribution's Place in the American Economy Since 1869* (New York: National Bureau of Economic Research, 1955).

6. See Alvin Toffler, *Future Shock* (New York: Random House, 1970), and Herman Kahn and Anthony J. Wiener, *The Year 2000: A Framework for Speculation on the Next 33 Years* (New York: Macmillan, 1967).

7. Speech by Fred J. Borch quoted in Philip Kotler, *Marketing Management* (Englewood Cliffs, New Jersey: Prentice-Hall, 1972), p. 466.

14

Applying evolutionary models to the retail sector

Keri Davies

Source: *International Review of Retail, Distribution and Consumer Research* 8(2) (April 1998): 165–181.

Abstract

Retail change has been an area which has interested academics for a number of years and numerous theories have been produced to model and predict change. Drawing upon current notions of evolutionary development, this paper proposes that there is an overall 'design space', which encompasses the 'possible' forms of retailing and which can be open to upheaval or catastrophic change when, for example, there is a major change in retail technology. This larger design space is moderated by local variation, based on social, cultural dimensions, etc. Mechanisms for describing change and competition within these spaces are proposed and discussed.

Keywords

Retail change, models, evolutionary models

Introduction: Existing models of retail change

Efforts to model retail change have been a feature of academic debate for many years. For example, Brown (1987) distinguishes between four main streams of thought:

Environmental theory   Such theories maintain that the structure of the retail system reflects changes in the surrounding economic, demographic, social, cultural and technological conditions of the marketplace. Some authors, such as Dreesman (1968), Hensel (1973), Markin and Duncan (1981), Etgar (1984), Klein and Roth (1987) and Roth and Klein (1993) have extended this into an ecological approach, arguing for some form of 'natural selection' within the economic environment.

Cyclical theory The most widely examined and respected area, cyclical theories claim that change occurs in an oscillatory manner, involving the repetition of earlier trends. The three principal contributions have been: The retail accordion (Hollander 1966); the retail life cycle (Davidson *et al.* 1976); and the wheel of retailing (Hollander 1960; Izraeli 1973; McNair and May 1978; Goldman 1978; Hollander 1980; Savitt 1984; Thomas *et al.* 1985; Sampson and Tigert 1994). The mechanisms behind these cycles is unknown, although suggestions have included a decline in management quality, trading up and so on.

Conflict theory When faced with the challenge of an innovator, established institutions must either respond or risk failure. The most well-known conflict theories have been the dialectical model (Gist 1968) and the action-reaction sequence put forward by Fink *et al.* (1971), which was applied to retailing by Stern and El-Ansary (1977).

Combined theories The environmental, cyclical and conflict-based theories are by no means unrelated, and a number of efforts have been made to combine the theories. Brown (1987: 25) highlights the 'spiral' model (Agergaard *et al.* 1970) in which each revolution of the wheel of retailing leaves the system on a 'slightly higher plane' compared to the previous revolution.

What this short preamble shows is that the retail sector is an area which academic theorizing has long suggested to be characterized by cyclicality (Brown 1990). This paper suggests that we extend our reach to look at some of the new models of the firm, with their emphasis on evolutionary theory. As with general economic theory, biological analogies have both possibilities and dangers. Markin and Duncan (1981) argue that the use of such analogies is better for descriptive and perhaps pedagogical reasons rather than in explanation and prediction. The reification of retail institutions and the 'bestowing' upon them of animal or human qualities and behaviour also has considerable problems, as, to be fair, is recognized by these authors. There are clear dangers in overplaying the ecological and environmental hand in terms of retail analogy. None the less, it is useful to address the issues because the analogies have widespread acceptance in retail teaching and, to a lesser extent, practice, and have a simplistic appeal. It is common to see references to the 'survival of the fittest', 'natural dominance', 'natural selection', 'triumph of the best', etc., and to read about the march of retail progress supplanting more 'primitive' retail forms. (Although Brown's point (1995c) about the wheel of retailing not going away until we stop talking about it is well taken.)

Endogenous growth, resource advantage and marketing decision making

The traditional neo-classical economics which have served as the underpinning for much marketing theory has worked on the assumption of diminishing returns. Put simply, as a firm expands, the theory suggests, it eventually hits a limit where costs per unit of output start to rise and unit profits fall. That limit may be, for example, the capability of its management or the size of its regional market, beyond which unit costs will rise. Each producer expands output until this zone of increasing costs is reached. No one firm can cover the market, so competition will thrive.

Unfortunately, many of these ideas, while useful, do not work in practice and neo-classical economists have had to patch them up and work with simplified, unrealistic situations. Alternative configurations have been mooted over the years but they have foundered on the difficulties of finding suitable analytical tools. Since the early 1980s two major changes have occurred. First, there has been the development of mathematical techniques able to capture some of the complexities of non-linear problems (Gleick 1987; Waldrop 1992). These have allowed economists to vary the data and the methods which they use to address problems – indeed, they have altered the sorts of issues which are seen as economic problems.

Second, and linked intimately with this, there has been a new stress on evolutionary economics and a cross-fertilization of ideas with the natural sciences (Boulding 1981; Nelson and Winter 1982). The notion that market competition is analogous to biological competition formed the basis of Walrassian economic theories and so has been part of economic thought for a long time. Business analyses which draw upon evolutionary theory suggest that change takes place in response to changes in the environment, including the activities of competing firms (Hodgson 1993).

What has been the new is the interest in the role of knowledge in economic affairs. Economists such as Paul Romer (Rivera-Batiz and Romer 1991; Romer 1994) and Paul Krugman (Krugman 1996) have added 'knowledge' back into neo-classical economic theory in order to make the theoretical production function more plausible. First, the new theories recognize that knowledge (e.g. about how to make things) can raise the return on investment. Second, whereas in the neo-classical theory technological progress just happens, in the new theories knowledge is a factor of production which, like capital, has to be paid for by forgoing current consumption. Economies and organizations have to invest in knowledge in the same way that they invest in machines. Third, since past investment in capital may make it more profitable to accumulate knowledge, the new theories admit the possibility of a virtuous circle in which investment spurs knowledge and knowledge spurs investment. This in turn implies that a sustained increase in investment can permanently raise a country's or a firm's growth rate (Anon 1992).

These models of 'increasing returns' have spurred exploration of why some companies and some products succeed and some fail. For example, Arthur (1989) argues that increasing returns are not found in all industries but that they are an integral part of modern, complex technologies. It is implicit in the work of those such as Romer that markets evolve, responding to changes in their environment. In a number of studies, Arthur has argued that, as this evolution takes place, and as two or more increasing-return technologies 'compete' for a 'market' of potential adopters, insignificant events may by chance give one of them an initial advantage in adoptions. One of two things may then happen: On the one hand, this technology may improve more than the others or, on the other, potential adopters may see the larger market as reducing their risks. Whichever route is followed, the one technology becomes more attractive to adopters and is further adopted and improved. Thus, a technology that by chance gains an early lead in adoption may eventually 'corner the market' even though later analysis may show it not to have been the 'best' of the available technologies (Arthur 1989, 1994). Commonly cited examples of the outcomes of such a process are the QWERTY keyboard (David 1985) and the VHS video format (Cohen and Stewart 1994).

This basic change in the ground of economic theory has begun to be reflected in efforts to re-conceptualize marketing theory. Dickson's model of a Dynamic Theory of Competitive Rationality placed the role of information and organizational learning firmly at the heart of buying behaviour and organizational response (Dickson 1992). More recently, Hunt and Morgan (1995) have brought forward their Resource-Advantage Theory of Competition in which organizational knowledge and, critically, the ability to use that knowledge are seen as additional to the resources, such as labour, which have been included in previous models. Following criticisms of the original paper (Deligönül and Cavusgil 1997), particularly of its apparently static approach (Dickson 1996), a revised model has appeared (Hunt and Morgan 1996, 1997). While the matrix which is developed from this theory has links to the competitive advantage models of Porter (1980), the underpinning is overtly evolutionary and even ecological (Hunt 1997).

In accepting these revisions into the marketing canon we have to be careful for two primary reasons. First, there is a considerable degree of doubt about the wisdom of applying biological analogies to economic and cultural issues (Jennings and Waller 1996; Hodgson 1996). This is an important issue which is too large to examine in detail here and which is unlikely to be resolved in the near future anyway. We can follow Dosi and Nelson on this:

> It is quite straightforward that one cannot construct a satisfactory theory of economic evolution simply by way of analogy with the biological model. Still, a reference to [the] major building blocks of the biological model might help in illustrating the specificities of evolution in the social domain.
>
> (Dosi and Nelson 1994: 155)

The second point relates to the ground chosen by those, such as Hunt and Morgan, who are looking to incorporate evolutionary theory from economics into marketing. As proponents of endogenous growth they are now arguing that their ideas have policy implications (Arthur 1996; Dickens and

Czinkota 1996) and so it is as well to be aware of those things which have been left out as well as those which have been included. The retail sector provides us with a useful area in which to test these ideas.

Evolutionary theory and retail change

In looking at retail change we should distinguish between the 'macro' scale, when the retail environment changes, and the 'micro' scale, when particular retail forms change to reflect the macro level changes. While this is a fairly obvious starting point, it is our contention that too many of the retail models mentioned above have tended to confuse the two scales. More of a worry, it is suggested that these same mistakes are to be seen in the models suggested by Hunt and Morgan for a more general marketing theory. This paper draws upon some of the recent writings on biological evolution, as opposed to ecology, which have also tried to distinguish between these two scales of analysis. In addition, by its very nature, evolutionary theory calls upon notions of change and development, and academics in this field have tried to explain a variety of regularities and cyclicalities.

'Macro' scale: The design space

Our starting point has to be the space within which retailing operates and which offers opportunities for, or constraints on, new developments; we shall refer to this is the 'design space' (Cohen and Stewart 1994; Dennett 1995). This space is comprised of many different facets; for example, Klein and Roth (1987) identified five distinct categories which, they argued, make up the retail environment and so affect retail development. These were:

1. the size of the aggregate population and its spatial distribution over a given region, which will determine the overall need for goods in an area;
2. the need structure for goods, which affects and is affected by family size, income allocation, etc.;
3. the total income of the region and the allocation of that income across the population;
4. technology, which has a major impact on both consumers and retailers;
5. government regulation, which can constrain or encourage both the supply and demand sides of the exchange process.

To these we would add a social/cultural facet which helps to determine whether retailers or consumers will actually be able to 'see' any particular portion of the available design space. The pattern of what is socially visible or invisible, what is seen as a shop (which is just one legitimate environment for selling among many possible environments) changes constantly (Brown 1995b).

Evolutionary theory suggests that change takes place in response to changes in the environment, including the activities of competing firms. Thus, Klein and Roth (1987) argued that, using the ecological perspective, retail structure at any point in time is a function of the past management decisions and of the environment, where the environment is, in turn, assumed to be beyond the control of individual decision makers. (We will concede this point for now, although followers of Lovelock's Gaia hypothesis may like to consider the means by which retail organizations might alter the environment to their own benefit – see also Marsden and Wrigley 1996.)

Theoretically, the design space contains (at any one time) all of the possible responses to the environmental conditions, including those permutations which have not appeared (or been recognized) for some reason or another. Hollander (1980: 82) captured this point neatly when he argued that retail theories of change need also to account for those forms of retailing that i) have never been tried; ii) have been tried but have not caught on; iii) were once popular but have now passed from the scene; iv) rely upon being different from conventional retailing to attract their customers.

Both Gould (1989) and Dennett (1995) suggest that, as the design space is huge, and because any change in the environment is likely to open up such a wide range of possibilities, we cannot predict which new forms will succeed or fail. Gould (1989) pushes this argument to its limit by arguing that, if we could rewind the 'tape of history' and replay it, the odds are stacked heavily against our obtaining the same outcome. This then is the biological analogue of Arthur's views on path dependency and 'lock-in' (although there are also links to concepts in the fields of chaos (Gleick 1987; Stacey 1993) and complexity (Prigogine and Stengers 1985; Waldrop 1992; Kauffman 1993; Cohen and Stewart 1994) with their emphasis on sensitivity to initial conditions).

Natural selection and economic fitness

The basic position from evolutionary biology is that under natural selection, animals (firms) which are not in tune with their environment struggle or die out, leaving the fitter, the better adapted animals to survive and pass on their form to future generations. This is a situation though where 'fitness' has a specific meaning.

> Much like the biological analogy, the theory of adaptation says that what survives is fit. This means only that what survives is fit now, i.e., the functions and services provided by the institution are deemed valuable by the marketing environment. Too often our ethnocentric notion of things leads us to conclude that 'what is, is right'.
>
> (Markin and Duncan 1981: 64)

There is another problem here though for those studying biological evolution: Namely, there are many situations where animals have body shapes or practices which appear to be maladaptive. Animals which die when mating would appear not to be 'fit'; similarly, the peacock's tail has been an often-used example of a body form which would seem to leave the bird less able to escape predators. A new emphasis therefore has come from the 'ultra-Darwinists', who look not to the survival of the animal but of the animal's genes (Dawkins 1989). Dawkins and others argue that, if a larger tail means that any one peacock gets to mate more often, then that is a useful adaptation. This has been a major insight into evolution and one which is now widely accepted. Dawkins has even suggested that there may be an analagous mechanism in social and cultural evolution – the 'meme'. A meme would be an idea, a saying or a ritual, able to propagate itself through a society, regardless of whether or not it is a 'good' or a 'bad' idea.

Ultra-Darwinism lays the stress on the individual and it is this stress which has, quite naturally, been picked up by those experimenting with evolutionary analogues in economics and marketing. In particular, the stress has been on the role of knowledge and information (memes) and how they can be utilized and passed within and between organizations. For example, Dosi and Nelson (1994: 162) have suggested that 'technologies' (particular practices or capabilities) may be seen as memes, with firms just acting as temporary carriers for competing technologies. This suggests that the same mechanisms operate at all scales and that, once one understands the mechanisms at the level of the individual (the organization), the mechanisms can be aggregated up to make the whole network (the economy). Thus, proponents of this view see retailers as 'fractal' organizations where the same basic principles (same use of technology) govern competition at different scales, such as competition between products for shelf-space, competition between stores in a local market and competition between firms in the regional, national or international market (John Dawson: personal communication).

However, we would argue that experience in the retail sector actually suggests that this is not the whole picture and we can now see this to be an echo of the arguments going on in evolutionary biology. The work of those such as Gould (1989) and Eldredge (1995) suggests that in evolution there is often no evidence of a lock-step evolution of animals and plants with changes in the environment. To be sure, there is slow change over long periods of time (where competition between genes may be important) but Eldredge argues that the most likely response when the local environment changes is for plants and animals to move, to migrate, with the conditions for which they are adapted. Instead of major evolutionary changes going on all the time, there are a long periods of stasis, punctuated by short periods of major upheaval. When change comes in a (relatively) short time scale, it comes at the species level, not the level of the individual. Those such as Eldredge argue, therefore, that there is a structure which is largely independent of competition at the level of the individual. Species represent combinations of traits suited to local environments and which co-evolve with other species, reflecting changes in their own relationship and in their wider environment. The complexity of species interaction is related to transfers and flows of energy in the local environment and goes beyond simple gene-based competition between individuals.

If we look to the retail sector, we can see that individual retail firms do try to adapt to their local environment – and here Hunt and Morgan's model with its stress on the use of knowledge may be relevant. That knowledge may allow them to change and adapt but, as Eldredge argues, it may also lead them to move (even to internationalize) in an effort to find a environment similar to that in which they first evolved. Unlike an animal, however, these firms may also compete in more than one environment: a corporation may have different retail formats for different customer groups, products or needs. One interpretation of this situation is to see firms applying their knowledge to different circumstances – the better they are at that, the more successful they will be.

But, our interpretation is that different forms represent different bundles of technology, different combinations of practices which need to be treated as separate and distinct from the practices at the level of the firm. Firms may survive for long periods of time, relying on their ability to learn and to apply knowledge. Firms evolve (generally relatively slowly) with the environment. Formats, on the other hand, compete at the local level and need to be adapted to the local social, cultural and economic environment. Instead of a life-cycle pattern, we see periods of stasis interspersed with short periods of upheaval during which the number and variety of formats changes (even though the firms involved may remain the same).

Change in the retail design space

Thus, we would argue that the underlying design space is actually far more stable than would be suggested by most contemporary accounts. When there is change in the design space, we would expect a reaction from the firms that exist within and (in part) comprise that environment. Some changes, such as the growth in mobility (car ownership), may make parts of the existing design space more accessible to both companies and customers; other changes, such as the development of the elevator and escalator, the introduction of self-service or computing technology, may actually enlarge the available design space. But it also takes longer than is usually believed for 'real' change to come about. For example, it has taken fully fifty years for the full effects of the move to self-service to unwind throughout the retail design space, affecting store location and design, products, customer habits, supply chain management, etc. Instead, in many instances, firms will expand or move elsewhere to find circumstances similar to those in which they evolved.

Two outcomes may be discernible from changes in the retail environment. First, despite the potentially large size of the design space, there are probably 'preferred' outcomes given the same set of initial conditions, not 'random' outcomes as argued by Gould (1989). Or, as Dennett (1995) puts it, while the range of outcomes from any interaction is theoretically vast, the actual range of possible outcomes (or design spaces) is actually much smaller. Evolution, therefore, is constrained by context (Cohen and Stewart 1994: 334); there are only so many meaningful ways in which to display products or to use computers in retailing, although the current methods may not be optimal, and not all of those may be socially acceptable (Roth and Klein 1993: 178). Thus, if Sam Walton had fallen under a bus at the age of four, we would not have had WalMart, but we would most likely still have large stores in suburban locations selling a wide range of goods at relatively low prices (see Peters 1992: 619).

Second, even short periods of severe environmental change may produce much more change in retail forms and practices than would occur over very much longer periods of slow environmental change. This is analogous to Gould's notion of 'punctuated equilibrium' (Gould 1989) or Thom's catastrophe theory (Woodcock and Davis 1980). During such periods of rapid change, predicting the outcome may be difficult because of the impact of very small differences in the initial starting positions.

When the environment is stable (change is slow and predictable), we could expect a system to converge on particular lines of thought (Arthur 1994) and for those lines to move towards their optimum. But, as Gould (1996) has reminded us, there may be a need to reintroduce a recognition of physical limits into arguments about evolution because growth cannot go on forever within a static environment. A large part of Gould's book is devoted to a discussion of the reasons why no recent hitter in American baseball has been able to emulate the feats of the pre-1939 era. His argument is that the rules of baseball have changed little in almost a century, providing a very stable environment, and so the players have come up against a very real physical barrier: Baseball hitters have actually got stronger, more professional and have better technologies at their disposal than ever before but they were already so close to their physical limit before 1939 that the marginal improvement has been quite small. Over the same period, pitchers and fielders have also improved (and they, starting from a lower base, had more space to play with before they reached the design limit) but now the overall level of performance is uniformly high. In effect, the squeezing out of mediocre play has raised the overall level of performance but it has also constrained the possibilities for exceptional or above average play.

It is possible to argue that similar features can be seen in retailing during periods when the design space is relatively stable. An innovative technique or product cannot be hidden and so can be copied. As a result, the general level of retail performance has increased in recent years and so the potential for outstanding performance has decreased – which is not to say that it cannot exist but that it becomes increasingly difficult to sustain. The norm becomes the achievement of short-term advantage with an ever-decreasing time lag before competitors imitate the new product or service. Basically, the number of axes on which retailers can distinguish themselves from the competitors has been cut; while this should be no bad thing overall for customers, an unfortunate side effect may be the oft-cited consumer complaint that all stores, shopping centres, towns, etc., look or feel the same.

Local optima and retail niches

A question which is raised by evolutionary theory is why, if and when the environment changes, the old forms of retailing often do not die out.

> Although the economic discipline concentrates on the idea of optimization and profit maximisation, it appears that many suboptimal outlets continue to exist in the market. This reality has been justified in many ways, including reference to non-economic goals of the decision-makers. A more realistic approach may be to consider a range of survival abilities where optimal profitability stands at one end point of the continuum and the minimal level for survival is at the other. This approach, while allowing many structures to exist in the same environment, carries with it an inability to predict which particular structure will survive.
>
> (Roth and Klein 1993: 177)

One way of allowing for this is through the notion of global optima versus local optima. We have already described the macro-scale as encompassing opportunities or constraints, such as the technology available to consumers and retailers but at the micro-scale there may be local variations in culture or economy which will affect the application of the larger trends. We could, for example, see the use of laser scanning, the development of large databases, changes in logistics technology or self-service as 'global' environments, available to all and tending to bring about (possibly 'catastrophic' or 'chaotic') change throughout the design space when first introduced. However, whether a supermarket is located in a free-standing store in the suburbs or in the basement of a city centre department store may be a local response to a local environment, as in the difference between St Louis and Singapore.

Thus, Cohen and Stewart (1994) and Dennett (1995) argue that something which is 'inefficient' (however defined) on a global scale may still survive and even prosper at the local level because it already occupies the local niche and is difficult to dislodge. For example, it is not surprising that some department stores have survived; the current global technology just cannot be applied effectively at the moment to some niches which are *already* occupied and which continue to serve a consumer need. The converse is that if department stores were a new product, they would almost certainly fail to gain a foothold and die out without a trace.

'Micro'-scale mechanisms of retail change

We have argued that adopting the notion of a design space from evolutionary theory will allow us to see the existing view of the retail environment as partial and too easily swayed by short-term changes. This has led us to concentrate on the wrong area when looking to model retail change (Klein and Roth 1987). Even using the design space idea, we still need to ask the question 'What is the mechanism for change?' at the micro-level. We will provide a two-part answer to this question: first, we don't know! Put simply, we cannot predict the specific mechanism for change for any particular situation or any particular time. To argue, as Roth and Klein do, that ecological models are failing because they cannot be used for prediction is to miss the point. We have no known way currently of predicting the outcomes of such complex systems with their chaotic responses to change, particularly during periods of sudden, rapid change (Stacey 1993; Kauffman 1993). We may achieve limited success but only by so constraining the object of our study as to nullify the usefulness of the answer. If we seek regularity and predictability over the richness of 'real' situations, then we get minimal prediction at the very real risk of losing all understanding (Brown 1995a, 1995c).

Second, we can't know! The specific mechanism used will vary depending upon the local environment or context. This is why so many of the existing models of retail change are so limited because they have chosen to elevate one mechanism (low price, wide assortment or management inertia) over others. *What we are seeing is not the cyclical repetition of the same mechanism but 'cycles' of decisions in response to change in the environment.* While the actual change may not be predictable, the pattern of reactions may be regular and cyclical.

So, it is argued here that different mechanisms are likely to be found depending upon the position in the 'cycle' of decisions (cf. Dosi and Nelson 1994). When there is an upheaval, a discontinuity in the environment, e.g. technological change, there is a change in the global design space with new areas/opportunities opening up and, probably, some existing areas being closed off or becoming less efficient to occupy. There will be a great deal of experimentation; new forms of retailing will be introduced but not all will survive. In addition to the environmental theories mentioned above, this would seem to have some links to the activities discussed by conflict theories.

Hannan and Freeman (1989), drawing on ecological theory, have suggested that two forms of firms and strategies are likely within any design space.

R-strategies   When change is rapid and discontinuous, an *r-strategy* is most likely; an opportunistic strategy, this calls forth many new formats (combinations of technologies) which maximize *the system*'s response to changes in the environment, although no one firm is guaranteed to survive. The ability of these firms to work under changing conditions is not a reflection of flexibility, but rather of high rates of founding to offset high mortality rates. R-strategists thus exploit new and ephemeral opportunities quickly, but at the expense of being poor at coping with larger rivals. These firms map out the new design space which is coming into being, trying different formats in different markets. As change slows and firms converge on a small number of designs, so another form of strategy takes hold.

K-strategies   When change is slow and predictable, a *K-strategy* is likely to ensue; larger firms or formats cover a larger part of the market and each individual has a good chance of surviving or even thriving in the face of dense competition. K-strategists have the ability to withstand rivals, but are slow at coping with or taking advantage of change. As the successful formats begin to emerge, so the eventual market leaders will move in and drive costs down by operating efficiently and covering the market widely. Such market leaders will tend to be k-strategy firms, which have either been able to make the switch from an r-strategy or have entered from other sectors (Hannan and Freeman 1989: 118–9). They are not necessarily offering low prices, although their adaptation to the new market conditions may offer consumers lower costs (taking into account both prices and the direct costs to customers such as transport, parking, etc.).

Paradoxically, what this means is that it is during periods when environmental change is slow and the design space is relatively stable that cyclical change of the sort described by the *wheel of retailing* is more likely to occur. And it also takes place because organizations, unlike animals and plants to a large degree, often react to market dominance in a positive, rather than negative, manner. Furthermore, we do not need to develop special mechanisms for the retail sector to describe these features. One possibility, as authors such as Porter (1980) and Ries (1996) have argued, is that competition in capitalist economies can be viewed as being based on either cost leadership or focus. To this we can add Hunt and Morgan's stress on firms being able to capitalize on these means of competition through their ability to use knowledge (Hunt and Morgan 1997) (but note that the introduction of change at the level of the format in reaction to changes in the global or local environment moves the Hunt and Morgan model from a largely static model to a more dynamic one).

When the design space is stable, the primary means of attacking the newly dominant k-strategy format is through focus (Ries 1996). A concentration on specific market segments will tend to lead to either lower costs (probably reflected in lower prices) or differentiation (probably reflected in higher prices). We can dispel, therefore, some of the problems raised by the *wheel of retailing* where authors have worried that, rather than low-price entrants, it is high-priced, high-quality formats which have been seen to attack the existing format. Note, however, that there is no implicit 'problem' with the existing format or the retail management. It is a dynamic of the marketplace that brings the 'attack' in these two specific areas, although whether or not they succeed will depend very much on local conditions.

If the innovation is successful, it is unlikely to destroy the original format completely because the latter usually continues to have some advantage with at least part of the customer base; now however the new format comes under the same sort of attack itself. Thus, following the introduction of self-service, car parking, refrigeration, etc., we have seen the department store (the one store for all needs) ousted by mass market retailers based on the application of these new technologies to food (supermarkets and hypermarkets) and non-food (variety stores). As the technology has been stable, competitors to these new forms have been forced to look to either further differentiation (smaller, specialist stores with wider ranges and higher prices) or lower costs (category killers with limited lines and low prices). When any format (niche) is large enough and attractive enough it will attract further competition which, again, has this very limited range of options with which to make its mark. This is not to deny that 'trading up' (expanding the niche) or mistakes by management do not occur but we should be very wary of using *post hoc* analysis to elevate these issues above the underlying forces of competition.

The longer the design space is stable, the more likely it is to become both fragmented (more 'attacks' have been made on existing niches) and yet more homogeneous in its use of technology (most players have got closer to the limits of the space and, as k-strategy firms, are less receptive to major upheavals). This represents the current position of much fixed store retailing in Western Europe and the USA, as shown, for example, by the vogue for loyalty cards and data mining which look for the slightest competitive advantage in abstruse variations in customer databases.

The scene would seem to be set for some form of upheaval or discontinuity, with the most likely candidate currently being the changes in communications technology which may allow electronic retailing to take place. If Hannan and Freeman are right, small and flexible firms are most likely to explore the new design spaces created by such a change; large retailers are not only slower to respond but also more closely bound to the existing design space and so less likely to see the new means of exchange which can be attained through the new space. However, once there is some stability in the design space, so large firms are likely to take over and some of these *may* be existing large retailers; the likelihood however is that most fixed store retailers will be unable to make the switch.

Conclusion

This paper has outlined some current evolutionary theory and attempted to show how this theory can be applied to retailing to overcome a number of the problems associated with the existing theories of retail change. It is not suggested that retailing can be 'modelled' exactly using models devised for biological evolution but that the underlying notions can illuminate some (at least) of the issues of change and stability which interest academics and practitioners alike.

References

Agergaard, E., Olsen, P.A. and **Allpass, J.** (1970) 'The interaction between retailing and the urban centre structure: A theory of spiral movement', *Environment and Planning*, 2: 55–71.

Anon (1992) 'Explaining the mystery', *The Economist*, 4 January: 15–8.

Arthur, W.B. (1989) 'Competing technologies, increasing returns, and lock-in by historical events', *The Economic Journal*, 99: 116–31.

Arthur, W.B. (1994) *Increasing Returns and Path Dependence in the Economy*, Ann Arbor, MI: University of Michigan Press.

Arthur, W.B. (1996) Increasing returns and the new world of business, *Harvard Business Review* (July–August): 100–9.

Boulding, K.E. (1981) *Evolutionary Economics*, Beverley Hills, CA: Sage.

Brown, S. (1987) 'Institutional change in retailing: A review and synthesis', *European Journal of Marketing*, 21(6): 5–36.

Brown, S. (1990) 'The wheel of retailing: Past and future', *Journal of Retailing*, 66: 143–9.

Brown, S. (1995a) *Postmodern Marketing*, London: Routledge.

Brown, S. (1995b), 'Sex n shopping: A "novel" approach to consumer research', *Journal of Marketing Management*, 11: 769–83.

Brown, S. (1995c), 'Postmodernism, the wheel of retailing and the will to power', *International Review of Retail, Distribution and Consumer Research*, 3: 387–414.

Cohen, J. and **Stewart, I.** (1994) *The Collapse of Chaos: Discovering Simplicity in a Complex World*, London: Viking.

David, P. (1985) 'Clio and the Economics of QWERTY', *Proceedings of the American Economic Review*, 75: 332–7.

Davidson, W.R., Bates, A.D. and **Bass, S.J.** (1976) 'The retail life cycle', *Harvard Business Review* (November–December): 89–96.

Dawkins, R. (1989) *The Selfish Gene*, 2nd edn, Oxford: Oxford University Press.

Deligönül, Z.S. and **Cavusgil, S.T.** (1997) 'Does the comparative advantage theory of competition really replace the neoclassical theory of perfect competition?' *Journal of Marketing*, 61(4): 65–73.

Dennett, D.C. (1995) *Darwin's Dangerous Idea: Evolution and the Meanings of Life*, London: Penguin.

Dickson, P.R. (1992) 'Toward a general theory of competitive rationality', *Journal of Marketing*, 56(1): 69–83.

Dickson, P.R. (1996) 'The static and dynamic mechanics of competition: A comment on Hunt and Morgan's comparative advantage theory', *Journal of Marketing*, 60(4): 102–6.

Dickson, P.R. and **Czinkota, M.** (1996) 'How the United States can be number one again: Resurrecting the industrial policy debate', *Columbia Journal of World Business*, 31(3): 77–87.

Dosi, G. and **Nelson, R.R.** (1994) 'An introduction to evolutionary theory in economics', *Journal of Evolutionary Economics*, 4: 153–72.

Dreesman, A.C.R. (1968) 'Patterns of evolution in retailing', *Journal of Retailing*, 44: 64–81.

Eldredge, N. (1995) *Reinventing Darwin: The Great Evolutionary Debate*, London: Phoenix.

Etgar, M. (1984) 'The retail ecology model: A comprehensive model of retail change', *Research in Marketing*, 7: 41–62.

Fink, S.L., Baek, J. and **Taddeo, K.** (1971) 'Organisational crisis and change', *Applied Behavioral Science*, 7(1): 15–37.

Gist, R.R. (1968) *Retailing: Concepts and decisions,* New York: Wiley.

Gleick, J. (1987) *Chaos. Making a New Science,* London: Abacus.

Goldman, A. (1978) 'Institutional change in retailing: An updated "wheel of retailing" theory', in A.G. Woodside, J. Taylor Sims, D.M. Lewison and J.F. Wilkinson (eds) *Foundations of Marketing Channels,* Texas: Austin Press, pp. 189–212.

Gould, S.J. (1989) *Wonderful Life: The Burgess Shale and the Nature of History,* London: Penguin.

Gould, S.J. (1996) *Life's Grandeur: The Spread of Excellence from Pluto to Darwin,* London: Cape.

Hannan, M.T. and **Freeman, J.** (1989) *Organizational Ecology,* London: Harvard University Press.

Hensel, J.S. (1973) 'Environmental change and the future structure of retailing', *Arizona Business,* 20: 14–20.

Hodgson, G. (1993) *Economics and Evolution: Bringing Life Back into Economics,* Cambridge: Polity Press.

Hodgson, G. (1996) 'Some responses to Jennings and Waller', *Journal of Economic Issues,* 30(4): 1163–8.

Hollander, S.C. (1960) 'The wheel of retailing', *Journal of Marketing,* 21(1): 37–42.

Hollander, S.C. (1966) 'Notes on the retail accordion', *Journal of Retailing,* 42: 29–40, 54.

Hollander, S.C. (1980) 'Oddities, nostalgia, wheels and other patterns in retail evolution', in R.W. Stampfl and E. Hirschmann (eds) *Competitive Structure in Retail Markets: The Department Store Perspective,* Chicago, Ill.: American Marketing Association, pp. 78–87.

Hunt, S.D. (1997) 'Resource-advantage theory: An evolutionary theory of competitive firm behaviour?', *Journal of Economic Issues,* XXXI(1): 59–77.

Hunt, S.D. and **Morgan, R.M.** (1995) 'The comparative advantage theory of competition', *Journal of Marketing,* 59(2): 1–15.

Hunt, S.D. and **Morgan, R.M.** (1996) 'The resource-advantage theory of competition: Dynamics, path dependencies, and evolutionary dimensions', *Journal of Marketing,* 60(4): 107–14.

Hunt, S.D. and **Morgan, R.M.** (1997) 'Resource-advantage theory: A snake swallowing its tail or a general theory of competition?', *Journal of Marketing,* 61(4): 74–82.

Izraeli, D. (1973) 'The three wheels of retailing: a theoretical note', *European Journal of Marketing,* 7: 70–4.

Jennings, A. and **Waller, W.** (1996) 'Cultural emergence reaffirmed: A rejoinder to Hodgson', *Journal of Economic Issues,* 30(4): 1168–77.

Kauffman, S. (1993) *The Origins of Order: Self-Organization and Selection in Evolution,* New York: Oxford University Press.

Klein, S. and **Roth, V.J.** (1987) 'Theory and retail change', paper presented to the Twelfth Annual Macromarketing Seminar, Montreal, 6–9 August.

Krugman, P. (1996) *Pop Internationalism,* Cambridge, MA: MIT Press.

McNair, M.P. and **May, E.G.** (1978) 'The next revolution of the retail wheel', *Harvard Business Review,* 56(5): 81–91.

Markin, R.J. and **Duncan, C.P.** (1981) 'The transformation of retailing institutions: Beyond the wheel of retailing and life cycle theory', *Journal of Macromarketing,* 1: 58–66.

Marsden, T. and **Wrigley, N.** (1996) 'Retailing, the food system and the regulatory state', in N. Wrigley and M. Lowe, (eds) *Retailing, Consumption and Capital,* London: Longman.

Nelson, R.R. and **Winter, S.G.** (1982) *An Evolutionary Theory of Economic Change,* Cambridge, MA: Harvard University Press.

Peters, T. (1992) *Liberation Management*, London: Macmillan.

Porter, M.E. (1980) *Competitive Strategy: Techniques for Analyzing Industries and Competitors*, New York: The Free Press.

Prigogine, I. and **Stengers, I.** (1985) *Order out of Chaos: Man's New Dialogue with Nature*, London: Flamingo.

Ries, A. (1996) *Focus, The Future of Your Company Depends on It*, London: HarperCollins.

Rivera-Batiz, L.A. and **Romer, P.M.** (1991) 'Economic integration and endogenous growth', *Quarterly Journal of Economics*, CVI(2): 531–56.

Romer, P.M. (1994) 'The origins of endogenous growth', *Journal of Economic Perspectives*, 8(1): 3–22.

Roth, V.J. and **Klein, S.** (1993) 'A theory of retail change', *International Review of Retail, Distribution and Consumer Research* 3(2): 166–83.

Sampson, S.D. and **Tigert, D.J.** (1994) 'The impact of warehouse membership clubs: The wheel of retailing turns one more time', *International Review of Retail, Distribution and Consumer Research*, 4(1): 33–59.

Savitt, R. (1984), 'The "wheel of retailing" and retail product management', *European Journal of Marketing*, 18(6/7): 43–54.

Stacey, R. (1993) *Strategic Management and Organisational Dynamics*, London: Pitman.

Stern, L.W. and **El-Ansary, A.I.** (1977) *Marketing Channels*, Englewood Cliffs, NJ: Prentice Hall.

Thomas, S.M., Anderson, R.E. and **Jolson, M.A.** (1985) 'The wheel of retailing and non-store evolution: An alternative hypothesis', paper presented to the Second World Marketing Congress, University of Stirling, 29–31 August.

Waldrop, M. (1992) *Complexity: The Emerging Science at the Edge of Order and Chaos*, London: Penguin.

Woodcock, A. and **Davis, M.** (1980) *Catastrophe Theory*, London: Pelican.

15

The retailing ecology model: a comprehensive model of retail change

Michael Etgar

Source: *Research in Marketing* 7 (1984): 41–62.

Abstract

This paper presents a model of change of retailing institutions. It incorporates the natural selection approach with economic and sociological approaches and develops an open system model based on the biological concepts of variation, selection, and retention.

I. Introduction

The continuous emergence of novel forms of retailing and of new retailing institutions is a major characteristic of the retailing scene. Following the supermarket revolution in the 1940s, the discounting in the 1950s, and the franchising in the 1960s, the 1970s have witnessed the introduction of hypermarkets, warehouse retailing, and catalog showroom retailing (Bucklin 1972), while the 1980s promise novel forms of electronic and computer-based retailing (Mason & Mayer 1981; Rosenberg & Hirschman 1980).

The most important issue is why some new retailing institutions succeed and survive in the retailing world while others fail and die. McNair and May recognize that basic phenomenon and claim that

> new institutions appear (e.g., supermarkets, regional shopping malls and discount department stores); older institutions decline (e.g., downtown department stores or specialized food stores such as butcher shops and fish-mongers) and sometimes completely vanish . . . (1976, p. 3).

The constant change and innovation in retailing has motivated marketing researchers to identify and formulate a number of models which purport to explain the rationale for retailing change and for emergence of novel retailing institutions. A review of this research tradition of retailing change suggests that we do have several useful concepts, ideas, laws, and principles.

These include, among others, the wheel theory (Hollander 1960), the accordion theory (Hollander 1966), the simplex-multiple-omniplex scheme (Regar 1964), the dialectic model (Gist 1968), and the life cycle model (Davidson et al. 1976).

However, what is missing is a comprehensive theory of retailing change. Such a theory is required to provide researchers with an integrative framework which can attempt to present jointly available knowledge. Development of such a framework promises several benefits. First, it provides a focal point for deductive empirical research. So far, retailing change has been primarily studied from the theoretical point of view. There were few attempts to empirically test the various models. Methodologists suggest that lack of a tradition of deductive reasoning based upon a conceptual body of knowledge is a sign of a relative theoretical weakness of a discipline (Hunt 1976; Sheth 1983). Thus, development of a comprehensive theory could advance the field by providing the framework required for deductive research.

Second, the comprehensive theory can alleviate the problem of reductionism which all the currently available models seem to suffer from. Reductionism refers to the "idea that the principles explaining one range of phenomena are adequate for explaining a totally different range of phenomena" (Hoult 1972, p. 267). Reductionism suggests that all the various aspects of retailing change should be explained by one model powerful enough to provide an appropriate conceptual framework to encompass all various aspects.

Analysis of the wheel-of-retailing model can provide one example of the reductionism problem. The model postulates that new retailing institutions emerge, offering a low price-low service retailing mix and competing with existing institutions which tend to concentrate on a high price-high service retailing mix. While this model seems to explain emergence at their time of some novel retailing organizational formats such as supermarkets and discount stores, the model does not explain emergence of other retailing institutions.

For example, Goldman (1975) has indicated that such important retailing institutions as department stores have not emerged with low price-low service offer, as the wheel theory proposed, but rather with high service-high price offer. The implication is that the wheel theory does not provide an explanation for the emergence of these important retailing institutions and, as such, cannot be considered comprehensive enough to encompass and explain retail change in general.

Similar observations can be made about franchise operations. Those also do not fit the service-price shift concept because the innovation here pertains to a completely different phenomenon—that of internal operation of retailing rather than to its marketing aspects. As such, none of the existing models will explain it.

The dialectic model provides another example of partial explanation of models of retailing change. It provides an explanation as to what happens to a retailing innovation once it appears on the retailing scene and how it becomes accepted in the retailing community; however, it does not enumerate how and why a specific retailing innovation appears and succeeds and why other innovations may fail. Thus, this model addresses itself only to a partial aspect of retailing change and not to the whole phenomenon.

Third, a comprehensive model can provide a framework into which concepts and constructs from several disciplines can be integrated. This will allow research carried out by different researchers to be correlated and permit communication among scholars operating with different research traditions.

Fourth, all the models developed so far in retailing are closed-system models. They view developments and changes in retailing as emanating from and being explained by the patterns of development of the retailing institutions themselves. As a result, closed-system models disregard the inherent dependency of any retailing system on its environment. Changes in retailing are expected to reappear on a predictable basis and are not linked to or explained by changes taking place outside the realm of the retailing institutions themselves.

This approach to retailing change has been attacked by several critics of retailing change theories (e.g., see Hunt 1976; Goldman 1975; Hollander 1980). Even Hollander, who expounded the wheel-of-retailing model, which is the most famous of the closed-system models, recognized the basic limitations of these models and the need to look beyond them for better explanations for retailing changes.

The purpose of this paper is to present a comprehensive model of retailing change. Before we present the model, several observations are in order:

First, the model is concerned with the macro level of analysis. It attempts to describe how retailing innovations appear, penetrate, and get established in a given society or economy. It is not intended to provide a blueprint for analyzing the development of a particular retailing establishment.

Second, the unit of analysis in this model is the retailing organizational form rather than an individual establishment. The theory analyzes how novel forms are born and survive.

Third, the proposed model is interdisciplinary and incorporates concepts and constructs developed in several disciplines. It is based in particular on conceptual frameworks developed by organizational theorists, marketers, and economists, and provides a comprehensive analytical framework of retailing change. The framework used for analysis in this paper is that of retailing ecology and is based on the biological concepts of the natural selection process.

An earlier attempt to apply the notion of natural selection to the retailing scene was made by Gist (1968). Duncan has used the framework to evaluate the responses of department stores to their environments (Duncan 1965). The notion, however, has not been carried far in application, primarily because the very mechanisms of selection and survival of novel retailing forms were not spelled out by the early researchers.

Since then, research carried out in economics, organization theory, and marketing has led to the development of conceptual tools which can assist us in understanding the natural selection process operating within the retailing scene. Therefore, it is possible now to design a comprehensive analytical framework which will deal with these issues.

Fourth, the model treats retailing change as a process. Such a process is composed of stages, each of which is explained in detail.

Finally, it adopts an open system approach to retailing change. Retailing change is viewed as a dependent variable which takes place and succeeds as a result of developments in retailing environments.

II. The retail ecology model

A. Definition of a retailing institution

Any scientific analysis of a phenomenon must begin with an exact definition of its units of analysis. This is also a necessary step for understanding retailing. Once such a unit is defined, one can proceed and classify the analyzed universe and provide frames of reference, points of view, and vocabulary that collectively form part of the foundation for comprehension and insight.

The retailing structure offers a variety of ways in which retailing institutions can be defined, classified, and analyzed; these include type of ownership, geographic location, level of sales, merchandising strategy, etc. (Mason & Mayer 1981). Researchers have attempted to provide lists of various categories, which often run into the dozens. Such a variety of available institutions suggests the need to first define a retailing institution.

B. The Retail organizational form

The retailing ecology model defines a retailing institution as an organizational form. *An organizational form* is a unique way in which various resources—human, financial, physical, and social—are combined to achieve certain goals set up for or by the organization. Aldrich defines an organizational form as reflecting three dimensions and views it as "a goal directed, boundary maintaining, activity system" (Aldrich 1978, p. 4). These three dimensions—*goals and strategies*, *boundaries*, or what is included and what is excluded out of the organization, and the *way it operates* (its activity system)—differentiate among different organizational forms.

Retailing diversity stems from the fact that different institutions develop different goals, boundaries, and activity systems. Retailers may differ as to markets they serve and their retailing strategy (goals), technology (activity systems), and composition (boundaries). Some retailers serve mass markets, while others serve selected markets; some encompass a large number of units, while others only a few; and some use labor-intensive technology, while others rely on capital-intensive technology.

C.   The notion of retailing change

Boulding suggests that organizations and the environment in which organizations exist are continually evolving:

> The organizations, institutions, ideas and techniques of one period permit the rise of new organizations, institutions, ideas and techniques which eventually may displace the former set almost entirely and which, in turn, permit the rise of further succession. We thus see human history as structurally a continuation of the immense drama of evolution (1953, p. 23).

A new retailing institution, then, can be defined as an organizational form which offers a novel mix of goals and strategies, boundaries, or technology. The change can take place along one of these dimensions, or it can occur simultaneously on several.

A retailing change is exhibited in a deviation from current modes of operation, popular in the industry in a specific period of time and in the introduction of a new model of operation which differs along one (or more) of these dimensions. Retailing diversity can be approached from three broad perspectives. One pertains to the format in which a retailing institution runs its *internal operations.* The second pertains to the formats with which retailing organizations interact with their customers and suppliers (*external formats*). The third encompasses both aspects jointly.

1.   Internal operations

Retailing institutions may vary in the format of their internal operations. Figure 1 indicates that such differences may reflect differences in the design of organizational boundaries as well as the use of different technologies within the organizational form. Retailing organizational forms may vary as to the number of units they encompass (single units vs. multiple-unit chains), geographic location (downtown vs. suburban, local and regional vs. national

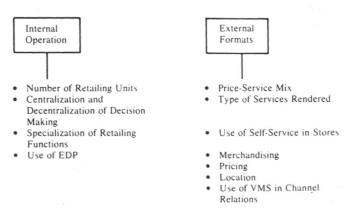

Figure 1 Characteristics of retailing variety

or international) and type of organization (corporation-owned vs. franchises or cooperatives).

Technologies used by retailing organizations may differ as well. Differences are encountered at three levels—the managerial or decision-making, merchandising management, and electronic data processing (EDP) levels. Thus, stores may differ as to the extent of centralization and decentralization of decision making. While in some retailing organizations buying and selling decisions are highly centralized, in others they are delegated to store or department levels.

Another technological difference among retailers concerns specialization in retailing functions. Separation of buying from selling functions has been a great innovation of the department stores and to large extent encouraged the development of mass merchandisers in general.

Merchandising management and the use of inventory controls and electronic data processing are other important factors differentiating among retailing forms.

2. *External formats*

Novel retailing institutions have appeared on the retailing scene also to offer new formats of interaction with customers. Offers of diverse retailing mix have given rise to novel forms of supermarkets, discount houses, catalog showrooms, etc.

A change in the retailing mix has been reflected in changes in various aspects of merchandising, pricing, service, and location. For example, the novelty of discount stores was basically their different margin and pricing policy. Supermarkets offered consumers a different pricing service mix in the form of self-service. Warehouse retailing has offered different lot sizes, suburban shopping malls offered convenience to suburban residents, etc.

Similarly, novel retailing organizations have also emerged, offering new ways of interacting with suppliers. Thus, franchisers or voluntary chains offer novel ways of organizing channel relations between the retailing unit and his suppliers, providing improved channel arrangements (McNair & May 1976).

3. *Joint changes*

However, often internal and external changes are tied in together so that one finds it difficult to identify which one plays, the predominant role in the new retailing organization. At the same new retailing organizational form, one can find a novel format of interacting with customers, i.e., a novel retailing mix offer unavailable at previously existing retailing institutions, as well as a new way of organizing the operation of the retailing organization.

Figure 2 presents a retailing institution change map. In it one can identify several retailing changes and categorize the nature of the inherent change proposed by these institutions at the time of their appearance. In the figure

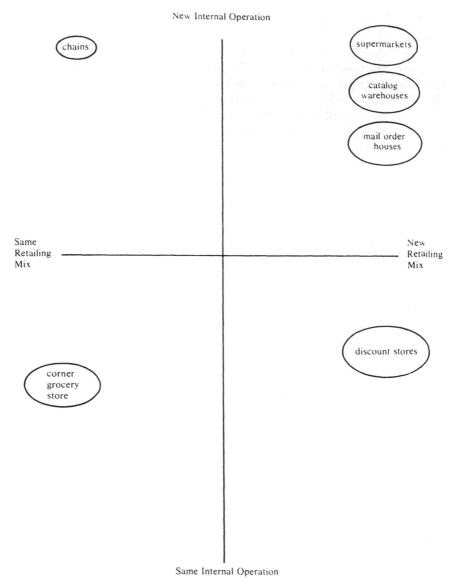

Figure 2 Potential strategies of retailing change

the horizontal axis presents a spectrum of novelty of retailing mix offered by the new institutions. At the left side of the map, one finds new institutions which offer the same retailing mix; on the right side, one finds institutions which offer new retailing mixes.

In the similar way the vertical axis indicates the extent of novelty offered by the new institution in terms of its internal operation. Above the horizontal line lay institutions offering new modes of internal operation; below the horizontal line lay institutions which offer the same format of internal operation.

Jointly, the map proposes that new retailing institutions can be divided into the three groups discussed above. In the right-hand upper quadrant one finds institutions which offer both novel retailing mix and novel forms of internal operation. In the left-hand upper quadrant one finds new institutions which offer new modes of internal operation but not a new retailing mix. In the right-hand lower quadrant one finds new institutions which offer new retailing mix but with the same modes of internal operation. Several examples are presented in the figure as well.

D. *Retailing change as a natural selection process*

Following a definition of a retailing form and of retailing change, we proceed with analyzing the rationale for retailing change. The approach taken in this paper is to consider retailing organizations as being involved in an evolutionary process through which retailing organizations best suited to their environment survive and succeed while those which do not fit are doomed to die and disappear from the retailing scene.

Survival of social institutions in general has been the topic of concern for social scientists who developed the evolutionary theory of natural selection of social institutions (Hawley 1950; Barzun 1958; Campbell 1969; Zachariah 1971). Both economists (Williamson 1975) and organization theorists (Aldrich 1978) have based their analysis of social institutions on the notion of the *natural selection* process, though each analyzed different survival mechanisms.

The evolutionary approach to retailing change proposes that emergence and survival of retailing institutions are governed by the biological rules of a natural selection process.

The theory of natural selection in retailing is a direct descendant of Darwin's theory of natural selection, which has been popularized in the phrase "survival of the fittest." Basically, Darwin's theory states that a species that most effectively adapts to its environment is most likely to survive and perpetuate its kind. Applying this theory to retailing, one can envision retailing institutions as economic species confronting their environments and competing over scarce resources.

The process encourages the survival of those retailing forms most suitable to respond to some specific environmental requirements, while those forms which cannot respond correctly grow weaker and fewer and eventually disappear. *Retailing changes are seen as planned or unplanned adaptive responses to threats* and opportunities *embedded in the environment surrounding the pertinent retailing structure.*

As indicated by students of organizations, the environment surrounding an organization has a tremendous impact on how it is structured and operated as well as on the goals it purports to seek (Hall 1977; Aldrich 1978). The environment serves as a source of inputs (manpower, products, physical and financial resources) for any organizational form; it also serves as the ultimate receiver of the outputs produced by the organization. Retailing organizations need to rely on their environments for similar purposes. In order to survive and succeed they need to be able to find customers to sell products to, suppliers to get products from, manpower, financing, etc.

Organizations manipulate their forms in ways which facilitate their response to and interaction with their environments. Organizations in other words attempt to "fit" their forms to the perceived environment. The form of the organization is thus contingent upon the environment.

In the long run, organizational forms can survive if they can provide adequate answers to the demands posed by their environment. While existing forms may strive to change their environments to fit their organizational needs, new forms will primarily emerge and succeed because of their ability to fit better than existing forms some environmental requirement(s). Thus, new retailing forms develop and emerge when an environmental niche, a distinct combination of resources and other constraints, emerges which is sufficient to support an organizational form.

III.   Stages of the process

The natural selection process postulates that new retailing institutions pass through three stages until they become established members of the retailing industry. At each stage, new retailing institutions can fail to survive. Only after passing through all three stages can they become established members of the retailing community. Their ability to survive at each stage depends therefore on their capacity to utilize mechanisms of survival available to them at each stage.

Broadly, the natural selection process can be divided into three sequential stages. Those are, respectively, the stages of *variation appearance, selection,* and *retention.* Each of these is discussed in detail.

A.   Variation

In order for the natural selection process to take place, it needs to start with the appearance of diverse species, in this case, of diverse retailing institutions. During a particular historical period several different retailing institutions may appear. The diversity can reflect differences in modes of internal operation, different modes of interacting with suppliers, and/or different strategies of appealing to customers. While the rationale for the appearance of diverse retailing institutional forms may vary, during each historical period these institutions are subjected to the selection process.

The retailing industry has traditionally exhibited low barriers to entry (Bucklin 1972), enabling new institutions to enter rather freely. Low barriers

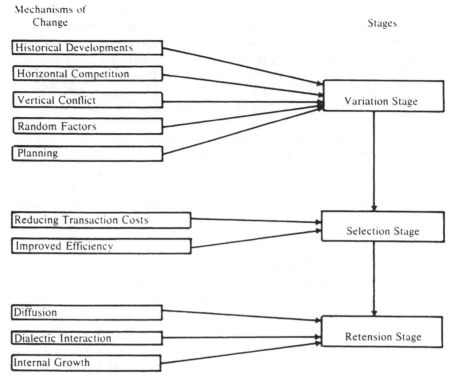

Mechanisms of
Change

Stages

Historical Developments

Horizontal Competition

Vertical Conflict

Random Factors

Planning

Variation Stage

Reducing Transaction Costs

Improved Efficiency

Selection Stage

Diffusion

Dialectic Interaction

Internal Growth

Retension Stage

Figure 3 Stages and mechanisms of retailing change

of entry reflect the relatively low levels of requirements of capital, human skills, or specialized resources typically needed to start a retailing operation. As a result, retailing has through all periods attracted entrepreneurs interested in trying their luck in offering something new.

This trend has been especially pronounced in the United States, where regulatory and legislative constraints have been even less pronounced than in other countries. Novel forms of retailing have been introduced constantly, offering a wide variety of retailing forms in each time period.

B. Selection

Of all the diverse organizational forms which exist in a given time period in an industry, only a subset is selected and survives while others fail and die. The process of selection is based on the fit of the organization with its environment. Organizations which better fit their environment survive and succeed; those that do not disappear sooner or later. Environmental fit, however, is a dynamic concept, because environments change, reflecting changes in technology, economic or social structure, or legal developments. As a result, changing environments induce constant changes in retailing.

Retailing forms which fit yesterday's requirements will not fit those of today, and those which fit those of today may not fit those of tomorrow.

The natural selection model refers to a tendency and does not mean an absolute but a relatively better fit. Some organizational forms may survive in spite of a seeming lack of fit, because of random factors. They may survive because of historical quirks or luck, or because they are insulated in one form or another from their environment and therefore can operate with impunity.

At the same time, some new form of retailing organization may not succeed at a given time even though it fits well the changes in the environment, again because of a variety of reasons. Luck and random events may often be blamed. Incompetent management may ruin an otherwise viable organization; excessive competition, lack of financial resources, or insufficient public recognition can all be blamed as well.

C. Retention

Selection of the most appropriate form of retailing does not ensure its survival in the long run, nor does it guarantee its dominance. To determine longevity, the process proceeds to the next stage, that of retention.

Retention is the mode through which successful organizational forms are retained and diffused in a given population. The retention mechanisms thus preserve the selected form and ensure its survival. Retention occurs when selected variations are preserved, duplicated, or otherwise reproduced so that the selected behavior is repeated on future occasions.

IV. Mechanisms of change

In order for the three stages to be activated, the natural selection process operates specific change mechanisms. At each stage, one finds one or more of the following mechanisms through which new retailing forms appear on the retailing scene, are selected (or rejected), and are eventually retained.

A. Mechanisms of the variation stage

At the variation stage, five distinct change mechanisms can be identified. These are *historical development, horizontal competition, vertical conflict, random factors, and planning*. Each contributes to the emergence in a particular historical period of a variety of diverse retailing institutions which compete with each other for consumer patronage.

1. Historical development

On many occasions, retailing institutions which operate in a given historical period reflect past historical developments. Historical developments may often create situations where retailing institutions which have not fitted their environment in the past have been dying out only to be reviewed as retailing conditions change again in their favor.

One example of such a development is the urban corner grocery store. With the population shift to the suburbs and strong competition from supermarkets, corner grocery stores were dying out in the 1960s and 1970s in the large cities of the United States. However, in the late 1970s and early 1980s, some urban areas like Manhattan in New York have experienced a revitalization of the corner grocery store as people moved back into the metropolitan core.

2. Horizontal competition

Horizontal competition among retailers operating in the same industry and appealing to the same market segment is another factor which generates retailing change. All organizational forms compete over external resources embedded in their environment (Pfeffer & Salancik 1978). For retailing firms, competition over customer patronage is the most important format to achieve control over crucial resources. In competing, each retailing form attempts to achieve *differential advantage* which would allow it to limit the threats posed by competing forms.

Retailing, as an industry, exhibits structural characteristics which limit the ability of retailing forms to achieve differential advantage through financial, legal, or technological barriers to entry (Bucklin 1972). Entry into the retailing industry is relatively easy. Though large firms abound in this industry, they do not maintain excessive control and cannot exclude competitors. The relative freedom to enter and to compete forces retailers to use retailing strategy as the major vehicle to achieve differential advantage. Those strategies require changes in the retailing structure through emergence of new institutions or the adoption of new strategies by existing institutions.

One attempt to explain retail innovation as a function of retail competition is to focus on its strategic implications for the innovator. Based on his study of steel distributors, Kriesberg (1969) had developed a model which links retailing innovation with the channel member's channel position. He postulated that retailing innovations are used by firms which come from outside a given industry to gain entry into it. The outsider firms, which Kriesberg denotes as transients, are more prone to innovation because they do not have vested interests in maintaining the current modes of operation.

3. Vertical conflict

Retailers are inherently parts of marketing channels, where they struggle for control with manufacturers, wholesalers, and other channel intermediaries. Conflict within the distributive channel is an all-pervasive phenomenon. (For a review of the role of conflicts in marketing channels, see Stern & El-Ansary 1981; also Etgar 1976b, 1979.)

One example of the role of vertical conflict in retailing innovation is provided by Etgar (1977) in his study of the property and casualty insurance industry. In that industry, conflict between insurance companies on one hand and the insurance agents on the other hand has not permitted the adoption of innovations and greater efficiency in distribution. To defend their prerogatives, insurance agents resisted computerization of insurance policies and payments and better channel organization. To regain control over the distributive channel, insurers had no choice but to develop novel retailing forms—exclusive agencies, direct writing, and retail store insurance selling. Thus, novel retailing forms emerged as a result of the conflict.

Galbraith (1952) has presented a theoretical framework which can provide an explanation of this phenomenon. He argued that, in marketing channels as in other social systems, the natural tendency is to retain a balance of power; whenever such a balance is disturbed, countervailing forces are activated to restore it.

In this way Galbraith explains the emergence of large-scale retailers. To him, these retailers emerged as a countervailing power in response to the emergence of large manufacturers. While Galbraith's explanation of the emergence of large-scale retailers was seriously challenged by researchers, the model provides a good explanation as to the impact that vertical relationships may have on retailing change.

4.   Planning and random factors

The variety of retailing institutions can also reflect conscious and *planned* efforts by some managers to introduce new retailing institutions which they believe will succeed in the market. Retail innovations successful in one country are introduced into another one. Thus, the supermarket concept, developed in the United States, was copied in Europe and all over the world with varying degrees of success. The concept of a hypermarket, on the other hand, was developed in France and imported into the United States.

Finally, one must point out to the potential impact of *random factors* on retailing development. New retailing institutions often may arise from a unique mixture of factors in an unrelated and unplanned way. They may reflect a unique experience of an individual, specific business opportunities available at a particular place and time, etc.

B.   Survival mechanisms

To survive beyond the emergence stage, retailing institutions must fit the requirements of their environments and devise a marketing strategy which will provide them with some relative advantages over competing retailing institutions.

The mechanisms which ensure survival of a retailing institution are embedded in its ability to *reduce transaction costs of some customer segment* or *improve efficiency*. Each of these are discussed separately.

1. Reduction in transaction costs

A transaction is a process through which consumers acquire the right to use and/or own a particular product. Consumer costs reflect the activities they are engaged in before, during, and after a transaction. Several attempts to model these activities have been made; consider, for example, the flowchart presented in Figure 4. According to it, consumers need to go through several stages to complete their consumption process, each involving use of their own resources. Such a process requires use of economic resources: consumers need to pay for the product itself as well as use their time and capital household goods (cars, refrigerators, etc.).

The major rationale proposed in this paper is that consumers' choice of retail institutions is primarily motivated by the desire to reduce costs. The notion of transaction costs has been developed recently by Williamson (1975, 1979, 1981a, 1981b) and spurred a substantial research effort in economics and organization theory, as well as in marketing (Etgar 1976a; Stern & Reve 1980).

Consumers can use less of their time and resources if they entrust shopping activities to others in return for remuneration. Manufacturers, retailers,

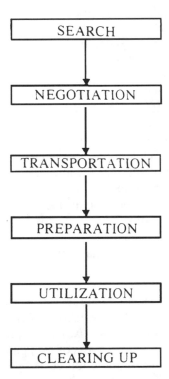

Figure 4 Stages of consumer consumption process
Source: Based on Etgar (1978)

and specialized entities can perform some of these activities on behalf of consumers. Consumers can reduce travel time by shopping at home, inventory maintenance by buying in smaller sizes, delivery time by demanding home delivery, etc. In each case, a retailer is required to perform a service. He needs to offer retail outlets closer to consumers' residential areas, offer smaller sizes and portions, home delivery, credit, etc. In each case, he will charge for his services accordingly.

In selecting a retailing store to patronize, consumers need to evaluate services offered and their price. Some consumers may prefer to perform the required services themselves, figuring that the costs they will incur are less than the service fee charged (in the form of higher retailer margins) by the retailers. Others may come to an opposite conclusion. They may envision that cost of use of their time and/or of their household resources exceeds such service fees and will find it more economicaly to "buy" these services from their retailers.

The decision as to what is more advantageous for a given group of consumers depends on the one hand on the margins charged by retailers for their services and on the other hand on the cost parameters for the consumers. Value of time, for example, may vary among consumers due to differences in their earning potential, leisure habits, family status, etc. (Becker 1965; Etgar 1978; Feldman & Hornick 1981). Costs of transportation, storage, etc, may depend on mobility and residential location, while costs of storage will depend on size of residence, usage rates, and usage quantities. Those in turn depend on a host of economic, demographic, and social factors such as income, family size, marital status, education, life-styles, etc.

Differences among consumers as to economic, demographic, and lifestyle characteristics lead to diversity in consumer cost parameters in their transactions. Different segments may appear with different preferences for retail services—margin ratios. While some consumers will prefer a high margin—high services mix, others will prefer the alternative.

Changes in consumer economic, demographic, and life-style characteristics affect the value of resources they use in their transactions. Increases in the value of time or transportation or storage costs for consumers will prompt them to shift some of the activities involved to retailers. Consumers may then seek retailing institutions that enable them to save shopping time, reduce transportation costs (by shopping over the phone or by mail, for example) or buy smaller-sized items.

Similarly, changes in consumer characteristics which reduce the value of time (e.g., women dropping out of the labor force), or transportation (due to increased mobility), or storage costs (when people move to large houses) will generate an opposite trend. As costs of shopping decline, consumers will attempt to reduce their total transaction costs by undertaking more of the relevant activities themselves and relieving retailers of their performance in return for lower prices.

Thus, the economic analysis of consumer shopping costs provides guidelines as to consumer retailing preferences. Supermarkets, discount stores, and food warehouses are all innovations which succeeded because they catered to a downward shift in consumer demand for retailing services. Due to demographic, social, and economic factors, substantial market segments arose who were ready to accept a tradedown and fewer retailing services if accompanied by a lower margin, and these stores provided such a mix (Schwartzman 1971). Similarly, department stores and convenience stores are examples of retailing answers for a demand for high-service, high-margin mixes (Goldman 1975).

2. *Improved efficiency*

The ability of a retailing institution to improve productivity is the second important mechanism of survival. Increased productivity provides a retailing institution cost savings, which in turn can be used to enhance the competitive advantages of the institution. A more efficient institution can offer the same service mix to consumers at lower prices, or offer a higher service mix at the same margins and prices, gaining an advantage over competitors in each case.

Major sources of improved productivity for retailers are *horizontal* and *vertical* economics of scale. To gain one or both kinds of economies requires novel types of retailing institutions in which modes of operation can be rearranged.

Horizontal economies of scale reflect economies embedded in the division of labor in retailing and in the use of large-scale technologies in material handling, storage, accounting, and promotion. Thus, separation of buying from merchandising functions and the establishment of specialized buyer departments has been a major source of economies of scale for chains. The chains and large-scale retailers could also use their size to introduce large-scale technologies and reduce the costs of operation and of the performance of the retailing functions. Survival of the mass merchandisers can in part, at least, be attributed to their horizontal economies of scale which allowed them to reduce costs of operation and gain competitive advantage.

Vertical economies of scale reflect better vertical channel function allocation within a channel, better transfer of information between different channel levels, and improved coordination (Bucklin 1971; Etgar 1976a). These economies have been the major incentive for the emergence of vertical marketing systems in the form of corporate, contractual, and administrative channels and their corresponding institutional expressions. Voluntary chains, retailer cooperatives, and franchising arrangements were all developed to utilize these benefits in diverse forms.

In many situations horizontal and vertical economies of scale are inseparable, and institutions develop to benefit simultaneously from both. What both offer for retailing is an opportunity to lower operational costs without necessarily lowering the level of retailing services, thus providing a distinct advantage over established retailing operations.

C. Retention mechanisms

The adoption of an innovation is a social process taking place in a given community. As a result, retention mechanisms are basically social processes reflecting the patterns of interaction prevalent in the specific community.

Adoption of a new retailing institution can take one of the following three forms. A new format can be adopted by entrepreneurs and managers in its *original* form and *diffused* into new areas or industries. In the second form, a *dialectic* interaction takes place. The novel form is adopted by existing institutions and modified to suit these. The result is a synergistic format which often incorporates characteristics of new and old retailing institutions. The third involves *internal* expansion, as the novel institution grows by internal growth and the original firm replaces the older institutions.

1. Diffusion process

Following early rural sociology studies of diffusion among farmers, extensive models of the diffusion process of novel ideas have been developed (Rogers & Shoemaker 1971). The underlying concept of the diffusion process is that different members of a community adopt an innovation at different times after it becomes available. For purposes of analysis, members of a community are classified as innovators, early adopters, early majority, late majority, and laggards according to when they adopt or have a propensity to adopt the innovation.

Empirical attempts to document the diffusion of retailing innovations are few. Kriesberg's study (1969) of steel distributors suggested that retail innovations are linked to the social position of retailers. Innovations are first adopted by marginal members of a given retailing community, and only later on are they adopted by other, more established members. Discounting and fast-food franchising are classic examples of this approach.

2. Dialectic mechanism

While the diffusion process involves adoption of a novel institution in its original form, and establishment of its reproductions, in many cases novel retailing procedures do not retain the original form but change it. The mechanism which governs retentions here is that of the dialectic process based on Hegelian thought (Gist 1968). Institutional change is viewed as a dialectic process in which there is conflict between a thesis, or the established institutional form, and the antithesis, the innovative institutional form. The conflict between the two is for domination of the particular industry. The conflict, however, does not result in the victory of one or the other. Rather, it leads to a fusive process in which a *synthesis* takes place. A new firm(s) emerges which combines characteristics of both of the original forms.

Alternatively, both of the original adversaries adopt some characteristics of their opponents and thus become more similar to each other. Examples of dialectic processes include the fight between supermarkets and food chain stores, with the end result being chains of supermarkets, and that between downtown department stores and suburban shopping centers. Here too a synthesis developed, with the department stores establishing branches in the suburban shopping centers, on the one hand, and merchants establishing downtown shopping malls, on the other hand.

3. Internal expansion

Biologists have noted that new species which are more adaptive to changing environments replace older, less suitable species through a biological process of birth and death. The older species which cannot cope well with their new environments die away; their death creates a vacuum, which is subsequently filled by novel species which expand and multiply. In retailing, retention of novel institutions often follows a similar process, through the force of competition for customer patronage. Novel, more suitable institutions often grow through internal expansion, replacing older institutions. One example is provided in the property and casualty insurance industry (Etgar 1977), There, over a period of 30 years, the superior format of distribution of insurance by exclusive agents propelled two companies, State Farm and Allstate, from nonexistence to control of over 40 percent of the market.

V. Conclusions

The analysis of existing models of retailing change suggests that their ability to explain past and present changes in retailing and the emergence of new retailing institutions is highly limited to subsets of the retailing change phenomenon. A more comprehensive model which explains various aspects of retailing change is needed. Such a model is presented in this paper. The model fuses the population ecology approach developed by organizational theorists with economic and organizational approaches to provide a comprehensive model of retailing change. The end result is a theoretical framework which is broad enough to explain all retailing changes involved in the emergence of new retailing institutions, from the department store to shopping via television. The model is an open system model which emphasizes the impact of the retailing environment on its institutional structure.

Retailing change is a process. It passes through three distinct stages—variation, selection, and retention—in which each new retailing innovation is tested for survival. Those innovations which pass all the stages become an acceptable retailing institution.

For marketers, the proposed model offers an analytical framework with which they can evaluate a particular retailing innovation—that is, see at which stage it is situated at each particular moment and which change mechanisms it uses. These perceptions will allow managers to understand better the change process which their particular institution undergoes. Managers will be able to realize the competitive advantages and disadvantages of their particular institution and their survival and growth potential.

For marketing researchers, the model presented provides a framework which can guide future empirical research. In particular, novel retailing institutions can be analyzed in terms of their ability to utilize the selection mechanisms presented in order to expand and grow.

References

Aldrich, H. E. *Organizations and environments.* Englewood Cliffs, N.J.: Prentice Hall, 1978.

Barzun, J. *Darwin, Marx, Wagner* (2nd ed.). New York: Doubleday Anchor, 1958.

Becker, G. A theory of the allocation of time. *Economic Journal,* 1965, *75,* (6) 493–517.

Boulding, K. *The organizational revolution.* New York: Harper and Row, 1953.

Bucklin, L. P. The economic base of franchising. In D. N. Thompson (Ed.), *Contractual marketing systems.* Lexington, MA.: Heath Lexington Books, 1971.

Bucklin, L. P. *Competition and evolution in the distributive trades.* Englewood Cliffs, N.J.: Prentice-Hall, 1972.

Campbell, D. Variation and selective retention in sociocultural evolution. *General Systems,* 1969, *16,* (1) 69–85.

Davidson, W. R., Bates. A. D., & Bass, S. T. The retail life cycle. *Harvard Business Review,* 1976, *54,* (November–December), 89.

Duncan, D. T. Responses of selected retail institutions to their changing environment. In P. D. Bennet (Ed.), *Marketing and Economic Development.* Chicago: American Marketing Association, 1965.

Etgar, M. The effect of administrative control on efficiency of vertical marketing systems. *Journal of Marketing Research,* 1976a, *13,* (February), 12–24.

Etgar, M. Channel domination and countervailing power in distribution channels, *Journal of Marketing Research,* 1976b, *13,* (August), 254–262.

Etgar, M. Three models of distributive change. In C. Slater (Ed.), *Macro-marketing: distributive processes from a societal perspective.* Boulder: University of Colorado, Bureau of Business Research, 1977.

Etgar, M. The household as a production function. In J. Sheth (Ed.), *Research in Marketing* (Vol. 1). Greenwich: JAI Press, 1978.

Etgar, M. Sources and types of intrachannel conflict. *Journal of Retailing,* 1979, *55,* (Spring), 407–19.

Feldman, L. & Hornick, J. The use of time: an integrated conceptual model. *Journal of Consumer Research,* March 1981, pp. 407–19.

Galbraith, J. *The American capitalism.* New York: Wiley, 1952.

Gist, R. R. *Retailing: concepts and decisions.* New York: Wiley, 1968.

Goldman, A. The role of trading up in the development of the retailing system. *Journal of Marketing,* 1975, *39,* (January), 54–62.

Hall, R. H. *Organizations: Structure and process.* Englewood Cliffs, N.J.: Prentice Hall, 1977.

Hawley, A. *Human ecology.* New York: The Ronald Press Co., 1950.

Hollander, S. C. The wheel of retailing. *Journal of Retailing*, 1960, *24*, (July), 37–48.
Hollander, S. C. Notes on the retail accordion. *Journal of Retailing*, 1966, *42*, (Summer), 29–40.
Hollander, S. C. Oddities, nostalgia, wheels and other patterns in retail evolution. In R. W. Stampfl & E. Hirschman (Eds.), *Competitive structure in retail markets; the department store perspective.* Chicago: American Marketing Association, 1980.
Hoult, T. F. *Dictionary of modern sociology.* Totowa, N.J.: Littlefield Adams & Co., 1972.
Hunt, S. D. *Marketing theory: Conceptual foundations of research in marketing.* Columbus, Ohio: Brid, 1976.
Kriesberg, L. Occupational controls among steel distributors. In L. W. Stern (Ed.), *Distribution channels: Behavioral dimensions.* Boston: Houghton Mifflin, 1969.
McNair, M. P. & May, E. G. *The evolution of retail institutions in the United States.* Cambridge, Mass.: Marketing Science Institute, 1976.
Mason, J. B. & Mayer, M. L. *Modern retailing: Theory and practice.* Plano: Texas Business Publications, 1981.
Pfeffer, J. & Salancik, G. R. *The external control of organizations.* New York: Harper & Row, 1978.
Regan, W. J. The stages of retail development. In Cox, A. & Shapiro (Eds.), *Theory in marketing* (2nd series). Homewood, Ill.: Irwin, 1964.
Rogers, E. M. & Shoemaker, F. F. *Communication of innovations* (2nd ed.). New York: The Free Press, 1971.
Rosenberg, L. J. & Hirschman, E. C. Retailing without stores. *Harvard Business Review*, (July–August 1980), pp. 103–112.
Schwartzman, D. The decline of service in retail trade. Pullman: Washington State University, Bureau of Economic and Business Research, 1971.
Sheth, J. An integrative theory of patronage preference behavior. Faculty Working Paper No. 808, College of Commerce and Business Administration, University of Illinois, Urbana, Champaign, 1983.
Stern, L. W. & El-Ansary, A. I. Marketing channels. Englewood Cliffs, N.J.: Prentice-Hall, 1981.
Stern, L. W. & Torger, R. Distribution channels as political economics: A framework for comparative analysis. *Journal of Marketing*, 1980, *44*, (Summer), 52–69.
Williamson, O. *Markets and hierarchies: Analysis and antitrust implications.* New York: The Free Press, 1975.
Williamson, O. Transaction cost economics: The governance of contractual relationships." *Journal of Law and Economics*, 1979, *22*, (2), 233–260.
Williamson, O. The economics of organization: The transaction cost approach. *American Journal of Sociology*, 1981a, *87*, (3), 548–577.
Williamson, O. The modern corporation: Origins, evolution, attributes. *Journal of Economic Literature*, 1981b, 19 (December), 1537–1568.
Zachariah, M. The impact of Darwin's theory of evolution on theories of society. *Social Studies*, 1961, *62*, (1), 69–76.

16

The wheel of retailing

Stanley C. Hollander

Source: *Journal of Marketing* 24 (1960): 37–42.

"The wheel of retailing" is the name Professor Malcolm P. McNair has suggested for a major hypothesis concerning patterns of retail development. This hypothesis holds that new types of retailers usually enter the market as low-status, low-margin, low-price operators. Gradually they acquire more elaborate establishments and facilities, with both increased investments and higher operating costs. Finally they mature as high-cost, high-price merchants, vulnerable to newer types who, in turn, go through the same pattern. Department-store merchants, who originally appeared as vigorous competitors to the smaller retailers and who have now become vulnerable to discount house and supermarket competition, are often cited as prime examples of the wheel pattern.[1]

Many examples of conformity to this pattern can be found. Nevertheless, we may ask:

(1) Is this hypothesis valid for all retailing under all conditions?
(2) How accurately does it describe total American retail development?
(3) What factors cause wheel-pattern changes in retail institutions?

The following discussion assembles some of the slender empirical evidence available that might shed some light on these three questions. In attempting to answer the third question, a number of hypotheses should be considered that marketing students have advanced concerning the forces that have shaped retail development.

Tentative explanations of the wheel

(A) *Retail personalities*

New types of retail institutions are often established by highly aggressive, cost-conscious entrepreneurs who make every penny count and who have no interest in unprofitable frills. But, as P. D. Converse has suggested, these men may relax their vigilance and control over costs as they acquire age and wealth. Their successors may be less competent. Either the innovators or their successors may be unwilling, or unable, to adjust to changing conditions. Consequently, according to this view, deterioration in management causes movement along the wheel.[2]

(B) Misguidance

Hermann Levy has advanced the ingenious, if implausible, explanation that retail trade journals, seduced by profitable advertising from the store equipment and supply industry, coax merchants into superfluous "modernization" and into the installation of overly elaborate facilities.[3]

(C) Imperfect competition

Although retail trade is often cited as the one type of business that approaches the Adam Smith concept of perfect competition, some economists have argued that retailing actually is a good example of imperfect competition. These economists believe that most retailers avoid direct price competition because of several forces, including resale price maintenance, trade association rules in some countries, and, most important, the fear of immediate retaliation. Contrariwise, the same retailers feel that service improvements, including improvements in location, are not susceptible to direct retaliation by competitors. Hence, through a ratchet process, merchants in any established branch of trade tend to provide increasingly elaborate services at increasingly higher margins.[4]

(D) Excess capacity

McNair attributes much of the wheel effect to the development of excess capacity, as more and more dealers enter any branch of retail trade.[5] This hypothesis rests upon an imperfect competition assumption, since, under perfect competition excess capacity would simply reduce margins until the excess vendors were eliminated.

(E) Secular trend

J. B. Jefferys has pointed out that a general, but uneven, long-run increase in the British standard of living provided established merchants with profitable opportunities for trading up. Jefferys thus credits adjustments to changing and wealthier market segments as causing some movement along the wheel. At the same time, pockets of opportunity have remained for new, low-margin operations because of the uneven distribution of living-standard increases.[6]

(F) Illusion

Professor B. Holdren has suggested in a recent letter that present tendencies toward scrambled merchandising may create totally illusory impressions of the wheel phenomenon. Store-wide average margins may increase as new, high-markup lines are added to the product mix, even though the margins charged on the original components of that mix remain unchanged.

Difficulties of analysis

An examination of the actual development of retail institutions here and abroad does shed some light on both the wheel hypothesis and its various explanations. However, a number of significant difficulties hinder the process.

(1) Statements concerning changes in retail margins and expenses are the central core of the wheel hypothesis. Yet valid information on historical retail expense rates is very scarce. Long-run changes in percentage margins probably do furnish fairly reliable clues to expense changes, but this is not true over short or intermediate periods. For example, 1957 furniture-store expense rates were about 5 percentage points higher than their 1949–1951 average, yet gross margins actually declined slightly over the same period.[7]
(2) Historical margin data are somewhat more plentiful, but these also have to be dredged up from fragmentary sources.[8]
(3) Available series on both expenses and margins merely note changes in retailers' outlays and receipts. They do not indicate what caused those changes and they do not report changes in the costs borne by suppliers, consumers, or the community at large.
(4) Margin data are usually published as averages that may, and frequently do, mask highly divergent tendencies.
(5) A conceptual difficulty presents an even more serious problem than the paucity of statistics. When we talk about "types" of retailers, we think of classifications based upon ways of doing business and upon differences in price policy. Yet census categories and other systems for reporting retail statistics are usually based upon major differences in commodity lines. For example, the "pineboard" druggists who appeared in the 1930s are a "type" of retailing for our purposes. Those dealers had cruder fixtures, charged lower prices, carried smaller assortments, gave more attention to turnover, and had less interest in prescriptions than did conventional druggists. Yet census reports for drugstores necessarily included all of the pineboards that maintained any sort of prescription department.

Discount houses provide another example of an important, but amorphous, category not reflected in census classifications. The label "discount house" covers a variety of retailers. Some carry stocks, others do not. Some have conventional store facilities, whereas others operate in office buildings, lofts, and warehouses. Some feature electrical appliances and hard goods, while others emphasize soft goods. Some pose as wholesalers, and others are practically indistinguishable from all other popular priced retailers in their fields. Consequently discount dealers' operating figures are likely to be merged into the statistics reported for other appliance, hardware, or apparel merchants.

Examples of conformity

British

British retailing provides several examples of conformity to the wheel pattern. The grocery trade has gone through several wheel-like evolutions, according to a detailed analysis made by F. G. Pennance and B. S. Yamey.[9] Established firms did initiate some changes and some margin reductions, so that the pattern is obscured by many cross currents. But the major changes seem to have been due to the appearance and then the maturation, first, of department-store food counters; then, of chain stores; and finally, of cut-price cash-and-carry stores. Now supermarkets seem to be carrying the pattern through another evolution.[10]

Jefferys also has noted a general long-run upgrading in both British department stores and chains.[11] Vague complaints in the co-operative press and a decline in consumer dividend rates suggest that wheel-like changes may have occurred in the British co-operative movement.[12]

American

Very little is known about retail margins in this country before the Civil War. Our early retail history seems to have involved the appearance, first, of hawkers, walkers, and peddlers; then, of general stores; next, of specialty stores; and finally, of department stores. Each of these types apparently came in as a lower-margin, lower-price competitor to the established outlets, and thus was consistent with the wheel pattern. We do not know, however, whether there was simply a long-run decline in retail margins through successive improvements in retail efficiency from one type to another (contrary to the wheel pattern), or whether each of the early types was started on a low-margin basis, gradually "up-graded," and so provided room for the next entrant (in accordance with the pattern).

The trends toward increasing margins can be more easily discerned in many branches of retailing after the Civil War. Barger has described increases over the years 1869–1947 among important retail segments, including department stores, mail-order firms, variety stores, and jewelry dealers. He attributes much of the pre-World War I rise in department-store margins to the absorption of wholesaling functions. Changes in merchandise mix, such as the addition of soda fountains and cafeterias to variety stores and the upgrading of mail-order merchandise, seem to have caused some of the other increases. Finally, he believes changes in customer services have been a major force in raising margins.[13] Fabian Linden has extended Barger's observations to note similar 1949–1957 margin increases for department stores, variety chains, and appliance dealers.[14]

Some other examples of at least partial conformity to the wheel pattern may be cited. Many observers feel that both discount-house services and margins have increased substantially in recent years.[15] One major discount-house operator has stated that he has been able to keep his average markup below 12%, in spite of considerable expansion in his facilities and commodity mix.[16] However, the concensus seems to be that this probably is an exception to the general rule.

A study of gasoline pricing has pointed out how many of the so-called "off-brand" outlets have changed from the "trackside" stations of pre-war days. The trackside dealers typically maintained unattractive and poorly equipped installations, at out-of-the-way locations where unbranded gasoline was sold on a price basis. Today many of them sell well-promoted regional and local brands, maintain attractive, efficient stations, and provide prompt and courteous service. Some still offer cut prices, but may have raised their prices and margins up to or above national brand levels.[17] Over time, many of the pineboard druggists also seem to have become converted to fairly conventional operations.[18]

Non-conforming examples

Foreign

In underdeveloped countries, the relatively small middle- and upper-income groups have formed the major markets for "modern" types of retailing. Supermarkets and other modern stores have been introduced in those countries largely at the top of the social and price scales, contrary to the wheel pattern.[19] Some nonconforming examples may also be found in somewhat more industrialized environments. The vigorous price competition that developed among Japanese department stores during the first three decades of this century seems directly contrary to the wheel hypothesis.[20] B. S. Yamey's history of resale price maintenance also reports some price-cutting by traditional, well-established British merchants who departed from the wheel pattern in the 1880s and 1890s.[21] Unfortunately, our ignorance of foreign retail history hinders any judgment of the representativeness of these examples.

American

Automatic merchandising, perhaps the most "modern" of all American retail institutions, departed from the wheel pattern by starting as a high-cost, high-margin, high-convenience type of retailing.[22] The department-store branch movement and the concomitant rise of planned shopping centers also has progressed directly contrary to the wheel pattern. The early department-store branches consisted of a few stores in exclusive suburbs and some equally high-fashion college and resort shops.

Only in relatively recent years have the branches been adjusted to the changing and more democratic characteristics of the contemporary dormitory suburbs. Suburban shopping centers, too, seem to have appeared first as "Manhasset Miracle Miles" and "Ardmores" before reaching out to the popular price customers. In fact, complaints are still heard that the regional shopping centers have displayed excessive resistance to the entry of really aggressive, low-margin outlets.[23] E. R. A. Seligman and R. A. Love's study of retail pricing in the 1930s suggests that pressures on prices and margins were generated by all types of retailers. The mass retailing institutions, such as the department and chain stores, that had existed as types for many decades were responsible for a goodly portion of the price cutting.[24] As McNair has pointed out, the wheel operated very slowly in the case of department stores.

Finally, Harold Barger has described the remarkable stability of over-all distributive margins during the years 1919–1947.[25] Some shifting of distributive work from wholesalers to retailers apparently affected their relative shares of the total margins during this period, but this is not the type of change contemplated by the wheel pattern. Of course, the stability Barger notes conceivably could have been the result of a perfectly smooth functioning of the pattern, with the entrance of low-margin innovators providing exactly the right balance for the upcreep of margins in the longer established types. But economic changes do not come in smooth and synchronized fashion, and Barger's data probably should indicate considerably wider oscillations if the wheel really set the mold for all retailing in the post-war period.

Conclusions

The number of non-conforming examples suggests that the wheel hypothesis is not valid for all retailing. The hypothesis, however, does seem to describe a fairly common pattern in industrialized, expanding economies. Moreover, the wheel is not simply an illusion created by scrambled merchandising, as Holdren suggests. Undoubtedly some of the recent "upcreep" in supermarket average margins is due to the addition of nonfood and other high margin lines. But in recent years the wheel pattern has also been characteristic of department-store retailing, a field that has been relatively unreceptive to new commodity groups.[26]

In some ways, Jefferys' secular trend explanation appears most reasonable. The tendency of many established retailers to reduce prices and margins during depressions suggests also that increases may be a result of generally prospering environments. This explanation helps to resolve an apparent paradox inherent in the wheel concept. Why should reasonably skilled businessmen make decisions that consistently lead their firms along seemingly profitable routes to positions of vulnerability? Jefferys sees movement along the wheel as the result of sensible, business-like decisions to change with prospering market segments and to leave the poorer customers to low-margin innovators. His explanation is supported by the fact that the vulnerability contemplated by the wheel hypothesis usually means only a loss of market share, not a loss of absolute volume. At least in the United States, though, this explanation is partially contradicted by studies showing that prosperous consumers are especially prone to patronize discount houses. Also they are equally as likely to shop in supermarkets as are poorer consumers.[27]

The imperfect competition and excess capacity hypotheses also appear highly plausible. Considerably more investigation is needed before their validity can be appraised properly. The wheel pattern developed very slowly, and very recently in the department-store field. Yet market imperfections in that field probably were greater before the automobile gave the consumer shopping mobility. Major portions of the supermarket growth in food retailing and discount-house growth in appliance distribution occurred during periods of vastly expanding consumption, when excess capacity probably was at relatively low levels. At the moment there is little evidence to suggest any clear-cut correlation between the degree of market imperfection and the appearance of the wheel pattern. However, this lack may well be the result of the scarcity of empirical studies of retail competition.

Managerial deterioration certainly must explain some manifestations of the wheel, but not all. Empires rise and fall with changes in the quality of their leadership, and the same thing seems true in business. But the wheel hypothesis is a hypothnesis concerning types of retailing and not merely individual firms. Consequently, the managerial-deterioration explanation holds true only if it is assumed that new people entering any established type of retailing as the heads of both old and new companies are consistently less competent than the first generation. Again, the fact that the wheel has operated very slowly in some fields suggests that several successive managerial generations can avoid wheel-like maturation and decay.

Notes

1. M. P. McNair, "Significant Trends and Developments in the Postwar Period," in A. B. Smith (editor), *Competitive Distribution in a Free, High-Level Economy and Its Implications for the University* (Pittsburgh: University of Pittsburgh Press, 1958), pp. 1–25 at pp. 17–18.

2. P. D. Converse, "Mediocrity in Retailing," JOURNAL OF MARKETING, Vol. 23 (April, 1959), pp. 419–420.

3. Hermann Levy, *The Shops of Britain* (London: Kegan Paul, Trench, Trubner & Co., 1947), pp. 210–211.

4. D. L. Shawver, *The Development of Theories of Retail Price Determination* (Urbana; University of Illinois Press, 1956), p. 92.

5. Same reference as footnote 1.

6. J. B. Jefferys, *Retail Trading in Great Britain, 1850–1950* (Cambridge: Cambridge University Press, 1954), various pages, especially p. 96.

7. Cited in Fabian Linden, "Department Store Operations," *Conference Board Business Record*, Vol. 14 (October, 1958), pp. 410–414, at p. 411.

8. See Harold Barger, *Distribution's Place in the American Economy Since 1869* (Princeton: Princeton University Press, 1955).

9. F. G. Pennance and B. S. Yamey, "Competition in the Retail Grocery Trade, 1850–1939," *Economica*, Vol. 22 (March, 1955), pp. 303–317.

10. "La Methode Americaine," *Time*, Vol. 74 (November 16, 1959), pp. 105–106.

11. Same reference as footnote 6.

12. "Battle of the Dividend," *Co-operative Review*, Vol. 36 (August, 1956), p. 183; "Independent Commission's Report," *Co-operative Review*, Vol. 38 (April, 1958), pp. 84–89; "£52 Million Dividend in 1957," *Co-operative Review* (August, 1958), pp. 171–172.

13. Same reference as footnote 8, p. 82.

14. See footnote 7.

15. D. A. Loehwing, "Resourceful Merchants," *Barron's*, Vol. 38 (November 17, 1958), p. 3.

16. S. Masters, quoted in "Three Concepts of Retail Service," *Stores*, Vol. 41 (July–August, 1959), pp. 18–21.

17. S. M. Livingston and T. Levitt, "Competition and Retail Gasoline Prices," *The Review of Economics and Statistics*, Vol. 41 (May, 1959), pp. 119–132 at p. 132.

18. Paul C. Olsen, *The Marketing of Drug Products* (New Brunswick: Rutgers University Press, 1948), pp. 130–132.

19. H. S. Hettinger, "Marketing in Persia," JOURNAL OF MARKETING, Vol. 15 (January, 1951), pp. 289–297; H. W. Boyd, Jr., R. M. Clewett, & R. L. Westfall, "The Marketing Structure of Venezuela," JOURNAL OF MARKETING, Vol. 22 (April, 1958), pp. 391–397; D. A. Taylor, "Retailing in Brazil," JOURNAL OF MARKETING, Vol. 24 (July, 1959), pp. 54–58; J. K. Galbraith and R. Holton, *Marketing Efficiency in Puerto Rico* (Cambridge: Harvard University Press, 1955), p. 35.

20. G. Fukami, "Japanese Department Stores," JOURNAL OF MARKETING, Vol. 18 (July, 1953), pp. 41–49 at p. 42.

21. "The Origins of Resale Price Maintenance," *The Economic Journal*, Vol. 62 (September, 1952), pp. 522–545.

22. W. S. Fishman, "Sense Makes Dollars," *1959 Directory of Automatic Merchandising* (Chicago: National Automatic Merchandising Association, 1959), p. 52; M. V. Marshall, *Automatic Merchandising* (Boston: Graduate School of Business Administration, Harvard University, 1954), pp. 108–109, 122.

23. P. E. Smith, *Shopping Centers* (New York: National Retail Merchants' Association, 1956), pp. 11–12; M. L. Sweet, "Tenant-Selection Policies of Regional Shopping Centers," JOURNAL OF MARKETING, Vol. 23 (April, 1959), pp. 399–404.

24. E. R. A. Seligman and R. A. Love, *Price Cutting and Price Maintenance* (New York: Harper & Brothers, 1932).

25. Same reference as footnote 8, pp. ix, x.

26. R. D. Entenberg, *The Changing Competitive Position of Department Stores in the United States by Merchandise Lines* (Pittsburgh: University of Pittsburgh Press, 1957), p. 52.

27. R. Holton, *The Supply and Demand Structure of Food Retailing Services, A Case Study* (Cambridge: Harvard University Press, 1954).

17

Notes on the retail accordion

Stanley C. Hollander

Source: *Journal of Retailing* 42 (1966): 29–40, 54.

The history of retail development seems to demonstrate an accordion pattern. Domination by general line, wide-assortment retailers alternates with domination by specialized, narrow-line merchants. Neither the pattern's universality nor its existence can be proven definitely (since there are no valid historical statistics on merchandise assortments), but many astute students of retailing history have discerned these rhythmic oscillations.

Margaret Hall and her associates speak, for instance, of "a characteristic cycle of evolution of retail trade."[1] Ralph Hower notes two such alternations, one in functions performed, the other (which is the one that concerns us at the moment) in merchandise assortments:

> Throughout the history of retail trade (as, indeed in all business evolution) there appears to be an alternating movement in the dominant method of conducting operations. One swing is toward the specialization of the function performed or of the merchandise handled by individual firms. The other is away from such specialization toward the integration of related activities under one management or the diversification of products handled by a single firm.[2]

Postwar emphasis on scrambling

Recently, however, marketing writers have tended to emphasize the movement toward wider, more scrambled assortments. This emphasis has been a natural one, since in these years the supermarket chains have invaded the nonfood field, the discounters have added soft lines, and the variety chains have moved into big ticket categories. Moreover, these scrambling tendencies have been the result of strong economic forces. Scrambling is not only attractive to the merchant who finds opportunities to add profitable lines from other fields; it is also attractive to the consumer who benefits from what Baranoff calls "concentrated variety" or the assembly of "everything under one roof."[3] E. J. McCarthy points out that scrambling is likely to continue because inflexibilities and rigidities in the practices of the retailers who are established in any one line create opportunities for invasion by outsiders.[4]

Thus there is considerable justification for many statements like the following that underline the tendencies toward mixing and broadening assortments. Marketing observers have many reasons for saying:

> Retailing is smack in the middle of a merchandise scramble, the likes of which it has never before experienced. . . . In short, everyone's in the act, and there's no end in sight.
>
> [There is a] broad trend among almost all chains toward giant one-stop store units carrying an enormous variety of merchandise classifications, and with stocks in each classification deep and, sometimes, broad.
>
> It sometimes seems that every retailer is trying to become a department store.
>
> The new center of retailing will probably be a highly efficient combination of the best features of all three: discounter, supermarket and department store. . . . If carried to its logical extension, this consolidation could go far beyond one store for three.[5]

Countertrends

Even though merchandise scrambling is one of the most prominent characteristics of contemporary distribution, retail history suggests the advisability of looking also at the forces conducive to specialization. For a long time now both the trade press and the popular journals have predicted the ultimate triumph of the "one-stop" store. For example, an 1892 editorial in *The American Grocer* declared under the title "The Sell-Everything System:"

> In these days of hurry and push, people do not like to have to go into six different shops for six different articles; they prefer to buy the lot at one shop, and the trader who gives them this facility will get their business.[6]

Yet in spite of many such predictions over the years, tendencies toward specialization also continued to appear. Thus, in 1906 *The Dry Goods Economist* commented on the remarkable development of limited line stores, such as ladies' waist shops, and in 1917 it declared:

> There was a time when the aim of the average department store seemed to be to handle as many varieties of goods as possible. . . . But the inclination to "spread out" in this direction seems to have passed its meridian, and instead of adding specialties in grindstones or coffins State Street merchants are today giving an intensive cultivation to the lines they already carry.[7]

Specialized merchants still constitute a large proportion of the total retail population. At least some of our attention should be directed toward the factors that have allowed this specialization to continue and even, at times, to grow. A modification of our original analogy may be somewhat helpful in this process. Instead of comparing retailing to an accordion, we might picture it as an orchestra or band of accordion players. At any one moment some of the players are compressing the music boxes while others are extending them. Moreover, at any time, some players (including those with compressed and those with extended accordions) are retiring from the orchestra, while still others (mainly with compressed instruments) are joining the band. Similarly changes in the retail population include both arrivals and departures of merchants offering various assortments as well as the expansion and contraction of assortments among the continuing firms.

In looking at this process of specialization, we may note at least three phenomena:

1. Attempted merchandise mixtures that proved unsuccessful. Examples of these include many as yet fruitless attempts to introduce general merchandise lines into gasoline service station retailing; attempts at selling haberdashery and women's wear accessories through vending machines; and a few abortive ventures, such as Ford-Wanamaker and Kaiser-Sears, at offering automobiles in department stores. Of course, any of these or other ventures might prove profitable at some point in the future, when either circumstances or the method of introduction might be more propitious. All we can say is that some attempts at expanding the accordions have, so far, encountered insurmountable limitations.
2. Cases in which established merchants actually dropped or discarded some of their conventional lines; for example, the discontinuance of major appliance lines by some department stores in the face of discount competition some years ago.
3. The perhaps more typical situation in which the conventional assortments continue to include a particular line, but an increasing share of the business goes to (new) specialists. Thus most merchants who normally sold greeting cards in the past are probably continuing to do so today, perhaps even more profitably than ever before. Yet specialized card shops are certainly enjoying a larger share of the market now than they did a few decades ago.

Drug trade

The retail pharmacy industry provides good illustrations of both phases of the accordion process. Before (and in many cases even after) the Civil War, physicians who dispensed as well as prescribed drugs, plus general merchants controlled most of the country's drug trade. There were druggists and apothecaries in some cities, but they were as much involved in the sale of textile dyestuffs, oils, and paints, as in dispensing *materia medica*. The physicians gave up first their open shops, in which anyone (whether a patient or not) could buy drugs; then ultimately they eliminated almost all dispensing, even to their own patients. The general merchants also surrendered a large part of the drug business to the druggists. Simultaneously the dyestuff, oil, and paint business splintered off from the drugstores.

However, the specialized nature of the drugstore was steadily diluted by the addition of sidelines and nonmedical items, including a great increase during the 1880's and 1890's in the proportion of stores equipped with fountains. General merchandise lines were added regularly, particularly during the 1920's and 1930's, as well as in more recent years. Thus drugstores again tended to become more general in nature, even as food supermarkets, discount department stores, and others added drug and health lines. But some offsetting contractions can also be noted. Both the number and the percentage of drugstores that have soda fountains have declined fairly steadily since World War II. Moreover, two types of specialized drugstores have recently come into increasing prominence. One is the discount drug unit which in many ways resembles the equally specialized pineboard operation of the '20's and '30's. The other, at the opposite end of the price spectrum, is the "professional" or "ethical" outlet, today often located in a medical building, where the proprietor concentrates almost entirely upon prescriptions and therapeutic items.[8]

Food trends

Some, although perhaps not as many, instances of contraction can be found in the grocery trade. One was a tendency at the turn of the century toward the elimination of soda fountains, lunch counters, and tearooms.[9] The full-scale retreat of the large mail-order firms and many department stores from the grocery business in the early 1900's provides a more significant example of contraction.[10] During the latter half of the last century, specialized dairy stores and specialized tea, coffee, and spice establishments took a good portion of the urban trade in those commodities away from the full-line groceries.[11] Many of the coffee and tea specialists attracted their customers through a combination of elaborate premium plans and low prices in a product sector where the conventional grocers had enjoyed exceptionally high markups. But they also drew their customers by offering much wider assortments of spices and teas than were available in the conventional stores, just as today's specialized franchised doughnut and ice cream stores use variety as the major drawing card.[12] The bantam supermarkets or convenience stores that are springing up all over the country constitute another type of specialization. These stores tend to sell items selected from many of the usual merchandise categories (and thus are a form of scrambling), but at the same time they limit their stock to high turnover items that the consumer usually buys without much advance planning.[13] Finally, the difficulties that some food chains encountered when they tried to introduce extensive soft goods assortments into the food stores suggests at least a possible current limit on scrambling in this field.

Other fields

The automotive branches of retailing demonstrate greater (although not totally unmixed) tendencies toward contraction. Although department stores and mail-order houses were major outlets for bicycles in the days when the cycle was an important form of transportation, and although there were some attempts at selling automobiles through general merchandise outlets, the basic pattern in the automobile business involved the development of specialized outlets. Similarly, subject to a few recent exceptions, the gasoline pump moved from the grocery and hardware store to the very limited-line filling station. Entenberg found that from 1929 to 1953, the department stores lost approximately 85 percent of their market share in tires, batteries, and automobile accessories, mainly to service stations and to automotive supply stores.[14] Similarly Leigh describes the tire business as passing from bicycle and carriage shops, garages, hardware stores, and general stores into the hands of specialized tire dealers.[15]

More recently the auto accessory dealers have added rather extensive hard goods lines while both department store and discount store merchants seem to be making successful forays into the t.b.a. field. So at least some of the auxiliary branches of automotive retailing may be moving into an expansion phase of the accordion.

Specialization has also appeared in many other trades. Although the book business has experienced much scrambling, partially through the absorption of giftware, greeting cards, and miscellaneous merchandise into the book-stores, and partially through the addition of book departments to department and discount stores, it is also developing a number of very limited-line stores. The American booktrade now includes a great many paperback stores and a growing number of business and technological book dealers, in addition to the older specialists in textbooks and religious publications. Shoe merchants, who once handled a full line of family footwear, have tended to divide into separate men's, women's, and children's outlets.[16] Fuchs reports that retail furriers gained a considerable share of total fur volume from 1939 to 1948 at the expense of department stores and full-line ready-to-wear specialty stores.[17] Furniture houses that feature only Early American or only Swedish Modern styles are now a well-entrenched part of that trade.

Many new limited-line stores are designed to cater to the consumer's recreational interests, and thus are perhaps a manifestation of a leisure-minded society. These stores include high-fidelity equipment shops, phonograph record stores, ski shops, marinas, and garden supply units.[18] In her analysis of changes in Boston's retail population, Eileen Schell found that many of the limited-line newcomers were specialized prepared food shops and lunch rooms including establishments that concentrated on pizza pies, submarine sandwiches, fish and chips, or chicken-in-the-basket. Other outlets were confined to particular new products, such as high-fidelity equipment, aluminum windows and doors, and self-service dry cleaning. She also found that the typical electrical appliance sales/repair shop had been replaced by one expanded type, the combination furniture-appliance store; one somewhat intermediate type, the large discount appliance store (which might carry a wider line but presumably deemphasized repairs); and two contracted types: the small, repair-oriented store, and the gas appliance outlet.[19]

The contraction of the accordion is by no means a purely American phenomenon. Jefferys, Hausberger, and Lindblad suggest that rising standards of living in Europe provide fertile ground for the support of specialized retailing.[20]

Even in England, where scrambling now seems to be the order of the day, several instances of the opposite process can also be noted. Some of the London department stores now seem to be compressing their activities. These stores, which once went much further than their American counterparts toward fulfilling William Whitely's objectives of being "Universal Providers," are now tending to curtail the undertaking, household moving, and catering services that had become a fairly conventional part of the department store trade. The British department stores have been losing ground to the specialized clothing chains during the last ten years or so.[21] And one of the most spectacular successes in all British retailing is the Marks and Spencer chain, which discarded many variety and junior department store lines to concentrate on popular priced household textiles, a somewhat limited clothing line that omits men's and boy's suits and coats, and as even more limited grocery and food assortment.

These examples of contraction, both American and foreign, could be multiplied several times over. However, it is more important to ask what are the forces that permit and encourage specialization.

Forces promoting contraction

The forces promoting contraction are numerous. They include the following.

1. *Noneconomic.* A considerable body of evidence suggests that many merchants, particularly small ones, want to devote their attention to a limited

offering. Some undoubtedly are anxious for the "quiet life" and do not wish to cope with the problems that expansion presents. Others derive more positive satisfaction from concentration. Apparently many small furriers, florists, and the like want to think of themselves and want to practice as craftsmen and artists in their trades, not as growth-minded businessmen. Many bookdealers and specialists in recreational equipment must have somewhat the same set of desires. Quite possibly, the pharmacists who set up "professional" (prescription and health products) shops find closer agreement between the self-images that led them into pharmacy school and their current activities than they would experience in retailing ice cream, toys, and cosmetics.[22] Of course, except for the very significant advantages that interest, "expertise," and enthusiasm yield, this set of motives mainly explains why some people want to set up specialized stores rather than why the economy supports those attempts.

2. *Restraints.* In a well-known article some years ago, Professor John Due suggested that the limits on scrambling arose out of voluntary restraints or what the economists now call "conjectural interdependence."[23] Due argued that small additions to the lines carried almost always involved only relatively minor marginal expenses for those retailers who had already made their basic investments and overhead commitments in their "normal" or "regular" lines. Hence retailers in one commodity field could usually sell a few attractive items from another field at lower prices and higher profits than could the retailers who normally dealt in that field. Thus there always was a temptation to raid each other's assortments, but this was held in check by implicit voluntary restraint because of fear of competitive retaliation.

   This explanation ignores personal differences in vulnerability to retaliation. A druggist may become so irate, for instance, that he will suggest that his colleagues ought to sell lettuce "to teach the grocers a lesson." But clearly fear of retaliation has not, and cannot, keep the supermarkets from selling health and beauty aids. The operating realities left the druggists powerless to punish the grocers. Nevertheless, especially in small communities, unwillingness to disturb the status quo at times must limit competitive invasions.[24] In at least one extreme case, in Cordova, Nebraska, the seven merchants who comprised the town's retail population explicitly agreed to refrain from invading each other's merchandise classifications.[25]

   Other restraints are imposed by outsiders. The legal straightjackets have been much more confining in Europe than in America, but even here nonspecialist outsiders are often forbidden entry into such fields as pharmaceutical and liquor retailing. Shopping center developers place some limits on the ways in which component stores can expand into each other's privileged fields. Suppliers and franchisers often encourage or force their dealers to specialize, perhaps in part to increase the dealers' dependence.[26] Thus a host of personal, political, and interfirm considerations help shape the composition of the retail orchestra. However, these factors are only part of the whole story, and we should also look at the fundamental supply and demand conditions affecting various types of retail service.

3. *Capacity.* Many new entrants as well as many continuing firms operate on a limited line basis because their capital and other resources do not seem to permit any considerable merchandise expansion. Conceivably one could maintain a wide, but shallow, assortment establishment on a relatively meager asset base. Some small general stores are of exactly this nature. But as a practical matter, competitive conditions often force each merchant to maintain a certain minimum stock within each conventional merchandise category in which he operates or intends to operate. Consequently the retailer who has only limited funds or limited managerial energies is often forced to choose between offering a restricted line and not operating at all.[27]

The capacity problem may also arise in a somewhat different context. The large firm that wants to expand through the absorption of additional functions, *i.e.*, vertical integration, may find its accordion position determined by the width of the offerings at what it considers to be the most difficult or the most important stage of its operations.[28] Thus shoe manufacturers who venture into retailing are usually more able, at least at the start, to operate shoe shops rather than department stores. A historical hypothesis might hold that manufacturers who have integrated forward tend to have narrower assortments than retailers who have integrated backwards.

4. *Costs.* Capacity and cost questions are closely related. Some instances of expansion simply put idle or underutilized capacity to work and thus reduce the average costs of handling each item. Other instances of expansion are likely to push the retailer onto the increasing portion of his cost curve. As Reavis Cox has pointed out in a somewhat different context:

> Diversification of product has the immediate effect of complicating almost all of the retailer's work. The number of items from which he must choose his inventory grows enough to increase the cost of selecting those he wants to offer his customers. Furthermore, he must enlarge his inventory, his display space, his accumulation of records, and so on. He may experience very serious effects.[29]

Of course the really significant question is whether costs grow at a faster rate than revenue when classifications are added to the store's assortment. A number of conceptual models have been prepared that show the effects, at different stages, of different cost and revenue functions, but we still have little empirical information to insert into those models.[30] Nevertheless, it is clear that some of the most significant advantages in large-scale retailing, including decision-making economies and purchasing advantages, flow from selling large quantities of each item stocked, rather than from selling many different items. For this reason, McClelland argues that specialized chains tend to operate from more favorable bases than do generalized individual department stores of equal sales volume.[31]

5. *The Market.* The complex pattern of consumer preferences provides a base for both expansion and contraction of the accordion. We really know very little about the shopping tastes and desires of various market segments. Clearly, some customers like stores with wide assortments, some prefer specialized stores, and some tend to divide their patronage in accordance with the item involved, the reason for purchase, the time and energy available for shopping, and other considerations. The expanded-line store does offer attractions that include the convenience of one-stop shopping and the recreational values of walking past dazzling assortments of goods. But in at least some purchasing situations these attractions are offset by some factors to which we shall now direct our attention. These are the factors that tend to help the stores with limited lines.

For example, the concept of incompatabilities and incongruities has been explored mainly in connection with location problems. This concept results in the advice, for example, that supermarkets should not be placed next to automobile repair shops.[32] The same line of thought, which fundamentally rests upon anticipated consumer rejection or distaste for particular combinations, is easily extendable to the mixture within the individual establishment. Essentially this means that certain combinations of goods are not feasible unless the unit is large enough to interpose considerable neutral space between the hostile products. The problem is comparable to the difficulties of selling men's suits if the department is located in a women's ready-to-wear area. Moreover, at least one set of studies found that shoppers are mainly attracted to stores with either very wide or very deep assortments. The shoppers in these studies rejected the "intermediate" and "indeterminate" stores.[33] The fact that the consumer dislikes certain combinations standing by themselves and also dislikes intermediate ranges of extension indicates several discontinuities in the expansion process. According to this viewpoint, it is difficult or inadvisable to attempt "just a little scrambling."

Yet sheer size, which is a possible and sometimes practical answer to the problem of "all or nothing" has its own disadvantages. Martineau, for example, found that a significant proportion of his interviewees expressed feelings of confusion and of being overwhelmed by the crowds and sheer size of large stores.[34] Another investigator reports that most of the people he studied said they would prefer a collection of specialty stores with greater variety to a single store offering a general assortment under one roof. He found that older people were particularly likely to complain of the time and effort required to search for goods in large establishments.[35] The large store experiences two further disadvantages as a result of its need for support from a large market. One, as noted by Doody and Davidson, is the loss of distinctiveness and differentiation that tends to occur when the store tries to cater to everyone. Scrambling intensifies this difficulty, since the attempt to sell a little bit of everything to everyone is almost an open invitation to banality and dullness.[36] The other basic difficulty of market outreach is the problem of consumer resistance to travel time and trouble. This difficulty also hampers the specialty shop unless it can cater to the unique needs of a nearby community, since a good many customers are usually required to support a deep selection within a single line.

Opportunities

Rising incomes, expanding consumer demands, urbanization and suburbanization, and transportation improvements are increasingly providing markets that will support highly specialized and, in many cases, highly differentiated retail ventures. The very growth and expansion of the large, scrambled units tends to create opportunities for smaller, more distinctive, and more focused enterprises.[37]

This certainly does not mean that the day of the large firm is over. A number of techniques permit specialization of units and subunits within the large corporation. Different stores under the same ownership, but not necessarily under the same name, can offer different things. Leasing out departments provides some of the advantages of specialization, while the division of the large establishment into shops and boutiques provides some of the others. Ingenious managements are learning ways to obtain many of the benefits of concentration while at the same time reaping most of the rewards of expansion.[38]

Nor does the current picture mean that scrambling is, in any sense, passé. The orchestra probably will never consist entirely of only expanded or only contracted accordions. Rather it suggests that the retail population will continue to resemble the composition of a well-designed shopping center. The developers of these centers have always recognized the way in which large, wide scale enterprises and small, specialized ones complement each other to provide the most attractive shopping combination. The specialized units must continuously adjust to find and fill consumer requirements that the scrambled stores cannot or do not satisfy. But such opportunities are likely to continue, and even increase, for a long time to come.

Notes

1. Margaret Hall, John Knapp, and Christopher Winsten, *Distribution in Great Britain and North America* (London: Oxford University Press, 1961), p. 23.

2. Ralph Hower, *History of Macy's of New York, 1858–1919* (Cambridge, Mass.: Harvard University Press, 1943), p. 73.

3. Seymour Baranoff, "Retailing as an Operating System," in Reavis Cox, Wroe Alderson, and Stanley Shapiro, eds., *Theory in Marketing*, 2d Series (Homewood, Illinois: Richard D. Irwin, Inc., 1964), p. 161.

4. *Basic Marketing* (rev. ed.) (Homewood, Illinois: Richard D. Irwin, Inc., 1964), p. 510.

5. Ed Gold, *The Dynamics of Retailing* (New York: Fairchild Publications, Inc., 1963), pp. 40–41; E. B. Weiss, "The Shrinking Headquarters Target," in S. H. Britt and Harper Boyd, eds., *Marketing Management and Administrative Action* (New York: McGraw-Hill Book Company, Inc., 1963), p. 445; E. A. Miller, "Can Independent Stores Survive in Tomorrow's Mass Merchandising Era?" JOURNAL OF RETAILING, Vol. 39 (Winter 1963–1964), 29; "Retailer Fusion: Who Will Win?" *Printers' Ink*, August 18, 1961.

6. January 20, 1892, p. 9.

7. "Specialization," April 14, 1906, p. 25; "Greatest Retail Street," *The Dry Goods Economist*, April 7, 1917, p. 151.

8. The material in this section is drawn almost entirely from Glenn Sonnedecker, *Kremers and Urdang's History of Pharmacy* (3d ed.) (Philadelphia, Pa.: J. B. Lippincott Company, 1963), Chap. 16.

9. See "Grocery Restaurant Fad," *Grocery World*, May 7, 1906, p. 13. It should be noted that these facilities were never offered in more than a small fraction of the stores in the country.

10. Boris Emmet and John E. Jueck, *Catalogues and Counters* (Chicago, Illinois: University of Chicago Press, 1950), pp. 228–29.

11. "Straight Talks to the Trade," *The American Grocer*, January 23, 1895, p. 7; "The Stroller's Column," *Grocery World*, February 20, 1905, p. 26.

12. See "Why Hickory Farms Goes to the Fair," *Business Week*, September 4, 1965, for a description of a successful franchising operation in cheeses, smoked meats, jellies, and candies.

13. "Snaring Sales While Others Sleep," *Business Week*, November 6, 1965, p. 129.

14. Robert Entenberg, *The Changing Competitive Position of the Department Store* (Pittsburgh, Pa.: University of Pittsburgh Press, 1957), p. 91.

15. W. Warren Leigh, "Automotive Tires," in Richard M. Clewett, ed., *Marketing Channels* (Homewood, Illinois: Richard D. Irwin, Inc., 1954), p. 125.

16. William Girdner, "Shoes," in Clewett, *op. cit.*, p. 300.

17. Victor Fuchs, *The Economics of the Fur Industry* (New York: Columbia University Press, 1957), pp. 80–81.

18. John E. Mertes, "The Adaptive Behavior of the Retailer: Historically Considered," *Iowa Business Digest*, March 1964, p. 5; E. B. Weiss, "The Return of the Specialty Store," *Advertising Age*, May 13, 1963, pp. 92–96. Many of the garden supply units Weiss discusses are free standing subdivisions of chain variety outlets.

19. *Changes in Boston's Retail Landscape* (New York: Retail Research Institute, National Retail Merchants Association, 1964), pp. 84–95.

20. *Productivity in the European Distributive Trades: Wholesale and Retail Aspects* (Paris: O.E.E.C., 1954), p. 68.

21. W. G. McClelland, *Studies in Retailing* (Oxford: Basil Blackwell, 1963), p. 13.

22. Much of the evidence on this set of attitudes is summarized by Bert C. McCammon, Jr., and Robert W. Little, "Marketing Channels: Analytical Systems and Approaches," in Grorge Schwarts, ed., *Science in Marketing* (New York: John Wiley & Sons, Inc., 1965), pp. 344–50. Also see Earl R. Quinney, "Adjustment to Occupational Role Strain: The Case of the Retail Pharmacy," *Southwestern Social Science Quarterly*, March 1964, pp. 367–76.

23. "A Theory of Retail Price Determination," *Southern Economic Journal*, January 1914, pp. 380–97.

24. See Stanley C. Hollander, *Restraints Upon Retail Competition* (East Lansing, Michigan: Bureau of Business and Economic Research, Michigan State University, 1965), pp. 71–73.

25. *The Gasoline Retailer*, October 19, 1960, p. 14.

26. See Bedros P. Pashigian, *The Distribution of Automobiles, An Economic Analysis of the Franchise System* (Englewood Cliffs, New Jersey: Prentice-Hall, Inc., 1961).

27. See Bob R. Holdren, *The Structure of a Retail Market and the Market Behavior of Retail Units* (Englewood Cliffs, New Jersey: Prentice-Hall, Inc., 1960), pp. 29–33.

28. See Richard H. Holton, "Is Integration in Retailing Stymied?" in Robert S. Hancock, ed., *Dynamic Marketing for a Changing World* (Chicago, Illinois: American Marketing Association, 1960), p. 544.

29. "Broad Social Forces and the 'Cost Squeeze' in Retailing," in Lynn H. Stockman, ed., *Advancing Marketing Efficiency* (Chicago, Illinois: American Marketing Association, 1959), p. 219. Although in the above discussion Cox was particularly concerned with the effects of diversification by manufacturers, the same or more severe results obtain when the retailer himself diversifies.

30. See W. J. Baumol and E. A. Ide, "Variety in Retailing," *Management Science* (October 1956), pp. 92–101; F. E. Balderston, "Assortment Choice in Wholesale and Retail Marketing," *Journal of Marketing* (October 1956), pp. 175–83; and Holton, *op. cit.* One of the most detailed analyses available appears in Holdren, *op. cit.*, pp. 165–69.

31. *Op. cit.*, pp. 4–5. To at least some extent both sets of advantages can be obtained by operating chains of department stores, but the opportunities for doing this are somewhat limited. See Hall, Knapp, and Winsten, *op. cit.*, p. 65.

32. Richard L. Nelson, *The Selection of Retail Locations* (New York: F. W. Dodge Corporation, 1958), pp. 66–78.

33. "Experimental Research in Consumer Behavior," *Cost and Profit Outlook* (Alderson and Sessions), February 1956; "Getting Inside the Shopper's Mind," *Business Week*, November 12, 1955, pp. 58, ff.

34. Pierre Martineau, "The Personality of the Retail Store," *Harvard Business Review* (January–February 1958), pp. 47–55.

35. Charles J. Collazo, Jr., *Consumer Attitudes and Frustrations in Shopping* (New York: Retail Research Institute, National Retail Merchants Association, 1963), pp. 43, 116.

36. Alton F. Doody and William R. Davidson, "Growing Strength in Small Retailing," *Harvard Business Review* (July–August 1964), pp. 72–73.

37. This concept is discussed at greater length in Wroe Alderson, *Marketing Behavior and Executive Action* (Homewood, Illinois: Richard D. Irwin, Inc., 1957), pp. 115–17; and in Edith T. Penrose, *The Theory of the Growth of the Firm* (New York: John Wiley & Sons, 1959). Also see Callazo, *op. cit.*, pp. 135–36.

38. E. B. Weiss, "The Return of the Specialty Store," *Advertising Age*, May 13, 1963, pp. 92–96.

The transformation of retailing institutions: beyond the wheel of retailing and life cycle theories

Rom J. Markin and Calvin P. Duncan

Source: *Journal of Macromarketing* 1(1) (1981): 58–66.

This paper reviews existing and accepted theories of retail institution growth and development, and incorporates them into the construction of an improved conceptual framework that adequately explains the evolution of retailing institutions. The framework emphasizes the role of environmental factors and highlights the potential contributions of functionalism, conflict theory, and the notions of evolution and adaptation.

Marketers have not systematically tackled the problems of institutional change and development that represent new frontiers for exploration (Bagozzi 1980, p. 56). This paper reviews existing and accepted theories of retail institutional growth and development, including the "wheel" and "life cycle" theories, and examines the logic and propositions upon which they are based. Its purpose is to incorporate these two approaches into the construction of an improved conceptual framework that adequately explains the evolution of retailing institutions. The framework emphasizes the role of environmental factors and highlights the potential contributions of functionalism, conflict theory, and the notions of evolution and adaptation.

Existing theories of retail institutional development and change

"Everything changes" observed the ancient Greek philosopher Heraclitus. It was he who pointed out that man cannot bathe twice in the same river for he is not the same man, nor is it quite the same river. Retailing and other marketing institutions also change, and the reasons for the transformation of retailing institutions remain one of the most intriguing and difficult problems in the marketing discipline.

With few exceptions, the popular theories of how and why retailing institutions change are cyclical theories which fall into either the "wheel of retailing" or the "life cycle" frameworks. Although most elementary marketing or retailing textbooks use these concepts, there is rarely serious criticism of these two theories, despite an acknowledged lack of empirical evidence to support them.[1]

The wheel of retailing

Malcolm P. McNair has offered the "wheel of retailing" as his theory of the growth and development of retailing institutions (McNair 1958). McNair contends that growth, development, change, and extinction follow this progression of more or less orderly activities:

1. A new innovator or operator emerges as low-cost institution—the low cost being attributed to some new procedure or system for eliminating or lowering operating expenses.
2. The new developer increases his market share via low prices and attracts numerous competitors who, in turn, emulate his procedures.
3. To differentiate one firm's offering from the others, and to hold the patronage of customers already attracted, the new innovators "trade-up" their goods and service offerings and this non-price competitive activity swells the operating expense ratio, and reduces the gross margin and, ultimately, profits as a return on investment.
4. A new innovator emerges under the umbrella of high costs and margins created by the now traditional operators; thus the wheel revolves and continues.

Arguments used to support the "wheel of retailing" theory as a viable explanation for the transformation of retailing institutions include: leadership senility, excess capacity, and market structure.

LEADERSHIP SENILITY   One view focuses upon the eroding effects of leadership incompetence or senility. New retail institutions, it is presumed, are the product of aggressive firms led by cost conscious, hard-charging entrepreneurs who are profit maximizers and who have little interest in unprofitable frills. However, as the firms leading the new wave of thinking become successful, they are made vulnerable because their leaders relax their vigilance and control over cost as they acquire age and wealth. The successors to these leaders-originators are perceived as less competent or unable to change with changing conditions (Converse 1959).

This argument has not been verified empirically, and the assertion itself may be logically inconsistent. Why should it be assumed that intelligent persons with the vision and ability to participate in the development of new institutions would be incapable of managing innovating firms successfully as challenges to their existence arise? Why should decision-makers progressively make decisions that would lead to their own vulnerability? At least, growth and earnings make possible the substitution of professional management for charisma's magic. Furthermore, leaders and those who possess leadership qualities are often "change agents" who deliberately work toward inducing change through creative thinking and innovation. And while nothing, not even leadership creativity, lasts forever, it is a transferable characteristic and can be acquired by others.

EXCESS CAPACITY   McNair, the originator and proponent of the wheel thesis, attributed the wheel effect to excess capacity. "Innovating forms of retail distribution, once they have caught on, tend to have higher utilization of plant capacity during the period of their early growth. The gradual erosion of this advantage through the growing competition of others of their own kind is part of the 'revolution of the wheel'" (McNair 1958, p. 23).

In some ways, this explanation represents another tribute to the presumption of management ineptness. Why should managers of innovating organizations build excess capacity into their operations, and why not cope with excess capacity by stringent price competition to drive out the marginal operators? Neither McNair nor others have addressed these questions.

THE NATURE OF THE MARKET STRUCTURE   It is often argued that retailing approaches a market structure of at least monopolistic competition or differentiated oligopoly and that given the nature of firm behavior in these market settings, the emphasis is on non-price rather that price competition. Thus, because of this tendency for non-price competition to occur, there exists a kind of ratchet process which may tend to put upward pressure on operating expenses and raise gross margin and price levels over time (Shawver 1956, p. 92).

While a pattern of escalating margins and prices is consistent with the wheel of retailing theory, this pattern may be more a reflection of astute decisions by innovating firms to trade-up or to adopt scrambled merchandising than a complete explanation of why and how retailing institutions develop and change over time. The tendency toward increasing margins has been investigated by Barger (1955) in the United States and Jefferys (1954) in Great Britain. Both researchers attributed margin increases to trading up, including the addition of services and broader assortment mixes, and these factors were ascribed to changing developments in the economy, namely the generally rising affluence and standard of living. Thus, trading up appeared to be a positive response to potentially profitable market opportunities rather than a defensive reaction by innovating organizations to impede the inroads of imitative competitors.

The tendency toward scrambled merchandising also created illusory impressions of the wheel phenomenon according to Hollander (1960). He argued that storewide average margins may increase as new, high margin lines are added to the product mix, even though the margins on the original components of that mix remain unchanged or increase slightly with increases in the general upward movement of the price level.

SUMMARY   There is neither strong logic nor empirical evidence to support the notion of a "wheel of retailing" as a theory of retail institutional change. It can be observed that not all retailing institutions in the United States began with the advent of low-cost, low-margin, price-oriented firms. Vending machine merchandising has always been a high-cost form of distribution, and many of the contemporary innovations such as boutique specialty stores, health food stores, mass market building supply stores, convenience food stores, and even catalog showroom stores are not, strictly speaking, just price oriented. Furthermore, there is little evidence of any revolution of the wheel because too few types ever become extinct.

Variations on the wheel: Related theoretical explanations

RETAIL ACCORDIAN   Hollander contended that the wheel of retailing was not very relevant as a theoretical explanation of growth, development, and change. Nonetheless, he did not abandon the concept completely because, while renouncing the name "wheel of retailing," he continued to promote the notion of cycles and rhythm under the guise of the "Retail Accordian" (Hollander 1966). His message, however, sounded familiar:

> The history of retail development seems to demonstrate an accordian pattern. Domination by general line, wide assortment retailers alternates with domination by specialized, narrow line merchants. (p. 29)

He added that neither the pattern's universality nor its existence can be proven definitely because of the lack of valid historical statistics on merchandise assortment.

Hollander later modified his theory and asserted that, instead of comparing retailing to an accordian, we might better compare it to an orchestra or band of accordian players. At any one time, he argued, some of the players are compressing the music boxes while others are extending them. Further, at any time, some players (including those with compressed and those with extended accordians) are retiring from the orchestra, while still others (mainly with compressed instruments) are joining the band. But with this statement, Hollander moves from a simple theory of assortment mixes to a larger notion—a theory of retail growth and development. Finally, he ends by suggesting that the retail population (the mix of retail store types and the nature of their assortment mixes) would continue to resemble the composition of a well-designed shopping center. In short, he implicitly acknowledges the need for diversity based upon demand consideration; a position to be advocated and expanded upon later in this paper.

MULTIPLE WHEELS   Israeli (1973) saw little value to a single "wheel of retailing" so he suggested that if one was not sufficient to explain growth, development and change of retailing institutions, then three wheels would be better. He asserted that McNair's original theory did not apply to innovators who penetrated the high end of the market, nor to the adaptive responses of established organizations. Rather than deal with these as "exceptions" to the theory, he preferred to incorporate such deviating cases into an expanded theory of institutional change. He believed this could be accomplished by perceiving the process as involving the patterned movement of three wheels of retailing. The first wheel represented innovators entering at the low end of the cost-margin continuum, the second wheel represented innovators entering at the high end, and the third wheel was for the established organizations around the middle.

There is some question why Israeli felt the need to suggest three wheels. The real crux of his argument, and one that might be developed into a meaningful theoretical framework, was that growth and change of retailing institutions is brought about by conflict and accommodation, a consequence of the dynamic process of competition through adaptation and imitation.

The retail life cycle

Another "theory" which purports to describe and explain retail institutional growth and development, and which has been reported frequently in the textbooks and literature of marketing, is that of the institutional life cycle. One group which has attempted to popularize the life-cycle notion (Davidson, Bates, and Bass 1976) contends that their theory extends the "wheel" theory because:

1. The wheel theory focuses too exclusively on changing cost and gross margin relationships as the key to understanding changing retail firm behavior and that the "wheel" focuses too limitedly on cost orientation as the basis for new retail firm innovation.
2. The wheel theory, they contend, was never really intended to determine the pace with which retail institutions rise and fall.

The retail life cycle theory has been described in detail elsewhere (Davidson 1970; McCammon 1973; Davidson, Doody, and Sweeney 1975). Briefly, the theory has four stages. The first stage is characterized by the emergence of a new retailing institution. The new concept is presumed to represent a sharp departure from existing retailing approaches. Its advantage(s) may stem from lower costs or from a greater ability in the art and science of stimulating customers, locational advantages, or in the product and assortment mix offered.

In the second stage of the institutional life cycle, both sales volume and profits experience high rates of growth. There is widespread expansion into new geographic territories by the new institutional development, and new entrants are rapidly attracted. Market share of the innovating firms increases steadily. However, by the end of this period, these favorable factors tend to be counterbalanced by cost pressures that arise from the need for a larger staff, more complex internal systems, more management controls, and the other presumed diseconomies of large scale multi-unit organizations.

In the maturity stage, market share declines. Managers face increasing difficulties in controlling their large organizations. Once again, the spectre of management ineptness arises. "Although they were excellent at maintaining the vitality and excitement of their organizations in the first two stages, they often lack the management skills necessary to direct large organizations in stable markets. Consequently, the quality of operations begins to slip" (Davidson, Bates, and Bass 1976, p. 92). Too much capacity, the same problem which McNair argued in his "wheel" theory, is seen as a problem also in the maturity phase of the institutional life cycle. Finally, management finds itself facing direct frontal assaults from new forms of distribution. Upstart challengers siphon off needed sales thus creating volume and profit problems.

The final stage is decline and death. Major losses of market shares occur, profits are thin and the institution is in the last phases of its extinction mode.

Like the "wheel of retailing " thesis, the retail life cycle is an intriguing metaphor but a questionable theory of institutional change. To some, the retail life cycle is seen as a natural developmental process and according to Davidson, Bates, and Bass, "executives can do little to counteract it" (1976, p. 96). We are thus led to believe that the process is inexorable, a fated end of economic and managerial determinism. Again, must we presume that entrepreneurs and managers who have the ability to bring new and innovative methods into existence will be incapable of sustaining them for any length of time after they become accepted? The institutional life cycle, like its product counterpart, is not an independent variable to which dynamic institutions led by innovating firms must conform. Rather, it is a dependent variable which is determined by marketing and managerial action (Dhalla and Yuspeh 1976).

The retail life cycle may also lead to false conclusions based upon a faulty time frame. It is difficult to specify the exact year in which a particular institution is established because most institutions have important historical antecedents that can be traced back a long way. Furthermore, it is difficult to reckon when a particular institution reaches maturity. Market data are confusing and sometimes contradictory. Different firms belonging to the same institutional classification reach maturity at different times, in different geographic regions, and many firms run counter to the predominant trends.

An expanded framework for explaining retailing institutional change: some relevant concepts

In general, cyclical theories of change seem unacceptable. They are too speculative, and they offer insufficient explanation of how or why change takes place. Cyclical and rhythm theories, including the wheel of retailing and the institutional life cycle, are simplistic and deterministically mechanistic. They fail to recognize that change can be explained only within the broader context of the society and culture in which the change occurs.

Any relevant and therefore meaningful theory relating to transformations of retailing (or other marketing) institutions should relate to modern notions of what retailing (or marketing) is and what retailing (or marketing) does. Realistic and modern theory should be related to the notion of exchange transactions (Bagozzi 1975). The conceptual approach proposed here is based upon the premise that retailing institutions exist in a dynamic state of interaction with their environment. Simply put, retailing institutions emerge, develop, and change in direct response to their market (environment) opportunities. Such an approach is multilinear in that it can take place in many different ways and change does not necessarily follow exactly the same direction in every society. It views the process of change as a "tendency," not as a universal law (Salmon 1971). The framework as shown in Figure 1, is holistic and it embraces the notions of functionalism, conflict, and ecological evolution, and adaptation.

Institutions defined

What is an institution and what purposes does it serve? Popular usage of the term institution embraces the notion that institutions are complex systems of action which serve some function for society (Bates and Harvey 1975, p. 287). An institution is more than an organization and more than a simple cultural pattern. It attracts support and legitimacy from its environment so that it can better perform its functions and services. The retailing institution, like other economic and social institutions, is comprised of a network of exchange relationships with a limited number of organizations. It fosters transactions for the purpose of gaining support, overcoming resistance, exchanging resources, structuring the environment, and transforming norms and values. For example, the appearance of voluntary chains was a response by wholesaling and retailing intermediaries to the competition of large chain stores. The success and survival of the voluntary chain is tied to the (economic and marketing) needs of independent retailers and final consumers on the one hand, and to the sponsorship and support of wholesalers and suppliers on the other. There exists, then, a complex set of interactions between retail institutions and their environments. The latter varies in readiness for or resistance to change, both over time and from place to place.

In the context of the present discussion, the institution is associated with the provision of a service which has economic value. It is assumed that general economic and social change alters the demand for the service. This alteration in environmental conditions brings about a disequilibrium between service demand and supply. In the process of realigning supply with demand, institutions adapt and evolve.

Institutions facilitate exchange through transactions

For a retailing institution to sustain its existence, a set of transactional and exchange relationships which ensure its access to resources, outlets for

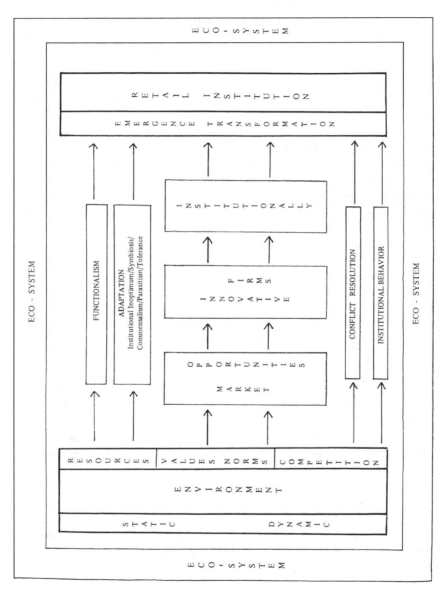

Figure 1

its products, and environmental support for its innovations must be established and maintained. Thus, a reciprocal and interactive relationship must
exist between the institution and its environment (Barth 1966). The object
of this behavior, from the standpoint of the retail institution, is to achieve
institutionality—meaning that the innovative norms and action patterns
become valued by the larger society and are incorporated into the behavior
of linked organizations and other groups. Institutionalization means that
the organization and its innovation are accepted and supported by the
external environment. Institutional acceptance, survival, growth, and all
transformations are a function of environmental opportunities and organizational linkages. This conceptualization points up the consideration most
critical for institutionalization—the establishment and maintenance of interdependencies which exist between an institution and other parts of society
(Esman 1972). An institution provides something in return for its inputs
whether it is tangible and immediate or not.

A theory of the transformation of retailing institutions is usefully built
around a functionalist theory and therefore the study of the transformations
of retailing institutions would, of logical necessity, be based upon the dictum
that form follows function, i.e., function determines structure (Alderson
1965). Retailing institutions act as socioeconomic pipelines. They consist of
interconnected activities produced in one part of the complex socioeconomic
system, through the behavior of actors, to other parts of the system. Such
institutions are also regarded as structures through which these functions
are produced. Retailing institutions are teleological: they emerge and grow
in accordance with the purposes they serve. The purposes which retailing
institutions attempt to serve are related to the desire for differential or comparative advantages.

Retail institutions, because they are human structures, must be subject to
the laws which guide and shape human behavior. To this end, such institutions obviously are affected by interpersonal transactions and, therefore, it
would follow that retail institutional behavior is affected by its consequences.
Retail institutional behavior which is not reinforced will be extinguished;
institutional behavior which is reinforced will be repeated in order to receive
further rewards.

Conflict as an integral part of change

Conflict as a part of the theory of change and transformation of retailing
institutions holds that change is caused by tensions between competing
interests in society. The beginning of the retail institution's transformation
is always the same. It is either a response to a distortion in the retailing/
marketing system created by the uncoordinated change of its components, or
it begins with a vision of a state of affairs preferred to the existing reality.
Economic and social change generates conflict which continuously calls for
modified or new institutions. Thus, for example, economic conditions in

combination with an increasing consumer willingness to provide for himself, has given rise to self-service automobile repair facilities.

Schumpeter recognized the importance of conflict brought about by new innovations in the form of new retailing institutions. Such innovative organizations create what he called a "big" disturbance because they "disrupt the existing system and enforce a distinct process of adaptation" (Schumpeter 1939, p. 101). For Schumpeter, the normal method of competition in which familiar types of organizations compete for the patronage of a given market by familiar methods is not the competition that counts (Bliss 1960). According to his theory, if there is "competition that matters" new institutions must find acceptance in the marketplace with new ways of organizing things, new sales-cost relationships, new methods of selling and, he might have added, a new perception of the market opportunity. In the case of retail trade, the competition that had mattered—that brought change through conflict and disturbance—has come in the form of the department store, the chain store, the mail-order house and, of course, the supermarket.

Much of the conflict of the marketplace is resolved through dialectical change which leads to merger (assimilation) or division (differentiation). The principal version of the dialectic is the mutual adjustment process, a form of compromise or accommodation or even a regression of two competing value systems embodied in two different institutional types such as full service, full line stores vs. limited service, limited line stores. Over time, the conflict between these two types may be temporarily resolved by each becoming more and more like the other. The market is a competitive and sometimes even hostile environment for new institutional innovations. Hence, the market must be developed. Innovators must anticipate environmental hostility to their presence, and even when this is minimal, they must expect that the other existing organizations may compete for control of the market. Markets, depending on these characteristics, may present a broad spectrum of generalized change readiness and change resistance, as well as receptivity and resistance to specific innovations.

The transformation of retailing institutions is an adaptation process

Perhaps one of the most meaningful and relevant propositions contributing to an understanding of the transformation of retailing institutions can be found in the theory of survival and adaptation, i.e., evolution via the survival of the fittest. It is an extension of Darwinian doctrine which emphasizes the value of functional processes in terms of survival value (Vanderpool 1973). The retail institution emerges, adapts, survives or declines in terms of how well it serves its purposes. Its purposes are judged by the environment of which it is a part. In effect, then, the theory states that retail institutions must adapt to changing external environments or risk being replaced by new institutions.

Such an adaptation and accommodation point of view would help to explain the diversity which exists in the number and type of retailing institutions in our own culture and it further explains why retailing systems show remarkable degrees of variation and differentiation in different cultures; namely, different environments spawn different kinds of retailing institutions. This is not only a Darwinian/ecological point of view, but it squares well with economic theory from the time of Adam Smith who asserted that "specialization and division of labor is limited by the extent of the market" (Stigler 1951). The institution's functions, which determine its structure, are conditioned by market forces. When market forces change, institutions are forced to accommodate and adapt.

When the change by individual firms becomes widely adopted by a significant number of firms, then the order or structure of the industry is likely to change and this in itself becomes a change in the institution. For example, the bundle of social, technological, and economic activities which characterize today's supermarkets are considerably different from the bundle of such activities that characterized the supermarkets of the 1940s. Cash-and-carry and self-service practices embodied in the early supermarkets caused radical change in the appearance and structure of retail food marketing.

Much like the biological analogy, the theory of adaptation says that what survives is fit. This means only that what survives is fit now, i.e., the functions and services provided by the institution are deemed valuable by the marketing environment. Too often our ethnocentric notion of things leads us to conclude that "what is, is right." We see too much stability and too little tendency for things to change. However, a longer-run perspective of things might lead us to conclude that, "what is, is wrong." It is wrong because it won't last and it won't last because of the entropic nature of things. There is, according to Norbert Wiener (1967), a statistical tendency in the universe for things if left alone, to run down, to deteriorate, to lose their distinctiveness —in short, to change. In this respect, it can be said that the single most important function of management is to control or forestall entropic tendencies to which every firm falls heir. Thus, as the environment changes, what was right becomes wrong and change works to create a new equilibrium or stability that is, especially in dynamic, sophisticated environments, short lived. Evolution is a process involving a continuing adaptation of the retailing institution to its surroundings. The kernels of evolution and adaptation are differentiation and merger. Differentiation is the process whereby latent or rudimentary characteristics take on distinct and variable forms, or give rise to new and more complex institutional types. Merger also promotes change as in the case of the department store which emerged as a result of the aggregation of a number of speciality shops.

In a dynamic environment, change is not the antithesis of equilibrium, because equilibrium is never attained, but is instead the very process of equilibration; change is the reason why retail institutions adapt and survive, and is also the process through which they occasionally break down.

Ecological systems analysis

The retailing institution and its environment form an ecosystem in which the parts interact and mutually affect one another. For a retailing institution to survive, it must maintain a degree of harmony with respect to its environment. Because its behavior affects the environment, and these effects are fed back into the socioeconomic system, it follows that a retailing institution must continually change and adapt in order to maintain a relatively constant survival relationship to its environment. For it is only by striving to achieve a form of equilibrium with the environment that long-term survival can be assured.

Two salient facts regarding success and survival of retailing institutions can be explained in terms of our ecological reasoning. Ecological analysis stipulates that each species or institution has *requirements* which are the total and indispensible conditions for the accomplishment of the goals and objectives of the institution. Such requirements may be sales, profit, and growth, while underlying these may be such essential factors as demand, everyday need, income, and propensity to consume.

Parallel to these requirements is the need for *tolerance*. Each institutional type within the ecosystem has a maximum and minimum intensity of elements or conditions that it can withstand without damage. Most importantly, requirements and tolerance are complementary and, in a sense, contrary phenomena. Some institutions (e.g., the general store) that show low requirements and high tolerance can utilize the resources (opportunities) of the environment to a high degree.

Finally, adaptation, the real secret of growth and survival, is the ability of the institution to cope with the conditions of its environment and to utilize its resources so as to maintain its ecological niche (or market share). This is achieved through an adjustment of its requirements and tolerances to the elements of the environmental habitat. Successful institutions (those that survive) would seem to have reasonably low requirements and exceedingly high tolerance, or else the elements of their environmental habitat change little if at all. Such retail institutions as the public market, the bazaar, and the fair which characterize tradition-bound, steady-state environments found in less developed countries, are prime examples of this phenomenon. Survival as the test of success often dictates flexibility and accommodation.

Usually, the more specialized and adapted a retailing institution is in a given evolutionary stage, the smaller is its potential for passing to the next stage. A particular institution may become overspecialized and so fail to progress, but its practices and methods may, in part, be adopted and implemented if they offer some advantages to other institutions. According to the theory of adaptation, the greater the differentiation and diversity of a given retail institution, the greater will be its responsiveness to change within the external ecosystem. An organism with insufficient variety cannot survive. However, the greater the degree of discontinuity of a new retail institution from established institutions, the higher the new institution's failure rate is likely to be. An entirely new institutional concept, requiring change in consumption patterns, is more likely to fail or to be unprofitable for a longer period of time while consumer learning occurs, than is a new institution incorporating only minor change.

The transformation of retail institutions as a result of their performance within an ecosystem offers some explanation of the process whereby various institutions participate in the nutritive elements of the environment. This suggests that there must be a sufficient market opportunity, or an environment characterized by a generally favorable set of circumstances and an acceptable probability of success. Market opportunities can be penetrated or approached in a number of ways. Thus, *Parasitism* implies that one of two organisms needs the other in order to subsist. Examples of this condition might be trading stamp companies in relation to retail store operations. *Symbiosis* is the association through contact of two or more species (institutions) involving some benefit to all. Firms comprising voluntary and cooperative chain structures are examples of symbiotic behavior in the vertical retailer network. *Commensalism* is a phenomenon which suggests that organisms belonging to different species must have nearly the same requirements, so that they may live together in the same habitat. Thus, the size of trade centers and the numbers and types of retailing institutions contained within the centers, will depend upon the extent of the market opportunity.

Finally, diversity of retailing institutions results primarily because no single type of retailing institution encounters in any given habitat or environment the optimum conditions for all its functions. Such a condition might very well be called the principle of the *institutional inoptimum*. While the inoptimum may characterize the individual type of institution, the total retailing system or network of all institutional types tends toward optimality through association, interaction, and organization. The principle of institutional inoptimality suggests that cooperation and association is as integral to survival and adaptation as is conflict.

Conclusions

A theory of retail transformations must deal with the alteration in patterns of retail institutional structure and functions over time. The process is universal but occurs at different rates and in different ways. Retail institutional behavior is affected by its consequences. Hence, institutional transformation is the dynamic result of the interaction of the institution with its environment, both of which exist in a state of interaction, the motive or impetus of which is exchange and transaction. The institutions' leaders, as change agents, are in large measure responsible for much of the transformation. Just as "man is his choices," retail institutional transformations are probabilistic resultants of both facilitative and obstructive decisions, the consequences of which are narrowed probabilities of planned and unplanned market or environmental adjustments. In retrospect, the most important lesson we can learn is that the most efficient way of understanding change in retailing institutions is to view change as a set of analytically separable processes or problems. It is unfortunately true that while there exists a mushrooming necessity for understanding and for explaining change, this necessity has not been greeted with immediate and effective attempts at developing new theories of change or challenging the limited and simplistic theories which are extant. It is hoped that perhaps this paper contributes some ideas which will stir others to respond.

Note

1. For one of the few critical evaluations of theories of change relating to retailing institutions, see Ronald R. Gist, *Marketing and Society*, New York: Holt, Rinehart and Winston, Inc., 1971. In *Competition and Evolution in the Distributive Trades* (1972), Bucklin chronicles the changes which have occurred in the distributive trades. While Bucklin discusses the wheel of retailing, he does not offer a serious challenge to its efficacy or its premises.

References

Alderson, Wroe (1965), *Dynamic Marketing Behavior*, Homewood, IL: Richard D. Irwin.

Bagozzi, Richard (1980), *Causal Models in Marketing*, New York: John Wiley & Sons.

—— (1975), "Marketing as Exchange," *Journal of Marketing*, 39 (October), 32–39.

Barger, Harold (1955), *Distribution's Place in the American Economy Since 1869*, Princeton: Princeton University Press.

Barth, Fredrich (1966), "The Analytical Importance of Transaction," in *Models of Social Organization*, Occasional Paper No. 23, London: Royal Anthropological Institute of Great Britain and Ireland.

Bates, Fredrick L., and Clyde C. Harvey (1975), *The Structure of Social Systems*, New York: Gardner Press.

Bliss, Perry (1960), "Schumpeter, the 'Big' Disturbance and Retailing," *Social Forces*, 39 (October), 72–76.

Bucklin, Louis P. (1972), *Competition and Evolution in the Distributive Trades*, Englewood Cliffs, NJ: Prentice Hall.

Converse, Paul D. (1959), "Mediocrity in Retailing," *Journal of Marketing*, 23 (April), 419–420.

Davidson, William R. (1970), "Changes in Distributive Institutions," *Journal of Marketing*, 34 (January), 9.

——, Albert D. Bates, and Stephen J. Bass (1976), "The Retail Life Cycle," *Harvard Business Review*, 54 (November–December), 89–96.

——, Alton F. Doody, and Daniel J. Sweeney (1975), *Retailing Management*, New York: The Ronald Press Company.

Dhalla, Nariman K., and Sonia Yuspeh (1976), "Forget the Product Life Cycle," *Harvard Business Review*, 54 (January–February), 102–122.

Esman, Millan J. (1972), "Some Issues in Institution Building," in *Institution Building: A Model for Applied Social Change*, D. Woods Thomas et al., eds., Cambridge, MA: Schenkman Publishing Company.

Gist, Ronald R. (1971), *Marketing and Society*, New York: Holt, Rinehart and Winston.

Hollander, Stanley C. (1966), "Notes on the Retail Accordian," *Journal of Retailing*, 42 (Summer), 29–40, 54.

—— (1960), "The Wheel of Retailing," *Journal of Marketing*, 24 (July), 37–42.

Israeli, Dov (1973), "The Three Wheels of Retailing," *European Journal of Marketing*, Vol. 7, No. 1, 70–74.

Jefferys, J. B. (1954), *Retail Trading in Great Britain, 1850–1950*, Cambridge: Cambridge University Press.

McCammon, Bet C., Jr. (1973), "The Future of Catalogue Showrooms: Growth and Its Challenge to Management," Marketing Science Institute Working Paper.

McNair, Malcolm P. (1958), "Significant Trends and Developments in the Postwar Period," in *Competitive Distribution in a Free, High Level Economy and its Implication for the University*, A. B. Smith, ed., Pittsburgh: University of Pittsburgh Press.

——, and Eleanor G. May (1976), *The Evolution of Retail Institutions in the United States*, Cambridge: Marketing Science Institute.

Roberts, Blaine, and Robert Holdren (1972), *Theory of Social Processes*, Ames: Iowa State University Press.

Salmon, William (1971), "Statistical Explanation," in *Statistical Explanation and Statistical Relevance*, Pittsburgh: University of Pittsburgh Press.

Schumpeter, Joseph (1939), *Business Cycles*, Vol. 1, New York: McGraw-Hill Book Co.

—— (1947), *Capitalism, Socialism and Democracy*, 2nd ed., New York: Harper and Bros.

Shawver, Donald L. (1956), *The Development of Theories of Retail Price Determination*, Urbana: University of Illinois Press.

Stigler, George J. (1951), "The Division of Labor Is Limited by the Extent of the Market," *Journal of Political Economy*, 59 (June), 185–193.

Vanderpool, Harold Y. (1973), *Darwin and Darwinism*, Lexington, MA: D. C. Heath and Co.

Wiener, Norbert (1967), *The Human Use of Human Beings*, New York: Avon Books.

Reilly's challenge: new laws of retail gravitation which define systems of central places

M. Batty

Source: *Environment and Planning A* 10(2) (1978): 185–219.

Abstract

This paper attempts a reformulation and generalisation of Reilly's (1931) law of retail gravitation. Reilly himself challenged workers in the field to produce new evidence which would refute or strengthen his law, and developments in spatial-interaction theory during the last decade are used here in taking up this challenge. A critique of Reilly's law sets the scene: by adopting a gravity model more general than the Newtonian model used by Reilly, it is shown how the limitations of the law with respect to hierarchy, spatial competition, locational size, and the symmetry of trade flows, are overcome. In particular the notion of Reilly's law as a special case of the market-area analysis originating from Fetter (1924) and Hotelling (1929) is demonstrated in terms of a theory of the breakpoint implying spatial price–cost indifference. Another approach, through entropy-maximisation and its dual problem, leads to similar conclusions with regard to prices, and it also serves to introduce multicentred spatial competition. These ideas are then generalised in several ways: through notions about the influence of prior spatial information, through concepts of consumer as well as producer market areas or fields, and through the implications of the analysis for the family of spatial-interaction models. A speculation on the relationship of price differentials to Tobler's (1975) interaction winds is made, and the paper is concluded with an application of these models to the definition of an urban hierarchy in the Reading subregion.

Introduction

William J Reilly, founder of the Institute for Straight Thinking and originator of the law of retail gravitation, posed a fascinating and irresistible challenge in his remarkable book first published nearly fifty years ago:

"If any reader finds that he has the facts in relation to a breaking point in any part of the United States that does not conform to this law, please let us know. For after analyzing this exceptional case, we should know more about the factors which cause abnormal behavior of retail trade influence. An exception to any general rule is usually surrounded by one or more obvious conditions that help to explain the exception. And sometimes, by demonstrating the effect of any unusual condition, it serves to strengthen, rather than to undermine, the fundamental law" (Reilly, 1931, pages 33–34).

In the half century since Reilly began his work, the role of science in social science has been transformed beyond the wildest speculations of those researching into social systems who lived in those times. In Reilly's own area of interest there has been an enormous increase in research activity devoted to explaining, interpreting, and testing the concept of gravitation in spatial systems, and the time now seems ripe to take up Reilly's challenge and to attempt to reassess his law in the light of these developments.

During this time, and especially in the last decade, social physics has been enriched by powerful and influential theories based on economic and statistical foundations, whose convergence in the ideas of utility and entropy has led to some quite remarkable insights. The implications of gravitation to accessibility, to spatial competition, and to economic rationality have been traced, and a unified theory appears to be in the making. Moreover a degree of mathematical consistency has been imposed on the field owing to the increasing use of derivations of gravitational phenomena from extremal principles, from optimisation theory. Applications have abounded and the wealth of literature resulting from these researches must surely affect the status of Reilly's law. Several important questions can be asked. How has Reilly's law withstood the test of time? But more important, can the flourishing new insights into spatial systems, originating from the approaches alluded to above, be used to produce new laws of retail gravitation, to reformulate Reilly's law, to generalise it, and perhaps to 'strengthen' it? This then is the central task of this paper. It is to be hoped that Reilly himself would approve, and although it is quite obvious that Reilly's law is hardly an iron one, the remarks to be made below are very much in the spirit of Reilly's original and pioneering work as presented in his book: ". . . yet the mind should be kept open and hospitable to any new evidence that might suggest a present exception to, or a future modification of, the law as we know it" (Reilly, 1931, page 33).

In this quest to provide a critique and reformulation of Reilly's law, the starting point will be a statement of the law as originally presented. But the treatment will adopt a notation and mathematical style more consistent with recent ideas in social physics. The critique of the law will follow: a brief discussion on the concept of laws, models, and hypotheses in social science is apposite but the dominating critique is based on the more substantive implications which flow from Reilly's work. In particular the law is much restricted in its relevance to central-place theory, and the main theme to be pursued in this paper is concerned with reformulating the law to explicitly deal with the notions of hierarchy, competition, and hinterland, so integral to central-place theory. The question of hierarchy is dealt with first: a simple reformulation of the effect of space through distance in Reilly's law leads to a much more general statement about market areas, which has strong similarities to the established theories of spatial competition originating from Fetter (1924) and Hotelling (1929). The explicit effects of competition in the reformulated law are then presented: in particular the development of optimisation frameworks based on entropy and utility lead to generalised gravity models in which competition, expressed as comparative spatial advantage, price, or accessibility arises quite naturally. A further extension of these ideas leads to optimisation frameworks capable of incorporating prior spatial information in which the effect of size in the central-place system is recognised. At this point it is useful to generalise the ideas further: the notion of producer and consumer fields, markets based on demand and supply orientation, is introduced, and the well-known typology of gravity models is reinterpreted in these terms. Before the paper is concluded with an application of these ideas to the urban hierarchy in the Reading subregion, a speculation on the relationship of the reformulated law to Tobler's (1975) concept of interaction winds and potentials is made. An evaluation of Reilly's law in terms of its reformulation, presented in empirical terms, forms the conclusion.

The law of retail gravitation: Reilly's original formulation

Reilly stated his law as follows: "Two cities attract trade from an intermediate town in the vicinity of the breaking point, approximately in direct proportion to the population of the two cities, and in inverse proportion to the squares of the distances to the intermediate towns" (Reilly, 1931, page 9). However, Reilly derived the law from more general considerations in which he began with no preconception as to the specific way in which population and distances formed these direct and inverse proportions, and it is with this more general form that this argument will begin.

First define some appropriate notation. In the model, places are classified according to whether they form the origin of consumer demand for goods, or whether they are points of supply, or of exchange, or are market centres. Then in conventional fashion assume there are N places of consumer demand notated by subscripts i and l, and M market centres or central places given by subscripts j and k. Then the general equation which Reilly adopted is given by

$$\frac{p_{ij}}{p_{ik}} = \left(\frac{P_j}{P_k}\right)^{\alpha}\left(\frac{d_{ik}}{d_{ij}}\right)^{\beta},\tag{1}$$

where p_{ij} and p_{ik} are the proportions of the whole of the trade from some place of consumer demand i taken up by centres j and k respectively, P_j and

P_k are the populations of j and k, and d_{ij} and d_{ik} are the distances from i to the centres j and k: α and β are constants to be derived empirically.

The equilibrium condition adopted by Reilly to define the breakpoint between centres j and k, that is, to define the hinterlands around i and k, is the condition which gives the point at which the proportions of trade flowing from i to j and k are equal. This condition can be written as

$$p_{ij} = p_{ik}. \tag{2}$$

Equation (2) implies that equation (1) is equal to unity, and thus it is clear that the equilibrium condition, the boundary condition between market areas, can be specified as

$$\frac{d_{ik}}{d_{ij}} = \left(\frac{P_k}{P_j}\right)^{\alpha/\beta}. \tag{3}$$

Reilly worked with equations (1) and (3) although he did not appear to derive the breakpoint, given by d_{ik} and d_{ij}, solely in terms of known variables. In fact, throughout this paper, explicit breakpoint equations will be used, and thus it is worthwhile explicitly solving equation (3) for d_{ik} or d_{ij}. However, as yet there are two unknowns, d_{ij} and d_{ik}, but only one equation, and thus it is necessary to express one or other of these variables in terms of known data. But there is the identity $d_{jk} \equiv d_{ij} + d_{ik}$, and it is possible to use this in equation (3) to solve for d_{ij} or d_{ik}. For example, to solve for d_{ij} it is necessary to substitute for d_{ik} in equation (3) in terms of $d_{ik} \equiv d_{jk} - d_{ij}$. Rearrangement of the result leads to the breakpoint equation for d_{ij},

$$d_{ij} = d_{jk} \left/ \left[1 + \left(\frac{P_k}{P_j}\right)^{\alpha/\beta}\right]\right.; \tag{4}$$

d_{ik} can be immediately derived using equation (4) in the distance identity equation. Equation (4) is implicit in Reilly's work although it is not apparent from his book that he actually used it to compute breakpoints.

A clearer and perhaps more satisfying way of deriving equation (4) is to postulate a model of retail trade and to use this in calculating the proportions of trade from any place i to any place j. The unconstrained gravity model is appropriate, and a form due to Anderson (1955), in which the influence of mass (in terms of population) on retail trade is raised to some power different from unity, can be used. Then

$$T_{ij} = K P_i^\gamma P_j^\alpha d_{ij}^{-\beta}, \tag{5}$$

where T_{ij} is the retail trade flowing from i to j, K is a scaling constant introduced to ensure some kind of normalisation, and γ, α, and β are parameters; other terms are as defined previously. Then the proportions of trade p_{ij} and p_{ik} can be calculated as

$$p_{ij} = \frac{T_{ij}}{\sum_j T_{ij}}, \quad \text{and} \quad p_{ik} = \frac{T_{ik}}{\sum_k T_{ik}}, \tag{6}$$

and the ratio of these proportions to give the balance of trade flow at i yields

$$\frac{p_{ij}}{p_{ik}} = \frac{T_{ij}}{T_{ik}} = \frac{KP_i^\gamma P_j^\alpha d_{ij}^{-\beta}}{KP_i^\gamma P_k^\alpha d_{ik}^{-\beta}} = \left(\frac{P_j}{P_k}\right)^\alpha \left(\frac{d_{ik}}{d_{ij}}\right)^\beta. \tag{7}$$

Equation (7) is the same as equation (1), and this illustrates quite cogently that Reilly's law must be treated as a *derived* condition from some model which must be initially defined and tested.

The estimation of α and β must therefore be regarded as part of the model calibration process, although it is possible to estimate α and β from the derived condition. Reilly in fact suppressed the explicit model in his analysis; from his discussion he appeared to guess α as being equal to unity, and on this basis he was able to compute β using very detailed data on the proportions of trade flow in the regions between a series of market centres. His analysis yielded values for β of between 1·5 and 2·5, and from these results he approximated β as 2. Of marginal interest here is the fact that Reilly's guess as to α being equal to unity appears to have been borne out in many more recent applications of retail-trade models (Batty, 1976; Coelho and Wilson, 1976). For $\alpha = 1$ and $\beta = 2$, the breakpoint equation, equation (4), becomes

$$d_{ij} = d_{jk} \left/ \left[1 + \left(\frac{P_k}{P_j}\right)^{1/2} \right] \right., \tag{8}$$

which is the well-known form embodying Reilly's law. As mentioned already it is not clear whether Reilly himself actually used equation (8) in determining the market areas presented in his book, although it is hard to see how he would have constructed these without it. In fact equation (8) was used by Converse in 1930 (quoted in Styles, 1969), and it is certain that Reilly would have known of its use. However, the earliest known (to this author) statement of the breakpoint equation (8) is by Strohkarck and Phelps (1948), and their article seems to have prompted Converse (1949) into publishing the fact that he had already been using equation (8) for some years.

A critique of the law: on hypotheses, theories, and models

To elevate the ideas embodied in the previous set of equations to the status of a law seems presumptuous to say the least. Reilly's law would hardly meet the stringent criteria to which well-known scientific laws accord. Indeed even

Lösch (1954) in his great book *The Economics of Location* is slightly sceptical in that he always refers to Reilly's law in inverted commas. Yet like all ideas, whether they become influential or not, they can only be judged and understood from their context. In 1930 it must have seemed amazing to men like Reilly that such clear regularities in human behaviour existed, and thus it is a little easier to see how the enthusiasm and optimism of those times led to such flamboyant conclusions and terminology. Reilly was not alone in his use of words such as law, for Fetter (1924) devised a somewhat similar "economic law of market areas", and what is most intriguing is that Fetter was well aware of the peril of calling any piece of knowledge a law: "The term 'law' surely should be applied sparingly and used not at all where such terms as principle, hypothesis, doctrine, or theory, may serve to describe the character of the generalization attempted" (Fetter, 1924, page 520). Yet Fetter went on to describe his ideas about market areas using the term 'law'. The rules of the game were clearly very different in the 1920s from those which operate today! But despite these differences in cultural conditions, a close analysis of Reilly's law reveals that it is a derived condition from a gravitational model which at best is of wide applicability, and at worst is of a trivial nature. And gravitational theory in social systems is still subject to such fundamental dispute.

In one sense Reilly's law can be seen as the final stage in a model-building process in which theory is being refined and tested. It is clear that any theory of the spatial system requires a model which provides the vehicle on which the theory or hypothesis is tested. In short the model provides the artificial environment which enables the theory to be translated into operational form. Clearly there is a loss of information between the various stages of this process, and, in some instances, model and theory seem remote. But it is the model which is fitted or calibrated to data in the quest to evaluate the relevance of the theory. In these terms then, the breakpoint equation, as given in equation (4) say, is a derived result from a model such as that in equation (5), which has already been calibrated and perhaps validated in some limited sense. If this derived result about breakpoints between market areas is then subjected to a separate and additional test based on independent data then this process of model-building can be regarded as providing a double test of the model. As such it would be a particularly strong test of the model, akin to testing the model on a different data base, at a different time, or in a different place. The derived condition about breakpoints can also be regarded as another means of presenting the model's predictions, and thus its derivative nature is clear. Reilly himself did not test the model, derive the breakpoint equation, and then test this condition. Instead he tested the breakpoint equation directly, and as such his work must be regarded as one of the first, albeit indirect, tests of the gravity model. Indeed as far as the author is aware there have been no complete tests of the model-building process just described. Models are usually tested directly or through the derived condition, but not both, and most of the tests of Reilly's law have been indirect tests of gravity models.

Reilly's law has been quite widely applied since its original statement, but there have been far fewer tests of its form. Researchers have been content to take the law at face value, and in marketing literature the law appears to have been applied quite religiously with little regard to its theoretical basis. For example, in the Haydock Park study (Kantorowich, 1964) no test of the law was used to check its appropriateness for defining retail-trade areas in North West England, although in this case it is fair to point out that an independent test, on the same data base, of a model consistent with Reilly's law revealed a value for β of 2·6 (McLoughlin et al, 1966). This result, and the fact that the related model results were similar statistically to predictions using Reilly's law, provided a partial justification of the use of the law in this case.

Reilly's law, besides being a derived condition from the unconstrained gravity model, can be regarded as an inversion of the model to yield a result relating to the spatial configuration of the system of interest—in this case, the hinterland of a central place. There have been other such inversions of gravity models. In particular Tobler et al (1970) have used such inversions to predict geobotanical distances, and Tobler and Wineburg (1971) have predicted the location of archaeological sites using this idea. In the urban-modelling field a good deal of work on zoning systems for such models has dwelt on such inversions: an example is given by Batty (1976). In this discussion the concept of derived conditions or inversions of models as yielding information about the configuration of the spatial system is a useful one. In a sense the hinterland or market area about a central place can be seen as a means of representing the basic spatial form generated from a complex set of spatial processes reflecting economic competition. Thus it is possible to take a variety of interpretations concerning such analysis: from viewing such analysis and the associated market areas as integral to the economic theory underlying central-place organisation, to viewing the concept of the market area purely as a presentational device.

One final point about testing Reilly's law must be made before the discussion shifts to more substantive issues. In principle it is possible to define breakpoints from available trade-flow data: that is, to define the breakpoint where observed flows T_{ij}^* and T_{ik}^* are equal (the asterisk denotes that the variable is an observed, not a modelled quantity). However, there are enormous practical difficulties in finding data sets which are fine enough to detect such points of equal flow. In short the problem is one of resolution in data collection, and it provides a reason for the fact that those, like Reilly, who have attempted to test the law of retail gravitation have used the model to predict the set of breakpoints in advance of collecting the data. The prediction gives a starting point for data collection, which is begun in the vicinity of the prediction and then moves outward in an effort to detect the real breakpoint. In this sense, the procedure used by Reilly to determine his law was really quite sophisticated.

These methodological points about using the model to determine hinterlands say nothing about the substantive theory on which the law is based. The law attempts to define a system of market areas about a given pattern of central places, and a cornerstone of central-place theory concerns the notion of *hierarchy*. The concept of hierarchy has received substantial attention in central-place theory in recent years, and the idea of a continuum rather than of distinct hierarchy has come to the fore (Beavon, 1977). Furthermore the notion that the hierarchy is an approximation to a lattice of overlapping market areas is appealing, and present research into central-place theory is concerned with such ideas.

The first major critique of Reilly's law, in substantive terms, concerns this idea of hierarchy. Reilly's law assumes that the hierarchy of central places is determined in advance. The form of the breakpoint equation is such that a breakpoint must exist between any two central places, and thus the system of central places used by the model must pertain to one specific level of hierarchy. This limitation has been recognised for a long time. Somewhat inevitably Lösch makes the point: "This law holds only for retail trade, only for two towns at a given time, and only in the neighbourhood of the line on which both towns are equally strong; which assumes that each town is large enough to exclude the other from its local market. That is to say, the pair must not be too unequal" (Lösch, 1954, page 411). Thus hierarchy is an input to the model, but it should be possible to use gravitational theory to predict the hierarchy. In short this limitation of the model could be resolved if the level of hierarchy of any town could be viewed as a consequence of fitting the model. Indeed, as will be shown later, this is possible in a rather obvious and simple way, and it revolves around the form in which distance, or more specifically transport cost, enters the model. In extending the model in this way, inevitable errors due to prior hierarchical definition are avoided.

A second important limitation of Reilly's law relates to the way in which *competition* or interdependence between places in the spatial system is treated. The law is only applicable to pairs of central places, and no relation to the wider system of central places is taken account of in the model. In short the law is based on a model of spatial competition reflecting duopoly. However, by using more recent gravitational theory in which these wider competitive effects are handled through constraints on movement, it is possible to take account of system-wide interaction when predicting the breakpoint between any two places. The various optimising frameworks used to derive gravity models are significant in this regard in that system-wide competition is related to accessibility and price. Moreover, by introducing such competition, the hierarchy predicted from the model becomes more structurally and economically sound.

Two additional and related limitations of the law must also be discussed. In its original form the distinction between origins and destinations, between points of consumer demand and supply, is in doubt. Population is used to measure the attraction of both kinds of place, and thus this *symmetry* appears to be ill-conceived, or at least a rather coarse approximation. The question of symmetry is tied up with the question of how the *size* of the central place appears in the model. In the following analysis it will be argued that size must be included in such models as prior information, and the question of symmetry relates to the differences between consumer and producer–supplier market areas or fields, which suggests that a certain intrinsic asymmetry must be present.

To summarise this substantive critique of Reilly's law, it can be argued that the law in its original form assumes that the hierarchy of the central-place system is known, that competition other than that between any pair of places is absent, that the measurement of size effects in terms of population is naive, and that the symmetry suggested by such measures is incorrect. The resolution of all these problems is possible and will be elaborated in the sequel. Furthermore it is hoped to demonstrate that the use of gravitational theory in defining central-place systems is valid, and that a macrostatistical approach to such problems is thus possible. This would not be possible, however, without the developments of the last decade, and it presents further evidence that gravitational theory and social physics has a somewhat deeper theoretical basis than its critics would wish us to believe. The first and perhaps the most important problem—that of hierarchy—will now be broached, and the following discussion will attempt to establish the similarity of the law to traditional theories of market-area analysis.

A generalised formulation: towards a theory of the breakpoint

The central and all-embracing difficulty with Reilly's law is that it is based upon a model which assumes that consumer demand for a product is infinite at the point of supply, at the central place. In terms of equation (5), as $d_{ij} \to 0$, $T_{ij} \to \infty$, and thus the estimation of demand in the vicinity of the origin is likely to be grossly misleading. This problem has however been recognised in traffic studies for many years. Indeed the inability of the traditional gravity model, in which deterrence was included in the form of an inverse power function, to model trips over small distances, led many researchers to suggest that the deterrence effect be based on a function which was positive and well-defined at the origin. Negative-exponential functions of distance have been a popular way of overcoming such problems and have also found favour in theoretical terms (Schneider, 1959; Wilson, 1970), and other researchers have gone further in arguing that it should be possible to define a function which can be zero at the origin: hence the use of the gamma function

(Tanner, 1961; March, 1971). Moreover the inverse power function can be derived from the negative-exponential, and thus it appears to be worthwhile to explore this more general function in terms of market-area analysis. A general form of interaction model can now be stated:

$$T_{ij} = \exp(-\mu_i - \lambda_j - \beta c_{ij}),\tag{9}$$

where the parameters μ_i and λ_j relate to the influence of consumer demand at i and of supply at j respectively on T_{ij}, and β is a parameter reflecting the effect of generalised spatial impedance c_{ij}. Note that the assumption that origins and destinations are measured using different variables, thus implying an intrinsic asymmetry, has been built into the model. Also note that the signs of μ_i, λ_i, and β, although specified as negative in the exponential, are arbitrary and are determined by calibration.

An immediate comparison of equations (5) and (9) is now possible. If it is assumed that c_{ij} and d_{ij} are comparable, it is clear that, as $d_{ij} \to 0$, equation (9) is well-defined and positive, whereas equation (5) tends to ∞. The implications for breakpoint analysis are obvious: when equation (5) is used, it is always possible to find a value of d_{ij} where $T_{ij} = T_{ik}$ and the breakpoint i lies directly between j and k; when equation (9) is used, however, there is the definite possibility that there exists a value of d_{ij} where i does not lie between j and k, that is, d_{ij} is negative or greater than d_{jk}. These notions are illustrated in figure 1 where two hypothetical trip frequency distributions are plotted over distance. The importance of using the negative-exponential function lies in its ability to generate negative breakpoint values. The obvious speculation is that a negative breakpoint value for d_{ij} is indicative that the centre j is at a lower order in the hierarchy than centre k. The implication is that centre k dominates centre j, that the trip frequency distribution associated with k embraces that associated with j. Thus hierarchy becomes something which can be predicted from the model. Of interest here is the fact that Lösch (1954) made a very similar point; indeed the diagram (figure 71, page 411) he used to show the encirclement of a small town by a large one has a similar structure to that of figure 1(b) in this paper.

The formal analysis of the breakpoint by use of equation (9) follows quite easily. The equilibrium condition implies that $T_{ij} = T_{ik}$, thus $\ln T_{ij} = \ln T_{ik}$, or from the model in equation (9),

$$-\mu_i - \lambda_j - \beta c_{ij} = -\mu_i - \lambda_k - \beta c_{ik}.\tag{10}$$

Equation (10) implies that at the breakpoint i, the basic indifference relation is

$$\lambda_j + \beta c_{ij} = \lambda_k + \beta c_{ik},\tag{11}$$

which can also be written in terms of differences,

$$c_{ij} - c_{ik} = \frac{1}{\beta}(\lambda_k - \lambda_j).\tag{12}$$

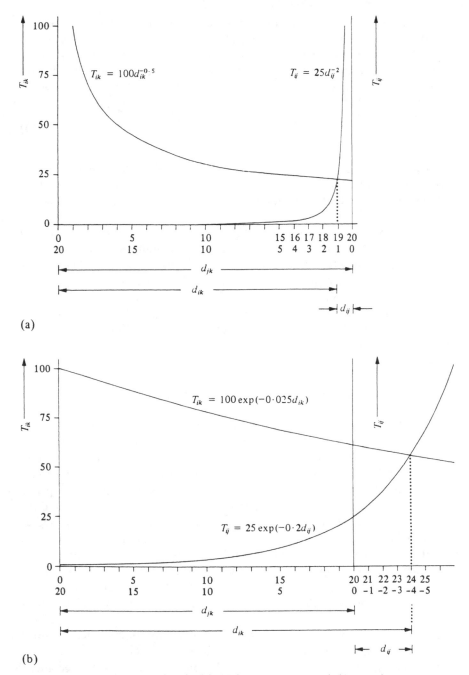

Figure 1 Breakpoints associated with (a) inverse-power and (b) negative-exponential gravity models

As in the derivation of Reilly's breakpoint equation, it is necessary to express one of the unknowns in equation (12) in terms of known information before it is possible to solve for c_{ij} or c_{ik}. Now since $c_{jk} \equiv c_{ij} + c_{ik}$, it is possible to solve for c_{ij} using this generalised travel-cost identity, and the resulting breakpoint equation is given as

$$c_{ij} = \frac{1}{2}\left[c_{jk} + \frac{1}{\beta}(\lambda_k - \lambda_j)\right]. \tag{13}$$

That equation (13) is more general than equation (4) is quite clear in that a comparison shows that equation (4) can never be negative whereas equation (13) can be; hence there exist implications for predicting hierarchical structure from equation (13).

The interpretation of equations (11) to (13) is quite fascinating, for they appear in the theory of spatial competition as defining the points of economic indifference between any two spatial markets. Equation (11) can thus be interpreted as defining the point i where the delivered prices of goods being sold at markets j and k are equal. Thus λ_j and λ_k can be interpreted as the FOB prices of goods at j and k, and β can be viewed as the cost of transport per unit distance, or the freight rate if $c_{ij} = d_{ij}$, as has been assumed. Note also that the argument does not assume that goods are literally transported as freight to the consumer: delivered price is the price which the consumer incurs when he picks up the goods, either at the market or at his place of origin. Equation (11) is basic to Fetter's (1924) work and it is used explicitly by Hyson and Hyson (1950). It is also used as the starting point by Hotelling (1929) in his seminal paper, and in fact the generalised breakpoint equation, equation (13), appears in Hotelling's paper as his equation (7). More general forms of the equation appear in the work of several mainstream locational theorists: for example, Isard (1956). The interpretation, from the breakpoint analysis, of the quantities μ_i, λ_j, and β as prices or costs, has some important implications for gravitational theory, and, as will be evident from the next section, similar conclusions can be arrived at through a rather different form of analysis involving nonlinear optimisation problems and their duals. To show that Reilly's law is really a special case of the wider theory of spatial competition, specifically the theory of spatial duopoly of Fetter (1924) and Hotelling (1929), it is necessary to be more explicit about the generalised model in equation (9). This analysis will now be described.

First it is necessary to note that the generalised travel impedance, c_{ij}, must be defined in terms of a transformation of distance. Then $\ln d_{ij} = c_{ij}$, and equation (12), the economic difference relation between markets, becomes

$$\ln d_{ij} - \ln d_{ik} = \frac{1}{\beta}(\lambda_k - \lambda_j). \tag{14}$$

In solving equation (14) for d_{ij}, first get rid of the logarithms, giving

$$\frac{d_{ik}}{d_{ij}} = \exp\left[\frac{1}{\beta}(\lambda_j - \lambda_k)\right],$$ (15)

and then substitute for d_{ik} from $d_{ik} \equiv d_{jk} - d_{ij}$, leading to the breakpoint equation

$$d_{ij} = d_{jk}\bigg/\left\{1 + \exp\left[\frac{1}{\beta}(\lambda_j - \lambda_k)\right]\right\}.$$ (16)

Note the correspondence between equation (5) and (9), and set $\lambda_j = -\alpha \ln P_j$; thus equation (16) can be written as

$$d_{ij} = d_{jk}\bigg/\left\{1 + \exp\left[\frac{\alpha}{\beta}(\ln P_k - \ln P_j)\right]\right\},$$ (17)

which is identical to equation (4). Of additional interest here is the fact that the price λ_j is assumed to be negatively related to the logarithm of size, thus possibly reflecting economies of scale in supply. There is a certain kind of economic sense to this point which will be explored later.

One final but fundamental point must be made before the whole economic basis of competition in the model is discussed, and this pertains to the question of hierarchy. It has been argued that whenever c_{ij} is negative this implies that centre k dominates centre j so powerfully that the two centres are at different levels in the hierarchy. This of course implies that $c_{ik} > c_{jk}$ which is another way of stating the same. In terms of equations (12) and (13), if $c_{ij} < 0$, this would imply that the normalised price differential $(\lambda_j - \lambda_k)/\beta > c_{jk}$. In other words the price of any good in centre j is too large for consumers to afford the transport cost of visiting the market to purchase the good. Thus these consumers would not patronise that centre, at least at the particular level of hierarchy associated with centre k. This is equivalent to saying that the price advantage of centre k is sufficient to swamp out any advantage which centre j might have had in terms of transport cost. The implication is that centre k would capture the market which centre j might potentially have held, owing to the lower prices charged by centre k. The point is made quite forcefully by Fetter: ". . . both markets can exist so long as the price difference of the two markets is less than the full freight difference" (Fetter, 1924, page 521). The corollary to Fetter's statement in terms of this paper is that if the price difference is greater than the freight difference, the market will no longer exist at that level in the hierarchy of markets, but at a lower level. This indeed is the rationale for much of this paper, but before it can be further explored it is necessary to show how an explicit competition between all centres, not just two as in the duopolistic case, can be introduced into the analysis.

Theoretical derivations: mathematical programmes, duals, prices, and accessibilities

So far the notion of hierarchy and its influence on the orientation of the central-place system has been introduced by generalising the model used to derive breakpoints. An explicitly economic interpretation in terms of spatial duopoly has been made in which it has been suggested that prices vary inversely with some characteristic of locational size, and that freight rates or transport costs modify the influence of distance. In terms of Reilly's law, for example, it was shown that price varies with the logarithm of the inverse of population. But this interpretation is somewhat dubious in that no explicit effects which structure the demand–supply equilibrium in space have yet been included. In short, competition apart from that between two centres is absent from the analysis. Yet in spatial-interaction theory a particularly well-developed equilibrium model exists, one which has been used for many years by traffic engineers, and one which can be derived quite cogently from statistical optimisation theory. It is this model and its derivation through optimisation which forms the starting point of this section, and it will lead to a more general and perhaps more intuitively and theoretically accept-able interpretation of the breakpoint equations. In the following analysis the derivation of gravity models is based on the maximisation of an entropy or information statistic measuring the amount of 'evenness' in the distribution of spatial demand, and thus the treatment follows Wilson (1970). However, it is quite possible to consider the analysis as one in which utility is being maximised (Beckmann, 1974), for at a certain level these ideas are inter-changeable. Nevertheless entropy maximisation will be adopted largely for pragmatic reasons; in the event the results are the same.

Consider the following programme. It is required to maximise an entropy S which is defined in terms of the variables T_{ij} which are to be estimated. S is given as

$$S = -\sum_i \sum_j T_{ij}(\ln T_{ij} - 1),\tag{18}$$

and equation (18) is to be maximised subject to two sets of accounting constraints on known activity at the origins and destinations, and subject to a constraint on the total distance travelled. Note that as before it is assumed that c_{ij} is measured in units of distance. The constraints are stated as

$$\left.\begin{array}{ll} \sum_j T_{ij} = O_i, & \forall_i, \\[2ex] \sum_i T_{ij} = D_j, & \forall_j, \text{ and} \\[2ex] \sum_i \sum_j T_{ij}c_{ij} = C. \end{array}\right\}\tag{19}$$

The maximisation is straightforward: form a Lagrangian $\mathcal{L}$ which is the objective function S augmented by the set of constraints in equations (19). Lagrangian multipliers μ_i, λ_j, and β associated with the three sets of constraints in equations (19) ensure that the first- and second-order conditions for a maximum are satisfied. Then

$$\mathcal{L} = S - \sum_i \mu_i \left(\sum_j T_{ij} - O_i \right) - \sum_j \lambda_j \left(\sum_i T_{ij} - D_j \right) -$$

$$\beta \left(\sum_i \sum_j T_{ij} C_{ij} - C \right). \tag{20}$$

Differentiation of equation (20) with respect to T_{ij} leads to

$$\ln T_{ij} = -\mu_i - \lambda_j - \beta c_{ij}, \tag{21}$$

from which the model for T_{ij} is easily derived as

$$T_{ij} = \exp(-\mu_i - \lambda_j - \beta c_{ij}). \tag{22}$$

Clearly the derived model in equation (22) is identical to that stated in equation (9), although it is clear now that a basis for interpreting the parameters μ_i, λ_j, and β exists in terms of constraints and Lagrangian multipliers. Needless to say the models in equations (9) and (22) were notated with this potential interpretation in mind.

There are a number of ways of solving the optimisation problem in equations (18) and (19). It is possible to operate on the Lagrangian directly and to set up an unconstrained problem soluble by standard methods. However, it is more usual to find forms for the parameters μ_i and λ_j and to set up some solution procedure on this basis. Moreover an interpretation for μ_i and λ_j then becomes possible. A substitution of the model in equation (22) into the first two sets of equations in (19) relating to origin and destination constraints, leads to

$$\exp(-\mu_i) = O_i \left[\sum_j \exp(-\lambda_j - \beta c_{ij}) \right]^{-1} \tag{23}$$

and

$$\exp(-\lambda_j) = D_j \left[\sum_i \exp(-\mu_i - \beta c_{ij}) \right]^{-1}. \tag{24}$$

It is clear that the Lagrangian multipliers μ_i and λ_j are spatially interdependent and vary with respect to the logarithm of the ratio of this interdependence to size. A slightly clearer interpretation of this interdependence is possible if the following definitions are made:

$$\exp(-\mu_i) = A_i O_i = O_i \left[\sum_j B_j D_j \exp(-\beta c_{ij}) \right]^{-1} \tag{25}$$

and

$$\exp(-\lambda_j) = B_j D_j = D_j \left[\sum_i A_i O_i \exp(-\beta c_{ij}) \right]^{-1}, \tag{26}$$

where $A_i = \exp(-\mu_i)/O_i$ and $B_j = \exp(-\lambda_j)/D_j$.

By use of equations (25) and (26), the model in equation (22) now takes on a familiar form

$$T_{ij} = A_i O_i B_j D_j \exp(-\beta c_{ij}), \tag{27}$$

and the usual procedure for solving for μ_i, λ_j, and β is based on fixing β, solving equations (25) and (26) for μ_i and λ_j, then varying β in some systematic manner, solving for μ_i and λ_j in equations (25) and (26) again, and so on. The solution of equations (25) and (26) is the basis of the so-called 'Furness' time-function iteration. Equations (25) and (26) also show that the way the masses at locations i and j enter the model is as a function of size and access. The terms A_i and B_j are inverse accessibility functions and have been called competition terms. A quasi-economic interpretation suggests that competition is the inverse of accessibility, for the higher the accessibility, the greater the tendency towards spatial monopoly. In a mathematical sense, A_i and B_j are weights on the amount of activity O_i and D_j which enable the complex balancing in the demand–supply equilibrium to be achieved, and these could be regarded as prices which 'ration' the flow of demand from consumers to suppliers; clearly such prices are a product of the computed equilibrium.

It is now worthwhile making explicit the breakpoint analysis by using the generalised model and the balancing factor/competition terms in equations (23) to (26). From equations (24) and (26),

$$\lambda_j = \ln \left\{ \left[\sum_i \exp(-\mu_i - \beta c_{ij}) \right] D_j^{-1} \right\} = \ln \left\{ \left[\sum_i A_i O_i \exp(-\beta c_{ij}) \right] D_j^{-1} \right\}, \tag{28}$$

and it is clear that price varies directly with the logarithm of the ratio of accessibility to size. The larger the accessibility for any fixed size of place, the greater is the ability of a place of that size to control the market, and the higher the price that it can set. For a fixed accessibility, the larger is the place, and the lower the price, owing to economies of scale. High accessibility implies a tendency towards monopoly and low competition, but it must be realised immediately that the accessibilities in this model are only relative. That is, the Lagrangian multipliers—the prices—are only unique up to an additive constant, and thus it is not possible to speculate on the absolute levels of access or prices generated by such models. The use of equation (28) in equation (13) leads to an explicit form for the breakpoint c_{ij} which includes accessibility or its inverse—competition. Then

$$c_{ij} = \frac{1}{2}\left\{c_{jk} + \frac{1}{\beta}\ln\left[\frac{D_j\sum_l\exp(-\mu_l - \beta c_{lk})}{D_k\sum_l\exp(-\mu_l - \beta c_{lj})}\right]\right\}$$

$$= \frac{1}{2}\left\{c_{jk} + \frac{1}{\beta}\ln\left[\frac{D_j\sum_l A_l O_l\exp(-\beta c_{lk})}{D_k\sum_l A_l O_l\exp(-\beta c_{lj})}\right]\right\}. \tag{29}$$

In terms of the breakpoint, the difference in travel costs is equal to the differences in prices, and thus the difference in distances from centres j and k to i is a weighted function of these price differences as in equation (12). Formally, by use of equation (26),

$$c_{ij} - c_{ik} = \frac{1}{\beta}\ln\left[\frac{B_j D_j}{B_k D_k}\right]. \tag{30}$$

Equation (30) is identical to the consumer surplus which is formed when the integral of the demand equation, equation (22), is evaluated with respect to a change in transport cost/distance c_{ij} (Neuberger, 1971). This line of analysis will not be taken further here but it is consistent with what follows in terms of the analysis of the dual of the entropy-maximisation programme.

Equation (29) includes system-wide competition explicitly, and, in comparison with Reilly's original equation for the breakpoint, the reformulated equation must surely yield results quite different from those using Reilly's law. The assumption of uniform accessibility which is implicit in Reilly's law seems untenable and is bound to produce very different results unless access covaries with size, in which case the access effect would be redundant. This is a distinct possibility in spatial systems because of spatial autocorrelation induced by boundary effects and/or by the phenomenon itself. Thus in previous applications of Reilly's law it is possible that accessibility has been included by default. It is interesting to examine the size of the market area when prices change, by using equation (29). If the price of the good at place j, λ_j, falls, the size of the market area increases. As price varies positively with access and negatively with size, a decrease in relative access, or an increase in size, or both would lead to a fall in price. Ceteris paribus, a large place with low access is likely to have a much larger trading area than a similarly sized place with high access. This type of result is frequently observed when the size of hinterland in rural farming regions is compared with that in metropolitan regions. There is also an implication in this analysis that lower prices are better for all consumers. In fact this type of conclusion is somewhat misleading because the analysis is only able to handle relative price levels. However, it is intuitively obvious that a more even distribution of prices would result if access levels were more even, and if places were uniformally sized (and spaced), and the implication is that such a situation would maximise the overall consumer surplus associated with the system. It is not appropriate to take this idea further here, but Williams and Senior (1977a) have embarked on a formal analysis of the problem which is completely consistent with these conclusions.

At this point it is necessary to take stock of the argument so far. Reilly's law has been reformulated in such a way that the breakpoint equation is able to yield information about the hierarchy of central places, owing to the fact that a model of demand has been used which is capable of simulating the dominance of one place over another. The breakpoint equation derived turns out to be the one used by Hotelling (1929) and others, and this leads to a conjecture that the price–cost indifference at the breakpoint is implied by the associated model in terms of its mass and deterrence functions. These prices and costs are further generalised when a more sophisticated model of demand–supply equilibrium is used which includes multicentred spatial competition. There is, however, a much clearer way of introducing these prices into gravity models. It is well-known in mathematical programming that every primal problem has a dual which in one sense is the inverse of the primal. Usually, if the primal is a maximisation problem, the dual is a minimisation problem. Moreover the Lagrangian multipliers which are used to effect the optimisation of a primal such as that in equations (18) and (19) are the variables to be selected in the dual. If the maximisation of entropy is regarded as being similar to the maximisation of utility, albeit in a rather coarse sense, then the minimisation problem of the dual can be seen as one in which the prices are to be chosen so that the total cost of locating and travelling in the system is at a minimum. Thus by appealing to duality theory the idea of prices appears quite naturally.

A rather ad hoc interpretation of the parameters μ_i, λ_j, and β can be made if the value of entropy at its maximum is examined. It is well-known that, at the optimum, changes in the value of S are related quite simply to the Lagrangian multipliers. Then

$$\frac{\partial S}{\partial O_i} = \mu_i, \quad \forall_i, \qquad \frac{\partial S}{\partial D_j} = \lambda_j, \quad \forall_j, \qquad \text{and} \qquad \frac{\partial S}{\partial C} = \beta.$$

In other words, when entropy or utility is at a maximum, the effects of perturbing this optimal value by marginal changes in the resources are the resource costs μ_i, λ_j, and β; hence their interpretation as prices, or more strictly as marginal costs or shadow prices. Note that although the multipliers μ_i have not yet been strictly defined as prices, they can be regarded as the rents or costs of locating in i, that is, the comparative advantage for consumers living at i. The question which arises from this discussion is whether or not a problem exists in which a total price can be minimised. This problem turns out to be the dual and will be sketched below.

Evans (1973) appears to have been the first to study extensively the idea of duals in optimisation approaches to gravity models, although the treatment here follows the more accessible work of Wilson and Senior (1974). The easiest way to form the dual is to expand the Lagrangian in equation (20) by using the model in equation (22), and to express the objective function as one of choosing the dual variables. This is the approach used by Balinski and Baumol (1968), although there are several other methods. The dual of the primal involving the maximisation of S consists of minimising an objective function Z,

$$Z = \sum_i \mu_i O_i + \sum_j \lambda_j D_j + \beta C + \sum_i \sum_j T_{ij}, \tag{31}$$

subject to

$$-\mu_i - \lambda_j - \beta c_{ij} = \ln T_{ij}, \quad \forall_{i,j}. \tag{32}$$

The problem can be solved by substituting T_{ij} from equation (32) into equation (31) and performing a standard unconstrained optimisation on the objective function. It is possible to think of $\ln T_{ij}$ as a kind of value or utility of travelling from i to j which must be equal to the costs incurred for that travel. This also gives a rationale for the breakpoint analysis because equation (32) has been used before to derive the breakpoint [see equation (10)]. It is possible to speculate on a more formal economic interpretation which clearly exists (Intriligator, 1971), but this is beyond the scope of this paper. Note also that it is often more convenient to solve the dual problem than the primal one owing to the former's lower dimensionality, and a great deal of mathematical-programming theory is devoted to this notion.

It is not possible to talk about the absolute level of Z in terms of absolute prices as noted earlier, but it is possible to speculate on the relationship of Z to S for different price distributions. For example, in the case where all prices were uniform this implies that spatial competition and accessibility are also uniform across the system. Such a situation can only result if each origin and each destination are the same as other origins and destinations respectively. A maximum of the maxima for the primal problem will, however, only result when the value of β is 0, which implies that there is no constraint on travel distance—that the cost of travel is zero. This situation has led Erlander (1977a) to speculate that there may be some absolute measure relating to such optimisation problems, in particular that the entropy S is a measure of system-wide accessibility. Such ideas are clearly of interest here but as yet they are rather ill-formed. When other prices in the dual are zero, this implies, by the Kuhn–Tucker complementary slackness conditions, that the associated constraint in the primal problem is absent or redundant.

Clearly such a result would only be coincidental were it to occur in a demand–supply equilibrium situation such as this. As $\beta \to \infty$, Evans (1973) and Senior and Wilson (1974) have shown that the cost constraint dominates, and the nonlinear programme becomes linear and equivalent to the linear-programming transportation problem. With the origin and destination constraints, trips are allocated from their point of origin to the nearest supplier. The dual variables μ_i and λ_j then take on the same interpretation as the familiar shadow prices in linear programming, and in this context can be created in similar terms (Senior and Wilson, 1974).

Two points must be made to conclude this section. The so-called doubly constrained equilibrium model has been discussed here, but it is clear that any other member of the family of spatial-interaction models could have been derived and developed for breakpoint analysis. These will be dealt with later. Furthermore the astute reader will have realised that all of the results so far pertaining to breakpoints between market centres could easily have been generalised to breakpoints between consumers. Not only do hinterlands or fields exist around suppliers at central places but they also exist around consumers. Despite the fact that this paper is largely concerned with the producer's or supplier's field, a note on consumer fields will be included later. But before these questions of symmetry are addressed, the problem of size will be formally studied. Size clearly enters the model as a function of the origin and destination constraints, but if these constraints are missing then size must be included in another way—through generalising the model to include prior information. This is the concept which will be discussed next.

The influence of prior spatial information

In many modelling problems, information which has been assumed in the theoretical context must somehow be taken into account. In the foregoing analysis all information was included in the constraints, but it is also possible to include such known information in the objective function. In spatial-interaction problems the influence of some prior knowledge about the interaction pattern can be incorporated by maximising an entropy function which measures the information difference between this prior pattern and the pattern to be estimated. Such functions involve the comparison of a prior distribution $\{T_{ij}^\circ\}$ with a posterior distribution $\{T_{ij}\}$, and the problem of defining an appropriate estimator for $\{T_{ij}\}$ now involves maximising a more general function of entropy, defined by

$$\tilde{S} = -\sum_i \sum_j T_{ij} \left[\ln \left(\frac{T_{ij}}{T_{ij}^\circ} \right) - 1 \right], \tag{33}$$

subject to the constraints in equations (19). The maximisation of $\tilde{S}$ is equivalent to the minimisation of $-\tilde{S}$ which is the expected information gain or information divergence defined by Theil (1972) and Kullback (1959). In maximising $\tilde{S}$ subject to the constraints, a new Lagrangian $\tilde{\mathscr{L}}$ is constructed which is the same as $\mathscr{L}$ but with $\tilde{S}$ replacing S. Differentiation of this leads to a minimally prejudiced estimate of T_{ij} in terms of known T_{ij}° and the constraints. Then

$$\ln \frac{T_{ij}}{T_{ij}^{\circ}} = -\mu_i - \lambda_j - \beta c_{ij} \tag{34}$$

and the spatial-interaction demand model becomes

$$T_{ij} = T_{ij}^{\circ} \exp(-\mu_i - \lambda_j - \beta c_{ij}). \tag{35}$$

The dual problem is the same as that given in equation (31) but with equation (34) rather than equation (32) forming the appropriate constraint.

Before the various Lagrangian multipliers are evaluated (which depend on the precise form of T_{ij}°), it is worth stating the new breakpoint equations which are now weighted by the prior information $\{T_{ij}^{\circ}\}$. Then at the point of price–cost indifference i,

$$\lambda_j + \beta c_{ij} - \ln T_{ij}^{\circ} = \lambda_k + \beta c_{ik} - \ln T_{ik}^{\circ}. \tag{36}$$

Ln T_{ij}° and $\ln T_{ik}^{\circ}$ clearly contribute to this price–cost argument, and the easiest interpretation is to assume that these quantities are based on some previous model of interaction which has the same form as, say, the doubly constrained model in equations (21) and (22). Then it is clear that equation (36) involves the sum of two sets of prices and costs, those associated with the new distribution and those with the old. In fact, if the prior–posterior model of equation (35) is given a definite temporal structure, then the price–cost indifference equation becomes the sum of all prices and costs associated with all previous distributions in time. Clearly the estimation of λ_j and β would reflect price and cost differences rather than absolutes. The distance-difference equation at the breakpoint, which is defined from equation (36), is

$$c_{ij} - c_{ik} = \frac{1}{\beta} \left[\ln \frac{T_{ij}^{\circ}}{T_{ik}^{\circ}} + (\lambda_k - \lambda_j) \right], \tag{37}$$

and the breakpoint equation becomes

$$c_{ij} = \frac{1}{2} \left\{ c_{jk} + \frac{1}{\beta} \left[\ln \frac{T_{ij}^{\circ}}{T_{ik}^{\circ}} + (\lambda_k - \lambda_j) \right] \right\}. \tag{38}$$

Various specific forms for equation (38) exist if assumptions are made about the prior distribution $\{T_{ij}^{\circ}\}$, and in the following discussion two main cases will be identified.

When the prior distribution is based on the mull hypothesis $\{T_{ij}^{\circ} = \text{con-stant}: \forall_{i,j}\}$, then equation (38) clearly collapses back to equation (13), for this prior information does not involve anything which helps to model the real distribution. Moreover if the distribution $\{T_{ij}\}$ is based on a model which gives the same estimates as $\{T_{ij}^o\}$, then equation (38) also reduces to equation (13). However, a more appropriate null hypothesis for spatial-interaction models is based on the assumption of spatial independence between origins and destinations. In such a case, T_{ij}^o is proportional to the origin and destination activity, that is,

$$T_{ij}^o = \frac{O_i D_j}{T}, \tag{39}$$

where T is the total trip demand in the system, that is, $T = \sum_i O_i = \sum_j D_j$. The substitution of equation (39) into equation (35) gives the model

$$T_{ij} = \frac{O_i D_j}{T} \exp(-\mu_i - \lambda_j - \beta c_{ij}). \tag{40}$$

The factors $\exp(-\mu_i)$ and $\exp(-\lambda_j)$ can be evaluated in the usual manner and are given by

$$\exp(-\mu_i) = T \left[\sum_j D_j \exp(-\lambda_j - \beta c_{ij}) \right]^{-1} \tag{41}$$

and

$$\exp(-\lambda_j) = T \left[\sum_i O_i \exp(-\mu_i - \beta c_{ij}) \right]^{-1}. \tag{42}$$

The use of the familiar definitions

$$a_i = \frac{\exp(-\mu_i)}{T} = \left[\sum_j b_j D_j \exp(-\beta c_{ij}) \right]^{-1} \tag{43}$$

and

$$b_j = \exp(-\lambda_j) = \left[\sum_i a_i O_i \exp(-\beta c_{ij}) \right]^{-1} \tag{44}$$

permits equation (40) to be rewritten in a more obvious form as

$$T_{ij} = a_i O_i b_j D_j \exp(-\beta c_{ij}), \tag{45}$$

and it is clear that the model in equation (45) is equivalent to the model in equation (27). In short the size variables O_i and D_j introduced as prior spatial information are redundant in a model in which demand and supply are constrained to meet these same quantities. But in a model where such constraints are missing, such variables can only be introduced as prior information. This is essential in models which are not totally constrained in the sense of equations (19). Because the models in equations (27) and (45) are equivalent, the breakpoint equations must be the same. This can easily be checked by substituting the independence assumption in equation (39) and the prices from equation (42) into equation (38) which can then be shown to be identical to equation (29).

For real differences to occur in terms of prior information affecting the breakpoint analysis, the prior model must be related to some kind of spatial interdependence. A particularly appealing prior model which incorporates the physical affects of the space—the true gravitational effects—is based on the Coleman–Zipf model (Batty and March, 1976). This particular model accounts for boundary effects and the effect of size, and is stated as

$$T_{ij}^o = KO_iD_jd_{ij}^{-1}, \tag{46}$$

where the scaling constant K is defined by

$$K = T\left[\sum_i \sum_j O_iD_jd_{ij}^{-1}\right]^{-1}. \tag{47}$$

The model can be stated directly by substituting equation (46) into equation (35), giving

$$T_{ij} = KO_iD_jd_{ij}^{-1}\exp(-\mu_i - \lambda_j - \beta c_{ij}), \tag{48}$$

and the balancing factors can be derived as

$$\exp(-\mu_i) = \left[K\sum_j D_jd_{ij}^{-1}\exp(-\lambda_j - \beta c_{ij})\right]^{-1} \tag{49}$$

and

$$\exp(-\lambda_j) = \left[K\sum_i O_id_{ij}^{-1}\exp(-\mu_i - \beta c_{ij})\right]^{-1}. \tag{50}$$

As in the previous case, set $a_i = K\exp(-\mu_i)$ and $b_j = \exp(-\lambda_j)$, and this gives the model

$$T_{ij} = a_iO_ib_jD_jd_{ij}^{-1}\exp(-\beta c_{ij}). \tag{51}$$

Equation (51) includes the effect of distance (when $c_{ij} = d_{ij}$) as a modified gamma function (March, 1971).

The breakpoint analysis is of considerable interest owing to the fact that distance enters the model from both prior and posterior considerations. The price–cost indifference equation is first stated as

$$\lambda_j + \beta c_{ij} - \ln D_j + \ln d_{ij} = \lambda_k + \beta c_{ik} - \ln D_k + \ln d_{ik}. \tag{52}$$

The solution of a transcendental equation such as (52) is immediately problematical; this can be overcome, however, if it is assumed that $c_{ij} = \ln d_{ij}$, and
if the correspondence between equations (9) and (48) is noted, and in such a
case equation (52) transforms to Reilly's original indifference equation with
$\alpha = 1$ and the parameter β of equations (14) to (17) as $\beta + 1$ in terms of
equation (52). In the same way, if it is assumed that d_{ij} has the form $\exp(c_{ij})$,
and again if the correspondence between equations (9) [or (22)] and (48) is
noted, then equation (52) reduces to the standard price–cost indifference
relation of the negative-exponential model with β of equation (29) equal to
$\beta + 1$ of equation (52). In both cases, breakpoint solutions can be derived
in the normal way owing to the fact that the deterrence effects of the prior
and posterior models are of the same form, and hence their parameters
are additive. When $c_{ij} = d_{ij}$, however, the breakpoint equation arising from
equation (52) after rearrangement and the use of equation (44) is given by

$$d_{ij} = \frac{1}{2}\left\{ d_{jk} + \frac{1}{\beta}\ln\frac{D_j}{D_k} + \frac{1}{\beta}\ln\frac{d_{ik}}{d_{ij}} + \frac{1}{\beta}\ln\left[\frac{\sum_l a_l O_l \exp(-\beta d_{lk})}{\sum_l a_l O_l \exp(-\beta d_{lj})}\right]\right\}. \tag{53}$$

The immediate reaction to equation (53) is to suggest that it may be solved
by iteration, with a first estimate of the breakpoints d_{ik} and d_{ij} from some
other theory such as central-place theory. As the term $\beta^{-1}\ln(d_{ik}/d_{ij})$ is likely
to be small in comparison with other terms, convergence is likely to be fast.
However, this assumes that d_{ij} is positive after the first iteration. If it is not
then the solution of equation (53) might have to be regarded as a once-for-all
affair.

   However, a more cogent rationale for the solution of equation (53) exists
if it is assumed that d_{ij} is first predicted from the prior model—the Coleman–
Zipf prior model—by use of Reilly's law. From equation (3) it is clear that
the ratio of prior breakpoint distances can be written as

$$\frac{d_{ik}}{d_{ij}} = \frac{D_k}{D_j}, \tag{54}$$

and substitution of equation (54) into equation (53) gives the new breakpoint
equation,

$$d_{ij} = \frac{1}{2}\left\{ d_{jk} + \frac{1}{\beta}\ln\left[\frac{\sum_l a_l O_l \exp(-\beta d_{lk})}{\sum_l a_l O_l \exp(-\beta d_{lj})}\right]\right\}. \tag{55}$$

This scheme clearly gives a once-for-all estimate which differs from the
previous scheme in that the effects of prior distance and size are assumed,
from Reilly's law, to cancel themselves out, thus leaving the breakpoint as

being solely determined by competition. Size however is included indirectly in equation (55) through competition. A precise conclusion as to the various merits of these schemes is not possible yet, for it will involve further theoretical work and an assessment of the implications for the empirical determination of breakpoints. In the example which is described at the end of this paper, prior spatial information has not been included, and the empirical development of these ideas awaits further work.

There is one final aspect to this question of prior spatial information to be explored, and this relates to whether or not the prior information is 'modellable'. In the previous discussion it has been assumed that models of such information are to be constructed, and in essence the derived model used for breakpoint analysis is one based on both prior and posterior assumptions. In such cases there is little difficulty in determining breakpoints because these can be modelled. However, if $\{T_{ij}^{\circ}\}$ were based on known data, a problem arises. The calculation of the breakpoint by use of, say, equation (38) requires a search over an extremely fine-grained data set in terms of the distribution of consumers so that a point can be found which makes equation (38) stable in some sense. In the event, iteration on equation (38) would probably be required, starting from the point where $T_{ij}^{\circ} = T_{ik}^{\circ}$. Such a procedure might, however, be impossible because, as mentioned before, the data may not be fine enough in its specification to enable such an iteration to proceed. Thus the use of known spatial information in contrast to assumed information is in doubt; and this too is another area for further research, especially as such solution procedures are critical to empirical work which seeks to identify the central-place system by use of all known information.

Consumer and producer fields: demand and supply in space

The analysis so far has been restricted to examining the hinterlands or fields around centres of supply or of production of services, and such producer fields identify the catchment areas within which the average or typical consumer finds it worth his while to purchase goods at the associated central place. Although the model used to determine spatial demand deals with all consumers, and reflects a situation where preferences vary in a systematic way, the resulting market areas of producer fields define areas over which the associated centres dominate in terms of the FOB prices charged and the transport costs incurred. Exactly the same kind of analysis can be developed for the area around a typical consumer, or more generally around a particular origin point of consumer demand. If it is assumed that a typical consumer has to pay a fixed rent for his locational advantage, then the line of rent–transport-cost indifference between any two origin points of consumer demand reflects the boundary between areas over which the consumer can dominate by paying higher prices for goods at centres. In short the associated consumer fields represent areas in which consumers living at the origin of the field can outbid other consumers at other origins, and thus the implication that the typical consumer belonging to that field purchases his goods at centres within the field. The point of economic indifference using the model in equation (9) [or (22)] is where $T_{ij} = T_{lj}$, i and l now relating to origins of consumer demand, and j to the breakpoint between these origins. Then from equation (21) it is clear that

$$\mu_i + \beta\tilde{c}_{ij} = \mu_l + \beta\tilde{c}_{lj}, \tag{56}$$

where the tilde above the spatial impedance term shows that the equation pertains to consumer fields. The breakpoint equation is obvious and can be derived in a similar manner to that presented earlier. If one notes that $\tilde{c}_{il} \equiv \tilde{c}_{ij} + \tilde{c}_{lj}$, it is possible to solve equation (56) for $\tilde{c}_{ij}$, thus yielding

$$\tilde{c}_{ij} = \frac{1}{2}\left[\tilde{c}_{il} + \frac{1}{\beta}(\mu_l - \mu_i)\right]. \tag{57}$$

The justification for interpreting μ_l and μ_i as rents payable for locational advantage is a product of this analysis as well as of the previous analysis using the dual of the entropy- or utility-maximising model. If $\tilde{c}_{ij} = \ln \tilde{d}_{ij}$ then equation (56) can be solved to give the traditional breakpoint equation,

$$\tilde{d}_{ij} = \tilde{d}_{il}\bigg/\left\{1 + \exp\left[\frac{1}{\beta}(\mu_i - \mu_l)\right]\right\}, \tag{58}$$

which yields the consumer field associated with Reilly's law.

Specific forms for the breakpoint equations depend upon the models used to simulate spatial demand. In the case of equation (57), use of the doubly constrained model given in equations (22) or (27) yields a consumer field in which access and size play similar roles to the same variables in producer fields. Then from equation (22) and its balancing factors in equations (25) and (26),

$$\tilde{c}_{ij} = \frac{1}{2}\left\{\tilde{c}_{il} + \frac{1}{\beta}\ln\left[\frac{O_i\sum_k B_k D_k \exp(-\beta\tilde{c}_{kl})}{O_l\sum_k B_k D_k \exp(-\beta\tilde{c}_{ki})}\right]\right\}, \tag{59}$$

and the same interpretations concerning size and accessibility as were developed around equation (29) can be made. Clearly the similarity between equations (29) and (59) is quite consistent with the symmetry of the gravity model in terms of its origins and destinations, although the use of different measures for origin and destination activity in equations (29) and (59) does also embody an intrinsic asymmetry. In contrast, by use of the unconstrained model in equation (5), the breakpoint associated with Reilly's law can be determined from equation (58). Then

$$\tilde{d}_{ij} = \tilde{d}_{il} \bigg/ \left[1 + \left(\frac{P_l}{P_i} \right)^{\alpha/\beta} \right], \tag{60}$$

which has the same structure as equation (4). No consumer hierarchy can be derived from equation (60), and no competition between places in the central-place system other than between i and l characterise the field. Equation (60) also displays the original problem of symmetry referred to in relation to Reilly's law. If the set of origins corresponds to destinations, that is, if every origin is a destination and vice versa, equation (4) is identical to equation (60); thus consumer and producer fields coincide, and any intrinsic difference between them disappears. In fact they are intrinsically different, as the following argument seeks to establish.

Although the two types of field are symmetrical in a mathematical sense, there is a major substantive difference between them. The distribution of suppliers or producers is usually regarded as a point distribution described in discrete terms, whereas the distribution of consumers is regarded as being continuous over the plane. This clearly is only a matter of degree, but it does represent the general notion that the number of suppliers is of an order of magnitude less than the number of consumers. In terms of the producer field, this area defines an actual catchment within which consumers are attracted by a certain centre, and the boundary line is defined in terms of the location of consumers. In principle at least, it is possible to have a data set giving the flow of consumers at location i to centres at j which is fine enough to effect the definition of the field. In contrast the consumer field has less real meaning. It can certainly be envisaged as a catchment within which consumers patronise certain centres, but the boundary line around the field cannot be defined by centres of supply. In other words this field could not be defined from data concerning consumer flows to centres, for it is assumed that the number of centres would be far too small to enable such definition to be made. Nevertheless in both cases the concept of a field is an abstraction of analytical use only, and the consumer field is no less a relevant concept in this context that the mean-information field used in diffusion studies (Hägerstrand, 1967).

The other question to be briefly noted is that of closure of the analysis in economic terms. Derived from the doubly constrained model are prices in the form of rents, prices of goods at market centres, and the cost of transport. Clearly these quantities are predictions which can be tested in the normal way if data concerning price distributions are available. However, in the case of prices which are locationally dependent, namely rents and the prices of goods, the values obtained are only unique up to the addition of an arbitrary constant. Therefore some adjustment is required and this is easiest to make in the case of rents which can be calibrated against some marginal or lowest rent observed (Senior and Wilson, 1974). A more speculative idea here would be to embed the model in some wider economic budgeting framework, and to assess the degree to which the constraints could be met in terms of ensuring that the rents, prices of goods, and transport costs met some overall constraint. This is a matter for future research, but it would help in providing a stronger basis for interpretation of the meaning of consumer and producer fields.

A typology of models based on consumer and producer fields

The critique of Reilly's law has been developed in relation to four features of the original model: its inability to handle the question of hierarchy, its narrow focus on spatial competition between pairs of centres rather than for all centres, its simplistic treatment of locational characteristics, and its undesirable symmetry in predicting interaction. Each of these limitations has been overcome in some way. Hierarchy has become explicit by adopting a form of spatial deterrence function which allows the domination of other centres by those centres supplying goods: competition, mass, and symmetry have been treated through notions of equilibrium constraints on interaction and of the prior influence of size. At this stage it is worthwhile drawing these strands together through an examination of different types of interaction model and the fields and breakpoint equations which they imply. A suitable range of models consistent with the idea of varying the degrees of constraint on the interaction pattern has been categorised by Wilson (1970) as a family, and this family will form the basis of the typology explored here. Moreover this discussion will be augmented by the use of negative-exponential functions and inverse power functions, both of which will describe spatial impedance, thus serving to highlight the difference between Reilly's original work and its reformulation in this paper.

In the following argument it will be assumed that the mass or size of the system originates in the various models as prior information. In terms of the previous discussion, prior spatial information will be incorporated by use of the maximisation framework implied by equations (33) to (35), and equation (39) in which $T_{ij}^{o} = O_{i}D_{j}/T$. In this form, the optimisation programme is often nonconvex, thus leading to problems if the model is first calibrated by optimising directly on the dual or primal model. However, as Erlander (1977b) has shown, a suitable transformation of the prior model T_{ij}^{o} in $\tilde{S}$ is able to make the problem equivalent to the original entropy—maximisation in equations (18) to (22). Here this is unnecessary, for it is the interpretation of the resulting models which is of interest, not their estimation. By use of $\tilde{S}$ as the function to be maximised, Wilson's family of interaction models can be generated by assuming different degrees of constraint on the origin and destination of activity. Generally four typical members of the family are studied: a model with no constraints on origins and destinations—an unconstrained model; a model with a full set of constraints on origins and destinations—a doubly constrained model; and models with constraints on origins or destinations, but not both together. The first two types of model—unconstrained and doubly constrained—have already been dealt with in some detail, and thus it is the singly constrained models which are of prime interest at this juncture. In fact, as multicentred spatial competition is a function of the degree to which the model is constrained, the unconstrained model originally used by Reilly is the least useful in that its spatial competition is based on duopoly, with centres taken two at a time. In contrast the doubly constrained model is likely to be the most satisfying in that competition is fully included as a feature of the demand–supply equilibrium. Moreover, in the unconstrained model, the consumer and producer fields can coincide if the origins and destinations are in one–one correspondence and if $O_i = D_j$ which $i = j$, for all i and j; this makes the model even less desirable.

Models which include constraints on origins or on destinations will include only those competitive effects due to these constraints, and the associated fields will be affected accordingly. For example, in the case of origin-constrained models the competition which is a feature of the model is based on the accessibility of the consumer to all centres. Consider the shopping model due to Huff (1963, 1964) and first developed by Lakshmanan and Hansen (1965) for Baltimore. This model has been widely applied in retail studies, and it is of interest to explore the fields and hierarchies associated with it. The model is stated as follows:

$$S_{ij} = C_i \frac{F_j^\alpha d_{ij}^{-\beta}}{\sum_j F_j^\alpha d_{ij}^{-\beta}}, \tag{61}$$

where S_{ij} is the number of shopping trips made from the centre of consumer demand i to centre j, C_i is the amount of demand generated at i, F_j is the shopping centre attractiveness at j (often measured by floorspace), and d_{ij}, α, and β are as defined previously. Clearly the model is origin- or demand-constrained in that

$$\sum_j S_{ij} = C_i, \tag{62}$$

and thus the competition involved relates to the consumers. In terms of the previous notation, $\exp(-\mu_i) = C_i / \sum_j F_j^\alpha d_{ij}^{-\beta}$ and $\exp(-\lambda_j) = F_j^\alpha$; then the consumer field is given by equation (58). An explicit development of this equation leads to

$$
\tilde{d}_{ij} = \tilde{d}_{il} \left/ \left[1 + \left(\frac{C_l \sum_k F_k^\alpha d_{ik}^{-\beta}}{C_i \sum_k F_k^\alpha d_{lk}^{-\beta}} \right)^{1/\beta} \right] \right. ,
\tag{63}
$$

from which it is clear that no hierarchy in terms of consumer fields can be predicted from the model owing to its use of the inverse power function. The real focus in this paper, however, is on producer fields, and in this case the breakpoint equation is given as

$$
d_{ij} = d_{jk} \left/ \left[1 + \left(\frac{F_k}{F_j} \right)^{\alpha/\beta} \right] \right. ,
\tag{64}
$$

which is the same field predicted from the use of Reilly's law.

These fields predicted from the demand-constrained shopping model are fairly obvious from the present line of argument, but seen in perspective the result concerning the producer fields is startling. Huff (1963) introduced the demand-constrained shopping model as a replacement for Reilly's law, and he argued that the model was in every sense superior. However, the model is quite consistent with Reilly's law, and had Reilly used Huff's model his results would have been the same. Most applications of shopping models, at least in the United Kingdom, have used inverse power functions and the constraints based on Huff's model in equation (61) (Batty and Saether, 1972), and the implication is that use of Reilly's law in all these case studies would have provided results quite consistent with those actually obtained. Indeed the test made by McLoughlin et al (1966) of Reilly's law which used the Huff model was bound to yield consistent results, and their point that "the close similarities in the results seem to be mutually reinforcing: the divergencies can be explained by differences in approach and working assumptions", seems obvious in the light of the present analysis. On the other hand had the widely used model been destination- (supply-) rather than origin-constrained, the derived producer field would have been based on competition between centres; and this would have produced results different and perhaps more relevant than those produced using Reilly's law or the demand-constrained model. This model will not be stated formally here. It is included in table 1 which is a summary of the various results in this paper for the family of models. In any case the logic used should now be sufficiently clear for the reader to anticipate its form.

Finally some evaluation should be made of the various models developed here for breakpoint analysis. The general implication is that the doubly constrained model is preferable in that this type of model is usually applied to a situation which must be regarded as being in demand–supply equilibrium. Unless there are good reasons for assuming that a central-place system is demand- or supply-orientated, the doubly constrained model is more useful

Table 1 Breakpoints associated with a family of gravity models and two types of deterrence function.

Type of model and field	Deterrence function	
	negative-exponential function:	*inverse power function:*
	$c_{ij} = \frac{1}{2}\left[c_{jk} + \frac{1}{\beta}(\lambda_k - \lambda_j)\right]$	$d_{ij} = d_{jk}\bigg/\left\{1 + \exp\left[\frac{1}{\beta}(\lambda_j - \lambda_k)\right]\right\}$
	$\tilde{c}_{ij} = \frac{1}{2}\left[\tilde{c}_{il} + \frac{1}{\beta}(\mu_l - \mu_i)\right]$	$\tilde{d}_{ij} = \tilde{d}_{il}\bigg/\left\{1 + \exp\left[\frac{1}{\beta}(\mu_i - \mu_l)\right]\right\}$
Unconstrained model		
producer field	$c_{ij} = \frac{1}{2}\left[c_{jk} + \frac{1}{\beta}\ln\left(\frac{D_j}{D_k}\right)\right]$	$d_{ij} = d_{jk}\bigg/\left[1 + \left(\frac{D_k}{D_j}\right)^{1/\beta}\right]$
consumer field	$\tilde{c}_{ij} = \frac{1}{2}\left[\tilde{c}_{il} + \frac{1}{\beta}\ln\left(\frac{O_i}{O_l}\right)\right]$	$\tilde{d}_{ij} = \tilde{d}_{il}\bigg/\left[1 + \left(\frac{O_l}{O_i}\right)^{1/\beta}\right]$
Origin-constrained model		
producer field	$c_{ij} = \frac{1}{2}\left[c_{jk} + \frac{1}{\beta}\ln\left(\frac{D_j}{D_k}\right)\right]$	$d_{ij} = d_{jk}\bigg/\left[1 + \left(\frac{D_k}{D_j}\right)^{1/\beta}\right]$
consumer field	$\tilde{c}_{ij} = \frac{1}{2}\left[\tilde{c}_{il} + \frac{1}{\beta}\ln\left(\frac{O_i A_i}{O_l A_l}\right)\right]$	$\tilde{d}_{ij} = \tilde{d}_{il}\bigg/\left[1 + \left(\frac{O_l A_l}{O_i A_i}\right)^{1/\beta}\right]$
Destination-constrained model		
producer field	$c_{ij} = \frac{1}{2}\left[c_{jk} + \frac{1}{\beta}\ln\left(\frac{D_j B_j}{D_k B_k}\right)\right]$	$d_{ij} = d_{jk}\bigg/\left[1 + \left(\frac{D_k B_k}{D_j B_j}\right)^{1/\beta}\right]$
consumer field	$\tilde{c}_{ij} = \frac{1}{2}\left[\tilde{c}_{il} + \frac{1}{\beta}\ln\left(\frac{O_i}{O_l}\right)\right]$	$\tilde{d}_{ij} = \tilde{d}_{il}\bigg/\left[1 + \left(\frac{O_l}{O_i}\right)^{1/\beta}\right]$
Doubly constrained model		
producer field	$c_{ij} = \frac{1}{2}\left[c_{jk} + \frac{1}{\beta}\ln\left(\frac{D_j}{D_k}\right)\right]$	$d_{ij} = d_{jk}\bigg/\left[1 + \left(\frac{D_k B_k}{D_j B_j}\right)^{1/\beta}\right]$
consumer field	$\tilde{c}_{ij} = \frac{1}{2}\left[\tilde{c}_{il} + \frac{1}{\beta}\ln\left(\frac{O_i A_i}{O_l A_l}\right)\right]$	$\tilde{d}_{ij} = \tilde{d}_{il}\bigg/\left[1 + \left(\frac{O_l A_l}{O_i A_i}\right)^{1/\beta}\right]$

for descriptive purposes, and this certainly extends to breakpoint analysis. The theme of this argument is more dubious if these models are to be used in forecasting, for then the picture changes, although another question of the suitability of these models in dynamics emerges. These notions are beyond the scope of this paper despite their importance and despite the need to explore the conditions under which each member of the family should be applied. To summarise these ideas, table 1 presents the various forms of model associated with each member of the family both for negative-exponential functions and inverse power functions, thus illuminating the contrast between Reilly's original work and the reformulation attempted here.

A speculation: on price differentials and interaction winds

Before the ideas of this paper are illustrated by some empirical work, it is worth speculating on the spatial form of this type of market-area analysis. Apart from the fact that the central-place hierarchy must be known in advance to use Reilly's law, the basic difficulty with the law is that it is based on a model which is symmetrical with respect to origins and destinations. The model generates identical flows from origins to destinations and vice versa: that is, if $O_j = P_j$ and $D_k = P_k$, then $T_{jk} = T_{kj}$ when it is assumed that distance is also symmetrical, $d_{jk} = d_{kj}$, which is normally the case. This problem is also clear from market-area analysis, which demonstrates that the consumer and producer fields coincide if this kind of symmetry is assumed. This problem of symmetry arises in another context, and it is of interest to explore this question for the results produced here might apply to this related problem. It is often required to build a model, based on gravitational principles, in which distances rather than trip interactions are to be predicted. For example it is possible to invert a gravity model to predict 'unknown' distances from known trips T_{jk}^*. The problem of symmetry arises immediately; in general, trips are asymmetrical in that $T_{jk}^* \neq T_{kj}^*$, thus the distances predicted show the same asymmetry $d_{jk} \neq d_{kj}$. However, by assumption it is required that $d_{jk} = d_{kj}$, and thus symmetrical models must be modified to enable this kind of prediction to be made. The problem is of critical importance in the geobotanical distance predictions made by Tobler et al (1970) and in the archaeological-site location problem studied by Tobler and Wineburg (1971).

Tobler (1975; 1976) has developed a method to handle this difficulty, and it is worth demonstrating this for the geobotanical distance problem which he and his colleagues have studied. The model used by Tobler et al (1970) in their study of plant migration in the New Zealand islands can be stated as

$$T_{jk} = K(P_j + P_k) \exp(-\beta d_{jk}), \tag{65}$$

where K is a scaling constant and the other variables are as defined previously. Note, however, that β, although a parameter interpretable as a freight rate or travel cost, does not have quite the same formal role as developed previously. Distances can be predicted, if known trips T_{jk}^* are available, by inverting equation (65) to yield

$$d_{jk} = \frac{1}{\beta} \ln \left[\frac{K(P_j + P_k)}{T_{jk}^*} \right], \tag{66}$$

where it is clear that in general $d_{jk} \neq d_{kj}$. To resolve this problem, Tobler (1975; 1976) introduced a directional effect, ρ_{jk}, which he calls an 'interaction wind' or current. This variable modifies the symmetric interaction by introducing an element of asymmetry, and Tobler argues that as ρ_{jk} increases, the flow T_{jk} must also increase, thus in the model it has the opposite effect to distance. Moreover Tobler requires that $\rho_{jk} = -\rho_{kj}$, which is a reasonable assumption in that a characteristic of the original symmetry in the model is preserved. The model of equation (65) can now be stated as

$$T_{jk} = K(P_j + P_k) \exp\left(\frac{-\beta d_{jk}}{r + \rho_{jk}}\right). \tag{67}$$

Note that r is a factor which introduces a positive displacement from the origin for ρ_{jk} and which might be required to ensure correct dimensionality.

The use of the same kind of logic in terms of distance inversion as that displayed above enables one to solve for ρ_{jk} in the following way. Equation (66) now becomes

$$\frac{d_{jk}}{r + \rho_{jk}} = \frac{1}{\beta} \ln\left[\frac{K(P_j + P_k)}{T^*_{jk}}\right], \tag{68}$$

and for the modified distance effect for the direction kj the equation analogous to (68) is

$$\frac{d_{kj}}{r + \rho_{kj}} = \frac{d_{jk}}{r - \rho_{jk}} = \frac{1}{\beta} \ln\left[\frac{K(P_j + P_k)}{T^*_{kj}}\right], \tag{69}$$

where the definitions $d_{kj} = d_{jk}$ and $\rho_{kj} = -\rho_{jk}$ have been used. From equations (68) and (69) it is possible to solve directly for ρ_{jk}, and the solution can be stated as

$$\begin{aligned}
\rho_{jk} &= r\left\{\frac{\ln T^*_{jk} - \ln T^*_{kj}}{2 \ln [K(P_j + P_k)] - \ln T^*_{jk} - \ln T^*_{kj}}\right\} \\
&= r\left\{\ln\left(\frac{T^*_{jk}}{T^*_{kj}}\right) \Big/ \ln\left(\frac{[K(P_j + P_k)]^2}{T^*_{jk} T^*_{kj}}\right)\right\}. \tag{70}
\end{aligned}$$

Without loss of generality, r can be set equal to some constant, say unity, by "a convenient choice of units" (Tobler, 1975). The concept of an interaction wind or current is a measure of the orientation of the spatial system over and above the pure effects of mass/size and distance. The value of ρ_{jk} is directly correlated with that of T^*_{jk}: that is, as T^*_{jk} increases so does ρ_{jk}. Furthermore the set $\{\rho_{jk}\}$ forms a force field based on forces other than gravitation, and associated with such a field is a vector potential. Tobler suggests forming the potential ρ_j from

$$\rho_j = \sum_{\substack{k=1 \\ k \neq j}}^{m} \frac{\rho_{jk}}{m-1}, \tag{71}$$

and ρ_j, suitably expressed in coordinate form as a direction vector, gives a summary of the strength of the force field at that location. Tobler's (1975) analysis then proceeds to explain the patterns associated with such potentials.

On a very general level it can be argued that the asymmetry associated with interaction is caused by spatial competition which in turn originates from the constraints imposed by the equilibrium. Thus the current ρ_{jk} could be seen as a function of differences in the accessibilities of different places. The speculation advanced here is that ρ_{jk} is proportional to the price differential $\lambda_k - \lambda_j$ which is a measure of difference in the competitive position of different suppliers in the supply-constrained gravity model. This is a particularly bold speculation which demands to be clarified immediately, for at face value the link between symmetric and asymmetric gravity models with which ρ_{jk} and $\lambda_k - \lambda_j$ are associated seems obscure. Symmetric gravity models imply that interaction takes place between like activities in different locations, whereas asymmetric models relate unlike activities. It is possible to derive such symmetric interaction by aggregating the asymmetric model over one of its activities. Thus symmetric models can be interpreted as interaction models at a higher level of sectoral aggregation, in that interaction takes place between similar activities but through the medium of other activities. For example, commodity flows between like industries could be derived by aggregating commodity flows between unlike industries. Linkages between retailers might thus be seen as a function of demand from consumers, and so on. In literal terms the flow between two suppliers j and k might then be taken as $T_{jk} = \sum_j T_{ij} + \sum_i T_{ik} = D_j + D_k = P_j + P_k$ (by use of previous definitions). However, it is likely that a deterrent effect would also operate on such higher level interaction, and thus the flow T_{jk} would be modulated by a function such as $\exp(-\beta d_{jk})$ or in this context $\exp[-\beta d_{jk}/(r + \rho_{jk})]$. It is clear that this analysis yields the symmetric model used by Tobler et al (1970), either in its unmodified form [equation (65)] or modified form [equation (67)]. The speculation that ρ_{jk} is related to the difference in competitive advantage of j and k measured by $\lambda_k - \lambda_j$ in the asymmetric model clearly has some basis in the logic of this argument.

To give some substance to these ideas, assume that ρ_{jk} is hypothesised as

$$\rho_{jk} = \frac{1}{\beta}(\lambda_k - \lambda_j) = c_{ij} - c_{ik}, \quad \forall_i, \tag{72}$$

or as the difference in prices expressed as the difference in radial distance between the market areas associated with j and k. Note that the β parameter converts prices into units of distance, and that the desired symmetry in $\rho_{jk} = -\rho_{kj}$ is also a feature of the hypothesis. Thus the asymmetry in market areas computed from breakpoint equation (13) forms the basis for introducing asymmetry into the symmetric gravity model. An appropriate form for the model can be written as

$$
\begin{aligned}
T_{jk} &= K(P_j + P_k) \exp[-\beta(d_{jk} - \rho_{jk})] \\
&= K(P_j + P_k) \exp(-\beta d_{jk} + \lambda_k - \lambda_j).
\end{aligned} \tag{73}
$$

As Tobler (1975) notes, the hypothesis that ρ_{jk} depends only upon characteristics at j and k is a feature of Somermeijer's (1971) model, and it leads to a particularly interesting estimation problem. Note also in equation (73) that as the quantity ρ_{jk} is already in units of distance, no origin displacement constraint r is required, and the effect can thus be added to distance directly. If it is assumed that λ_k and λ_j are unknown then it is possible to solve for these quantities by using known flow data and from the assumption that $d_{jk} = d_{kj}$. Then from equation (73) it is clear that

$$
\lambda_k - \lambda_j = \frac{1}{2} \ln\left(\frac{T^*_{jk}}{T^*_{kj}}\right), \quad k \neq j. \tag{74}
$$

Equation (74) gives $m(m - 1)$ equations in m unknowns, and thus it is possible to estimate the values of λ_j statistically by some sort of least-squares method, say. Furthermore it would then be possible to test the hypothesis as to how close the values of λ_j predicted statistically were to those associated with the supply-constrained gravity model. From the argument advanced here, there is some justification for thinking that the values of λ_j predicted from the supply-constrained model would be useful in detecting the required asymmetry in the gravitational field. And what is more, an interpretation of their meaning in economic terms already exists.

In the manner of Tobler (1975) it is possible to construct the vector potential from the force field ρ_{jk}. However, the quantities λ_j are already in potential form as logarithms of the ratio of access to size; thus the potential ρ_j is clearly proportional to λ_j as the following equation shows:

$$
\rho_j = \sum_{\substack{k=1 \\ k \neq j}}^{m} \frac{\rho_{jk}}{m - 1} = -\frac{\lambda_j}{\beta} + \frac{1}{\beta(m - 1)} \sum_{\substack{k=1 \\ k \neq j}}^{m} \lambda_k. \tag{75}
$$

The last term on the right-hand side of equation (75) is constant. Clearly the potential ρ_j is proportional to the price λ_j converted into units of distance. Note that as λ_j is arbitrary up to an additive constant, the additional constant term is irrelevant. λ_j is the logarithm of the per-unit accessibility of place j, that is, the logarithm of the access of j divided by the activity at j. In some cases it may be necessary to omit the size effect from λ_j on the basis that this has already been included in the interaction equation. However, this is easily done and makes little difference to the argument.

Finally, as evidence of the positive effect of the ρ_{jk} field, a direction potential $\vec{\rho}_j$ can be constructed in coordinate form. Then, if the coordinates of j and k are given by (x_j, y_j) and (x_k, y_k), the direction vector $(\vec{x}_j, \vec{y}_j)$ can be computed from

$$\left. \begin{array}{l} \vec{x}_j = \dfrac{1}{n-1} \displaystyle\sum_{\substack{k=1 \\ k \neq j}}^{m} \left[\dfrac{\rho_{jk}}{d_{jk}} (x_k - x_j) + x_j \right], \quad \text{and} \\[20pt] \vec{y}_j = \dfrac{1}{n-1} \displaystyle\sum_{\substack{k=1 \\ k \neq j}}^{m} \left[\dfrac{\rho_{jk}}{d_{jk}} (y_k - y_j) + y_j \right]. \end{array} \right\} \tag{76}$$

The use of this vector field in demonstrating the orientation of the central-place system will be examined in the empirical work which now follows.

Applications: the urban hierarchy as a function of access, competition, and price differentials

A suitable conclusion to the ideas introduced in this paper as well as an essential element in taking up Reilly's challenge, involves an application of the methods presented here to an actual problem of defining the central-place system. The example to be discussed is based on the pattern of service trips in the Reading subregion as observed in 1966. The set of origin and destinations zones are in one-one correspondence, and the origin and destination activities have been defined from a suitable aggregation of the trip matrix. Twenty-three centres are identified, and it is proposed to show the differences between market areas defined using Reilly's original equations and the areas produced by application of two versions of the more general gravity model: the unconstrained and doubly constrained models. Use of the more general model enables an explicit hierarchy of centres to be derived, and specific emphasis will be placed on the market areas associated with these hierarchies and on the price differentials which are implied in their determination. Problems of constructing market areas from the breakpoint equations will be broached, and the use of Tobler's (1975) interaction winds to give some orientation to the configuration of central places also helps to explain the structure of the system. In every sense the application presented here is a caricature of a real problem: the problem is a relatively simple one for demonstrating the methods of the paper, and there are many loose ends of application still to be tried up. Nevertheless the results reported here do enable a fairly clear view to be formed of the success or otherwise of these ideas.

To emphasise the illustrative nature of the application, it is sufficient to note the difficulty in constructing market areas from breakpoint predictions. In the previous discussion it has been assumed that the breakpoint predictions are made between each pair of centres in the system. However, in none of the models presented here are the properties of the physical nature of the map of the system accounted for. In short, the breakpoints produced do not assume a planar map in which the adjacency or contiguity of centres is preserved. Thus it is not possible to construct or reconstruct a set of market areas which preserve the properties of the planar map from the breakpoint equations. The distances computed are necessarily inconsistent with the spatial form of the system because adjacency has nowhere been accounted for in the predictions. If it is not necessary to express the breakpoints as a map of market areas, the problem never arises, but for obvious reasons a planar map of market areas must be constructed even if it is only by way of a visual check of the results produced. Thus the contiguity or adjacency of centres comprising the map must somehow be implied. There are two ways of doing this. The first, which has been used by Tobler and Wineburg (1971), is more ambitious in that some statistical fitting and scaling technique is used to transform the set of predicted distances into a consistent set of breakpoints. The second is easier in that it is assumed that only those links between adjacent centres are used in the breakpoint analysis, thus preserving the properties of the planar map for all the predictions. Thus breakpoints are only computed for the arcs of the planar graph which form the dual of the original map. The second approach has been adopted here despite the possibility that the market areas constructed according to these assumptions might be misleading. Clearly what is really required is the use of a whole class of local map projections which transform nonplanar data into planar form in the most appropriate way. This is obviously beyond the scope of the present paper, but in the further empirical development of these ideas such techniques are essential.

The study area, its centres and their associated zones over which the point data has been collected, and the planar map and its dual are presented in figures 2(a), 2(b), and 2(c). An immediate difficulty with Reilly's law is now clear, for, in applying the law to the arcs of the graph, the set of market areas produced will have a similar spatial structure to the original set of zones. This is due to the fact that a positive breakpoint occurs on every link or arc in the graph. Moreover the simplification caused by only considering adjacent links is quite severe: some 55 links from a possible total of 253, that is, about 22% of possible links, are used in constructing the market areas. Thus 78% of information predicted by the breakpoint equations has to be disregarded. The market areas defined by using Reilly's original inverse-square

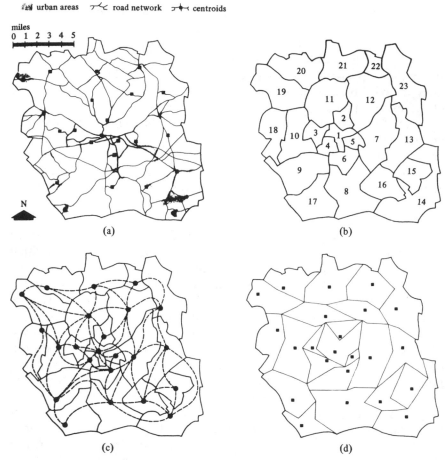

Figure 2 Centres, zones, contiguity relations, and market areas based on Reilly's law in the Reading subregion: (a) the structure of the Reading subregion; (b) the spatial units; (c) the planar graph of contiguity, and its dual; and (d) the hinterland boundaries based on Reilly's law

equation given previously as equation (8), with the populations of j and k measured by destination activity, are shown in figure 2(d). Besides all the simplifications necessary so far, the construction of these market areas involves further assumptions. It is not possible to construct convex market areas—Thiessen polygons—without omitting more breakpoint information (Haggett et al., 1977), and thus nonconvex market areas have been drawn, starting at the centre of the region, linking breakpoints directly where possible, and using vertices of already constructed polygons whose breakpoints are common to centres of the market area under construction. The map produced is by no means unique but not much visual license is necessary, and the resulting configuration appears reasonable. In figure 2(d) it is clear that the market areas associated with larger centres are larger than the original zones in figure 2(b), and the larger peripheral zones with smaller centres yield smaller market areas. The domination of Reading [1 in figure 2(b)] is also clear, but the fact that the market areas produced are so much based on the original planer map is incontrovertible evidence that Reilly's law is limited empirically as well as theoretically.

The reformulated breakpoint equation associated with the more general gravity model and given previously in equation (13) is slightly easier to interpret than the original Reilly breakpoint equation. The initial stage in the analysis relates to inferring the hierarchy from the set of predicted distances: this hierarchy can be handled in the first instance as a tree, or as a lattice of overlapping trees, and thus it is possible to generate some analysis prior to the construction of market areas. The two models applied—unconstrained and doubly constrained—had to be calibrated to yield appropriate values of the Lagrangian multipliers which would reflect constraints on the models' structures. The β parameter was calculated by use of a search by golden section over a predetermined range of parameter values (Batty, 1976), and in the case of the doubly constrained model this search was nested within a Furness procedure which yielded the values of μ_i and λ_j used to effect the origin and destination constraints. The values of β computed from the calibration were 0·0339 for the unconstrained model and 0·0522 for the constrained model. The lower the value of β the greater the amount of travel generated by the model, and thus one would expect that there would be a greater tendency for some centres to dominate others when β was low. This is clearly seen from equation (18) where the displacement of the breakpoint from the midpoint of c_{jk} is clearly related to the value of β: that is, as β falls, the displacement increases. In the case of the unconstrained model the displacement is purely a function of the size differences between centres, whereas in the case of the doubly constrained model it is the unit-accessibility difference which determines the breakpoint.

In deriving the hierarchy from the breakpoint equations, use can be made of the fact that a set of directional relations which is formed by taking differences between certain characteristics which pertain to the elements of the set, must obey the property of transitivity. In this context, if c_{ij} is negative in equation (13) then this implies that centre k *dominates* centre j in that the market area associated with k overlaps or encircles j. In the same way, if centre j dominates some other centre l, in that the breakpoint from l towards j is negative, then by transitivity it is clear that centre k also dominates j. This is due to the fact that the set of relations is based on price differentials, and if the price differences between k and j and between j and l lead to relations of dominance then the difference between k and l must also have the same characteristic. Thus when the hierarchy is constructed these transitive relations between levels in the hierarchy can be assumed in the normal way. The construction of the hierarchy from the set of breakpoint data is particularly simple. Between any two centres j and k, if c_{jk} is negative a binary matrix is formed with the appropriate (j, k)-entry equal to 1; if c_{jk} is positive, the relevant entry is then 0. Then this matrix is summed over its columns to determine the outdegree of (the number of ones in) each row. This number gives the degree of dominance of a particular centre j. When the outdegree is 0, the centre is not dominated by any others, and the centre belongs to the highest order of the hierarchy. The next step is to delete from the binary matrix the relevant rows and columns pertaining to the highest-order centres, and to then repeat the operation of calculating outdegrees. This identifies the set of second-order centres, and the whole procedure is then iterated until all the remaining centres have outdegrees of zero. This then forms the lowest level of the hierarchy.

From the derived ranking of centres, the lattice is constructed as follows. The first-order centres dominate certain second-order centres, and arrows showing this domination are drawn. Then the third-order centres are considered, and arrows showing the domination of first- and second- over third-order centres are drawn unless the relation from first- to second- to third-order centre is transitive, in which case an arrow from second- to third-order centre suffices. This procedure is repeated for all lower-order centres in the hierarchy until the complete structure has been formed. Clearly with a large problem some automation might be required, and it would also be necessary to 'unravel' the resulting lattice for presentation purposes. None of this is very difficult and standard programs exist to effect it; here, however, the hierarchy is simple enough to construct by hand. The two hierarchies from the unconstrained and constrained models are shown in figures 3(a) and 3(b), and it is immediately clear that these more general models are able to predict quite distinct hierarchical structures. The structure pertaining to the unconstrained model is richer than that of the constrained, and it shows all the characteristics alluded to earlier: overlapping fields, transitive relations, and relations between nonadjacent levels of hierarchy—orders of centres. Furthermore the results obtained are intuitively acceptable: in the unconstrained problem Reading (1), Wokingham (15), and Henley (22) are first-order centres with Reading clearly dominating the region; in the doubly constrained problem Reading still dominates, Wokingham does to a lesser extent, and the peripheral centres become independent of the market area centred on Reading.

The construction of market areas associated with these hierarchical structures is, however, quite tricky. The same rules as used previously permit the construction of the market areas around first-order centres, but, when it comes to second- and lower-order centres, some data on breakpoints may have been used already to enable definition of high-order areas. In such cases an arbitrary decision has been made using the midpoint between two centres as breakpoint, and clearly this involves a little more visual license than

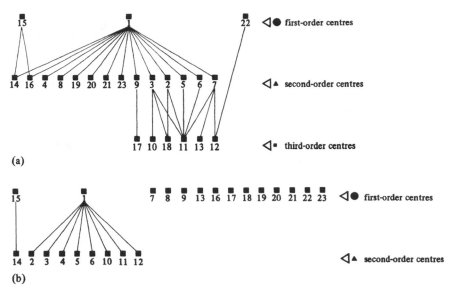

Figure 3 Hierarchies of central places associated with (a) unconstrained and (b) doubly constrained gravity models in the Reading subregion

was used before. Nevertheless the two market-area systems associated with figures 3(a) and 3(b) are shown as figures 4(a) and 4(b). Overlap makes the map of the unconstrained market-area system more difficult to read, especially as two of the second-order fields based on centres 5 and 6 are truncated. In the case of the constrained model, the first-order market areas are easier to construct. Fortunately the dominated centres are all spatially adjacent and thus the map in figure 4(b) has been constructed in exactly the same way as figure 2(d). Figure 4 also contains information relating to price differentials plotted as nondirectional and directional potentials. In figures 4(c) and 4(d) the interpolated and smoothed potential surface based on equation (75) is plotted for the unconstrained and constrained models respectively. This potential is in effect a measure of the difference between the mean price in the system, excluding the price at the given location, and the price at the given location itself. The lower the price, the greater the competitive spatial advantage, and thus the larger this potential, the greater the advantage. In face these prices are transformed into distance terms through the equations for the breakpoint [see equations (12) and (13)], and thus they reflect average breakpoint differentials. In terms of the unconstrained model these differentials are based on size, whereas in the doubly constrained model they are based on unit accessibility. The fact that lower prices imply lower per-unit accessibility and that Reading, for example, has the lowest per-unit accessibility in the system, changes the usual interpretations of accessibility. Such a

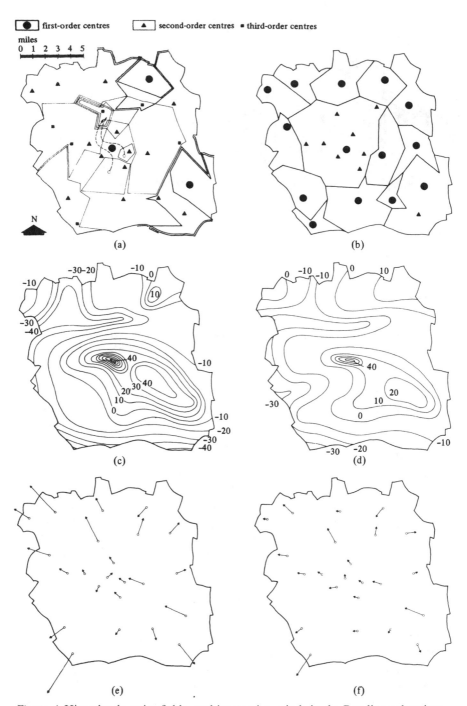

Figure 4 Hinterlands, price fields, and interaction winds in the Reading subregion: the hinterlands based on the (a) unconstrained and (b) constrained models; the fields of price differentials for the (c) unconstrained and (d) constrained models; and the interaction winds from the (e) unconstrained and (f) constrained models

point is clearly outside the scope of this paper but it is of interest in further research (Williams and Senior, 1977b).

Finally these breakpoint differentials have been plotted as directional vectors in figures 4(e) and 4(f). These are computed from equations (76) and they suggest the dominant direction of influence in the system. This is clearly from centre to periphery, apart from the southeast quadrant of the region where the influences of Reading and Wokingham considerably complicate the pattern. Of interest is the fact that the length of the vector gives some indication of the strength of the dominating force, and it is clear from this that centre 17 is the most dominated in the hierarchy Furthermore these interaction winds also reflect the asymmetry in the system over and above pure gravitational effects. A comparison of the two sets of results in figure 4 suggests that both models imply the same central-place structure in terms of hierarchy and orientation. However, the constrained model produces a less clear picture than the unconstrained, but both show the dominance of Reading, the complex pattern on the Reading–Wokingham axis, and the peripheral importance of Henley. Clearly comparisons with the market areas derived by use of Reilly's law show very different configurations which are much more intuitively and theoretical acceptable in terms of traditional central-place theory.

Conclusions

The ideas of this paper represent only a beginning in the use of gravitational model in central-place theory. This is evidenced by the richness of the empirical work of which much more could have been made, but, in the spirit of the speculative approach adopted, these refinements must be left to further research and application. Any conclusions to a paper such as this, which explicitly takes up a challenge to existing work, must attempt to evaluate whether or not the challenge has been met. In terms of Reilly's law it is clear that the generalisation and reformulation of the idea by use of the generalised gravity model is able to embrace a host of additional characteristics and to meet the law's most basic limitations: the ability to derive hierarchical structure and the relation to Hotelling's (1929) price–cost indifference equation, and the extension of the law from spatial duopoly to oligopoly through to notion of equilibrium constraints reflecting the interdependence of all centres—these are essential aspects of a relevant theory which can be tested empirically. And, what is more, the brief excursion into empirical work shows that these ideas appear to be well-founded.

Yet there are many rough edges to this research, some of which are clearly manifest from the empirical work. In particular the construction of market areas, which are necessarily planar, from nonplanar data on breakpoints is fraught with difficulties, and reveals once again the more fundamental problem that the real nature of physical space is not treated by such gravitational models. A further difficulty relates to the construction of the hierarchy: as a structure this can be derived using a straightforward technique of graph reduction, but the breakpoint equations provide too little information to map the nested and often overlapping system of market areas associated with such a structure. Yet the price theory which underlies the hierarchical interpretation of these gravitational models, although bare developed, adds a richness to this macrostatistical approach which has previously been lacking. In particular the relationships between prices and accessibilities or indices of spatial competition leads to a fascinating interpretation of the way different central places relate to one another at different levels of the hierarchy.

Traditional central-place theorists will surely object to this 'macro' approach, with its emphasis on size, access, and distance as the major determinants of hierarchy, but objections that this theory fails to get to grips with the differentiation of the product traded at different centres might be met by disaggregation of the models used here. Such disaggregation is a highly developed aspect of modern spatial-interaction theory (Wilson, 1970), and, although not necessarily leading to greater theoretical insights, it can provide interesting notions about the competitiveness of different products and centres in space. Moreover it is not intended in any way that the ideas produced here should replace any part of central-place theory; indeed the notions appear to complement traditional theory. Nevertheless one can draw from this analysis some useful conclusions which extend traditional ideas. The notion of a strict hierarchy and its generalisation to a continuum, which has dominated the theory for many years, seems limited: empirical work reveals that overlapping trade areas are likely to be the rule rather than the exception, and that certain centres might take on different orders when associated with different centres and market areas in the system. These ideas are quite consistent with the arguments outlined in this paper.

One final note of caution seems appropriate. In attempting to meet Reilly's challenge, the necessary starting point has been gravitational models of social systems, and the general limitations of such models are well-known; it is only possible to go so far with such approaches, and the somewhat speculative nature of this argument reinforces the point. However, it does appear that gravitational models and central-place theory, which have been close in spirit but apart in theory and practice for so long, might converge through recent developments in spatial-interaction theory. It is hoped that the speculations advanced here might contribute a little to this wider goal.

References

Anderson T R, 1955 "Inter metropolitan migration: a comparison of the hypotheses of Zipf and Stouffer" *American Sociological Review* **20** 287–291

Balinski M L, Baumol W, 1968 "The dual in nonlinear programming and its economic interpretation" *Review of Economic Studies* **35** 237–256

Batty M, 1976 *Urban Modelling: Algorithms, Calibrations, Predictions* (Cambridge University Press, Cambridge)

Batty M, March L, 1976 "The method of residues in urban modelling" *Environment and Planning A* **8** 189–214

Batty M, Saether A, 1972 "A note on the design of shopping models" *Journal of the Royal Town Planning Institute* **58** 303–306

Beavon K S O, 1977 *Central Place Theory: A Reinterpretation* (Longman Group, London)

Beckmann M J, 1974 "Entropy, gravity and utility in transportation modelling" in *Information, Inference and Decision* Ed. G Menges (D Reidel, Dordrecht, Holland)

Coelho J D, Wilson A G, 1976 "The optimum location and size of shopping centres" *Regional Studies* **10** 413–421

Converse P D, 1949 "New laws of retail gravitation" *Journal of Marketing* **14** 379–384

Erlander S, 1977a "Accessibility, entropy and the distribution and assignment of traffic" *Transportation Research* **11** 149–153

Erlander S, 1977b "Entropy in linear programs: an approach to planning" report LiTH-MAT-R-77-3, Department of Mathematics, Linköping University, Linköping, Sweden

Evans S P, 1973 "Some applications of optimization theory in transport planning" unpublished Ph D thesis, Research Group in Traffic Studies, University College London, London

Fetter F A, 1924 "The economic law of market areas" *Quarterly Journal of Economics* **38** 520–529

Hägerstrand T, 1967 *Innovation Diffusion as a Spatial Process* (University of Chicago Press, Chicago, Ill.) translated from the original published in 1953

Haggett P, Cliff A, Frey A, 1977 *Locational Methods* (Edward Arnold, London)

Hotelling H, 1929 "Stability in competition" *Economic Journal* **39** 41–57

Huff D L, 1963 "A probabilistic analysis of shopping center trade areas" *Land Economics* **39** 81–90

Huff D L, 1964 "Defining and estimating a trading area" *Journal of Marketing* **28** 34–38

Hyson C D, Hyson W P, 1950 "The economic law of market areas" *Quarterly Journal of Economics* **64** 319–324

Intriligator M D, 1971 *Mathematical Optimization and Economic Theory* (Prentice-Hall, Englewood Cliffs, NJ)

Isard W, 1956 *Location and Space Economy* (MIT Press, Cambridge, Mass)

Kantorowich R H (Ed.), 1964 "Regional shopping centres in North West England" Department of Town and Country Planning, University of Manchester, Manchester

Kullback S, 1959 *Information Theory and Statistics* (John Wiley, New York)

Lakshmanan T R, Hansen W G, 1965 "A retail market potential model" *Journal of the American Institute of Planners* **31** 134–143

Lösch A, 1954 *The Economics of Location* (Yale University Press, New Haven, Conn.) translated from the original published in 1940

McLoughlin J B, Foot D H S, Nix C K, 1966 "Regional shopping centres in North West England. Part 2: a retail shopping model" Department of Town and Country Planning, University of Manchester, Manchester

March L, 1971 "Urban systems: a generalised distribution function" in *London Papers in Regional Science 2: Urban and Regional Planning* Ed. A G Wilson (Pion, London) pp 157–170

Neuberger H, 1971 "User benefit in the evaluation of transport and land use plans" *Journal of Transport Economics and Policy* **5** 52–75

Reilly W J, 1931 *The Law of Retail Gravitation* (Pilsbury, New York), republished in 1953

Schneider M, 1959 "Gravity models and trip distribution theory" *Papers and Proceedings of the Regional Science Association* **5** 51–56

Senior M L, Wilson A G, 1974 "Explorations and syntheses of linear programming and spatial interaction models of residential location" *Geographical Analysis* **6** 209–237

Somermeijer W, 1971 "Multi-polar human flow models" *Papers of the Regional Science Association* **26** 131–144

Strohkarch F, Phelps K, 1948 "The mechanics of constructing a market area map" *Journal of Marketing* **13** 493–496

Styles B J, 1969 "Principles and historical development of the gravity model" in *Gravity Models in Town Planning* Eds R L Davies, B J Styles, Lanchester Polytechnic, Coventry, England

Tanner J C, 1961 *Factors Affecting the Amount of Travel* TP-51, Road Research Laboratory (HMSO, London)

Theil H, 1972 *Statistical Decomposition Analysis* (North-Holland, Amsterdam)

Tobler W, 1975 "Spatial interaction patterns" report RR-75-19, International Institute for Applied Systems Analysis, Laxenburg, Austria

Tobler W, 1976 "Spatial interaction patterns" *Journal of Environmental Systems* **6** 271–301

Tobler W, Mielke H, Detwyler T, 1970 "Geobotanical distance between New Zealand and neighboring islands" *Bioscience* **20** 537–542

Tobler W, Wineburg S, 1971 "A Cappadocian speculation" *Nature (London)* **231** 39–42

Williams H C W L, Senior M L, 1977a "A retail location model with overlapping market areas: Hotelling's problem revisited" *Urban Studies* **14** 203–205

Williams H C W L, Senior M L, 1977b "Accessibility, spatial interaction and the evaluation of land use–transportation plans" paper presented at the International Conference of Spatial Interaction Theory and Planning Models, Basted, Sweden

Wilson A G, 1970 *Entropy in Urban and Regional Modelling* (Pion, London)

Wilson A G, Senior M L, 1974 "Some relationships between entropy maximizing models, mathematical programming models, and their duals" *Journal of Regional Science* **14** 207–215

20

Retail location theory – the legacy of Harold Hotelling

Stephen Brown

Source: *Journal of Retailing* 65(4) (1989): 450–470.

Sixty years ago Harold Hotelling's seminal paper, "Stability in Competition," was published in The Economic Journal. *Known to generations of students as the locational problem faced by ice-cream vendors on a beach, Hotelling's "principle of minimum differentiation" has generated a prodigious amount of academic research. This paper reviews Hotelling's much criticized conceptualization and explores alternative theoretical explanations of the agglomeration of similar retail firms. It also examines the extent to which the principle of minimum differentiation has stood the test of time and assesses both Hotelling's contribution to retail location theory and the likely direction of future research activity.*

Introduction

It has often been said that the three most important properties of a retail store are location, location, and location (Dickinson 1981; Jones and Simmons 1987). Like most of retailing's aphorisms, this is not entirely true; all sorts of other factors besides location influence the success or failure of retail outlets (Davidson et al. 1988; Mason and Mayer 1987). Location, nevertheless, is crucial. As Ghosh and McLafferty (1987) point out,

> It is through the location that goods and services are made available to potential customers. Good locations allow ready access, attract large numbers of customers, and increase the potential sales of retail outlets. In the extremely competitive retail environment, even slight differences in location can have a significant impact on the market share and profitability. Most importantly, since store location is a long-term fixed investment, the disadvantages of a poor location are difficult to overcome.

Given its significance, the issue of retail location has generated a prodigious amount of academic contemplation, conceptualization, and indeed contention (for a review see Craig et al. 1984; Wrigley 1988). Central place theory, bid rent theory, and "the law of retail gravitation" are perhaps the most familiar theoretical contributions, but equally important is Harold Hotelling's (1929) "principle of minimum differentiation." Known to generations of students as the problem of ice-cream vendors that contrive to cluster together in the center of a beach, the principle of minimum differentiation provides a simple and easily remembered illustration of the agglomerative bent of similar retail firms. The department stores of Boulevard Haussmann in Paris, the outfitters of London's Oxford Street, the electrical retailers of Akihabara in Tokyo, and the theaters and cinemas of Broadway are among the better known examples of this phenomenon. But the clustering of similar outlets is a truly universal trait, ranging from the hamburger alleys and automobile rows of most American cities to the pronounced clusters of goldsmiths and banana sellers in the periodic markets of the third world.

Although the principle of minimum differentiation is widely and irrevocably associated with the agglomeration of retail outlets in general and jostling ice-cream vendors in particular, the reality of the concept—as originally formulated and subsequently developed—is quite different from the popular myth. Apart from the fact that Hotelling never mentioned ice-cream vendors or allowed his sellers to leap-frog each other in order to capture the prime, central locations in the market, his seminal study was *not even addressing the issue of retailing location*, incredible though this now seems.

Given the widespread misconceptions about the principle of minimum differentiation; the recent and dramatic revival of interest in the concept among economists; and, perhaps most appropriately, the fact that this year is the sixtieth anniversary of the publication of Hotelling's original paper, it is arguable that the time is now ripe for an examination of his regularly referenced but rarely read contribution to retailing thought. Accordingly, this paper will review, in a nontechnical fashion, the often highly technical literature on the principle of minimum differentiation, noting that contrary to popular perception, the concept does not in fact explain the agglomeration of similar retail firms. The paper then goes on to examine the alternative theoretical approaches to the clustering phenomenon and describes some of the important conceptual advances that have taken place as a result of the introduction of agglomeration economies, uncertainty reduction, and multipurpose shopping behavior. Finally, the paper will endeavor to assess both Hotelling's contribution to location theory and identify some potentially fruitful avenues of future research activity.

Stability in Competition

In his classic paper "Stability in Competition," Harold Hotelling was, as noted above, not directly concerned with retail location. He was actually trying to show that price stability was possible in the case of two-firm competition (duopoly) without resort to collusion. The then received wisdom from Cournot (1897), Bertrand (1883), Edgeworth (1925), and others, maintained that as all buyers patronize the cheapest seller, a price cut by one firm would capture the entire (spaceless) market. This gives rise to price instability as the competitors undercut each other, except of course when prices are driven down to cost.

Hotelling, however, challenged this view, arguing that in practice a price cut by one firm would only result in the loss of a few customers to the other, because many purchasers prefer to do business with a supplier despite small differences in prices. These preferences, he contended, stem from a variety of factors including the sellers' respective standards of in-store service, merchandise mix, quality of goods, methods of doing business, and even the religious or political persuasions of both seller and buyer. Most importantly for the model that he went on to develop and, indeed, for subsequent spatial analysis, customer behavior was held to be influenced by the cost of transportation and the relative locations of purchaser and purveyor.

Dealing initially with two profit maximizing firms, selling identical products (with zero production costs) at f.o.b. prices, from *fixed locations* in a bounded linear market where transport rates are constant, demand is completely inelastic and identical, utility maximizing consumers are evenly distributed, bear the costs of distribution, and patronize outlets solely on the basis of delivered prices, Hotelling showed that an equilibrium existed where neither outlet could increase profits by altering its prices.

Having thus demonstrated price stability in noncollusive, duopolistic competition, albeit under highly restrictive assumptions, he argued that if *one* seller is free to relocate, it would maximize its hinterland (and hence its profits) by setting up shop adjacent to the other on the "long" side of the market. If, as Chamberlin (1933) subsequently noted, both sellers are footloose, a process of mutual leap-frogging to the longer side of the market ensues. The upshot of this is the classical back-to-back arrangement in the center of the market, not the socially optimum pattern of two spatially dispersed firms at the market's quartiles.

There is more to the principle of minimum differentiation, however, than the agglomeration of duopolists in the center of a bounded linear market under conditions of inelastic demand and uniform population density. Elaborating his finding, Hotelling (1929) maintained that the clustering phenomenon is discernible on a plane as well as a linear market and could be established when consumers are unevenly distributed. What is more, it holds good when more than two sellers are involved and it also helps explain the standardization of most aspects of daily life including furniture design, house styles, fashion trends, education systems, and the policies of political parties. It is, in short,

> a principle of the utmost generality. It explains why all the dime stores are
> usually clustered together, often next door to each other; why certain

towns attract large numbers of firms of one kind; why an industry, such as the garment industry, will concentrate in one quarter of a city. It is a principle which can be carried over into other differences than spatial differences. The general rule for any new manufacturer coming into an industry is, "Make your product as like the existing products as you can without destroying the differences." It explains why all automobiles are so much alike and tend to get even more alike . . . It explains the importance of brand names in commercial, social, and even religious life . . . and . . . it also explains the importance of advertising, for a great part of advertising is little more than an attempt to establish a brand name in the minds of the public (Boulding 1966).

Subsequent research

Elaborations of the principle of minimum differentiation

Since Hotelling's pioneering contribution, the principle of minimum differentiation has generated a considerable amount of research effort, which, broadly speaking, can be divided into three categories. The first involves the examination of the universality of the conceptualization. It has been applied, with varying degrees of success, to television programming (Steiner 1961; Webster and Wakshlag 1983), the electoral process (Downs 1957; Wittman 1983; Enelow and Hinich 1984; Osborne and Pitchik 1986; Ginsberg et al. 1987), department store retailing (Nielsen 1966; Goldman 1975, 1978), transportation provision (Evans 1987; Foster and Golay 1986), fiscal policy (Lindbeck and Weibull 1987), the study of labor markets and wage rates (Schulz and Stahl 1985; Nakagome 1986) and, from a marketing standpoint, perhaps most importantly, to new product development and product positioning strategies (Dixit and Stiglitz 1977; Shaked and Sutton 1982; Bonanno 1987). Empirical examples of the last named include Swann's (1985) study of the microprocessor industry and Shaw's (1982) analysis of UK fertilizer manufacturing, though the bulk of this work is theoretical (Eaton and Kierzkowski 1984; Paloff and Salop 1985; Eaton and Grossman 1986).

The second extension of the principle of minimum differentiation concerns Hotelling's original point of departure, the application of classical price theory in space and, in particular, with conjectual variations in competitive pricing (see for example, Hobbs 1986; Ohta 1980, 1981; Nelson and McCarl 1984; Macleod et al. 1987). Implicit in the Hotelling model is an assumption of zero conjectural variation; in other words, that the competitors set prices without reference to each other and that when one alters its prices the others refrain from retaliatory action. Alternative conjectures, however, include the Loschian, where all firms price identically and if one makes an adjustment the others match it; the Greenhut–Ohta, wherein pricing is discriminatory and action by one competitor results in an equal and opposite reaction from its rivals; and the Stackelbergian, where a dominant competitor acts as price leader and the others follow suit (Losch 1954; Greenhut and Ohta 1975; Von Stackelberg 1952). Much of the recent research (and vigorous debate) in this area surrounds the short and long-term ramifications of these price conjectures, or combinations thereof, and the intractable question of whether spatial pricing in competitive circumstances gives rise to higher or lower prices than under monopoly conditions (Capozza and Van Order 1977, 1978; Treble 1980; Norman 1981; Spulber 1984; Watson 1985; Anderson 1987; Fik 1988).

The third and, from a retailing perspective, perhaps the most significant development of the principle of minimum differentiation involves the location of economic activities in space and, in this respect, the research record has not been kind to Hotelling's conceptualization, nor indeed to his extensions of the principle. Chamberlin (1933), for example, challenged Hotelling's suggestion that a third seller would locate next to the first two in the center of the market. To do so would deprive the centrally located supplier of its hinterland and thus initiate an unstable leap-frogging process as each competitor attempts to capture the prime exterior sites. Given Hotelling's assumptions, Chamberlin argued, the introduction of a third firm results in two sellers locating at the quartiles with the other somewhere in between (see Eaton 1972; Shaked 1975, 1982). Moreover, more than three firms—and up to 256 have been examined—results not in a large, centrally located agglomeration of suppliers but, at best, a dispersed pattern of paired establishments (Lerner and Singer 1937; Eaton and Lipsey 1975; Okabe and Suzuki 1987). This phenomenon has been termed the "principle of local clustering" (Eaton and Lipsey 1975).

Likewise, extending the argument from a bounded linear market to a two-dimensional frame of reference lends scant support for Hotelling's agglomerative hypothesis. Anticipating the English translations of the works of Christaller (1966) and Losch (1954), Lewis (1945) demonstrated that given an even spread of customers in a two-dimensional market, each firm will be equidistant from its neighbors in the socially optimal center of a hexagonal market area. This result has been corroborated in a variety of alternative market shapes including a network (Wendell and McKelvey 1981; ReVelle 1986) and the circumference of a circle (Shaked 1975; Hannesson 1982), though others have argued that the propensity to cluster is determined by the length, not the shape of the market (Eaton 1972; Kohlberg and Novshek 1982).

If investigations of the number of sellers and the shape of the marketplace clearly contradict the principle of minimum differentiation, the case for an unevenly distributed population is more supportive (Chamberlin 1933; Devletoglou 1965; White 1975; Ali and Greenbaum 1977). It is generally acknowledged that Hotelling/type clustering can occur if the population is sufficiently concentrated (Shilnoy 1981; Greenhut et al. 1986; Neven 1986;

Lederer and Hurter 1986), though this, of course, does not explain the agglomeration of similar retail firms *within* shopping districts (Ghosh and McLafferty 1987).

Analysis of Hotelling's assumptions

Just as the generalizations of Hotelling's model have failed to withstand close scrutiny, so too a relaxation of its initial highly restrictive assumptions proves unfortunate for the principle of minimum differentiation. It must be said, however, Hotelling recognized that a modification of several of his assumptions, most notably that of inelastic demand, would result in a tendency towards dispersal. This point has since been demonstrated under conditions of both linear (Smithies 1941; Devletoglou 1965; Hartwick and Hartwick 1971) and rectangular demand (Lerner and Singer 1937; Gannon 1972; Economides 1984). In the case of the former, demand declines regularly with distance from the point of supply, whereas in the latter a price ceiling or reservation price is assumed to exist. Another important influence (noted again by Hotelling) on the propensity to cluster is the cost of transportation and it has been shown that when freight rates are high or are met by the seller, a dispersed pattern of outlets transpires. Alternatively, agglomeration is encouraged by low freight rates or when costs are paid by the consumer (Gannon 1973; D'Aspremont et al. 1979; Heal 1980; Ghosh 1983).

The spatial consequences of duopolistic competition also depend upon the attitudes, expectations, and behavior of the combatants. As outlined earlier, Hotelling anticipated zero conjectural variation, but a number of early investigators noted that a wide variety of reactions to the spectre of competition were possible, ranging from collusion or indifference, to tooth and nail conflict in either locational or pricing terms, or both (Zeuthen 1933; Palander 1935; Lerner and Singer 1937; Losch 1954).

With regard to location-only reactions, Gannon (1972, 1973) has shown how an aggressive response to the competitive behavior of the other participant, or simply fear of retaliation, persuades sellers to keep well apart. Complacent behavior, on the other hand, or the expectation of a subdued response encourages agglomeration. Drezner (1982), likewise, argues that if a firm is motivated by a desire to capture the trade of its competitors or, conversely, wishes to protect its existing business, the most appropriate locations are, respectively, immediately adjacent to or as far as possible from the competing firm. Furthermore, under the more realistic assumptions of fixed locational choice and free entry, it pays sellers to increase their number of outlets or products (Teitz 1968; Prescott and Visscher 1977; Salop 1979), expand production capacity (Eaton and Lipsey 1979a), or locate sufficiently far apart (Hay 1976; Hannesson 1982; Bonnano 1987) to deter the entry of competitive firms. A spatially dispersed, socially optimum pattern of retail outlets is thus the inevitable outcome (Eaton and Lipsey 1975; Rothschild 1979).

Although most investigations of the assumptions of the principle of minimum differentiation have concentrated upon location-only issues, attempts have also been made to combine locational adjustment with competitive pricing behavior. This approach to the Hotelling model considerably complicates matters however (Graitson 1982). Apart from the sheer variety of pricing options open to competitors, it has long been noted (Palander 1935; Lerner and Singer 1937) and formally demonstrated (D'Aspremont et al. 1979), that the clustering of two sellers in the center of the market is impossible under conditions of competitive pricing. Behavior simply reverts to the previously described Cournot–Bertrand scenario of instability in competition and indefinitely fluctuating prices (Beckmann and Thisse 1986).

In an attempt to circumvent this problem, a number of rules of engagement have been adopted by latter day investigators of spatial competition. These include two-stage rather than simultaneous location and pricing decisions (Carruthers 1981; Economides 1986; Neven 1985), the use of a quadratic distance function (D'Aspremont et al. 1979), the introduction of waiting time to smooth out price discontinuities (Prescott and Visscher 1977; Kohlberg 1985) and the imposition of a no-undercutting price constraint (Eaton and Lipsey 1975; Novshek 1980), though the last named, in fact, does not resolve the problem (Macleod 1985). Such manipulations, however, are largely unnecessary as, according to Webber (1974), the prices existing under zero conjectural variation turn out to be exactly the same as those made under the assumption of perfectly informed competitors with infallible foresight. Nevertheless, as a rule, the combination of competitive pricing behavior and an ability to relocate serves only to disperse the combatants once again, leading Economides (1984) to advocate the existence of a "principle of maximal differentiation."

Besides the key assumptions concerning location, pricing, transportation costs, consumer behavior, conjectural variations, market shape, and number of competitors, a host of other factors have been explored within the context of the Hotelling model (Graitson 1982). In the majority of cases these studies do not corroborate the concept of clustering, though the retailing of differentiated products—which are not therefore in direct competition—proves an important exception to the rule (Gannon 1977; Williams and Senior 1977; Kennedy and Copes 1978; DePalma et al. 1985; Gabszewicz and Thisse 1986). Despite this interesting finding, the published record hitherto has not been kind to the principle of minimum differentiation. Aside from some evidence of pairing, usually on the peripheries of the market, the bulk of studies support Eaton and Lipsey's (1979b) conclusion that,

> the Hotelling model is not able to explain the local clustering of firms
> . . . Indeed, once the assumptions are relaxed very slightly in the direction
> of realism, Hotelling's model predicts that no two firms should be clustered
> together.

Agglomeration and uncertainty

The principle of minimum differentiation and its derivatives are thus incapable of explaining the much-observed, and statistically proven (Kivell and Shaw 1980), clustering of similar retail firms, except on the very rare occasions when real-world conditions closely replicate the assumptions of the model. One such occasion was provided by the development of the western Canadian fur trade between 1787 and 1835 when two major organizations, the Hudson's Bay Company and the North West Company, competed vigorously for this new and lucrative business (Freeman and Dungey 1981). Besides the duopolistic situation, demand was effectively inelastic as Indian trappers were totally dependent upon the trading posts for European manufactured goods and had no alternative outlet for their furs. Moreover, as routeways extended along the rivers of the interior and canoe was the main mode of transport, the market was virtually linear. In their efforts to exploit this business opportunity, the rival companies not only established trading posts in very close proximity, but they also leapfrogged each other in their desire to capture potentially strategic locations. In fact, such was the rivalry, that it rapidly degenerated into violence, price cutting, and lavish gift-giving, most notably alcohol, to attract Indian custom. Order was only restored after 1821 when the two companies were merged and the network of trading posts rationalized.

Instances of the principle of minimum differentiation in action are few and far between however, and even the foregoing dramatic example could be challenger on points of detail. The fact of the matter is that Hotelling's conceptualization, as originally presented and subsequently developed, has little explanatory power and, arguably, should be excised from retailing's theoretical canon, at least in its initial form.

The principal reason for the failure of the principle of minimum differentiation is the simple fact that it is predicated upon essentially negative premises —that clustering is socially wasteful and bad for business, whether through collusion or destructive competition in both locational and pricing terms. The concept thus fails to recognize the existence of agglomeration economies, the *positive* externalities or cost reducing benefits that flow from spatial propinquity (see Isard 1956; Papageorgiou 1979; Mulligan 1984a). It is increasingly acknowledged, however, that agglomeration does more than simply reduce the cost of doing business through intra-center economies of shared car parking, lighting, security services, maintenance, advertising and promotion; it also provides an all-important means of uncertainty reduction (Pascall and McCall 1980; Goldstein and Gronberg 1984; Daniels 1985). Indeed, this re-laxation of the traditional assumption of perfectly informed—and thus completely certain—decision makers has provided a major fillip for the models of spatial competition and a means of resurrecting the principle of minimum differentiation (Papageorgiou and Thisse 1985; DePalma et al. 1985, 1987).

The earliest attempts to introduce uncertainty into spatial competition employed the concepts of game theory wherein simultaneous location decisions are made by competitors who are unaware of the others' behavior but are nonetheless rational, profit-maximizing, fully informed, and capable of calculating precisely the outcomes of their actions (Isard 1956; Stevens 1961). Such assumptions, as Simon (1959) points at, require reasoning powers even more fantastic than those of economic man; despite recent advances, most notably in scenario planning (see for example Ghosh and Craig 1983, 1984, 1986; Ghosh and McLafferty 1982) and the not infrequent casting of spatial competition problems in game theoretic terms (Shaked 1982; Economides 1986; Hurter and Lederer 1985), even its strongest advocates acknowledge that game theory is difficult to adapt to real-world situations (Eliasberg and Chatterjee 1985; Moorthy 1985). After all, many real-world retail locational decisions are made on the basis of intuition, hunch, or rudimentary rules of thumb, all of which are characterized by imperfect information and high levels of uncertainty (Guy 1980; Rogers 1987).

By introducing uncertainty and risk reducing behavior into the Hotelling problem and realistically assuming a once-and-for-all locational choice, Webber (1972) has shown that the inevitable outcome is an agglomeration of sellers at the center of the market. What is more, this conclusion holds good when the initial assumptions of homogeneous market, duopolistic competition, inelastic demand, no economies of scale and so on, are relaxed, though the rigor and methodology of Webber's analysis has since been called into question (Dean and Carroll 1977; Mai 1981, 1984). Agglomeration, however, is not simply a least-risk reaction to competitive threat. On the contrary, the existence of a seller successfully exploiting a specific site serves notice to others that market potential exists at that location (Stahl and Variana 1978; Brown 1979). Imperfectly informed firms are thus drawn to locations where their rivals appear to thrive, or as Pascall and McCall (1980) put it.

> adrift in a sea of uncertainty, what could be more logical than heading towards those islands which have demonstrably provided salvation to similar and earlier swimmers.

Agglomeration, furthermore, is socially beneficial in that it reduces the travel and search costs of imperfectly informed consumers (McLafferty and Ghosh 1987). Indeed, consumers' attempts to reduce uncertainty through information search have attracted considerable attention from economic modellers (Lippman and McCall 1979, 1981). Several scholars have shown that when consumers are uncertain and consequently prone to acquire information about prevailing prices, quality, and variety of goods, it pays retailers of the same type to locate in close proximity (Stuart 1979; Stahl 1982a, 1982b; Gabszewicz and Garella 1986, 1987).

Uncertainty reduction through comparison shopping behavior has been under empirical investigation for many years (Katona and Mueller 1954;

Nelson 1958; Newman 1977; Brown 1988), though Eaton and Lipsey (1979b) were the first to introduce it formally into the Hotelling model. By (exogeneously) imposing the constraint that consumers visit two stores before making a purchase, they showed how multi-outlet clusters of similar firms emerge and, moreover, that profits are much greater in agglomerated than isolated locations. The increase in competition that results from spatial proximity is more than offset by the additional demand that agglomeration generates (Wolinsky 1982). The propensity to agglomerate, however, is heavily influenced by the variability of consumer demand. In other words, retailers of goods with highly variable demand (for example, antiques) are very likely to cluster together, whereas sellers of merchandise of predictable and therefore less uncertain demand are more likely to be driven apart (for example, grocery stores). The model, in short, captures reality (Kivell and Shaw 1980).

Evaluation, extensions, and future research

By introducing uncertainty reduction through comparison shopping into the Hotelling model and stressing the positive side of retail agglomeration, recent developments in spatial competition theory have done much to revitalize the principle of minimum differentiation. Indeed, the models are not only more realistic than hitherto, but they are compatible with inductively derived generalizations like Nelson's (1958) much vaunted "theory of cumulative attraction." It would appear that after decades of scholarly stricture, the principle of minimum differentiation has been restored to its rightful place as a milestone in retail location theory.

Seminal though it is, Hotelling's model only addresses one aspect of agglomeration, the clustering of similar retail firms, be they department stores, burger bars, ice-cream vendors or whatever. Most shopping districts, however, are characterized not only by clusters of similar retail outlets, but by a congeries of stores selling dissimilar products. In fact, this shortcoming of the principle of minimum differentiation was highlighted in one of the earliest critiques of the Hotelling model. Having noted that stores selling similar products tend to group in order that people might shop, Chamberlin (1933) argued that,

> stores of quite different types cluster together so that buyers may make many purchases in one district . . . and herein lies the explanation of most of the concentration actually found in retail trading.

This issue, the relationship between multipurpose shopping behavior and the agglomeration of dissimilar retail outlets, has been tackled with considerable vigor in recent years, albeit within the context of central place studies (McLafferty and Ghosh 1987; Thill and Thomas 1987). As with analyses of the principle of minimum differentiation, these models vary considerably in their assumptions and approaches (Hensher 1976; O'Kelly 1983; Bacon 1984; Thill 1985). In some, the rate of multi-purpose shopping is imposed exogenously (Eaton and Lipsey 1982; Foster and Brummell 1984; Mulligan 1984b), whereas in others it arises endogenously from the conditions of the model and the relative location of centers (Ghosh and McLafferty 1984; McLafferty and Ghosh 1984, 1986; Ghosh 1986). Assumptions range from quantity discounts for retailers' bulk purchasing behavior (McLafferty and Ghosh 1987) and outlets selling more than one line of merchandise (Thill 1986) to variations in consumer storage costs (Harwitz, Lentnek, and Narula 1983), population densities, and shop rentals (Kohsaka 1984, 1986a). The models, moreover, have been developed in a variety of geographical settings including a line (Eaton and Lipsey 1982), an area (McLafferty and Ghosh 1984, 1986, 1987), the circumference of a circle (Thill 1985, 1986) and a circular city (Kohsaka 1986b). Yet despite these differences in approach, it is increasingly recognized that modelling multipurpose shopping behavior provides, for the first time, a formal explanation of the well documented fact that dissimilar retail outlets cluster together within recognizable shopping districts and, most importantly from the perspective of this paper, for the existence of several outlets selling the same type of goods within a single center.

Recent advances in central place studies are thus highly compatible with recent developments of the principle of minimum differentiation. The former provides a rationale for several outlets of the same kind in a single shopping district and the latter helps explain the agglomeration of the outlets therein. The coalescence of these two subfields of location theory have yet to be integrated formally, though significant progress has been made of late (Stahl 1982b; Wolinsky 1982; McLafferty and Ghosh 1987).

There is, however, another issue which has hitherto been virtually ignored by analysts of spatial competition. The frequently observed clustering of similar (or dissimilar) retail outlets may be a reflection of all sorts of influences besides agglomeration economies, uncertainty reduction through comparison shopping, or multipurpose shopping behavior. It may simply be the result of inertia—locational decisions made some time in the past but having no present-day significance (Bloomstein, Nijkamp, and Van Veedendaal 1980). It may be a manifestation of cultural forces, such as the caste system which underpins clusters of similar business types in Indian towns (Janaki and Sayed 1962). It may represent the outcome of managerial decision making, whereby sellers are not given freedom of locational choice but allocated specific sites, as in traditional African markets (Hodder 1962; Ukuw 1969) and planned shopping centers (Jones 1969; Beddington 1982). Or, it may be an example of institutional influences, such as the part played by guilds and town councils in determining the retail geography of medieval market places and modern shopping districts respectively (Nelson 1958; Davis 1966; Davies and Bennison 1978).

The models of spatial competition thus ignore important supply side influences upon the location of retail outlets. Indeed, despite their increasingly realistic assumptions (regarding consumer behavior, shop numbers, market shape, pricing policies, etc.), the fact is that most models of spatial competition are posited within an unfettered micro-economic environment that is untouched by zoning regulations, political interference, the investment activities of financial institutions, and the well documented vagaries of the property market (Harvey 1973; Johnston 1977). Though long on rigor, it is arguable that the models of spatial competition remain somewhat short on reality at present. This represents, by the same token, a significant opportunity for future research activity.

Conclusion

In the sixty years since its publication, the principle of minimum differentiation has generated a considerable amount of research activity. Almost without exception, these studies show that once the assumptions of the model are relaxed in the direction of realism, it predicts dispersion not agglomeration and is therefore incapable of explaining the frequently observed, and statistically proven, clusters of similar retail outlets. In recent years, however, the conceptualization has been transformed by the introduction of uncertainty and risk reducing behavior. The even spacing of firms that occurs under certainty is replaced under uncertainty by the more conservative policy of clustering. These advances thus corroborate the findings of manifold pattern studies and the voluminous literature on consumer search and information seeking behavior (Newman 1977; Brown 1988). The basis upon which agglomeration occurs, however, is at odds with Hotelling's original model (or, to be more precise, the popular perception of Hotelling's seminal study). If the apocryphal ice-cream sellers cluster together today, it is not as a consequence of identical costs, products, customers etc., but because they are uncertain about the level of demand for their wares and, moreover, because they realize that sunbathers prefer to compare prices and flavors before purchase. The arrival of a hot-dog seller, however, considerably complicates the competitive landscape, though the real challenge to spatial theorists lies in the incorporation of the influence of the owners and developers of the beach and, of course, the decisions of the relevant zoning authority.

References

Ali, M. M., and S. I. Greenbaum (1977), "A Spatial Model of the Banking Industry," *The Journal of Finance*, **32** (4), 1283–1303.
Anderson, S. (1987), "Spatial Competition and Price Leadership." *International Journal of Industrial Organisation*, **5**, 369–398.

Bacon, R. W. (1984), *Consumer Spatial Behaviour: A Model of Purchasing Decisions Over Space and Time*, Oxford, England: Clarendon Press.

Beckmann, M. J., and J. F. Thisse (1986), "The Location of Production Activities," in P. Nijkamp (ed.), *Handbook of Regional and Urban Economics, Volume I*, Amsterdam: North Holland, 21–95.

Beddington, N. (1982), *Design for Shopping Centers*, London: Architectural Press.

Bertrand, J. (1883), "Revue de la theorie mathematique de la richesse sociale et des researches sur les principes mathematiques de la theorie des richesses," *Journal des Savants*, **48**, 499–508.

Bloomstein, H., P. Nijkamp, and W. Van Veedendaal (1980), "Shoppers' Perceptions and Preferences: A Multi-dimensional Attractiveness Analysis of Consumer and Entrepreneurial Attitudes," *Economic Geography*, **56**, 155–174.

Bonnano, G. (1987), "Location Choice, Product Proliferation and Entry Deterrence," *Review of Economic Studies*, **54** (1), 37–45.

Boulding, K. E. (1966), *Economic Analysis, 4e*, New York, NY: Harper & Row.

Brown, D. M. (1979), "The Location Decision of the Firm: An Overview of Theory and Evidence," *Papers of the Regional Science Association*, **43**, 23–29.

Brown, S. (1988), "Information Seeking, External Search and 'Shopping' Behaviour: Preliminary Evidence from a Planned Shopping Center," *Journal of Marketing Management*, **4** (1), 33–49.

Capozza, D. R., and R. Van Order (1977), "Pricing under Spatial Competition and Spatial Monopoly," *Econometrica*, **45** (6), 1329–1338.

—— (1978), "A Generalized Model of Spatial Competition," *American Economic Review*, **68** (5), 896–908.

Carruthers, N. (1981), "Location Choice when Price Is Also a Decision Variable," *Annals of Regional Science* **15** (1), 29–42.

Chamberlin, E. H. (1933), *The Theory of Monopolistic Competition: A Re-orientation of the Theory of Value*, Cambridge, MA: Harvard University Press.

Christaller, W. (1966), *Central Places in Southern Germany*, Englewood Cliffs, NJ: Prentice-Hall. Translated by C. W. Baskin.

Cournot, A. (1897), *Researches sur les principes mathematiques de la theorie des richesses*, New York, NY: Macmillan. Translated by N. Bacon.

Craig, C. S., A. Ghosh, and S. McLafferty (1984), "Models of the Retail Location Process: A Review," Journal of Retailing, **60** (1), 5–36.

Daniels, P. W. (1985), *Service Industries: A Geographical Appraisal*, London: Methuen.

D'Aspremont, C., J. J. Gabszewicz, and J. F. Thisse (1979), "On Hotelling's 'Stability in Competition,'" *Econometrica*, **47** (5), 1145–1150.

Davidson, W. R., F. J. Sweeny, and R. W. Stampfl (1988), *Retailing Management, 6e*, New York, NY: John Wiley.

Davies, R. L., and D. J. Bennison (1978), "Retailing in the City Centre: The Characters of Shopping Streets," *Tijdschrift voor Economische en Sociale Geografie*, **69**, 270–285.

Davis, D. (1966), *A History of Shopping*, London: Routledge and Kegan Paul.

Dean, R. D., and T. M. Carroll (1977), "Plant Location under Uncertainty," *Land Economics*, **53** (4), 423–444.

De Palma, A., V. Ginsburgh, and J. F. Thisse (1987), "On the Existence of Location Equilibria in the 3-firm Hotelling Problem," *Journal of Industrial Economics*, **36** (2), 245–252.

——, Y. Papageorgiou, and J. F. Thisse (1985), "The Principle of Minimum Differentiation Holds under Sufficient Heterogeneity," *Econometrica*, **53** (4), 767–781.

Devletoglou, N. E. (1965), "A Dissenting View of Duopoly and Spatial Competition," *Economica*, **32** (May), 140–160.

Dickinson, R. A. (1981), *Retail Management*, Austin, TX: Austin Press.

Dixit, A. K., and J. E. Stiglitz (1977), "Monopolistic Competition and Optimum Product Diversity," *American Economic Review*, **67** (3), 297–308.

Downs, A. (1957) *An Economic Theory of Democracy*, New York, NY: Harper and Row.

Drezner, Z. (1982), "Competitive Location Strategies for Two Facilities," *Regional Science and Urban Economics*, **12** (4), 485–493.

Eaton, B. C. (1972), "Spatial Competition Revised," *Canadian Journal of Economics*, **5** (2), 268–278.

——, and R. G. Lipsey (1975), "The Principle of Minimum Differentiation Revisited: Some New Developments in the Theory of Spatial Competition," *Review of Economic Studies*, **42** (1), 27–49.

—— (1979a), "The Theory of Market Preemption: The Persistence of Excess Capacity and Monopoly in Growing Spatial Markets," *Economica*, **46**, 149–158.

—— (1979b), "Comparison Shopping and the Clustering of Homogeneous Firms," *Journal of Regional Science*, **19** (4), 421–435.

—— (1982), "An Economic Theory of Central Places," *The Economic Journal*, **92** (March), 56–72.

Eaton, J., and G. M. Grossman (1986), "The Provision of Information as Marketing Strategy," *Oxford Economic Papers*, **38** (Nov.), 166–183.

——, and H. Kierzkowski (1984), "Oligopolistic Competition, Product Variety, Entry Deterrence and Technology Transfer," *Rand Journal of Economics*, **15** (1), 99–107.

Economides, N. (1984), "The Principle of Minimum Differentiation Revisited," *European Economic Review*, **24** (3), 345–368.

—— (1986), "Minimal and Maximal Product Differentiation in Hotelling's Duopoly," *Economics Letters*, **21** (1), 67–71.

Edgeworth, F. (1925), "The Pure Theory of Monopoly," in *Papers Relating to Political Theory, Volume 1*, London: Macmillan, 455–469.

Eliashberg, J., and R. Chatterjee (1985), "Analytical Models of Competition with Implications for Marketing: Issues, Findings and Outlook," *Journal of Marketing Research*, **22** (Aug.), 237–261.

Enelow, J., and M. J. Hinich (1984), *The Spatial Theory of Voting*, Cambridge, England: Cambridge University Press.

Evans, A. (1987), "A Theoretical Comparison of Competition with Other Economic Regimes for Bus Services," *Journal of Transport Economics and Policy*, **21** (1), 7–36.

Fik, T. J. (1988), "Spatial Competition and Price Reporting in Retail Food Markets," *Economic Geography*, **64** (1), 29–44.

Forster, J. J. H., and A. C. Brummell (1984), "Multi-purpose Trips and Central Place Theory," *Australian Geographer*, **16**, 120–127.

Foster, C., and J. Golay (1986), "Some Curious Old Practices and Their Relevance to Equilibrium in Bus Competition," *Journal of Transport Economics and Policy*, **20** (2), 191–216.

Freeman, D. B., and F. L. Dungey (1981), "A Spatial Duopoly: Competition in the Western Canadian Fur Trade 1770–1835," *Journal of Historical Geography*, **7** (3), 250–270.

Gabszewicz, J. J., and P. Garella (1986) , " 'Subjective' Price Search and Price Competition," *International Journal of Industrial Organisation*, **4** (3), 305–316.

—— (1987), "Price Search and Spatial Competition," *European Economic Review*, **31** (4), 827–842.

Gabszewicz, J. J., and J. F. Thisse (1986), "On the Nature of Competition with Differentiated Products," *The Economic Journal*, **96** (March), 160–172.

Gannon, C. A. (1972), "Consumer Demand, Conjectual Interdependence and Location Equilbria in Simple Spatial Duopoly," *Papers of the Regional Science Association*, **28**, 83–107.

—— (1973), Central Concentration in Simple Spatial Duopoly: Some Behavioral and Functional Considerations," *Journal of Regional Science*, **13** (3), 357–375.

—— (1977), "Product Differentiation and Locational Competition in Spatial Markets," *International Economic Review*, **18** (2), 293–322.

Ghosh, A. (1983), "Competition and Cooperation Among Itinerant Traders," *Geographical Analysis*, **15** (1), 1–13.

—— (1986), "The Value of a Mall and Other Insights from a Revised Central Place Theory," *Journal of Retailing*, **62** (1), 79–97.

——, and C. S. Craig (1983), "Formulating Retail Location Strategy in a Changing Environment," *Journal of Marketing*, **47** (Summer), 56–68.

—— (1984), "A Location Allocation Model for Facility Planning a Competitive Environment," *Geographical Analysis*, **16** (1), 39–51.

—— (1986), "An Approach to Determining Optimal Locations for New Services," *Journal of Marketing Research*, **23** (Nov.), 354–362.

Ghosh, A., and S. L. McLafferty (1982), "Locating Stores in Uncertain Environments: A Scenario Planning Approach," *Journal of Retailing*, **58** (4), 5–22.

—— (1984), "A Model of Consumer Propensity for Multi-purpose Shopping," *Geographical Analysis*, **16** (3), 244–249.

—— (1987), *Location Strategies for Retail and Service Firms*, Lexington, MA: Lexington Books.

Ginsburg, V., P. Pestieau, and J. F. Thisse (1987), "A Spatial Model of Party Competition With Electoral and Ideological Objectives," in A. Ghosh and G. Rushton (eds.), *Spatial Analysis and Location Allocation Models*, New York, NY: Van Nostrand Reinhold, 101–117.

Goldman, A. (1975), "The Role of Trading-up in the Development of the Retailing System," *Journal of Marketing*, **39** (Jan.), 54–62.

—— (1978), "Institutional Changes in Retailing: An Updated 'Wheel of Retailing' Theory," in A. G. Woodside et al. (eds.), *Foundations of Marketing Channels*, Austin, TX: Lone Star Press, 189–211.

Goldstein, G. S., and T. J. Gronberg (1984), "Economies of Scope and Economies of Agglomeration," *Journal of Urban Economics*, **16** (1), 91–104.

Graitson, D. (1982), "Spatial Competition a la Hotelling: A Selective Survey," *Journal of Industrial Economics*, **31** (1/2), 13–25.

Greenhut, M. L., C. C. Mai, and G. Norman (1986), "Impacts on Optimum Location of Different Pricing Strategies, Market Structures and Consumer Distributions Over Space," *Regional Science and Urban Economics*, **16** (3), 329–351.

Greenhut, M. L., and H. Ohta (1975), *Theory of Spatial Pricing and Market Areas*, Durham, NC: Duke University Press.

Guy, C. M. (1980), *Retail Location and Retail Planning in Britain*, Westmead: Gower.

Hannesson, R. (1982), "Defensive Foresight Rather than Minimax: A Comment on Eaton and Lipsey's Model of Spatial Competition," *Review of Economic Studies*, **59**, 653–657.

Hartwick, T. M., and P. G. Hartwick (1971), "Duopoly in Space," *Canadian Journal of Economics*, **4** (4), 485–505.

Harvey, D. (1973), *Social Justice and the City*, London: Edward Arnold.

Harwitz, M., B. Lentnek, and S. C. Narula (1983), "Do I Have to Go Shopping Again? A Theory of Choice With Movement Costs," *Journal of Urban Economics*, **13** (2), 165–180.

Hay, D. A. (1976), "Sequential Entry and Entry-deterring Strategies in Spatial Competition," *Oxford Economic Papers*, **28** (2), 240–257.

Heal, G. (1980), "Spatial Structure in the Retail Trade: A Study in Product Differentiation With Increasing Returns," *Bell Journal of Economics*, **11** (2), 565–583.

Hensher, D. A. (1976), "The Structure of Journeys and the Nature of Travel Patterns," *Environment and Planning-A*, **8**, 655–672.

Hobbs, B. F. (1986), "Mill Pricing Versus Spatial Price Discrimination Under Bertrand and Cournot Spatial Competition," *Journal of Industrial Economics*, **35** (2), 173–191.

Hodder, B. W. (1962), "The Yoruba Rural Market," in P. Bohannan and G. Dalton (eds.), *Markets in Africa*, Evanston, IL: Northwestern University Press, 103–117.

Hotelling, H. (1929), "Stability in Competition," *The Economic Journal*, **39** (March), 41–57.

Hurter, A. P., and P. J. Lederer (1985), "Spatial Duopoly With Discriminatory Pricing," *Regional Science and Urban Economics*, **15** (4), 541–553.

Isard, W. (1956), *Location and Space Economy: A General Theory Relating to Industrial Location, Market Areas, Land Use, Trade and Urban Structure*, Cambridge, MA: MIT Press.

Janaki, Y. A., and Z. A. Sayed (1962), "The Geography of Padra Town," Baroda, India: University of Baroda Press, Geographical Series No. 1.

Johnston, R. J. (1977), "Concerning the Geography of Land Values in Cities," *South African Geographer*, **5** (April), 368–397.

Jones, C. S. (1969), *Regional Shopping Centres: Their Location, Planning and Design*, London: Business Books.

Jones, K., and J. Simmons (1987), *Location, Location, Location: Analysing the Retail Environment*, Toronto, Ontario: Methuen.

Katona, G., and E. Mueller (1954), "A Study of Purchase Decision," in L. H. Clark (ed.), *Consumer Behavior: The Dynamics of Consumer Reaction*, New York, NY: New York University Press.

Kennedy, P., and P. Copes (1978), "Product Differentiation and Centralization of Production," *Journal of Regional Science*, **18** (3), 323–335.

Kivell, P. T., and G. Shaw (1980), "The Study of Retail Location," in J. A. Dawson (ed.), *Retail Geography*, London: Croom Helm.

Kohlberg, E. (1985), "Equilibrium Store Locations When Consumers Minimise Travel Time Plus Waiting Time," *Economics Letters*, **11** (3), 211–216.

——, and W. Novshek (1982), "Equilibrium in a Simple Price-location Model," *Economics Letters*, **9**, 7–15.

Kohsaka, H. (1984), "An Optimization of the Central Place System in Terms of the Multi-purpose Shopping Trip," *Geographical Analysis*, **16** (3), 250–269.

—— (1986a), "An Analysis of Two-center Competition," *Journal of Regional Science*, **26** (1), 179–188.

—— (1986b), "The Location Process of Central Place System Within a Circular City," *Economic Geography*, **62**, 254–266.

Lederer, P. J., and A. P. Hurter (1986), "Competition of Firms: Discriminatory Pricing and Location," *Econometrica*, **54** (3), 623–640.

Lerner, A. P., and H. W. Singer (1937), "Some Notes on Duopoly and Spatial Competition," *Journal of Political Economy*, **45** (2), 145–186.

Lewis, W. A. (1945), "Competition in Retail Trade," *Economica*, **12**, 202–234.

Lindbeck, A., and J. W. Weibull (1987), "Balanced-budget Redistribution as an Outcome of Political Competition," *Pubic Choice*, **53** (3), 273–297.

Lippman, S. A., and J. J. McCall (1979), *Studies in the Economics of Search*, Amsterdam: North-Holland.

—— (1981), "The Economics of Uncertainty: Selected Topics and Probabilistic Methods," in K. J. Arrow and M. D. Intriligator (eds.), *Handbook of Mathematical Economics*, Amsterdam: North-Holland, 211–284.

Losch, A. (1954), *The Economics of Location*, New Haven, CT: Yale University Press. Translated by W. H. Woglom and W. F. Stolper.

Macleod, W. B. (1985), "On the Non-Existence of Equilibria in Differentiated Product Models," *Regional Science and urban Economics*, **15** (2), 245–262.

——, G. Norman, and J. F. Thisse (1987), "Competition, Tacit Collusion and Free Entry," *The Economic Journal*, **97**, 189–198.

Mai, C. C. (1981), "Optimum Location and the Theory of the Firm Under Demand Uncertainty," *Regional Science and Urban Economics* **11**, 549–557.

—— (1984), "Location and the Theory of the Imperfectly Competitive Firm Under Demand Uncertainty," *Southern Economic Journal*, **50** (4), 1160–1170.

Mason, J. B., and M. L. Mayer (1987), *Modern Retailing: Theory and Practice, 3e*, Plano, TX: Business Publications Inc.

McLafferty, S. L., and A. Ghosh (1984), "A Simulation Model of Spatial Competition With Multi-purpose Trips," *Modelling and Simulation*, **15**, 477–482.

—— (1986), "Multi-purpose Shopping and the Location of Retail Firms," *Geographical Analysis*, **18** (3), 215–226.

—— (1987), "Optimal Location and Allocation with Multi-purpose Shopping," in A. Ghosh and G. Rushton (eds.), *Spatial Analysis and Location Allocation Models*, New York, NY: Van Nostrand Reinhold, 55–75.

Moorthy, K. S. (1985), "Using Game Theory to Model Competition," *Journal of Marketing Research*, **22** (August), 262–282.

Mulligan, G. F. (1984a), "Agglomeration and Central Place Theory: A Review of the Literature," *International Regional Science Review*, **9** (1), 1–42.

—— (1984b), Central Place Populations: Some Implications of Consumer Shopping Behavior. *Annals of the Association of American Geographers*, **74** (1), 44–56.

—— (1985), "Consumer Demand and Multi-purpose Shopping Behavior," *Geographical Analysis*, **15** (1), 76–81.

Nakagome, M. (1986), "The Spatial Labor Market and Spatial Competition," *Regional Studies*, **20** (4), 307–312.

Nelson, C. H., and B. A. McCarl (1984), "Including Perfect Competition in Spatial Equilibrium Models," *Canadian Journal of Agricultural Economics*, **32** (March), 55–70.

Nelson, R. L. (1958), *The Selection of Retail Locations*, New York, NY: Dodge.

Neven, D. (1985), "Two Stage (Perfect) Equilibrium in Hotelling's Model," *Journal of Industrial Economics*, **33** (3), 317–325.

—— (1986) "On Hotelling's Competition with Non-uniform Customer Distributions," *Economics Letters*, **21**, 121–126.

Newman, J. W. (1977), "Consumer External Search: Amount and Determinants," in A. G. Woodside et al. (eds.), *Consumer and Industrial Buying Behavior*, New York, NY: North Holland, 79–94.

Nielsen, O. (1966), "Developments in Retailing," in M. Kjaer-Hansen (ed.), *Readings in Danish Theory of Marketing*, Amsterdam: North-Holland, 101–115.

Norman, G. (1981), "Spatial Competition and Spatial Price Discrimination," *Review of Economic Studies*, **58**, 97–111.

Novshek, W. (1980), "Equilibrium in Simple Spatial (or Differentiated Product) Models," *Journal of Economic Theory*, **22**, 31–326.

Ohta, H. (1980), "Spatial Competition, Concentration and Welfare," *Regional Science and Urban Economics*, **10** (1), 3–16.

—— (1981), "The Price Effects of Spatial Competition," *Review of Economic Studies*, **58**, 317–325.

Okabe, A., and A. Suzuki (1987), "Stability of Spatial Competition for a Large Number of Firms on a Bounded Two-Dimensional Space," *Environment and Planning/A*, **19**, 1067–1082.

O'Kelly, M. E. (1983), "Multipurpose Shopping Trips and the Size of Retail Facilities," *Annals of the Association of American Geographers*, **72** (2), 231–239.

Osborne, M. J., and C. Pitchik (1986), "The Nature of Equilibrium in a Location Model," *International Economic Review*, **27** (1), 223–237.

Palander, T. (1935), *Beitrage zur standortstheorie*, Uppsala, Sweden: Almquist and Wiksells Boktryckeri.

Papageorgiou, G. J. (1979), "Agglomeration," *Regional Science and Urban Economics*, **9** (1), 41–59.

Papageorgiou, Y. Y., and J. F. Thisse (1985), "Agglomeration as Spatial Interdependence Between Firms and Households," *Journal of Economic Theory*, **37** (1), 19–31.

Pascal, A. H., and J. J. McCall (1980), "Agglomeration Economies, Search Costs and Industrial Location," *Journal of Urban Economics*, **8** (3), 383–388.

Paloff, J. M., and S. C. Salop (1985), "Equilibrium With Product Differentiation," *Review of Economic Studies*, **52** (1), 107–120.

Prescott, E. C., and M. Visscher (1977), "Sequential Location Among Firms With Foresight," *Bell Journal of Economics*, **8** (2), 378–393.

ReVelle, C. (1986), "The Maximum Capture or 'Sphere of Influence' Location Problem: Hotelling Revisited on a Network," *Journal of Regional Science*, **26** (2), 343–358.

Rogers, D. (1987), "Shop Location Analysis," in E. McFadyen (ed.), *The Changing Face of British Retailing*, London: Newman Books, 74–83.

Rothschild, R. (1979), "The Effect of Sequential Entry on Choice of Location," *European Economic Review*, **12**, 227–241.

Salop, S. (1979), "Monopolistic Competition With Outside Goods," *Bell Journal of Economics*, **10**, 141–156.

——, and J. Stiglitz (1976), "Bargains and Ripoffs: A Model of Monopolistically Competitive Price Dispersion," *Review of Economic Studies*, **44**, 493–510.

Schulz, N., and K. Stahl (1985), "On the Non-Existence of Oligopolistic Equilibria in Differentiated Product Spaces," *Regional Science and Urban Economics*, **15** (2), 229–243.

Shaked, A. (1975), "Non-existence of Equilibrium for the Two-dimensional, Three Firms Location Problem," *Review of Economic Studies*, **42** (1), 51–56.

—— (1982), "Existence and Computation of Mixed Strategy Nash Equilibrium for 3-firms Location Problem," *Journal of Industrial Economics*, **31** (1/2), 93–96.

——, and J. Sutton (1982), "Relaxing Price Competition Through Product Differentiation," *Review of Economic Studies*, **49** (1), 3–13.

Shaw, R. W. (1982), "Product Proliferation in Characteristics Space: The UK Fertilizer Industry," *Journal of Industrial Economics*, **31** (1/2), 69–92.

Shilnoy, Y. (1981), "Hotelling's Competition With General Customer Distributions," *Economics Letters*, **8**, 39–45.

Simon, H. A. (1959), "Theories of Decision-making in Economics and Behavioral Science," *American Economic Review*, **49**, 253–283.

Smithies, A. (1941), "Optimum Location in Spatial Competition," *Journal of Political Economy*, **49**, 423–439.

Spulber, D. F. (1984), "Competition and Multiplant Monopoly With Spatial Nonlinear Pricing," *International Economic Review*, **25** (2), 429–439.

Stahl, K. (1982a), "Location and Spatial Pricing Theory With Non-convex Transportation Cost Schedules," *Bell Journal of Economics*, **13** (2), 575–582.

—— (1982b), "Differentiated Products, Consumer Search and Locational Oligopoly," *Journal of Industrial Economics*, **31** (1/2), 97–114.

——, and P. Varaiya (1978), "Economics of Information: Examples in Information and Land-use Theory," *Regional Science and Urban Economics*, **8**, 43–56.

Steiner, P. (1961), "Monopoly and Competition in Television: Some Policy Issues," *Manchester School of Economic and Social Studies*, **29** (2), 107–131.

Stevens, B. H. (1961), "An Application of Game Theory to a Problem in Location Strategy," *Paper and Proceedings of the Regional Science Association*, 7, 143–157.

Stuart, C. (1979), "Search and the Spatial Organisation of Trading," in S. A. Lippman and J. J. McCall (eds.), *Studies in the Economics of Search*, Amsterdam: North-Holland, 17–33.

Swann, G. M. P. (1985), "Product Competition in Microprocessors," *Journal of Industrial Economics*, **34** (1), 33–53.

Teitz, M. B. (1968), "Locational Strategies for Competitive Systems," *Journal of Regional Science*, **8** (2), 135–148.

Thill, J. C. (1985), "Demand in Space and Multi-purpose Shopping: A Theoretical Approach," *Geographical Analysis*, **17** (2), 114–129.

—— (1986), "A Note on Multi-purpose Shopping, Sales and Market Areas of Firms," *Journal of Regional Science*, **26** (4), 775–784.

——, and I. Thomas (1987), "Toward Conceptualizing Trip Chaining Behavior: A Review," *Geographical Analysis*, **19** (1), 1–17.

Treble, J. G. (1980), "Pricing Under Spatial Competition and Spatial Monopoly: A Comment," *Econometrica*, **48** (5), 1327–1328.

Ukuw, U. I. (1969), "Markets in Iboland," in B. W. Hodder and U. I. Ukuw, *Markets in West Africa*, Ibadan: Ibadan University Press, 113–250.

Von Stackelberg, H. (1952), *The Theory of Market Economy*, London: William Hidge. Translated by A. T. Peacock.

Watson, J. K. (1985), "A Behavioral Analysis of Negative Price Reactions in Spatial Markets," *Southern Economic Journal*, **51** (3), 882–885.

Webber, M. J. (1972), *The Impact of Uncertainty Upon Location*, Cambridge, MA: MIT Press.

—— (1974), "Free Entry and the Locational Equilibrium," *Annals of the Association of American Geographers*, **64** (1), 17–25.

Webster, J. G., and J. J. Wakshlag (1983), "A Theory of Television Program Choice," *Communication Research*, **10** (4), 430–446.

Wendell, R. E., and R. D. McKelvey (1981), "New Perspectives in Competitive Location Theory," *European Journal of Operational Research*, **6**, 174–182.

White, L. J. (1975), "The Spatial Distribution of Retail Firms in an Urban Setting," *Regional Science and Urban Economics*, **5** (3), 325–333.

Williams, H. C. W. L., and M. L. Senior (1977), "A Retail Location Model With Overlapping Market Areas: Hotelling's Problem Revisited," *Urban Studies*, **14**, 203–205.

Wittman, D. (1983), "Candidate Motivation—A Synthesis of Alternative Theories," *American Political Science Review*, **77** (1), 142–157.

Wolinsky, A. (1982), "Retail Trade Concentration Due to Consumers' Imperfect Information," *Bell Journal of Economics*, **13**, 275–282.

Wrigley, N. (ed.) (1988), *Store Choice, Store Location and Market Analysis*, London: Routledge.

Zeuthen, F. (1933), "Theoretical Remarks on Price Policy: Hotelling's Case With Variations," *Quarterly Journal of Economics*, **47**, 231–253.

21

Retail location at the micro-scale: inventory and prospect

Stephen Brown

Source: *Services Industries Journal* 14(4) (1994): 542–576.

Although the issue of retail location has attracted a great deal of academic attention, the bulk of this literature pertains to the national, regional and urban scales of analysis. An equally important, but comparatively neglected, consideration is micro-scale retail location; that is, location within planned shopping centres and unplanned shopping districts. This article reviews the literature on retail location at the micro-scale, summarises the current state of knowledge and sets out a future research agenda.

Introduction

It has often – perhaps too often – been said that the three secrets of success in retailing are location, location and location [Ghosh, 1990; Davies and Harris, 1990; Pearson, 1991]. Important though the other elements of the retail marketing mix undoubtedly are, the most sophisticated store designs, meticulous merchandise planning procedures, imaginative advertising campaigns, astute pricing policies and competent sales personnel all come to naught if a retailer's locational strategy is flawed. What is more, whereas errors in pricing, promotions, merchandise planning and so on can be comparatively easily adjusted, mistaken locational decisions are not readily rectified – indeed for some they can prove fatal – and only then at considerable expense, disruption and damage to a retailer's carefully nurtured reputation [Ghosh and McLafferty, 1987].

In keeping with its standing as a key component in the retailing mix, the locational issue is subject to intensive investigation and continual improvement [e.g. Ghosh and Ingene, 1991]. Although intuitive approaches to locational decision taking are still surprisingly prevalent [Simpkin, Doyle and Saunders, 1985; Anderson, Parker and Stanley, 1990], recent years have seen several sophisticated additions to the locational analyst's toolkit. Thanks to the virtual ubiquity of powerful, low cost computing facilities, a wide range of spatial databases and analytical techniques are now available [Beaumont, 1988; Goodchild, 1991; Curry, 1993]. Whether developed in-house or purchased from specialist providers like CACI and Pinpoint, these databases typically comprise a geographically organised (geocoded) amalgam of information from the population census statistics, postcodes file and surveys of shopper behaviour and buying power. They thus provide rapid, low cost means of assessing, profiling and comparing market opportunities, screening potential sites and defining catchment areas. This information, furthermore, is compatible with the new generation of store location models, such as SLAM, ILACS or FRANSYS, which facilitate the evaluation of multi-outlet networks operated by a single retail chain [Simpkin, 1989; Goodchild, 1984; Ghosh and Craig, 1991].

Despite the latter-day advances in location modelling and geographical information systems, the outcome of locational decisions ultimately rests on *micro-scale* considerations; that is, the appropriateness or otherwise of the precise location *within* the chosen city centre, regional shopping centre, inner city arterial, secondary shopping district, retail warehouse park or whatever. Indeed, it has often been said – though perhaps not often enough – that a few yards can make all the difference between success and failure in retailing [Parkes, 1987; Dewar and Watson, 1990]. The issue of micro-scale location, however, remains comparatively neglected by retailing researchers. True, the need for detailed study of retail location at the micro-scale has often been stressed [Shepherd and Thomas, 1980; Dawson, 1980; Potter, 1982; Breheny, 1988] and ample empirical evidence attests to its importance [Hansen and Weinberg, 1979; Hise *et al.*, 1983; Anderson, 1985]. Yet, compared to the extraordinarily voluminous literature on retail location at the national, regional and urban scales of analysis, the micro-scale placement of retail outlets within planned shopping centres and unplanned shopping districts has attracted relatively little academic discussion.

In an attempt to draw attention to this important, if somewhat neglected, research issue, this study will endeavour to bring together the extant literature on micro-scale retail location. It does so by, firstly, identifying and evaluating the available theoretical frameworks and associated empirical studies of shop patterns; secondly, exploring demand side analyses of within-centre shopper movement and behaviour; thirdly, highlighting the often imperceptible influence of supply side factors like town planning policies and the shopping centre development industry; and, fourthly, attempting to summarise the current state of knowledge on micro-scale retail location and set out a future research agenda. Before commencing the review proper, however, it is important to note that, despite its reputation as a 'cinderella' subject, the micro-scale literature is far from negligible. Its 'important but overlooked' status is entirely *relative* to the academic attention lavished on retail location at the meso- and macro-scales. As shall become apparent, a surprising amount of published material actually exists, though it tends to be scattered among a wide variety of academic specialisms – economics, geography, marketing, psychology, town planning and traffic engineering, to name but the most prominent.

Theoretical context

If the literature on micro-scale retail location had to be summarised in a single word, that word would probably be agglomeration. Above all else, the spatial arrangement of retail outlets *within* shopping districts exhibits a tendency for similar 'types' of establishment – those selling similar categories of merchandise or orientated toward a similar target market – to cluster together into distinctive sub-areas. The department stores of Boulevard Haussmann, the outfitters of Oxford Street and the theatres and cinemas of Broadway are some of the best known examples of this phenomenon, but the agglomeration of analogous trade types is one of the most ubiquitous features of the commercial environment and a truly universal trait. It has been observed in suburban shopping centres [Jones, 1969; Maitland, 1985], traditional African markets [Miracle, 1962; Ukuw, 1969], Third World cities [Sendut, 1965; Beaujeu-Garnier and Delobez, 1979] and also times past. Nystrom [1930], for instance, noted 'natural groupings' of similar retail businesses in the centres of nineteenth-century American cities; Hassan [1972] has described the spatial proximity of retailers of books, incense, textiles and utensils in the Islamic cities of the late Middle Ages; and Davis [1966, p.108] cites an account of seventeenth-century Cheapside when it 'was beautiful to behold the glorious appearance of goldsmiths' shops . . . which in a con- tinuous course reached from the Old Change to Bucklesbury, exclusive of four shops only of other trades in all that space'.

Not unnaturally, the agglomerative tendencies of similar retail outlets and the intra-centre spatial arrangement of these clusters of activity have attracted a considerable amount of theoretical discussion and associated empirical analysis. The conceptual touchstones are two long-established and much-debated models, *the principle of minimum differentiation* and *bid rent theory*. Although different in many respects, both concepts are predicated on positivist, neoclassical premises, which presuppose, essentially, that there is an identifiable order in the material world, that people are rational, utility maximising decision-makers and that economic activity takes place in a freely competitive manner. The theories, what is more, are deductively de- rived and normative in ethos. In other words, they are based on stated, often highly simplified assumptions, not empirical observation, and as a result describe patterns of retail activity that ought to occur, given the underlying assumptions, not ones that necessarily do. That said, the models are by no means totally divorced from reality. On the contrary, they have given rise to numerous empirical investigations (the results of which are somewhat mixed but broadly supportive of the hypothesised patterns of retail activity) and several inductively derived attempts to combine and integrate the concepts into a more general *combination theory*.

The principle of minimum differentiation

Although it is perhaps less well known than macro-scale locational concepts like central place theory and spatial interaction theory, Harold Hotelling's [1929] principle of minimum differentiation provides the conceptual foundations for the study of micro-scale retail location. Dealing initially with two profit maximising firms, selling identical products (with zero production costs) at f.o.b. prices from fixed locations in a bounded linear market where transport costs are constant, demand is completely inelastic and identical, utility maximising consumers are evenly distributed, bear the costs of distribution and patronise outlets solely on the basis of delivery prices, Hotelling demonstrated that an equilibrium existed where neither outlet could increase profits by altering its prices. He argued, moreover, that if one seller is free to relocate, it would maximise its hinterland (and hence its profit) by setting up shop adjacent to the other on the 'long' side of the market. If, as Chamberlin [1933] subsequently noted, both sellers are footloose, a process of mutual leapfrogging to the longer side of the market ensues, the upshot of which is a distinctive clustered arrangement in the centre of the market.

Since Hotelling's pioneering contribution, the principle of minimum differentiation has been applied to all manner of marketing phenomena, ranging from television programming and pricing conjectures to new product development [Brown, 1989; Ingene and Ghosh, 1991]. However, possibly as a result of its traditional textbook portrayal as the 'problem' of ice cream vendors on a beach, the concept is often taken to pertain to retail location at the micro-scale. In this respect, indeed, the associated empirical record lends considerable weight to Hotelling's agglomerative hypothesis. Shop pattern studies undertaken in a number of different countries, using a variety of statistical techniques and referring to a comprehensive cross-section of retail trade types, agree that sellers of the same category of merchandise (food, clothing, motor car dealers and so on) tend to cluster tightly together [Rogers, 1969; Lee, 1974; Okabe, Asami and Miki, 1985]. A number of empirical analyses also attest to the fact that compatible but contrasting store types (restaurants and cinemas, grocers and florists etc.) exhibit marked intracentre agglomerative tendencies [Ratcliff, 1939; Parker, 1962; Brady, 1977].

Although Hotelling's clustering hypothesis appears to enjoy a high degree of empirical support, the agglomerated outcome of his model is a consequence of its initial assumptions concerning market conditions and competitor behaviour. Such conditions are rarely encountered in the real world, though the development of the western Canadian fur trade provides a fascinating exception to the rule [Freeman and Dungey, 1981], and, inevitably, this has prompted many attempts to relax the model's highly restrictive assumptions [e.g. Lerner and Singer, 1937; Devletoglou, 1965; Eaton and Lipsey, 1975]. Almost without exception, however, these adjustments give rise, not to the anticipated agglomerated pattern, but to *dispersed* spatial arrangements of competing firms. Apart from some evidence of pairing when large numbers of outlets are involved [Okabe and Susuki, 1987], the bulk of studies support Eaton and Lipsey's [1979, p.422] conclusion that, 'the Hotelling model is not able to explain the local clustering of firms . . . Indeed, once the assumptions are relaxed very slightly in the direction of realism, Hotelling's model predicts that no two firms should be clustered together'.

In recent years, however, the Hotelling model has been rehabilitated somewhat. This has been achieved through, firstly, the incorporation of agglomeration economies, positive externalities or cost reducing benefits that flow from spatial propinquity [Thill and Thomas, 1987; Fujita and Smith, 1990]; secondly, relaxing the traditional assumption that retailers and consumers are perfectly informed, and thus certain about the outcomes of their actions [Pascal and McCall, 1980; de Palma, Ginsburgh and Thisse, 1987]; and, thirdly, permitting these uncertain consumers to gather information and minimise costs by indulging in multi-purpose, multi-stop and comparison shopping behaviours [Fujita, Ogawa and Thisse, 1988; Ingene and Ghosh, 1990]. The upshot of these modifications is that the principle of minimum differentiation is once again capable of describing the much observed and statistically proven clustering of competitive and compatible retail outlets within unplanned shopping districts and planned shopping centres, though the conditions under which agglomeration occurs is somewhat at odds with Hotelling's original conception.

Bid rent theory

Although the principle of minimum differentiation has traditionally been associated with micro-scale retail location, the same cannot be said for bid rent theory, or at least not with the same conviction. It was originally developed at the macro-scale (regional/urban), and with respect to all manner of land use categories (residential, industrial, commercial, etc.), though it has since been applied with some success to retail land uses in general and micro-scale settings in particular. Dating from the celebrated agricultural model of von Thünen [1826], bid rent theory emphasises the paramount importance of accessibility to the patterning of urban land uses [see Jones, 1991; Thrall, 1991]. As the city centre is the focal point of transportation networks, it is the most accessible location in an urban area and consequently offers maximum market potential and optimum access to sources of labour and customers. Competition takes place for this, the most desirable of locations, and land goes to the highest bidders, those that can derive the greatest utility from the most central locations. Rents, therefore, are highest in the very centre of the city centre and decline with distance from the core area [Balchin, Kieve and Bull, 1988].

The need for a central location, however, varies between different categories of retail outlet and this affects the level of rents they are willing to bid for sites increasingly eccentric to the core. Assuming, as before, the existence of uniformly priced travel which is equally easy in all directions, a free market in property, perfectly informed, profit maximising buyers and sellers etc., bid rent curves can be constructed for each retailing function, their angle reflecting the sensitivity of that activity to changes in accessibility. Desiring to attract custom from the entire urban area and, as a result, requiring the most central sites of all, high order retailing functions such as department and speciality stores are prepared to bid the highest rentals, though the amount they are willing to pay falls off rapidly with distance. Low order retail functions, on the other hand, are more willing to trade off the accessibility of the primary shopping streets for the lower rentals available in secondary or peripheral shopping thoroughfares, and their bid rent curves are correspondingly shallower. Bid rent theory, in other words, postulates a concentric arrangement of intra-centre land uses with department stores and speciality retailers in the centre of the city centre and grocery stores and convenience goods retailers on the outer fringe [Scott, 1970]. A broadly similar model of the internal structure of suburban shopping districts has also been posited [Garner, 1966; Chudzynska, 1981].

Given its implausible assumptions of, amongst others, a monocentric city, accessibility that is maximised in the city centre and declines equally in all directions, a free market in property and the presence of a multiplicity of independent, rational, fully informed, utility maximising buyers and sellers, it is hardly surprising that the bid rent model has been subject to severe academic criticism [Harvey, 1974; Ball, 1979, 1985]. The empirical record, however, lends considerable support to the concentric zonation prediction, though the patterns are less clear cut in practice than they are in theory. Whether based upon land value or land use data, or utilising qualitative or quantitative analytical procedures, shop pattern studies undertaken in the centres of several American [Rannells, 1956; Weaver 1969], European [Davies, 1972a; Friedrichs and Goodman, 1987], African [Davies, 1965; Beavon, 1970], Asian [Khan and Uddin, 1967; Bellett, 1969] and Antipodean [Scott, 1959; Alexander, 1974] cities, concur that the retailing component of the city centre comprises a centrally located core devoted to high order functions and a peripheral fringe occupied by low order outlets and space extensive retailing establishments [Davies, 1976].

This intra-centre zonation, it must be emphasised, is not confined to western city centres, nor is it an artifact of the recent past. It has been reported in the market places and shopping parades of the developing world [Beaujeu-Garnier and Delobez, 1979], within the retailing assemblages at the exits of US interstate highways [Norris, 1987], in the centres of nineteenth-century European cities [Shaw, 1988] and the market towns of medieval England [Carter, 1983]. Indeed, its prevalence is nowhere better illustrated than in the recent emergence of 'suburban downtowns' in major US metropolitan areas, where, despite the ostensibly planned environment, competitive bidding for the most accessible micro-scale locations has become increasingly apparent [Buckwalter, 1989; Hartshorn and Muller, 1989]. When all is said and done, even the sternest critics of bid rent theory recognise that the pattern of retail land use it predicts provides a reasonably accurate reflection of reality [Harvey, 1973; Johnston, 1977; Whitehand, 1987].

Combination theories

The concentric pattern of retail land use described by bid rent theory and the agglomerative proclivities enshrined in the principle of minimum differentiation do not, of course, operate in isolation. In fact, many empirical studies of micro-scale retail location, ranging from western city centres to traditional Moroccan souks, have noted that a combination of specialised clusters of activity and broad zonation from core to periphery tends to obtain in practice [Fogg, 1932; Scott, 1959; de Blij, 1962]. A number of attempts, therefore, have been made to develop significant combination theories of this state of affairs, though in sharp contrast to the deductively derived, neoclassical premises of both bid rent theory and the principle of minimum differentiation, these frameworks are almost without exception the outcome of inductive reasoning.

An early and much cited example of such theorising is the 'coreframe' model of Horwood and Boyce [1959]. Derived from a detailed literature review and land use surveys of the centres of eleven US cities, this model maintained that central areas comprised: firstly, an inner 'core' dominated by vertical development, pedestrian movement, internal linkages and an extreme concentration of shops, offices and other intensive land uses; and, secondly, an outer 'frame' which tended to be horizontally developed, motor vehicle orientated, externally linked and characterised by semi-intensive clusters of specialist land uses like wholesaling, light industry, transportation termini and automobile sales. Subsequent analyses in the United States [Horwood and McNair, 1961], Canada [Campbell, 1970], Germany [Hartenstein and Staack, 1967], Australia [Alexander, 1974] and the United Kingdom [Davies, 1976] have lent empirical weight to the concept and concluded that it has considerable descriptive and, indeed, prescriptive value [Davies, 1984].

Influential as it proved to be, the core-frame model – and its analogues [e.g. Davies, 1965; Herbert and Thomas, 1982] – was formulated with respect to a wide range of land use categories and thus tended to discuss retailing in crude aggregate terms. Another equally important but retail specific combination theory is Davies' [1972b] 'complex' model of city centre retailing. This not only incorporates the concentric zonation and specialist clusters of bid rent theory and the principle of minimum differentiation respectively, but also adds an arterial or linear component, which represents, in effect, a spatial manifestation of the countervailing forces of agglomeration and dispersion. Ostensibly an intra-centre adaptation of Berry's [1963] seminal typology of urban retail structure – though its roots are actually much older – empirical tests of Davies 'complex' model have proved remarkably successful. It was first employed to describe the central shopping district of Coventry [Davies, 1972a] and has since been successfully applied, albeit with a number of minor methodological and taxonomic adjustments, to the central areas of Newcastle-upon-Tyne [White, 1975], Stockport [Potter, 1982], Belfast [Brown, 1987a] and the west end of London [Davies, 1976].

Demand side analyses

Close though the correspondence appears to be between the normative predictions of the above theories and the associated empirical evidence culled from studies of intra-centre shop patterns, it is incorrect to infer that the latter, in some way, 'proves' the former – quite the reverse. Extant spatial patterns of retail activity may result from any number of processes (inertia, cultural factors etc.) other than the behaviours of the utility maximising decision takers and so on of the bid rent and PMD models. While the commonplace clustering of (say) booksellers within the central area of many European cities may well reflect consumers' desire to reduce uncertainty through shopping around, this behavioural process cannot be deduced from the study of spatial patterns alone. As Scott [1970] rightly points out, 'the immediate juxtaposition of . . . shops is not necessarily more indicative of the economies to be derived from agglomeration than the juxtaposition of residents is indicative of neighbourliness'.

In these circumstances, it is not surprising that attempts have been made to address the demand side of the locational equation; in other words, to examine empirically and model the micro-scale movements of consumers within planned and unplanned shopping centres. Broadly speaking, these studies can be subdivided into three major categories: *empirical-behavioural*, *cognitive-behavioural* and *conceptual*. The first focuses entirely upon overt, acted-out consumer behaviour, the second concentrates upon consumers' (covert) mental processes and appraisals of retailing milieux whereas the third endeavours to derive meaningful behavioural generalisations by drawing upon both overt and, to a lesser extent, covert investigations.

Empirical-behavioural

Although micro-scale retail location is reputed to be a comparatively underdeveloped field of study, the empirical-behavioural literature is far from negligible. Dating from the early years of the present century, when pedestrian counts for store location purposes first commenced [Hurd, 1903; Brisco, 1927], this consists largely of analyses of shopper behaviour within a variety of retailing environments, ranging from regional shopping centres to neigh-bourhood parades, in contrasting countries and employing all manner of research techniques [e.g. Bennison and Davies, 1977; Boal and Johnson, 1968; Churchman and Tzamir, 1981; Parker and McLaughlin, 1988]. Yet despite these major differences in milieux and methodology, the principal findings of such studies are remarkably consistent.

The first of these is the influence of magnet or attractor stores. Although the nature of the magnet many vary from environment to environment – department stores dominate in traditional town and city centres, supermar-kets hold sway in neighbourhood shopping complexes and restaurants do likewise in festival malls etc. – the studies of micro-spatial shopper behaviour are as one in the key, customer-generating function of the magnet stores and the all-important influence they exert on shopper circulation patterns. To cite but two examples, a questionnaire survey of 1470 shoppers in central Newcastle-upon-Tyne, concluded that consumer movements were largely determined by the locations of the 13 major department and variety stores and Granger Market, which together accounted for 80 per cent of all 3193 reported purchases [Davies and Bennison, 1978]. In Canada, meanwhile, a study of shopper behaviour in the Whyte Center, an unplanned commercial agglomeration in inner city Edmonton, found that the bulk of consumers patronised either the Safeway supermarket or an Army and Navy depart-ment store – and many visited both [Johnson, 1978].

The second fundamental finding concerns the customer interchange that tends to occur between shops of a similar or compatible trade type. This tendency is amply illustrated by Toyne's [1971] detailed year-round examina-tion of shopper behaviour in central Exeter, which revealed that the vast majority of inter-outlet linkages comprised movements from one outfitter, shoe shop, furniture retailer, cafe or whatever to another outfitter, shoe shop, furniture retailer and so on. Equally prominent were inter-type link-ages between complementary retail establishments like supermarkets and greengrocers, greengrocers and bakers and shoe shops and outfitters. By far the best known study of shopper interchange, however, was that undertaken over 30 years ago by Nelson [1958]. After examining the shop-to-shop move-ments of around 100,000 customers in a host of planned and unplanned shopping centres in the US, he assembled his celebrated 'compatibility' tables in which retail business types were deemed to be highly compatible if between 10 and 20 per cent of the customers of both establishments were interchanged, moderately compatible if between 5 and 10 per cent interacted, slightly compatible if between 1 and 5 per cent of shoppers were shared and incompatible if very little customer interchange occurred. Another deleterious category was also devised, though no details on its calculation were supplied.

The third principal finding of the empirical-behavioural perspective pertains to the effects of entry and exit points on consumers' subsequent circulation patterns. As most intra-centre shopping trips commence and conclude at a car park, bus stop, railway terminus or, in certain cities, underground station, the precise location of these facilities has a major influence on the nuances of micro-spatial shopper movement, as indeed do alterations in the provision of transportation termini [Morris and Zisman, 1962]. This point is exemplified by the above mentioned longitudinal studies of shopper movement in central Newcastle-upon-Tyne [Bennison and Davies, 1980; Howard and Davies, 1986]. In the mid-1970s, the nature and geographical extent of consumers' within centre circulation behaviour was very closely related to the spatial arrangement of the three main bus stations. These activity patterns, however, were transformed by the opening of the Metro light rail system in 1982. The construction of the centrally located Monument station in particular ensured that shopper movements became increasingly confined to the core shopping area of Northumberland Street and Eldon Square. Although retailers in the primary shopping thoroughfares undoubtedly benefited from this change, the shopping streets on the peripheries of the city centre suffered severe downturns in trade as a consequence.

The final key finding of the studies of micro-scale consumer behaviour is the frictional effect of distance. Despite the fact that the distances involved are often comparatively short, shoppers appear determined, in line with Zipf's [1949] famous principle, to minimise the expenditure of effort [Johnston, 1973]. In the United States, for instance, the complaint is increasingly being heard that the new generation of mega-scale shopping developments – West Edmonton Mall, Mall of the Americas etc. – is proving just too large for comfort with shoppers being forced to walk what are deemed to be 'excessive' distances [Rogers, 1987; Turchiano, 1990]. Similar charges have recently been laid at the (widely separated) doors of European megacentres [Howard and Reynolds, 1991; McGoldrick and Thompson, 1992], though a friction of distance effect is apparent within even the smallest shopping milieux [Johnston and Kissling, 1971]. Indeed, numerous commentators have concluded that a maximum inter-outlet walking distance exists, with 200 metres being perhaps the most frequently cited spatial limit [Nelson, 1958; Gruen 1973; McKeever and Griffin, 1977].

Cognitive-behavioural

The wellspring of the cognitive-behavioural school of thought is unquestionably Kevin Lynch's [1960] seminal study of city centre images in the United States. By means of interviews, conducted tours and, most significantly for the body of research that was to follow, requiring respondents to draw freehand sketch maps of the locality in question, he managed to elicit the mental constructs of the downtown area held by citizens of Boston, Los Angeles and Jersey City. Although the details of the Lynchian 'mental mapping' methodology have been subject to considerable subsequent criticism [Pocock and Hudson, 1978], his investigations stimulated a spate of similar sketch map studies and the mental maps of many city centres have since been investigated. These include Washington DC [Zawawi, 1970], Chicago [Saarinen, 1977], Toronto [Jones and Simmons, 1987], Berlin [Sieverts, 1967], Amsterdam, Rotterdam and The Hague [de Jonge, 1962], Bristol [Smith, Shaw and Huckle, 1979] and, once again, Newcastle-upon-Tyne [Davies and Bennison, 1978]. Despite the inevitable variations from study to study, most analyses agree that retailing facilities figure prominently in mental representations of the city centre. Shop elements featured strongly in Lynch's [1960] pioneering investigation and over 90 per cent of the respondents to de Jonge's [1962] study of central Rotterdam mentioned the Lijnbann, the major shopping street. Similarly, Sieverts [1967] was able to distinguish between primary and secondary cognitive shopping streets in Berlin, whereas the undergraduate interviewees in Newcastle described some streets in terms of the particular retailing specialisms found therein, as did students in Toronto [Davies and Bennison, 1978; Jones and Simmons, 1987]. Most significantly perhaps, large stores and transportation termini have consistently emerged as important cognitive features in individual images of the city centre [Goodey, 1973; Matthews, 1980; Jansen, 1989].

Consumers' mental representations of retailing at the micro-scale thus appear to lend weight to the principal empirical-behavioural revelations, though the images themselves are far from Elucidean. As a rule, Lynchian style sketches tend towards normalisation, in that complex shapes are rearranged into patterns of straight lines and right angles, and simplification, through the omission of many minor details. The extent of normalisation and simplification, however, depends upon the 'legibility' of the locality; in other words, the simplicity/complexity of the city's spatial configuration and thus the degree to which it can be readily organised into a coherent cognitive pattern [see Marchand, 1974].

Important though mental mapping and similar exercises, such as 'cognitive distance', have proved [see Golledge and Timmermans, 1990], consumer cognitions are not confined to inventories of imperfect information about the micro-scale spatial arrangement of retailing facilities. They also comprise evaluations of, attitudes towards and emotional involvements with the shops and shopping centres that make up their retailing schemata. Indeed, as patronage decisions are determined, at least in part, by consumers' likes, dislikes, attitudes and so on, it is not surprising that such appraisive issues have been studied at length. The bulk of these analyses, however, refer to shopping centres as a whole or individual retail outlets (cf. the vast store image literature), though there are a limited number of micro-scale exceptions to the rule. These include studies of consumer attitudes towards contrasting shopping streets and shopping centres within the same city centre [Allpass and Agergaard, 1979; Smith and Dolman, 1981], attitudes towards the same street before and after pedestrianisation and refurbishment programmes [Roberts, 1989], and attitudes towards different sub-areas *within* the same shopping street [Moles, 1979].

Just as contrasts in *consumers'* attitudes are apparent, so too *retailers* differ in their intra-centre assessments. An attitude survey of 1000 plus retail organisations in the centre of Belfast, for example, revealed that the micro-spatial cognitions of store managers were dominated; firstly, by the customer attracting ability of nearby magnet stores; secondly, the compatibility or incompatibility of adjacent shop types (outlets belonging to the same retail trade were especially favoured); thirdly, the importance of proximate transportation facilities (car parks, bus stops) and potential sources of custom (office blocks, schools); and, fourthly, by a cognitive distance decay effect, wherein 200 metres was the maximum perceived distance over which one retail outlet could generate spin-off trade for another [Brown, 1987b]. Broadly similar findings have been reported in surveys of retailer attitudes in Holland [Timmermans, 1986], Germany [Heinritz and Sittenauer, 1991] and Singapore [Wing and Lee, 1980].

Behavioural generalisations

Despite the many and varied research procedures employed and retailing environments examined by students of micro-scale consumer behaviour and cognition, the above analyses nonetheless concur on the importance of magnet stores, the friction of distance effect, the positioning of points of ingress and egress and the customer interchange that occurs between complementary outlets. This has prompted several attempts to formulate meaningful models of micro-scale consumer behaviour. Perhaps the best known and certainly the most widely cited of these behavioural generalisations are the various locational 'rules' that R. L. Nelson [1958] derived from his extensive surveys of consumer shop-to-shop movement.

In an attempt to encapsulate the substantial volumes of shopper interchange between retail establishments selling related categories of merchandise (theatres and restaurants, outfitters and jewellers etc.), Nelson [1958, p.66] posited his 'rule of retail compatibility', which states that,

> two compatible businesses in close proximity will show an increase in business volume directly proportionate to the incidence of customer interchange between them, inversely proportional to the ratio of business volume of the larger store to that of the smaller store and directly proportionate to the sum of the ratios of purposeful purchasing to total purchasing in each of the two stores.

Similarly, consumers' apparent desire to compare the offerings of several stores before purchase, especially for items where price, pattern, quality and fashion are important considerations, prompted the proposal of the 'theory of cumulative attraction'. This contends that, 'a given number of stores dealing in the same merchandise will do more business if they are located adjacent, or in proximity to each other than if they are widely scattered' [Nelson, 1958, p.58].

Although Nelson's generalisations have been subject to severe criticism [Applebaum and Kaylin, 1974; Okabe and Miki, 1984], the empirical record lends substantial weight to their veracity. As noted earlier, several studies have highlighted the extensive customer interchange that occurs between compatible and competitive retail outlets, and shown, moreover, that the volume of interchange is strongly influenced by the distance between the establishments concerned [Hawes and Lewison, 1984; Bromley and Thomas, 1989; McNeal and Madden, 1987].

These countervailing forces of compatibility (or attraction) and distance are encapsulated in a familiar and much-used macro-scale behavioural generalisation, the gravity model or spatial interaction theory [Haynes and Fotheringham, 1984; Fotheringham and O'Kelly, 1989]. One of the earliest micro-scale adaptations of the gravity model was Morris and Zisman's [1962] study of pedestrian movement in Washington DC. They argued that the volume of customers city centre retail establishments attracted from adjoining office blocks and other places of employment was directly proportional to the size of the retail outlets (and the office blocks) and inversely proportional to the square of the distances between them. A similar model, which also took the locations of transportation termini into account was employed by Ness, Morall and Hutchinson [1969] to estimate journey to work and lunchtime pedestrian movements in downtown Toronto. Other applications include the entropy maximising procedure advanced by Scott [1974], Butler's [1978] less than totally successful attempt to adapt this framework to the movement of shoppers in central Liverpool and Rutherford's [1979] comprehensive analysis of the spatial behaviour of 11,632 individuals in downtown Chicago, which produced a 'reasonable replication of observed trip patterns' (p.57). More recently, Hagishima, Mitsuyoshi and Kurose [1987] have used spatial interaction theory successfully to simulate the micro-scale movements of shoppers in Fukouka City, Japan, though they found that the model, as Rutherford discovered in Chicago, underestimated pedestrian flows in several main streets due to the large traffic volumes generated by transport termini therein.

Apart from spatial interaction theory, other attempts have been made to develop models of micro-scale consumer movement [see May, Turvey and Hopkinson, 1985]. These include the O-D (origin-destination) procedures beloved by traffic planners [Barrett, 1972; Thornton, McCullagh and Bradshaw, 1992], analyses of the relationship between land uses and pedestrian flows [Behnam and Patel, 1977; Sandrock, 1988] and, most notably, the trip chaining models of Borgers and Timmermans [1986a,b]. The last of these comprised a Monte Carlo simulation of the destination choice, route choice and stopping behaviour of 345 shoppers in the centre of Maastricht, Holland. Although the model provided a 'satisfactory' correspondence between predicted and observed pedestrian movement, more recent research suggests that the decision heuristics employed by shoppers are strongly influenced by the complexity of the extant retailing environment and the idiosyncrasies of the individual location [van der Hagen, Borgers and Timmermans, 1991].

Supply side studies

While it is true, as Craig, Ghosh and McLafferty [1984:12] point out, that 'the aggregate choices of consumers shape the overall pattern of retail activity', it is equally undeniable that the patronage decisions of consumers are themselves shaped by the locational choices of retail organisations and analogous supply side decision takers. Thus the distinctive agglomerations of (say) cattle dealers within the marketplaces of the developing world or estate agents and building societies in British city centres may well be a manifestation of consumers' desire to compare the offerings of several competing establishments before purchase. In reality, however, the placement of the stallholders or purveyors of property services is often an outcome of the locational policies adopted by the marketplace administrators and local town planners respectively. These retail establishments, in other words, are not free to choose their locations but are allocated sites according to the preferred spatial arrangement of the appropriate legislative authority. True, the legislators may have devised their optimal layout on the basis of theoretical principles or in an attempt to simplify the consumer's task. Nevertheless, the fact remains that the spatial pattern of cattle dealers or property service outlets is primarily a manifestation of the supply side of the locational equation.

Of all the manifold supply side influences upon retail location perhaps the most important, and certainly the most thoroughly investigated, are: firstly, the policies of shopping centre developers; secondly, the spatial strategies of multiple retail organisations; and, thirdly, the controls of central and local government and equivalent administrators. Although a substantive literature exists in each of these areas, detailed micro-scale considerations remain, as ever, *comparatively* few in number.

Shopping centre development

From a micro-scale standpoint, perhaps the most important aspect of the planned shopping centre is the fact that – as the 'planned' epithet implies – it is a totally controlled environment in which everything is pre-ordained by the developer and designer, and manipulated to maximise customer expenditure and ultimately the returns of the owners and investors. Contrary to the assumptions of land value theory and so on, a free market in property does not obtain. The 'highest and best use' of any given location within a centre is determined by some combination of developer, property consultant and letting agent, *not* by the workings of the bid rent mechanism. Similarly, the intra-centre circulation of shoppers is an effect not a cause of the micro-spatial placement of the centre's occupants. In fact, it has often been asserted that the shopping centre ideal is a controlled flow of pedestrians past as many of the outlets as possible [Martin, 1982; Northen, 1984; Abratt, Fourie and Pitt, 1985].

In the quest for the shopping centre grail of controlled pedestrian flow, a host of 'principles' of tenant placement have been posited. These comprise such well-known rules of thumb as: place the magnet stores at opposite ends of the mall and line the intervening space with smaller outlets; ensure that the main entrances and anchor stores are sufficiently far apart to pull shoppers past the unit shops; avoid culs de sac if at all possible, as they inhibit the free flow of shoppers; place service outlets on the side malls close to the entrances and exits; keep pet shops and dry cleaners away from food shops, and food shops separate from outfitters; and, achieve an even distribution of shoppers in multi-level centres through the judicious arrangement of escalators and eating facilities and by manipulating the tier at which consumers enter the complex [Dawson, 1983; Casazza and Spink, 1985; Maitland, 1990].

Useful though these rules of tenant placement have proved, they are the outcome of a long and expensive trial and error process [Beddington, 1982]. As such, they are subject to fashion effects and have given rise to sterile and specious debate. A consensus, for example, has long been lacking over the efficacy of placing similar types of outlet, such as fashion or food retailers, or stores of comparable quality levels, in close spatial proximity within the centre. Shopping centre developers in the United States have been variously advised to separate similar shop types in order to maximise consumer movement within the centre, thereby increasing their exposure to its attractions [Rouse Company, 1969; Stambaugh, 1978; McKeever and Griffin, 1977], and to cluster compatible shop types in order to ease the shopper's task and to enable certain areas of the centre to become magnets in their own right [Smith, 1956; Berman, 1970; Gruen, 1973]. A zonal compromise between the two extremes has also been suggested and this appears to be the preferred approach at present, at least in the larger regional, super-regional and mega-regional schemes [Jackson and Johnson, 1991].

Although it is easy to condemn the shopping centre industry for its continuing reliance upon the received wisdom of tenant placement, it must be appreciated that the placement process, constrained as it is by the financial plan and overall design, is a highly complex undertaking [Gosling and Maitland, 1976]. Equally importantly perhaps, the comparatively few published studies that there are lend weight to the saws of tenant placement [see Anderson, 1985; Sim and Way, 1989; Brown, 1992]. Guthrie [1980a,b], for example, conducted a multiple regression analysis of the sales figures of 848 stores in ten US regional centres and concluded that certain locations within the malls performed substantially better than others. Central courtyards and corner sites proved to be the best overall locations in the selected shopping complexes, though mid-mall and ground floor situations also produced above average sales performances. Somewhat surprisingly, locations adjacent to anchor stores tended to underperform, as, rather less surprisingly, did sites in the side malls. Of all the micro-scale options, however, culs de sac were by far the worst performers. Stores in these dead ends averaged as little as 53 per cent of the sales figures of equivalent establishments in superior spatial settings. Besides his analysis of broad sub-areas within regional shopping centres, Guthrie explored the extent to which similar types of retail store benefited from geographical juxtaposition. He found: firstly, that clusters of ladieswear outlets have substantial synergistic effects; secondly, that menswear outlets gain considerably from close geographical proximity; and, thirdly, that retailers of menswear and ladieswear mix well. Agglomeration, in short, pays dividends.

Retailers' spatial strategies

Just as the planned shopping centre has attracted considerable academic attention, so too an extensive empirical literature exists on the spatial strategies of individual retail firms and the diffusion of innovative retailing institutions [Allaway, Mason and Black, 1991]. These include analyses of regional and off-price shopping centres in the USA [Cohen, 1972; Lord, 1985], hypermarkets in Europe [Dawson, 1984] and retail organisations as diverse as McDonalds [Aspbury, 1984], Macys [Laulajainen, 1987], Marshall Field [Laulajainen, 1990] and Marks and Spencer [Bird and Witherwick, 1986].

Useful though such studies have proved, however, they have tended to overlook the competitive aspect of retailers' spatial strategies. With the possible exceptions of market leaders, such as Toys R Us or IKEA, and the unreal multiple retailers of most neoclassical models [Teitz, 1968; Ghosh and Buchanan, 1988], very few organisations can afford to ignore their competitors when taking locational decisions. Indeed, several competitor orientated spatial strategies can be identified, most notably 'avoidance', 'matching' and 'predation'. The avoidance approach, which, as the name implies, simply involves keeping away from the competition, is exemplified by the growth of variety stores in the central belt of Sweden [Laulajainen and Gadde, 1986], branch banks in Charlotte, North Carolina [Lord and Wright, 1981] and the development of the Kwik Save discount grocery chain in Great Britain [Sparks, 1990]. A matching or competitor-seeking stance, by contrast, has been pursued by co-operative retailing organisations in Finland [Laulajainen, 1981], fast food restaurants in Atlanta [Pillsbury, 1987] and Filene's speciality department store chain in Boston [Cohen and Lewis, 1967]. Safeway, meanwhile, was once renowned for its predation approach which comprised buying up all the available sites in a market, thereby pre-empting its competitors, or by locating in very close proximity to established supermarkets and precipitating a price war, thus driving out the rival [West and von Hohenbalken, 1984]. A similar strategy of 'keeping out the competition' has been deduced from longitudinal studies of the spatial patterns of convenience stores and petrol stations in Denver and Hong Kong [Lee and Koutsopoulos, 1976; Lee and Schmidt, 1980].

As with so much of the locational literature, most of the above investigations of retailers' spatial strategies have been conducted at the meso- and macro-scales of analysis. Yet micro-scale considerations are vitally important and are clearly taken into account by retail organisations. It is not unusual, after all, to find several branches of the same chain or conglomerate retailing organisation in the same shopping district or centre. There are two branches of Marks and Spencer, six branches of Benetton, three branches of Burger King and eighteen outlets belonging to the Burton Group alone in Oxford Street, London, for example, and the West Edmonton Mall is similarly endowed [Johnson, 1991]. Micro-scale locational decisions, moreover, are often taken with regard to competitive or complementary establishments. In Britain, 'as close as possible to Marks and Spencer' remains a widely espoused spatial strategy [Peters, 1990] and a 'parasitic' approach, where firms locate themselves in very close proximity to outlets in entirely different sectors of the retail industry (supermarkets adjacent to drug stores, for instance), has been reported on numerous occasions [Cohen and Lewis, 1967; Berman and Evans, 1991]. For example, the chairman of T & S Stores, a chain of some 600 discount convenience stores, has recently stated that he prefers to site his outlets 'next to shops which have a high customer flow such as bakers or greengrocers, rather than banks or building societies' [Thornhill, 1992, p.14]. Beavon [1970], Brown [1987b] and Brous [1981] have also described how the micro-locational decisions of retail organisations in South Africa, Great Britain and the United States respectively are made with reference to propinquitous outlets, especially major magnet stores. Yet anecdotal evidence aside this issue has been all but neglected by students of spatial strategy hitherto and must be considered a major priority for future research.

Government and administrative influences

Important though the foregoing supply side factors have proved, the location of retailing activities is not simply a reflection of the tenant placement policies of shopping centre developers, nor an artefact of the spatial machinations of multiple retailers intent on optimising branch networks whilst confounding their competitors. It is also attributable to the locational policies or the locational outcomes of the policies of central and local governments and other legislative authorities, such as the administrators of marketplaces in the developed, developing and indeed ancient worlds.

As discussed in detail by several commentators [Boddewyn and Hollander, 1972; Dholakia and Dholakia, 1978], the retail industry is subject to a plethora of direct and indirect policy controls, some of which have micro-scale locational implications. In the United Kingdom, for instance, these include the Betting, Gaming and Lotteries Act of 1963 and the Town and Country Planning Use Classes Orders of 1972 and 1988. The former controls the number, appearance and location of betting shops, which are prohibited in close proximity to churches, schools or premises patronised by persons of 'known bad character'. The latter serve to permit or prohibit proposed changes of land use, such as from 'shop' to 'office' or, more specifically, from certain types of retail outlet to others (e.g. bookseller to bank, or grocer to hot food facility). The upshot of these micro-scale interventions, according to Davies and Bennison [1987], is that the internal spatial organisation of British shopping districts is more a manifestation of retail planning policies than the market forces the plans were designed to accommodate.

In the United States, furthermore, the territorial exclusivity clauses of franchise agreements are subject to state and federal law [Stern and El-Ansary, 1988], zoning ordinances are ubiquitous, albeit circumventable [Kane and Belkin, 1981] and, to cite arguably the best known example, the tenant mix planning procedures of shopping centre developers have attracted detailed government scrutiny. In the early years of the shopping centre industry the emerging concept of a controlled tenant mix was accompanied by the addition of a variety of 'restrictions and exclusives' clauses to centre leases. Introduced at the insistence of the all-powerful anchor stores, these 'inducement' clauses allowed the magnets effectively to determine the merchandise range, pricing policy, space allocation and precise location within the complex of the centre's other occupants [ICSC, 1974; Cutler and Reilly, 1976]. Equally commonplace were covenants concerning store opening hours, permitted advertising and promotional activities, membership of the merchant's association and the prohibition of other branches of the same organisation within a specified radius of the centre [see Cooper, 1975; Mason, 1975; Mallen and Savitt, 1979]. Such restraints of trade attracted the attention of the FTC which issued, after a landmark investigation of leasing practices at Tyson's Corner regional shopping centre, a series of consent decrees relating to proscribed activities [Savitt, 1985].

Although the spatial organisation of British shopping districts and American shopping centres cannot be understood without an appreciation of the regulatory context, the degree of administrative control in the western world pales by comparison with that exercised in the fixed and periodic markets of the developing and ancient worlds. Whether it be the *souks* of Kuwait City [Al-Otaibi, 1990], the *tamus* of Sabah [Burrough, 1978], the *tianguis* of Mexico City [Pyle, 1978], the *raun* of New Guinea [Ward *et al.*, 1978], the *zoma* of Madagasgar [Donque, 1966] or the *nien-shih* of T'ang dynasty China [Braudel, 1982], the internal spatial organisation of these urban, rural, formal and informal marketplaces leaves very little to chance and is often minutely controlled [Moore, 1985]. Once again, however, the predominant micro-scale organising principle is the clustering of sellers of similar wares and the separation of purveyors of incompatible merchandise. It has been observed in the markets of Manila [McIntyre, 1955], Madras [Lessinger, 1985], Mali [Harts-Broekhuis and Verkoren, 1987] and pre-conquest Mexico [Berdan,

1985], the medinas of Morocco, Algeria and Tunisia [Troin, 1990; Thompson, 1982; Miossec, 1990], the forums of ancient Rome [Allix, 1922], the fairs and marketplaces of medieval Europe [Alexander, 1970; Moore, 1985] and many more besides.

Current status and future prospects

This article has endeavoured to demonstrate that, although minute by meso- and macro-scale standards, the literature on micro-scale retail location is far from negligible. It is, admittedly, scattered throughout a diverse mix of academic specialisms such as marketing, geography, economics, psychology, operations research, urban planning, architecture, estate management and regional science. The material, moreover, is characterised by definitional and methodological disputation, whether it be the most appropriate procedures for delimiting shopping districts, the comparative advantages of nearest neighbour analysis or quadrat analysis in the statistical assessment of shop patterns, the existence or otherwise of mental maps, the bogus calibration and spatial non-stationarity problems of the gravity model, or, simply, disentangling the relationship between the spatial patterns of retail activity and the processes of supply and demand which appear to give rise to them.

Yet despite the above methodological differences and marked variations in approach – be it theoretical and associated shop pattern analysis, demand side led or supply side orientated – the micro-scale literature exhibits a surprisingly high degree of commonality. Summarised in Table 1, retail location at the micro-scale is characterised by centripetal and centrifugal tendencies, and the interaction or combination of these two opposing forces. Centripetal tendencies are inherent in the theoretical underpinnings provided by the principle of minimum differentiation, the empirically observable and all but universal clusters of specialised retail activities (bookshops, electrical goods suppliers, kola nut dealers etc.), consumers' demonstrable desire to compare the wares of several competing outlets before purchase and the policy of 'matching', clustering or locating adjacent to outlets of a similar trade type/quality level widely espoused by shopping centre developers,

Table 1 Retail location at the micro-scale: approaches and insights

	Centripetal	*Centrifugal*	*Combination*
Theory	principle of minimum differentiation	bid rent theory	complex model
Pattern	cluster	dispersed	linear
Demand	comparison	multi-purpose	convenience
Supply	match	mix	intercept

town planners and retail organisations respectively. Centrifugal tendencies, on the other hand, are implicit in bid rent theory (in that competition for the prime central locations pushes lower order retailing functions progressively to the peripheries of unplanned shopping districts), the mixed pattern of shop types that characterises most non-specialist shopping districts and centres, consumers' everpresent preference for variety, a choice of *different* shop types within easy reach, and, not least, the belief long held by many retailers, developers and planners that direct competition is best avoided or kept at arms' length and that a balanced and carefully managed 'mix' of compatible shop types is always preferable to the uncertain (and invariably agglomerated) outcome of the free play of market forces.

Centripetal and centrifugal forces, of course, do not act in isolation and, as exemplified by Davies' 'complex' model of city centre retailing, attempts have been made to strike a meaningful balance between the two. Thus the linear component of the complex model can be viewed as the spatial manifestation of the countervailing tendencies towards agglomeration and dispersal, insofar as it combines the clustering of retail outlets on an edge-of-town-centre arterial and their spatial extension alongside it. Similarly, shoppers' overarching desire for convenience and effort minimisation underpins *both* their comparison shopping activities (e.g. several shoe shops in close spatial proximity) and their multi-purpose trips for different items (indeed, the wide range but limited assortment offered by hypermarkets and department stores represents the same principle under a single roof). Likewise, it is arguable that the supply side equivalent of this phenomenon is the parasitic or interceptor location, where a retail outlet is interposed (as a consequence of the organisation's spatial strategy or the activities of a surrogate supply side decision taker) between the consumers' point of entry into the shopping environment and their primary or ultimate destination, usually the magnet store.

Given the high degree of commonality in the literature, irrespective of the diverse approaches adopted by individual researchers, it is tempting to conclude that micro-scale retail location is characterised, above all, by the agglomeration of similar shop types and the dispersal of these clusters throughout the said shopping district. Indeed, as a basic organising principle, this appears to have much to commend it. The reality of micro-scale retail location, however, is rather less straightforward, in that – theoretical assumptions notwithstanding – all retailing outlets are not created equal. Even though they may belong to the same trade 'type', retail establishments differ enormously in terms of size, reputation, range of goods, pricing policy, service quality, promotional activity, customer pulling power and so on. In fact, much of the attraction of a specialist retailing cluster derives from these non-locational differences between the various neighbouring outlets. After all, if every establishment offered precisely the same goods, at exactly the same prices and so on, there would be nothing to choose between them and no reason to compare their wares. Indeed, shop pattern studies have shown that when outlets of the same type are comparatively undifferentiated – e.g. CTNs – there is a tendency towards spatial dispersal.

In other words, the legitimacy of the entire body of micro-scale locational literature rests ultimately on the veracity of 'trade type' taxonomies. Although long established and still in widespread use, such classifications invariably fail to withstand close scrutiny. Apart from the advent of 'scrambled merchandising', which has prompted many commentators to question the continuing relevance of trade type distinctions *per se* [Dawson, 1982; Dawson and Sparks, 1986; O'Brien and Harris, 1991], the number of categories in the classification and the subtlety, or otherwise, of their gradation can prove equally problematical. The frequently noted clustering of 'food' outlets, for example, disguises the fact that individual butchers or greengrocers tend to avoid locations adjacent to direct competitors, but are often situated in close proximity to compatible 'food' purveyors like bakeries, grocers and so on. The characteristics of the classification, in short, influence the outcome of the empirical analysis, whether it be the study of shop patterns, consumers' store-to-store movements or the placement policies of town planners and shopping centre developers.

Thus, although Table 1 represents an attempt to transcend trade type considerations by summarising the theoretical (and associated pattern analysis), demand side and supply side approaches, it must also be appreciated that the realities of micro-scale location are by no means as clearly delineated as the table suggests. Centrifugal and centripetal tendencies not only overlap, as noted above, but the relationship between the various components is multifaceted and reflexive. It is, for example, an oversimplification to assume that the spatial pattern of retailing is an *outcome* of the forces of demand and supply. The reality, of course, is that the patronisation and locational decisions of consumers and retailers (or their supply side surrogates such as urban planners, shopping centre developers and marketplace administrators) are influenced if not determined by extant patterns of retail activity. Likewise, land use planners and so on plan on the basis of existing conceptualisations such as the core-frame model or, at a different scale, central place theory, and which determine in turn the spatial patterns of retailing activity. In other words, the processes of supply and demand, the geography of retailing and theoretical insights are intimately intertwined. The study of micro-scale retail location is thus entangled in what Giddens [1990] terms the 'double hermeneutic', where the very existence of a concept (or classification) influences and alters the phenomena to which it pertains.

Just as the relationships between demand, supply and the spatial arrangement of retail outlets are not definitive, neither is our understanding of retail location at the micro-scale. Despite the enormous literature that already exists on the subject of retail location generally and, to a much lesser extent, the specifics of the micro-scale, there remains ample scope for additional research activity within each of the theoretical (and associated pattern analysis), demand side and supply side traditions. With regard to the first of these, recent years have witnessed enormous strides in the study of bid rent theory and the principle of minimum differentiation. Multi-stop and multi-purpose shoppping behaviours, dynamic dimensions, uncertainty reduction and a host of other more realistic assumptions have been successfully incorporated within the models. Set against these normative insights, however, latter-day shop pattern analyses have been less than impressive. The bulk of the empirical 'tests' of the bid rent, PMD and 'complex' models are 20 to 30 years old (e.g. Berry's [1963] classic Chicago study and Davies' [1972a] landmark analysis of Coventry). Given the enormous changes in the spatial structure of retailing since then, it may be worthwhile attempting to address, once again, the most basic of questions: is the bid rent model still applicable to the spatial organisation of urban retailing and the micro-geography shopping districts? Do stores of the same retail trade and of similar quality levels still cluster together within planned and unplanned shopping centres? Is the complex model still applicable to the internal spatial organisation of central shopping districts or have latter-day planning interventions rendered it all but redundant?

In a similar vein, the empirical, cognitive and conceptual variants of the demand side perspective have much to offer today's micro-scale research workers. The empirical-behavioural approach, for instance, remains beset by a basic methodological problem concerning the lack of correspondence between consumers' observed and reported behaviour [Shepherd and Thomas, 1980]. Researchers have traditionally utilised the latter technique, which is substantially cheaper if less reliable than the former, though asking retail managers to provide insights into micro-scale shopper movement may provide a cost-effective alternative [Heinritz and Sittenauer, 1991]. On the cognitive side, moreover, mental mapping exercises relevant to retailing have hitherto been confined to central business districts or, on occasion, the internal layout of individual retail outlets [Sommer and Aitkens, 1982]. Consumers' cognitions of planned suburban shopping environments have yet to be fully explored, as indeed have retailers' [though see Foxall and Hackett, 1992]. Likewise, despite widespread agreement on the principal characteristics of micro-scale shopper behaviour, attempts to model the movements of shoppers within centres remain few and far between. There are, admittedly, a number of important exceptions to this oversight, but as Baron [1991, p.3] has recently and tantalisingly pointed out 'if you can find a workable model of pedestrian flows in shopping centres, you can make a fortune'.

Last but not least, the supply side of the intra-centre locational equation is in particular need of further investigation. As discussed above, micro-scale factors manifestly impinge upon the spatial strategies of retail organisations, yet this issue has hardly featured in the locational literature. The rules of thumb employed in the internal spatial organisation of planned shopping centres are also comparatively under-researched, as are the specific micro-scale effects of legislative change. A final component of the locational canon that has been sorely neglected by retailing researchers is the unique character of the micro-site (i.e. the individual site as opposed to the location's situation relative to the whole shopping centre or district). The significance of site specific factors like street layout, alignment, aspect, slope, pavement width, prevailing wind, foot frontage, visibility, proximity to car parking, pedestrian crossings, street corners and so on were recognised and discussed at length over 60 years ago [Pyle, 1926; Parkins, 1930]. Yet the bulk of the subsequent micro-scale literature has overlooked these essentially idiographic elements in the search for meaningful generalisations. Generalisations, moreover, that in many cases comprise uncritical adaptations of concepts developed at the macro- and meso-locational scales (bid rent theory, spatial interaction theory etc.). It is arguable, therefore, that until such times as students of micro-scale location come up with meaningful concepts of their own, the subject will continue to languish as an 'interesting but ignored' component of the retailing mix.

Conclusion

It has often been said that a few yards can make all the difference between success and failure in retailing. This article has reviewed the literature on retail location at the micro-scale, arguing that theoretical, demand side and supply side approaches can be discerned. The theoretical approach comprises two long-established, normative conceptualisations, bid rent theory and the principle of minimum differentiation, various inductively derived attempts to integrate the two into a plausible combination theory and a body of associated empirical research which is broadly supportive of the hypothesised spatial patterns of retail activity. Demand side studies range from the analysis of consumer movements within planned and unplanned shopping centres and mental mapping exercises, to micro-scale adaptations of the gravity model and analyses of the much-lauded locational dicta of R. L. Nelson. Supply side perspectives include the tenant placement policies practised by owners and developers of planned shopping centres, the micro-scale locational strategies of conglomerate retailing organisations and, not least, the (often imperceptible) influence of government legislation and analogous administrators.

Albeit small in meso- or macro-scale terms, the subject of micro-scale location has generated a surprisingly sizeable literature, though it is scattered across a number of academic specialisms from economics to architecture. There is, none the less, ample scope for additional research activity within each of the theoretical, demand side and supply side schools of thought. If, however, the study of micro-scale location is to develop beyond its current status of 'interesting but ignored', a meaningful reformulation of long-established but increasingly outmoded trade type taxonomies is urgently required, as are attempts to develop models and theories that are macro-scale specific rather than straightforward applications of macro-scale concepts. Further research, as they say, is clearly necessary.

References

Abratt, R., J. L. C. Fourie and L. F. Pitt, 1985, 'Tenant Mix: The Key to a Successful Shopping Centre', *Quarterly Review of Marketing*, Vol.10, No.3.

Alexander, D., 1970, *Retailing in England During the Industrial Revolution*, London: Athlone Press.

Alexander, I. C., 1974, *The City Centre: Patterns and Problems*, Nedlands: University of Western Australia Press.

Allaway, A. W., J. B. Mason and W. C. Black, 1991, 'The Dynamics of Spatial and Temporal Diffusion in a Retail Setting', in A. Ghosh and C. A. Ingene (eds.), *Spatial Analysis in Marketing: Theory, Methods and Applications*, Greenwich: JAI Press.

Allix, A., 1992, 'The Geography of Fairs: Illustrated by Old-World Examples', *Geographical Review*, Vol.12.

Allpass, J. and E. Agergaard, 1979, 'The City Centre – For Whom?', in I. Hammarstrom and T. Hall (eds.), *Growth and Transformation of the Modern City*, Stockholm: Swedish Council for Building Research.

Al-Otaibi, O., 1990, 'The Development of Planned Shopping Centres in Kuwait', in A. M. Findlay, R. Paddison and J. A. Dawson (eds.), *Retailing Environments in Developing Countries*, London: Routledge.

Anderson, C. H., T. H. Parker and S. R. Stanley, 1990, '1990 Site Selection Study: Summary of Results', paper presented at Applied Geography Conference, Charlotte, October.

Anderson, P. M., 1985, 'Association of Shopping Centre Anchors with Performance of a Non-anchor Speciality Chain's Stores', *Journal of Retailing*, Vol.61, No.2.

Applebaum, W. and S. O. Kaylin, 1974, *Case Studies in Shopping Centre Development and Operation*, New York: International Council of Shopping Centres.

Aspbury, G. F., 1984, 'The Geography of Franchise Expansion: An Illinois Example', *Bulletin of the Illinois Geographical Society*, Vol.26, No.2.

Balchin, P. N., J. L. Kieve and G. H. Bull, 1988, *Urban Land Economics and Public Policy*, Basingstoke: Macmillan.

Ball, M., 1979, 'A Critique of Urban Economics', *International Journal of Urban and Regional Research*, Vol.3, No.3.

Ball, M., 1985, 'The Urban Rent Question', *Environment and Planning A*, Vol.17, No.4.

Baron, S., 1991, 'No Accounting for Shoppers?', *O R Insight*, Vol.4, No.1.

Barrett, R., 1972, 'Moving Pedestrians in a Traffic-Free Environment', *Traffic Engineering and Control*, Vol.14.

Beaujeu-Garnier, J., and A. Delobez, 1979, *Geography of Marketing*, London: Longman, translated by S. H. Beaver.

Beaumont, J. R., 1988, 'Store Location Analysis: Problems and Progress', in N. Wrigley (ed.), *Store Choice, Store Location and Market Analysis*, London: Routledge.

Beavon, K. S. O., 1970, *Land Use Patterns in Port Elizabeth: A Geographical Analysis in the Environs of Main Street*, Cape Town: Balkema.

Beddington, N., 1982, *Design for Shopping Centres*, London: Butterworth Scientific.

Behnam, J. and B. G. Patel, 1977, 'A Method for Estimating Pedestrian Volume in a Central Business District', *Transportation Research Record*, Vol.629.

438   *The evolution and development of retailing*

Bellett, J., 1969, 'Singapore's Central Area Retail Pattern in Transition', *Journal of Tropical Geography*, Vol.28, No.1.

Bennison, D. J. and R. L. Davies, 1977, *The Movement of Shoppers Within the Central Area of Newcastle-upon-Tyne*, Department of Geography, Seminar Papers No.34, Newcastle: University of Newcastle-upon-Tyne.

Bennison, D. J. and R. L. Davies, 1980, 'The Impact of Town Centre Shopping Schemes in Britain', *Progress in Planning*, Vol.14.

Berdan, F., 1985, 'Markets in the economy of Aztec Mexico', in S. Plattner (ed.), *Markets and Marketing*, New York: University Press of America.

Berman, B., 1970, 'Location Analysis within Regional Shopping Centres', in D. J. Rachman (ed.), *Retail Management Strategy: Selected Readings*, Englewood Cliffs: Prentice Hall.

Berman, B. and J. R. Evans, 1991, *Retail Management: A Strategic Approach*, New York: Macmillan, fifth edition.

Berry, B. J. L., 1963, *Commercial Structure and Commercial Blight: Retail Patterns and Processes in the City of Chicago*, Department of Geography, Research Paper No.85, Chicago: University of Chicago.

Bird, J. and M. E. Witherwick, 1986, 'Marks and Spencer: The Geography of an Image', *Geography*, Vol.71, No.4.

Boal, F. W. and D. B. Johnson, 1968, 'Nondescript Streets', *Traffic Quarterly*, Vol.22.

Boddewyn, J. J. and S. C. Hollander, 1972, *Public Policy Toward Retailing: An International Symposium*, Lexington: D. C. Heath.

Borgers, A. and H. J. P. Timmermans, 1986a, 'City Centre Entry Points, Store Location Patterns and Pedestrian Route Choice Behaviour: A Microlevel Simulation Model', *Socio Economic Planning Science*, Vol.20, No.1.

Borgers, A. and H. J. P. Timmermans, 1986b, 'A Model of Pedestrian Route Choice and Demand for Retail Facilities within Inner-city Shopping Areas', *Geographical Analysis*, Vol.18.

Brady, J. E. M., 1977, 'The Pattern of Retailing in Central Dublin', unpublished MA thesis, Dublin: University College Dublin.

Braudel, F., 1982, *The Wheels of Commerce*, London: Collins, trans. S. Reynolds.

Breheny, M. J., 1988, 'Practical Methods of Retail Location Analysis: A Review', in N. Wrigley (ed.), *Store Choice, Store Location and Market Analysis*, London: Routledge.

Brisco, N. A., 1927, *Principles of Retailing*, New York: Prentice-Hall.

Bromley, R. D. F. and C. J. Thomas, 1989, 'The Impact of Shop Type and Spatial Structure on Shopping Linkages in Retail Parks', *Town Planning Review*, Vol.60, No.1.

Brous, P., 1981, 'The Chain Store Looks at the Future', in G. Sternlieb and J. W. Hughes (eds.), *Shopping Centres USA*, Centre for Urban Policy Research, New Jersey: Rutgers.

Brown, S., 1987a, 'The Complex Model of City Centre Retailing: An Historical Interpretation', *Transactions, Institute of British Geographers*, Vol.12, No.1.

Brown, S., 1987b, 'Retailers and Micro-Retail Location: A Perceptual Perspective', *International Journal of Retailing*, Vol.2, No.3.

Brown, S., 1988, 'Information Seeking, External Search and "Shopping" Behaviour: Preliminary Evidence from a Planned Shopping Centre', *Journal of Marketing Management*, Vol.4, No.1.

Brown, S., 1989, 'Retail Location Theory: The Legacy of Harold Hotelling', *Journal of Retailing*, Vol.65, No.4.

Brown, S., 1992, 'Tenant Mix, Tenant Placement and Shopper Behaviour in a Planned Shopping Centre', *Service Industries Journal*, Vol.12, No.3.

Buckwalter, D. W., 1989, 'Effects of Competition on the Patterns of Retail Districts in the Chattanooga, Tennessee, Metropolitan Area', *Southeastern Geographer*, Vol.29, No.1.

Burrough, J. B., 1978, 'The Tamus of Sabah', in R. H. T. Smith (ed.), *Market Place Trade – Periodic Markets, Hawkers and Traders in Africa, Asia and Latin America*, Centre for Transportation Studies, Vancouver: University of British Columbia.

Butler, S., 1978, *Modelling Pedestrian Movements in Central Liverpool*, Working Paper 98, Institute for Transport Studies, Leeds: University of Leeds.

Campbell, N., 1970, 'An Application of the Core-Frame Concept to the CBD, London, Ontario, in Three Dimensions', *Ontario Geography*, Vol.5.

Carter, H., 1983, *An Introduction to Urban Historical Geography*, London: Edward Arnold.

Casazza, J. A. and F. H. Spink, 1985, *Shopping Centre Development Handbook*, Washington DC: Urban Land Institute, second edition.

Chamberlin, E. H., 1933, *The Theory of Monopolistic Competition: A Re-orientation of the Theory of Value*, Cambridge: Harvard University Press, eighth edition.

Chudzynska, I., 1981, 'Locational Specialisation of Retail Trade Functions in Warszawa', *Environment and Planning A*, Vol.13, No.8.

Churchman, A. and Tzamir, Y., 1981, 'Traffic Segregation and Pedestrian Behaviour in a Shopping Centre', *Man-Environment Systems*, Vol.11.

Cohen, S. B. and G. K. Lewis, 1967, 'Form and Function in the Geography of Retailing', *Economic Geography*, Vol.43, No.1.

Cohen, Y. S., 1972, *Diffusion of an Innovation in an Urban System: The Spread of Planned Regional Shopping Centres in the United States, 1949–1968*, Department of Geography, Research Paper 140, Chicago: University of Chicago.

Cooper, M. B., 1975, 'Shopping Centre Lease Agreements: Participants and Perceptions of Selected Operating Policies', in H. W. Nash and D. P. Rodin (eds.), *Proceedings: Southern Marketing Association 1975 Conference*, Mississippi: Mississippi State University.

Craig, C. S., A. Ghosh and S. McLafferty, 1984, 'Models of the Retail Location Process: A Review', *Journal of Retailing*, Vol.60, No.1.

Curry, D. J., 1993, *The New Marketing Research Systems*, New York: Wiley.

Cutler, E. R. and J. R. Reilly, 1976, *The Anti-trust Aspects of Restrictive Covenants in Shopping Centre Leases*, New York: International Council of Shopping Centres.

Davies, D. H., 1965, *Land Use in Central Cape Town: A Study in Urban Geography*, Cape Town: Longmans.

Davies, G. J. and K. Harris, 1990, *Small Business: The Independent Retailer*, Basingstoke: Macmillan.

Davies, R. L., 1972a, 'The Retail Pattern of the Central Area of Coventry', in *The Retail Structure of Cities*, Occasional Publication No.1, London: Institute of British Geographers.

Davies, R. L., 1972b, 'Structural Models of Retail Distribution: Analogies with Settlement and Land Use Theories', *Transactions, Institute of British Geographers*, Vol.57, No.1.

Davies, R. L., 1976, *Marketing Geography: With Special Reference to Retailing*, Corbridge: Retail and Planning Associates.

Davies, R. L., 1984, *Retail and Commercial Planning*, London: Croom Helm.

Davies, R. L., and D. J. Bennison, 1978, 'Retailing in the City Centre: The Characters of Shopping Streets', *Tijdschrift voor Economische en Sociale Geografie*, Vol.69, No.5.

Davis, D., 1966, *A History of Shopping*, London: Routledge and Kegan Paul.

Dawson, J. A., 1980, 'Introduction', in J. A. Dawson (ed.), *Retail Geography*, London: Croom Helm.

Dawson, J. A., 1982, *Commercial Distribution in Europe*, London: Croom Helm.

Dawson, J. A., 1983, *Shopping Centre Development*, London: Longman.

Dawson, J. A., 1984, 'Structural-Spatial Relationships in the Spread of Hypermarket Retailing', in E. Kaynak and R. Savitt (eds.), *Comparative Marketing Systems*, New York: Praeger.

Dawson, J. A. and L. Sparks, 1986, 'Issues for the Planning of Retailing in Scotland', *Scottish Planning Law and Practice*, Vol.18.

De Blij, H. J., 1962, 'The Functional Structure and Central Business Direct of Laurenço, Marques, Mocambique', *Economic Geography*, Vol.38, No.1.

De Jonge, D., 1962, 'Images of Urban Areas, their Structures and Psychological Foundations', *Journal of the American Institute of Planners*, Vol.28.

De Palma, A., V. Ginsburgh and J.-F. Thisse, 1987, 'On the Existence of Location Equilibria in the 3-Firm Hotelling Problem', *Journal of Industrial Economics*, Vol.36, No.2.

Devletoglou, N. E., 1965, 'A Dissenting View of Duopoly and Spatial Competition', *Economica*, Vol.32, May.

Dewar, D. and V. Watson, 1990, *Urban Markets: Developing Informal Retailing*, London: Routledge.

Dholakia, N. and R. R. Dholakia, 1978, 'A Comparative View of Public Policy Toward Distribution', *European Journal of Marketing*, Vol.12, No.8.

Donque, G., 1966, 'Le zoma de Tananarive: étude géographique d'un marche urbain', *Madagascar Revue de Géographie*, Vol.8.

Eaton, B. C. and R. G. Lipsey, 1975, 'The Principle of Minimum Differentiation Revisited: Some New Developments in the Theory of Spatial Competition', *Review of Economic Studies*, Vol.42, No.1.

Eaton, B. C. and R. G. Lipsey, 1979, 'Comparison Shopping and the Clustering of Homogeneous Firms', *Journal of Regional Science*, Vol.19, No.4.

Fogg, W., 1932, 'The Suq: A Study in the Human Geography, of Morocco', *Geography*, Vol.17, Nov.

Fotheringham, A. S. and M. E. O'Kelly, 1989, *Spatial Interaction Models: Formulations and Applications*, Dordrecht: Kluwer.

Foxall, G. R. and P. Hackett, 1992, 'Consumer Perceptions of Micro-Retail Location: Way Finding and Cognitive Mapping in Planned and Organic Shopping Environments', *International Review of Retail, Distribution and Consumer Research*, Vol.2, No.3.

Freeman, D. B. and F. L. Dungey, 1981, 'A Spatial Duopoly: Competition in the Western Canadian Fur Trade, 1770–1835', *Journal of Historical Geography*, Vol.7, No.3.

Friedrichs, J. and A. C. Goodman, 1987, *The Changing Downtown: A Comparative Study of Baltimore and Hamburg*, Berlin: de Gruyter.

Fujita, M., H. Ogawa and J.-F. Thisse, 1988, 'A Spatial Competition Approach to Central Place Theory: Some Basic Principles', *Journal of Regional Science*, Vol.28.

Fujita, M. and T. E. Smith, 1990, 'Additive-interaction Models of Spatial Agglomeration', *Journal of Regional Science*, Vol.30, No.1.

Garner, B. J., 1966, *The Internal Structure of Retail Nucleations*, Northwestern University Studies in Geography, No.12, Department of Geography, Evanston: Northwestern University.

Ghosh, A., 1990, *Retail Management*, Hinsdale: Dryden.

Ghosh, A. and B. Buchanan, 1988, 'Multiple Outlets in a Duopoly: A First Entry Paradox', *Geographical Analysis*, Vol.20, No.2.

Ghosh, A. and C. S. Craig, 1991, 'FRANSYS: A Franchise Distribution System Location Model', *Journal of Retailing*, Vol.67, No.4.

Ghosh, A. and C. A. Ingene, 1991, *Spatial Analysis in Marketing: Theory, Methods and Applications*, Greenwich: JAI Press.

Ghosh, A. and S. McLafferty, 1987, *Location Strategies for Retail and Service Firms*, Lexington: Lexington Books.

Giddens, A., 1990, *The Consequences of Modernity*, London: Polity Press.

Golledge, R. G. and H. Timmermans, 1990, 'Applications of Behavioural Research on Spatial Problems I: Cognition', *Progress in Human Geography*, Vol.14, No.1.

Goodchild, M. F., 1984, 'ILACS: A Location-Allocation Model for Retail Site Selection', *Journal of Retailing*, Vol.60, No.1.

Goodchild, M. F., 1991, 'Geographic Information Systems', *Journal of Retailing*, Vol.67, No.1.

Goodey, B., 1973, *Perception of the Environment*, Centre for Urban and Regional Studies, Occasional Paper 17, Birmingham: University of Birmingham.

Gosling, D. and B. Maitland, 1976, *Design and Planning of Retail Systems*, London: Architectural Press.

Gruen, V., 1973, *Centres for the Urban Environment: Survival of the Cities*, New York: Van Nostrand Reinhold.

Guthrie, P. R., 1980a, 'Statistical Survey Reveals Effect on Sales of Store Location Inside Mall', *Shopping Centre World*, Vol.9, May.

Guthrie, P. R., 1980b, ' "Zone" Location in Mall May Affect Sales Performance', *Shopping Centre World*, Vol.9, June.

Hagishima, S., K. Mitsuyoshi and S. Kurose, 1987, 'Estimation of Pedestrian Shopping Trips in a Neighbourhood by Using a Spatial Interaction Model', *Environment and Planning* A, Vol.19, No.9.

Hansen, M. H. and C. B. Weinberg, 1979, 'Retail Market Share in a Competitive Market', *Journal of Retailing*, Vol.55, No.1.

Hartenstein, W. and G. Staack, 1967, 'Land Use in the Urban Core', in W. F. Heinemeijer, M. van Hulten and H. D. de Vries Reilingh (eds.), *Urban Core and Inner City*, Leiden: Brill.

Harts-Brockhuis, E. J. A. and O. Verkoren, 1987, 'Gender Differentiation among Market-traders in Central Mali', *Tijdschrift voor Economische en Sociale Geografie*, Vol.78, No.3.

Hartshorn, T. A. and P. O. Muller, 1989, 'Suburban Downtowns and the Transformation of Metropolitan Atlanta's Business Landscape', *Urban Geography*, Vol.10, No.4.

Harvey, D., 1973, *Social Justice and the City*, London: Edward Arnold.

Harvey, D., 1974, 'Class-monopoly Rent, Finance Capital and the Urban Resolution', *Regional Studies*, Vol.8.

Hassan, R., 1972, 'Islam and Urbanisation in the Medieval Middle East', *Ekistics*, Vol.33, Feb.

Hawes, J. M. and D. M. Lewison, 1984, 'Retail Site Evaluation : An Examination of the Principle of Accessibility', in R. W. Belk (ed.), *A.M.A. Educators' Proceedings*, Chicago: American Marketing Association.

Haynes, K. E. and A. S. Fotheringham, 1984, *Gravity and Spatial Interaction Models*, Beverly Hills: Sage.

Heinritz, G. and R. Sittenauer, 1991, 'Linkage Behaviour and Mix of Goods and Services in Shopping Centres: Observations in the PEP, Munich', paper presented at IGU Commission, *Geography of Commercial Activities Conference*, Munich, Aug.

Herbert, D. T. and C. J. Thomas, 1990, *Urban Geography: A First Approach*, London: Wiley.

Hise, R. T. J. P. Kelly, M. Gable and J. B. McDonald, 1983, 'Factors Affecting the Performance of Individual Chain Store Units: An Empirical Analysis', *Journal of Retailing*, Vol.59, No.2.

Horwood, E. M. and R. R. Boyce, 1959, *Studies of the Central Business District and Urban Freeway Development*, Seattle: University of Washington Press.

Horwood, E. M. and M. D. McNair, 1961, 'The Core of the City: Emerging Concepts', *Plan*, Vol.2, No.2.

Hotelling, H., 1929, 'Stability in Competition', *Economic Journal*, Vol.39, March.

Howard, E. B. and R. L. Davies, 1986, *Contemporary Change in Newcastle City Centre and the Impact of the Metro System*, CURDS, Discussion Paper No.77, Newcastle: University of Newcastle-upon-Tyne.

Howard, E. B. and J. Reynolds, 1991, 'Understanding the Challenge of the UK Regional Shopping Centre', in R. A. Thurik and H. J. Gianotten (eds.), *Proceedings of the Sixth World Conference on Research in the Distributive Trades*, The Hague: Institute for Small and Medium-Sized Business.

Hurd, R. M., 1903, *Principles of City Land Values*, New York: The Record and Guide, 1924 reprint.

ICSC, 1974, *Anti-trust Update: The Shopping Centre Industry and Anti-trust Laws*, New York: International Council of Shopping Centres.

Ingene, C. A. and A. Ghosh, 1990, 'Consumer and Producer Behaviour in a Multipurpose Shopping Environment', *Geographical Analysis*, Vol.22, No.1.

Ingene, C. A. and A. Ghosh, 1991, 'Conclusions', in A. Ghosh and C. A. Ingene (eds.), *Spatial Analysis in Marketing: Theory, Methods and Application*, Greenwich: JAI Press.

Jackson, E. L. and D. B. Johnson, 1991, 'The West Edmonton Mall and Megamalls', *Canadian Geographer*, Vol.35, No.3.

Jansen, A. C. M., 1989, ' "Funshopping" as a Geographical Notion, or: The Attractiveness of the Inner City of Amsterdam as a Shopping Area', *Tijdschrift voor Economische en Sociale Geografie*, Vol.80, No.3.

Johnson, D. B., 1978, 'The Unplanned Commercial Nucleation as a Regional Shopping Centre', in P. J. Smith (ed.), *Edmonton: The Emerging Metropolitan Pattern*, Western Geographical Series, Vol.15, Department of Geography, Victoria: University of Victoria.

Johnson, D. B., 1991, 'Structural Features of West Edmonton Mall', *Canadian Geographer*, Vol.35, No.3.

Johnston, R. J., 1973, *Spatial Structures*, London: Methuen.

Johnston, R. J., 1977, 'Conceiving the Geography of Land Values in Cities', *South African Geographer*, Vol.5, April.

Johnston, R. J. and C. C. Kissling, 1971, 'Establishment Use Patterns within Central Places', *Australian Geographical Studies*, Vol.9.

Jones, C. S., 1969, *Regional Shopping Centres: Their Location, Planning and Design*, London: Business Books.

Jones, D. W., 1991, 'An Introduction to the Thünen Location and Land Use Model', in A. Ghosh and C. A. Ingene (eds.), *Spatial Analysis in Marketing: Theory, Methods and Applications*, Greenwich: JAI Press.

Jones, K. G. and J. Simmons, 1987, *Location, Location, Location*, Toronto: Methuen.

Kane, H. E. and E. H. Belkin, 1981, 'Legal and Land Use Tissues: Suburb versus Central City', in G. Sternlieb and J. W. Hughes (eds.), *Shopping Centres USA*, Centre for Urban Policy Research, New Jersey: Rutgers.

Khan, F. K. and A. S. Uddin, 1967, 'The City Centre of Chittagong', *The Original Geographer*, Vol.11, No.1.

Laulajainen, R., 1981, 'Three Tests on Locational Matching', *Geografiska Annaler*, Vol.63B., No.1.

Laulajainen, R., 1987, *Spatial Strategies in Retailing*, Dordrecht: Reidel.

Laulajainen, R., 1990, 'Defense by Expansion: The Case of Marshall Field', *Professional Geographer*, Vol.42, No.3.

Laulajainen, R. and L-E. Gadde, 1986, 'Locational Avoidance: A Case Study of Three Swedish Retail Chains', *Regional Studies*, Vol.20, No.2.

Lee, Y., 1974, 'An Analysis of Spatial Mobility of Urban Activities in Downtown Denver', *Annals of Regional Science*, Vol.8, No.1.

Lee, Y. and K. Koutsopoulos, 1976, 'A Locational Analysis of Convenience Food Stores in Metropolitan Denver', *Annals of Regional Science*, Vol.10.

Lee Y. and C. G. Schmidt, 1980, 'A Comparative Location Analysis of a Retail Activity: The Gasoline Service Station', *Annals of Regional Science*, Vol.14, No.2.

Lerner, A. P. and H. W. Singer, 1937, 'Some Notes on Duopoly and Spatial Competition', *Journal of Political Economy*, Vol.45, No.2.

Lessinger, J., 1985, '"Nobody here to yell at me": Political Activism among Petty Retail Traders in an Indian City', in S. Plattner (ed.), *Markets and Marketing*, New York: University Press of America.

Lord, J. D., 1985, 'The Malling of the American Landscape', in J. A. Dawson and J. D. Lord (eds.), *Shopping Centre Development: Policies and Prospects*, London: Croom Helm.

Lord, J. D. and D. B. Wright, 1981, 'Competition and Location Strategy in Branch Banking: Spatial Advoidance or Clustering?', *Urban Geography*, Vol.2, No.3.

Lynch, K., 1960, *The Image of the City*, Cambridge: MIT Press.

Maitland, B., 1985, *Shopping Malls: Planning and Design*, London: Construction Press.

Maitland, B., 1990, *The New Architecture of the Retail Mall*, London: Architecture Design and Technology Press.

Mallen, B. and R. Savitt, 1979, *A Study of Leasing Practices and Retail Tenant Selection and Restriction in Shopping Centres in Canada*, Research Branch, Bureau of Competition Policy, Ottawa: Department of Consumer and Corporate Affairs.

Marchand, B., 1974, 'Pedestrian Traffic Planning and the Perception of the Urban Environment: A French Example', *Environment and Planning A*, Vol.6, No.5.

Martin, P. G., 1982, *Shopping Centre Management*, London: Spon.

Mason, J. B., 1975, 'Power and Channel Conflicts in Shopping Centre Development', *Journal of Marketing*, Vol.39, April.

Matthews, M. H., 1980, 'The Mental Maps of Children: Images of Coventry'a City Centre', *Geography*, Vol.65.

May, A. D., I. G. Turvey and P. G. Hopkinson, 1985, *Studies of Pedestrian Amenity*, Institute for Transport Studies, Working Paper 204, Leeds: University of Leeds.

McGoldrick, P. J. and M. G. Thompson, 1992, *Regional Shopping Centres: In-town Versus Out-of-Town*, Aldershot: Avebury.

McIntyre, W. E., 1955, 'The Retail Pattern of Manila', *Geographical Review*, Vol.45, No.1.

McKeever, J. R. and N. M. Griffin, 1977, *The Community Builder's Handbook*, Washington DC: Urban Land Institute.

McNeal, J. U. and C. S. Madden, 1987, 'Retail Failure: A Site Selection Perspective', *Southwest Journal of Business and Economics*, Vol.4, No.3.

Miossec, J-M., 1990, 'From Suq to Supermarket in Tunis', in A. M. Findlay, R. Paddison, and J. A. Dawson (eds.), *Retailing Environments in Developing Countries*, London: Routledge.

Miracle, M. P., 1962, 'African Markets and Trade in the Copperbelt', in P. Bohannan and G. Dalton (eds.), *Markets in Africa*, Evanston: Northwestern University Press.

Moles, A. A., 1979, 'The Human Perception of Urban Streets', *Planification Habitat Information*, Vol.94, April.

Moore, E. W., 1985, *The Fairs of Medieval England: An Introductory Study*, Toronto: Pontifical Institute of Medieval Studies.

Morris, R. L. and S. B. Zisman, 1962, 'The Pedestrian Downtown, and the Planner', *Journal of the American Institute of Planners*, Vol.28, No.3.

Nelson, R. L., 1958, *The Selection of Retail Locations*, New York: Dodge.

Ness, M. P., J. F. Morrall and B. G. Hutchinson, 1969, 'An Analysis of Central Business District Pedestrian Circulation Patterns', *Highway Research Record*, Vol.283.

Norris, D. A., 1987, 'Interstate Highway Exit Morphology: Non-Metropolitan Exit Commerce on I-75', *Professional Geographer*, Vol.39, No.1.

Northen, R. I., 1984, *Shopping Centre Development*, London: Spon.

Nystrom, P., 1930, *The Economics of Retailing*, New York: The Roland Press.

O'Brien, L. and Harris, F., 1991, *Retailing: Shopping, Society, Space*, London: David Fulton.

Okabe, A., Y. Asami and F. Miki, 1985, 'Statistical Analysis of the Spatial Association of Convenience-Goods Stores by Use of a Random Clumping Model', *Journal of Regional Science*, Vol.25, No.1.

Okabe, A. and F. Miki, 1984, 'A Conditional Nearest-Neighbour Spatial-Association Measure for the Analysis of Conditional Locational Interdependence', *Environment and Planning A*, Vol.16, No.2.

Okabe, A. and A. Suzuki, 1987, 'Stability of Spatial Competition for a Large Number of Firms on a Bounded Two-Dimensional Space', *Environment and Planning A*, Vol.19, No.8.

Parker, A. J. and M. McLoughlin, 1988, *Shoppers in Dublin: Grafton Street*, Dublin: Research Report 88/3, Centre for Retail Studies, University College Dublin.

Parker, H. R., 1962, 'Suburban Shopping Facilities in Liverpool', *Town Planning Review*, Vol.33.

Parkes, C., 1987, 'Problems Facing Out-of-Town Shopping Developers', *Financial Times*, Thursday, 18 June.

Parkins, A. E., 1930, 'Profiles of the Retail Business Section of Nashville, Tenn., and their Interpretation', *Annals of the Association of American Geographers*, Vol.20.

Pascal, A. H. and J. J. McCall, 1980, 'Agglomeration Economies, Search Costs and Industrial Location', *Journal of Urban Economics*, Vol.8, No.3.

Pearson, T. D., 1991, 'Location! Location! Location! What is Location?', *The Appraisal Journal*, January.

Peters, J., 1990, 'Managing Shopping Centre Retailer Mix: Some Considerations for Retailers', *International Journal of Retail and Distribution Management*, Vol.18, No.1.

Pillsbury, R., 1987, 'From Hamburger Alley to Hedgerose Heights: Toward a Model of Restaurant Location Dynamics', *Professional Geographer*, Vol.39, No.3.

Pocock, D. C. D. and R. Hudson, 1978, *Images of the Urban Environment*, London: Macmillan.

Potter, R. B., 1982, *The Urban Retailing System: Location, Cognition and Behaviour*, Aldershot: Gower.

Pyle, J., 1926, 'The Determination of Location Standards for Retail Concerns', *Harvard Business Review*, Vol.4, April.

Pyle, J., 1978, 'Tianguis: Periodic Markets of Mexico City', in R. H. T. Smith (ed.), *Market Place Trade – Periodic Markets, Hawkers and Traders in Africa, Asia and Latin America*, Centre for Transportation Studies, Vancouver: University of British Columbia.

Rannells, J., 1956, *The Core of the City: A Pilot Study of Changing Land Uses in Central Business Districts*, New York: Columbia University.

Ratcliff, R. U., 1939, *The Problem of Retail Site Selection*, School of Business Administration, Ann Arbor: University of Michigan.

Roberts, J., 1989, *Talking About Walking*, London: TEST.

Rogers, A., 1969, 'Quadrat Analysis of Urban Dispersion: 2. Case Studies of Urban Retail Systems', *Environment and Planning*, Vol.1, No.2.

Rogers, D. S., 1987, 'America's Shopping Centres: A Mid-life Crisis?', *Retail and Distribution Management*, Vol.15, No.6.

Rouse Company, 1969, *Amalgam Mall: A Case Study in the Development of a Regional Shopping Centre*, New York: International Council of Shopping Centres.

Rutherford, G. S., 1979, 'Use of the Gravity Model for Pedestrian Travel Distribution', *Transportation Research Record*, Vol.728.

Saarinen, T. F., 1977, *Maps in Minds: Reflections on Cognitive Mapping*, New York: Harper and Row.

Sandrock, K., 1988, 'Heuristic Estimation of Pedestrian Traffic Volumes', *Transportation Research*, Vol.22A.

Savitt, R., 1985, 'Issues of Tenant Policy Control: The American Perspective', in J. A. Dawson and J. D. Lord (eds.), *Shopping Centre Development: Policies and Prospects*, London: Croom Helm.

Scott, A. J., 1974, 'A Theoretical Model of Pedestrian Flow', *Socio-Economic Planning Sciences*, Vol.8.

Scott, P., 1959, 'The Australian CBD', *Economic Geography*, Vol.35.

Scott, P., 1970, *Geography and Retailing*, London: Hutchinson.

Sendut, H., 1965, 'The Structure of Kuala Lumpur', *Town Planning Review*, Vol.36.

Shaw, G., 1988, 'Recent Research on the Commercial Structure of Nineteenth-Century British Cities', in D. Denecke and G. Shaw (eds.), *Urban Historical Geography: Recent Progress in Britain and Germany*, Cambridge: Cambridge University Press.

Shepherd, I. D. H. and C. J. Thomas, 1980, 'Urban Consumer Behaviour', in J. A. Dawson (ed.), *Retail Geography*, London: Croom Helm.

Sieverts, T., 1967, 'Perceptual Images of the City of Berlin', in W. F. Heinemeijer, M. van Hulten, and H. D. de Vries Reilingh (eds.), *Urban Core and Inner City*, Leiden: E. J. Brill.

Sim, L. L. and C. R. Way, 1989, 'Tenant Placement in a Singapore Shopping Centre', *International Journal of Retailing*, Vol.4, No.1.

Simpkin, L. P., 1989, 'SLAM: Store Location Assessment Model: Theory and Practice', *Omega*, Vol.7, No.1.

Simpkin, L. P., P. Doyle and J. Saunders, 1985, 'UK Retail Store Location Assessment', *Journal of the Market Research Society*, Vol.27, No.2.

Smith, G. C. and N. K. Dolman, 1981, 'Consumer Responses to Alternative Retail Environments in Nottingham's Central Area', *East Midland Geographer*, Vol.7/8.

Smith, G. C., D. J. B. Shaw and P. R. Huckle, 1979, 'Children's Perception of a Downtown Shopping Centre', *Professional Geographer*, Vol.31, No.2.

Smith, P. E., 1956, *Shopping Centres: Planning and Management*, New York: National Dry Goods Association.

Sommer, R. and S. Aitkens, 1982, 'Mental Mapping of Two Supermarkets', *Journal of Consumer Research*, Vol.9, No.2.

Sparks, L., 1990, 'Spatial Structural Relationships in Retail Corporate Growth: A Case Study of Kwik Save Group PLC', *Service Industries Journal*, Vol.10, No.1.

Stambaugh, D., 1978, 'Proper Tenant Mix: How to Put It all Together', *Shopping Centre World*, Vol.7, No.4.

Stern, L. W. and A. I. El-Ansary, 1988, *Marketing Channels*, Englewood Cliffs, Prentice Hall.

Teitz, M. B., 1968, 'Locational Strategies for Competitive Systems', *Journal of Regional Science*, Vol.8, No.2.

Thill, J-C. and I. Thomas, 1987, 'Toward Conceptualising Trip Chaining Behaviour: A Review', *Geographical Analysis*, Vol.19, No.1.

Thompson, I. B., 1982, *The Commercial Centre of Oran*, Geography Department, Occasional Papers No.9, Glasgow, University of Glasgow.

Thornhill, J., 1992, 'Why Location Counts', *Financial Times*, Thursday 27 Feb.
Thornton, S. J., M. J. McCullagh and R. P. Bradshaw, 1992, 'Pedestrian Flows and Retail Turnover', *British Food Journal*, Vol.93, No.9.
Thrall, G. I., 1991, 'Production Theory of Land Rent', *Environment and Planning A*, Vol.23, No.8.
Timmermans, H., 1986, 'Locational Choice Behaviour of Entrepreneurs: An Experimental Analysis', *Urban Studies*, Vol.23, No.2.
Toyne, P., 1971, 'Customer Trips to Retail Business in Exeter', in K. J. Gregory and W. C. D. Ravenhill (eds.), *Exeter Essays in Geography*, Exeter: University of Exeter Press.
Troin, J-F., 1990, 'New Trends in Commercial Locations in Morocco', in A. M. Findlay, R. Paddison and J. A. Dawson (eds.), *Retailing Environments in Developing Countries*, London: Routledge.
Turchiano, F., 1990, 'Farewell Field of Dreams: "Build it and they will come" Era Ends for Shopping Centres', *Retailing Issues Letter*, Vol.2, No.9.
Ukuw, U. I., 1969, 'Markets in Iboland', in B. W. Hodder and U. I. Ukuw, *Markets in West Africa*, Ibadan University Press: Ibadan.
Van der Hagen. X., A. Borgers and H. Timmermans, 1991, 'Spatio-Temporal Sequencing Processes of Pedestrians in Urban Retail Environments', *Papers in Regional Science*, Vol.70.
Von Thünen, J. H., 1826, *Der Isolierte Staat in Beziehung auf Landwirtschaft und Nationa lokonomie, 1. Teil*, Hamburg: Perthes.
Ward, R. G. D. Howlett, C. C. Kissling and H. C. Weinand, 1978, 'Maket Raun: The Introduction of Periodic Markets to Papua, New Guinea', in R. H. T. Smith (ed.), *Market Place Trade – Periodic Markets, Hawkers and Traders in Africa, Asia and Latin America*, Centre for Transportation Studies, Vancouver: University of British Columbia.
Weaver, D. C., 1969, 'Changes in the Morphology of Three American Central Business Districts 1952–1966', *Professional Geographer*, Vol.21, No.6.
West, D. S. and B. von Hohenbalken, 1984, 'Spatial Predation in a Canadian Retail Oligopoly', *Journal of Regional Science*, Vol.24, No.3.
White, P. G., 1975, *The Composite Structure of the Central Area*, Newcastle: University of Newcastle-upon-Tyne, Department of Geography, Seminar Papers No.30.
Whitehand, J. W. R., 1987, *The Changing Face of Cities: A Study of Development Cycles and Urban Form*, Oxford: Basil Blackwell.
Wing, H. C. and S. L. Lee, 1980, 'The Characteristics and Locational Patterns of Wholesale and Service Trades in the Central Area of Singapore', *Singapore Journal of Tropical Geography*, Vol.1, No.1.
Zawawi, M., 1970, 'Perception of Downtown: A Case Study of Washington DC,' unpublished MA thesis, Washington DC: George Washington University.
Zipf, G. K., 1949, *Human Behaviour and the Principle of Least Effort*, Cambridge: Harvard University Press.

22

New laws of retail gravitation

P. D. Converse*

Source: *Journal of Marketing* 14 (1949): 379–384.

The original law of retail gravitation stated that two cities attract trade from an intermediate town in the vicinity of the breaking point approximately in direct proportion to the populations of the two cities and in inverse proportion to the squares of the distances from these two cities to the intermediate town.[1] This is expressed in the following formula (No. 1):

$$\frac{Ba}{Bb} = \left(\frac{Pa}{Pb}\right)\left(\frac{Db}{Da}\right)^2$$

where Ba is the proportion of the trade from the intermediate city
    attracted by city A
Bb is proportion attracted by city B
Pa is population of city A
Pb is population of city B
Da is distance from intermediate town to city A
Db is distance from intermediate town to city B

To illustrate, Farmer City is 25 miles from Champaign-Urbana (with a 1940 population of 37,366) and 27 miles from Bloomington-Normal (with a 1940 population of 39,851). So

$$\frac{Ba}{Bb} = \left(\frac{39,851}{37,366}\right)\left(\frac{25}{27}\right)^2 = .915.$$

Bloomington-Normal attracts .915 times as much trade as Champaign-Urbana. If $Ba/Bb = .915$ then the relative percentages can be derived by dividing .915 by 1.915. This gives 48 per cent to Bloomington and 52 per cent to Champaign-Urbana.[2] A survey of consumers in Farmer City in 1942 found that Bloomington-Normal and Champaign-Urbana attracted trade from Farmer City in the proportion of 45 per cent to the former and 55 per cent to the latter.

This formula is of considerable value in connection with another formula derived at the University of Illinois some years ago which determines the boundaries of a trading center's trade area. The formula (No. 2):

$$\text{Breaking point, miles from } B = \frac{\text{Miles between } A \text{ and } B}{1 + \sqrt{\dfrac{\text{Population of } A}{\text{Population of } B}}}.$$

Where *A* is the larger town and *B* the smaller town

Using this formula the boundaries of a town's trade area are determined.[3] Then the first formula is used for towns near the area's boundary to determine how the trade *should* be divided between the two trading centers. The formula is based on average conditions found in a number of tests or surveys. A trading center town may do better or worse than the average. It may be determined by use of the formula that town *A* should attract 55 per cent and *B* 45 per cent of the trade leaving the intermediate town for towns *A* and *B*.

However, to determine how a town is actually holding its own against competing towns, surveys must be made in the territory along the boundaries of the town's trade area. Such a survey may, for example, find that town *A* attracts 45 per cent and town *B* 55 per cent of the trade going to the two towns from a territory where it should be split evenly. This is a poor showing for *A*, and apparently means that the retailers in *B* are doing a better merchandising job. There may, of course, be other factors such as more traffic congestion in *A* than in *B*, poorer roads to *A*, or mountains to be crossed in reaching *A*.

The second formula may be used to determine a town's normal trade area, in a very few minutes, without any field work. All that is needed is a highway map, the population figures, and ability to extract a square root. The law was formulated to apply to fashion goods, or shopping goods (apparel and household furniture and furnishings), but within limits may be applied to other types. Once the trade area is determined, the merchants know where to concentrate their merchandising efforts, and the newspapers know the territories which they should cultivate intensively. To illustrate, a department store was advertising over a considerable area. Its attention was called to the formula for determining the town's trade area. The area was computed and the store found that it was spending much of its advertising appropriation outside its trade area. By concentrating its advertising inside the trade area, it experienced a considerable increase in sales with no increase in advertising expenditures.

Determining the loss of trade by a town

The accepted law of retail gravitation deals with the trade attracted by trading center towns from intermediate towns near the boundaries of the trade areas of two trading centers. That is, it has to do with the division among outside towns of the trade lost by a given town. But what about the amount of trade retained and lost by a town? Can we find a formula to predict the proportion of trade a town will retain and the proportion it will lose? The present article deals with this problem. There are only two factors in the method used—population of the towns involved and the distance between them. If there is a fairly definite pattern in the way a smaller town divides its trade between two larger near-by towns, should there not also be a definite pattern in the way the consumers of a town divide their purchases between home town stores and the stores in a near-by town? By a near-by town we mean one close enough and large enough so that an appreciable amount of trade is lost to it.

In order to test this idea we used the same approach that was used in deriving Formula No. 1. In our trade area studies at the University of Illinois, we have surveyed the consumers in more than 100 towns. In these we know how the fashion goods trade is divided between the home town and other towns. That is, we know *Ba* and *Bb* in Formula No. 1. We know the populations of the various towns and the distances between them.

We let town *B* in the original equations represent the home town, and solved for *Db*. We then solved the equation in 100 cases involving the trade leaving 48 towns. We used towns with populations of over 1,000, on the ground that these towns had stores carrying at least limited stocks of fashion goods.

See Table 1. *Db* (*x* in the table) was found to be usually close to 4, which is the inertia-distance factor. This factor reflects the inertia that must be overcome to visit a store even a block away. The results of our tests support the new formula fully as well as Reilly's data supported Formula No. 1.

The formula is then:

$$\frac{Ba}{Bb} = \left(\frac{Pa}{Hb}\right)\left(\frac{4}{d}\right)^2$$

Ba, proportion of trade going to the outside town
Bb, proportion of trade retained by the home town
Pa, population of the outside town
Hb, population of the home town
d, distance to the outside town
4, inertia factor

The last four factors are now known, and the equation can be solved for the split in trade between the larger and smaller towns.

Table 1 Computation of Inertia-Distance Factor in Purchases of Fashion Goods for Home Towns and Larger Towns in Illinois—100 Tests

For the 100 tests:

Median	3.9 miles
Mean	4.5 miles

East Central Illinois Towns			Miscellaneous Surveys*			Kankakee Area		
Home Town	*Other Town*	x	*Home Town*	*Other Town*	x	*Home Town*	*Other Town*	x
Gibson City	Champaign	1.0	Clinton	Springfield	3.0	Coal City	Kankakee	1.2
Onarga	Champaign	3.2	Clinton	Decatur	4.1	Lowell	Gary	2.9
Taylorville	Decatur	3.2	Clinton	Bloomington	4.3	Lowell	Hammond	3.0
Farmer City	Bloomington	3.3				Manteno	Joliet	3.0
Tuscola	Decatur	3.4	Clinton	Champaign	3.3	Lowell	Crown Point	3.1
Tuscola	Mattoon	3.4	Clinton	Decatur	4.4	Kentland	Watseka	3.5
Farmer City	Champaign	3.5	Clinton	Bloomington	5.1	Watseka	Danville	4.6
Arcola	Mattoon	3.8				Coal City	Joliet	4.8
Onarga	Kankakee	3.8	Shelbyville	Mattoon	3.8	Wilmington	Kankakee	5.2
Gibson City	Bloomington	3.9	Shelbyville	Decatur	6.7	Watseka	Kankakee	5.9
Clinton	Decatur	4.1				Onarga	Champaign	6.3
Taylorville	Springfield	4.2	Bement	Monticello	3.8	Lowell	Kankakee	7.6
Clinton	Bloomington	4.3	Bement	Champaign	7.9	Manteno	Kankakee	7.7
Monticello	Decatur	4.7	Bement	Decatur	17.6	Kentland	Lafayette	7.9
Tuscola	Champaign	5.6				Wilmington	Joliet	9.0
Monticello	Champaign	6.2				Onarga	Kankakee	10.1
Hoopeston	Danville	6.9						
Bement	Decatur	9.0						

Average value 4.3
Median value 3.85

Average value 5.4
Median value 5.0

Central Illinois Towns

Farmer City	Decatur	3.1
Pontiac	Peoria	3.3
Farmer City	Bloomington	4.1
Fairbury	Peoria	4.2
Farmer City	Clinton	4.5
Gibson City	Champaign	4.5
Lincoln	Springfield	4.5
LeRoy	Bloomington	4.7
Bloomington	Peoria	4.9
Fairbury	Pontiac	5.3
Gibson City	Bloomington	5.7
Farmer City	Champaign	5.9
Pontiac	Bloomington	6.3
Gibson City	Peoria	6.8
El Paso	Bloomington	6.8
Fairbury	Bloomington	7.0
El Paso	Peoria	7.6

Average value 4.7
Median value 4.5

Bloomington Area

Lincoln	Decatur	1.6
LeRoy	Champaign	2.1
Lincoln	Bloomington	2.5
Lincoln	Peoria	2.7

Crab Orchard Area (Southern Illinois)

Herrin	West Frankfort	1.6
Carbondale	Murphysboro	1.8
Murphysboro	Carbondale	1.9
Christopher	West Frankfort	2.0
West Frankfort	Herrin	2.1
Benton	West Frankfort	2.1
Carterville	Carbondale	2.3
Johnston City	Marion	2.3
Marion	West Frankfort	2.6
Johnston City	West Frankfort	2.8
Christopher	Herrin	2.9
Carterville	Herrin	3.0
Carterville	West Frankfort	3.0
Murphysboro	West Frankfort	3.2
Zeigler	West Frankfort	3.3
Johnston City	Herrin	3.5
Zeigler	Herrin	3.7
Marion	Herrin	3.8
DuQuoin	Carbondale	4.0
Carbondale	West Frankfort	4.4
Pinckneyville	Herrin	7.3
Pinckneyville	West Frankfort	7.9

Average value 3.3
Median value 2.95

Rockford Area

Beloit	Rockford	2.4
Rochelle	DeKalb	2.9
Marengo	Belvidere	3.1
Dixon	Rockford	3.4
Belvidere	Rockford	3.5
Harvard	Woodstock	3.7
Harvard	Rockford	4.2
Oregon	Dixon	4.8
Rochelle	Rockford	4.9
Marengo	Elgin	5.7
Oregon	Rockford	5.8
Marengo	Rockford	5.9

Average value 4.2
Median value 3.95

* The commodities included in these surveys differed from those listed by area.

To illustrate, Benton, Illinois, has a population of 7,372 and is 7 miles from West Frankfort, which has a population of 12,383. A survey showed that Benton's trade was divided 87 per cent to Benton and 13 per cent to West Frankfort. Thus

$$\frac{13}{87} = \left(\frac{12,383}{7,372}\right)\left(\frac{x}{7}\right)^2 \qquad \text{Solving, } x = 2.1 \text{ miles.}$$

In this case the inertia-distance factor of trading at home is below the average. This means that Benton does better than the state average or the average in the Crab Orchard area (Table 1) in keeping its trade at home. The figure of 2.1 suggests that Benton has somewhat better stores than most surrounding towns of its size. Crab Orchard consumers have a greater tendency to trade at home than do the consumers in the central and northern parts of the state. Possible explanations of this are a larger proportion of relatively low-income families, since upper-income families shop out-of-town more than low-income families. The fact that most of the trading centers in the Crab Orchard area are of about the same size probably means that one finds the assortments in other trading centers little if any larger than in one's home town. If so, there is more incentive to shop in other towns in areas where the other towns are larger and the stores have larger assortments of goods from which to make selections.

New law of retail gravitation

The new law may be stated: a trading center and a town in or near its trade area divide the trade of the town approximately in direct proportion to the populations of the two towns and inversely as the squares of the distance factors, using 4 as the distance factor of the home town.

This new law has several uses. It can be applied to satellite towns or other towns inside the trade area of a larger town. It gives an approximate measure of how the trade is divided without making a survey. Surveys can be made to check actual results against predicted or "average" results. The merchants of the smaller town by comparing the results of the survey with the predictions of the formula have a standard and so know "how they are doing" in competition with larger towns.

If a small town loses a considerable amount of trade to two or more larger towns, the proportion lost to these towns should be determined by using multiples of 4 to obtain a total inertia factor. If Doeville loses trade to two larger towns, we would use 8 as the inertia factor. If Doeville loses trade to three, we would use 12, and if to four towns we would use 16. We have experimented with this method and it appears to work satisfactorily.

There is still the amount of "transient" trade to be considered. So far comparisons have been made only between towns reasonably close together. Consumers make a considerable number of purchases in towns outside their normal trading orbit, in towns which they visit only occasionally. People go to towns to visit friends or relatives, or on business, and make some purchases in these towns. Wives accompany husbands on business trips and "shop" while their husbands are transacting their business. People make purchases while on vacation trips. Some towns lose more transient business than they gain and some gain more than they lose. On the whole we would say that small towns have a net loss on transient trade while larger towns and resort towns have a net gain. It may be that a study of trade movement from a number of towns will enable a fairly definite factor to be established to measure it.

If so, one could predict the proportion of trade a town would retain, how much it would lose to surrounding trading centers, and its net gain or loss of transient trade.

When town *A* is much larger than home town

It has been found in our Illinois studies that Formula No. 1 predicts the movement of trade with a relatively high degree of accuracy when town *A* is not more than 20 times the size (population) of town *B*. When the difference in population is greater than 20, the accuracy of prediction appears to drop. When the larger town has 50 or 100 times the population of the smaller town, the formula definitely gives too much weight to population. In our studies we have tried to compensate for this when computing the division of trade between Chicago or St. Louis and other towns by using the cube of the distance. We do not have enough data as yet to measure the accuracy of this adjustment. We do know that the traffic congestion and parking difficulties in our large cities are causing a definite decentralization of retail trade.

Large cities have more than one shopping district carrying complete assortments of fashion goods. Such cities apparently do not attract trade in direct proportion to their total populations. It may be that they attract trade in proportion to the population trading in the central retail district.

The inertia factor for Chicago is considerably lower than the inertia factor in central Illinois. This means that the small towns lose much less trade to Chicago than predicted by the law of retail gravitation using the squares of the distances (Formula No. 1). This increased inertia against going to Chicago (or reduced inertia against shopping at home) may result from traffic congestion and parking difficulties in Chicago (or cost of train and taxicab fares). Or it may result from the decentralization of retail shopping areas in Chicago. It is possible that Chicago attracts trade in proportion to the population shopping in the downtown or Loop area and not in proportion to the total population of the city.

To ascertain the inertia-distance factor for smaller towns in northern Illinois in competition with Chicago, we set up and solved equations for the towns where we have made surveys. The inertia-distance factor was found to be 1.5. See Table 2.

Summary of formulas

The original (No. 1) formula:

$$\frac{Ba}{Bb} = \left(\frac{Pa}{Pb}\right)\left(\frac{Db}{Da}\right)^2.$$

From this was derived the formula (No. 2) for bounding trade areas:

Boundary or Breaking Point Distance from town $B =$
$$\frac{\text{Distance between towns } A \text{ and } B}{1 + \sqrt{\dfrac{\text{Population of } A}{\text{Population of } B}}}.$$

New Formula No. 3 for determining division of trade between two towns:

$$\frac{Ba}{Bb} = \left(\frac{Pa}{Hb}\right)\left(\frac{4}{d}\right)^2.$$

Table 2 Computation of Inertia-Distance Factor in Purchases of Fashion Goods for Towns in Northern Illinois and Chicago

Home Town	X
Kankakee	.4
Onarga	.6
Gibson City	.9
Rochelle	1.3
Belvidere	1.3
Marengo	1.4
Tuscola	1.5
Dixon	1.6
Harvard	1.6
Pontiac	1.6
Oregon	1.7
Beloit (Wisc.)	1.9
Rockford	3.4
Average value	1.5
Median value	1.5

Formulas Nos. 4 and 5 for a small town and a large metropolitan center:

$$\frac{Ba}{Bb} = \left(\frac{Pa}{Pb}\right)\left(\frac{Db}{Da}\right)^3 .$$

$$\text{Distance from } B = \frac{\text{Distance between towns } A \text{ and } B}{1 + \sqrt[3]{\dfrac{\text{Population of } A}{\text{Population of } B}}} .$$

New Formula No. 6 for small town vs. Chicago:

$$\frac{Ba}{Bb} = \left(\frac{Pa}{Hb}\right)\left(\frac{1.5}{d}\right)^2 .$$

Notes

* I am indebted to Miss Janice Olbrich, Research Assistant in Marketing, and the staff of the Bureau of Economic and Business Research for statistical assistance in this study, and to my colleague, Professor Robert Mitchell, for reading and criticizing the manuscript.

1. William J. Reilly, *The Law of Retail Gravitation* (New York: William J. Reilly, 1931).

2. *Ba + Bb* = 100 per cent (total trade leaving Farmer City for Champaign-Urbana and Bloomington-Normal). We can solve for *Ba* by merely substituting value of *Bb* in terms of *Ba* to reduce equation to one unknown.

3. In some instances the total volume of fashion goods sales (sales of general merchandise, clothing, and furniture stores) may be a better measure than population figures.

23

A retail market potential model

T. R. Lakshmanan and Walter G. Hansen

Source: *Journal American Institute of Planners* 31 (1965): 134–143.

The authors explore possible equilibrium distributions for large retail trade centers in the Baltimore metropolitan area. Possible sites for centers are selected on general planning grounds and tested for feasibility and "balance." Balance is determined in terms of the volume of business attracted by each center in relation to its size. By repeated trials, it is established that there exists a balanced distribution in which the size of centers is related to their drawing power, which in turn depends on the distribution of purchasing power projected for the area and the transportation facilities and for trip-makers. This land use model is intimately related to transportation models, by the balanced distribution of retail outlets turns out to be the minimum cost pattern for trip-makers. This land use model is intimately related to transportation models, by way of network tracing and a gravity model trip distribution theory. It represents a departure from some of the restrictions of central place theory (as illustrated in the article by Berry in this issue).

The study reported in this paper is concerned with the investigation of one regional development form—the Metrotown Plan for Baltimore. The Metrotown concept is, to some extent, a reformulation of the ideals and spatial structure expressed in the British New Towns, in accordance with the realities of contemporary patterns of living, work, and circulation in the United States. It envisages a regional system of suburban towns deployed radially and in rings around the city of Baltimore. Each Metrotown is viewed as a physically cohesive community, with a population of 100,000–200,000, broad and varied choices of housing densities, considerable employment opportunities, a full scale retail and service hub, and attractive recreational and cultural opportunities.[1]

This study is one of a series of related studies that investigate the scale, composition, and location of Metrotown Centers. It addresses itself to one component of the town center: the retail core. It investigates the possibility that the large commercial cores envisaged in the Metrotown Center concept can be realized. Stated differently, assuming the continuation of current policies and growth trends in the Baltimore region, what potential exists for large commercial centers? How many centers? What sizes? What locations? When?

In the first part of the paper, the development and testing of a market potential model is described. The second part of the paper is concerned with the specification of criteria to evaluate the retail potential in the future. The final part of the paper presents the conclusions developed relative to the feasibility, location, and sizes of retail centers for the future.

A market potential model

Retail activities are oriented to the consumer. A reasonable premise of the model would be that the size and the number of retail establishments in an area is a function of the number of consumers, or more appropriately their aggregate purchasing power. Stated differently, within a metropolitan region, which can be considered for the present purpose as an economic and spatial entity, the total sales generated at all the shopping centers must equal the total available consumer expenditures for retail goods.[2] However, the sales at any given retail center will be a function of the consumer expenditures in the "surrounding" area.

It is in the definition of the "surrounding" area that the present formulation differs from most approaches to this problem. Since customers bear the burden of costs of movement—economic, temporal, or psychic—to the retail center, the actual locations of the retail centers are influenced by the intricate patterns of consumer movements for retail goods. Generally, there is a desire to minimize these costs of movement on the part of the consumer.[3] This overall tendency has persuaded market analysts to assume that a consumer, confronted with a choice among several alternative shopping centers, will *inexorably* choose the nearest center. This heuristic assumption permits the delineation of trade area—primary and secondary—boundaries, with the enclosed consumer expenditures allocated through other sub-assumptions to the individual shopping centers. Such a procedure is no more accurate than the highly questionable assumption of closed market areas around retail centers. Empirical studies have demonstrated that there is, instead, a continuum of market orientation of consumers to shopping centers.[4] From a behavioral point of view it has also been asserted that shoppers engage in an information-seeking process, which, over a period of time, tends to attract them to different centers in some constant proportion.[5] Further, the traditional definition of the "surrounding region" as a closed market area is operationally inflexible for the evaluation of alternate spatial patterns of retail activity attempted in this study.

The present formulation, consequently, asserts that the location or sales potential of a retail center is not to be viewed as a function of the purchasing power of an arbitrary spatial slice of the region. More realistically, it describes a situation of overlapping competition between shopping centers and develops a mathematical framework for measuring it.

Essentially, the model states that the sales potential of a retail center is directly related to its size. This follows from the observation that a large center offers a wider range of goods and attracts consumers from a wider area than a smaller center would in the same location. Further, the sales potential of a center is directly related to its proximity to the number and prosperity of the consumers. The larger and closer the consumer shopping dollars available, the greater the sales potential. Finally, the model states that the sales potential of a center is related to how disposed it is to competing shopping facilities. The further away other shopping facilities are spatially, the greater the sales potential of a center.

These relationships are expressed in a mathematical form, using the familiar gravity model framework shown below.[6]

$$S_{ij} = C_i \frac{\dfrac{F_j}{d_{ij}^\alpha}}{\dfrac{F_i}{d_{ij}^\alpha} = \dfrac{F_j}{d_{ij}^\alpha} \cdots \dfrac{F_n}{d_{in}^\alpha}} = C_i \frac{\dfrac{F_j}{d_{ij}^\alpha}}{\displaystyle\sum_{k=1}^{n} \dfrac{F_k}{d_{ik}^\alpha}} \tag{1}$$

where S_{ij} = Consumer retail expenditures of population in zone i, spent at zone j

C_i = Total consumer retail expenditures of population in zone i

F_j = Size of retail activity in zone j

d_{ij} = Distance (in driving time) between zone i and zone j

α = An exponent applied to the distance variable

The above model[7] states the retail center in zone j (F_j) attracts consumer dollars (S_{ij})

a) in direct proportion to the consumer expenditures, C_i,

b) in direct proportion to its size F_j,

c) in inverse proportion to distance to the consumers (d_{ij}^α), and

d) in inverse proportion to competition $\left(\displaystyle\sum_{k=1}^{n} \dfrac{F_k}{d_{ik}^\alpha} \right)$

Equation (1) can be modified to state the consumer expenditures available in all zones of the region that would probably be spent in zone j (retail centers F_j).

$$S_j = \sum_{i=1}^{n} C_i \frac{\dfrac{F_j}{d_{ij}^\alpha}}{\displaystyle\sum_{k=1}^{n} \dfrac{F_k}{d_{ik}^\alpha}} \tag{2}$$

where S_j = Total sales in retail center F_j

Equation (2) sums up the sales from every zone at zone j. It implies that there is no trade area boundary but a shopping interaction between all zones, though this may fall off sharply with distance.

This model, though new to market potential studies, has been extensively used in traffic studies in many urban areas in the United States. These studies have used operational definitions for the variables meaningful for traffic analysis and found it a good predictor of shopping travel patterns.

The relevance of the model to the real world was verified by applying it to the current shopping patterns in terms of dollar sales and shopping trips in the Baltimore region. The size of retail activity was expressed in terms of square feet of shopping goods floor space. The consumer expenditures were the product of zonal population and per capita shopping goods expenditures. A spatial parameter called the Friction Factor $F\left(=\dfrac{1}{d_{ik}^{\alpha}}\right)$, obtained from the Baltimore Metropolitan Area Transportation Study shopping goods traffic model was also used.

With all the variables measured, standard computer programs developed for traffic studies were used to generate sales in dollars that were attracted to all zones that had shopping goods floor space. A comparison of the annual sales generated by the model and the actual annual sales confidentially obtained for six large shopping centers showed a good fit.

The sales comparisons, though encouraging, were possible for only six centers. To provide a more thorough check on the model, an estimation of shopping goods trips was made. This was felt to be a valid check of a model, for previous studies have clearly shown a direct relationship between retail sales and trip generation.[8] The number of shopping goods trips that actually left every residential zone was obtained from origin-destination survey data. These trips correspond to the consumer expenditures that went from every zone to different shopping goods centers in the previous estimation. Using the shopping goods floor space as an attractor, these trips were allocated to the various shopping centers. From the origin–destination (O–D) survey it was also possible to obtain the number of shopping goods trips actually attracted to each center.

A comparison between actual (O–D) shopping person trips and those generated by the model showed that the model did a reasonable allocation ($r^2 = 0.91$).

The sales comparison at the central business district (CBD) was inconclusive owing to the unaccountability of purchases made by workers and visitors. However, the shopping trip comparison was extremely gratifying (only about 5 percent difference).

(Actual) O–D Shopping Trips to CBD = 17466
Model Shopping Trips to CBD = 16425

Summing up, the comparison of the actual and estimated patterns of current shopping sales and trips in the Baltimore region demonstrates that the model performs reasonably well. The noticeable variations appear to be a measure of the inevitable abstraction in any model formulation as well as data problems. The market potential model was, consequently, accepted for application.

Model application—data requirements and output

The market potential model formulated and tested in this study is essentially a tool for estimating the market potential of each retail center in a metropolitan region. To be used as an estimating tool, the model requires a description of the urban area in terms of:

a) shopping goods demand by small area
b) supply of competing shopping goods facilities
c) spatial links between the retailers and the consumers.

All these three components of the retail spatial structure have to be specified before the model can be used for estimating sales of *each* center in the urban area for a required point in time, say 1970 or 1980.

The demand for shopping goods is represented by the consumer purchasing power in the region. To compute the demand for shopping goods for a future year, projections of population and per capita expenditures are prerequisites. This study used the zonal population projections developed in a recent study by the Baltimore Regional Planning Council.[9] These projections resulted from the application of mathematical models that made two basic assumptions: a) existing trends in the residential site selection process would continue, and b) existing policies—zoning, public works, and so on—in the region would continue. No policies relating to the metrotown program entered into these projections. Thus, the distribution of consumers in 1970 and 1980 assumed as inputs to the market potential model would reflect the *probable effect of existing policies.*

The per capita shopping goods expenditures for 1970 and 1980 were developed through the application of an econometric model.[10]

The projections of per capita expenditures by zone used the income projections developed in the previously cited study by the Baltimore Regional Planning Council. Thus, both the population and income projections used in the study imply the continuation of existing policies.

The supply of "existing" facilities refers to the shopping goods retailing units described by size and location in the region in any year for which the model is to be applied. To apply the model for a future point in time, say 1970 or 1980, the size and location of the shopping goods facilities had first to be assumed for that year. The model could then allocate the total consumer expenditures for shopping goods to the various assumed and existing shopping centers. Therefore, use of the model is a trial and error process. Thus, the model framework is not a locational but an evaluative scheme.

Generally, models of intraurban location determine locations of shopping facilities, given the distribution of retail demand and the distributive effects of the transportation system. The market potential model used in this study, however, accepts locations of shopping facilities as *inputs* and then estimates their sales levels. Since alternative location-size patterns can be assumed, this model offers a technique for estimating the consequences of alternative patterns of growth of shopping goods facilities.

In practice, alternate assumptions of the sizes and locations of shopping facilities in addition to the existing facilities today were made. The market potential or sales level of each of the centers in the region in each of the alternatives was then obtained from the model.

A key variable of the model is the consumer–retailer interaction space. The operational definition used for the variable was the driving time between the consumer's zone and the retailer's zone. An application of the model to 1970 or 1980 requires, consequently, the zone-to-zone travel times on the 1970 and 1980 highway networks. This data input leads to assumptions concerning the highway networks in 1970 and 1980.

Here again, the assumption built into the model is that current policies will continue. The Baltimore Regional Planning Council prepared a map showing the future highway networks that represented a composite of existing policies. Inside the BMATS area, the recommendations of the recent Wilbur Smith Study were incorporated. In the rest of the region outside the BMATS area, the highways proposed in the Maryland Needs Study were assumed to exist.

Given a description of the three components of the retail spatial structure —demand, supply, and buyer-seller interaction space—the model output provides the following measures for each alternative:

1. The probably sales levels at *each* center—"existing" and "future."
2. The average trip length for shopping goods for the system as a whole.
3. The consumer dollars from each residential zone that are spent at each shopping center.

Criteria for evaluation of retail potential

To use the various alternatives and the corresponding sales estimates to identify the locational opportunities for large shopping centers, two broad sets of criteria were formulated. The first set of criteria assessed any alternative at the individual location level. These were broad criteria to evaluate the probable investment decisions of individual developers.

The evaluation problem in this study is broader in scope, however, than that of an individual developer interested in a specific location. It involves the consideration of rigidities in the existing commercial pattern. For instance,

what would be the impact of a large new shopping center on the performance (or sales level) of a nearby existing shopping center? Therefore, the
second set of criteria enlarged the scope of evaluation from an assessment of
individual centers to an evaluation of an interrelated system of centers in the
whole region. In other words, how do the "new" (assumed) shopping centers
evaluated by the first set of criteria and the existing set of regional centers
"add up" as a regional pattern? Do the regional patterns assumed provide
comparable levels of service in different parts of the region to the consumers?
Further, are the regional patterns of centers evaluated in relation to all the
above questions a reasonable "simulation" of the market processes? These
are ticklish questions and the judgment criteria related to them are by no
means easy to establish. But they are very relevant questions and the criteria
developed in the study appear, in our opinion, to be the most reasonable in
this regard.

All the criteria used in this study are explicitly set down below. The
rationale for their use is developed in some detail.

Size of centers

It was stated earlier that this study investigates the potential for large
shopping centers to form the cores of Metrotown Centers. This raises the
question of an operational definition of a large center. The definition adopted
in this study was in terms of a minimum size for a shopping center to be
considered as a metrotown core.

The specification of a minimum size must, of course, be related to the
observable trends in retailing. A number of factors seem to contribute to the
increase in the scale of a shopping center. For one thing, as the population
and income per capita increase in a region, the distribution plant in the
retailing sector becomes utilized more fully and possible economies of scale
increase. As the retail establishments increase in size, they also tend to cluster
together and offer a wider range of goods and associated services to induce
the consumers away from other clusters. Further, as these clusters of establishments develop and increase the size of their market, the probability
of new specialty goods stores coming in with special bundles of goods
increases.[11] As a result, though there are limits for the increase in size of the
individual establishments, the clusters of establishments—shopping centers
—have been growing in size. However, the increasing searching costs of
the consumers in large centers as well as the competition of other clusters
may pose restrictions on the indefinite increase in scale of a shopping center.
The time costs imposed on a consumer looking for a shopping good increase
rapidly with increase in the size of the shopping center. Conceivably, these
costs could increase in a system of very large centers to a point where
consumers may prefer smaller centers.

The shopping goods floor space in a center would, of course, vary with its
location and with the number of consumers in the part of the region where it

would be dominant. Consequently two minimum sizes related to location in the region were postulated for consideration of shopping centers as Metrotown Center potential. In the more densely settled portions of the region, the minimum size of centers to be considered was assumed to be 450,000–500,000 square feet of shopping floor space. In the areas of thinner development, a lower minimum of 250,000–300,000 square feet of shopping goods floor space was postulated. Exceptions to these rules were outlying older recognized communities such as Aberdeen and Westminster.

A locational decision is made by a shopping center developer when a minimum expected return is assessed at a particular location relative to returns available at known alternate locations. There appears to be a minimum expected return on a shopping center considered necessary by developers before locational decisions are made. This minimum return is defined here in terms of annual sales per square foot.[12]

Sales per square foot vary by the type of store in a regional shopping center. Thus, the department stores sell, on an average, $59 per square foot while the variety stores sell $27; jewelry shops $55, and shoe stores $40–$45.[13] In the Baltimore region, the sales per square foot for all shopping goods stores in a regional center in 1963 ranged from $45 to $53.[14] The shopping goods establishments aggregated over the entire Baltimore region averaged $44 per square foot.

This study assumed that new shopping goods aggregations are viable when the sales per square foot obtained from the model run were at least $50–$55. This minimum value is in line with the data reported above and with current thinking among some leading practitioners in the field of marketing.

The sales per square foot estimated for any location at one point in time is related to the size of center that is assumed. When our study indicated that a shopping center would sell less than $50 per square foot, a reduction of its size in the next trial indicated that the same location would be workable at a smaller size. Thus, this criterion helps to determine the scale at which a shopping center is viable.

In addition, this criterion aids in assessing the impact of a large new center on an existing center. Since the sales level at an existing center can be obtained, it is easy to measure the drop in its performance when competition is "offered" in the form of an assumed center nearby. Judgments can then be made about the size and location of new shopping centers that could be added close by without depressing sales at the existing center below minimum levels.

Other criteria for prediction

The use of the economic feasibility criterion at given locations will only indicate which centers are viable in 1970 and 1980 at sizes chosen. It will not show whether the set of "future" centers tested in any subregion or in the entire region are a reasonable approximation of the probable commercial development as a result of market processes. Such an evaluation is not easy to make, but some indications may be obtained by considering simultaneously the set of centers tested in a subregion under any assumed alternative. Two such criteria were developed.

First, the sales per square foot of shopping centers estimated in any alternative were aggregated by transportation districts. The underlying assumption is that if a group of shopping centers in a transportation district achieve very high sales per square foot (say over $75), consumers in these and surrounding districts are poorly served. High sales per square foot in such areas would result either in an increase in the size of the centers or in the development of new stores nearby to serve the consumers. The implication for our analysis is that if some alternative patterns indicate high sales per square foot for a number of transportation districts in a subregion, those alternatives are poor descriptions of the probable future shopping pattern in that subregion. Therefore, in such subregions, more shopping goods floor space would be assumed and the evaluation procedures would be repeated. This criterion is useful as a corrective in the iterative strategy of setting up alternatives to "approximate" the probable future patterns of shopping goods growth.

The second criterion was the average length of shopping trips. This is a gross measure of the "system efficiency" of an alternative. In any alternative, if the assumed centers are tested at locations eccentric to population distribution, the average length of the shopping goods trip will increase. As indicated later, the average trip length increased 15 percent (1.5 minutes) over present-day levels in one alternative. If the total number of shopping trips is considered, this would involve a very considerable increase in time spent on shopping trips in the region. An alternative pattern was evaluated as efficient in terms of how close its average trip length was to the present-day level. Generally, a 5–7 percent variation from the current average trip length for the region was considered reasonable.

Application of criteria and evaluation of retail potential

The first step in the estimation of retail potential is the development of alternative patterns of possible future retail development. The development of alternative patterns was basically a trial and error process. Initially, it involved allocating the estimated total regional demand for additional shopping goods by 1970 and 1980 to specific locations in a few exploratory alternatives. The probable sales levels at all centers estimated by the model for such alternatives were then evaluated against the stated criteria to provide guidelines for the formulation of more "realistic" alternatives. The formulation and analysis of the preliminary alternatives and the feedback nature of the preliminary analysis will be presented first.

A prerequisite to the formulation of alternatives is an estimation of future regional demand for shopping goods in the region. The projected growth of consumer expenditures on shopping goods in the region for 1962–70 and 1970–80 was treated as potential demand and expressed in floor space for the respective time periods.[15] Based on analysis of current trends, 78 percent of the regional floor space demand was assumed as nucleated retail center potential.

To allocate the regional demand estimated above in the form of alternatives, a set of 67 potential locations was specified by the Regional Planning Council.[16] Each of these locations was treated as a potential candidate for Metrotown Centers and tested in this study for retail potential.

Initially, two hypotheses—"concentration" and "dispersion" of retail development—were assumed. In the first alternative all the growth by 1970 was assumed to take place within the inner beltway (identified as 1970 alternative 1). The second assumption was that most of the growth is likely to skip the more densely settled inner beltway area and locate in the less developed outer beltway area (1970 alternative 4). The 1970 consumer shopping expenditures were then distributed with the model to all shopping centers— "existing" and "future"—in each of these two alternatives.

The sales per square foot of shopping centers by transportation districts were computed and mapped for both alternatives as well as for 1963. The map for 1963 showed that the areas with sales levels of over $75 per square foot—areas of poor retail service—are minimal. The few such pockets are mainly peripheral low-density areas. The main thing to realize is that except for these few pockets, the system of shopping goods centers today provides good retail service throughout the region. In contrast, in 1970 alternative 1 indicates that the "concentration" provides a low level of retail service for large peripheral sections. It will also be indicated below that the sales performance of the various centers varied from $30 to $150—an unlikely occurrence in the market process. Conversely, in 1970 alternative 4, the level of retail service in the outer areas of the region is good, but large areas of the densely populated inner parts of the region are poorly served. In addition, the average trip lengths for these alternatives were 11.8 and 11.4 minutes—a 10 percent increase over current levels.

The major conclusion from this preliminary evaluation was that both these "pure" alternatives are poor descriptions of likely future development. Composite patterns that combine features of both these alternatives were consequently set up for further evaluation.

Throughout the course of this study, 25 alternatives (14 for 1970 and 11 for 1980) were set up and evaluated. This evaluation is a complex process involving several dimensions of interpretation: the relation of size to performance in several alternatives for the same center; the sensitivity of a center to competition nearby; the interrelation of all centers in a subregion; and the assessment of subregional levels of retail service by alternative. Space limitations do not permit a detailed description of all the evaluations performed; however, the following selected examples will indicate the procedures used and the typical findings.[17]

The basic framework of the evaluation was the subregion. It involves the recognition of six overlapping subregional markets. This framework permits the retail centers in each subregion to be viewed as serving one market, which is overlapped by service of some centers in the adjoining subregion. Recognition of the subregions is a device of *evaluation only* and does not affect the sales estimation procedures which still assume a market continuum implicit in the use of the model.

For each of the six subregions, four graphs—two for 1970 and two for 1980—were prepared. For each point of time, the two graphs were: a) Comparative success of centers in the subregion (Figure 1); b) Comparative

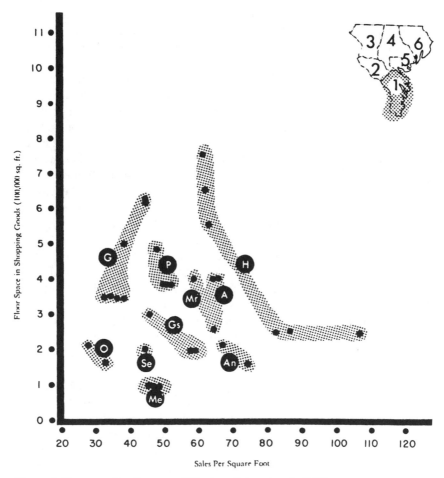

Figure 1 Comparative Success of Centers Subregion 1, 1970

"system" performance in subregion (Figure 2). Both these graphs are plots of sales per square foot versus size of centers for selected alternatives. Figure 1 involves connecting the points in all alternatives for each center. This shows clearly the relation between size and corresponding performance—a measure of depth of market and effect of nearby competition.

The second graph, Figure 2, involves connecting the plots of all the centers for each alternative. It gives a visual measure of the performance range of different centers within the subregion. In Figure 2, the very wide range of sales per square foot among centers in subregion 1 for alternatives 1 and 4 is striking. If a center such as 0 could generate only very low sales, it would either not be built or it would go out of business. If a center such as H generated over $80 per square foot, either its size would be increased or

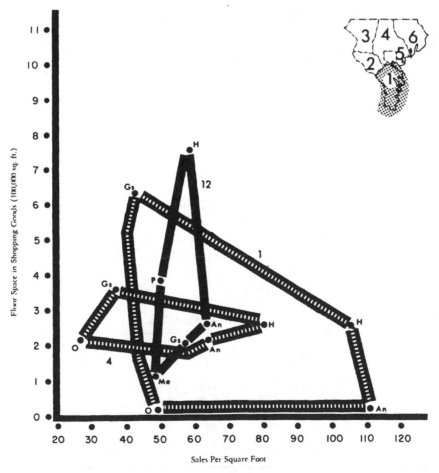

Figure 2 Comparative "System" Performance Subregion 1, 1970

competition would be generated nearby. The market process is more truly indicated by alternative 12, where all the centers have sales ranging from $43 to $65 per square foot.

It is of interest to recall that alternatives 1 and 4 were the exploratory alternatives providing poor levels of retail service and with high values of average trip length. Alternative 12 on the other hand provided better retail service and lower trip length.

Evaluation of a similar nature involving the "system efficiencies" and the probable potential of individual locations was carried out for all locations in all subregions. Out of this evaluation emerged two preferred systems of centers. In terms of the criteria used, clear preference of one pattern over the other could not be established.

Retail growth patterns and implications

The nature of the regional commercial growth pattern indicated by the preferred system of centers can be described in two ways.

One

Table I provides a statistical summary of commercial growth. The inner belt area is the ring around the inner beltway where most of the present suburban nucleated shopping centers are located. The outer belt corresponds to the area around the proposed outer beltway and beyond. The satellite communities refer to old established peripheral communities such as Westminster, Belair, and Annapolis.

It is interesting to note the shifting of the axis of major growth from the inner belt to the outer belt between 1970 and 1980. Up to 1970, the inner belt accounts for half of the total growth, while the outer belt is expected to get 60 percent of the next decade's growth. The satellite communities

Table I Projected Growth of Shopping Goods Floor Space

| | 1962–1970 | | 1970–1980 | | Percent of Total Growth | |
	million sq. ft.	Percent	million sq. ft.	Percent	1962–1970	1970–80
Inner belt	1.90	50	1.04	26	66	34
Outer belt	1.36	36	2.44	60	38	62
Satellite community	0.54	14	0.56	14	50	50

tend to have a constant rate of growth throughout the time period studied, indicating their relative isolation from the wave of metropolitan expansion during this period.

Put another way, the inner belt is expected to experience two-thirds of its growth before 1970 while the outer belt area will get two-thirds of its growth during the following decade.

Two

The patterns of probable retail growth in the belt area have very important subregional variations. These subregional variations provide important guides to commercial policy. Thus it was possible to discover that three large existing commercial centers in the region have considerable potential for growth. In addition, three new locations hold out great possibilities of growth. Two other existing centers appear to suffer from poor location or slow growth in their markets. Since this study was based on data that assumed continuation of current policies and trends, the findings have a relevance beyond the Metrotown concept.

Conclusion

It may be recalled that this study was prompted by the desire to test out a key component—large commercial cores—of the multi-use centers envisaged in the Metrotown concept. Accordingly, all the locations identified by the Regional Planning Council as potential candidates for Metrotown Centers were evaluated for their retail potential. This evaluation, assuming the continuation of existing trends and policies, identified the potential for large-scale retail activity at a number of these locations. It was found that, under existing policies, market forces seem to point to the development of several retail centers of the scale envisaged in the Metrotown Concept. By 1970, nine commercial centers could be cores of Metrotown Centers; six more could approach this size by 1980. This implies that a key component of the Metrotown Center appears to be consistent with the operation of urban growth processes.

The market potential model, though developed in response to a specific planning problem, has a more general application. In this study, the continuation of existing land and highway policies were assumed and the evaluation criteria were relevant to the needs of a "New Town" retail core. The model can be applied equally well with different assumptions of metropolitan policies and various evaluative criteria related to other forms of commercial organization. The estimating procedures are fully computerized and compatible with data being produced by the metropolitan studies under way in many American cities.

Notes

1. Baltimore Regional Planning Council, *Metrotowns for the Baltimore Region: A Pattern Emerges*, Technical Bulletin No. 4 (June, 1962).

2. The following formulation assumed that purchases by residents in establishments outside the region are balanced by the sales made to visitors in the region.

3. Hence the desire of the retailer to choose sites of high accessibility so as to reduce these "costs of friction." See R. M. Haig, "Toward an Understanding of the Metropolis," *Quarterly Journal of Economics*, XL (May, 1926), 402–34.

4. See Alan M. Voorhees, Gordon B. Sharpe, and J. T. Stegmaier, *Shopping Habits and Travel Patterns*, Urban Land Institute Technical Bulletin No. 24 (Washington, D.C., 1955).

5. David L. Huff, *Determination of Intraurban Retail Trade Areas* (Los Angeles: University of California, Real Estate Rescarch Program, 1962).

6. The gravity model was first applied by Reilly to separate the market areas of two cities competing for customers in a hinterland. See William J. Reilly, *The Law of Retail Gravitation* (New York: W. J. Reilly Co., 1931).

7. This model can be meaningfully applied if the region is divided into a large number of zones.

8. See Donald E. Cleveland and Edward A. Mueller, *Traffic Characteristics at Regional Shopping Centers* (New Haven: Yale University, Bureau of Highway Traffic, 1961), Figure 47.

9. Baltimore Regional Planning Council, *A Projection of Planning Factors for Land Use and Transportation*, Technical Report No. 9 (1963).

10. For details of this model, see Alan M. Voorhees and Associates, *Forecasting Consumer Expenditures: An application to the Baltimore Region*, Baltimore Metrotown Evaluation Technical Report No. 1 (Washington, D.C., December, 1963). For 1960, $C_{ij} = 2.3 Y_i^{.573}$; for 1970, $C_{ij} = 2.30 (Y_i + 109)^{.573}$; and for 1980, $C_{ij} = 2.30 (Y_i + 238)^{.573}$ where C_{ij} = per capita shopping goods expenditures and Y_i = estimated mean income

11. Richard H. Holton, "Scale Specialization and Costs in Retailing," Berkeley: University of California, 1962, p. 5 (Mimeographed.)

12. The use of this measure assumes returns for investment to be the same for different production functions of different retail establishments. Thus the payoffs between sales levels and costs such as rent levels are ignored (they may be uncovered in the subsequent site analysis). Further, the assumption is made that merchandising and advertising differentials will not be significant and location vis-a-vis consumers is most relevant.

13. These data are drawn from Urban Land Institute, *The Dollars and Cents of Shopping Centers, Part 2* (Washington, D.C., 1962), Appendix A.

14. This information is drawn from confidential information obtained from the Sales Tax Department for a set of six regional shopping centers for 1963.

15. On the assumption of an average $55 return per square foot.

16. Available land, existing commercial nucleation, general locations fixed in previous Metrotown studies, and disposition to areas of population growth were some of the factors guiding the choice of these locations.

17. For a detailed description, see Alan M. Voorhees and Associates, Baltimore Metrotown Evaluation Technical Report No. 3 (June, 1964).

24

A stated choice model of sequential mode and destination choice behaviour for shopping trips

H. J. P. Timmermans

Source: *Environment and Planning A* 28 (1996): 173–184.

Abstract

Stated preference and choice models currently used in urban planning are focused on predicting single choices. In this paper the intention is to extend these modelling approaches to the case of sequential choice behaviour. Design strategies and model specifications that allow one to predict sequential choice are discussed. The approach is illustrated in a study of sequential mode and destination choice behaviour for shopping trips. The research findings suggest that the proposed approach may be a valuable extension of currently available stated preference and choice methods to analyse more complex forms of decisionmaking.

1 Introduction

Choice models based on the revealed choices of individuals have traditionally received most attention in travel choice modelling in general and prediction of shopping trips in particular. There are numerous examples of research projects in which spatial interaction or multinominal logit models have been applied to observed spatial shopping patterns (for instance, see Barnard, 1987; Black et al, 1985; Fotheringham, 1988a; 1988b; Guy, 1987; McCarthy, 1980; Recker and Kostyniuk, 1978; Recker and Stevens, 1976; Richards and Ben-Akiva, 1974; Timmermans, 1981a; 1981b; 1984a; 1984b; 1984c; Weisbrod et al, 1984).

Recently, increasing attention has been given in the transportation and urban planning literature to deriving models from individuals' responses to hypothetical choice alternatives observed in (quasi-)laboratory experiments (Louviere, 1988). Individuals are typically presented with a series of hypothetical travel alternatives constructed according to the principles of the design of statistical experiments and are requested to express their strength of preference for each alternative. These overall preference measures are then decomposed into the part-worth utilities associated with the attribute levels used to describe the travel alternatives. This approach, which has been called 'conjoint analysis' (for example, Green and Srinivasan, 1978) or 'decompositional multiattribute preference modelling' (for example, Timmermans, 1984a), has become known in the transportation literature as 'stated preference analysis' (Kroes and Sheldon, 1988). Stated preference models have recently been applied in a variety of contexts, such as preference for bus services (Bradley et al, 1989; Timmermans and Overduin, 1981), competition between rail and coach services (Louviere et al, 1981), preferences for rail services (Anderson P B, et al, 1986; Dinwoodie, 1989), the effects of area licensing proposals (Hensher and Louviere, 1979), valuation of travel time (Hensher and Truong, 1985), route choice behaviour (Bovy and Bradley, 1985; Bradley and Bovy, 1984), and choice of car parking facilities (Axhausen and Polak, 1991).

Most of the stated preference methods applied in urban planning and transportation science that have appeared in the literature rely on the ranking or rating of data on hypothetical travel alternatives. Consequently, the models that are developed are preference models rather than choice models, the aim being to predict preferences as opposed to choices. Because the aim of much applied research is to predict the likely consequences of transport policy decisions in terms of market shares and consumer choice behaviour, additional assumptions are required to relate the estimated preference function to subsequent choice behaviour. In early applications, almost invariably a deterministic choice rule was employed in which each individual was assumed to choose the travel option with the highest predicted preference or utility score.

Estimated market shares are predicted by aggregating the simulated choices. More recently, probabilistic choice rules have been applied in which choice probabilities are a function of (differences in) utility scale values (for example, see Green and Krieger, 1988; Timmermans and Van der Heijden, 1984). The best known of these probabilistic choice rules are the Bradley-Terry-Luce model (Bradley and Terry, 1952; Luce, 1959) and the logit model. Alternatively, the exploded logit model (Chapman and Staelin, 1982) may be used, which is based on the Luce and Suppes ranking choice theorem. Applications of this model can be found in, for instance, Moore (1988; 1989; 1990).

Given the rigorous and often limited assumptions underlying these probabilistic choice rules, Louviere and Woodworth (1983) suggested choice data be used directly. Their approach differs from that taken in stated preference methods in that the hypothetical travel options are placed into choice sets. Subjects are asked to choose an option rather than to rank or rate the travel options in terms of overall preferences. Consequently, a choice model rather than a preference function is estimated. Different design strategies may be used, but often orthogonal fractional factorial designs are constructed because these are the most efficient. The multinomial logit model typically is used to represent the observed choice data. If the number of travel options among which individuals will choose is constant (say, N), and each travel option has M attributes with L levels, choice designs that satisfy the multinominal logit model can be constructed by designing an L^{NM} main-effects, orthogonal fractional factorial experimental design to create joint combinations of attribute levels. Often a constant travel option is added to each choice set to fix the origin of the utility scale. Individuals are requested to select one travel option from each choice set or to allocate some fixed set of resources (for example, trips) to the available travel options. Applications of this approach in travel demand modelling include that by Louviere and Hensher (1982).

The stated choice approach, however, is not necessarily restricted to the multinominal logit model. More complicated models can be estimated by using the principles underlying this approach. Substitution models that avoid the property of independence from irrelevant alternatives (IIA) of the multinominal logit model can be estimated by introducing the attribute levels of competing travel options into the utility function of the travel option of interest. Violations of the IIA property are present if these cross-effects are statistically significant. Borgers, Van der Waerden, and I have illustrated this approach in a model of destination choice (see Timmermans et al, 1991). Likewise, the effects of varying choice set composition and size, and choice set constraints on travel choice behaviour, can be estimated by including availability effects in the specification of the utility function. Estimation of such models requires one to construct choice sets of varying size and composition, 2^N designs being a potential candidate (Anderson D A, et al, 1992).

Clearly, much progress has been made recently in developing stated preference and choice models of travel demand. Nevertheless, a shortcoming of all these models is that they predict single choice behaviour. That is to say, mode or single destination choice is predicted as a function of choice attributes. Existing approaches do not allow one to predict sequential choice behaviour. Therefore, if stated choice models are to become an alternative to the nested logit model of revealed choice behaviour, existing modelling approaches must be extended.

My objective in this paper is to extend stated choice models to allow the estimation of sequential choice behaviour. I present a design strategy that allows the efficient estimation of models of sequential choice behaviour, and I illustrate the approach in the context of the choice of sopping centres, given the choice of transport mode. To accomplish this goal, the remainder of the paper is organised as follows. First, in section 2, the modelling approach that allows one to estimate models of sequential choice behaviour is outlined. Then, in section 3, the approach is illustrated by using sequential mode – shopping centre choice as an example. Finally, in section 4, the implications of the results for current and future research in travel choice modelling are discussed.

2   Modelling sequential choice behaviour

The theoretical assumptions underlying the suggested approach are similar to those underlying decompositional choice models. It is assumed that shopping centres and transport modes can be represented in terms of a set of attributes that describes their positions on these choice dimensions. Individuals are assumed to derive a utility from each attribute level and to integrate their part-worth utilities into an overall utility or preference according to some combination rule. Further, it is assumed that the combination rule that individuals apply in the integration process can be uncovered in quasi-laboratory situations by presenting participants with a series of hypothetical shopping centres or transport modes and observing their responses. These hypothetical choice alternatives should be constructed according to the principles of the design of statistical experiments. Appropriately designed experiments allow one to estimate the applied utility function. If individuals are presented with choice sets of varying size and composition, or with choice sets of fixed size and consisting of choice alternatives of different attribute levels, and are asked to choose the one alternative they like most, the resulting choice data may be used to estimate simultaneously the utility function and the choice model that they apparently used in generating their responses. Obviously, the choice design that is constructed should allow the estimation of the assumed choice model. Orthogonal, main-effects, fractional factorial designs allow the efficient estimation of the multinominal logit model.

How can this approach be extended to model sequential choice behaviour? One way to test for dependence in sequential choices is to include the attribute levels of the choice alternatives available in the previous choice step in the specification of the utility function of the choice alternatives at the present choice occasion. If these cross-effects are not statistically significant, the attribute levels of the choice alternative selected at the previous step of the sequential choice process will not influence the choice probabilities at the present step. Similarly, significant cross-effects indicate dependencies in the sequential choice process. This sequential model can be compared in terms of predictive ability with an independence model that can be constructed by developing separate models for each step of the sequential choice process and multiplying the resulting choice probabilities.

To estimate the model of sequential choice behaviour efficiently, all experimental designs constructed to develop a choice model for each choice and the design to estimate the cross-effects should be orthogonal. This can be accomplished by constructing a single orthogonal fractional factorial design. Suppose that at the first step of the choice sequence individuals have to choose between two transport modes, each described by three two-level attributes. Suppose also that they have to choose between two shopping centre profiles at the second step of the choice sequence, each described in terms of three three-level attributes. Then, orthogonality within and between the successive steps of the choice sequence is preserved if a fraction of the $2^6 \times 3^6$ factorial design that allows the estimation of the assumed choice model is constructed. The six columns of the design representing two-level attributes can be used to estimate the submodel of mode choice. Likewise, the six columns representing three-level attributes can be used to estimate the submodel of shopping centre choice. All twelve columns are required to estimate the model of sequential choice behaviour.

Parameter estimation is not different from conventional stated choice models. Different estimation techniques such as maximum likelihood and generalised least squares analysis (for example, see Louviere and Timmermans, 1990) may be used. In the present study, parameter estimation was based on the reweighted least squares method (Jenrich and Moore, 1975; Woodworth and Louviere, 1985).

3 The study

3.1 Study area and sample

The field research was conducted in Eindhoven, a major city in the south of the Netherlands. Self-completion questionnaires were distributed to a random sample of respondents. Respondents were told about the objectives of the survey and requested to return their responses in a self-addressed envelope to Eindhoven University of Technology. The questionnaire consisted of two parts. In the first part, a set of questions concerning respondents' shopping choice behaviour and cognition of shopping centres was asked; the second part concerned an experimental task which was constructed to examine respondents' sequential choice of transport mode and shopping centre. The results reported in this paper are based upon the second part of the questionnaire. A total of 750 questionnaires were distributed, of which 167 were returned. This is a response rate of 22.3%.

3.2 The design and experimental task

In order to estimate the sequential choice model, the following steps are required. First, the attributes that are supposed to influence the choice behaviour of interest need to be identified. Then, in the second step, each of the selected attributes is defined in terms of attribute levels. These attribute levels are then combined according to the principles of the design of statistical experiments. Usually, a fractional factorial design which allows one to estimate all main effects is selected. This approach is used in most applications of stated preference methods in the transportation literature. However, if choices rather than preferences are examined, the attribute profiles constructed according to the selected statistical design need to be placed into choice sets. One possible approach is to construct choice sets that satisfy the multinominal logit model. As already described in section 1, if the number of choice alternatives among which individuals will choose is constant (say, N), and each choice alternative has M attributes with L levels, choice sets that satisfy the multinominal logit model can be constructed by designing an L^{NM} main-effects, orthogonal fractional factorial experimental design. Choice sets created in this way have a fixed number of (travel) alternatives, but the positions of these alternatives on the selected attributes vary from choice set to choice set (for example, see Louviere and Woodworth, 1983). The respondents' task then is to indicate which one choice alternative in each set they would be most likely to choose, or, alternatively, to allocate some fixed amount of resources (for example, trips) among the choice alternatives. These choices are then aggregated across respondents to produce relative frequencies of choice. Iteratively reweighted least squares analysis or other appropriate techniques can then be used to estimate the parameters of the choice model.

In the present study, shopping centres were characterised in terms of four attributes: size, price, parking facilities, and distance. These attributes were chosen because they have proven to be major determinants of consumer spatial shopping behaviour (for example, see Timmermans, 1993). Size, price, and distance were varied in terms of three attribute levels. The attribute of parking facilities was dichotomised. Hence, a 2×3^3 full factorial design would describe all possible combinations of attribute levels. The attributes and their levels are listed in table 1.

Table 1 Attributes and their levels

Attribute	Level	Attribute	Level
Transport mode:		Shopping centre:	
Car		size	small; mainly groceries
parking costs (Fl h^{-1})	free		medium; most types of stores available
	1		large; a lost of choice
	2	price	many discount stores
travel time (min)	5		average price level
	10		expensive
	15	parking facilities	ample parking
Bus			available parking spaces often occupied
return fare (Fl)	6	distance (km)	<1
	4		1–3
	2		3–5
travel time (min)	10		
	15		
	20		
frequency of service	every 15 min		
	every 30 min		

Because I have assumed that transport mode choice influences the choice of shopping centre, the modes need also to be described in terms of attribute levels. Two modes were selected: car and bus. In this case, alternative specific utility functions were assumed. The car was described in terms of parking costs and travel time, whereas the bus was represented by three attributes: fare, travel time, and frequency. Parking costs, fare, and travel times were all three-level attributes; frequency was a two-level attribute. These attributes and their levels are also listed in table 1. Hence, a total of 2×3^4 (162) attribute combinations or profiles were possible.

The principle underlying the present approach is that both components of the sequential choice process (transport mode and shopping centres) under investigation should be estimated independently. A 2×3^4 subdesign describing the transport modes allows one to estimate the choice of transport mode. Similarly, a $2^2 \times 3^6$ design, consisting of two descriptions of hypothetical shopping centres in terms of generic attributes, allows the estimation of a model of shopping centre choice. These two subdesigns should be combined to estimate these two models independently. More specifically, a fraction of the resulting $2^3 \times 3^{10}$ full factorial design was selected to estimate the sequential choice model. This fraction consisted of 36 treatments. Each treatment consisted of two transport mode options, varied in terms of two or three attributes, and two shopping centre options, each described in terms of four attributes. A constant base alternative described as 'none of these' was added to each choice set.

Respondents were asked first to choose between the two transport modes or 'none of these'. Then, they were requested to choose the hypothetical shopping centre they were most likely to patronise, given their choice of transport mode.

3.3 Results

The ultimate aim of the present research project was to estimate and test a stated choice model of sequential mode and shopping centre choice. It was assumed that the choice of shopping centre may be influenced by the choice of transport mode. To assess the performance of the model, its predictive success was compared with that of an alternative model in which it is assumed that these two types of choice behaviour are independent. Thus, three different choice models were estimated:

(a) a model of mode choice behaviour, derived from the orthogonal fraction of the 2×3^4 subdesigns, which uses alternative specific utility functions;
(b) a model of shopping centre choice, based upon an orthogonal fraction of the $2^2 \times 3^6$ subdesigns, which uses generic attributes;
(c) a model of sequential choice behaviour derived from the orthogonal fraction of the $2^3 \times 3^{10}$ full factorial design, consisting of 36 choice sets.

The performance of model (c) was compared with the performance of a model of independence that resulted from multiplying model (a) with model (b). A multinominal logit model was assumed to represent the choice process in all three cases.

To estimate the choice models, the attribute levels need to be coded. Different coding schemes, such as dummy coding, effect coding, or orthogonal polynomial coding, may be used. The choice of coding scheme will not affect the goodness of fit of the choice model, but it will influence the parameter estimates and their interpretation, their standard errors, and the correlations, if any, in the design matrix. In the present study, effect coding was used. Consequently, the parameter estimates reflect differences from the mean utility. Effect coding implies that for any attribute with K levels, $K - 1$ indicator variables are constructed. $K - 1$ attribute levels are coded by a 1 on one of the indicator variables, and by zeros on the remaining indicator variables. The Kth attribute level is coded by -1 on all $K - 1$ indicator variables. The dependent variable of the model consists of the relative choice frequencies that are obtained by aggregating separately the responses across respondents for each choice alternative and choice set. Iteratively reweighted least squares analysis was used to find the parameters of the choice models.

The results of the parameters estimates that predict transport mode choice behaviour are presented in table 2. A number of interesting observations can be made with respect to these results. First, both alternative specific parameters are negative, suggesting that the propensity to choose car or bus for shopping is lower than the propensity to choose any other means of transportation. This finding reflects the fact that the majority of shopping trips in the Netherlands indeed are made on foot or by bicycle. The spatial distribution of retail facilities allows consumers to act in this way. Because of strong urban planning regulations, all neighbourhoods have at least one small shopping centre that provides all convenience goods; and walking distance to such centres rarely exceeds more than 500 m. As expected, the utility for the bus is in turn less than the utility for the car. Although the provision of public transport in Eindhoven is satisfactory, the bus is chosen less frequently for probably because the time it would take to wait for the bus is more than the time it takes to walk to the shopping centre.

Second, it can be seen in table 2 that all estimated parameter values are in the anticipated directions. Utility for using the car for shopping increases monotonically with decreasing parking costs. The utility of the bus increases with decreasing fares at an increasing rate. Its utility also increases with a higher frequency of service. Utility for travel time decreases with increasing time for both car and bus. Respondents seem more sensitive to the travel time of the bus compared with the travel time of the car. It should be noted, however, that most parameter estimates are not statistically significant beyond conventional probability levels, with the exception of the alternative specific constants: the free parking attribute level and the F16 fare attribute level. This suggests that consumers apparently prefer walking or cycling, no matter what the actual attribute levels of the car and bus, to go shopping.

Table 2 Parameter estimates of the multinomial logit model of transport mode choice

Attribute	Parameter	Standard error	t-value
Car:			
Constant	−0.237	0.04	−5.52
Parking costs (Fl h⁻¹)			
free	0.200	0.06	3.36
1	−0.057	0.06	−0.95
2	(−0.143)		
Travel time (min)			
5	0.036	0.06	0.60
10	−0.004	0.06	−0.07
15	(−0.032)		
Bus:			
Constant	−2.574	0.11	−23.60
Return fare (Fl)			
6	−0.357	0.16	−2.17
4	−0.060	0.16	0.41
2	(0.297)		
Travel time (min)			
10	0.092	0.41	0.64
15	0.053	0.41	0.36
20	(−0.145)		
Frequency of service			
every 15 min	0.055	0.10	0.53
every 30 min	(−0.055)		

Note: The figures in parentheses are not estimated but are calculated so that the estimates sum to 1.

The simple multinominal logit model provided an 88% improvement over the null model. This improvement is significant beyond the 5% probability level. The correlation coefficient between predicted and observed choices was 0.914.

The model estimated to represent consumer choice of shopping centre was also a simple multinomial logit model. It contained four generic attributes: size, price, parking facilities, and distance. In table 3 I present the estimated parameter estimates, their standard errors, and associated *t*-values. It can be seen that all parameters are statistically significant beyond the 5% probability level and that all are in the are in the anticipated directions. The utility of a shopping centre increases as its size increases. Utility also increases with decreasing prices and it decreases at an increasing rate with increasing distance. Respondents' choices are most influenced by price, followed by distance, and size, as indicated by the range in estimated parameters. It can also be seen from table 3 that utility for a shopping centre increases if ample parking is available.

Table 3 Parameter estimates of the multinomial logit model of shopping centre choice

Attribute	Parameter estimate	Standard error	t-value
Constant	1.047	0.078	15.75
Size			
small	−0.502	0.06	−9.06
medium	0.193	0.06	3.70
large	0.409		
Price			
discount	0.750	0.06	13.48
average	0.555	0.06	10.00
expensive	−1.305		
Parking			
ample	0.353	0.04	9.50
often occupied	−0.353		
Distance (km)			
<1	0.571	0.06	10.18
1–3	0.130	0.06	2.33
3–5	−0.701		

The goodness of fit of this choice model was satisfactory. The correlation between observed and predicted choices was 0.970; the improvement in log-likelihood over the null model was 89.431%.

The results of the model sequential choice that predicts the probability of choosing a shopping centre as a function of shopping centre attributes and attributes of the transport mode chosen at the previous step of the choice process are presented in table 4. It can be seen that none of the transport mode attributes is statistically significant. Thus, it seems that the choice of transport mode does not influence shopping centre choice. Moreover, the parameters of the distance categories are not significant. This may suggest that the evaluation of distance categories differs considerably between respondents choosing different transport modes. All other parameter estimates run in the theoretically expected directions. This finding gives further support to the validity of the results. The correlation between predicted and observed choices is 0.98. The estimated sequential choice model exceeds the null model by 87.1% in terms of the likelihood ratio.

Another way to assess the sequential choice model is to compare its predictive ability with the predictive success of an independence model that is obtained by multiplying the transport mode choice model with the shopping centre choice model. In table 5 I present a summary of some of the goodness-of-fit statistics that were calculated. Thus, these statistics indicate which of these two models predicts best the observed market shares for combinations of transport modes and shopping centres. Inspection of table 5 indicates that, regardless of the goodness-of-fit statistic, the proposed sequential model

Table 4 Parameter estimates for the model of sequential choice

Attribute	Parameter estimate	Standard error	t-value
Constant	4.037	0.38	10.75
Shopping centre choice:			
Size			
small	−0.645	0.08	−7.39
medium	0.264	0.08	3.23
large	0.381		
Price			
discount	0.641	0.08	7.44
average	0.614	0.09	6.89
expensive	−1.255		
Parking			
ample	0.581	0.06	9.41
often occupied	−0.581		
Distance (km)			
<1	0.007	0.09	0.08
1–3	1.692	0.09	1.83
3–5	−1.699		
Transport mode effect:			
Car:			
Parking costs (Fl h^{-1})			
free	0.133	0.57	0.23
1	−0.015	0.56	−0.03
2	−0.128		
Travel time (min)			
5	0.154	0.58	0.27
10	0.019	0.57	0.03
15	−0.173		
Bus:			
Return fare (Fl)			
6	−0.034	1.17	−0.02
4	−0.160	1.17	−0.09
2	0.194		
Travel time (min)			
10	−0.107	1.17	−0.06
15	0.318	1.17	0.18
20	−0.211		
Frequency			
every 15 min	0.236	1.12	0.193
every 30 min	−0.236		

produces the best results. For example, Pearson's product-moment correlation coefficient between predicted and observed choice frequencies of combinations of transport mode and shopping centre is 0.977, whereas its value is only 0.715 if these frequencies are predicted by multiplying transport mode probabilities with shopping centre probabilities under the assumption of independence. Thus, from a predictive viewpoint, the proposed sequential model provides satisfactory results.

Table 5 Goodness of fit of the choice models

Statistic	Independence model	Sequential model
Correlation coefficient	0.715	0.977
Robinson's agreement	0.841	0.987
Theil's inequality coefficient	0.356	0.035
Mean absolute error	0.119	0.036
Minimum discrimination		
information index	9.843	1.497

4 Conclusions and discussion

In this paper I have explored the potential for estimating sequential choice models by using principles of stated choice methods. I have shown how discrete choice experiments may be used to derive models of transport mode and shopping centre choice and I have suggested design strategy that retains orthogonality properties within and between choice sets for elements of the choice sequence. It allows the efficient estimation of discrete choice models for each step in the choice sequence and for the sequential choice model.

The application of the suggested model of sequential choice behaviour was illustrated in the context of choice of shopping centre, given the choice of transport mode. I am not necessarily arguing that these choices are made in that order. This conceptualisation was required to develop the experimental task that was presented to the respondents. In fact, the suggested modelling approach allows one to test for the assumed structure in the choice sequence. The results of the present application suggested that choice of shopping centre is largely independent of choice of transport mode. Still, the predictive success of the sequential choice model exceeds the predictive success of a model of independence if one wishes to predict combinations of transport mode and shopping centre choice.

The results of the application and the ease of implementing the experiment leads me to conclude that this type of sequential choice model is easy to develop in cases of a moderate number of choices and attributes. Experimental designs that allow the estimation of the suggested type of model are readily available or can be easily constructed. It is also clear that these sequential models can be estimated from simple mail surveys and that the experimental task is easy to understand. Future research should test the limits to the suggested approach in terms of the number of attributes that can be included in the utility function and in terms of the extension of the suggested approach to problems of simultaneous choice. I hope to report on such developments in the near future.

Acknowledgements

The author thanks Peter Van der Waerden for his programming assistance.

References

Anderson D A, Borgers A, Ettema D, Timmermans H J P, 1992, "Estimating availability effects in travel choice modeling: a stated choice approach", in *Transportation Research Record, Number 1357: Planning and Administration* (National Academy Press, Washington, DC) pp 51–65

Anderson P B, Moeller J, Sheldon R J, 1986, "Marketing DSB rail service using a stated preference approach", in *Proceedings of the PTRC 14th Annual Summer Meeting* (PTRC, London) Seminar M, pp 263–270

Axhausen K W, Polak J W, 1991, "Choice of parking: stated preference approach" *Transportation* **18** 59–81

Barnard P O, 1987, "Modelling shopping destination choice behaviour using the basic multinomial logit model and some of its extensions" *Transport Reviews* **7** 17–51

Black W C, Ostlund L E, Westbrook R A, 1985, "Spatial demand models in an intra-brand context" *Journal of Marketing* **49** 106–113

Bovy P H L, Bradley M, 1985, "Route choice analysed with stated preference approaches", paper presented at the Transportation Research Board Annual Meeting, Washington, DC; copy available from P Bovy, Faculty of Civil Engineering, Delft University of Technology, Delft

Bradley M, Bovy P H L, 1984, "A stated preference analysis of bicyclist route choice", paper presented at the PTRC Annual Summer Meeting, Brighton, 10–13 July; copy available from P Bovy, Faculty of Civil Engineering, Delft University of Technology, Delft

Bradley M, Kroes E, Sheldon R, Widlert S, Gärling T, Uhlin S, 1989, "Preferences for bus and underground services in Stockholm", paper presented at the fifth World Conference on Transport Research, Yokohama, 10–14 July; copy available from T Gärling, Department of Psychology, University of Göteborg, PO Box 14158, S-40020 Göteborg

Bradley R A, Terry M E, 1952, "Rank analysis of incomplete block designs I: the method of paired comparisons" *Econometrica* **39** 324–345

Chapman R G, Staelin R, 1982, "Exploiting rank ordered choice set data within the stochastic utility model" *Journal of Marketing Research* **19** 281–299

Dinwoodie J, 1989, "A sated preference approach to forecasting suburban retail demand in eastern Plymouth", paper presented at the PTRC Conference, University of Warwick, September; copy available from J Dinwoodie, Department of Shipping and Transport, Polytechnic South West, Plymouth Polytechnic, Plymouth

Fotheringham A S, 1988a, "Consumer store choice and choice set definition" *Marketing Science* **7** 299–310

Fotheringham A S, 1988b, "Market share analysis techniques: a review and illustration of current US practice", in *Store Choice, Store Location and Market Analysis* Ed. N Wrigley (Routledge, London) pp 120–159

Green P E, Krieger A M, 1988, "Choice rules and sensitivity analysis in conjoint simulators" *Journal of the Academy of Marketing Science* **16** 114–127

Green P E, Srinivasan V, 1978, "Conjoint analysis in consumer research: issues and outlook" *Journal of Consumer Research* **5** 103–123

Guy C M, 1987, "Recent advances in spatial interaction modelling: an application to the forecasting of shopping travel" *Environment and Planning A* **19** 173–186

Hensher D A, Louviere J J, 1979, "Behavioural intentions as predictors of very specific behaviour" *Transportation* **8** 167–182

Hensher D A, Truong T P, 1985, "Valuation of travel time savings" *Journal of Transport Economics and Policy* **9** 237–261

Jenrich R I, Moore R H, 1975, "Maximum likelihood by means of nonlinear least squares" *American Statistical Association Proceedings of the Statistical Computing Section* 57–65

Kroes E P, Sheldon R J, 1988, "Stated preference methods" *Journal of Transport Economics and Policy* **22** 11–25

Louviere J J, 1988, "Conjoint analysis modelling of stated preferences" *Journal of Transport Economics and Policy* **22** 93–119

Louviere J J, Hensher D A, 1982, "Design and analysis of simulated choice or allocation experiments in travel choice modeling" *Transportation Research Record* number 890, 11–17

Louviere J J, Timmermans H J P, 1990, "Hierarchical information integration applied to residential choice behavior" *Geographical Analysis* **22** 127–145

Louviere J J, Woodworth G, 1983, "Design and analysis of simulated consumer choice or allocation experiments: an approach based on aggregate data" *Journal of Marketing Research* **20** 350–367

Louviere J J, Henley D H, Woodworth G, Meyer R J, Levin I P, Stoner J W, Curry D, Anderson D A, 1981, "Laboratory simulation versus revealed preference methods for estimating travel demand models" *Transportation Research Record* number 794, 42–51

Luce R D, 1959 *Individual Choice Behavior* (John Wiley, New York)

McCarthy P S, 1980, "A study of the importance of generalised attributes in shopping behaviour" *Environment and Planning A* **12** 1269–1286

Moore L, 1988, "Stated preference analysis and new store location", in *Store Choice, Store Location and Market Analysis* Ed. N Wrigley (Routledge, London) pp 203–224

Moore L, 1989, "Modelling store choice: a segmented approach using stated preference analysis" *Transactions of the Institute of British Geographers: New Series* **14** 461–477

Moore L, 1990, "Segmentation of store choice models using stated preferences" *Papers of the Regional Science Association* **69** 121–131

Recker W, Kostyniuk L, 1978, "Factors influencing destination choice for the urban grocery shopping trip" *Transportation* **7** 19–33

Recker W, Stevens R, 1976, "Attitudinal models of modal choice: the multinomial case for selected nonwork trips" *Transportation* **5** 355–375

Richards M, Ben-Akiva M, 1974, "A simultaneous destination and mode choice model for shopping trips" *Transportation* **3** 343–356

Timmermans H J P, 1981a, "Spatial choice behaviour in different environmental settings: an application of the revealed preference approach" *Geografiska Annaler B* **63** 59–67

Timmermans H J P, 1981b, "Multiattribute shopping models and ridge regression analysis" *Environment and Planning A* **13** 43–56

Timmermans H J P, 1984a, "Decompositional multiattribute preference models in spatial choice analysis: a review of some recent developments" *Progress in Human Geography* **8** 189–221

Timmermans H J P, 1984b, "Decision models for predicting preferences among multiattribute choice alternatives", in *Recent Developments in Spatial Data Analysis: Methodology, Measurement, Models* Eds G Bahrenberg, M M Fischer, P Nijkamp (Gower, Aldershot, Hants) pp 337–355

Timmermans H J P, 1984c, "Discrete choice models versus decompositional multi-attribute preference models: a comparative analysis of model performance in the context of spatial shopping-behaviour", in *London Papers in Regional Science 14: Discrete Choice Models in Regional Science* Ed. D E Pitfield (Pion, London) pp 88–102

Timmermans H J P, 1993, "Retail environments and spatial shopping behavior", in *Behavior and Environment: Psychological and Geographical Approaches* Eds T Gärling, R G Golledge (Elsevier, Amsterdam) pp 342–377

Timmermans H J P, Overduin T, 1981, "Informatie integratie en vervoermiddelkeuze" *Verkeerskunde* **31** 321–325

Timmermans H J P, Van der Heijden R E C M, 1984, "The predictive ability of alternative decision rules in decompositional multiattribute preference models" *Sistemi Urbani* **5** 89–101

Timmermans H J P, Borgers A, Van der Waerden P J H J, 1991, "Mother logit analysis of substitution effects in consumer shopping destination choice" *Journal of Business Research* **23** 311–323

Weisbrod G E, Parcells R J, Kern C, 1984, "A disaggregate model for predicting shopping area market attraction" *Journal of Retailing* **60** 65–83

Woodworth G G, Louviere J J, 1985, "Fitting large scale multinomial logit models via iteratively reweighted least squares", paper presented at the Operations Research Society of America/The Institute of Marketing Services Marketing Science Conference, Nashville, TN; copy available from J J Louviere, Department of Marketing, University of Sydney, Sydney